Contents

Illustrations

Maps

Figures

Tables

Box

Preface

China's Political System, Fourth Edition, describes and analyzes China's political system, taking as its *leitmotif* the efforts of successive leaderships to harmonize elements of the country's unique and impressive indigenous culture with formulas for industrialization and modernization that originally evolved in the West. The nineteenth-century paradigm "Chinese learning for the essence; Western learning for practical use" resonates with Mao Zedong's injunction to "walk on two legs"—the modern and the traditional—and Deng Xiaoping's search for "socialism with Chinese characteristics." Over the past two decades, other and related themes have become prominent in Chinese politics. As the leadership of the People's Republic shifts emphasis from revolutionary ideals to the more mundane business of governing and from a socialist planned economy to a market-based system, the question of how much of its communist heritage it should retain also arises. Elements of re-traditionalization co-exist with trends toward modernization and globalization. The intended audience for *China's Political System* is upper-level undergraduates in political science and history or simply interested persons who want to learn more about China. The author hopes that this will be an enjoyable experience; academic jargon has been minimized.

A brief summary of the different ways in which Chinese politics and history have been analyzed is followed by brief overviews of the traditional Chinese system, its breakdown, and the rise of communism, followed by a more detailed treatment of the characteristics and major events of the communist era. Because politics has permeated virtually every sphere of Chinese society since 1949, an analysis of how politics has impinged on these different spheres form the major building blocks of the text—economics; the legal system; the military; literature, art, and journalism; and so forth. Although the list of topics that might be considered is long, the academic semester is limited; hence, the number of chapters has been set at 15, or approximately one for each week of the average semester. Resisting the urge to be encyclopedic has meant not providing separate chapters for topics that some might prefer, such as ideology, human rights, and the role of women, which are treated as subthemes in other chapters. A concluding chapter integrates these different areas, assesses the successes and failures of the Chinese communist system, and sketches out possible scenarios of the future. Suggestions for additional reading—five, on the advice of my editor—appear at the end of each chapter. A list of websites for current information on China appears at the end of the volume.

The Fourth Edition has been updated to include developments through early 2003. The leadership and policy changes resulting from the 16th Party Congress and 10th National People's Congress are introduced, as are recent legal and economic developments and the results of the 2000 national census. There is expanded coverage of changing relationships among central, provincial, and local governments as well as the impact of enhanced citizen participation in the political process. More transnational comparisons have been provided, as has additional information on human rights, expanding military capabilities, foreign policy developments, and the treatment of ethnic minorities. Efforts have been made to tie China's economic, politial, and social currents more closely together.

The author very much appreciates the advice of many people, including Eric Stano, Allison McNamara, and Cristine Maisano of Longman, Ken Harrell of Shepherd Incorporated, and fellow China-watchers John Copper, Edward Dreyer, Bruce Gilley, Tom Gold, Baogang Guo, Bill Heaton, Michal Korzec, Cheng Li, Jim Nafziger, Stan Rosen, James Seymour, Tim Trampedach, Al Willner, and Suisheng Zhao. I have also greatly profited from the collective discussions of the Chinapol email group chaired by Rick Baum. Special thanks to Boris Pritcher of the University of Miami School of Business's computer laboratory for his expert assistance in the preparation of the volume's charts and tables.

June Teufel Dreyer
Coral Gables, Florida

About the Author

June Teufel Dreyer is Professor and Chair of the Department of Political Science at the University of Miami, Coral Gables, Florida, and a commissioner of the congressionally-established U.S.-China Economic and Security Review Commission. She is the author of *China's Forty Millions: Minority Nationalities and National Integration in the People's Republic of China* (Harvard University Press); and editor of *Chinese Defense and Foreign Policy* (Paragon House), and *Asian-Pacific Regional Defense* (Paragon House).

To the memory of my parents,
Anna Elizabeth Waldhauer
Paul Albert Teufel

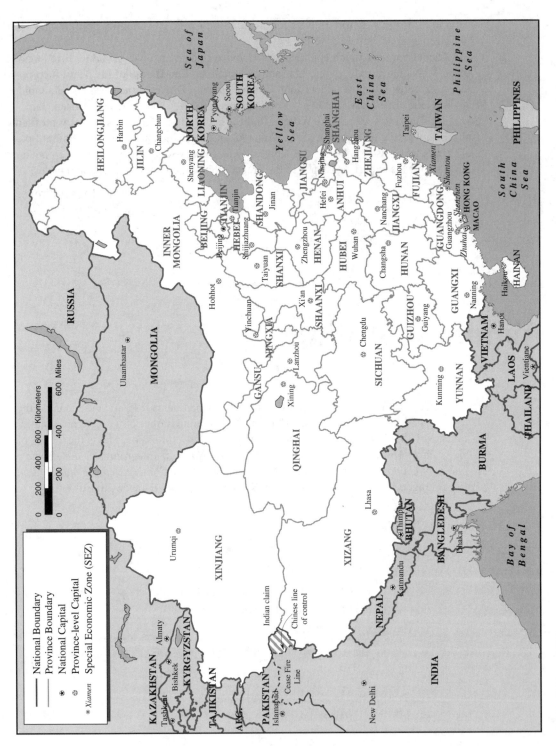

Political Map of China

CHAPTER

1 Introduction

Modernization and Chinese Civilization

Inheritors of the world's oldest continuous civilization, the Chinese can be justly proud of their achievements. Early creation of a written language, development of elaborate techniques of silk-weaving and wet rice cultivation, and invention of the compass and gunpowder are but a few of the more outstanding of these accomplishments. Thus the Chinese had good reasons for feeling secure in their image of themselves as the Middle Kingdom, *Zhongguo*, or that entity at the fringes of which the less favored groups of humanity existed.

The arrival, beginning in the sixteenth century, of Westerners who desired trade and wanted to spread their religious beliefs was therefore seen as an unwelcome intrusion into the peace and harmony of the empire. The Chinese government summarily rebuffed Western overtures, since it was obvious that ignorant barbarians could not contribute significantly to the well-being of the Celestial Empire and might even cause genuine harm. However, the Westerners were persistent. They defeated the Chinese with relative ease in a series of armed confrontations, beginning with the Opium War of 1839–1842.

This posed a problem for the heretofore self-confident Chinese elite. It is easy to reject another country's culture as inferior, there being no universally accepted criteria by which to measure aesthetic values. Military superiority, however, could be judged on the battlefield, and in this area the Middle Kingdom proved decidedly deficient. Continued military inferiority jeopardized the survival of both the empire and its esteemed culture. It therefore became a matter of great importance to the Chinese government to build the country's defenses to the point where Western intrusions need no longer be feared.

One solution that occurred to a number of people was that China should learn the barbarians' military secrets, in order to use them against the enemy. In addition to seeming perfectly reasonable, this solution could be (and was) rationalized by calling upon the authority of China's first and leading military strategist, Sun Zi. Writing in the fourth century B.C., Sun Zi had advised "Know yourself, know your enemy, win ten thousand battles." At the same time, however, this precept raised a fundamental dilemma in the minds of many of the intelligentsia: Could one sustain the belief in the superiority of one's own civilization while borrowing from another's? If so, how much could be borrowed before one lost one's own culture? What actually was the essence of what one might call Chineseness? And, faced with a stark choice of saving one's culture at the risk of sacrificing the empire to the barbarians or sacrificing one's culture in order to save the empire from the barbarians, what should the answer be?

These and other related questions were heatedly debated by some of China's most brilliant minds. Initially, most of them deemed it acceptable to borrow military techniques only. This type of imitation was not unprecedented: Several times in the past the Chinese had copied barbarian ways of war. The idea of fighting from horseback, as opposed to using horse-drawn chariots, had come from China's nomadic neighbors to the north. At a somewhat later date the stirrup, which enabled mounted warriors to shoot backward, was adopted from Turkic invaders. Nevertheless, even in this area, borrowing from foreigners had been quite limited.

Western military techniques were, however, more elaborate. Their acquisition required, among other things, the creation of factories, foundries, and a system of raw-material procurement on a much larger scale than had ever been attempted before. The desirability of adopting these, too, was eventually rationalized, as epitomized by the late-nineteenth-century slogan "Chinese learning for the essence [*ti*]; Western learning for practical use [*yong*]." Unfortunately, certain difficulties emerged in putting this *ti-yong* ideology into practice. For example, the establishment of the factory system entailed fundamental changes in social organization. Its needs for a mobile labor force, specialized production, and the like necessitated major modifications in the Confucian family system, the educational curriculum, and many other areas. Western learning, it was later discovered, had an essence of its own.

By the end of the nineteenth century, a new generation began to reject many aspects of the Confucian tradition that most earlier Chinese thinkers had considered the essence of their civilization. Sun Yat-sen, an iconoclast, a Christian, and a medical doctor, sought to strengthen and modernize China in ways he considered compatible with the characteristics of the culture. The philosophy (or, more properly, ideology) Sun attempted to substitute for Confucianism was the Three Principles of the People: People's Nationalism, People's Democracy, and People's Livelihood. He explicitly stated that his inspiration had been Abraham Lincoln's government "of the people, by the people, and for the people."

The imperial government was overthrown in 1911, a victim of its own ineptitude as well as of the revolutionaries' efforts. However, Sun died before the movement he founded, which came to be known as the Kuomintang (KMT, or Chinese Nationalist Party), could come to power. His successor as head of the KMT, Chiang Kai-shek, was able to wrest control of the central government from a variety of warlords and almost immediately restored large elements of Confucianism to official ideology. Withal, China remained poor and weak in relation to the Western powers and Japan. Within a few decades the KMT government fell, due to a combination of its internal weaknesses, a bloody and draining war with Japan, and a communist insurgency.

One reason a number of Chinese intellectuals found communism appealing as a solution to their country's problems is that it purported to be a scientific, culturally neutral process that would occur naturally in the course of historical development. In other words, adopting communism did not have to be understood as borrowing something from the West. That its creator, Karl Marx, was very definitely a Westerner, who drew most of his examples from the Western experience and in fact believed that history had "gone to sleep" in Asia, was conveniently overlooked. To these intellectuals, the Bolsheviks' seizure of power in Russia indicated that communism might be made relevant to China as well. The Bolsheviks' success had refuted Marx's contention that the communist revolution would occur first in a highly industrialized society; perhaps, then, it could happen in China as well. Even so, to apply an ideology based on an appeal to industrial workers to an overwhelmingly peasant-based society like China's necessitated a fundamental reworking of Marxism.

Mao Zedong was well aware that even a theory that purported to be culturally neutral must come to terms with the culture in which it operated. As early as 1938 he declared

> A communist is a Marxist internationalist, but Marxism must take on a national form before it can be applied. There is no such thing as abstract Marxism, but only concrete Marxism. What we call concrete Marxism is Marxism that has taken on a national form, that is, Marxism applied to the concrete struggle in the concrete conditions prevailing in China and not Marxism absolutely used.[1]

Later Mao declared that it was necessary to "make the past serve the present and foreign things serve China."[2]

The way in which Mao sought to deal with the Chinese cultural context involved a bitter attack against *official*, or high, culture and a glorification of the culture of the *masses*, or low culture. The term for official, *guan*, became one of opprobrium; the bureaucrats of the People's Republic are called by a different name: *ganbu*, or cadres. History was revised to emphasize the contributions of ordinary folk. Thus a placard on the Ming tombs near Beijing advises just how many of the masses toiled in their construction rather than dwelling on the grandeur of the emperors who are buried there. And folk art, such as paper-cutting, was praised and encouraged, while art forms associated with the upper classes, such as richly embroidered silks and delicate paintings on gilt, were criticized. However, the distinction between high and low cultures is not clear-cut, and the upper classes certainly held no monopoly on backward thoughts and practices. Hence, choosing which items from China's past to serve China's present was not an easy task. There were bitter disagreements on which elements to keep and which to discard, and several changes in the official party attitude.

As for making foreign things serve China, Marx provided little help. He was primarily a theorizer and had few concrete suggestions on how to make his theories operational in the day-to-day administration of a state. For guidance here, Chinese communists quite naturally looked to the example of the first and, for several decades only, communist state, the now-defunct USSR. What they received were Leninist and Stalinist interpretations of Marx that had been influenced both by the worldviews of the Soviet leaders and by their perceptions of the needs of the Soviet Union. Even in the early years of the People's Republic of China (PRC), Mao Zedong and other leaders cautioned against blindly copying the experience of the USSR and urged adapting the Soviet experience to Chinese reality. But, since the Soviet Union was the PRC's only important ally and aid-donor in these early years, it was almost inevitable that the Soviet model would be closely imitated.

A realization of the limitations that the experience of the relatively sparsely populated and capital-intensive USSR would have for the densely populated and labor-intensive PRC was an important reason for the Great Leap Forward of 1958. This daring socioeconomic break with the Soviet model attempted to modernize the PRC by making use of China's advantages (such as its abundant labor power) and certain traditional techniques (such as herbal remedies and acupunctural medicinal approaches). The culture of the masses was lauded to a much greater degree, with some elements of what had been regarded as acceptable heirlooms from the past summarily discarded. The Great Leap Forward's message was radically egalitarian. It tried to implement Marx's definition of communism, "from each according to his ability, to each according to his need." Lacking incentives to work hard, too many people discovered ways to work less. For these and other reasons, production levels fell and, almost immediately, the country was plunged into yet deeper poverty and weakness. Production fell to levels that prevailed during the early years of the communist government, but with a substantially larger number of people among whom to divide what was produced. Millions died of hunger or malnutrition-related diseases. This particular effort to implement a Chinese version of modernity had failed disastrously.

By 1962, after many of the Great Leap Forward's more ill-advised measures had been reversed or modified, the PRC regained its pre–Great Leap Forward production levels. Returning along with recuperating production levels were some of the phenomena that had induced Mao to begin the Great Leap Forward: greater disparities in income levels,[3] officials using their positions for financial gain, marriages contracted for economic reasons, traditional superstitious practices, and gambling. The latter three, though definitely part of China's folk culture, were clearly not acceptable in making the past serve the present.

In 1966 Mao unleashed the Great Proletarian Cultural Revolution, another massive effort to purge the country of Soviet, other Western, *and* traditional influences. In its zeal to purify the country of both foreign and decadent old influences, the Cultural Revolution radicals had to make some odd compromises. For example, totally reworking Chinese opera to remove decadent themes, including banning traditional musical instruments, meant performing it to a piano accompaniment. On being questioned as to how this fit in with purging culture of decadent Western elements, Madame Mao replied, "We have liberated the piano."

The Cultural Revolution's message was, like that of the Great Leap Forward, egalitarian and strongly antihierarchical, but to an even greater degree. Those who dressed better or ate better than others were believed to have been affected by Western bourgeois liberal or Soviet revisionist poison. A large number of people became the targets of brutal attack. Normal work activities were seriously disrupted in some areas, though the overall effect on production was not nearly as much as during the Great Leap Forward. Social and political problems were, however, far greater. Although the violence of the Cultural Revolution had abated by late 1968, many of its policies remained for many years thereafter.

Mao's death in 1976 led indirectly to Deng Xiaoping's accession to power and to the repudiation of many of Mao's more radical policies. Deng's "second-generation leadership" abandoned Mao's emphasis on class struggle and social transformation in favor of creating prosperity for society as a whole. His reputation as an anti-ideological pragmatist had been the cause of Deng's being purged during the Cultural Revolution. He immediately announced that his priority was to modernize China and that his method would be to proceed on the basis of "seeking truth from facts." By modernization Deng appeared primarily to mean industrialization and the attainment of higher living standards for the population. While explicitly acknowledging the need for greater personal freedom and pluralism in the decision-making process, Deng appeared to regard these as necessary in order to give people incentive to work harder rather than because he believed in freedom as a value in itself. Similarly, Deng announced that he would support the introduction of the rule of law, which is normally considered another concomitant of democratization in the West. But his rationale was less civil-libertarian than because he believed that a legal system was necessary to resolve disputes, both between people and among businesses, before the wheels of production could hum smoothly. Modernization was not to be construed as slavish copying of the capitalist states, but as a process of building "socialism with Chinese characteristics."

No precise definition of socialism with Chinese characteristics has ever been given. While stating that he had no intention of abandoning socialism, Deng was explicit that it was acceptable to be rich, as long as one became rich through one's own diligence and hard work rather than by inheriting wealth or getting it through speculative activities or personal connections. Moreover, he added, it was not necessary for everyone to become rich at the same time. It is clear that Deng, like so many of his country's previous leaders during the past century and a half, was in search of wealth and power—a common slogan of nineteenth-century reformers—for his country: to make China equal or superior to the Western states in a manner compatible with Chinese reality. Unlike the nineteenth-century reformers, Deng did not proclaim the necessity to select the best from East and West. But his policies, which included that of the Open Door to the West, encompassed importing advanced scientific and technical equipment, and sending Chinese students abroad to acquire the ability to produce and improve upon this equipment. Though Deng's final goal of a prosperous, economically modernized China was not unlike that of Mao, the two men differed in important ways. Faced with making a choice between equality and prosperity, Mao had a tendency to favor equality, and Deng prosperity.

Under Deng, the profit motive was restored. Factories were allowed to retain their earnings beyond a certain amount to be paid to the central government, and peasants were free to sell on the free market whatever they raised beyond a fixed quota to be delivered to the government. Given these opportunities, a number of people prospered to a degree that would have been unthinkable only a few years before. A wider variety of consumer goods appeared in the stores and the country's gross national product began a period of rapid growth. At the same time, however, other people were left behind. Sometimes this was because they were inept farmers or indifferent workers. Often, unfortunately, they were not able to take advantage of the new opportunities due to factors beyond their control. Farmers who held poorer land, or who could not procure adequate supplies of seed and fertilizer, might actually become poorer regardless of how hard they worked. The state's investment policies favored coastal areas, on the very sound assumption that those were the places that would most readily produce a quick return on investment capital. But at the same time, these policies discriminated against residents of the PRC's vast and more needy hinterland.

The new policies also generated inflationary pressures, to the detriment of those who lived on fixed incomes. These included the large number of state employees as well as students and the elderly. While businesspeople and farmers could raise prices to keep up with the rising cost of living, these groups could not. Those who prospered under the new system were the envy of those who did not, and jealousy—the red-eye disease, as Chinese call it—became more prominent. Deng had deemed it acceptable for some to become rich before others, but he had also tacitly sanctioned becoming poorer. In order to increase the

PRC's efficiency and prosperity as a whole, unprofitable factories and businesses were to be allowed to go bankrupt. The system of guaranteed employment could no longer be sustained, he declared. "The iron rice bowl" was to be broken. Understandably, people worried about the disappearance of their safety net.

These concerns were expressed privately and hesitantly at first. As the decade wore on, citizens began to take advantage of the less stringent controls over freedom of expression that Deng considered necessary to provide economic incentives. Letters to the editors of newspapers, journal articles, and even protest marches became more common. Concerned with rising levels of civil disorder, Deng seemed to back away from earlier promises of liberalization, and advanced the theory of "neoauthoritarianism," meaning that the PRC needed firm guidance from above in order to continue its development. Partially obscured by the shock and horror of the Chinese government's brutal suppression of the demonstrations of 1989 was the message that large numbers of the PRC's people were dissatisfied with important elements of Deng's plan to build socialism with Chinese characteristics. There is widespread agreement about what is wrong with the present model but little consensus on what to replace it with.

After the demonstrations of the spring of 1989, the government made a number of adjustments to economic policy to try to deal with the people's grievances, while at the same time restricting their ability to express their concerns. It also blamed the demonstrations on a small handful of counterrevolutionaries who had been misled by foreign bourgeois liberalism. This was followed by a major propaganda effort to convince people that such Western concepts as privatization of enterprises and property, the separation of powers, and the theory of checks and balances were inappropriate to China. A number of Chinese disagree, feeling that only when China adopts such concepts will it be able to become a strong and prosperous power. Although much about China has changed in the past 150 years, these debates are remarkably similar in tone and substance to those of the nineteenth century. The *ti-yong* argument was again advanced: One cannot have Western-style economic development (the practical manifestations) without the underlying freedoms (the essence) that make economic development possible.

However, coexisting with desires for more freedom were profound feelings of uneasiness over the culture of materialism that Western capitalism was believed to have brought with it. Some people turned to religion, including faiths of Western origin, for solace. Others looked back into the Chinese past for antidotes. There was renewed interest in both Buddhism and Confucianism as alternatives to Western commercialism. Having observed the deficiencies of Marxism as the motivating force for modernization, some intellectuals began to search the past for ways to insert a uniquely Chinese element into the Chinese revolution. As these developments were taking place, Jiang Zemin chose to press forward with economic reforms and a modest increase in personal freedoms. For a variety of reasons, some of which were international and beyond Jiang's control, these reforms proved difficult to implement. A dissonant chorus of advice, ranging from those nostalgic for Maoism to advocates of popular direct elections, was emboldened by economic difficulties. The search for a formula that will permit the modernization of the PRC in a manner compatible with Chinese reality continues.

This book examines efforts to achieve modernization in the Chinese context. There are, to be sure, a variety of different opinions on what constitutes modernity. Several of these theories of modernization, and their implications for the Chinese case, are discussed in some detail in subsequent chapters. Briefly, some individuals concentrate on the end goals of modernization, such as control over destiny, individual autonomy, and the acquisition of material goods. Others, including all of the leaders of the PRC so far, would define modernization more narrowly, in terms of increased levels of industrialization and higher living standards. Yet a third group favors a broader definition, including additional factors such as the commercialization of agriculture, increased urbanization, the spread of mass literacy and improved education, the development of mass communication, and promotion based on merit. As people acquire a new sense of being able to influence their own destinies they will demand a larger share of political power, and the modernized system will accommodate these demands. This author uses the broader definition, believing that in practice it is extremely difficult to achieve industrialization and higher living standards in the absence of commercialized agriculture, urbanization, mass literacy, mass communications, and a merit system. Certainly the experience of China so far seems to bear this out.

Theories of Analysis of Chinese Politics

In recent years, far more sources of information have become available to foreign analysts. Even so, there is much we do not know. The restricted nature of the dissemination of information in the People's Republic of China has caused problems for the analysis of its political decisionmaking. Typically, when examining political systems analysts use a model that describes the society to be examined as an *environment*. Individuals resident therein are influenced by the environment in various ways and respond to it accordingly. They may have concerns or grievances that they wish to be addressed. An effective way to do this is to aggregate these demands through the formation of interest groups. These demands are termed *inputs* and are presented to the government, which has the job of *conversion* of the demands into *outputs*, or decisions. The legislature writes laws, the executive carries them out, and the judiciary settles disputes arising in connection with the impact of the laws on those affected. These outputs then affect the environment through the *feedback loop*. Here they may give rise to another set of inputs. For example, in the early 1990s, many people in the United States became concerned with the cost of medical care for the elderly. Interest groups such as the Gray Panthers lobbied, or brought inputs, to the legislature, which converted the demands into a new health care bill for the elderly. However, many elderly people were dissatisfied with the way in which the burden of paying for these medical costs was allocated. The feedback of this dissatisfaction resulted in the aggregation of new demands on government, and the law was rescinded.

Trying to apply this scheme of analysis to Chinese politics, yields very unsatisfactory results, particularly during the Maoist era. To start with, it is difficult to identify the interest groups. One may assume that they are similar to those in societies we are more familiar with: workers, farmers, doctors, the elderly, minority groups, and so forth. Certainly there exist within the PRC what the Chinese communist government calls *mass organizations*. Groups such as women, workers, peasants, writers, and doctors each have their own mass organization. But these organizations are very tightly controlled by the government specifically so that they support the agenda developed by the Chinese Communist Party

(CCP) rather than articulating demands that would benefit their own memberships. The Chinese Medical Association does not demand that health care fees be raised, and Chinese trade unions will urge their members to complete this year's production quota quickly rather than call for shorter working hours or better pension plans. Hence these organizations have not functioned very well as interest groups.

Similar difficulties arise in applying other parts of the model described above. The Chinese party and government structures can be described in detail (and are, in Chapter 5). But how decisions are made remains a mystery. Politburo meetings are not televised except on ceremonial occasions, and politburo members do not give interviews about the differences of opinion that arise in their discussions. The memoirs of elderly or deceased leaders are sometimes published but have a suspiciously unreal tone and scrupulously follow the current party line, no matter what period in the past the writer is discussing. Who, then, decides how much money and attention shall be allocated in what amounts to which sectors of the society? In the absence of more specific information, foreign analysts sometimes resort to ambiguities such as "the party has decided." But the CCP is a large and unwieldy organization with 65 million members, so it is unlikely that the party as such really decides anything. Other analysts write as if the country's leader makes all the decisions: "Jiang Zemin has revamped the economic system. . . ." or "Hu Jintao has ruled that. . . ." The PRC is a huge country, with many problems calling for resolution each day. No one person can actually make all these decisions. *The party* and *Hu* are used here as shorthand: meaningful in the general sense, but potentially misleading unless one realizes that there is a great deal more to the decision-making process than embodied in these names alone.

Because we do not know a great deal about the internal workings of Chinese politics, people have been obliged to "read the tea leaves"—make educated guesses on the basis of the facts available to them. Particularly in the early years of the communist regime, when hard facts were much more scarce than they are at present, analysts resorted to such tactics as looking at photographs of the National Day parade and other ceremonial occasions to see who stood next to whom, and who was missing. Sometimes this indicated that someone had fallen out of favor (he was standing farther from the center of the leadership group than before) or been purged (he was not present on the parade's reviewing stand at all). Differences of opinion often arose on what one might conclude from this. If, for example, several people who were associated with leftist causes were missing for a long period of time, analysts expected that to be correlated with the implementation of moderate policies in the country.

This, however, would be unusual. More typical was that *one* person China-watchers *thought* was associated with a particular policy would not be seen in public for perhaps a month or two. One might conclude that he had been purged. On the other hand, and given the advanced ages of many leaders in the PRC, it was at least as plausible to assume that he died of natural causes. This, too, had its pitfalls, since the dearly departed might suddenly reappear in apparent good health. He or she may have been recuperating from a non-life-threatening disease, escaping Beijing's less-than-salubrious climate for a while, or taking a discreet investigation tour of the provinces. Sometimes analysts were able to corroborate their hunches with gossip from within China, but even here they remained on shaky ground. Like many countries in which the citizens do not trust their news media, the PRC has a lively and vivid gossip network. Frequently, however, it turns out to be wrong:

The then-octogenerian Deng Xiaoping was unreliably reported to be dead at least three times in the 1980s and one time to have been the victim of a bloodless coup d'état by the military organization he commanded. He died in 1997, of natural causes. Dating from the time that Deng allowed greater access between China and the outside world, more sources began to become available. Some foreigners were, and are, granted access to Chinese archives and other data. Journalists and scholars have been able to establish contacts with knowledgeable individuals who are willing to share their opiinions. The Chinese press itself now expresses diverse opinions, albeit carefully and at risk of official sanctions.

Both in the past when data were scarce and in the present era of many sources, there have been a variety of different views about the PRC. When people start out with different basic assumptions, no matter how impeccable their processes of reasoning and how clear the facts, they will end with different conclusions. These differing basic assumptions account for many of the disagreements among China-watchers.[4] In addition, analysts differ in the particular angle from which they approach Chinese politics—economic development, for example, being more important to some and human rights considerations to others. Essentially, there have been three periods in the analysis of PRC politics. The first set of theories was fostered in the earliest years of the communist government; the second, by the events of the Cultural Revolution; and the third by Deng Xiaoping's reforms.

Theoretical Analysis in the Early Years of the PRC

Initially, the leading paradigm for the analysis of Chinese politics was the totalitarian model.[5] A one-party (the CCP) state headed by a strong leader (Mao) imposes its ideology (communism) on the citizenry, which owes total and unswerving loyalty to it. Organizations such as family, professional group, or religion, which might perform a mediative role between the citizen and the state are weakened, co-opted, or destroyed. The motivation behind this is to atomize the individual: to isolate her or him from any influence except that of the ruling party and its ideology.

Decisions were seen as made consensually within a basically harmonious party elite dominated by Mao. Opinion groups might exist within the elite, but they were believed to shift in response to specific problems and to have no motivating force behind them. A variant on this view, the *generational school*[6] argued that there was a common generational viewpoint based on shared personal and political experiences. *Generation* was defined not as chronological age but in terms of the year in which an individual joined the communist party. Adherents to this line of analysis divided the early history of the CCP into twelve periods, each characterized by a crisis—such as a KMT attempt at exterminating the CCP or the outbreak of war with Japan. Those who joined the party at such a time were assumed to be responding to the crisis, which would therefore predispose them to certain political outlooks. By seeing who joined the party during which period and checking this list against which generations hold which levels of positions in the leadership hierarchy, one might be able to predict policy interests and predispositions.

For example, the first two generations to have joined the communist party were almost all born and raised in the central Yangtze Valley provinces, came from peasant backgrounds, had very little formal education, and had not traveled much outside China. Hence they were assumed to have xenophobic tendencies: suspicious of foreign powers, and probably against close relations with them, no matter how benign their intentions toward China. The political focus of these generations was likely to be local or regional. Militarily, they would favor defending China by means of small-unit, irregular tactics such as those provided by guerrillas and local militias.

By contrast, the third and fourth generations entered the party at a time of increasing specialization and division of labor between the party and the army, and within the party and army themselves. After November 1931, the party had a special school to train military officers. It also began to put more emphasis on technology and less on guerrilla tactics. The people who joined the CCP during this period came from a larger number of geographical areas than did the first two generations. They tended to be better educated and were more likely to have traveled outside China. Adherents of the generational school of analysis saw them as more oriented to the national scene than to local areas. They were likely to be less suspicious of people who are not from their own native place, more cosmopolitan, and more open to alliances with other countries. Thus, a shift from a leadership composed mainly of the first two generations to a leadership that is predominantly from the third and fourth generations ought to correlate with greater emphasis on professional specialization and more internationalist policies. Those who entered the CCP at the time of close relations between the PRC and the USSR in the 1950s, and who studied there, could be assumed to be pro-Soviet in their outlook. An important rationale for offering Chinese students educational opportunities in the United States has been that they will return to the PRC with a good impression of the United States, which will aid Sino-American relations someday when these young people have become leaders of their country.

In a general sense, there was a good deal to recommend this line of analysis. The first two generations do seem to have been more inward-looking than the second two, although it might be argued that there were few alternatives available, given the fact that it was necessary to mobilize members—a local/regional task rather than an international one—during the early days of the party's existence. Later, the party's championing the idea of resistance to Japan became a useful technique for drawing supporters. This could be construed as seizing an opportunity once it became available rather than creating a mind-set conditioned by when one joined the CCP.

Also, while some important members of the first-generation CCP ruling elite did come across as xenophobic and suspicious of foreigners, others did not. Mao, poorly educated, from the central Yangtze Valley, and not well traveled, has indeed been portrayed as distrustful of the outside world and preoccupied with China's domestic concerns. But this did not preclude him from concluding an alliance with the Soviet Union in 1950 or from approaching the United States at the end of the 1960s. Again, circumstances rather than a mind-set seem to have been operative. It should also not be forgotten that the other towering figure of the first generation, Zhou Enlai, was a consummate cosmopolitan. Since many people will belong to each generation, there will not be unanimity among them. A persistent minority can sometimes change the common viewpoint of the majority, and changing circumstances can alter political perceptions as well. Former Chinese premier Li Peng, who studied for several years in the USSR, can be seen as pro-Russian in some ways. However, it is not necessarily the case that study in a given country will create warm feelings about it: One might have come away from the Soviet Union having made some close friends there, but at the same time convinced from firsthand observation that the country's political and economic systems were not worth emulating. Hence, analytical schemes that depend on knowing the percentages of high-ranking positions held by a given generational group can be misleading.

A generational form of analysis is still applied, but in this latter-day view, it refers to the period during which a particular leadership group holds power. Hence, the elite during the Mao years is considered the first generation and, when Deng was paramount leader, the second generation. Jiang Zemin and his cohort constituted the third generation, and Hu Jintao, the fourth. Although it is acknowledged that there may be differences of opinion among them, a common mind-set is still assumed. For example, foreign commentary on the leadership that emerged after the 1989 Tiananmen incident dwelt on the officially released picture of eight octogenarians who were assumed to have similar views on the need to suppress dissent and rein in the economy. It predicted that not until these "eight immortals" passed from the scene could meaningful political change be expected. Although members of the group did pass away, the hoped-for political changes did not materialize. Currently, some analysts hypothesize, such change will occur when the fifth generation, better educated and with more exposure to the outside world than their predecessors, takes charge.

Yet another theory of analysis, the *strategic interaction school* saw the crucial issue motivating Chinese politics as the PRC's struggle for great-power status. Strategic interaction analysts believed in the importance for the present day of China's humiliation in the nineteenth century by foreign powers, including the so-called unequal treaties that were forced on it and the territorial concessions China was forced to make. Hence—and this represents a rather large assumption—China's main goal at present is to erase, or at least compensate for, that memory. China's behavior can be explained in terms of trying to gain the respect, even the fearful respect, of the great powers.

Although this school starts from a historically conditioned premise, the humiliations of the nineteenth century, specific cultural–historical factors actually play very little part in its analytical scheme. It assumes that China is a rational international actor, capable of making reasonable judgments about goals and the options and costs associated with those goals. China is also seen as having broad geographical constraints from which no government—be it communist, capitalist, or vegetarian in ideology—can escape. The country is, quite simply, viewed as aiming to attain the maximum political–military power status at least cost. Implicitly, an important task of analysis for this school is identifying China's major enemy at a given time. China is generally viewed as dealing with at least four other major power blocs: the United States, the Soviet Union (now the former Soviet Union or FSU), Japan, and Western Europe.

Much of this scheme of analysis is unobjectionable. Many of the founding members of the CCP did feel keenly the humiliations visited on their ancestral land by foreign powers, and one of their motivations was to build a China capable of withstanding external pressures. This has not been completely forgotten. A series of meetings commemorating the 150th anniversary of the Opium War were held (not coincidentally, one suspects) on the first anniversary of the Tiananmen incident. Speakers used the occasion to denounce Western imperialism and blame China's humiliation on the fact that the communist party had not yet been founded. A politburo member opined that the significance of the Opium War was that it showed that opposing imperialism and loving one's country did not preclude learning from foreign countries things that are useful for China.[7]

However, there are problems in applying the strategic interaction scheme to the analysis of Chinese politics. One is that it provides no role for ideology and culture. Any government is assumed to act the same, weighing the options presented by its territorial imperatives in a cold, calculating manner in order to attain success in its international relations. That culture and ideology may shape the government's perception of what might be a sensible response to an event is not taken into account. For example, culturally conditioned concerns with possible loss of face might motivate the Chinese government to react in a manner that would strike the Finnish or Peruvian government as illogical.

Another conceptual problem with the strategic interaction school is that it assumes that the country possesses what one might call a corporate personality. It may be convenient to say that "China" takes a certain action or feels a certain way, but to do so risks creating the image of a monolithic entity, neglecting the possibility that there are groups of Chinese who prefer one policy option and others who favor another. For example, there is considerable evidence that Mao Zedong met substantial resistance to his late-1960s plan for rapprochement with the United States. A number of high-ranking officials were adamantly opposed to coming to terms with capitalism, arguing that the Soviet Union, for all its faults, was at least a socialist state and was therefore preferable to the United States as a strategic partner. Were American policymakers to assume, consonant with the strategic interaction analysis, that there was a corporate Chinese personality that was firmly in favor of leaning toward the United States, they might be seriously misled.

A third criticism of the strategic interaction school is that it gives too much weight to foreign policy. The average Chinese, like her counterpart elsewhere in the world, is apt to be more concerned with wages, health care, and the children's educational opportunities than whether her country receives proper respect within the United Nations. And the Chinese leadership has a great many domestic problems to cope with that preclude its dealing exclusively, or even predominantly, with foreign policy matters.

In sum, the Chinese elite continues to be concerned with maintaining and enhancing what they consider to be their nation's rightful place in the world. This was seen in the outrage expressed when Beijing was not chosen as the site of the year 2000 Olympic games, and in the importance the government placed on China becoming a founding member of the World Trade Organization. (Beijing was later chosen to host the 2008 games, and the PRC entered the World Trade Organization in 2002.) Old age has removed the generation that felt most keenly the humiliations visited on their country by external powers, and they have already succeeded in winning for China the respect of those powers. Nonetheless, party and government have found that reminders of China's "century of shame" can evoke powerful patriotic emotions among the population when it wishes them to back a strong foreign policy stand.

Another commonly heard theory during this period, which continues to have adherents today, might be called the *China-is-China-is-China school*. It assumes that communist China's economic landscape, psychological mind-set, and bureaucratic processes are basically the same as those of imperial China. The paramount leader is similar to the emperor in what he may or may not do: unlimited in many ways, but also constrained by his fellow old revolutionaries or, later, his fellow politburo standing committee members, who perform the function of nobles; his wife (who may have a political agenda of her own); and the bureaucracy, which is seen as behaving much like the mandarinate that preceded it. Parallels are found between Confucianism and communism, although adherents to the China-is-China-is-China school generally argue that ideology is of secondary importance: All Chinese governments will eventually act in a similar fashion because of the force of tradition and the necessity to deal with a large population, scarce arable land, and water-control problems.

There is a good deal to recommend this line of analysis. Mind-sets developed over centuries are not erased by a revolution, and there are relatively few ways in which to allocate modest amounts of cultivable land to an enormous population in a manner that they will be comfortable with. Mao's personal physician reported that Mao read Chinese history books rather than Marx when preparing strategies.[8] He referred to his time with the chairman as "life in Mao's imperial court,[9] noting that Mao occasionally even referred to himself as the emperor.[10] In planning to seize power after her husband's death, Mao's wife consciously saw herself as a latter-day Wu Zetian, China's only female empress, even to the extent of ordering copies of Wu's gowns for herself.[11]

Chinese citizens who are not members of the elite are also prone to finding parallels with the past. Even though ordinary folk knew nothing of Madame Mao's gown-ordering, they frequently compared her to ambitious empresses of the past; after she was purged, cartoons regularly depicted her in the embroidered gowns, elaborate hairstyles, and long fingernails of deceased royalty. Deng Xiaoping, however, was less frequently referred to as emperor and even then, it would appear, the term was intended metaphorically rather than literally. Jiang Zemin and Hu Jintao are not seen in imperial terms at all.

As for the policies thus engendered, it is unfortunately not always possible to clearly distinguish the genesis of a policy as tradition versus communist ideology. For example, the prosperity and well-being of the common people were important to both Confucius and Karl Marx. The problem with the China-is-China-is-China school is that although there *are* parallels between imperial and contemporary China, they *are* incomplete. Accepted too rigidly, these parallels are misleading. In addition to the commonalities between Confucius and Marx, there are also significant differences. For Confucius, the peasant was the backbone of the empire; Marx spoke of "rural idiocy." Confucian philosophy aimed at the attainment of a Great Harmony, to be achieved by properly ordering relationships, with the emperor at the pinnacle of a gradually descending hierarchy, each member of which was to set an example for those below. Marx championed egalitarianism.

Confucius was unconcerned with the ownership of the means of production or the idea of progress. For Marx, in contrast, ownership of the means of production is the key to social, political, and economic dominance. His Great Harmony is to be achieved through violent revolution from below. In yet another contrast between traditional and modern-day China, the PRC leadership accepts the concept of national sovereignty. Failure to take these important differences between past and present China into consideration will limit the usefulness of one's analysis.

Theories Engendered by the Cultural Revolution

The view of a basically harmonious elite group implicit in the above models was shaken by the outbreak of the Cultural Revolution in the mid-1960s. As leaders once believed to be united in the pursuit of a strong communist state began to battle each other both verbally and physically, foreign analysts quickly reassessed their theories. *Factional models* gained credence. In Andrew Nathan's classic statement of this view,[12] factions are based on "clientelist ties." These are cultivated essentially through the constant exchange of goods and favors and result in relationships that involve unwritten but nonetheless well-understood rights and obligations among faction members.

Factions are assumed to be incapable of building sufficient power to rid the political system of rival factions, and therefore to have little incentive to try to do so. The most important concern of a faction is to protect its own base of power while opposing accretions of power by any other faction. Since today's enemy may have to be tomorrow's ally, factional alliances cannot remain stable. It is therefore impossible for factions to make ideological agreement a primary condition for alliance with other factions. There is an ongoing struggle for office and influence: In order to stay in the game, factions must often cooperate with those with whom they have recently disagreed.

Nathan believes that pre–Cultural Revolution China did approximate the factional model, though admitting that lack of data makes it impossible to identify the faction leaders. He sees Mao Zedong's decision to launch the Cultural Revolution as breaking the rules of factionalism: By calling on students—the so-called Red Guards—to destroy the other factions, Mao was mobilizing new sources of power from outside the elite. The rest of the factional elite tried to resist Mao's extra-party offensive, demobilize the Red Guards, and restore the factional conflict system of the first 15 years of the regime. In essence, they succeeded. After the defeat of the fourth mobilization of the Red Guards in September 1967, there was no longer any hope of using the Guards to purge the party center of factionalism.

Nathan critiques his own model, pointing out that it simplifies by considering only one of many constraints that mold behavior: the organizational. Ideological and cultural constraints are ignored. Insufficient data make it impossible to decisively accept or reject the model even within the confines of the organizational sphere. Also, the model does not explain why people adopt a factional framework, how long they will adhere to it, or why they persist in disagreeing with one another at all.

A variation on Nathan's theory, the *central-regional school* also accents personal affiliations and loyalty in its analysis of Chinese politics. Adherents point out that, despite the unifying force of the imperial institution and an elaborately conceived hierarchy of central government, China has nonetheless had a long history of localism. The capital city was far away, communications were poor, and the imperial bureaucracy was thinly spread. The cultural milieu that one related to has typically not been China as a whole but rather one's village, clan, and province, in descending order of importance. As habitués of Chinese restaurants already know, the various Chinese provinces have distinctive styles of preparing food. They also have very different artistic styles and musical traditions. Different dialects may actually be mutually unintelligible, even where the speakers live in close proximity to one another. The *minnan* and *minbei* tongues of Fujian province are probably the most striking example of this.

Chinese culture also includes a strong element of personal loyalty. One relates to one's superior on grounds of personal feelings, rather than obeying because of the position that he or she holds. In turn, he or she takes care of you in terms of security and serves as a mentor in more than career terms. Superiors may, for example, help subordinates to find a spouse or perform intermediary functions to settle a dispute having nothing to do with the workplace.

Analysts who favor the central-regional school often see the Chinese communist military, the People's Liberation Army (PLA), as the framework within which these loyalties have developed. In the process of coming to power, the Chinese communists developed five so-called field armies. Since the CCP's road to power was through the rural hinterland, and since Japanese and Kuomintang armies occupied a number of contiguous areas, communication among the different field armies was sporadic. Hence, they developed essentially independently of each other, with relatively little interaction. There were relatively few transfers of people from one field army to another.

For several years after the communist victory in 1949, China was divided into six regions for administrative purposes. In each of these, a given field army predominated (one of the field armies controlled more than one region). When transfers occurred, people often went in groups, serving as "hostages" or "ambassadors" from one field-army system to another. In other words, the previously existing loyalty network was maintained. The field-army hypothesis sees political behavior in China as a balance-of-power process involving five major interest groups, the field armies, with the central elite acting essentially as a power broker.

This theory, too, seems to have some validity in explaining past political behavior. Lin Biao's rise to power at the time of the Cultural Revolution was accompanied by the promotions of a number of members of his Fourth Field Army and far fewer promotions than fairness would seem to demand for members of other field armies. After Lin's fall from power, many of those who had risen with him were purged, with a larger number of promotions for those from other field armies. The balance of power among the field armies that had existed prior to the Cultural Revolution was essentially re-created after Lin's death in 1971. Central-regional theorists interpret these events as the Fourth Field Army trying to destroy the balance of power and dominate the military-political hierarchy. Other field armies resisted what they perceived as an attack on their territories, combining to force Lin out and reestablish the balance of power.

However, the statistical evidence bolstering the field-army interpretation is not as clear-cut as it might initially appear. First of all, we simply do not know the field-army affiliation of a large number of PLA commanders and commissars. Second, there is a problem with how to factor in the approximately 15 percent of those people of the total whose field-army affiliation we know who have served in more than one field army. Third, the occasional transfers of officers from one field army into the bailiwicks of others can be as easily explained on the basis of random selection processes as by a conscious effort to achieve a balance of power among the military regions.

Although a purge of high-ranking Fourth Field Army officers did occur after the fall of Lin Biao, a number of Fourth Field Army people retained their important posts. And several of those purged with Lin were from other field armies. The fact that the dismissals began at the top suggests that Mao and other leaders were more concerned with the loyalties of the military people at the central government level than the regional level. Finally, however convinced one may be that the field-army analysis is a satisfactory explanation of what happened during the Cultural Revolution, it is no guarantee that field armies remain reliable predictors of loyalty affiliations in the twenty-first century. Ties formed during the communist party's rise to power in the 1930s did not appear to closely bind officers who were born in the 1950s.[13]

Interestingly, a letter drafted by seven military figures who opposed the use of the PLA against the demonstrators at Tiananmen in 1989 was signed by members of all field armies. Deng, who was from the Second Field Army, found himself strongly supported by Yang Shangkun, whose association is with the Fourth Field Army. He apparently did not get the support of the minister of defense, a man whose career had waxed and waned in exact parallel with Deng's own for the past half-century and who belonged to Deng's own Second Field Army. To be sure, it is possible to expand the scope of the central-regional school of analysis beyond the field-army hypothesis. If forces loyal to President and General Yang Shangkun gained power as a result of the Tiananmen incident (and indeed Yang's younger brother *was* promoted within the central government structure, while other Yang associates received important positions in a reshuffle of military region command during the spring of 1990), then anti-Yang forces will be assumed to be growing as well, aiming to restore a kind of pre-Tiananmen balance. This, too, came to pass. In 1992, amid rumors that the Yang family was making plans to seize power after Deng's death, the Yangs' ties with the military were severed and a number of their protégés were removed from positions of power. But expanding the scope of the school in this manner takes the argument away from a central government mediating among regional factions, and assumes that the factional dispute occurs first at the central level and then spreads into the regions.

Another variant of factional analysis, the *political-cultural school*, holds that the central issue in the PRC's politics is China's struggle to assimilate Western technology without destroying its own cultural traditions. In a general sense, this is a problem faced by all developing countries: how to modernize and industrialize without Westernizing and losing one's cultural "soul." The problem has been especially painful for China, since the country has traditionally been unusually culture-proud. Analysts who adhere to this scheme of analysis see China as sharply divided within itself among groups in various stages of modernization. These groups differ from one another in the level and amount of what they are willing to accept from the West and how much they feel must be rejected. There is conflict among the groups, and political-cultural analysts feel that this conflict explains a great deal, if not most of, Chinese political behavior.

There is some validity to this line of analysis. Even a cursory check of the Chinese communist press over the last half-century will reveal the existence of conflicts that are dichotomized in precisely this manner. There are frequent references to the "struggle between the two camps," the "counterrevolutionaries versus the socialists," the Maoists versus the revisionists, and so forth. Ideologues of the early 1990s accused Western countries of plotting to subvert China through a campaign of "peaceful evolution." Among those deemed to have been subverted were those considered far too Westernized. Some playwrights, for example, had suggested that Chinese culture should be discarded and replaced with that of the West. One of their productions, *River Elegy*, is discussed in Chapter 12.

Experts formerly referred to these disputes as the red-expert conflict, with *red* symbolic of those who adhere quite rigidly to ideology and *expert* referring to technocrats who are willing to borrow Western techniques to a significant degree. As Marxism faded, so did the usage of the term "red." The debate turned back toward the nineteenth century dilemma of what to absorb from foreign countries and what of the Chinese tradition—however that is defined—to retain. Although the term "red" may be passé this basic dichotomy remains.

As with the other methods discussed here, there are problems with the political-cultural line of analysis. First, it was the reds who were most fanatic about *attacking* Chinese cultural traditions, including, at various points, Confucian philosophy, Buddhist temples and other religious establishments, and even the nearly sacred family system. The leftist distaste for traditional culture was particularly noticeable during the Cultural Revolution and, to a somewhat lesser extent, the Great Leap Forward. Red attitudes toward Westernization are equally negative. Rather than preserving Chinese culture, they seek to substitute what they perceive as the culturally neutral socialist society, or homogeneous proletarian society, envisioned by Marx. In recent years, most reds have accepted the necessity to borrow technology: It, after all, can be rationalized as culturally neutral as well. By contrast, technocrats do not *necessarily* espouse borrowing from the West anything but technology.

To be sure, there are leading pro-democracy scientists such as Fang Lizhi, the celebrated dissident physicist who took refuge in the United States embassy when he was accused of fomenting the 1989 demonstrations in Beijing. However, there are also many skilled scientists who labor diligently in their laboratories during working hours but are serious students of calligraphy, devout Buddhists, and obedient Confucian sons and daughters while at home. At least in the past, one could also find skilled technocrats who, although they might look upon time spent in ideological study as time wasted, nonetheless considered themselves good communists. In other words, the dichotomy implied by this line of analysis is rarely so neatly drawn in reality.

A second difficulty in conceptualizing Chinese politics according to the political-cultural school is that it is often impossible to know whom to classify in which group. Partly this is a matter of lack of data. Partly it is because the same people who have been classified by the Chinese media as in one group may get shifted to another group a short time later. Sometimes circumstances have led the person to change his or her position; sometimes the party line will have changed, leaving the person on the wrong side of an issue. For example, during the Cultural Revolution, defense minister Lin Biao led the campaign to study the thoughts of Chairman Mao. He was lauded as a leading leftist, and was typically identified as "Chairman Mao's closest comrade in arms." Indeed, the constitution of 1969 named Lin as Mao's heir apparent. By 1971 Lin had been accused of trying to kill Mao and the media referred to him as China's leading rightist. When queried on this apparently complete about-face, the media explained that Lin had been "left in appearance, right in essence." Later, when the party line shifted to being antileftist, Lin was again described as a leftist.

Lin's case is just one instance, albeit the most spectacular example, of many. The important point is that it is of limited value to give people labels like left and right, or conservative and radical, that may not describe their behavior patterns, or even their political beliefs, in any meaningful way. Clearly, this limits the usefulness of the political-cultural school as a tool of analysis.

Yet another form of factional analysis is that of the *bureaucratic politics school*. For those who espouse this methodology, the crucial question is to identify which part of the PRC's bureaucratic organization has decisive power over the direction and scope of sociopolitical change. This might be a certain ministry, or one part of the armed forces, or some department within the party organization. The underlying premise of this line of analysis is that Chinese political behavior is the result of interorganizational bargaining for budgets, status, and power.

This is certainly a phenomenon noticeable in other countries where more information is available, and it is highly likely that this type of competition exists within the PRC. The problem is that, given the information that we have, it is very difficult to tell who the major players are in this bureaucratic bargaining game, and what stakes they are playing for. In the wake of the Cultural Revolution, the air force was repeatedly criticized for harboring "leftist" sentiments, but this was a highly unusual period and analysts continue to differ on what was really happening within the air force's high command.[14] There is some evidence of jurisdictional disputes between ministries on various issues. For example, an especially vigorous crackdown on crime in the mid-1980s was rumored to be the result of a turf fight between the newly created ministry of state security and preexisting public security forces on which of them could cope better with the rising crime rate. More recently, there is evidence of similar disagreements between central and provincial levels on the demarcation of their sphere of control. In the 1990s there were reports of a bureaucratic tug-of-war between the central government in Beijing and the Guangdong provincial government over which of them should play the major role in running Hong Kong after it reverted to Chinese control in 1997.

However, these are at best vague clues as opposed to analytical schemes. It would be helpful to be able to examine the relative shares of the budget allocated to each organization and department over a substantial period of time. Not having the necessary supporting data limits the usefulness of the bureaucratic politics school as a tool of analysis.

The *palace politics school* focuses almost exclusively on the issue of who will succeed to the top position within the Chinese leadership. It assumes an ongoing struggle among a number of people who wish to put themselves in line for the succession, or at least move themselves closer to it. Adherents see this struggle as personality-oriented rather than rooted in policy disagreements, fighting within the bureaucracy, or based on geographical constraints or generations. The players are individuals rather than groups although they do form factions and induce people who are loyal to them to help advance their cause.

The PRC has endured a number of power struggles in the relatively short time since its founding. As the story of Lin Biao indicates, some of them have been quite melodramatic. Unlike several of the other schools discussed earlier, the manifestations of palace politics interactions are fairly easily discernible. It is difficult to try to position oneself for the succession to high office without attracting attention. Even before the 1989 Tiananmen incident, many Chinese regarded president Yang Shangkun as a politically ambitious manipulator who wished either to succeed Deng Xiaoping as paramount leader of China or to have his younger half-brother do so. The credibility of these rumors was enhanced when, after Tiananmen, the younger half-brother was named secretary-general of the Central Military Commission and a member of the party secretariat.

Unfortunately, it is not usually possible to ascertain what would be more helpful to our understanding of decision making in Chinese politics: the manner in which these promotions are achieved. And even at the very top of the hierarchy, we do not generally know the loyalties of more than a few people. The lower one descends in the power structure, the more difficult it becomes. Therefore we were uncertain, for example, of the size and strength of the Yangs' power base both at the height of their power in 1989–1991 and after their purge in 1992. It also seems to be possible for some individuals to survive when not associated with the party line and without a strong power base. The classic example here is former premier Zhou Enlai, who over the years had taken many policy positions that were different from those favored by Mao. He was never purged and was actively involved in the administration of the country until his death in 1976.

Because someone has been successful in positioning himself for the succession, however, does not necessarily mean he will actually succeed to the top position. Lin Biao was removed from the succession in 1971, Hua Guofeng in 1976, Hu Yaobang in 1987, and Zhao Ziyang in 1989. Hu Jintao, an heir apparent who actually did become party general secretary at the sixteenth party congress in 2002, seemed painfully aware of the danger of his position, avoiding interviews and keeping a scrupulously low profile. Aware that he could be a target for other ambitious people, Hu's rare public statements were strongly supportive of his superior, Jiang Zemin. Even so, Jiang is believed to be responsible for the creation of a Shanghai faction which may be able to circumscribe or even usurp Hu's ability to govern (see Chapter 6). In sum, knowing who has been a successful player of palace politics does not allow us to predict China's next leader with any certainty.

Another theory specifically based on the experience of the Cultural Revolution was that the PRC was moving backward toward a *cellular economy*. The general weakening of administrative power and loosening of controls caused by the Cultural Revolution had encouraged individual localities and enterprises to develop along self-sufficient lines. According to its leading explicator, Audrey Donnithorne,[15] the Chinese economy had bifurcated. One sector was composed of a myriad of small, discrete units and strongly decentralized. It served the basic requirements of workers and peasants, and was largely run on principles of self-reliance. The other, comparatively centralized, dealt with research and production for military purposes. Considerable friction might result if, as Donnithorne correctly predicted, the central government exerted pressure to regain control and break down this cellular arrangement. The concept of the cellular economy would, however, reappear in the 1990s as part of theories of fragmented authoritarianism (see p. 21).[16]

The cellular theory has limitations. While local levels have indeed gained power vis-à-vis the center in recent years, they are increasingly being integrated into the world market. Simultaneous fragmentation and globalization result in a very different picture from that of Donnithorne's nearly self-sufficient traditional Chinese village. For example, localization could be seen in the fierce land-use rights struggle that broke out in a remote village in Yunnan in the mid-1990s. But the us-versus-them arguments, however cellular they appeared, had been engendered by the huge profits that could be realized by selling the speciality mushrooms that the area produced to gourmets in Japan.[17]

Post-Mao Theories of Analysis

Deng Xiaoping's accession to power in the late 1970s brought a diminution of the extreme overt manifestations of factional struggle. The abatement of strife was accompanied by Deng's introduction of major changes in political and economic structure. Foreign scholars were given greater access to China, and had more sources of information available to them. The combination of these factors again caused analysts to rethink their theories of Chinese politics. As the party moved toward the establishment of a market economy and away from ideological rigidity, scholars put forth a *pluralist* paradigm.[18] Adherents believe that, as the totalitarian state establishes itself, the need for terrorism and mass mobilization subsides. Political competition can begin, albeit within a fairly narrowly drawn system of political controls. The atomization of individuals is only a temporary phenomenon: social groups, not necessarily the same as had existed before the communist government came to power, arise and begin to articulate and otherwise pursue their common interests. Their activities may not be organized in the same ways as interest group activities in liberal democratic régimes, but they are based on group identities and interests nonetheless. The more that a totalitarian system tolerates this pluralistic competition, the more group politics will pervade bureaucratic institutions, and the more originally totalitarian systems will approximate liberal régimes. Eventually, convergence may take place.

Those who favor this paradigm cite evidence that a *civil society* is emerging in China, in which citizens feel free to voice their dissatisfactions with party, government, and individual leaders. They form associations and groups which, while in general loyal to party and government, at the same time seek to press them for changes consonant with the agendas of their constituents. Economic development, and particularly the economic decentralization that fosters this development, is generally seen as crucial. People who have become accustomed to making their own economic decisions will soon demand to make political and social choices, since these are often closely intertwined with economic decisions.

Citizens of the PRC have indeed become more publicly assertive in recent years, and groups such as student unions and work units have sometimes attempted to defy government orders. This was most conspicuous in the mobilization and deployment of groups around Tiananmen Square in the spring of 1989. However, as the government's brutal suppression of the demonstrations showed, democracy is not the necessary outcome of this assertiveness. Certainly the political situation that followed the overthrow of communism in the Soviet Union does not give rise to optimism that democracy is a natural successor to authoritarianism.

While adherents of pluralism view incidents such as the suppression of the 1989 demonstrations as no more than temporary setbacks in the inexorable march toward liberalism and a civil society, other analysts argue that fundamental differences exist within the society that make such an evolution unlikely. The theory of *communist neo-traditionalism* put forth by Andrew Walder[19] agrees with adherents of pluralism that communist societies are characterized by competition and conflict at all levels, and that people have a choice of means through which to pursue their interests. At the same time, it affirms the validity of two major features of the totalitarian model. First, neo-traditionalists agree that there are distinctive communist institutions that make organized control possible and, second, they argue that these forms of organization shape patterns of association and political behavior in distinctive ways.

However, in contrast to the totalitarian emphasis on disincentives to resistance caused by fear and the absence of alternatives to the existing government and ideology, neo-traditionalism emphasizes the incentives offered for compliance. Walder notes that political loyalty is rewarded systematically, with career opportunities, favored treatment in the distribution of scarce resources, and such other favors that officials in communist societies are uniquely able to dispense. In addition, the enforcement of the party's ideology has the unintended but important consequence of creating a highly institutionalized network of patron-client networks. These associations are composed of party loyalists and activists who trade their support for the party in exchange for preferential career opportunities and other rewards. Instead of social atomization and the destruction of social ties that are not subordinated to the party, instrumental-personal ties develop. Through them, individuals circumvent formal regulations to obtain official approvals, housing, and other public and private goods controlled by low-level officials.

Neo-traditionalism disagrees with the pluralist view that the "real" political and social forces are group forces: the social network rather than the group is its main structural concept. It rejects convergence theories, arguing that the evolution of Chinese communism will result in a historically new system of institutionalized clientelism—in effect, a neo-traditional pattern of authority based on citizens' dependence on social institutions and their leaders. Others take this line of analysis further, describing an already partially evolved model of *fragmented authoritarianism* involving policy-making through protracted bargaining between the top leaders and their bureaucracy, particularly in the provinces. Through their control over personnel appointments, the military, and key economic resources, the central authorities are able to influence the behavior of cities and provinces. Still, the decentralization of the economy has given these entities a certain ability to resist the central authorities as well. Hence, analysis should focus on the relationship between the center and the provinces and localities.[20]

Conclusions

As has been seen, each of these theories seeks to explain the formal and informal rules under which the Chinese leadership operates, how they organize themselves to deal with differences of opinion, how resources are mobilized in support of a given end, and what benefits accrue to the winners and what sanctions are meted out to the losers. Their emphases differ, encompassing history, culture, ideology, personal power struggle, organizational theories, and the supremacy of domestic or foreign policy factors. Some seem more relevant at a particular point in time than others; none seems to have been an accurate predictor for the entire post-1949 period. Although each theory has something to recommend it, none is without deficiencies. No single model can explain elite political behavior sufficiently and one should be skeptical of analyses which are based exclusively on any one of them. While no one method of analysis is perfect, the various different factors that are collectively central to them provide us with a list of useful variables to bear in mind when examining Chinese politics. Indicators such as the relative balance of state and society and that between the central government and lower-level units; leaders' family background, level of education, foreign travel, date of entry into the party, service in particular geographic areas and/or ministries, and long association with particular persons, provide valuable data for analysis and the inherently imperfect art of prediction.

Notes

1. Mao Zedong, "On the New Stage," in *Selected Works of Mao Tse-tung*, 5 vols. (Beijing: Foreign Languages Press, 1965–1977), vol. 2, pp. 195–211.

2. Quoted in *China Update* (New Haven, Conn.: The Yale-in-China Association, Winter 1990), p. 7.

3. This occurred despite the fact that high-level party cadres' salaries were cut twice, first in 1959, and again in 1961. The amounts of their salaries notwith-standing, high-level cadres had access to goods that money could not buy. And, in the context of official controls over economic activities being weakened in the name of survival, some people managed to turn the situation to their advantage better than others.

4. William Whitson, *Chinese Military and Political Leaders and the Distribution of Power in China, 1956–1971* (Santa Monica, Calif.: The RAND Corporation,

R-1091-DOS/ARPA, June 1973), pp. 5–36, contains an interesting discussion of several of these schools.

5. The classic explication of this model is found in Carl J. Friedrich and Zbigniew Brzezinski, *Totalitarian Dictatorship and Democracy*, 2nd ed. (New York: Praeger, 1965).

6. Donald W. Klein's "The 'Next Generation' of Chinese Communist Leaders," *China Quarterly*, no. 12, October–December 1962, pp. 57–74, exemplifies this method of analysis.

7. Li Ximing, quoted by *Xinhua* (Beijing), June 4, 1990, in United States Department of Commerce, *Foreign Broadcast Information Service: China* (hereafter *FBIS-CHI*), June 6, 1990, p. 17.

8. Li Zhisui, *The Private Life of Chairman Mao* (New York: Random House, 1994), p. 440.

9. Ibid., p. 637.

10. Ibid., p. 480.

11. Ibid., p. 586.

12. Andrew Nathan, "A Factional Model for CCP Politics," *China Quarterly*, No. 53, January–March 1973, pp. 34–66.

13. The clearest articulation of the central-regional school method of analysis is found in Chapter 12 of Whitson's *The Chinese High Command* (New York: Praeger, 1973). William Parish's "Factions in Chinese Military Politics," *China Quarterly*, no. 56, October–December 1973, pp. 667–699, contains a rebuttal of many of Whitson's points.

14. See Jin Qiu, *The Culture of Power: The Lin Biao Incident in the Cultural Revolution* (Stanford, CA., 1999, Stanford University Press) and Larry Wortzel's analysis thereof in *Journal of Asian Studies*, November 2000, pp. 998-999, for two different views.

15. Audrey Donnithorne, "China's Cellular Economy: Some Economic Trends Since the Cultural Revolution," *China Quarterly*, no. 52, October–December 1972, pp. 605–619.

16. Avery Goldstein, "The Study of Political Elites and Institutions in the PRC," *China Quarterly*, no. 139, September 1994, p. 724.

17. Emily T. Yeh, "Forest Claims, Conflicts, and Commodification: The Political Ecology of Tibetan Mushroom-Harvesting Villages in Yunnan," *China Quarterly* (London), March 2000, pp. 264–278.

18. Jerry F. Hough, *The Soviet Union and Social Science Theory* (Cambridge, Mass.: Harvard University Press, 1977). Deng Xiaoping's reforms made Hough's theory seem applicable to China.

19. Andrew G. Walder, *Communist Neo-Traditionalism: Work and Authority in Chinese Industry* (Berkeley: University of California Press, 1986).

20. Harry Harding, "State of the Field: The Contemporary Study of Chinese Politics: An Introduction," *China Quarterly*, no. 139, September 1994, pp. 700–701. The term "fragmented authoritarianism" was coined by professor Kenneth Lieberthal of the University of Michigan. See also the other essays on this topic in the same issue by Elizabeth Perry, Avery Goldstein, and Peter Moody.

Suggestions for Further Reading

Bruce J. Dickson, "Threats to Party Supremacy," *Journal of Democracy*, January 2003.

Andrew Nathan, "A Factional Model for CCP Politics," *China Quarterly*, no. 53, January 1973, pp. 34–66.

Minxin Pei, "Contradictory Trends and Confusing Signals," *Journal of Democracy*, January 2003, pp. 73–81.

Andrew J. Walder, *Communist Neo-Traditionalism: Work and Authority in Chinese Industry* (Berkeley: University of California Press, 1986).

William Whitson, *Chinese Military and Political Leaders and the Distribution of Power in China, 1956–1971* (Santa Monica, Calif.: The RAND Corporation, R-1091-DOS/ARPA, June 1973).

Gongxin Xiao, "The Rise of the Technocrats," *Journal of Democracy*, January 2003, pp. 60–65.

2 The Chinese Tradition

In order to understand the problems faced by Chinese modernizers, it is important to have some sense of the tradition that provides the focus for their efforts. Many members of the post-1949 leadership group had vivid memories of imperial China. While these have become fewer and fewer as the years pass, even those who do not hold the empire in living memory have had to deal with its legacy. No chapter—indeed, no multivolume work— can hope to cover the richness and complexity of Chinese civilization adequately. Here we simply sketch a few of the important points, to give the student of present-day China a better feel for the context within which the leadership had to operate.

Basic Characteristics

First, China was *one of the earliest sites inhabited by organized groups of human beings*. In the cold, dry soil of the Yellow River basin in north China, archaeologists have discovered skeletal remains, tools, and pottery dating from neolithic times. The rest of the area now referred to as China was inhabited by what would later be referred to as barbarians. This small core group gradually spread out to take control of an area whose contours are roughly similar to those of present-day China. Migration generally occurred in a southerly direction, along cultivable river banks, rather than toward the less hospitable north, with the original inhabitants either being absorbed or pushed into less fertile areas.

This raises the question of what characteristics set the Chinese or, as they normally refer to themselves, the Han, apart from their neighbors of other ethnic groups. These were possession of the sophisticated agricultural techniques necessary for *wet rice cultivation* and *silk production*. Ironically, due to marked climatic changes, neither can now be carried out in the areas in which they were originally developed. The Han also developed a sophisticated written language at an early date. Indeed, Chinese may be the *world's oldest continuously used script*. Egyptian hieroglyphics were developed considerably earlier, about 3000 B.C., but fell of general use in the third century A.D. and disappeared entirely in the sixth century.

The records of Chinese civilization are quite good. *An early and sustained interest in history and chronology* is another characteristic that sets Han China off from its neighbors. India, for example, also developed a highly sophisticated civilization, but one that was relatively little concerned with chronology. Originally, some of the earlier parts of traditional Chinese history were thought to be legendary. An essentially accidental discovery

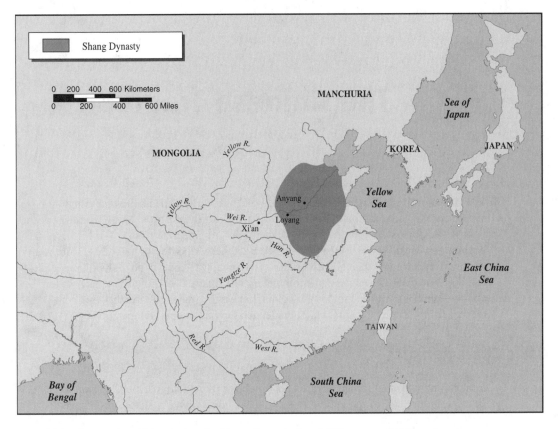

MAP 2.1A   Bronze Age China during the Shang Dynasty (ca. 1523 B.C.–ca. 1028 B.C.)

indicated that at least one of these supposedly mythical dynasties, the Shang, actually existed. In the 1920s, some Westerners noticed that a traditional medicine shop in north China was selling bones incised with Chinese characters. Though oddly rendered, the characters were still recognizable as their modern-day counterparts. Curious, the Westerners purchased the bones and began to study them. Extensive research and testing confirmed that the inscriptions dated from Shang times, about 1500 B.C. It seems unlikely that the existence of a still earlier dynasty, the Xia, will be confirmed.

Chinese chronologies have proved amazingly precise. They have been verified, for example, by checking the eclipses and sightings of comets mentioned in Chinese records against when mathematical calculations say they must have occurred. Halley's comet was observed regularly in China from 240 B.C. on, and may have been the comet recorded in 611 and 467 B.C. By 444 B.C., Chinese astronomers had calculated the length of a year to be 365¼ days, a remarkable achievement given the technology of the times.[1]

Not simply accurate record-keepers, the Chinese also had a well-developed *theory of history: the dynastic cycle.* According to it, although a golden age of perfection existed in the distant past, history was now cyclical. A dynasty was set up by a moral man in order

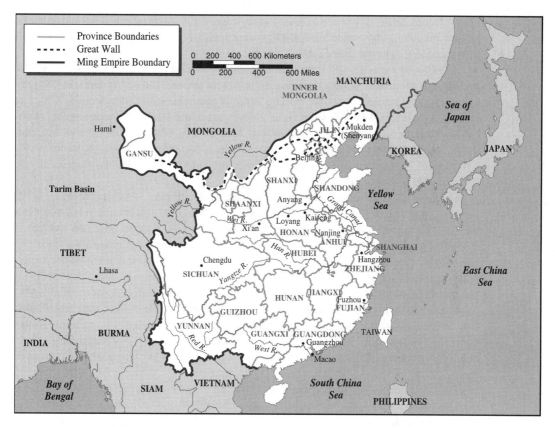

MAP 2.1B   Ming Dynasty (1368–1644). Note the tremendous expansion of territory.

to rectify existing evils. The ruler rules basically through presenting an example of virtue to be emulated by his people, and the man who is best qualified to rule is he who is most moral. The first few emperors will fit this example, working very hard. After that, decline will begin to occur: emperors will become more pleasure-loving and less virtuous.

A restoration, or midcourse correction, is possible. But eventually the moral quality of the rulers will decline again, and the dynasty will deteriorate still further. Portents are one indicator of the onset of decay: the appearance of comets and/or instances of plagues of insects, drought, floods, and barbarian invasions. Those who are unjustly ruled will raise rebellions and, when the quality of the emperor is poor enough, one of them—presumably the rebellion led by the most moral man—will succeed. Its leader will found a new dynasty.

Unfortunately, in China as elsewhere, the existence of a theory influences one's perception of reality. In this case, the theory of history provided a mold for the writing of history: The last emperor of a dynasty is always portrayed as bad. There is also a belief that a short, brutal, and efficient dynasty will be succeeded by a longer, benevolent one. The dynasty became the unit of history, and most dynasties had a separate official volume devoted to them, with administrative organization, major personalities, and events recorded in meticulous detail. There are at least twenty-four of these dynastic histories, depending on how many one chooses to accept. They were typically compiled by the scholar-elite of the succeeding dynasty. (See Figure 2.1.)

Philosophy was also an important element of the Chinese tradition. From about 500 to 300 B.C. there was a period of vigorous debate among various schools of thought, known as the Hundred Schools era. The name is not to be taken literally: The Chinese, who used the decimal system from earliest times, are using *hundred* as a convenient shorthand for a large number. Two millennia later Mao Zedong employed the idea of contending philosophies in a brief attempt at allowing people to express their true opinions on the best form of government. He enjoined his compatriots to "let one hundred flowers bloom, let a hundred schools of thought contend."

One of these schools was called *Confucianism*, after the Westernized name of its founder, Master Kong. His prescription for the well-ordered society included emphasis on hierarchical relationships: child subordinate to parents, wife to husband, subject to ruler, and so forth. The kingdom is the family writ large, with the emperor as father to his people. The Confucian ruler was a sage–king, a highly moral man whose exemplary behavior would inspire the people he ruled to emulate him. Confucius's ideal was the multigeneration family living together under the same roof, with its members paying respect to their common ancestors. Performance of these and other rites was important to Confucius, leading some foreigners somewhat misleadingly to refer to Confucianism as ancestor worship. Confucius was also strongly proagriculture and anticommerce, regarding the entrepreneur as someone who exploited what the labor of the peasantry produced. He also believed in "graded love," wherein one was expected to care more deeply for those people nearest one in the family, less so for those more distant. His notion of law was similarly hierarchical, with different rules for different classes of people.

Another school was *Mohism*, named for its founder, Mo Zi. The Mohists were more egalitarian in outlook, sounding much like modern-day advocates of democracy on many issues. They envisioned a state organization that measured everything in terms of its utility to all people. Mohists vehemently objected to aggressive war, though they produced skilled warriors and impressive tactics for defensive conflicts. They called for simplicity and frugality on the part of all people. Universal love, by which was meant equal regard for all other human beings, was also a central tenet of Mohism and contrasted sharply with the Confucian outlook. Laws were to apply equally to all people. Mohists wanted the responsibility for power placed in the hands of the most able people, whom they expected would act according to the desires of the masses. However, they did not specify the mechanisms through which this might be done. Mo Zi was greatly honored in his day, and his teachings were no less influential than those of Confucius. Nonetheless, the school seems to have died out by the first century A.D.

A third school, the *Daoists*, believed (and still do believe, since the school has a number of adherents even today) that a well-ordered society must be in harmony with The Way (*dao*). They hold that nature dictates all and that the way to order life is to do nothing contrary to nature. Striving for power and material goods is to be eschewed, as

FIGURE 2.1   The Chinese Dynasties

Five Emperors (mythical)	
Xia (mythical)	ca. 1994 B.C.–ca. 1523 B.C.
Shang (or Yin)	ca. 1523 B.C.–ca. 1028. B.C.
Zhou	ca. 1027 B.C.–256 B.C.
Qin	221 B.C.–207 B.C.
Western (Earlier) Han	202 B.C.–9 A.D.
Xin	9–23
Eastern (Later)	25–220
The Three Kingdoms	220–265
Shu, 221–263	
Wei, 220–265	
Wu, 222–280	
Western Jin	265–317
Eastern Jin	317–420
Former (Liu) Song	420–479
Southern Qi	479–502
Liang	502–557
Chen	557–589
Northern Wei	386–535
Eastern Wei	534–550
Western Wei	535–556
Northern Qi	550–577
Northern Zhou	557–581
Sui	590–618
Tang	618–907
Five Dynasties + Ten Kingdoms	907–960
Later Liang, 907–923	
Later Tang, 923–936	
Later Jin, 936–947	
Later Han, 947–950	
Later Zhou, 951–960	
Liao	907–1125
Northern Song	960–1126
Xixia	990–1227
Southern Song	1127–1279
Jin	1115–1234
Yuan	1260–1368
Ming	1368–1644
Qing	1644–1911

is travel: The key to understanding The Way is within oneself. According to one Daoist sage, the ideal situation is to sit in one's own village, listening to the barking of the dogs in the next village but never to visit that neighboring village. Intensely quietistic, Daoists meditate in order to search for The Way. An often-quoted Daoist slogan is that "the best form of action is inaction"; a Daoist ruler would accomplish everything by doing nothing.

Legalists, with the eminent Lord Shang as their principal spokesperson, insisted that the well-ordered state depends on a clearly enunciated rule of law which the state must enforce regardless of who might commit a crime. They advocated posting the laws of a city outside its gates, so that all who entered would be aware of proper standards of behavior. In distinct contrast to Confucius's image of the sage–king eliciting proper behavior from his subjects by providing them a role model, the Legalists did not expect the people to do good by themselves. Rather, the ruler would, through the use of rewards and punishments, make sure that they could do no wrong. Legalist philosophy provided the guiding principles for the Qin dynasty (221–207 B.C.). Although the Qin is not fondly remembered by Chinese tradition, the system of governmental organization and criminal law of the next two thousand years are basically of Legalist derivation.

The *Logicians*, or School of Names, vigorously debated the meaning of absolute versus relative terms. Despite an intense and ongoing interest in philosophy, China never developed a system of logic. In fact, the very name in use today, *loji*, is borrowed from the West. But the logicians seemed to be groping toward a system of logic, as exemplified the "Discourse on the White Horse" by its leading practitioner, Gongsun Long. Its main proposition is the assertion that "a white horse is not a horse," indicating the realization that adding the adjective *white* qualified the universal concept *horse*. The Logicians believed that only when names had been properly defined could any proper system of government and laws be set forth.

Yin–yang theory provided China with a cosmology. *Yang*, originally meaning sunshine, came to represent masculinity, activity, heat, brightness, dryness, and hardness, while *yin* was associated with femininity, passivity, cold, darkness, wetness, and softness. The interaction of these two primary principles was believed to produce all of the phenomena of the universe. Yin and yang are complementary, so that when one extreme is reached the other principle begins to assert itself. The greatest of successes contains within itself the seeds of its own destruction, just as the sun at midday is on the verge of giving way to night. The diagrammatic representation of the yin–yang interaction is depicted on the present-day South Korean flag. Yin–yang theorists were concerned with divining the future through interpreting the configurations of the so-called eight trigrams, each one made up of combinations of three divided or undivided lines. They also devised prescriptions for good health through eating certain foods, some classified as hot and others as cold. Yin–yang principles had a startling, if brief, popular revival in the United States during the 1960s.

Various folk religions incorporating other forms of geomancy also flourished during this time. One popular belief was that the *feng–shui*, or spirits of the winds (*feng*) and water (*shui*), had to be placated or disaster would ensue. A shaman would be brought in to determine the best site for a building or a grave, in order to make sure that ill fortune would not befall those who commissioned the structure.

Buddhism is not properly a part of the Hundred Schools, since it arrived in China somewhat later, in the second century A.D. But, in the sense that it did contend for power with the others, it is appropriate to consider Buddhism with them. Unlike the other schools, which are indigenous to China, Buddhism had its origins in India. Although there are many different sects of Buddhism, there is general agreement among them that human suffering arises from the individual's ignorance of the nature of things. From this ignorance comes the craving for and cleaving to life, which binds the individual to the eternal Wheel of Life and Death, from which he can never escape. Through enlightenment comes emancipation, or *nirvana*. This search for *nirvana* is essential to Buddhism.[2]

Eventually, Confucianism won out over its rivals and became accepted as the state philosophy. However, in the process it was fundamentally influenced by the other schools. For example, yin–yang symbolism was absorbed by Confucianism. Elements of Buddhism and Daoism figure prominently in the neo-Confucianism that emerged during the Song dynasty (A.D. 960–1279), and feng–shui was incorporated as well. In addition to borrowing elements from other philosophies, Confucianism was not exclusivist. One could be a Confucian scholar, take time out for Daoist contemplation, and also be a practicing Buddhist. This basic tolerance did not hold true for all faiths, as will be seen later. It is important to remember that Confucianism is not a religion in the usual sense of the word. Its concerns are with statecraft and with the proper relationships among human beings. Heaven is mentioned only once, when one of Master Kong's disciples states that heaven hears as the people hear and heaven sees as the people see. As a philosophy, it is unconcerned with the supernatural or with life after death. Confucius is revered as a great teacher rather than worshiped as a god. (See Figure 2.1.)

The Governmental Structure of Traditional China

The governmental structure that arose out of these debates over statecraft and ethics was impressive in its degree of centralization and attention to a variety of the problems of administration. At the top was the emperor, who theoretically reigned supreme. In fact, his decision-making powers were constrained by a number of factors, including the force of tradition, his own Confucian education, and the rest of the court structure.

The court structure included the empress and her family, who sought to have their members appointed to important and lucrative positions and might even try to seize the throne. There were also a large number of concubines, who similarly tried to advance themselves and their families through using their charms on the emperor. Providing the emperor with an heir was an excellent way to enhance one's status in court, although it often caused problems for one's relationships with the empress and with other concubines. There was also typically a large eunuch population within the palace compound. In order to make sure that the imperial sons and heirs were really the children of the emperor, only eunuchs were permitted in the parts of the palace where women lived. Since eunuchs were allowed substantial freedom of movement, which the palace ladies were not, a eunuch and a woman might ally for mutual benefit. The eunuch would provide a palace lady with information crucial to the advancement of her career in return for material and status

benefits if she succeeded. Eunuchs could and did lead the imperial heir into a life of dissolution, opening the way for another woman's son to be named heir apparent. They might
also administer poison to their lady's rival or to the rival's son.

The imperial bureaucracy was an elaborate hierarchy staffed by those who had
passed the civil service examinations. From the fourteenth century onward, the pinnacle of
the bureaucracy was the so-called Six Boards, corresponding to ministries in contemporary bureaucracies. Their respective administrative purviews also sound contemporary:
The Board of Personnel made civil service appointments to those who passed the examination system; the Board of Revenue collected taxes; the Board of Rites supervised the examination system, state festivals, and government-sponsored schools; the Board of War
appointed military officers from those who had passed the separate military examination
system; the Board of Punishment provided the court system, and the Board of Works was
in charge of building, irrigation, and "the produce of mines and marshes"—mostly salt, a
government monopoly.

A seventh entity, the Censorate, was a uniquely Chinese institution. It existed to criticize the other organs of government, including the emperor. Censors had to be extremely
courageous; they received no immunity by virtue of their position. Some were flogged to
death by order of the ruler who was angered by their complaints. Others might receive the
gift of a silken cord or a lump of raw opium from the emperor, thus conveying the imperial
desire that they commit suicide. That so many censors were willing to take these risks
speaks highly both for them as individuals and for the system that produced them.

Local government also had a well-articulated structure. Below the central government were the provinces. By the eighteenth century there were eighteen provinces in
China proper. Since then, more have been carved out of border districts that originally had
other forms of administration. Provinces were divided into prefectures, which were in turn
divided into counties, townships, and villages or hamlets. The county level was normally
the farthest down that the imperial bureaucracy reached. By the time of the Qing dynasty,
a typical county might be composed of several hundred thousand people. Supervising so
many people, spread over a wide area, with roads that were typically few in number and
poor in quality, and without modern communications, was exceedingly difficult. The
county magistrate had a staff of assistants, but they were far too few to actually administer
the area under their jurisdiction. The county magistrate therefore had to seek the help of
prominent local people and organizations.

In effect, then, the magistrate governed by supervising the local power structure,
which was not part of the imperial bureaucracy. There was a tendency to preside passively,
intervening only when it seemed absolutely necessary. Should the magistrate deem the situation important enough to do so, there were a number of measures at his disposal. These
ranged from dispensing informal advice to calling in military forces to maintain order or
gain compliance with imperial orders. The local worthies on whom the magistrate relied
were typically members of a class known as the gentry. These were people of some wealth
and social cultivation. They might be wealthy and therefore able to provide a son or sons
with an education so that they might succeed at the examination system, or an originally
poor family who had a bright son who had managed to pass the examinations, become an
official, and make his family wealthy. Other people in whose good graces it was necessary
for the magistrate to keep were the informal hierarchy of elders that every village had.

Yet another organization that might help the administration at local-government level was the *baojia*. In good Confucian fashion, the head of every household was responsible for the conduct of his family members. Since families tended to be large and multi-generational, this was often quite a responsibility. Every hundred households formed a *jia*, with one head of household as its head, and every ten *jia* a *bao*, again with a designated head. Each of these was responsible to those above him in the hierarchy for the conduct of those below him. Although the incumbents could be punished for breach of responsibility, none was paid for his efforts. This informal mutual security system did not always work: If one can be punished for something one's subordinates do, there are essentially two choices. First, one can try hard to keep potential troublemakers in line. Second, one can try to conceal what the troublemaker does. Often the second choice proved easier than the first.

Concealment was also the hallmark of the secret societies. These groups had fanciful names like the Triads, the Yellow Turbans, the White Lotus, or the Fists of Righteous Harmony. Members were initiated in an elaborate ceremony that included such mystic rites as chanting, dancing, and animal sacrifice. They claimed a Robin Hood role but tended to finance it by running Mafia-like protection operations. Secret societies were adept at resisting whatever aspects of central authority they did not like, such as tax increases. Not confined to particular local areas, they often had branches in other counties and provinces. When angered at imperial actions or mismanagement, they might stage large rebellions. Secret societies were influential in toppling several dynasties.

Bandit groups operated in similar fashion, preying on travelers or demanding protection money from merchants and peasants. The larger their numbers, the more noticeable they became, of course, and sometimes the magistrate was compelled to use force to deal with them. Imperial officials had no doctrine of hot pursuit, nor did they have any real incentive to resort to it: Bandits chased out of a magistrate's bailiwick became someone else's problem. Bandits thus preferred to operate from border areas, which had several advantages. They were far from the county seat and the magistrate's dwelling. Roads in border areas tended to range from sparse to nonexistent, and the bandits had the advantage of knowing the terrain. Also, should the pursuing force get too close, the bandits could quickly flee into another administrative area. Members of secret societies and bandit groups led lives of high adventure and as a result became a favorite topic of vernacular novelists. The young Mao Zedong, an avid reader of such novels, employed some of the bandits' techniques in overthrowing the Chinese government of his day.

Faced with the enormous task of governing a large area with limited resources, the county magistrate tried to accommodate the informal power structure so that it would look to his superiors as if his district were peaceful and prosperous. In accordance with Confucian philosophy, lack of peace and prosperity would indicate that the magistrate was not setting a virtuous example and hence he might be removed. The upper levels of the bureaucracy were not completely unaware of these factors but had their own superiors to answer to. Various devices were tried to reduce the collusion between the magistrate and the local power structure. One method was fairly frequent transfers. Another was the "law of avoidance," whereby a magistrate was never posted to the area from which he came, so that his judgment would not be compromised by Confucian obligations to take care of his family members properly. This did not prevent the local power structure from being able to circumvent or modify central government directives with reasonable frequency: The empire was too large, and the bureaucracy too small, to expect a high degree of compliance. In the words of a popular Chinese saying, "Heaven is high, and the emperor is far away."

The resulting system of local-level government, though very informal, was surely not democratic, since the power structure was governed by rigid norms of authority and status. It was not even true decentralization, since all local power was conditional on the approval of higher levels. Nor was it really local autonomy, since a higher level of government could intervene if it decided to. It would probably be most accurate to say that basic-level traditional Chinese government was an operating arrangement, undertaken largely for reasons of administrative efficiency and conservatism, in which local authorities were encouraged to control their own areas, provided they did so effectively and without violation of imperial requirements. Gentry and other wealthy individuals, large clan groups, merchant and crafts guilds, and even secret societies could thus exercise great power over their subordinates and members. Possibly they could even influence the magistrate. But their power could go only so far as a direct challenge to the magistrate's power. At this point, a higher level would have to be brought in to deal with that challenge.

Although the bureaucracy could be almost nonexistent at the local level, it was quite top-heavy. There were many officials in the capital city, few of them with intimate knowledge of conditions in the countryside. For this reason, the bureaucracy tended to be out of touch with the people, a problem that the Chinese communists would later take considerable pains to rectify. In common with bureaucracies everywhere, it also had a tendency toward rigidity, with consequent stultifying effects on society. In the Chinese case, a major contributing factor to this rigidity was the imperial examination system.

The Examination System

From the time of the Tang dynasty (A.D. 618–906) onward, Chinese officials were selected on the basis of a competitive civil service examination. Candidates were tested on how well they had memorized the Confucian classics and internalized the code of ethics embodied therein. The tests were given on several levels, with special examination halls consisting of a series of individual cubicles constructed in many larger cities. The applicant brought his own food—he might be there for three days—and was provided with a standard writing brush and ink and a passage from the classics. Then the cubicle was sealed, leaving the candidate to write an essay on the passage in his best literary style, under eight headings referred to as legs. Every effort was made to prevent cheating, with monitors supervising the cells. The applicants' papers were copied over before being presented to the examiners, lest the examiners be unduly influenced by the candidates' calligraphy. Those few who passed, less than one percent of the Chinese population, gained enormous prestige.

The examination system had a number of advantages. First, it produced intelligent officials who had thoroughly internalized the Confucian ethic. Second, it provided the people, including those who did not pass, with an orthodox belief system that was important for the management of the empire. Third, the system rewarded merit, providing a channel of social mobility for the ambitious, even commoners, that was based on widely accepted moral principles rather than wealth, birth, brute force, or royal whim.

There were disadvantages as well, many of them recognized by high-ranking officials who had succeeded within the system. One Song dynasty (960–1279) statesman strongly urged that the principles of astronomy, ancient and modern laws, and political economy be included in the examinations. He and others criticized the excessive emphasis on memorization and the writing of couplets. In later times the term *eight-legged essay* became a synonym for rigid, banal, stereotyped, and irrelevant. The degree of equality the examination system provided was less than perfect: Despite the existence of a number of ways in which a poor child could gain access to education, the children of the wealthy were more likely to have better teachers and better environments for learning. And women were completely excluded from the competition. Nonetheless, the creation of the examination system was a remarkable achievement, especially when one considers how the various political entities of Europe were being governed during the Tang dynasty. Despite its imperfections, the examination system served China well for many years.

Literature and Art

China produced art of great variety and subtlety that was prized throughout the known world. Examples have been recovered from the ruins of Pompeii and elsewhere in the Roman Empire. Somewhat later, Chinese pottery began to be exported to Indonesia. During the eighteenth and nineteenth centuries, a vogue for chinoiserie swept Europe and the United States. Traditional China also produced a number of fine novels, on topics ranging from the ribald to the introspective.

Interestingly, there is no tradition of literary and artistic protest. China produced no equivalent of *The Vision of Piers Plowman*, with its biting critique of status differentiations, or Hieronymous Bosch, whose paintings satirized corruption within the established church. Aesthetics were nearly monopolized by the scholar-official class, who painted and wrote poetry essentially as hobbies.

Society held those who painted for a living in low esteem; culture was the triumph of the amateur ideal over that of professionalism. According to the *Analects*, Confucius said "the accomplished scholar is not a utensil."[3] It is worth noting that the great flowering of vernacular drama in China occurred during the Yuan dynasty, when the Mongols suspended civil service examinations for 78 years; the theater became a way for the literati to compensate for their waning social prestige and wounded pride.[4] To be sure, one can find examples of literature being used for protest purposes.[5] For the most part, however, the elite protested through the established political channels—oral and written protests to the emperor—while the lower classes expressed their grievances by rebelling.

The Role of Law in Traditional China

Confucian teachings also suffuse the legal system of traditional China. As noted above, Confucius did not believe in a uniform code of justice for all. A gentleman was assumed to be guided in his conduct by knowledge of the correct moral principles (*li*), while only the uneducated needed punishments (*fa*). Note that education, and not birth, is the basis of gentility. Since differences were believed to be inherent in the nature of things, only through the harmonious operation of these differences could a fair social order be achieved.

The idea of law as relative to one's status rather than as an absolute standard produced some rules that sound strange to Western ears. For example, how many bearers a person could have for his sedan chair was regulated by law, as was how much jewelry could be worn, and with what designs. It was never possible to enforce these laws completely. Nor was punishment ever completely done away with, even for high-ranking officials. There are instances of ministers being put to death, possibly on the reasoning that if their conduct was too outrageous, they could not be treated as gentlemen anymore. More commonly, however, officials who fell from favor were dismissed and sent to posts on the periphery of the empire, which presumably minimized the harm they could do. As mentioned previously, there were also ways to suggest that an official commit suicide—which he generally did.

The influence of Confucian views on the importance of family was also reflected in the legal system. Crimes against family members were punished more heavily than those against outsiders, with patricide regarded as the ultimate horror. While the notion of the imperial system as a family writ large, with the emperor as the father of his people, is in most respects a reasonable and workable one, it did cause certain problems. Confucius never made clear what should happen when loyalty to one's family conflicted with loyalty to the emperor. The situation was not supposed to arise, since one's parents' desires were not supposed to conflict with one's official duties. Unfortunately, such situations did arise, and with some regularity. The system tried to minimize these conflicts by various techniques. The law of avoidance, whereby officials were not to be posted to their family seats, has already been mentioned. Also, the law provided that officials be granted leave for the observance of the elaborate mourning rites demanded by Confucianism (a year in the case of a deceased father), which involved wearing special clothing, eating only certain foods, and the preparation of an elaborate funeral ceremony.

These codes notwithstanding, most matters were never brought to law courts at all. There was no concept of what the Western world knows as torts; in order to bring a legal action, one had to accuse someone of a crime. The system recognized parents' authority to control and punish their children; disputes between family members were settled in accordance with an individual's status within the kin group.

In addition to the notion that disputes ought to be settled within the family rather than consigned to strangers, there was another important reason that most disputes were not brought to the courts: To do so was an expensive and risky venture. Bribery was the accepted way to influence one's case. Frequently, the county magistrate served as judge, and even were he scrupulously honest, his various subordinates would have to be paid in order to persuade them to present the case, the magistrate having many other matters to attend to. This practice of payments, known as "squeeze," existed at all levels of government. Everyone seems to have taken for granted that squeeze would have to be paid, and the practice was not considered corruption until the fee grew exorbitant. It was understood that the bureaucrats involved had inadequate salaries and had obligations to their own families.

As to law in the higher sense, there were no guarantees against the exercise of imperial power. Government could initiate, regulate, adjudicate, and repress as it saw fit. Elites did assume a *moral* obligation to provide just and responsive government, but there were no constitutional or legal safeguards to back up the obligation. Enforcement depended upon, first, the bureaucratic recruitment process, which was supposed to ensure that only men of superior virtue would be chosen, and second, the bureaucracy's own supervisory system. The latter was really a case of self-regulation, since bureaucrats would have to agree to remove one of their number whom they believed was not exercising his responsibilities properly.

The traditional political system was essentially free to accumulate and exercise total power, although, to its great credit, it never made the fullest use of this right. An elaborate system of checks and balances was developed despite the absence of a constitutional framework. It aimed not at safeguarding human rights but at preventing one faction or group of bureaucrats at the imperial court from annihilating the other. This informal check-and-balance system was sanctioned by custom, not law. It did not preclude one individual from seizing power, but it greatly increased the difficulty of anyone actually doing so.

Although people at the highest levels of leadership were expected to conform to a rigid moral code, they seemed relatively indifferent to what went on at the lower levels so long as there was peace. Efforts were made to indoctrinate the population at large with the Confucian ethic through such means as sponsoring public lectures, ceremonies, and schools to teach filial piety, respect for elders and superiors, peaceful and industrious conduct, and observance of the law. However, neither the efforts made nor the results achieved were especially impressive. In the vast countryside, people were generally neither positively loyal to the existing government nor actively opposed to it, but simply concerned with the problems of their own daily lives.

The Military

By 500 B.C. China had produced one of the world's greatest military strategists, Sun Zi, whose *Art of War* is required reading in modern military academies. However, with a few salient exceptions, most notably the Yuan (Mongol) dynasty, the military was not held in high regard during imperial China. A popular saying was "As one does not use good iron to make nails, one does not use good men as soldiers." If the ruler were virtuous, the people would be prosperous and content, and there would be no need for a strong military. If the people were not prosperous and content, then the ruler must be at fault, and it might be necessary to make changes at the top.

Hence the army tended to be strong at the beginning of a dynasty, having been used to overthrow the previous incumbents. Then it would be allowed to decay because it was no longer needed. There was no navy to speak of, since China was attacked from the sea only by occasional pirates. Even then, the strategy adopted was often simply to move the coastal population inland. Some military presence was considered necessary at all times because of the need to deal with barbarian incursions.

Scholar-officials tended to usurp military command functions, especially in periods of dynastic decline, and always did their best to undercut military officers, who were usually not literate. This also can be seen as motivated by a belief in the supremacy of amateurism over professionalism. It was, however, more than this. There was a tendency for the official class to want to wrest control of all areas that might rival their dominant influence. This same tendency is noticeable in the campaign the scholar-officials waged against the impressive sea voyages of the early Ming dynasty. These were run by eunuchs, who gained a great deal of imperial favor through the voyages. Ultimately, the scholar-officials succeeded in stopping them completely.

The Barbarian Problem

The term *barbarian* is used here to mean any non-Han Chinese group that interacted with the Han. Some of these groups were quite cultivated, although most were not. The Han referred to them by a variety of terms, many of which had pejorative connotations. Unlike the Han, a number of these groups had great respect for the military, and produced some formidable fighting forces. This was particularly true of the northern groups such as the Uygurs, Kazakhs, and Mongols. Since members of these groups did not accept Confucian precepts, the Han could not expect that the presence of a virtuous ruler on their own throne would deter the barbarians' depredations. A military force had to be maintained in order to deal with them.

Various techniques were devised to deal with the barbarians in order to minimize the need for battle. One was to buy them off through such devices as giving them official titles, with salaries, and making them responsible for peacekeeping in their areas. Another was to play one militant group off against another, a stratagem known as "using barbarians to control barbarians." Of course, the barbarians were also able to make alliances with each other against the Chinese.

On occasion, barbarians conquered all or part of Han China and set up their own dynasties. This was accepted to the degree that the conquerors accepted Chinese cultural norms and assimilated themselves to Confucian precepts. The Yuan dynasty, founded by Mongols who strenuously resisted adapting to the existing system, was short-lived and most Chinese regard it as unsuccessful. In contrast, the Manchus' Qing dynasty, whose leaders displayed considerable ingenuity in functioning as Confucian rulers while avoiding assimilation, lasted more than twice as long and was, until its last half-century, far better regarded.

Foreigners could even command Chinese armies in battle, as did An Lushan, a Sogdian, during the Tang dynasty, and Frederick Townsend Ward, an American, in the nineteenth century. Culturalism rather than nationalism characterized the Chinese empire: What mattered was not birth or race, but rather one's willingness and ability to conform to accepted standards of ethics, behavior, and dress.

Interpretations of Chinese History

The question arises how to characterize this impressive and complex society. One view, that of Karl Marx, is that of China the unchanging. In his words, history went to sleep in Asia. Clearly, this is untrue. Artistic styles, technology, administrative techniques, and even Confucian philosophy were modified over time. Change may have come more slowly than in certain periods of European history, but there definitely was change.

A second view was held by Marxists, disciples of Karl Marx who revised his opinions and applied his categories for Western society to China. These involve a historical progression from primitive communism, wherein small hunter-gatherer groups share the results of their foraging, to slave society, in which some groups conquer others and use them in forced labor. Eventually, slave societies pass over into feudal societies characterized by land that is held in fiefs and serfs who are bound to the land through oath and lack of other alternatives. Industrialization then occurs, leading to the bourgeois-capitalist stage of society, in which workers are exploited by capitalists, who monopolize ownership of the means of production. The workers rebel and inaugurate socialist society, in which they collectively own the means of production. The final stage, communism, is achieved when allocation depends on "from each according to his ability, to each according to his need." At this point, the state will have become unnecessary and will simply wither away.

It is interesting to compare Marx's theory with China's reality. Unfortunately, hunter-gatherer groups cannot be expected to leave written records. Although the stage of primitive communism may well have existed, it cannot be proved. During the Shang dynasty, whence our earliest records come, slaves do seem to have existed, as indeed they did during the Han and in certain other periods. However, the presence of slaves does not characterize a society as a slave society unless a major portion of society's work was done by them. This was never the case in China.

Feudal society definitely did exist, though prior to the time the Hundred Schools of Thought contended. There was a noble class, which was responsible for raising armies from among their serfs. The nobles rode in chariots, wore armor, and had an elaborate code of ethics that has been compared to chivalry. And, just as in Western feudalism, the king was rather weak vis-à-vis a coalition of his nobles. However, feudal society was already in an advanced state of decay by the time of the Hundred Schools period, in the latter part of the Zhou dynasty. Throughout Confucius's writings, there are laments that the rules of etiquette are being ignored.

The next dynasty, the Han, began to institute bureaucracy. Nobles were paid in rice for their service to the state rather than being granted fiefs. Land began to be bought and sold. As a result of these developments, China could no longer be called feudal. Yet, if Marx's categories of development are to be applied to China, feudalism should have been succeeded by the bourgeois-capitalist stage. It was not, really, as even Marxists agree. There are a few indicators, they argue, that China might have been becoming bourgeois-capitalist. One can see the slow rise of a money economy. A protobanking system was also developed wherein money could be held on deposit in one city and drawn upon elsewhere. This enables Marxists to conclude that China went through a rather long period of being "semifeudal"—almost two thousand years. Marxists also argue that China was on the verge of entering the bourgeois-capitalist stage when Western imperialism intruded, destroying the sprouts of capitalism in order to colonize the country.

A third view is that Chinese society is an example of Oriental despotism, sometimes also referred to as hydraulic society. It is most closely associated with a German scholar, Karl Wittfogel, who argues that, of all the factors necessary for the successful cultivation of crops in a preindustrial society, only water (as opposed to temperature and surface) can be controlled through human effort.[6] The need for irrigation and flood control means that a large quantity of water must be channeled and kept within bounds. Dikes must be built and maintained, canals must be dredged regularly, and information relevant for navigation compiled and distributed. This can be done only through the use of mass labor. Moreover, the labor force must be coordinated, disciplined, and led. Effective water management requires an organizational web that covers the whole, or at a minimum the dynamic core, of the country's population. Timekeeping and calendar making are likewise essential for the success of hydraulic economies: Crops must be planted, irrigated, and harvested within fairly narrowly defined periods of time. Systematic observation, careful calculations, and dissemination of results are needed.

In consequence, those who control this network of laborers, calculators, and disseminators are well positioned to wield supreme political power. The resulting régime will be decisively shaped by the leadership and social control required by hydraulic agriculture. The state will be stronger than the society, and those outside the ruling apparatus are essentially enslaved to it; hence China needs a strong central government. This contrasts sharply with multicentered societies such as existed in medieval Europe and Japan and with their modern democratic incarnations, where the need for water control was never so crucial. In these countries, Wittfogel argues, the state was effectively checked and restrained by other strong and competing organizations, such as the church, craft and merchant guilds, and private owners of land and industrial capital. Such political systems offer vastly greater protection to the individual and also provide a basis for adaptive and progressive social change. By contrast, the fate of hydraulic societies such as China is apt to be slow stagnation.

Critics have charged that Wittfogel's analysis overemphasizes the importance of water control. They point out that the emperor and his officials viewed the collection of taxes, the administration of justice, and the conducting of annual sacrifices to heaven and earth as matters of far higher priority.

A fourth view is that China became modern during the midpoint of the Tang dynasty, about A.D. 850. This is known as the Naito hypothesis, after Naito Konsan, the Japanese scholar who first articulated it. As previously discussed, the term *modernization* can be defined in a number of ways. Naito's major criterion is that of social mobility: In a modern society, one rises through merit, as opposed to inheriting one's status. This actually did happen in the mid-Tang dynasty, thanks to the widespread institutionalization of the examination system during that period. At about the same time one begins to find military leaders who had been common soldiers of peasant background, as opposed to the aristocratic warriors who predominated in feudal society. Vernacular literature also spread, supplementing Confucian treatises and Buddhist sutras. The position of the commoner improved.

There is no doubt that all of these phenomena took place, as Naito points out. However, one may argue that China did not necessarily become modern because of them. A bureaucracy chosen by merit does not in itself confer modernity on a state. According to Max Weber, the eminent sociologist of bureaucracies, the hallmark of modernity is functional specificity: Bureaucrats have specific tasks such as supervision of engineering projects and preparation of the state budget. The first group would have been trained in bridge-building and dam construction, the second in statistics. This ran counter to the primacy of amateurism over professionalism in the Chinese bureaucracy. The examination system trained generalists, not specialists. What it tested was one's ability to expound on the Confucian classics, not one's ability to build public works or analyze statistics. However, one should point out that there is a consensus that nineteenth-century Great Britain was a modern state. Yet its bureaucrats were also trained as generalists: A background in Greek and Latin classics was considered excellent preparation for future leaders.

Another argument against the Naito hypothesis is that, whereas modernity includes the ability to rise through merit within a hierarchy, success in the Chinese bureaucracy was heavily dependent on whom one knew. One was also supposed to help out those who passed the examinations the same year one did and, assuming one was able to rise within the official hierarchy, their children as well. A counterargument is that the phenomenon of promotion on the basis of connections, whether one's own or one's relatives and their friends, is scarcely unknown in modern Western societies. And the perception of obligation to help members of one's peer group is the very essence of the "old school tie" in Britain and the *Burschenschaft* in Germany. The crucial element that kept China from modernity is less likely to have been the absence of a modern bureaucracy than the country's lack of industrialization.

Implications for Industrialization

The question of what factors are necessary for the industrialization of a country has been carefully examined by a number of social scientists and, not surprisingly, there is less than total agreement among them. A standard list of prerequisites for industrialization include:

1. Capital from the sale of commercially marketable agricultural surpluses that can be invested in manufacturing
2. Legal codes to protect businesses and their personnel
3. The concept of progress
4. A positive attitude toward science
5. Geographic mobility, to take advantage of manufacturing and other opportunities as they arise[7]

As we have seen, Confucianism was a rich and varied tradition. There were different interpretations of the classics over the years, and the original philosophy absorbed elements from other philosophies and religions. However, in all its phases, regardless of time or dynasty, Confucianism had a proagriculture, anticommercial bias. Peasants were considered the producers of wealth; that is, food. Merchants were regarded as nonproductive parasites on society: dishonest folk who sought to make a profit out of other people's work through such schemes as buying at a low price at one time of year or in one area and selling at higher prices at another time or place. Clearly, neither Confucius nor his disciples saw any value in the entrepreneurial function.

In those states that have succeeded in industrializing, the basis for industrialization has been the harnessing of capital derived from a commercially marketable agricultural surplus to manufacturing purposes. The Confucian attitude toward merchants and their activities made this virtually impossible. The socially sanctioned outlet for money derived from the sale of produce was investment in land. The goal was gentry status, not merely in terms of substantial landholdings but also to pass the examination system or have a son or close relative do so. Also, in addition to being anticommerce, Confucius was not favorably disposed to the rule of law as we know it; hence no codes that could regulate business transactions grew up. Merchants did exist, the Confucian attitude toward them notwithstanding, but they could not protect themselves to a sufficient extent to compete with officialdom. Business activities were inhibited by the need to pay bribes or taxes, often to the point of unprofitability.

A third basic ingredient of industrialization, the concept of progress, was also absent in traditional China. There was no motivation to strive toward a better age. Confucius perceived the golden age as in the past, during the period that preceded the Warring States era (443–221 B.C.). History after this golden age was seen as a series of cycles, as in the dynastic cycle. The virtue of rulers and the prosperity of the country would wax and wane in the manner depicted by yin-yang symbolism. This is not to say that change did not take place, since it certainly did. But change was not regarded as a good thing in itself, and the eternal perfectibility of the society was not expected. The aim was not progress, but harmony, as represented by the Chinese character for king: three horizontal lines, representing heaven, earth, and man, joined by a vertical stroke through the middle (王). The king, through his virtue, aligns heaven, earth, and man in equilibrium.

Science, the fourth prerequisite for industrialization, was regarded as unimportant and unnecessary. As is well known, the Chinese made some remarkable discoveries, including the compass and gunpowder, many years before they were invented in the West. In medieval times, their shipbuilding techniques were far superior to those of the West. These skills made long voyages possible, of which those of the early Ming dynasty are the best known. Confucius was not against science, but viewed exploration and invention as trivial: It was more important to cultivate one's moral virtue.

Confucius's emphasis on the veneration of ancestors also inhibited geographic mobility. It was incumbent on one to keep up the ancestral graves, and the village occupied an almost mystic point of reference for its inhabitants. This did not prevent some Chinese from venturing far and wide: prosperous Chinese merchant communities grew up in such places as Cambodia, Singapore, and Indonesia many hundreds of years ago. But, generally speaking, Chinese tradition did not encourage geographic mobility. And even those who migrated great distances often set aside sums of money to ensure that their remains were sent back to the ancestral home for proper burial.

Confucianism might, of course, have adapted to industrialization. One could easily look at medieval Europe, with its religiously mandated prohibition against lending money at interest and fatalistic belief that, because human misery was divinely ordained, nothing could be changed, and conclude that Christianity must permanently prevent industrialization. In the event, however, such adaptation did take place in Europe but did not take place in China, leading a number of scholars to speculate on why.

One intriguing hypothesis for China's slow technological development is that progress was held back by a *high-level equilibrium trap* (see Figure 2.2). According to this theory, through a number of interlocking causes, the input-output relationships of the late-traditional economy had assumed a pattern that was almost incapable of change through internally generated forces. In both technological and investment terms, agricultural productivity per acre had nearly reached the limits of what was possible without industrial-scientific inputs, and the increase of the population had therefore steadily reduced the sur-

Output

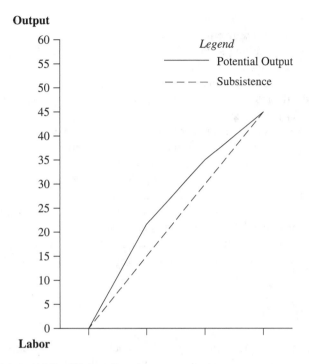

Labor

FIGURE 2.2   High-Level Equilibrium Trap

This chart illustrates the effects of a quasi-ceiling in late-traditional Chinese farm technology. The solid line shows Potential output for a given input of labor using the best Premodern methods; the dotted line shows the proportion of output needed for the subsistence of a given labor force. With land constant, potential surplus shrinks, first relatively, Then absolutely, as the labor force grows. At the farthest end of the chart, adding inputs no longer results in increased output. This trap can be broken out of only through the use of industrial-scientific inputs.
Source: Adopted from Mark Elvin, *The Pattern of the Chinese Past* (Stanford, Calif: Stanford University Press, 1973), p. 313.

plus product above what was needed for subsistence. A falling surplus per head of population means a reduction in effective demand per person for goods other than those needed for bare survival (see Figure 2.2). Premodern water transport was close to a similar ceiling of efficiency, and few possibilities existed for increasing demand for goods by reducing transport costs.

For these technological reasons, the rising price of food in periods when population pressure on land was becoming severe could not induce a higher output of grain except by migration and the opening up of new land. Migration did indeed take place. It was the chief means whereby the Chinese economy grew in quantitative terms, but there was almost no qualitative change. If the huge size of the traditional economy had any implications for technological change, they were probably negative. Any significant change in input-output relationships would have involved enormous amounts of materials and goods. For example, Britain's consumption of raw cotton tripled between 1741 and the early 1770s, when effective machine-spinning of cotton fiber first began. For China to have tripled consumption in a thirty-year period would have been beyond the cotton-producing ability of the entire eighteenth-century world.

With falling surplus in agriculture, and hence falling per capita income and per capita demand; with cheapening labor but increasingly expensive resources and capital; with farming and transport technologies so good that no simple improvements could be made, the rational strategy for peasant and merchant alike argued not for labor-saving machinery but for economizing on resources and fixed capital. Large but nearly static markets did not tend toward creating the systemic bottlenecks that might have prompted technological creativity. Merchants dealt with temporary shortages by more creatively using cheap transport. This is the essence of the *high-level equilibrium trap* explanation.[8]

A related theory, called *involutionary commercialization*, also hypothesizes that China's large population was a major factor in the country's failure to modernize. With the size of farms shrinking as population pressure grew, peasants turned to commercialized crop production and handicrafts, which required much more intensive labor input than grain production. Total output value grew, but at the cost of lower marginal returns per workday. The peasants marketed not for capitalist profit, which could have been reinvested, but for sheer survival. And economic growth was not accompanied by economic development.[9]

Conclusions

A brief summary of the many points touched on in this chapter may be helpful. First, some contemporary Chinese analysts notwithstanding, China was not feudal in the usual sense of the word, nor had it been for almost two millennia. Second, there was a good deal of social mobility in traditional China—an unusual amount for a premodern society. Hard physical labor and diligent study had raised a number of paupers or their sons into the official class. Third, China was not unchanging, although changes tended to come slowly and within the context of tradition.

Fourth, history was perceived as cyclical rather than as marching progressively onward. Fifth, the Chinese state was culturalistic rather than nationalistic. Acceptance into the society depended less on an individual's ethnic background than on his ability to assimilate Confucian principles. Sixth, the imperial bureaucracy was hierarchically arranged and subdivided according to function. However, it did not extend down to the level of local government. Seventh, the individual was subordinated to his or her family group. The empire was conceived as a family writ large, with the emperor as a benign, if authoritarian, father.

Eighth, scholars, administrators, and even the emperor himself were expected to follow an ethical rather than a legal code of conduct. Western-style individualism and the supremacy of law never became established, nor did the personal freedom under law represented by Western civil liberties and institutions of private property. It should be noted that legal safeguards of personal liberty are relatively recent even in the West, and still far from perfect. Ninth, traditional China was based on noncommercial agriculture and ruled by a powerful bureaucracy. Although it was politically centralized, China was economically decentralized. Its structures were sanctioned by customs and ethical beliefs rather than religion or law. When traditional China lived up to its ideals, it was quite a good system.

Notes

1. See L. Carrington Goodrich, *A Short History of the Chinese People,* 3rd ed. (New York: Harper, 1959), p. 30, for a concise description of these and other achievements.

2. For those desiring more information on Chinese philosophy, Fung Yu-lan's *A Short History of Chinese Philosophy* (New York: Macmillan, 1948) is highly recommended.

3. See Joseph R. Levenson, *Modern China and Its Confucian Past* (New York: Anchor Books, 1964), Chapter 2, for a discussion of this ideal as it relates to painting.

4. Goodrich, p. 187.

5. Burton Watson's "Chinese Protest Poetry: From the Earliest Times Through the Sung Dynasty," *Asia,* no. 17, Winter 1969–1970, pp. 76–91, contains some excellent examples of these. I am indebted to Dr. James D. Seymour of Columbia University's East Asian institute for calling this source to my attention.

6. See Karl Wittfogel, *Oriental Despotism: A Comparative Study of Total Power* (New Haven, Conn.: Yale University Press, 1957), for a detailed explanation of this theory.

7. See, for example, Barrington Moore, *Social Origins of Dictatorship and Democracy* (Boston: Beacon Press, 1966).

8. Mark Elvin, *The Pattern of the Chinese Past* (Stanford, Calif.: Stanford University Press, 1973), pp. 312–315.

9. This is the central argument of Philip C. C. Huang's *The Peasant Economy and Social Change in North China* (Stanford, Calif.: Stanford University Press, 1985).

Suggestions for Further Reading

Mark Elvin, *The Pattern of the Chinese Past* (Stanford, Calif.: Stanford University Press, 1973).

Fung Yu-lan, *A Short History of Chinese Philosophy* (New York: Macmillan, 1948).

L. Carrington Goodrich, *A Short History of the Chinese People,* 3rd ed. (New York: Harper, 1959).

Philip C. C. Huang, *The Peasant Economy and Social Change in North China* (Stanford, Calif.: Stanford University Press, 1985).

Joseph R. Levenson, *Modern China and Its Confucian Past* (New York: Anchor Books, 1964).

CHAPTER

3 Reformers, Warlords, and Communists

The New Invasion

By the nineteenth century, China was not a society that was living up to its ideals. Tax assessments had been fixed while the population and its needs expanded rapidly, meaning a curtailment of the amounts available for public works. Poor management had caused popular discontent; domestic rebellion became a problem. As noted in Chapter 2 these were important indicators of a downturn in the dynastic cycle. When the West, newly commercially developed and eager for markets, arrived and demanded trade privileges that Chinese officialdom had no desire to grant, the Westerners were seen as a third indicator of dynastic decline: barbarian invasion.

It was not considered important that, whereas previous barbarians had arrived by land, these new ones came by sea. The "new" barbarians' strange appearance—hairy, with big noses and florid complexions—and odd customs (one state was rumored to be ruled by a woman; another allegedly had a leader who reverted to being a commoner after four or eight years) were the subject of incredulous gossip. But Westerners as such were not seen as a serious threat. Minor concessions were granted, as they had been to other barbarians in times past. It was believed that foreign countries could not get along for a single day without tea and rhubarb, so His Majesty graciously bestowed the privilege of acquisition on them. Since the articles they brought in return were considered toys—elaborate clocks, for example—that were not needed by the Celestial Empire, China could simply cut off this privilege should the barbarians become too demanding. Officials downplayed the possibility of military threat. Among other misconceptions, it was believed that the barbarians' ships could be set afire by soldiers applying torches to the vessels' waterlines.

While the imperial government saw itself as graciously granting some of these inferior beings' annoying demands, Westerners chafed under what they regarded as arrogant behavior and petty restrictions. These became increasingly irritating. Trade was confined to one small area, to which they had no right of residence, and they could not communicate directly with the imperial government. Western merchants and their governments made a number of requests, including the opening of a number of ports to trade, access to China's hinterland, and the right to station an ambassador in the capital city. From the Beijing government's point of view, the barbarians had become too demanding. Particularly upsetting was their preferred method of payment for Chinese goods: opium. The drug was not new to China; it was raised domestically and used medicinally. Elderly people might also light up a pipe to ease the aches and pains that came with advanced years. Addiction existed, but on a relatively small scale.

This changed dramatically with the arrival of foreign opium. More and more Chinese smoked ever larger amounts. In addition to its deleterious effects on the health of the population, foreign opium caused financial problems for the government. The large net outflow of silver from China to pay for the opium had serious consequences. A scarcity of silver meant that its price rose relative to copper. Since peasants used copper currency for their everyday transactions but still had to pay their taxes in silver, the increasing value of silver meant that peasants were paying steadily higher taxes. This in turn meant less prosperity, more unrest, and a greater likelihood of rebellion—a further slide down the slippery slope of dynastic decline.

The imperial government pleaded with the Western powers, to no avail. The foreign intruders pointed out that China raised opium itself and that demand would simply be served by domestic sources if they stopped selling the drug. The court then decided on more drastic action. In 1839, an imperial commissioner at Guangzhou (Canton) seized nearly three million pounds of British raw opium and flushed it out to sea. This provided the Westerners with a cause for war, with concomitant opportunities to force concessions from the imperial government. In 1840, a British fleet arrived, equipped with modern steam-driven vessels and long-range guns, demolishing the Chinese defenses. This was the most decisive defeat the Qing (Manchu) dynasty had ever received, though worse were yet to come. The settlements ending the Opium War of 1839–1842 gave the foreigners substantial concessions in trade, tariffs, right of residence, extraterritoriality, most favored nation status, and redress for damages. Britain was also given Hong Kong island. This was the first of the so-called unequal treaties, discussed in Chapter 1 in connection with the strategic-interaction school.

The Chinese court spent the next decade doing its best to avoid compliance with the treaties it had signed. After 1851 it was chiefly concerned with a serious domestic uprising, the Taiping rebellion, and continued to temporize on the matter of treaty compliance. Wearying of these obfuscatory tactics, the British and French seized on a fairly minor incident in 1856 to recommence hostilities. These ended when a joint Anglo-French force marched on Beijing, forcing the emperor to flee. The 1860 Treaty of Beijing—actually a series of treaties, since through the most favored nation clause other nations participated in concessions won by the victors—constituted the second set of unequal treaties. The Chinese government had wasted more than two decades in responding to the barbarians. Clearly, something would have to be done.

The Self-Strengthening Movement

When a response came, it was well within tradition. The empire was judged to be suffering because its adherence to Confucian tradition had deteriorated. Restoration of traditional principles would arrest this decay, strengthen the empire, and make possible a midcourse correction to the dynastic cycle. This was the basis for the Tongzhi restoration, 1862–1874. *Tongzhi*, meaning "unified government," is the reign title of the emperor who ruled during these years. It would have been considered impolite to call the emperor by his actual name; a reign title was chosen to embody the aspirations held for the period. By analogy, Franklin Roosevelt would be referred to as the New Deal president and Lyndon Johnson as the Great Society president in preference to using their names.

The Tongzhi restoration was conceived as a self-strengthening movement conducted within the parameters of Confucian tradition. Although there were differences of opinion among officials on precisely what to do, most argued that it would be acceptable to borrow Western military techniques. This was sanctioned by traditional China's preeminent military strategist, Sun Zi, through his "Know yourself, know your enemy, win ten thousand battles" maxim, and the Chinese had in fact occasionally borrowed military techniques from barbarians in the past, as already noted. The defeats by Westerners had made this seem imperative to most officials. In addition, since "barbarian handling" had long been regarded as a legitimate concern and is certainly also sanctioned by Sun Zi's maxim, studying Western diplomacy could be considered a logical extension of past practices. One would study the Westerners in order to better manipulate the Westerners.

The slogan of the self-strengthening movement was "Chinese culture [*ti*] for the foundation, Western learning for practical use [*yong*]," as has been discussed in Chapter 1. One who disagreed completely with this was an eminent Manchu authority on the Confucian classics, Woren. He argued that Western learning had a *ti* of its own that would eventually displace the Chinese essence. Better, he argued, to sacrifice the empire to retain Confucian principles than subvert those principles for which the empire stood. However, this became a less and less common view.

There is no doubt that a great many things *were* accomplished during the Tongzhi restoration:

- The Grand Canal and some lesser canals that had been allowed to silt up, essentially through mismanagement, were dredged and reopened.
- A new and generally successful tax was instituted to ease the government's revenue problems. Called *likin,* a tax of one thousand, it was too small to make avoidance worthwhile and so proved easier to collect than other taxes.
- New, regionally based armies and navies were founded, funded by customs revenues and *likin.* Efforts were made to recruit literate gentry as officers and healthy young peasants as volunteers. Arsenals and shipyards were founded, again on regional bases, to supply the new armies with better weapons. Officers of the new armies were warned against corrupt practices such as padding the payrolls with the names of deceased or nonexistent soldiers and keeping the money that should have been paid to their actual troops.
- A school for the study of foreign languages was set up.
- A coal mine was opened.
- A proto-foreign office was set up. None had existed before, since all other countries were considered too inferior to warrant it.
- Army officers were sent to Germany to study military science.
- A group of students was dispatched to the United States to study at Yale University.

However, despite all these efforts, the Tongzhi restoration, judged as a whole, was a failure. This failure is all the more obvious when viewed alongside the success of Japan.

China's neighbor to the east had felt the pressure of the West even later than China. It was much smaller than China; it was much poorer in natural resources and had a similarly Confucian bias against commerce. In fact, large parts of Japanese culture, including the written language, had been borrowed from China. Although it was not widely recognized at the time, some of Japan's apparent disadvantages had advantageous aspects as well: Being smaller meant that new ideas and new technologies could be disseminated more quickly than in China's far-flung domains. And, because the Japanese had borrowed major parts of their culture from China, they were less averse to borrowing from the West.

Beginning from 1868, several years later than China, Japan also undertook a restoration: the Meiji restoration. The two restorations shared a common Chinese character: The reign title *Meiji* means "bright government," the *zhi* of Tongzhi being pronounced *ji* in Japanese. Within a few decades, the same decades as the self-strengthening movement in China, Japan managed to raise itself to major-power status. In 1894–1895, it defeated its much larger neighbor with ridiculous ease. China's defeat in the Sino-Japanese confrontation is taken as a symbolic date marking the failure of the restoration program.

Why did the Tongzhi restoration fail while the Meiji restoration succeeded brilliantly? One scholar believes the explanation lies in the greater fiscal strength of the Meiji state compared to China, and also because in Japan, unlike China, there were no strong Western interests that blocked or undermined the success of industrialization policies.[1] Another answer may be that the Chinese program genuinely aimed at a restoration, whereas the Japanese were in essence cloaking a revolution in traditional garb, the better to obtain compliance. Trying to make China into a strong modern nation through restoring Confucian principles was doomed to failure, because Confucianism was incompatible with the requirements of a modern nation.[2] It was not even nationalistic, but rather cultural. Other factors, such as anticommercialism, the relatively low regard with which technology and practical matters in general were held, and the belief that the golden age lay in the past, have been discussed in Chapter 2.

To be sure, the Tongzhi restoration did make some changes, carefully rationalized as being compatible with tradition, and therefore cannot be too starkly contrasted with the Meiji restoration on this matter. It was how the reforms worked themselves out that was crucial, and here many of them were rejected definitively, portending the certain defeat of the self-strengthening movement. For example, officials understood well the need for efficient communications for administrative purposes, as can be seen in their great concern for maintaining the speed of the traditional courier service, but they could not see the need for faster communication. When foreigners suggested building railroads and telegraph networks to speed communications, the officials replied that the existing system was fast enough for them. The only reason to send messages more quickly would be to facilitate commercial transactions. Since commerce was despicable, there was no need for railroads or telegraphs.

Most officials seem to have regarded railroads and telegraphs as toys: useless exotica from abroad. They thoroughly enjoyed playing with models, but the idea of putting up functioning systems horrified them. After repeatedly being refused permission to build a telegraph, a foreign consul suggesting building one that would connect only treaty ports, in order to circumvent the official objection that the telegraph system would adversely affect China. At the same time, unfortunately, building the system in this way would reduce much of its value to China. The consul was eventually permitted to proceed with construction, providing that all the lines were immersed in water and all the terminals were on ships.

One official built a miniature railroad on the grounds of his estate, and spent hours watching with fascination as the cars raced around the tracks. But he refused to approve the construction of a full-sized system. In 1876, a railroad was eventually built, connecting Shanghai with a city about ten miles away. There was tremendous resistance from the local population: The *feng-shui* (see Chapter 2) had been violated, and the noise scared their livestock. Hens, they reported, had refused to lay eggs. Eventually, the Chinese governor-general had to buy the railroad from the British, who had built it, and destroy it. Meanwhile, the Meiji government was appropriating funds to connect all of Japan's major cities with a rail net.

The steamship company that had been established as part of the self-strengthening movement also failed dismally. Set up under the principle that merchants would run the company under official supervision (a concession to the prerogatives of the official class, as well as a recognition of the inferior position of the commercial class), it seemed to be doing quite well at first. However, the company was bled to death when its initial profits, which should have been reinvested, were instead invested in land or in unproductive goods. Confucius would have approved, but Adam Smith would not have.

The Tongzhi restoration's educational mission failed as well. After the students had been at Yale for a few years, they were sent to meet with the newly appointed supervisor of the mission. When the boys were ushered into his presence they failed to perform the *ketou* (kowtow) of deference, as called for by traditional manners. Taking this as indicative that studying Western things had caused them to neglect Chinese tradition, the supervisor arranged to have the mission recalled.

The common theme of these examples is that borrowing from the West was considered acceptable so long as it did not interfere with Chinese tradition. Unfortunately, this attitude *did* interfere with China's self-strengthening. It should be pointed out that unswerving adherence to tradition was in itself untraditional. Chinese tradition had never been rigid and unbending, changing somewhat—albeit slowly—in response to the needs of the time. Neither manners nor technology remained the same from dynasty to dynasty. Tradition had never been a blind charge on the Chinese. It was not an imperative *we must*, but a guide: "How could a reasonable person do otherwise?" Thus, many of those who styled themselves traditionalists were in reality doing violence to Chinese tradition.

Confucianism might certainly have adapted. Drastic changes have occurred in many another ideology through such means as "heretics" who provide radical reinterpretations of the official canon, or others who reason that, if the great founder of the philosophy were alive today, she or he would surely have spoken differently. Possibly the shock of discovering how different the West was, and how great an adaptation China would have to make, was a factor in the inability of the leadership to adapt. Had a smaller amount of borrowing been called for, the adaptation might have taken place. This takes the problem back before the Qing, to the turning inward of China after the cessation of the sea voyages of the early Ming. Had China kept in better contact with the rest of the world, adaptation could have taken place more gradually. Responsibility for this lies with the official class.

Another factor lay in the dynastic leadership—or lack thereof. The Tongzhi emperor came to the throne as a child of five, succeeding his highly incompetent father. Though nominally in charge during the restoration that bears his name, the real "emperor" was his mother, Cixi. Originally a lower-ranking concubine, the empress dowager had been the only palace lady to bear her sickly master a male child. Cixi was intelligent, competent, and utterly ruthless—a set of qualifications generally believed to be shared by many highly successful world leaders. However, the empress dowager had to expend most of her energies fighting off plots against her. In terms of dealing with foreigners and the problems they presented, she was at a further disadvantage: Being a woman, she was unable to leave the palace and therefore had to get most of her information from eunuchs. However, under a Qing law imposed some years before in order to curtail the eunuchs' power, they also were prohibited from leaving the palace grounds. Though eunuchs had considerably more freedom of movement than the empress dowager, there were real limitations on their ability to provide the information she needed for proper decision-making. What they did tell her was often biased in terms of their own interests as well.

China's defeat in the Sino-Japanese war was a devastating blow. One problem was that China's navy was composed of several different regionally based naval fleets without a unified command. In addition, widespread corruption had diverted large sums of money meant for naval modernization. The empress dowager herself had ordered a marble boat to be constructed on the lake of her summer palace outside Beijing. It might have been argued that the empress dowager, by not living up to Confucian principles, had doomed the restoration—among other things, she had certainly not set an example of frugality. But in fact the Sino-Japanese war put an end to the idea of reform through Confucianism. With China's weaknesses further exposed by the humiliating defeat, there followed a period of scrambling for concessions by a number of foreign powers, including England, France, Italy, Germany, Russia, and Japan. Years of effort to improve China's situation had resulted in making it worse than ever.

Reform and Revolution

While the first generation of reformers had been full of confidence and almost arrogant about their chances for success, the second generation had no such confidence. Most of them felt strongly that *China* would have to be saved at all costs, even if it meant drastically changing or discarding Confucianism. This change of priorities marks an important step away from culturalism and toward nationalism. Yet another, still nascent at this time, was a tendency to blame China's problems on the fact that non-Chinese occupied the throne.

One of the most interesting of the second generation of reformers was a scholar named Yan Fu. Reading and translating the works of many Western philosophers into Chinese, he originally aimed at a compromise between Western thought and that of traditional China. Yan became much influenced by Herbert Spencer's theory of social Darwinism, which applies Darwin's concept of survival of the fittest to nations. Spencer's ideas seemed most relevant. Many Chinese scholars during the last quarter of the nineteenth century did entertain doubts as to their country's survivability. Eventually, Yan Fu came to the rather devastating conclusion that the Confucian faith could not be preserved, and that in fact there was a fundamental flaw in the entire *ti-yong* dichotomy: Western civilization contained an essence of its own, of which the coveted items for practical use were manifestations. Interestingly, this was the same argument the ultraconservative Woren had made some years before. However, Yan's conclusion was entirely different. Whereas Woren had urged categorical resistance to Westernization in order to preserve the Chinese essence, Yan Fu concluded that Westernization would have to take place to save China.

Yan Fu also criticized Confucius's belief that self-interest is the ultimate source of evil, believing with British utilitarian philosopher Jeremy Bentham that the goal of the state was to effect the greatest good for the greatest number of individuals. He argued that freedom was the crux of the Western *ti* and that it released human energy, with the wealth and power of the state the goal to which this energy must be applied. Western public spirit, Yan argued, came from promoting the constructive self-interest of the individual, releasing individual energies that would be applied to collective goals. Changes in law, he noted, were not as important as changes in the heart.[3] Again, this shows his opinion that the *ti* had to be replaced in order to have a beneficial effect on the *yong*.

The Reformers

As is not uncommon when there is widespread dissatisfaction with the status quo, those who wished to change it divided into three broad categories: the reformers, the reactionaries, and the revolutionaries. The most famous of the reformers was Kang Youwei (1858–1927). Born into an old, aristocratic Cantonese family of successful scholars, Kang had passed the first level of the imperial examination system while still quite young. At the same time, he was passionately interested in Western studies, especially science. Kang visited Hong Kong and Shanghai, and was impressed by the honesty and efficiency of the governments Westerners had set up there. He did not neglect classical studies while pursuing Western learning, and soon passed the second level of the examination system.

Armed with his new status, Kang began to write to the emperor on the need for reform. After Tongzhi's death in 1874, Cixi had chosen her husband's six-year-old nephew to succeed him. He reigned as the Guangxu emperor (1875–1908) and functioned as little more than her puppet during his childhood. As time went on, the empress dowager gradually took less interest in the affairs of government, and Guangxu gained in stature. While Guangxu's officials were shocked at the frank manner in which Kang addressed the emperor and the boldness with which he advocated reform, the emperor himself reacted well to Kang and his ideas. Perhaps he was actually flattered, since it was quite unusual for people to pay so much attention to him as opposed to the empress dowager. Guangxu even agreed to receive Kang in person, a rare privilege. It also meant that Kang could expound his views without fear of being misquoted.

Kang Youwei's technique for reforming China was to entirely reinterpret Confucius. He claimed, among other things, that the golden age Confucius looked back to had never really existed. Rather, it was a utopia that Confucius had contrived in order to give China a goal to strive toward. Kang thus cleverly, if not entirely convincingly, incorporated the idea of progress into Confucius. In his book *A Study of Confucius as a Reformer* and elsewhere, Kang propounded the thesis that Confucius was a progressive. He dismissed as forgeries those ancient writings that conflicted with his point of view. Clearly, his plan was to find support for Western ideas within the Chinese tradition so that traditional Chinese, who would otherwise be unable to accept ideas from the West, could do so with a clear conscience.

In 1898, Kang managed to persuade the emperor to promulgate a daring set of reforms. Called the Hundred Days Reforms because they were in effect for only that period of time, they included:

- A revamping of the examination system. Questions were to be chosen from current problems rather than the Confucian classics.
- The establishment of a bureau of agriculture, industry, and commerce in Beijing.
- The abolition of sinecure positions. There were a number of these at the time: For example, the official in charge of grain transportation had no responsibility for any kind of transportation, and the official in charge of the salt monopoly had no salt fields to supervise.
- A regular foreign office would be established, to succeed the proto-foreign office set up under the Tongzhi restoration.

Unfortunately, Kang had persuaded only the emperor of the wisdom of these reforms. The empress dowager, the nobles, and the officials, including those who controlled military power, had never even been consulted about these changes, much less consented to them. Clearly the empress and nobility had had their prerogatives trampled on. Moreover, since the officials had devoted considerable time and energy to advancing themselves through the classical examination system, it was understandable that they felt their positions threatened by Kang's reforms. There was broad agreement that both Kang and the emperor would have to be dealt with. Rumors of Guangxu's ill health began to circulate, and the empress dowager, with a great show of reluctance, stepped in to conduct government affairs again. With the help of a leading military commander, Yuan Shikai, a coup d'état was effected. Though Kang himself escaped to Japan, a number of his followers were executed. Guangxu was put under the equivalent of house arrest and the reforms were rescinded.

The Reactionaries

As might be expected, the failure of the Hundred Days Reforms weakened the reform movement while strengthening more extremist forces of ultraconservatism and revolution. The ultraconservatives made their move first. Many Qing officials began to support, at least tacitly but sometimes openly, a violently xenophobic movement. The literal translation of the movement's Chinese name is "Fists of Righteous Harmony," but Westerners soon began referring to it as the Boxers because the ritual calisthenics its members practiced somewhat resembled shadow boxing.

The Boxers' leader believed he had received a command from the Jade Emperor, a Daoist deity, to kill all foreigners. The fact that a number of reformers were enjoying a safe haven in Japan contributed to the Boxers' antiforeign feelings. In addition to performing ritual calisthenics, Boxers chanted incantations, believing that these made their bodies invulnerable to bullets. They stalked and murdered Western missionaries, Chinese Christians, and foreign officials, often horribly mutilating them. The empress dowager played a delicate game: While encouraging the Boxers covertly, she publicly deplored their actions.

Eventually, in 1900, the Qing government declared war on the foreign powers, and the Boxers laid siege to the foreign legation sector in Beijing. They were not able to break through, but conditions became very difficult for the residents. The siege was lifted nearly two months later when an allied force from eight foreign nations marched into Beijing. Its arrival forced Cixi to flee from the capital in a crude cart, dressed as a peasant. Through no fault of her own, the empress had not been outside the imperial palace since she was a teenager. The condition of the Chinese countryside therefore came as a shock. This experience, the death of many prominent ultraconservatives, and the humiliating settlement exacted by the foreign powers left the empress dowager with little choice but to institute reforms.

In 1901 Cixi ordered her subjects to "adopt the strong points of foreign countries in order to make up China's shortcomings," criticizing those who limited themselves to studying the foreigners' written and spoken languages and to the manufacturing of machines. She characterized languages and manufacturing techniques as "the skin and hair of Western technology, but not the fundamental source of Western government."[4] Over the next two years many of the reforms Kang Youwei had called for in 1898 were instituted, including the establishment of a regular foreign office and the abolition of many sinecure positions. The traditional examination system was ended altogether in both its civil and military forms. Old-style Confucian academies were converted into Western-style universities, and students were encouraged to go abroad to learn. Provinces were told to establish Western-style military academies to produce the officers heretofore recruited through the military examination system. A ministry of education and ministry of police were established. However, many people feel that the reforms came too late. Moreover, the empress dowager was now an elderly woman who nonetheless remained wary of grooming any strong leader to take her place. In 1908, realizing that her end was near, Cixi had the Guangxu emperor poisoned and arranged for yet another small child to assume the throne. The next day she died. In 1911 the dynasty itself fell.

The Revolutionaries

Sun Yat-sen, leader of the forces of revolution, was born to a poor family in Guangdong province, not far from Hong Kong, about 1866. His elder brother went to Hawaii as a common laborer, prospered, and sent for his sibling. Sun was sent to one of the most expensive and prestigious Western-style schools in Honolulu, where he excelled in English and declared his intention to become a Christian. Not pleased with Sun's conversion, his brother sent Sun back to China, where he promptly destroyed the idols in the village temple. After this unheard-of act of civic desecration, Sun's father packed him off to Hong Kong, where he formally became a Christian and took his medical degree. He also began to advocate the overthrow of the Qing.

In 1894, shortly after the outbreak of the Sino-Japanese War, Sun founded his first revolutionary society, the *Xingzhong Hui* (Revive China Society) with some friends. It advocated establishing schools to educate the masses, newspapers to help them become good citizens, and industries to improve their standard of living. Members were asked to buy ten-dollar "shares," with the assumption that they would recoup on their investments. Among those who joined was a financially successful American-educated Chinese businessman named Charles Jones Soong and his wife. The Soongs and Sun Yat-sen became good friends; later Sun would marry one of the Soong daughters.

Sun's would-be revolutionaries tried to smuggle arms and dynamite into China from Hong Kong but failed. A number of the society's members were caught and executed. Sun managed to escape not only this but several other efforts to apprehend him. He began to travel around the world raising money to support the revolution, mainly from among Overseas Chinese communities. In the process, he had a series of adventures beside which most spy novels pale by comparison. At one point he grew a luxuriant mustache and successfully posed as a Japanese, evading capture by Qing secret agents. In 1897 he was caught in London and imprisoned on the top floor of the Chinese legation there, pending the Qing government's authorization of the money necessary for his passage back to certain death in China. Ironically, the very inefficiency that Sun railed against saved his life. While the wheels of Qing bureaucracy creaked slowly away, Sun gained the trust of the chambermaid. Convinced that the government was planning to kill him because he was a Christian, she carried a message to one of Sun's former medical school professors, smuggling it out of the legation in a coal scuttle. Finding the British government uninterested in interfering with internal Chinese affairs, the professor turned to London's yellow press. Their sensationalized story of a persecuted Christian to whose plight Her Majesty's Government remained utterly indifferent created sufficient official embarrassment that Sun was eventually released. The incident had also made him a celebrity.

Sun continued his fund-raising activities and refined his ideology. In 1905 he founded a new organization, the *Tongmeng Hui*, or Alliance Society, later to become the *Kuomintang* (KMT) or Nationalist Party. It had four slogans: drive away the Manchus, recover China for the Chinese, establish a republic, and equalize land ownership. In recognition of the strength of horizontal rather than vertical ties in society, Sun described his country as a "sheet of loose sand," with the individual particles rolling over each other in response to external forces. His new organization was intended to weld them together to form a counterforce capable of resistance to these pressures.

The organization's members spent the next several years enlisting support from Overseas Chinese, students and intellectuals, military officers, and secret societies. In 1911, in the Yangtze River port of Wuhan, one of the *Tongmeng Hui*'s homemade bombs exploded by accident. With the location of their arsenal thus revealed, the society's members had to fight to protect themselves. This provided the spark for the overthrow of the Qing dynasty: As news of the Wuhan uprising spread, it roused others to action in many different parts of the country. Sun himself was in the United States at the time. He had been sent a coded telegram telling him about the revolution, but did not have the key with him, and first heard about the uprising when he purchased a newspaper at the Denver railway station.[5]

The Qing court, alarmed, turned for help to Yuan Shikai, the general Cixi had used to put down the Hundred Days reforms in 1898. However, the court, fearing that Yuan had become too powerful, had dismissed him in 1909, on totally specious grounds of ill health. The general therefore had little incentive to rush into the fray and informed the court that unfortunately his ill health prevented him from commanding armies. Meanwhile,

Manchus were being massacred throughout China. After extensive bargaining with both the court and the revolutionaries, Yuan exacted his compromise. The Republic of China was founded, with Yuan Shikai as president.

The 1911 revolution was better at tearing down than building up. The dynasty had been weak and corrupt, with its intellectual and ethical underpinnings badly deteriorated. What to replace it with was another matter. The abolition of the traditional examination system had meant the end of the scholar-official class that had provided such an important support for the dynasty. It also undermined the basis of the gentry class, which had been an important factor in the stability of the countryside. Since a new bureaucracy did not rush in to perform the functions the gentry had, there was a virtual administrative vacuum in the countryside. Modern students attended Western-style universities in China's major cities. There was an outflow of intellectuals from the countryside and, as a consequence, less understanding of the problems of China's rural areas—which then constituted about 90 percent of the country—than had been the case before. The gap between the Westernized city-dweller and the Chinese peasant widened, compounding the problems of government. The connection between civilian government and the military had also deteriorated. There were no more scholar-officials to command armies, and the professional officers turned out by the new provincial military academies founded by the empress dowager's decree were more likely to feel loyal to their regional commanders than to the central government.

While peasants raised their crops in much the same way their ancestors had, intellectuals gathered in university common rooms and urban teahouses to discuss ideologies. Meanwhile, Sun Yat-sen's infant KMT could not provide a check on Yuan Shikai, who grew increasingly autocratic. When, in 1915, Yuan tried to make himself emperor, the provincial governors, many of whom were also military officers, balked. Whereas previously they had supported Yuan against the KMT, they now made common cause with the KMT in opposition to Yuan's imperial designs. Interestingly, this unusual coalition was joined by an influential group of reformers who had resisted the idea of overthrowing the Qing. While the notion of restoring the dynastic system was not yet dead, it was clearly moribund. Yuan died in 1916, still president but a broken man. The question of who was to succeed him was dominated by the efforts of various military governors. China thus entered an era of warlordism.

The most obvious characteristic of warlordism is war, with capturing Beijing serving as the prize in an ultimately ruinous game. First, since Beijing had been the imperial capital, being in control of it conferred a certain prestige as well as access to such central government machinery as was still functioning. And second, foreign nations, in the absence of a stable government, had decided to deal with whoever was in charge of the government in Beijing as the legal government of China. This gave the incumbent legitimacy, not to mention access to customs revenue and foreign loans. The incentive for the leader in Beijing to contract foreign loans in order to strengthen himself against his enemies was very strong. However, contracting these loans had the simultaneous effect of increasing China's already large foreign debt as well as the pressures that foreign governments could put on the country.

Foreign governments were not, of course, confined to dealing with the person in charge of Beijing, and often had dealings with, and made loans to, several warlords. Since one of the charges leveled against the Qing was that it capitulated to foreign pressure, the new situation was not only no improvement but actually regressive.

Warlordism was regressive in other ways as well. It was by nature divisive, thereby weakening the strength of the country as a whole. The warlord system was also a distinct disincentive to production and commerce. Taxes might be levied at each section of a road controlled by a different warlord. Two or more warlords might also control different portions of a railroad, causing potential traffic bottlenecks because one warlord was unwilling to allow certain goods to fall into the hands of a rival. In the winter of 1925, for example, residents of Beijing were starving for want of food and fuel. The reason was that the warlord of Henan, who was supposed to be a subordinate and close ally of the warlord of Beijing, had refused to allow anything to be shipped in over the Beijing-Hankou railway.

Several warlords were competent governors with carefully thought-out plans for their areas, including literacy programs, economic development schemes, sanitation codes, and strict regulations against opium smoking, gambling, corruption, and even littering. As a whole, however, the warlord era was not good for China.

While the decade after the 1911 revolution was unsatisfactory from the point of view of solving many of the problems on the revolutionaries' agenda, it was an exciting time intellectually. Translations of many of the West's leading political philosophers became available, and heated discussions took place on how relevant their theories were to China. Chinese who had studied abroad returned, contributing their observations and experiences to the discussions.

After World War I began, Western economies regeared for war production, with concomitant benefits for the Chinese economy. There was a great expansion in the number of factories in China's major cities, and industrial production rose. Many of these products were exported to meet increased demand from the belligerent countries. Preoccupied with the war effort, Western powers eased their pressures on China. Unfortunately for China, however, Japanese pressure increased markedly without the West to intervene on behalf of China. Many of China's new industries were in fact Japanese owned and managed. And in 1915, Japan presented the Chinese government with a long list of demands that indicated it had far greater ambitions than factory ownership. If implemented, they would have made China into a quasi-colony.

Chinese intellectuals were impressed by Woodrow Wilson's Fourteen Points, especially those promising self-determination and the return of territories seized by force against the will of the people. When it began to look as if the Allies would be victorious, China joined them in a declaration of war, sending a large number of laborers to Europe to aid in the war effort. This further exposed a number of young Chinese, including Deng Xiaoping and Zhou Enlai, to Western influences. Allied victory was expected to mean, at the very least, the return of the area in Shandong province that China had been forced to lease to Germany.

The merits and drawbacks of differing social and political systems were debated in a number of newly founded journals. Neither capitalism nor communism seemed to have much appeal, the latter because Marx himself felt it inappropriate for any but the most developed countries. Anarchism had many advocates—including, at one point, the young Mao Zedong. Most intellectuals were sympathetic to socialist ideas in one form or another. Bertrand Russell, the well-known British socialist, visited China to lecture on his theories and was enthusiastically received. John Dewey, an American philosopher known for his views on the value of pragmatism, also went to China and had an even greater success. Like Russell, Dewey favored reforms but stressed that rapid changes risked counter-productive disruptions. He saw problems as discrete entities that should first be carefully outlined and researched, then attacked one by one. Once the effects of solving one problem had been coped with, society could move on to dealing with another. Progress would take place slowly, with the emphasis on building up rather than tearing down. Dewey's most famous Chinese disciple, Hu Shi, put forth the slogan "More Study of Problems and Less Talk of Isms."

The general feelings of hope and optimism that pervaded this period received a rude shock on April 30, 1919, when the results of the Versailles conference to formally end World War I were announced. Rather than returning Shandong to China, the Versailles Treaty had awarded it to Japan, which had also been on the victorious side in the war and claimed Shandong as its prize. The Japanese had in fact already conquered the territory from the Germans in 1914. To the disgust of many at home, the Chinese delegate to the Versailles conference had acquiesced in this abomination, undoubtedly because he felt himself powerless to do anything else. Yet another shock was finding out that, during the war, the Chinese government had secretly agreed to most of the humiliating Twenty-One Demands Japan had presented it with in 1915. The Versailles Treaty destroyed the faith that many of the new intelligentsia had put in the West.

On May 4, several thousand students demonstrated in Beijing. A scuffle with police resulted, with some injuries. One student subsequently died of his wounds, setting off a nationwide strike in which the students were joined by merchants and other members of the new urban middle class. Work strikes, antigovernment harangues, and boycotts of Japanese goods continued for six weeks; Japanese nationals were accosted and beaten. Finally, on June 12, the Chinese cabinet resigned. If the Versailles Treaty had disillusioned Chinese intellectuals about the West, the May Fourth movement showed them what a group of dedicated activists could accomplish. The May Fourth generation was a generation in revolt against many aspects of its culture, and the movement had results in a number of fields, including an attack on the Confucian family system and an impetus to the vernacular written language.[6] It also resulted in a rejuvenated KMT and in the founding of the Chinese Communist Party (CCP). Since the KMT and the CCP were to co-exist, usually not peacefully, in differing but always complicated relationships for many years, it is important to understand these interactions as well as the plans each had for China.

The Kuomintang

While Yuan Shikai's successors jockeyed for power in northern China, Sun Yat-sen's KMT supporters made their way to Guangzhou, capital of Sun's home province of Guangdong and contiguous to Hong Kong. There they set up a provisional military government, with Sun as generalissimo. At this point, the KMT government did not look much different from those of the warlords elsewhere in China, save that Sun had no military experience. Factionalism within the party made it difficult to accomplish anything. Sun, though a superb orator, lacked basic organizational skills and had become increasingly irritable with dissent. The KMT's future looked none too bright.

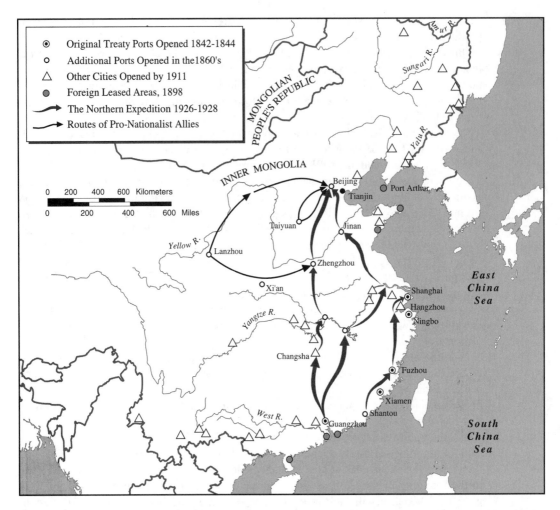

MAP 3.1   The Northern Expeditions of the Kuomintang. These expeditions, from 1926 to 1928, unified most of China under the Nationalist (Kuomintang) government of Chiang Kai-shek, inaugurating the Nanjing decade. Warlord armies continued to hold power on the periphery.

After the Bolshevik revolution in 1917, the new Soviet government began to cast about for ways to help spread world revolution, and Sun Yat-sen came to its attention. Certain of his ideas, such as the primacy of economic relations and his frequent references to the common people and the need to improve their livelihood, sound properly socialistic. Representatives of the Communist International (Comintern) made initial overtures to Sun as well as to several warlords, and one of them, Adolph Joffe, conferred at some length with him. The Soviets saw immediately that what the KMT needed was reorganization, which they offered to provide.

After some negotiation, the Sun-Joffe Manifesto was signed in January 1923. In it Sun recognized the desirability of friendship with, and help from, the Soviet Union. Joffe acknowledged that there was no necessary connection between Soviet help and the adoption of communist ideology. Members of the CCP were to join the KMT as individuals, in the so-called Bloc Within of what was to be the First United Front.

Within a month the Soviets began to supply Sun Yat-sen with money and arms, and Comintern advisers were reorganizing the KMT along Leninist lines. Fundamentally, this involved reconstituting the KMT so that it could be the one party ruling a one-party state, while also taking Sun Yat-sen's ideas into account. What emerged is known as the five-*yuan* system, in which the familiar Western-style triad of legislature, executive, and judiciary is supplemented by an examination *yuan* and a control *yuan*. The former was to supervise a thoroughly modern civil service examination and the latter to investigate improprieties in government, much as the Censorate had done in imperial China. Sun, the iconoclast (and, in fact, a man who knew little about Chinese tradition), had seen fit to breathe new life into two ancient institutions.

Sun and his supporters wrote a new constitution that gave Sun almost dictatorial powers. However, his actual power continued to be contingent on the loyalty of various military groups. Here, too, Soviet advisers provided help. They suggested founding a military academy, with the goal of training loyal, indoctrinated officers so there would be no need to rely on warlord, regional, or mercenary troops. The Whampoa Military Academy duly came into existence. Its first commander was Sun's deputy, Chiang Kai-shek, and somewhat later Zhou Enlai was appointed political commissar.

The Comintern representatives did not neglect propaganda activities and proved themselves consummate public-relations experts. Sun was already an excellent speaker, able to present complex abstract ideas in a nonacademic way that audiences found spellbinding. The Comintern representatives simply worked on ways to present his message better. In the process, they were able to package Sun and sell him to the Chinese public. In 1924, they arranged for him to give a series of lectures, which became and remains the bible of the KMT. Called the *San Min Zhu Yi*, or Three Principles of the People, it is also the title of the national anthem of the Republic of China. The book itself is somewhat disorganized and illogical, partly because it is a faithful reflection of Sun's somewhat disorganized and illogical thought.[7] Derived from a series of lectures, the book was rushed immediately into print without taking the time to iron out contradictions. Sun's advisers deemed it more important to get the book out quickly than to work carefully on the manuscript.

The Three Principles are people's nationalism, people's sovereignty, and people's livelihood; Sun explicitly links them with Abraham Lincoln's government by the people, of the people, and for the people. Before the 1911 revolution, Sun had used nationalism to mean opposition to the Manchu government. Blaming the Manchus for China's problems and demanding a "real" Chinese (that is, Han) government represented an important step away from the culturalism (adherence to Confucian norms and the Chinese language) that had characterized the Chinese tradition. Sun's precept was ethnically based and closer to Western nationalism.

After the fall of the Manchu dynasty, Sun changed the content of people's nationalism to mean opposition to foreign imperialism. Incredibly, he tried to scare the Chinese into nationalist consciousness by predicting that the country would die out for lack of population. People's sovereignty is to be achieved by introducing the rights of initiative, referendum, and recall so that people will be able to check the excesses of government. His analogy is of a child working a light switch: The child may not understand the principles of electricity (governance) but knows when light (a specific leader) is desired or not. Unfortunately, the processes of initiative, referendum, and recall are rather difficult for a child to organize and are not generally considered a huge success in the West, where they were invented.

People's livelihood is the principle in which Sun appears closest to left-wing thought. Yet he is no Marxist, rejecting the idea that material forces determine history. He also describes Marx as a social pathologist rather than a social psychologist, in that he is describing the evils of the capitalist system rather than the capitalist system itself. Sun feels that capitalism should be reformed rather than destroyed.

Basically, the KMT proved very good pupils of the Soviets' public-relations techniques, though not of their social ideals. Sun's widow, Soong Qingling, was the inheritor of his more left-wing thoughts. Espousing the communist cause, she lived on in communist China until her death in the 1980s. The Three Principles of the People—their specific interpretations somewhat revised, perhaps, to soften their criticisms of Marx— and Sun himself are held in esteem in China today.

Sun Yat-sen died in 1925 and was succeeded by Chiang Kai-shek. Chiang was able to use his headship of the Whampoa Military Academy to mobilize support for his succession. The Whampoa clique, as it came to be called, would form the core of Chiang's support throughout his tenure on the mainland. Chiang proceeded to inaugurate the Northern Expedition, a military campaign that aimed at bringing all of China under KMT rule. This it did, at least in the formal sense. In December 1928 the KMT took control of Beijing, thereby becoming the acknowledged legitimate government of China. But victory had been obtained at a cost, which was to infinitely increase the problems of governance. While some warlords had been conquered, others had been co-opted. This amounted to their being confirmed as governors in the provinces they had ruled, with a good deal of autonomy from the KMT central government and Chiang. Naturally this weakened the authority of the KMT. Also in the course of the Northern Expedition, Chiang had definitively ended his united front with the communists, who as a result became a party in overt opposition (see Chapter 4).

Chiang also jettisoned large portions of the more left-wing aspects of KMT ideology and rehabilitated Confucius. In 1927, KMT propaganda described the principles of Confucius as despotic and having the effect of oppressing the people and enslaving their thoughts. Straw effigies of Confucius were burned in the streets. In 1928, Chiang ordered his military officers to spend their leisure time in the study of the Confucian classics. Confucius's birthday became a national holiday, and government protection was accorded to Confucian temples. In 1934, Chiang inaugurated the New Life Movement, based on the four Confucian virtues of *li* (the rites), *yi* (righteousness), *lian* (integrity), and *chi* (sense of shame). These concepts are by nature abstract, and seemed even more vague in the twentieth-century context. Ninety-six rules were issued to apply them, including injunctions against eating noisily, spitting, smoking, and bad posture, and admonitions to kill rats and flies, be punctual, and use native products.[8]

The KMT also tried to revive the gentry class. Chiang sent a letter to provincial officials centering around a theme in the Confucian *Analects*: When the wind moves, the grass bends. The message was that the prestige of the local establishment should provide the wind of authority to back up central-government messages and to influence the common folk to comply. The *baojia* system was also revived, in order to assist in local control.

Though a loyal disciple of Sun, Chiang was a very different person. Born in 1887 to a prosperous salt-merchant family in Zhejiang, he had a classical education followed by study at the military academy of the Japanese army. Whereas Sun moved easily, both culturally and linguistically, among China, Hong Kong, Japan, England, and the United States, Chiang had relatively little foreign travel or knowledge of foreign languages. His brief experiences in Japan and, later, the Soviet Union, seemed to deepen his consciousness of being Chinese rather than to broaden his horizons. Chiang was not a traditionalist in the sense that the nineteenth-century reformers had been. Like Sun Yat-sen, he had married a daughter of Charles Soong. Unlike Sun, Chiang was not a Christian, although he converted in deference to the wishes of his bride and her family and thereafter attended church services regularly. Soong Mei-ling, a graduate of Wellesley College's class of 1917, played an important role in interpreting the West for her husband and in interpreting the KMT in the West. Chiang was an enthusiastic advocate of industrialization and railroad-building; the main centers of KMT support were in large industrial cities and included China's newly emerging middle class. Chiang also made considerable use of foreign advisers.[9]

Nonetheless, Chiang Kai-shek's ideas were formed much more within the Chinese tradition than Sun's, and found their most typical expressions in the language and formulas of the past. The failures of the KMT government on the mainland are unconnected to these expressions and formulas. Indeed, the KMT moved its five-*yuan* government, Confucian precepts, and industrialization strategy to Taiwan, where modernization within a steadily changing tradition has enjoyed great success.[10] If Chiang's eclectic blend of the old and new cannot directly be credited with this success, neither can his formula be said to have hindered it.

The mandate of heaven was not to belong to the KMT for very long before it passed to the Chinese Communist Party. The process by which this occurred, and the implications for modernization and tradition, are the subject of the next chapter.

Notes

1. Frances V. Moulder, *Japan, China, and the Modern World Economy: Toward a Reinterpretation of East Asian Development Ca. 1600 to Ca. 1918* (Cambridge, U.K.: Cambridge University Press, 1977), passim and pp. 200–201.

2. This is the argument made by Mary C. Wright in *The Last Stand of Chinese Conservatism* (Stanford, Calif.: Stanford University Press, 1957).

3. Benjamin Schwartz, *In Search of Wealth and Power: Yen Fu and the West* (Cambridge, Mass.: Harvard University Press, 1964), pp. 48–80.

4. Ssu-yu Teng and John K. Fairbank, *China's Response to the West: A Documentary Survey 1839–1923* (Cambridge, Mass.: Harvard University Press, 1954), p. 196.

5. On the life of Sun Yat-sen see Lyon Sharman, *Sun Yat-sen: His Life and Its Meaning* (Stanford, Calif.: Stanford University Press, 1934), and Harold Z. Schiff-rin, *Sun Yat-sen and the Origins of the Chinese Revolution* (Berkeley: University of California Press, 1970).

6. Chow, Tse-tsung, *The May Fourth Movement: Intellectual Revolution in Modern China* (Cambridge, Mass.: Harvard University Press, 1960).

7. See Sun Yat-sen, *San Min Chu I* (Shanghai: The Commercial Press, 1926).

8. Keiji Furuya, *Chiang Kai-shek: His Life and Times*, trans. Chun-ming Chang (New York: St. John's University Press, 1981), pp. 434–436.

9. William Theodore de Bary, ed., *Sources of Chinese Tradition* (New York: Columbia University Press, 1960), pp. 796–797.

10. See, for example, John F. Copper, *Taiwan: Nation-State or Province?*, 4th edition (Boulder, Colo.: Westview Press, 2003) and Denny Roy, *Taiwan: A Political History* (Ithaca, New York: Cornell University Press, 2003).

Suggestions for Further Reading

Chow Tse-tsung, *The May Fourth Movement: Intellectual Revolution in Modern China* (Cambridge, Mass.: Harvard University Press, 1960).

Harold Z. Schiffrin, *Sun Yat-sen and the Origins of the Chinese Revolution* (Berkeley: University of California Press, 1970).

Benjamin Schwartz, *In Search of Wealth and Power* (Cambridge, Mass.: Harvard University Press, 1964).

Ssu-yu Teng and John K. Fairbank, *China's Response to the West: A Documentary Survey 1839–1923* (Cambridge, Mass.: Harvard University Press, 1954).

Mary C. Wright, *The Last Stand of Chinese Conservatism* (Stanford, Calif.: Stanford University Press, 1957).

4 The Communist Road to Power

The Early Years: 1919–1923

The founding of the Chinese Communist Party (CCP) was a result of the convergence of two events: the victory of the Bolsheviks in Russia in 1917 and the rising wave of nationalism in China in the wake of the Versailles settlement in 1919. Neither was a sufficient cause in itself. Issues of the most prestigious intellectual journal of the time, *Xin Qingnian* (*New Youth*), that appeared just before the Versailles settlement contained several articles critical of Karl Marx's thought. Apart from any doubts about its validity in other areas of the world, the authors considered Marxism inapplicable to China because the country's proletarian class was so small. *New Youth*'s next issue, which was compiled after the Versailles Treaty and during the May Fourth movement, took a completely different tack. In effect, the post–World War I settlement had vindicated Marx: The bourgeois capitalist states had behaved in exactly as exploitative a fashion as one might predict from his writings.

One author, Li Dazhao, argued that China was actually a part of the world proletariat. His reasoning was that China was at the mercy of foreign imperialists who were exploiting all the Chinese people in a manner similar to that in which the capitalists exploited their own workers—by owning the means of production and seizing the workers' surplus value for themselves. Having thus determined that most of China could be considered proletarian, Li was able to bridge the gap between Marx's writings and China's reality.[1] Happily, the Chinese term for proletariat, borrowed from the Japanese, translates as "propertyless class," a convenient ambiguity that could be stretched to apply to many peasants as well.

The fact that Marx described his developmental scheme as scientifically based and culturally neutral was also appealing. Chinese who felt both humiliated by the West and disgusted with its behavior had no desire to borrow from it. Marx, by contrast, was highly critical of the political and economic systems of the West. He argued that what appear to be *national* characteristics are in reality the characteristics of *bourgeois* society. Abolishing capitalist rule would open the way for the emergence of a common proletarian culture in which the exploitation of one group by another would just not occur. Moreover, Marx promised immediate results, which seemed much preferable to the time-consuming gradualism advocated by people like John Dewey. An apocalyptic revolution would simply sweep away problems. Additionally, the founding of the Soviet Union in what had been regarded as one of Europe's most industrially backward areas—and much of whose territories were located in Asia—seemed to indicate that China could have just such an apocalyptic revolution despite its lack of industrialization.

Many of the intellectuals associated with *New Youth* became converted to communism, including its editor, Chen Duxiu. He had been a dean at Beida, China's most prestigious university, until March 1919, when conservative pressure led to his removal. Li Dazhao, author of the article mentioned above and likewise a professor at Beida, was also persuaded of the wisdom of a Marxist course for China. So were several less prestigious figures, including a clerk at the Beida library, Mao Zedong.

Mao was born in 1893 to a rich peasant family in Hunan. His strict father sent him to a Confucian academy for a classical education. Resistant from the outset, young Mao hid bandit novels behind the Confucian texts and read them instead. He also refused to consummate the marriage his father, following traditional practices, had arranged for him. One of his earliest writings, prompted by the suicide of a young woman who chose death rather than agree to an arranged marriage to a man she did not love, concerned the evils of the traditional family system. Mao was also intensely concerned with the plight of his country, and devoted much thought to discovering the reasons for China's weakness. Another of his early writings castigates the traditional distaste for physical labor. A lifetime of indolence, Mao argued, creates weaklings; a nation of weaklings is a weak nation. In the wake of the Bolshevik revolution and the May Fourth movement, Mao found in Marx a quick solution to strengthening China.

The suddenness of the conversion of this group had important implications for the future development of communism in China. Its members had never systematically studied Marxism. There was no Marxist-social democratic tradition in China, and there had been no appreciable Marxist influence on the thought of intellectuals before 1918. Early Chinese communists were thus quite unlike European and Russian Marxists, who had typically spent years studying and debating the fine points of Marxist theory before they decided to participate in the kinds of activities indicated by the communist worldview. The group around Chen and Li first became committed to a course of *political* action, a Marxist-style revolution, and only quite a bit later accepted even the basic assumptions of the Marxist worldview—for example, Marx's internationalism. Communism's appeal to Chinese intellectuals was that it provided an immediate solution for *China*.[2] Marx's course of *economic* action was, of course, even more remote from Chinese reality.

This means that the *New Youth* group responded to the message of the Bolshevik revolution almost completely outside the framework of Marxist categories of thought. Also, since its members had no strong attachments to Marxist formulations, they found it quite easy to change these formulations to fit the needs of the Chinese situation. This gave Chinese communism a certain amount of flexibility. At the same time, it opened the way to debates on what was orthodox and what was not; one person's idea of creative adaptation of the sacred texts may be another person's definition of revisionist heresy.

For the moment, this was not a major problem. On July 1, 1921, twelve people arranged to meet quietly in Shanghai's French quarter, where they were less likely to be harassed by the Chinese authorities. They took the additional precaution of holding their meeting at a private girls' school whose pupils were away on summer holiday. Here the CCP was formally founded, choosing Chen Duxiu as its first head. The delegates argued about such questions as whether to cooperate with the bourgeoisie, and if so, how much. A consensus was reached that the party should work toward the eventual achievement of a dictatorship of the working class but must be prepared to cooperate with other parties during a transitional period. The length of this transitional period was not specified. Meanwhile, the CCP must lead the bourgeois-democratic movement and give immediate priority to the organization of trade unions in China. The members also agreed to make full use of the experience and example of the Soviet Union.

At this point in the deliberations a suspicious-looking character appeared at the school, inquiring about a man who allegedly lived three houses away. The delegates left immediately, just ahead of the arrival of police. Thinking quickly, the twelve set out for a nearby lake, where they purchased picnic supplies, rented a boat, and continued their meeting undisturbed.

The Period of Soviet Control: 1923–1931

Chen Duxiu had always regarded labor organization as the primary task of his newly founded party and was pleased with the results of the CCP's initial efforts. Railway workers proved enthusiastic converts, and other unions were founded at Anshan, China's largest iron works, and at one other iron factory of substantial size. By the end of 1922, Chen was optimistic about creating an upsurge of proletarian support for the communist cause. Thus, the signing of the Sun-Joffe Manifesto in January 1923 came as an unpleasant shock. Its provisions for a united front between the CCP and the KMT seemed to undermine the successes that previous work had had. The blow was not appreciably softened by Comintern advisers telling the CCP leaders that they would not actually be surrendering the CCP's independence, since party members were to join the KMT only as individuals (see Chapter 3). The united-front decision appeared both unnecessary and unwise.

Rebuked by a Comintern representative for his illusions regarding the achievement of socialism in China, Chen apparently decided to acquiesce. Of perhaps even greater importance in changing Chen's mind was the brutal suppression of a railway strike in February of the same year. The powerful Beijing-Hankou Railway Workers Union was suppressed by an even more powerful warlord, with numerous deaths and the arrest of many union organizers. The Chinese labor union movement entered into a period of decline.

The uneasy "Bloc Within" or First United Front between the KMT and CCP continued until 1927, with the Soviet leadership maintaining that after Chiang Kai-shek and his bourgeois-democratic party had served their purpose—the reunification of China—they would be discarded. In Stalin's metaphor, the Comintern's plan was to squeeze Chiang out like a lemon and then dump him into the dustbin of history. Unfortunately for Stalin and the CCP, Chiang was well aware of the plans for him, and when the Northern Expedition reached Shanghai, it became clear that *he* intended to place the *CCP* in the dustbin. With the help of the Green Gang, a secret society heavily involved in the workings of the Shanghai stock market, Chiang very nearly succeeded. A "white terror" of frightening proportions was unleashed in China's urban areas, with anyone suspected of having any sympathy for communism liable to arrest and execution. Among the victims was Mao Zedong's beloved second wife.

With communists and their relatives and friends being slaughtered, it was no longer possible to pretend that a united front existed. In a cruel irony, Chen Duxiu was removed as head of the CCP on Soviet orders, because he had "misunderstood" the policy of the united front. His replacement, Qu Qiubai, was ordered to stage uprisings in the cities. Stalin had discovered a "revolutionary upsurge" in China that would allow the CCP to carry on urban insurrections without the cooperation of the KMT. This course of action appeared even more unrealistic than the united front, since the CCP did not have an army. In fact, it was Stalin who had ordered that they should not have an army, although there appears to have been no disagreement within the CCP on the matter. Its members associated militarism with the warlords, whom they considered their and China's enemies.

Armed insurrections were duly carried out in various areas. The insurrection attempted at Nanchang, the capital of Jiangxi province, in August 1927 marks the first organized use of military force by the communists. A second occurred in Shantou, on the south China coast. Mao Zedong was actively engaged in these activities, but with a much different focus. His aim was to take advantage of the peasants' rising discontent with their landlords and officials rather than, as envisioned by Marx, working with the urban proletariat. Mao led a so-called Autumn Harvest uprising in his home province of Hunan. None of these efforts succeeded.

The final failure was that of the Canton (Guangzhou) Commune, in December 1927. Since they did not have uniforms, communists had chosen to distinguish themselves from those they were fighting by wearing red kerchiefs or armbands. When they realized they were losing, the communists ripped off these identifying badges and threw them away. Unfortunately, the red dye had run freely out of the kerchiefs and armbands but proved almost impossible to get off the skin. Eyewitnesses tell of government troops ripping open people's jackets to check for telltale stains and bayoneting those who did not pass the test. Later, horse-drawn carts made the rounds of the city to collect the corpses.

The Canton uprising received worldwide press coverage and was a failure of such magnitude that Stalin was forced to reconsider the party line. Rather than take responsibility for the debacle himself, Stalin chose to blame Qu Qiubai. Qu was accused of "putschism" and replaced by Li Lisan, who was again charged with securing an urban base for the CCP. Li had had a stunningly successful career as a labor organizer and was moreover one of the few CCP members who actually had a proletarian background. However, it proved impossible to establish this urban base, Li's impressive credentials notwithstanding. The brutality of the White repression had made it very dangerous for workers to even express sympathy for the communist cause, much less overtly support the CCP. Moreover, the party leadership had failed the workers cruelly. In addition, the KMT was itself making reforms, including supporting the organization of trade unions. Communists castigated these as "yellow" unions designed to distract the proletariat's attention from preparing for the revolution which alone could save it. Workers, however, viewed the unions as a safer way to press for more benefits. Meanwhile, party membership had dwindled to about 15,000. This dedicated hard core met in small, highly secret groups in industrial cities. Li Lisan, using Shanghai as his base, tried his best to travel to and coordinate with them.

The Jiangxi Soviet: 1931–1934

After the failure of his Autumn Harvest uprising, the Comintern had removed Mao from all his party posts. Not only had the uprising failed to succeed, it had also run counter to the party line of organizing the proletariat rather than the peasants. Mao withdrew to a remote area on the border between Jiangxi and Fujian, founding what would later come to be known as the Jiangxi soviet. An area whose mist-shrouded mountains have the surrealistic beauty favored by Chinese landscape painters, it was home to both Daoist sages engaged in contemplation and outlaw groups who specialized in less spiritually motivated activities. Indeed, it was precisely the setting of the bandit novels that had so intrigued Mao as a boy.

Here Mao established a rural base area. He was aided by a ragtag army led by a reformed opium addict with some military training, Zhu De; they cooperated with bandits and secret societies, some of whose members agreed to serve in what was then known as the Red Army. Both base area and army began to grow, with the growth of the army directly related to the expansion of the base area. It was during this time that Mao articulated his philosophy that "political power grows out of the barrel of a gun," adding that the party must always control the gun instead of the gun controlling the party. At Jiangxi also Mao began to work out the principles that would later become known as People's War. Acting on traditional Chinese wisdom that "the army is the fish and the people are the water; the fish cannot swim without the water," Mao tried to enlist the entire population in support of the military. The military was to pay a fair price for anything it took from the people; harassment of civilians could be, and sometimes was, punished with death. The techniques of guerrilla war were developed, with slogans such as "Enemy advances, we retreat; enemy retreats, we pursue."

The rudiments of administration were set up: government offices, schools, and medical facilities. While the soviet's constitution proclaimed it a "democratic dictatorship of the proletariat and peasantry," in reality, the CCP monopolized power, with not even the semblance of a coalition. Also, its proletariat was confined to village artisans and handicraftsmen.

A radical-sounding land reform law was also less than it seemed. Landlords and rich peasants managed to retain political authority by declaring their loyalty to the new regime. Hence they were able to control the implementation of land reform, either completely avoiding having their land confiscated or arranging to have the best land allocated to themselves. This did not satisfy the poor peasants, whose continuing demands led to repeated redistributions. More than once the government had to stop a redistribution in order to save crop production. The Jiangxi soviet exerted relatively tenuous control over the scattered mountain areas that were nominally under its jurisdiction.[3]

Mao's soviet faced external problems just as troublesome as those of internal management. There was a good deal of interference from the CCP's politburo in Shanghai. Li Lisan's attitude toward the growth of the Red Army and the Soviet areas was that it was acceptable only so long as these were led by the urban proletariat. Li's and the Comintern's notion that cities could be encircled and taken from the countryside during this period was highly unrealistic. In that it implied that the proletariat would have to be rescued by a peasant army, the idea was also a negation of the leading role of the proletariat. It does indicate the extreme concern with which the CCP sought to maintain a link, however tenuous, with the proletariat in whose name the revolution was to be fought. During the summer of 1930 Li Lisan, in a desperate effort to secure an urban base, ordered an attack on Changsha, the capital of Hunan province. The effort failed, and Li Lisan, like Qu Qiubai before him, was criticized for putschism. Li confessed his errors and agreed to visit Moscow for a period of study, so that he might improve his revolutionary analytical capabilities.

At this point formal leadership of the CCP Central Committee passed to a group of people known as the "Returned Student" group or "the Twenty-Eight Bolsheviks." They were young CCP members who had studied at Moscow's Sun Yat-sen University; Mao and his supporters considered the group almost as out of touch with Chinese reality as their Soviet mentors and tried to ignore them insofar as possible. In 1931, Mao officially established his Jiangxi soviet. In 1932–1933, Chiang's repression forced the Central Committee to move its headquarters from Shanghai to the Jiangxi soviet. Some of the returned student group received influential positions there, consonant with Mao's tendency during this period to absorb rather than eliminate rivals. However, their leader, Wang Ming, Mao's chief nemesis within the group, was sent back to Moscow as China's delegate to the Comintern. Other rural soviets existed in addition to that at Jiangxi, but the Jiangxi soviet was by far the most important.

The Central Committee's relocation to the Jiangxi soviet marks a formal end to the CCP's urban link, and also a sharp drop in the degree of the USSR's control over the CCP. The pretense to an urban base and the degree to which the Soviet Union exercised control over the communist movement in China had, of course, been weakening for some years. Comintern advisers lamented that, despite their best efforts, what had started out as a proletarian revolutionary movement had degenerated into a typical Chinese peasant rebellion. Perhaps they remembered with a pang a nineteenth-century observer's comment that the Chinese were the most rebellious of people but the least revolutionary—in the sense that their rebellions aim at modest readjustments rather than fundamental changes in the political and economic systems. Such disillusionment with the CCP led Stalin to refer to the Chinese communists as "margarine communists" or, at other times, "radish communists": red on the outside but white within.

To summarize the important events of the Jiangxi period, first, it saw the development of the technique of building up rural base areas from which to begin the takeover of China and the abandonment of the technique of urban insurrection to achieve this end. Second, a regular army was created to aid this task. Third, the CCP became increasingly independent of ideological direction from the Soviet Union. And fourth, Mao Zedong rose to a position of de facto preeminence in the CCP although he was not yet formally acknowledged as its leader.

The Long March: 1934–1935

Chiang Kai-shek had not forgotten about the communists who fled to the countryside. In addition to trying to eradicate CCP cells in urban areas, Chiang attempted to encircle and destroy the rural soviets. What began as one encirclement campaign in November 1930 grew into five, the first two fairly perfunctory. Partly this was because the KMT had underestimated the CCP. But the KMT was also riven by factionalism, and its co-opted warlords did not always obey Chiang's orders. The third encirclement campaign, in 1931, might well have succeeded had the Japanese not chosen this moment to step up their pressure on China.

Having killed the warlord of northeast China, the Japanese army seized the three northeastern provinces and in 1931 set up a puppet kingdom called Manchukuo (Manchu country). The Qing emperor who had been deposed in 1911 was enthroned as its ruler, but was surrounded by Japanese advisers. In consequence, Chiang Kai-shek withdrew his troops from Jiangxi and moved them to Shanghai because of the perception that an all-out war with Japan was imminent. Chiang knew that he had no chance to win a confrontation with the superbly trained and highly motivated Imperial Japanese Army. He succeeded in avoiding war, albeit suffering damage to his image in the process. In terms of avoiding unnecessary bloodshed, Chiang's decision had been correct. But it angered many patriots who were already hypersensitive to the humiliations of foreign pressures on China. Chiang argued that the Japanese were but a disease of the skin, while the CCP represented a more serious internal problem. He also reasoned, quite correctly, that eventually the Japanese and the Americans would go to war and that the United States would prevail, thereby curing the skin disease. Hence, Chiang turned his attention back to the communists. Preparations were made for a fourth encirclement campaign.

Meanwhile, there were differences of opinion within the CCP on how to handle the encirclement campaigns. Mao's techniques of highly mobile guerrilla warfare predominated in the first three and appear to have been blamed for the near-annihilation of the Jiangxi soviet during the 1931 campaign. During the fourth encirclement campaign, CCP military leaders advocated a strategy of defense beyond the borders of the soviet, as opposed to Mao's technique of trying to lure the enemy deep into his territory and attacking its troops there. This turned out to be ill-advised, since it intruded on the turf of a number of landlords and turned them against the communists. Whereas previously their attitude had been that the KMT and CCP were equally bad, the landlords now decided to support the KMT. During the fifth encirclement campaign, Chiang devised a strategy of building blockhouses in an ever-tightening circle around the soviet. It was landlord control of the *baojia* system that provided the manpower to build the blockhouses.

CCP defenses were no match for the blockhouse strategy, and the population of the Jiangxi soviet was feeling increasingly beleaguered. There were acute shortages of medicine, cloth, kerosene, and salt, the last being more important than it might seem. Salt was needed for preserving food in the absence of refrigeration. It also helped to stabilize body fluids in the meat-scarce diets of most of the population. However, as the KMT's net grew tighter, it became apparent that the blockhouses were not being built in a complete circle according to plan. Here again the piecemeal way in which the KMT had reunified China inhibited its strategy. To the east and north of the Jiangxi soviet, units who were loyal to the KMT built blockhouses as ordered. But areas to the south and west of the Jiangxi soviet were controlled by warlords who wanted to overthrow Chiang. They built no blockhouses and kept their military forces concentrated in county seats.

This gap in the blockhouse circle allowed the communists to break out, abandoning the Jiangxi soviet and beginning the arduous trek across China that is known to history as the Long March. In October 1934, an estimated 100,000 men and 35 women, one of them Mao's pregnant third wife, crossed Jiangxi province and entered Hunan. Later communist writings have glorified the Long March, alleging that the marchers met strong resistance and were all but wiped out along the route. They also allege that the reason for the march was to fight Japan. Western scholarship indicates that about 70 percent of the troops deserted rather early on.[4] There is no question that fear of annihilation by the KMT rather than a desire to fight Japan motivated the Long March.

Although subsequent efforts at deification have embroidered the heroics involved in the Long March, the fact that even a small percentage of the members of the group survived is in itself a triumph over adversity. The KMT's efforts at annihilation en route were a decidedly minor part of the CCP's problems. Chiang Kai-shek had to be concerned with keeping up the strength of his own troops vis-à-vis potential warlord rivals. He therefore tried to destroy the Red Army with minimal involvement of his own units. In several instances, warlords who did not wish to weaken themselves by fighting the communists simply withdrew and allowed the Long Marchers to pass through. However, other hazards awaited the CCP. The march had begun in October and passed through wild, mountainous terrain during the coldest months of the year. The locals were generally not hospitable. Often they were members of ethnic minorities who had been pushed into marginal lands by the expansion of the Han Chinese state (see Chapter 1) and were quite resentful of the Han. The marchers were set upon by Yi snipers with rifles, had boulders rolled down on them by Tibetans as they filed through narrow mountain gorges, and were attacked by expert Muslim cavalrymen who despised infidels.

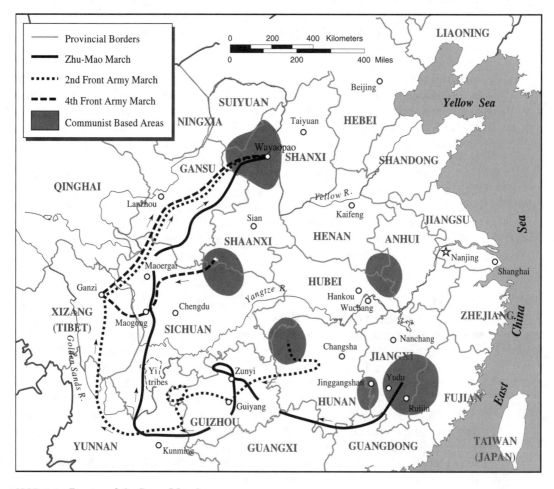

MAP 4.1   Routes of the Long March

The progress of the Long March was not helped by the fact that its leaders had no clear destination in mind. Having failed in an attempt to link up with another, smaller soviet in northern Hunan province, the march turned west to Sichuan. In January 1935 the exhausted survivors decided to rest in a desolate area of Guizhou province called Zunyi. It was here that Mao Zedong, whose career had suffered as a result of the poor results his military strategy had yielded in 1931, called for an enlarged conference of the CCP's politburo. Supported by several of the party's important military figures, he emerged as the dominant figure in the politburo. The Zunyi conference was the great turning point of Mao's career. Although the wisdom of his decisions would sometimes be challenged, he remained the party's dominant figure until his death in 1976.

Sichuan proved unattainable as a base area as well, and after more wandering about in the southwest, the march turned north. The ragged band managed to cross the Yangtze River, the symbolic dividing line between north and south China, by dressing some of their number in KMT uniforms and commandeering boats. The nadir of the Long March was the passage through the grasslands of northern Sichuan. The terrain was freezing cold and swampy; grass grew higher than people; the marchers could not see where they were going; and there was no food. The natives were armed, familiar with the terrain, and hostile. An American missionary who visited the area two years later recalled seeing numerous piles of whitened human bones. Finally, in October 1935, almost exactly a year after the Long March began, the survivors straggled into northern Shaanxi, where a small communist base area already existed, centered on the city of Yan'an. There are no accurate figures on the number of survivors, but it is thought to be between 7,000 and 10,000—less than 10 percent of those who left Jiangxi a year before. Since this number includes some people who became impressed with the communists en route and joined the Long March while it was in progress, the number of original marchers who survived is even smaller.

The Xi'an Incident: 1936

The area the communists entered had been the cradle of Chinese civilization 2,000 years earlier. It had also been home to three major dynasties. Since then, however, the region had fallen into decline. Its forest cover had been destroyed, and the depredations of erosion were severe. The fine, yellow loess soil that remained was fertile, but rainfall was both sparse and sporadic. Having no lumber to build houses, people lived in caves hollowed out of loess. The soil was so light that it rose in clouds when disturbed by a passing cart or animal. Those areas where traffic was frequent had become canyons just the width of the vehicles that traversed them, with walls that might reach forty feet in height. Travelers described the scene as yellow as far as the eye could see: hills, roads, rivers, and houses. There was even a persistent yellow haze in the air.

Already desperately poor, Shaanxi province was suffering from a famine when the Long March arrived. This being October, it would have been too late to plant crops even under the best of circumstances; hence the emigrants' first winter was enormously difficult. It would have been difficult for even the most optimistic observer to predict a bright future for the Yan'an base area.

Both the inhabitants and their technology seemed primitive, even by comparison with rural Jiangxi. The peasants required much more indoctrination by the communists before they could begin to understand the party's message. One propagandist recalled his frustration in trying to explain the concept of exploitation to bewildered people who stubbornly insisted that that was the way things had always been and always would be. With difficulty, the party reconstituted the institutions of government it had established in Jiangxi. Schools, a military academy, health care facilities, and social clubs were set up. A campaign to confiscate landlords' land was begun, though the communists cooperated with other elements in the local power structure, including secret societies. Meanwhile, Chiang Kai-shek was making plans for a sixth encirclement campaign.

Largely, it would seem, to save themselves, CCP leaders had been trying to convince local warlords that it would be best to reconcile their differences in order to fight the Japanese. One of those who was receptive to this message was Zhang Xueliang, son of the warlord the Japanese had killed in the process of setting up their client state of Manchukuo. The idea of avenging his father's death and reclaiming his territory had obvious appeal to Zhang. China's students and intellectuals were also very much in favor of mounting a strong resistance to Japan, as did those who, for vested interests of their own, found Chiang's unwillingness to attack Japan a convenient issue on which to criticize him.

On December 4, 1936, Chiang Kai-shek flew to Xi'an, the capital of Shaanxi, to supervise the attack on the communists. On December 12 he was kidnapped. Chiang, hearing noise from the break-in during the middle of the night, fled over the wall surrounding his residence and was eventually found next morning in his nightshirt, minus his false teeth. These events and the role of Zhang Xueliang's troops in carrying out the deed are accepted as fact. However, other details, such as whether the CCP colluded in planning the kidnapping, are murky. Certainly Zhang and the party had common cause, and certainly the CCP was involved in the negotiations with the KMT over Chiang Kai-shek's release. Chiang, it will be remembered, had a number of rivals within the KMT, and some of them had no particular desire to have him released.

After several weeks of intense bargaining, an agreement was reached, with Chiang returning to his capital at Nanjing on Christmas Day 1936. He had agreed to cease his attacks on the communists, to guarantee their "democratic rights," to summon a broadly based conference to unite for "national salvation," to make immediate preparations to resist Japan, and to improve the people's livelihood. The CCP in turn agreed to stop its armed insurrections aiming at overthrowing the KMT, to rename the workers' and peasants' democratic government it had set up at Yan'an as a special region of the Republic of China, to place the Red Army under the jurisdiction of the National Revolutionary Army, to discontinue its policy of confiscating landlords' land, to join in the anti-Japanese united front, and to institute a democratic system based on universal suffrage in the areas under its control.

The Second United Front: 1936–1941

Thus began the period known as the Second United Front. Since the anti-Japanese war effort involved a joint effort between the KMT and the CCP but not individuals from one party joining the other as had been the case with the First United Front, it is also called the

Bloc Without. However unwillingly, Chiang Kai-shek had been placed at the head of a movement to resist Japan and gained much stature as a patriot.

The CCP immediately renamed its soviet the Shaanxi-Gansu-Ningxia (Shaan-Gan-Ning) Special Region of the National Government, and party members expanded their organizing activities in the parts of those three provinces the region encompassed. Various other names were changed in order to conform to the concept of the united front. The Red Army was renamed the Eighth Route Army to indicate that it was now part of the KMT military system. Remnants of forces left behind in central China when the Long March began formed the New Fourth Army. The Red Army Academy was renamed the Resist Japan Academy. Social clubs, variously named Lenin Clubs or Workers' Clubs, now became Salvation [from Japan] Rooms.

In addition to the benefit of reducing Chiang Kai-shek's attacks against it, the Xi'an settlement had other positive effects for the CCP. Patriots applauded the party's initiative to organize resistance to Japanese pressures, and many Chinese students made the long journey to Yan'an to participate in the resistance movement. The need to resist seemed all the more pressing when, in 1937, the Japanese began full-scale war against China. The incredible, often carefully calculated, cruelty of the Japanese assault was documented by foreign photographers and played an important part in mobilizing world opinion on the side of China's struggle.

At a more mundane level, the party's agreement to modify its land redistribution plans enabled it to reach out to a wider spectrum of the population. CCP functionaries experimented with, and gained expertise in, the techniques of household registration and tax collection. They were also able to provide the base area with a stable currency, an achievement that would later prove crucial. The population of the Shaan-Gan-Ning base area grew rapidly, from an estimated six hundred thousand in 1938 to about a million and a half in 1944. As it had in the Jiangxi soviet, military power proved the spearhead for party expansion. Since high-ranking CCP leaders typically held leading military positions as well, the issue of whether the party controlled the gun or vice versa was moot. The majority of these leaders had no formal military education, but sheer day-to-day existence in an environment surrounded by hostile forces—landlords, some of whom had their own armies, plus the KMT and the Japanese—provided excellent on-the-job training.

The circumstances surrounding the Xi'an agreement did nothing to allay the distrust that the CCP and KMT had for each other, and it would appear that each was more concerned with the other than with fighting the Japanese. For example, by 1938 the Eighth Route Army had moved into Shandong province, beyond the limit the KMT government had assigned to it, and the New Fourth Army began organizing the population in the Jiangsu–Zhejiang–Anhui area, which was also beyond the scope of the agreement. Chiang Kai-shek became quite annoyed, with adverse effects on the functioning of the united front.

Meanwhile, the CCP began functioning as a legitimate government. While Shaan-Gan-Ning was not the party's only base area, it was the only one where conditions were stable enough to allow the CCP's programs to be carried out with any consistency. Other areas, often located behind Japanese lines, had to be concerned with survival as a first priority. These bases took general direction from Yan'an, but since they had only minimal ability to communicate with Yan'an, exercised a significant degree of autonomy.

The techniques of *mass mobilization*, already seen in earlier CCP efforts to organize workers and, subsequently, peasants, were further developed and refined during the Yan'an period. The party, partly because of Leninist influence and partly because of the persecution to which it had been subjected, was a secretive, elite organization. Yet it wanted to encourage popular participation in its programs. One of the ways in which this was done was to create *mass organizations*, structured to channel the energies of specific groups within the population. There were, for example, a women's group, a youth organization, and peasant and merchant federations. Party organizers who were knowledgeable about the problems of these specific groups and their feelings and perceptions conducted educational activities on behalf of the party with these groups. The goal was to have the entire population, including the lowest levels, involved in and supporting CCP programs.

The first of these programs to be carried out after the formation of the united front was *elections*. These had enormous significance both domestically and internationally. Even before the 1911 revolution, many Chinese intellectuals had come to believe that powerful nations were democratic nations, and that the holding of competitive elections was an important component of democracy. Foreign observers were impressed that a communist party would encourage and permit free elections, thereby contributing to the impression that CCP members were communists of a different and infinitely preferable sort.

The election law called for universal, direct equal suffrage by secret ballot to all those over sixteen years of age, regardless of social class. Rhetoric stressed Sun Yat-sen's Three Principles of the People rather than Marxist-Leninist class struggle. In what became known as the "three thirds" system, the communists promised that party members would hold no more than one-third of the elective offices. One-third would go to nonparty members who were considered "leftist progressives," and the final third to those classified as middle-of-the-road in their views. Sometimes this was interpreted as one-third CCP, one-third KMT, and one-third nonparty; occasionally even those classified as "rightists" or "diehards" were allowed to run, though such people never collectively attained a full third share.[5]

Mass organizations were encouraged to nominate and campaign for their candidates. Discussion meetings were held in the villages and townships, with the aim of getting people to discuss local issues, formulate suggestions for the new government, and state their opinions on the candidates. For peasants who had never participated in elections before (indeed, some of them had never *heard* of the concept) this was an important educational technique.

Actual balloting took place at the end of a four-day meeting in one of the more important district towns, in an atmosphere resembling a county fair. There were performances by children's groups, athletic competitions, and potluck picnics in addition to reports by government officials. Since it was difficult to implement the electoral law's provision for a secret ballot with a largely illiterate electorate, voting was sometimes done by a show of hands. Various other options were devised, including dropping beans into jars that had been placed behind the candidates' backs. However, the government thus elected was not the sole decision-making authority. It shared that responsibility with the party, the bureaucracy, the military, and mass organizations in a manner that almost certainly assured that the party's voice was the decisive one.

Although the process described above is far from that of the ideal democracy, most observers credited it with being a remarkable achievement under the circumstances. Elections also represented an important advance in the party's ability to mold popular sentiment.

Land redistribution was another important part of the party's program during the Yan'an period. Under the provisions of the united front, this had to be done in a restricted fashion. It had been agreed that the lands of all anti-Japanese soldiers and those involved in anti-Japanese activities would not be confiscated. This allowed even large landlords to escape redistribution by simply having one son enlist in the Red Army. However, it would seem that the redistribution that did take place succeeded in destroying large concentrations of wealth and reducing the numbers of poor peasants. A number of problems remained. For example, the party's program did not deal with the problem of rationalizing landholdings. Households might own a number of widely scattered plots, which took time and energy to commute to and limited the utility of machines that might be better used in a larger, consolidated plot. Nor did the party's program improve productivity, or prevent an elite group from reemerging. Nonetheless, the measures taken seem to have been quite popular with the peasantry, while at the same time not alienating members of the local elite whose support and talents the party wished to retain.

Control of *education* was a means of getting the party's message to a large number of people as well as teaching them things that would facilitate economic development. Although the number of primary schools increased greatly after 1937, nearly all were in district capitals. The pupils tended to have families who could afford to send them there, and the curriculum was not really relevant to rural life. Parents viewed education for their children as desirable but perceived success as having the children become officials and move out of the village rather than bringing their new skills home with them.

The party attempted to deal with these problems through a series of experiments in popular education operating on the principle of "management by the people, with assistance by the government." This shifted the responsibility from party officials and professional teachers to village leaders and grass-roots activists, who presumably knew better what was needed and what techniques would work. Night schools, half-day schools, and winter schools (to take advantage of the slack season for peasants) were experimented with. A *xiaxiang* (to-the-village) movement sent some of the educated youth who had come to Yan'an for patriotic reasons to the villages to teach the peasants. Equally important from Mao's point of view was what these educated urban youth would learn from the peasants: an appreciation of the problems that 90 percent of China's population faced. The new schools were also expected to help overcome the gap between urban and rural areas, and between mental and manual labor. They were an effort to unite thought and action.

At the apex of the educational hierarchy were institutions like the Resist Japan University (*Kangda*), the Higher Party School, and, for ethnic minorities, the Yan'an Nationalities Institute. Here bureaucrats and party activists were trained. Here also, however, one sees an effort to break down class barriers. Urban students were paired with those of peasant backgrounds to get them to exchange skills and learn to work with one another. Students were asked to build their own classrooms, raise their own food, mend their own clothes, and even knit their own socks. Still, increasing specialization was taking place.

Broadly speaking, two political impulses and leadership styles co-existed somewhat uncomfortably in the base area. The first, revolutionary, emphasized mass struggle and broad political participation. Its proponents tended to be illiterate peasants with leadership ability who were concerned with eliminating oppression and instituting social justice in their specific areas. The second, bureaucratic, stressed stable administration. Its proponents tended to be better educated and more concerned with patriotism and the future of the country as a whole. They were also likely to be more committed to the united front and to modernization. Their outlook tended to be closer to that of classic Western liberalism than to the Marxist-Leninist worldview. In addition, the base area was growing rapidly and its population becoming increasingly diversified. This complicated the tasks of administration and called for yet higher levels of specialization.

The means chosen to deal with the disparate impulses and centrifugal forces that were increasingly prominent in the Yan'an base area was a *zhengfeng*, or rectification, campaign. It would become the forerunner of larger, more spectacular mass movements after the founding of the PRC. The object was to create a party with common interests and a unified will. Peasant activists who were almost exclusively concerned with rural reorganization and urban intellectuals whose primary motivation was anti-Japanese had to be brought together under a common program if the party was to succeed. Not surprisingly, this program would be Marxist. Since knowledge of Marxism was actually not widespread, and most of the expertise was concentrated at the higher levels of the party, much study was required.

Those who participated—and several thousand people did so—were divided into small groups and given study materials. Many of the documents had been written by Mao; others were strongly influenced by him or contained interpretations of Marx that he favored. While aiming at orthodoxy, the campaign certainly did not construe orthodoxy as rigidity. Indeed, under conditions of guerrilla warfare, and because of the isolation of many villages and the differing circumstances they faced, blind adherence to party directives would have been suicidal. Mao sharply criticized those who studied Marx and Lenin as religious dogma, asking his listeners rhetorically how they could tell the difference between dogma and dog shit. Dog shit, he answered, was useful; it could fertilize the fields. But dogmas were of no use at all.

Another of Mao's concerns was to make the theory of Marxism relevant to the Chinese situation. If theory could not be put into practice, then there was something wrong with the theory and it would have to be revised. This presumably was a reply to critics, such as the 28 Bolsheviks who had pointed out that there were discrepancies between the Marxist-Leninist texts and the procedures of the base areas. While agreeing that a communist is a Marxist internationalist, Mao argued that Marxism had to take on a national form before it could be applied. Explicitly calling for "the sinification of Marxism," he called for "an end to writing eight-legged essays on foreign models."[6] For those who were imbued with Western liberal values and insisted on literature and art for the sake of literature and art, and on the supremacy of the creative impulse, Mao also had scathing words. All art and literature had a class character, he insisted. Proletarian art and literature must not be divorced from the masses, and must motivate them to struggle to change their environment.

The organizational techniques employed in the *zhengfeng* movement show their planners' grasp of the principles of small group dynamics. Documents were read and discussed, with group leaders and members criticizing deviant points of view so that errant members could correct themselves. Mao compared the process to a doctor dealing with a sick person: the object was to save the patient, not to cure him to death. The healing process was not normally a gentle one, with the sessions typically deserving their name of "struggle sessions." Group pressure was brought to bear against the "ill" person, with the understanding that when he changed his mind and came around to the correct point of view, his standing within the group would be restored. The underlying assumption here is that education can be effective in transcending self-interest and class background.

Yet another technique developed during the Yan'an period was the concept of the *mass line*. No matter how successful a *zhengfeng* campaign might be in uniting leaders on the basis of correct views, it would mean little if the masses were not brought along in this consensus. Fundamentally, the motivation behind the mass line was antibureaucratic: Cadres were warned not to divorce themselves from the common people and their concerns. "Commandism"—that is, the giving of orders rather than persuading people to do the right thing—was to be avoided. Again, education is placed in a pivotal role. Occasionally, the masses may not want to behave in the proper manner ("It sometimes happens that the masses objectively need some reform but are not yet subjectively awakened to it and willing or determined to bring it into effect").[7] With time and indoctrination, they will adopt the proper view. The essence of the mass line is interaction between the bureaucracy and its constituents: "from the masses, to the masses."

The significance of the Yan'an era is that it provided the party with experience in actually administering a territory. This was an enormous benefit, and one not commonly available to movements that seek the overthrow of an existing regime. Techniques of taxation, allocation of resources, education, and popular participation were developed and refined.[8] While Yan'an provided a blueprint for the future development of China, it would later be charged that Mao Zedong had become too rigidly attached to the "lessons of Yan'an," and unwilling to face the fact that techniques that had worked well in the 1930s and 1940s had become counterproductive by the 1960s and 1970s. Nonetheless, the Yan'an spirit is part of the founding myth of Chinese communism and continues to be honored, particularly in periods of ideological and economic uncertainty. A May 1990 meeting to inaugurate the China Society for Study of the Yan'an Spirit defined that spirit not in terms of the techniques enumerated previously but as self-reliance, plain living, and hard struggle. Speeches at the meeting noted that, although the problems facing the party and the nation were different today than in Yan'an, studying the period could yield valuable lessons and "make the past serve the present."[9]

The stunning success of the CCP at Yan'an compared to its relative lack of success during the Jiangxi period has led to speculation on the reasons for this. One explanation is that the communists were able to appeal to the patriotic spirit of the peasantry better than the KMT. The CCP was helped immeasurably in this endeavor by the tremendous cruelty that characterized the Japanese occupation, and also by the fact that the Japanese were more firmly ensconced in the areas of north China near the communist base areas than they were in the areas of south central and south China to which the KMT had fled. Thus the party was able to win over the peasantry in the course of the struggle against Japan.[10] An alternative explanation downplays the nationalism of the peasants, crediting instead the appeal of the party's economic reforms.[11] Leaving aside the question of which cause attracted the most people, the two explanations are not mutually exclusive. It is possible that some people responded primarily to the CCP's anti-Japanese message, others to its economic program, and still others to both.

Civil War and Victory: 1941–1949

The united front remained nominally in force during the war with Japan, despite severe strains. In 1939, for example, 300 communist guerrillas who moved into Shandong in violation of the Xi'an agreement were massacred,[12] presumably on Chiang Kai-shek's orders. The presence of the New Fourth Army in central China, which was legal, was also of concern to the higher levels of the KMT. These troops provided the CCP with a strategic presence in the Yangtze delta, one of the country's richest food-production areas. It was also the site of a large industrial center, although the latter was controlled by Japan during the war. Chiang Kai-shek became increasingly uncomfortable with this situation and, in January 1941, ordered the New Fourth Army to withdraw north of the Yangtze. When, after a month, no withdrawal had taken place, KMT troops attacked, killing more than 3,000 members of the New Fourth Army. Cooperation between KMT and CCP against the Japanese, which was minimal at best, became still more perfunctory. Following what became known as the New Fourth Army Incident, Chiang ordered a cessation of subsidies that had been paid to the communist government under the united front agreement and began a blockade of the Yan'an base area.

An American diplomat resident in China's wartime capital of Chongqing noted that the news of Japan's attack on Pearl Harbor in December 1941 was celebrated as a holiday by both communists and KMT, since it meant that now the United States would declare war on, and presumably defeat, their common enemy. This, of course, left the two more free to fight each other.[13] The United States, now formally fighting on the same side as China, gave Chiang Kai-shek's government substantial sums of money to aid it in fighting Japan. There was little accountability, and much of the aid appears to have found its way into the pockets of high-ranking government officials. Foreign observers were struck by the contrast between the opulent living style of KMT leaders in Chongqing despite the poverty all around them, and the spartan, relatively egalitarian conditions that characterized the Yan'an base area.

Meanwhile, the population suffered horribly under the Japanese occupation. Imperial forces had a ready answer to Mao's notion that the people were the water and the army the fish: Drain the pond. The "three alls"—kill all, burn all, destroy all—were ruthlessly applied in areas where the Japanese met resistance. Those not killed might be marched long distances away from their homes to serve as forced laborers and prostitutes, or to become the subjects of grotesque medical experiments. Such measures discouraged popular resistance to the occupation but also created deep hatred of the Japanese, which the CCP took clever advantage of. Japanese control of China may be envisioned in terms of a net, with the enemy in charge of major cities, roads, and rail lines. The rural areas formed the interstices of the net. Japanese troops could, and did, move quickly into the countryside when they perceived a threat. But China is a far larger country than Japan, with a population many times as large, and Japanese troops had to fight in numerous other areas of the Asian-Pacific hemisphere. No matter how efficient and well trained, the emperor's troops could not be everywhere at once. Quietly and often unnoticed, communist organizers took over many of the interstices, especially in north China. They reinstituted the *baojia* system as part of this effort.

The use of hitherto secret atomic bombs against Hiroshima and Nagasaki brought Japan's surrender more quickly than most people had expected, causing certain difficulties for the change of power in China. Chiang Kai-shek insisted that the Japanese surrender to his representatives rather than those of the CCP and had the Americans transport his troops to the north, where the KMT had only a minimal presence, to do so.

The Soviet Union, also on the winning side and, for reasons of geographic proximity, the first Allied power on the scene, managed to delay this process. At the same time, the USSR quietly ordered its troops to dismantle whatever they could find of value in Manchuria, home of China's most advanced heavy industry, and bring it to the Soviet Union. Much of this industry had been built by the Japanese. The Soviets also turned over huge stocks of Japanese weapons to the CCP. Now the civil war was on in earnest.

Chiang, again using American transport, moved his troops into north China. His predilection for choosing the commanders who were most loyal to him rather than the commanders who were most competent to direct battles against the communists proved unwise. The KMT did enjoy some successes. In 1947, for example, it captured Yan'an, thus formally bringing an end to the Yan'an period. But it also lost several key battles, along with large quantities of American-supplied weapons and vehicles. The morale of KMT troops suffered badly.

Military encounters were but one facet of the shifting power equation. Inflation is a common phenomenon at the end of wars, as pent-up purchasing power seeks to buy scarce consumer goods. Dealing with inflationary pressures requires the kind of strong, united, and scrupulously honest government that the KMT was not. Because it did not act quickly or decisively, exchange rates began to vary widely between city and city, with speculators moving from one urban area to another to take advantage of these variations. There was corruption reaching into the highest levels of government, including some members of Chiang Kai-shek's family. Strenuous efforts by dedicated and honest officials to damp down the inflation proved futile.

Runaway inflation is apt to disadvantage urban areas most seriously, since rural areas can more easily conduct barter exchanges in food and other crucial commodities. Unfortunately for the KMT, urban areas had provided its original base of support, and that support now slipped away. Meanwhile the CCP, ensconced in its largely rural base areas, was relatively little inconvenienced by the inflation. CCP morale had never been higher, and several KMT-affiliated warlords defected to the communist side. One of these was the general in charge of Beijing. His switch in allegiance was of great import, both strategically and symbolically.

On October 1, 1949, Mao Zedong rode through the streets of Beijing in a captured American jeep and, ascending the rostrum at Tiananmen Square, proclaimed the founding of the People's Republic of China. Though a number of battles remained to be fought in south China, the end of the civil war was foreordained. The mandate of heaven had passed to the Chinese Communist Party.

Notes

1. Maurice Meisner, *Li Ta-chao and the Origins of Chinese Marxism* (Cambridge, Mass.: Harvard University Press, 1967).

2. Benjamin Schwartz, *Chinese Communism and the Rise of Mao* (Cambridge, Mass.: Harvard University Press, 1951), pp. 23–27.

3. Conrad Brandt, Benjamin Schwartz, and John K. Fairbank, *A Documentary History of Chinese Commu-*nism (Cambridge, Mass.: Harvard University Press, 1952), pp. 217–219.

4. See William Whitson, *The Chinese High Command* (New York: Praeger, 1973), pp. 275–276.

5. Mark Selden, *The Yenan Way in Revolutionary China* (Cambridge, Mass.: Harvard University Press, 1971), pp. 161–162, 167; Lyman Van Slyke, *Enemies and Friends: The United Front in Chinese Communist*

History (Stanford, Calif.: Stanford University Press, 1967), pp. 142–146.

6. Translated in Stuart R. Schram, *The Political Thought of Mao Tse-tung* (New York: Praeger, 1969), p. 112.

7. Ibid., p. 318.

8. Selden *passim* describes this period in detail.

9. See the various speeches reprinted in *Renmin Ribao* (Beijing), June 29, 1990, p. 3.

10. This is the argument of Chalmers Johnson in *Peasant Nationalism and Communist Power, 1937–1945* (Stanford, Calif.: Stanford University Press, 1962).

11. See Donald Gillin, " 'Peasant Nationalism' in the History of Chinese Communism," *Journal of Asian Studies*, vol. 23, no. 2, February 1964, pp. 271–277.

12. Brandt et al., p. 240.

13. See John Melby, *Mandate of Heaven: Record of a Civil War 1945–1949* (Toronto: University of Toronto Press, 1968).

Suggestions for Further Reading

Donald Gillin, " 'Peasant Nationalism' in the History of Chinese Communism," *Journal of Asian Studies*, vol. 23, no. 2, February 1964, pp. 271–277.

Chalmers Johnson, *Peasant Nationalism and Communist Power, 1937–1945* (Stanford, Calif.: Stanford University Press, 1962).

John Melby, *Mandate of Heaven: Record of a Civil War 1945–1949* (Toronto: University of Toronto Press, 1968).

Benjamin Schwartz, *Chinese Communism and the Rise of Mao* (Cambridge, Mass.: Harvard University Press, 1951).

Mark Selden, *The Yenan Way in Revolutionary China* (Cambridge, Mass.: Harvard University Press, 1971).

5 PRC Politics Under Mao: 1949–1976

Consolidation of Power: 1949–1955

Mao Zedong was under no illusions that the revolution had been won when the CCP took power on the mainland; he explicitly compared the founding of the People's Republic of China to the first step on a new Long March. Victory had come more quickly than even the optimists had predicted. During the later stages of the war, the communists' troops' main challenge was not fighting the KMT troops, who were in full retreat, but running after them. Some soldiers jokingly referred to this as "the battle with the feet." Still, CCP leaders were aware that they had not won the hearts and minds of the majority of the population. The next few years may be characterized as the party's efforts to legitimize its power.

A first step was the establishment of the organs of government. In the fall of 1949, the CCP convened a meeting of over twelve hundred "persons from all strata of society" called the Chinese People's Political Consultative Conference (CPPCC). In addition to CCP members, delegates included representatives of assorted patriotic associations and minor political parties, including the China Democratic League and the KMT Revolutionary Committee. The latter had broken away from the main body of the KMT some years earlier in protest against some of its policies. Also attending were several warlords, a few former members of the KMT, prominent lawyers, doctors, professors, social workers, artists, members of ethnic minorities, and religious leaders. There appear to have been two criteria for receiving an invitation to the CPPCC. First, the invitees had to be influential with a sizable number of people either because, like the warlords, they held a great deal of power or because, like the religious leaders and the professional experts, they were highly respected. Second, the individual had to have indicated that he or she agreed with the idea of social change. Given the economic and social chaos in China at the time, this second criterion was not difficult to meet.

The rationale for this type of meeting is to be found in a creative adaptation of Marx written by Mao several years before, called "On the New Democracy." In it, Mao argues that since China was still colonial and semifeudal, its principal enemies were imperialism and semifeudal forces. Thus, all other forces, even the bourgeoisie, should unite against these enemies in a democratic dictatorship of several revolutionary classes under the leadership of the proletariat. In this way, China could pass through the bourgeois-democratic phase called for by Marx while preparing the conditions for the socialist revolution. The CPPCC would serve as the vehicle to initiate this dictatorship.

The CPPCC, its disparate composition allowing the CCP's carefully organized voice to dominate, passed a document called the Common Program. It would function as a proto-constitution until elections could be held and a more legitimate constitution agreed upon. The program declared that China was a democratic dictatorship of four classes: the working class, the peasant class, the petty bourgeoisie, and the national bourgeoisie. The petty bourgeoisie included such people as tradesmen, peddlers, and owners of small shops. The national bourgeoisie was understood to mean persons of more substantial means who were considered patriotic: They had not collaborated with the Japanese or been suborned by any other foreign power.

Under the leadership of the working class and the CCP, the People's Democratic Dictatorship would suppress those lackeys of imperialism: the landlord class, the bureaucratic capitalist class, and the KMT reactionaries.[1] Those who could be re-educated would be dealt with leniently; those who could not or would not would be dealt with ruthlessly. The CPPCC also adopted a flag symbolic of this class structure: red, with four small gold stars representing the four classes surrounding the large gold star of the CCP. The design of the flag has also been officially described as the large star representing the dominant Han nationality and the smaller stars standing for the more important minority groups— Tibetans, Mongols, Manchus, and Muslims.

The decision to include the bourgeoisie in the coalition allowed the adoption of parliamentary forms, since China was judged to be in the bourgeois-democratic phase of the revolutionary process. It also provided the theoretical basis for a new united front. Unlike the two previous united fronts, this was composed of several different *classes* instead of an alliance of the CCP and the KMT. Its job was to promote the unity of all the people against the nonpeople, the category composed of big landlords, capitalists, and those who had collaborated with foreigners. While democratic in theory, this alliance was to be under the dictatorship of the workers and peasants in the institutional form of their party, the CCP.

Class labels were assigned to everyone, with a certain amount of arbitrariness. Many bourgeois who considered themselves very patriotic might have cooperated with foreigners, sincerely believing that what they were doing was good for China as well as for themselves. One person's judgment of patriotic cooperation might be another person's verdict of treasonous collaboration. Also, a number of peasants had a landlord or person of some wealth in their background. As one peasant about to be assigned a bad class label argued poignantly to party officials, given the fact that marriages entailed the payment of expensive bride prices from the groom's family and the provision of dowries by the bride's, the sort of really poor peasant family favored by communist propaganda would have been unable to arrange a match and was apt to have died out as a result.

To make matters worse, class labels were not only assigned for life, they were hereditary. This caused problems when the children of bad classes wished to get married, apply for jobs, or seek educational opportunities. Such hereditary designations cannot be considered Marxist, since if a person no longer controls the means of production, he or she cannot be considered a member of the exploiting class. They do not even seem properly Maoist since, as we have seen, Mao emphasized the value of persuasion and education in molding socialist attitudes. Hereditary class designations are decidedly antimodern—in fact, feudal. As time went on, they were increasingly irrelevant to the Chinese context, since former landlords became the exploited class and party members took charge of the means of production (albeit on behalf of the collective) and prospered thereby. Why, then, did the CCP not undertake a new class analysis? Quite clearly, it was because this would risk alienating its main supporters.[2]

Meanwhile, the party set about creating unity among those it had designated "the people." A series of mass campaigns was begun in order to build up popular enthusiasm behind a common cause. The first of these was a 1950 campaign to "Resist the United States and Aid Korea." In addition to allowing the leadership to support its socialist brethren in North Korea and castigate its chief enemy, the United States, the theme was an excellent one in terms of building a sense of national unity against an external threat. As previously mentioned, many Chinese had stronger loyalties to clan, village, and province than to the nation. This made it difficult to coordinate responses to external aggression. Unity and patriotism would allow the leadership to give concrete form to Sun Yat-sen's sheet of loose sand.

This campaign, and others like it, took place in a celebratory atmosphere. Workers received time off to attend and were given small flags to wave; children in brightly colored costumes performed traditional dances. The military paraded, to the accompaniment of bands. Stirring speeches were punctuated with firecrackers and concluded with a display of fireworks. The new symbols of loyalty were much in evidence: the national flag and large pictures of Mao Zedong.

Other, less dramatic efforts at unity were also undertaken. The party attempted to impose a common spoken language (standard Mandarin, which the new régime, understandably having no desire to honor the mandarins, referred to as "the national language" or "common speech" in official documents). China is a land of many dialects, some of them mutually unintelligible even when the groups who speak them live in close proximity. Attachment to one's dialect is one indication of localism; imposing a standard that everyone was required to learn was one way of breaking down local barriers.

The party also took charge of printing and distributing mass-circulation magazines and newspapers using a written language that was closer to actual spoken Chinese than the literary language that had been used by the official class. This had been one of the demands of the May Fourth generation. Publications written in this "new" form were much easier to read, and hence the party's message could be absorbed more easily. Since the magazines and some of the newspapers were distributed nationwide, they also contributed to unity. At least in theory, Chinese all over the country would be reading the same things. The plethora of currencies that had existed in China prior to the communist takeover was also standardized.

A second mass campaign, which began a few months later, had the counterrevolutionaries as its main focus. Secret societies and anticommunist groups were searched out and, to the extent possible, destroyed. The nonpeople were identified, brought to mass meetings, and struggled against. Repentance might save one, but there were nonetheless a number of executions after the mass meetings had assessed guilt. Drug dealers, war profiteers, big landlords, pimps, and prostitutes were among the victims. Efforts were made to be more lenient with the less culpable who might have been forced into their illicit trades through poverty. There were programs to train beggars and prostitutes for other professions, and cold-turkey rehabilitation for drug addicts. The methods were crude but effective. Official sources indicate that there were 800,000 executions; other estimates run up to 10 million. Party leaders defended the process as necessary: "A revolution is not a dinner party," and "to make an omelet, one must break some eggs." Meanwhile, a generally successful effort was made to convince people that the new government was *for* the people.

The third major campaign, begun in 1951, is known as the *sanfan*, or "three antis": anti-corruption, -waste, and -bureaucracy. Its main targets were the cadres (as the CCP called officials, in preference to the old term for bureaucrat that they despised) of party and state organs. There was concern within the ruling elite that a number of opportunists had joined the CCP when its victory was assured, with the motive of profiting themselves and their careers rather than because they had sincerely espoused the party's goals. Other party and state cadres, they worried, had become corrupted by the new opportunities that supervising activities in postwar China offered them. The *sanfan* aimed at purging party and government of careerists.

At first, outside observers viewed the campaign through the perspective of the eighteenth-century revolution in France: The Chinese revolution was devouring its own children. Later, opinion changed, and the *sanfan* came to be seen as a manifestation of party health rather than sickness. The attack on deviations and weaknesses within its own ranks was seen as increasing CCP strength and discipline. A few months later, in January 1952, a *wufan* or "five anti" campaign began, with its target the bourgeoisie. The *sanfan* had revealed that most party and government corruption occurred in agencies that dealt with economic matters and had ties with the bourgeoisie. Hence it was decided to attack them as well. The five antis were anti-bribery, -tax evasion, -fraud, -theft of government property, and -theft of state economic secrets. Since the two movements overlapped so closely both in time and targets, they are sometimes referred to as the *sanfan-wufan*, or three-anti–five-anti campaign.

Also during the first years after it came to power, the party worked hard to restore the economy and bring it under party control. This included ending the inflation, rebuilding and expanding the infrastructure, instituting land reform, and preparing for collectivization. These will be discussed in detail in Chapter 7. It is important to remember, however, that changes in the political party line were often made with economic goals in mind.

Establishing the Organs of Power

For the first few years after the communist takeover, China was divided into six large regions under the administration of Military Administrative Committees, later to be known simply as Administrative Committees. Since China is so large, and because communications at the time were quite primitive, organizations such as these made sense in terms of allowing the CCP to consolidate its power. There is some evidence that the leadership was worried about the existence of centrifugal forces within these large areas. For example, the leaders of the Northeast and Shanghai regions were both removed on grounds that they had colluded to set up "independent kingdoms" (that is, bureaucracies that could evade Beijing's control), but precisely how far the central leaders thought these regional powerholders intended to go has never been made clear. Although central-regional tensions were a concern during this period, we have too little information to assess how serious a problem they were.

Consonant with the concept of a people's democratic dictatorship, the communist party is and has been the only meaningful party in China since 1949. Also in line with people's democratic dictatorship, a complete state apparatus was set up as well, after basic-level elections had been held in 1953 and a constitution was ratified in 1954. Thus there are two parallel hierarchies, the party and the government, with interlocking memberships (see Figures 5.1 and 5.2). This type of structure is quite different from the Western concept of political parties competing for control of the organs of government. Westerners, noting the overlap in leadership positions at the top of the hierarchy—leading government offices are almost always held by leading party members—are often puzzled by the apparent redundancy of the system. The answer to why two organizations exist where one would seem adequate is that the party is supposed to provide spiritual and ideological input for policies, and the government is supposed to execute the policies provided by the party by working out the administrative details thereof and supervising the routine decisions that follow from it. The party's will is, at least in theory, supreme.

Though given no formal decision-making role in either party or government hierarchy, the military has been a key political actor as well. However, as will be seen in Chapter 9, the dividing line between military and nonmilitary in the PRC was not sharply demarcated. This was especially true in the early years of its existence. Since members of the elite frequently held leading positions in party, government, and military at the same time, or moved from positions in one hierarchy to another and back again, this was not a case of the military, as a discrete institution, exercising influence over the party or the state.

Chinese political institutions are modeled on those of the former Soviet Union but are not exact duplicates. There is nothing comparable to the Soviet of Nationalities in the PRC, and China's constitution, unlike that of the former USSR, does not allow the PRC's constituent units the right to secede.

The highest organ of state, at least in theory, is the National People's Congress (NPC). It is empowered to enact laws, ratify treaties, and select the president and vice-president. Although the presidency and vice-presidency are held by important and frequently powerful people, the offices themselves are largely ceremonial. NPC members are influential within their communities and, like candidates at every other level of the state hierarchy, are individuals who are considered acceptable to the party. It is not necessary that they belong to the CCP, although many of them do. Unlike the American Congress, the NPC has no fixed size, though typically there are two to three thousand members. In recent years, the NPC has become more assertive (see Chapter 6). Nonetheless, its unwieldy size plus the fact that the NPC meets infrequently means that power is delegated. There is a Standing Committee of the NPC with perhaps 150 members, which is still rather large for interactive debate. It meets fairly frequently, seemingly to explain party policy to the more important nonparty officials. The organ that performs most administrative work is the State Council, headed by a powerful premier assisted by several vice-premiers. Again, there is no fixed number of vice-premiers. The various ministries and commissions are responsible to the State Council.

Below the NPC in descending order of importance are provincial or municipal people's congresses, county or city people's congresses, township people's congresses, and basic-level people's representatives. Below the State Council, also in descending order, are people's governments at each level.

It is, of course, the party hierarchy that is more important. A National Party Congress, again a very large body, elects—at least in theory—a central committee (CC). The CC has no fixed size, although typically it will have about 150 full members, who vote,

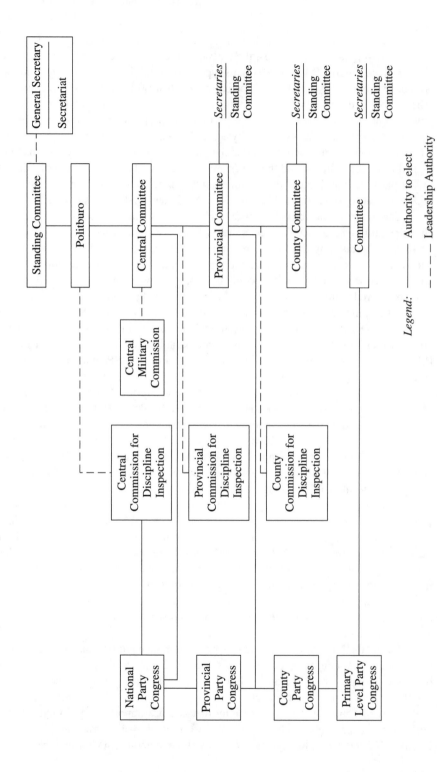

FIGURE 5.1 Organization of the Chinese Communist Party
Source: Adapted from the Constitution of the Chinese Communist Party, 1982.

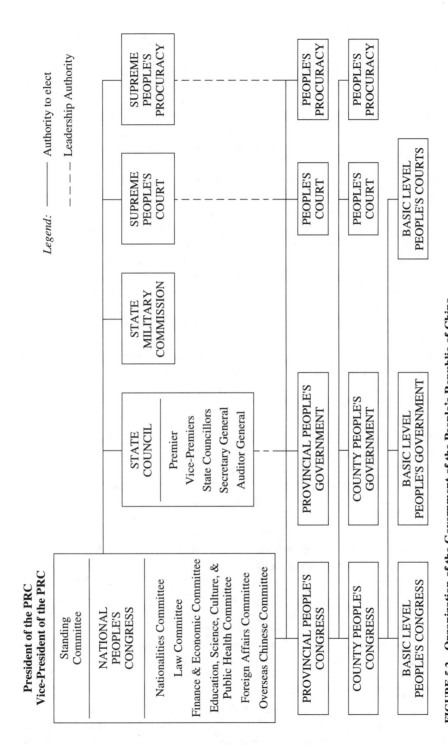

FIGURE 5.2 Organization of the Government of the People's Republic of China
Source: Adapted from the Constitution of the People's Rebulic of China, 1982.

and 125 nonvoting alternates. The CC has a secretariat, selected from among its members, which in turn supervises the descending hierarchy of provincial party and municipal committees, and so on down to basic-level party organizations.

CC members in theory choose a politburo of perhaps fifteen members, and it in turn selects five to seven of them as members of the politburo Standing Committee. These individuals, and particularly the chair of the Standing Committee, are considered the most powerful people in China. While the chair normally exercises enormous authority, he is not, and never has been, a totalitarian dictator. It would be more accurate to describe him as first among almost-equals. Decision-making appears to take place through coalition formation among Standing Committee members; the voice of the chair is generally, but not always, decisive.

The process by which lower levels elect higher levels, who in turn make decisions to be passed down along the hierarchy, is called democratic centralism. In reality, individuals are chosen rather than elected in free competition, and higher levels appear to choose members for lower levels rather than vice versa. Although all congresses in China claim to be organs of popular political power, only the basic-level congresses are directly elected by the people. Other levels are formally elected by the level just below.[3] As will be seen in Chapter 6, this may be changing.

After the establishment of the institutions of state power, the CPPCC did not pass out of existence, but remained as the organ of the united front. Typically, the party congress will meet first and changes, which have been formulated earlier by the politburo Standing Committee, will be ratified with little debate. Then the National People's Congress will convene and endorse the party congress's decisions. Lastly, the CPPCC will meet and do the same thing.

The relative stability of party and government organs during the last several decades belies the political battles that have swirled around them. From 1956 to 1977, no party congress served its full five-year term, and neither did any of the central committees appointed by the party congresses. The Eighth Central Committee, by contrast, served almost eight years beyond its term. On the government side, the National People's Congress did not even convene in thirteen of the thirty years it was formally in charge, and did not meet for one entire eight-year period between 1966 and 1974. One head of state, Liu Shaoqi, whose term would have officially ended in January 1969, was deposed in October 1968, not by the National People's Congress, which was the only organ legally entitled to do so, but by a plenary session of the party central committee, which did not have a quorum. In 1976, Hua Guofeng was appointed prime minister and Deng Xiaoping removed as deputy prime minister, both of these being government positions, by the *party* politburo, with no attempt at constitutional legitimization. Deng returned to power, and in 1985 retired several members of the politburo at a party conference, apparently because he feared the opposition of the constitutionally designated body, the party central committee. And from 1989 on, Deng, the universally acknowledged paramount leader of China, held *no* leadership position in party or government. In the 1990s, procedures gradually became more regularized.

The party made considerable efforts to draw the average individual into the political process. Mass organizations were founded, just as they had been in Yan'an. There is a Communist Youth League, a trade union federation, a women's organization, and a medical association, to name just a few of the more important. To reach the individual on a still more personal level, a device based on small study groups was instituted. In the rural areas this was done through the production team, and in urban areas through the *danwei*, or work unit. These were further broken down into *xiaozu*, or small groups, of eight to fifteen people. Based on the model developed at Yan'an, the most common form of the *xiaozu* was the political study group, in which members engaged in long discussions of study materials under the guidance of a group leader. Under the rubric of "criticism and self-criticism," each member was required to express his or her views, criticize himself, and submit to the criticism of others in the group.

The *xiaozu* was of use to the party in a number of ways. First, it gave cadres a forum through which to personally transmit party policy to the average citizen. Second, it placed policy changes in the context of face-to-face discussion, enhancing the possibilities for personal persuasion. Third, since the *xiaozu* normally consisted of people who lived near and worked with each other, it could exercise strong pressures for conformity within the group. Since group conformity was highly valued by Chinese tradition, the CCP could use this predilection to its advantage in gaining unanimous acceptance for policy changes. Fourth, the small group could give individuals a sense of participation in the political process, as well as providing a channel of information for the party on those individuals who showed stubborn or deviant tendencies. Finally, the small group was a method of strengthening the weak vertical integration of Chinese society—the leadership's ability to mobilize popular sentiment behind its policies being an important means to giving structure to the society Sun Yat-sen had described as a sheet of loose sand.

All of this, of course, assumes that the group functions according to plan. It did not always do so. Cadres complained of "individualism" and "particularism" among small-group members who stubbornly resisted accepting an unpopular party policy. Many people were simply bored, and attended the meetings physically while mentally tuning out their content. Even the politically unsophisticated could comprehend that they were being manipulated. Moreover, long periods of time spent in political study meant less time to spend in economically profitable activities. And frustrated cadres often resorted to behavior referred to in party documents as "formalism" and "commandism." By 1956, there was a noticeable trend toward ritualism rather than true participation in the small groups.[4] The device became moribund in the post-Mao period.

The Hundred Flowers Period: 1956–1957

During the first few years after liberation, there was fairly broad agreement within the Chinese population on goals, and the party did a reasonably good job of implementing them. Railroads were rebuilt and irrigation systems put back in order. The cities, which had been short of food, were better supplied. Inflation was halted and the currency revalued. Land reform was carried out.

By about 1955, however, tensions and stresses had begun to emerge. The mass collectivization of agriculture, handicrafts, private commerce, and industry had proved not nearly so popular as land reform. A much larger number of people perceived themselves as disadvantaged by the collectivization than during land reform and made their views known in a variety of ways. A repression campaign against certain writers led to a decline in both the quality and quantity of what was written, to the dismay of party leaders.

Mao Zedong realized that these tensions existed and was concerned to do something about them. Elsewhere in the communist world after the death of Stalin, popular discontent had boiled over into rioting in several areas. The Chinese leadership seemed to agree with the analyses made elsewhere that an important cause for these outbursts was that dissension had been repressed for too long.

The Hundred Flowers was Mao's attempt to do something to ease the tensions within Chinese society. In May 1956, he made a speech that included the phrase "let a hundred flowers bloom; let a hundred schools of thought contend." The second half of the slogan is a reference to the numerous philosophies that vied for preeminence in the Warring States period two thousand years before. The hundred flowers metaphor seems to have been coined by Mao himself, the assumption being that criticism would have the end result of strengthening socialism, because in the end truth wins out. In the course of debate, more people will become convinced that socialism is true precisely because the controversies will have forced them to think carefully about various options. This sounds remarkably like ideas advanced by the British utilitarian philosopher John Stuart Mill, though there is no evidence that Mao was familiar with Mill's writings.

Mao's speech was made to a group of party leaders and was never published. What we know of it comes from references to the speech that appeared in the Chinese press. These indicate that there were limits within which free speech was to be encouraged. Pornography was explicitly forbidden, as were attitudes such as "The moon in America is rounder than the moon in China" and "Let's all play mahjongg and to hell with state affairs." The assumption was that differences of opinion would not be serious because they would be examples of what Mao referred to as "nonantagonistic contradictions" (that is, those which do not need to be dealt with by coercive means) within the people.

At first, the result of this call for debate was a deafening silence. A well-known anthropologist hinted at the reason with an oblique reference to fear of "early spring weather"—which encourages buds to bloom but is inevitably followed by a frost that kills the flowers. In February 1957, Mao made another speech, not published at the time. Quotations and excerpts that appeared in the press indicate that this second effort went considerably further in encouraging freedom of speech. Backed up by party pressures, it did yield results. Initially, the criticism was mild. Intellectuals asked for a larger role for the CPPCC and democratic parties, and for the right to import more foreign periodicals that were relevant to their work.

Later, the citizenry became bolder, indicating that it now interpreted the still-unpublished second speech as sanctioning freedom of expression. Criticism escalated in ways that the leadership found shocking. Students at China's leading university, Beida, designated a particular wall as the place to vent their feelings, and covered it with "big-character" posters highly critical of the party. A Tianjin engineer complained that the communists had promised China a revolution but given it no more than a change of dynasties. A journalist wrote that the party had quickly become estranged from the masses, and that most of its members were "flatterers, sycophants, and yes-men." A professor pointed out that Marx and Lenin had constantly revised their theories and opined that they would not be pleased to learn that people with petty bureaucratic minds (the CCP leaders) were applying their doctrine so rigidly.

Peasants complained that the cooperatives were no good and demanded their land back. Workers proclaimed that the wage system was irrational, and voiced their annoyance at being required to "volunteer" to work overtime without pay. Some people even said they had been better off under the KMT. Ethnic minority groups advocated splitting off from China and founding independent states.

Contrary to the party's hopes, this was not the kind of criticism that would be conducive to unity. In fact, it seemed to be pointing toward disunity and centrifugal forces. Mao's February 1957 speech, entitled "On the Correct Handling of Contradictions Among the People," was finally published, but some passages appear to have been added. Among other things, it was noted that certain criticisms were not to be considered as fragrant flowers, but rather had been reclassified as noxious weeds in the garden of socialism. As antagonistic contradictions, they would have to be uprooted and destroyed.

The frosty weather that would kill the hundred flowers began in June 1957, and took the form of yet another mass campaign. Known as the Anti-Rightist Campaign, it had identified more than 300,000 people as rightists by the end of the year. Many of China's brightest and most dedicated intellectuals were among them. Rather than being encouraged to use their skills in economics, engineering, and astrophysics to help develop China, they had their careers ruined. Jail, reform through labor, or banishment to rural areas (the latter being to acquaint them with the "real" China, thus enabling them to understand the country better, while breaking down the sharp distinction between city and countryside) were among the punishments meted out. Promising futures were destroyed and families split. Some who had been branded rightists divorced, or were divorced by, their spouses in an effort to minimize the stigma on the rest of the family. Others committed suicide; a few were executed.

Could the Hundred Flowers campaign have been cleverly contrived from the first to ferret out malcontents? Initially, foreign analysts felt that it was not. They believed that party optimists, including Mao, were genuinely convinced that the campaign would solidify a unified population behind the party and ratify its plans for collectivization. Ideological hard-liners within the party would have had from the beginning real doubts about the wisdom of this course, and would have reminded the optimists of this when criticism escalated. Mao then espoused the hard-line position by rewriting his speech and allowing it to be published. Unity would then be obtained by weeding out the dissident "rightists."[5] However, more recent analysis cites a presumably authentic document indicating that the Hundred Flowers had an entrapment motive. In a letter circulated to higher party cadres in mid-May 1957, Mao states:

> Things are just beginning to change. The rightist offensive has not yet reached its peak. [The rightists] are still very enthusiastic. We want to let them rage for a while and climb to the very summit.[6]

The Great Leap Forward and Its Aftermath: 1958–1961

Among the more radical members of the leadership, a number of factors converged to create a mood of impatience with the status quo. The Hundred Flowers campaign seemed to disprove the idea that China could move gradually toward socialism, with people's attitudes inevitably moving toward acceptance of socialist goals. Furthermore, there was increasing dissatisfaction with the speed at which progress was taking place. Grain production in 1957 had risen only 1 percent vis-à-vis a population growth of 2 percent. Collectivization had been introduced in 1955–1956, and there were concerns that staying too long at the intermediate stage this represented might make it harder to advance to the next stage.

There was also a growing realization of the limitations that the Soviet model could have for China. The USSR had sent a number of advisers to the PRC after its founding, to assist in fields as varied as economics and ethnology. While there is no evidence that these advisers attempted to apply inappropriate Soviet experiences rigidly to the Chinese situation, they had an understandable tendency to think in terms of the categories and procedures they knew best. Since labor shortages were characteristic of the USSR, while labor surpluses were more typical in China, the Soviet tendency to substitute capital for labor did not work well in the PRC. Chinese leaders wished to put the country's huge population to work to increase production. Consistent with Mao's long-standing belief that Marxism must be made compatible with the society to which it was applied, the Great Leap Forward would implement communism in a way compatible with Chinese characteristics.

There was also a growing conviction that China's problems should be attacked by levels larger than cooperatives and villages. The leadership was in addition concerned with the growth of bureaucracy, feeling that increases in production were being held back by a morass of officially generated red tape. As well, new status differences were becoming evident. These were antithetical to the egalitarian ideas with which the party had come to power. A separate but related factor was Mao's deeply felt desire to reduce differences between the city and the countryside. Partly this was influenced by Marxist ideology.

Particularly in his earlier writings, Karl Marx had been very much concerned with reversing the alienation of man from the product of his labor that the specialization inherent in the factory system had caused. In the communist society he envisioned, someone could be a craftsman part of the day and by turns a fisherman, hunter, and literary critic at other times. Mao Zedong, as well as many non-Marxist Chinese of this era, had been concerned with the urban-rural gap in their own country for many years. Mao seems to have felt the gap particularly keenly. The product of a rural upbringing, he had been looked down on by various CCP leaders, including the Returned Student group, both because of his relative lack of sophistication and because of his emphasis on the peasants. They had referred to him disparagingly as a *tugong*, or "earth/dirt communist." Mao felt strongly that there should not be a dichotomy between the ideologically pure (i.e., communists) and the technocrats, who were assumed to be infected with bourgeois ideology: China needed people who were "both red and expert." The Great Leap thus contained a radically egalitarian message.

It was also Mao's conviction that international forces were favorable to a bold step forward at this time. In October 1957, the Soviet Union had launched Sputnik, the world's first satellite, and had made breakthroughs in intercontinental ballistic technology earlier in the year. Mao, who often wrote poetry and was fond of using poetic metaphors in his speeches, was moved to commemorate these developments in a heavily publicized speech arguing that "the east wind is prevailing against the west wind." He urged all progressive forces, including the Soviet Union, to take advantage of these favorable developments and march boldly onward.

Not surprisingly, the vehicle chosen to seize the moment was a mass campaign, in this case the Great Leap Forward. However, how exactly the Great Leap was decided upon has been the subject of much scholarly controversy. One analyst notes that Liu Shaoqi, whose bureaucratic orientation and sober nature made him a very different personality from Mao, delivered the speech that started the movement, although he would later be identified as having opposed the Leap.[7] A second scholar argues that Liu supported the movement, though for completely different reasons from Mao: Whereas Mao believed in the power of unleashed mass energy, Liu had organizational reasons for believing that the Great Leap could succeed. He also wanted to support Mao for reasons of self-interest.[8] Yet a third scholar, noting inconsistencies in this presentation of Liu, suggests that further research is needed on the relationship between Mao and Liu at this time.[9] A fourth, extremely controversial view, holds that Mao essentially ratified the views of the winning faction in a bureaucratic battle.[10] Mao's physician opined that we may never know what part the major actors played in formulating the Leap, since Mao's lieutenants, including Liu, displayed sycophantic enthusiasm, which may or may not have masked their true feelings.[11]

The early stages of the Leap involved experiments with larger-scale units of organization during the agricultural slack season of winter 1957–1958. Several cooperatives were encouraged to work together on projects such as dam building and other water-control work. The idea was to rely on local people and resources in preference to asking for state aid. Photographs of thousands of peasants scraping out tons of earth with crude shovels and even rice bowls in order to build dams appeared in newspapers in China and around the world. Outsiders' image of China changed from one of a sheet of loose sand to that of an army of ants, attacking enormous problems through group organization and sheer force of numbers. One author even entitled his study of Mao *Emperor of the Blue Ants*, the color being a reflection of the baggy blue jackets and pants that nearly all Chinese wore during this period.

In industry, hortatory slogans appeared on factory walls, urging the workers on to new goals. At first these were realistic: for example, "Overtake England in steel production in fifteen years" was a plausible target. Although the PRC's 1957 production of steel was well below that of Great Britain, Chinese levels had been rising while Britain's steel production remained essentially the same. Also, Britain is a much smaller country than China. Hence, the PRC could reasonably be expected to draw even with England within fifteen years. However, the time period of the slogan was progressively reduced from ten years to five and even, in a couple of areas, to three years. The slogan "More, better, faster, and cheaper" appeared everywhere. A visiting Soviet scientist recalled seeing such a banner over the door of a maternity hospital where, given China's enormous population, he found it most inappropriate.

There was also an intensification of a campaign, begun somewhat earlier, to send young urban intellectuals (defined at that time as those who had graduated from at least junior middle school) to the countryside to "take root, flower, and bear fruit." Known as the *xiaxiang*, or "sent-down" youth, they were expected to share their intellectual knowledge with the peasants while at the same time learning agricultural techniques that would enable them to raise more food for China. This fit in well with Mao's desire to reduce the differences between city and countryside. In general, however, it did not fit in well with the desires of either peasants or urban youth. Though it would have been dangerous to protest publicly, peasants resented having thrust upon them large numbers of youth who were unused to hard physical labor and ignorant of farm work. The *xiaxiang* youth tended to abhor the rigors of country living and farm chores, and to miss both their families and the amenities of city life.

Another slogan associated with the Great Leap Forward is "walk on two legs," with one leg representing the modern (as, for example, heavy industry with its need for expensive machinery, or, in the health field, up-to-date Western medical procedures) and the other leg representing the traditional (labor-intensive spinning and weaving techniques in the textile industry, and traditional Chinese medicine in the health field). The scientific method and research projects of all sorts were castigated as bourgeois. Correct political views and peasant wisdom were extolled; "bourgeois scientific objectivism" was ridiculed.

In August 1958, large-scale agricultural units called communes were formed by combining several cooperatives. The economic implications of these will be discussed in detail in the following chapter. Politically and sociologically as well, the communes entailed enormous changes. Backyard blast furnaces were intended to teach peasants the rudiments of industrial techniques, thereby helping to reduce the differences between city and countryside, and also to solve the problem of getting steel to the rural areas. This had been a problem because of poor transportation networks in the countryside. There was an attack on private property; peasants had to give up not only their private plots but, in many cases, personal possessions like wristwatches and jewelry.

Work points as a measure of income were abandoned in favor of the communist formula "from each according to his ability, to each according to his need." In addition to its appeal to ideological orthodoxy, this formula would free bookkeepers of the necessity to record work points so that they too could spend more time in the fields. People were to eat at mess halls so that they did not have to waste time cooking, and incidentally so that the state could control how long they spent at meals. Theoretically, there would also be less waste if one cooked in large quantities. Housewives were to be freed from working at home by providing nurseries for their children, so that they too could become productive. Old people were to enter "happiness homes for the aged." In some areas, there were direct attacks on the nuclear family; even married workers were to live in dormitories that were segregated by sex.

New agricultural techniques were mandated as well, including use of a double-wheeled, double-bladed plow, planting seeds more closely together and deeper than before, and utilizing land heretofore regarded as unsuitable for crops. While a few brave individuals protested the folly of some of these ideas, most had been cowed into silence by the antirightist campaign. For a party that prided itself on implementing the slogan "from the masses to the masses," this was the very antithesis of the mass line.

For a while it seemed that the enthusiasm of the Chinese people knew no bounds. There were stories of activists who arrived at work "on the backs of green frogs" (at first break of day), of elderly and sick people who toiled eighteen hours in the fields to show their love for Chairman Mao, and of agricultural production that tripled the previous year's harvest. Such tales did not last too long. The resolution on setting up communes was introduced on August 29, 1958; by October there began to be reports of party officials meeting to discuss "certain problems" that had arisen in the course of the Great Leap Forward.

The November issue of the party's theoretical journal *Red Flag* contained an article entitled "Have We Already Reached the Stage of Communism?" It may fairly be described as an exercise in how to sound enthusiastic about the Great Leap Forward while actually trying to damp down the enthusiasts. After some discussion, the author concludes that "we" have not yet reached communism and that therefore it would be appropriate to modify the practice of "from each according to his ability, to each according to his need" to what he called the "half-supply" system of "from each according to his ability, to each according to his work." The real reason, of course, was that most people had reacted to the previous formulation by not working very hard. Some were responding to unreasonable pressures by passive resistance; others actively engaged in sabotage by destroying property and killing their animals rather than turn them over to the state.

In December, it was announced that Mao would not stand for reelection as chairman of the PRC, though he retained his top party post. The stated reason was that he wished to spend more time in theoretical study and writing. The actual reason appears to have been that the failures of the Great Leap Forward had increased the power of a less ideologically hard-line faction within the party. Liu Shaoqi was elected to assume the post vacated by Mao. The Wuhan resolution introduced by the party central committee in that month also called for "doing away with blind faith," established definitively that China was in the stage of socialism rather than communism, and confirmed the "half-supply" system.

This and other subsequent directives dismantled much of the Great Leap Forward. For example, mess halls were told to improve the variety of food that was served, and their size was reduced. Their clients often had to spend so long traveling from their jobs to the mess halls that any economies gained from serving large numbers of people were lost by lengthening commuting time to and from the halls. The decision of whether to leave children at nurseries permanently was left to parents, who were guaranteed the right to bring their children home with them at any time. No elderly person was to be forced to enter a "happiness home"; if she or he wished to stay with relatives who were amenable to the arrangement, the state would not interfere. People were also to be guaranteed the right to eight hours of sleep each night. Private plots were returned as well, along with the right to keep a few pigs and chickens. The unit of accounting was no longer to be at commune level, but at that of the brigade—the former cooperatives, where it had been at the beginning of the Leap. Not long after, it devolved still further, to the level of the team.

Liu's replacement of Mao as head of the PRC government did not end dissatisfaction within the elite. Although it was officially announced that the Chairman had resigned because he wanted more time to think and write, Mao was in fact extremely annoyed with Liu. According to Mao's physician, Mao had been angry with Liu Shaoqi and Deng Xiaoping since mid-1956, holding them responsible for propagating principles that were anathema to him at the eighth party congress in September of that year. These principles included (1) supporting the idea of collective leadership; (2) removing Mao Zedong's thought as the country's guiding ideology; and (3) criticizing Mao's "adventurism." The physician believes that Mao spent the next decade trying to reverse these principles, ultimately launching the Cultural Revolution to do so.[12] The descending economic spiral continued to exacerbate differences of opinion among them, and in August 1959, at a party meeting held at Lushan, it was officially admitted that many of the accomplishments claimed for the Great Leap Forward were false. The defense minister, marshal Peng Dehuai, chided Mao for his role in planning the Leap. Though Peng had meant his remarks as constructive criticism, the angry Chairman sacked Peng for his bravery, replacing him with marshal Lin Biao. Mao, however, remained a low-key presence during the next several years.

Remedial measures could not bring immediate improvement. Crop damage is not undone overnight; decimated animal populations, particularly in the case of large animals who have few offspring, took several years to recover. Internationally, there were problems as well. China's repudiation of the USSR model, and Mao's urging the Soviet Union to take a stronger ideological line, had been done in such a way as to anger the Soviet leadership. In 1960, the USSR withdrew its advisers. Many left with their plans and blueprints, leaving scientific research projects incomplete and factories half-built.

Even the weather was uncooperative. Some areas suffered from drought, others from floods, typhoons, and plagues of insects. While some people saw this as the equivalent of the seven biblical plagues and others as a manifestation of the mandate of heaven, there were man-made causes as well. One reason for the plague of insects was a prior mass campaign against sparrows that managed to kill many other types of birds as well, thereby removing the natural predators of various types of insects. Some of the floods were due to the collapse of dams and dikes that had been poorly built by people who were not skilled in construction techniques.

Bourgeois expertise, whether red or not, began to seem desirable again. In terms of Max Weber's paradigm for modernization, the Great Leap's attack on specialization and expertise was antithetical to the modernization the leadership hoped to achieve. Indeed, it appears as a Luddite attack on modernization, with disastrous effects to the society as a whole. In this parlous state, the value of redness paled by comparison to the value of expertise. It was just such a realization that must have prompted the then-party secretary-general Deng Xiaoping to remark, "It does not matter whether it is a black cat or a white cat, so long as it catches mice." The capitalist and communist systems and their results rather than cats and mice were widely assumed to be what Deng meant by his comment. With actual physical survival at stake, people resorted to desperate measures. Making do, rather than ideological orthodoxy of any sort, was the imperative of the time.

The years 1959 through 1961 are known as the "three lean years." There were widespread shortages of nearly everything: food, clothing, fuel, and even paper. An African student at a Chinese university recalled his surprise at seeing an otherwise demure young lady lift her skirt high above her waist before sitting down. He later discovered that, since the cloth ration was so low, she was trying to make the garment's thin cotton material last for another year. The party's rationing system is in fact credited with preventing many more deaths than the famine might otherwise have claimed. Many years later, official sources admitted that 8 million people had died of causes related to the Great Leap Forward. Unofficial sources estimated the figure at between 12 and 20 million. Whatever the actual number the CCP, having expended years of effort attempting to win the loyalty of skeptics and the uncommitted, had lost considerable prestige with the masses in whose name it claimed to govern.

The Socialist Education Movement: 1962–1966

By 1962, production levels had returned to their pre–Great Leap levels. In October, the party Central Committee met, with Mao Zedong appearing in a more prominent role than he had for some time. The meeting's official communiqué contained references to class struggle, "opportunistic ideological tendencies within the party," and "the spontaneous tendency toward capitalism." The situation that lay behind these rather abstract words became clearer when the Taiwan government released a series of documents obtained when a group of its frogmen-commandos staged a raid on a commune near the Fujian coast. Called the Lianjiang Documents after the commune from which they were obtained, they describe a situation believed to be fairly typical of the early 1960s in China.

The documents reveal the existence of considerable concern with so-called unhealthy tendencies, among which were

- A "spontaneous tendency toward capitalism," meaning that peasants preferred to make money on their own rather than on behalf of the collective
- Relaxed social controls that had allowed gambling, speculative activities, and abandonment of the farmlands
- Revived "feudal practices," including religious observances, marriages contracted for economic reasons, spiritualist scams, and even sorcery
- A decline in cadre morale, with cadres complaining that the efforts necessary to fulfill their responsibilities far exceeded the rewards; many wanted to resign
- Cadre misappropriation of public funds for private use

The next several years saw a major effort to correct these unhealthy tendencies and reintroduce socialist orthodoxy through another mass campaign, the Socialist Education Movement.

One measure adopted in the campaign was to send higher-level cadres down to work in the countryside, grouped into work teams. There was a feeling that isolation of the cadres from the masses had caused many of the country's present problems. By living and working with the people they allegedly served, cadres could better understand their problems and therefore deal with them more effectively. By early 1963 the experiences gained thereby were summarized and the Socialist Education Movement began to take shape as a systematic campaign.

In May 1963 the party issued a document known as the Draft Resolution of the Central Committee on Some Problems in Current Rural Work or, more simply, the First Ten Points. It called for the formation of Poor and Lower Middle Peasant Associations to oversee management at the commune and brigade levels and carry out the four cleans. This entailed the cleaning up of accounts, granaries, properties, and work points.[13] At the same time, however, the associations were told to avoid interfering in routine administrative affairs. The distinction between interfering to find corruption and not interfering with routine administrative affairs was, needless to say, difficult to make. In order to make cadres spend more time in production and less on administrative work, the number of work points they could claim for the performance of administrative tasks was greatly reduced—to 1–2 percent from 4 percent or even, in extreme cases, 10 percent. Cadres were also given minimum numbers of days they needed to spend in productive labor, ranging from 60 for county-level cadres to 180 for those at the brigade level.

The next two years saw successive efforts to refine this effort to reimpose ideological orthodoxy without harming production. In September 1963, the Central Committee issued what became known as the Later Ten Points, and in June 1964 the Eighteen Points. This was followed in September 1964 by the Revised Draft of the Later Ten Points and by the Twenty-Three Points in January 1965. These and other documents caused no small amount of confusion. People remained bewildered by the scope of activities of the Poor and Lower Peasant Associations, as mentioned above. They were also unable to distinguish between legitimate sideline occupations, which the party approved of as a way to increase production, and "spontaneous capitalist tendencies," which it condemned.

What *is* clear from a careful reading of these successive documents is the leadership's growing pessimism that the unhealthy tendencies could be corrected soon: Longer and longer time frames are proposed. A hardening of the class line is also obvious, with a greater tendency to view problems as antagonistic (requiring struggle and violent methods to resolve) rather than nonantagonistic and capable of solution through persuasion and education. There were hints that the errant lower-level cadres had protectors at higher levels. In 1964, a new "politics takes command" campaign was introduced, and the PLA was held up as a model of political and ideological virtue for all Chinese to emulate. The cult of Mao study began to be propagated nationwide, and on a feverish pitch. At the same time, the targets to be struggled against began to be found at higher and higher levels in the party and government hierarchies. While there is no direct link between the Socialist Education Movement and the convulsive Cultural Revolution that followed it, the latter can be seen as a logical extension of the former.[14]

The Cultural Revolution: 1966–1976

The Years of Upheaval: 1966–1969

In November 1965, a young party official from Shanghai named Yao Wenyuan published a scathing article that is usually taken to mark the beginning of the Cultural Revolution. Yao attacked a historian-playwright, Wu Han, for "using the past to ridicule the present" in his works (see Chapter 12). This was followed by attacks on another writer, Deng Tuo, with whom Wu had collaborated on a column called "Three Family Village" for the newspaper *Beijing Daily*. The two men also contributed to a magazine called *Front Line*. Since most of the PRC's newspapers and periodicals, including these, did not circulate outside the mainland, nonresidents had never seen the material being criticized. One example of "Three Family Village" was entitled "Great Empty Talk." It complained that "some people," because they are experienced in public speaking, can talk endlessly on any subject. Yet, after they have finished, nobody can remember what it was they said. The column warned that if this technique of empty talk were taught to the younger generation, and if experts in it were cultivated among youth, things would go from bad to worse. The authors said that, to illustrate their point, they would take the example of a "neighborhood boy" who imitated the expressions of great poets and who had written many great empty talks, including:

> The heaven is our father
> The earth is our mother
> The sun is our governess
> The east wind is our benefactor
> The west wind is our enemy.

The neighborhood boy was unquestionably Mao, and the great empty talk was party propaganda in general. Meanwhile, there was yet another escalation of the cult of Mao study, with the study of his thoughts being credited for all sorts of accomplishments—from operating on cancerous tumors to raising watermelons to winning table-tennis tournaments.

At the same time, all other culture, both Western and traditional Chinese, became suspect for its bourgeois and/or feudal content. Chinese opera was considered as tainted as Bizet and Wagner. Hence "The East Is Red," a song praising Mao, became one of the few safe things to sing. Books other than the works of Mao disappeared from bookstores. A pocket-diary-size selection of Mao's quotations chosen by defense minister Lin Biao and bound in red plastic became a runaway best-seller, albeit in the near-total absence of competing works. Because of its size, the Little Red Book could be kept highly visible on one's person at all times as a symbol of loyalty, and even held aloft and waved on appropriate occasions. Another useful talisman was the Mao button, a small metal pin embossed with the image of The Great Helmsman, which could be pinned on one's jacket. Since these came in a variety of shapes and designs, some people took to pinning on several dozen badges at a time, hoping for a multiplier effect on this evidence of their loyalty to the Chairman.

While it was possible to view Yao's attack as directed against the particular culture of a few disgruntled intellectuals, his sally was actually a good deal more than that. In addition to being a historian and playwright, Wu Han was vice-mayor of Beijing. Deng Tuo was a secretary of the Beijing Party Committee, and the *Beijing Daily* and *Front Line* were official publications of the Beijing Party Committee. The hint made in the course of the Socialist Education Movement that officials at higher levels were protecting ideologically deviant subordinates now had concrete referents. The attacks, led, curiously—or so it seemed at the time—by the official military newspaper, *Liberation Army Daily*, then moved on to ask who was behind the "black gang" of Wu Han and Deng Tuo. No answer was given, although it was noticed that Peng Zhen, the mayor of Beijing and a ranking member of the party politburo, had not been seen in public or otherwise heard from in several months.

Nor had Mao been seen in public. In the West, rumors circulated that he might be dead or very sick and that the deification campaign had been plotted by those who hoped to succeed him. These rumors apparently convinced Mao that he should appear in public. Mao chose to return to the city of Wuhan in July 1966, for a swim in the Yangtze River. The real intent of the swim was to demonstrate Mao Zedong's health, although the official account went a bit far in claiming that the portly, chain-smoking 73-year-old had covered nine miles in 65 minutes, thus breaking all world records by a wide margin. Mao was, moreover, in no particular hurry; he was described as having stopped several times along the way to teach other swimmers some new strokes. Suspicious foreigners also opined that the official photograph might have been contrived, because the Chairman's face did not look wet, and the angle at which his head met the water did not seem proper. Since the press release quoted several of those present as saying "our respected and beloved leader Chairman Mao is in such good health," those who initially suspected that Mao was ill were now convinced that his condition was severe.

In August, Mao called out the Red Guards, young people who would enforce revolutionary purity. They were to be the children of the so-called five pure classes: workers, poor and lower-middle peasants, soldiers, party officials, and revolutionary martyrs. Mao wrote a big-character poster calling on activists to "bombard the headquarters" of established authority and struggle against the powerholders who were following the capitalist road. There was a clear implication that Liu Shaoqi, the man who had displaced Mao as head of government in the wake of the Great Leap Forward, was the chief capitalist roader. In addition to attacking established authority, the Red Guards were admonished to attack the "four olds": old ideas, culture, habits, and customs. In order to "exchange revolutionary experiences," they were encouraged to travel.

Seemingly instantly, Red Guard groups fanned out all over China. Millions decided that Beijing was the proper place to exchange revolutionary experiences, jamming transportation systems and causing health and sanitation problems. Others who had been *xiaxiang* to the countryside in past years felt that revolutionary experiences could best be exchanged by returning to the families and urban areas they had come from. Hundreds of thousands returned to already-crowded Shanghai and other major cities.

Possible ulterior motives notwithstanding, the young Guards proved extremely zealous. Among their demands were that blood banks draw their supplies only from those of pure class background, that Tiananmen (Gate of Heavenly Peace) Square be renamed East Is Red Square, and that traffic light colors be reversed, so that red, the color of revolution, could signify "go" rather than "stop." In accordance with Mao's orders, the Guards did indeed drag out many powerholders. The proof of their decadent capitalist leanings was often little more than possession of foreign liquor or their penchant for meals composed of a large number of dishes. Any association with the Soviet Union, which was believed to have perverted true Marxism-Leninism, was also very dangerous. Liu Shaoqi and a number of others were declared "revisionists" (as opposed to Mao, who was declared a genius since he had creatively adapted Marxism to the Chinese context) and castigated as "China's Khrushchev," after the despised leader of the Soviet Union. The Guards also ransacked museums and religious institutions, destroying their contents—all egregious manifestations of the Four Olds—and generally made a nuisance of themselves.

The Red Guards were far from homogeneous or united. While the idea that they should be of pure class background fit well with the campaign against the Four Olds, since the "olds" were associated with the overthrow of the old feudal-bourgeois classes, the children from bad family backgrounds protested at their exclusion from the movement. How, they wondered, could one be "red by birth?" Mao's original mandate had in effect asked the children of powerholders to purge the powerholders. When it became clear that the struggle was not producing the desired results, he began to use the children of impure backgrounds against party leaders whom he held responsible for the Red Guards' erroneous line. Hence, two different kinds of Red Guard organizations existed, one more likely to defend the established powerholders than the other.[15]

At the elite level, power shifted from the party organization to a group called the Cultural Revolution Small Group, containing among others Yao Wenyuan, several other Shanghai radicals, and Mao's wife Jiang Qing. Jiang, who had been active in left-wing theatrical circles in Shanghai during her youth, had become involved with Mao at Yan'an. Shortly thereafter, the wife who had made the Long March with him was sent off to Moscow "for her health." Since the USSR's capital was not known for either its salubrious climate or the excellence of its medical facilities, chances are that she, like Mao's defeated rival Wang Ming, was sent there to get her out of the way. It was rumored that there was considerable discomfort within the Yan'an leadership with this situation, and that in return for their acquiescence Jiang had had to promise to stay out of politics. Her activities during the Cultural Revolution have thus been interpreted as motivated by revenge. In addition to the Small Group and the party organization, the People's Liberation Army (PLA), led by defense minister Lin Biao, emerged as a powerful actor in the Cultural Revolution. The significance of the attacks in *Liberation Army Daily* and of Lin's editing the little book of Mao's quotations now became more apparent.

By the late summer of 1966, the principle of "free mobilization of the masses" was adopted: The elite, having reached a stalemate in their conflict with each other, drew in the masses, using official ideology to do so. Both party and government bureaucrats and the Small Group maneuvered to achieve control over the mass organizations. At the level of the ordinary citizen, mass involvement meant that all sorts of long-suppressed latent tensions in society rose to the surface. Tens of millions of people who had been socially conditioned by the party's previous mass campaigns responded enthusiastically. The Cultural Revolution entered a new, more radical phase. Possession of the Little Red Book and Mao badges, or a documentary record that one had been supportive of the party and Chairman Mao, did not necessarily protect one. One's enemies could, and did, claim that this amounted to an outward show of support to conceal the disloyalty within. They referred to this ploy as "waving the Red flag in order to oppose the Red flag." The atmosphere of the Cultural Revolution was militantly egalitarian: Anyone who had had authority over anyone else could be accused of being a corrupt powerholder. A large number of people were tortured or driven to suicide. Liu Shaoqi died when, desperately ill, he was denied medical care. Party secretary-general Deng Xiaoping's son, driven to jump out a window by his Red Guard tormentors, was crippled for life. Deng himself was tortured and removed from office.

In January 1967, the Small Group succeeded in establishing the Shanghai Commune, on the real or imagined model of the Paris Commune during the French Revolution. It was to emphasize the spontaneity of the masses without cadre participation. Unfortunately for the radicals, it proved unworkable. Chaos ensued as radicals in other areas tried to copy the Shanghai example. Premier Zhou Enlai, who had emerged as the leader of the party/government faction, gave the impression of being unconcerned with whether radicals or conservatives seized power, so long as production could proceed normally. Production was definitely not proceeding normally at this time, with railroad traffic disrupted and factories becoming battlegrounds for rival groups of workers. By February, Zhou seemed to have convinced Mao to opt for a more moderate policy. The formation of new bodies called revolutionary committees, which would assume both party and state functions, was ordered. The CPPCC and its functions were not mentioned. As the organ of the united front, which radicals had attacked because it represented collaboration with impure classes, the CPPCC simply disappeared. Revolutionary committees were to be composed of a three-way alliance of representatives of the revolutionary masses, revolutionary cadres, and revolutionary PLA members.

The radicals, believing that the emphasis on regularizing production meant selling out their principles, referred to this as the "February Adverse Current" and began their counterattack in mid-March. Several other shifts were to occur in what became a power struggle among the Small Group, the PLA, and a group of bureaucrats around Zhou Enlai. Though Mao's sympathies appeared to lie with the radicals, he was not above curbing their activities when it seemed wise and went to great lengths to publicly show his affection for Lin Biao. The two were photographed arm-in-arm, with the caption describing Lin as "Chairman Mao's Closest Comrade in Arms." Zhou Enlai seemed to have formed a coalition with Jiang Qing's radicals, despite their ideological and policy differences. He protected the Small Group against the PLA, perhaps because he wanted to maintain the balance between the two, with himself as mediator. The Small Group in return restrained the Beijing radicals from attacking Zhou.

As time went on, the PLA gained power over the Small Group. Mao gave the military authority to use force against any attempt to seize its weapons, and told it to unify the various warring factions. Lin Biao was designated Mao's heir apparent. With at least the facade of peace being made among some of the factions, revolutionary committees were set up in 1967 and on into 1968. On July 31, 1968, Mao sent a gift of mangoes to a workers' group stationed at Qinghua University, thereby symbolizing his support of the workers in their factional struggle with the students. The PLA moved onto campuses to maintain order. Thus the violent phase of the Cultural Revolution came to an end.

In October, the central committee, or what was left of it, met. Its major decision was to expel Liu Shaoqi from the party and from all his posts in party and government. The draft of a new party constitution was also agreed upon. Formally accepted in April 1969, it contained an unusual article designating Lin Biao, by name, as Mao Zedong's successor. Approximately half of the politburo could be considered Lin's supporters; even his heretofore politically inactive wife became a member. The Small Group was also prominently represented. Mao and Zhou Enlai were members as well.

At the middle and lower levels of the power structure—provincial level and on down—a number of old cadres who had originally been targets of the Red Guards returned or remained in positions of importance. They had neither forgotten nor forgiven their erstwhile tormentors. The "revolutionary masses," on behalf of whom the Cultural Revolution had allegedly been waged, were at best admitted selectively to the lowest levels of power, where they were under the careful surveillance of those they had accused of revisionism and taking the capitalist road. Some of them were actively persecuted.

If the Great Leap Forward had been antithetical to modernization, the Cultural Revolution was still more so. Its attacks on specialization and routinization of procedures ran directly counter to the modernization paradigm. While it may be argued that Mao opposed bureaucratism rather than bureaucrats and elitist snobbery rather than specialization per se, it proved very difficult in practice to uncouple one from the other.

Though falling considerably short of its goals, the Cultural Revolution had a number of other consequences. Rather than establishing greater egalitarianism, the revolution had removed many long-serving leaders while replacing them with new ones, dubbed "helicopter people" for their rapid ascent upward. The relationships of authority were destroyed in some areas and badly weakened in others. The party and certain ministries had all but ceased to function. Meanwhile, the role of the military in general and of Lin Biao in particular had been greatly enhanced. Production had declined, though the drop was by no means as precipitous as during the Great Leap Forward. There were drastic effects on the educational system (see Chapter 10), and both foreign and traditional influences on culture had been sharply reduced. What would take the place of that which had been damaged or destroyed was not yet clear. A large number of lives and careers had been damaged, too. Miraculously, some people emerged from the Cultural Revolution with their faith in the party intact. However, many others blamed the country's leadership for what had happened, thereby further weakening the CCP's legitimacy.

Reconstruction: 1970–1976

After the turmoil of the Cultural Revolution, a rebuilding process began. The year 1970 saw the revival of party organs; revolutionary committees remained, but functioned as governmental bodies replacing the people's congresses. Foreign policy also began to return to normal, with staff members posted to other countries as they had been before the revolution began.[16]

Behind the scenes, a fierce power struggle was being waged within the disparate coalition that had survived the holocaust. The main contenders were Lin Biao and his faction within the military; the Cultural Revolution Small Group, including Jiang Qing, which had its power base in Shanghai; and the less ideological party and government bureaucrats around Zhou Enlai. The prize was survival, and also the succession to Mao. Mao Zedong's health had been the subject of speculation for some years. The fact that he did not show up at several Red Guard rallies in late 1967 had been considered noteworthy enough that Jiang Qing, who attended in his place, had seen fit to tour Tiananmen Square in a jeep, announcing repeatedly through a bullhorn that Chairman Mao was in "robust" health. Whatever the truth of this, he seemed to decline in the early 1970s, with visiting diplomats summoned from their beds in the middle of the night or plucked from a visit to the Great Wall by helicopter in order to take advantage of Mao's lucid moments. While Mao's sympathies lay with the Small Group ideologues, he did not automatically side with them.

The first victim of the power struggle was Lin Biao, who made no public appearances after June 1971. He was later officially declared dead in a plane crash that occurred in Mongolia in September of that year. Lin was allegedly fleeing to the Soviet Union— China's archenemy at the time—after his plot to kill Chairman Mao was discovered. The "official" story exists in a number of versions, with numerous discrepancies among them that have never been resolved. Nor is there a convincing explanation of why Lin would want to kill the man he was constitutionally mandated to succeed. Many analysts believe that Lin was actually removed by his rivals, Zhou and the Small Group, possibly with help from non-Lin-affiliated factions of the PLA. Whatever the circumstances, Lin was deleted from the power equation, and more than 130 of his subordinates disappeared as well. The succession struggle now had only two major contenders: Jiang Qing's Shanghai hardliners and Zhou Enlai's less ideological bureaucrats.

The Tenth Party Congress, held in August 1973, saw the rehabilitation of some leading pre–Cultural Revolution bureaucrats, including former party secretary-general Deng Xiaoping. Deng quickly regained positions of prominence, including the directorship of the PLA's general staff department and a vice-premiership. He was regarded as Premier Zhou's leading protégé. Also re-emerging at this time were a number of military men not associated with Lin who had opposed the Cultural Revolution, generally from field armies different from Lin's. These rehabilitations have been seen as representing a victory for Zhou Enlai and for non-Fourth Field Army military leaders.

At the same time, the Cultural Revolution Small Group began to fight back hard, launching a mass campaign to "Criticize Lin Biao and Confucius," in which Confucius was widely understood to mean Zhou Enlai. The main charge against "Confucius" was that he was a "restorationist"—that he wanted to return China to its pre–Cultural Revolution state. Zhou, a master manipulator whose methods were often so subtle that their full extent may never be known, countered the Small Group's attack in various ways. Always outwardly friendly to Jiang Qing, he suggested that she contact an American woman to write her biography. Jiang did so, discussing matters which her enemies later used against her, alleging that she had confided "state secrets" to foreigners.[17] Satirical cartoons appeared depicting Jiang Qing as, among others, the empress dowager Cixi.[18] The implied commonality was that both had usurped the prerogatives of leadership that rightly belonged to their husbands.

Another method used by the radicals, who realized that they had few supporters in the military, was to build up the militia as a counterweight to the PLA. Militia units functioned as vigilante units in a number of cities, enforcing a left-wing line. Zhou's group meanwhile cultivated the PLA. As head of its general staff department, Deng Xiaoping was well positioned to do so.

In the end, the relative health of senior leaders rather than clever planning determined the succession, at least in the short run. Zhou Enlai, who had been suffering from a particularly painful form of cancer for several years, died in January 1976. Though always eclipsed by Mao's cult of personality, Zhou was genuinely beloved by millions of Chinese. His loss was deeply mourned by huge numbers of average people though, one imagines, by no one more so than his now-vulnerable protégé, Deng Xiaoping. On the next observance of the traditional Chinese festival of *Qingming*, or the sweeping of the graves, in April, Zhou's supporters flocked into Tiananmen Square with floral wreaths commemorating their deceased hero. There was also a large demonstration in favor of Deng and, allegorically, against Mao. According to the official, pro-Maoist account, demonstrators shouted that the people had had enough of "Emperor Qin Shi Huang" (the autocratic, egotistical emperor of the Qin dynasty) and made various "counterrevolutionary" and "rightist" demands. Foreign observers confirmed that the demonstrators had denounced Emperor Qin Shi Huang—Mao—and that they had demanded democracy.

At the height of the demonstration, there were an estimated hundred thousand people in the square. Although the sincerity of the pro-Zhou Enlai sentiment is not in doubt—many of the mourners were openly weeping—it is quite plausible that the demonstration was suggested by Deng for reasons of self-interest. If so, the plan backfired. "The party"—presumably meaning the Cultural Revolution Small Group—sent the militia and some public security and PLA units into Tiananmen Square to suppress the "counterrevolutionaries." This they did: Several people were killed and a large number were injured.[19]

Deng was blamed for instigating the demonstration and stripped of all of his party and government posts. His removal from the succession cleared the way for the Shanghai Gang of Four to take over. However, to nearly everyone's surprise, this did not happen.

Though ill and near his end, Mao Zedong decided to entrust the succession not to the ideologues but to Hua Guofeng, who did not appear to belong to either the reform or the hardline group. Considered a compromise choice, he had been a party secretary in his and Mao's native province of Hunan. The seriously weakened Chairman purportedly called Hua to his bedside and whispered to him, "With you in charge, my heart is at ease."

Mao's health continued to deteriorate. On July 28, 1976, one of history's most devastating earthquakes hit the Tianjin-Beijing area of northeast China, claiming many hundreds of thousands of lives. Its occurrence seemed portentous. In classical Chinese, one does not use the usual character for death to write of the passing of an emperor. The proper ideograph depicts the fall of a mountain, and means "cataclysm" or "earthquake." A few weeks later, on September 9, Mao died.

Notes

1. Translated in Stuart R. Schram, *The Political Thought of Mao Tse-tung* (New York: Praeger, 1969), pp. 456–457.

2. This point is made by Richard Kraus in *Class Conflict in Chinese Socialism* (New York: Columbia University Press, 1981), pp. 52–54.

3. James R. Townsend, *Political Participation in Communist China* (Berkeley: University of California Press, 1967), p. 105.

4. See Martin King Whyte, *Small Groups and Political Rituals in China* (Berkeley: University of California Press, 1974), and Townsend, pp. 174–218.

5. For more detailed information on this period, see Mu Fu-sheng (pseud.), *The Wilting of the Hundred Flowers* (New York: Praeger, 1963).

6. Cited in John Byron and Robert Pack, *Claws of the Dragon* (New York: Simon and Schuster, 1992), drawing on a study of this period by the respected Chinese journalist Dai Qing. I am indebted to Steven Mosher of the Claremont Institute and Professor John Copper of Rhodes College for calling this to my attention.

7. Translated in Robert R. Bowie and John K. Fairbank, *Communist China 1955–1959: Policy Documents with Analysis* (Cambridge, Mass.: Harvard University Press, 1965), pp. 479–483.

8. See the argument presented in Roderick MacFarquhar in *The Origins of the Cultural Revolution, vol. 2, The Great Leap Forward, 1958–1960* (New York: Columbia University Press, 1983), pp. 51–90.

9. See Thomas Bernstein's review of MacFarquhar's book in *China Quarterly*, no. 95, September 1983, p. 549.

10. David Bachman, *Bureaucracy, Economy, and Leadership in China: The Institutional Origins of the Great Leap Forward* (Cambridge, U.K.: Cambridge University Press, 1991); for a criticism of Bachman's thesis, see Alfred L. Chan, "Leaders, Coalition Politics, and Policy Formulation in China: The Great Leap Forward Revisited," *Journal of Contemporary China*, no. 8, Winter–Spring 1995, pp. 57–78; for Bachman's answer to Chan, see David Bachman, "Chinese Bureaucratic Politics and the Origins of the Great Leap Forward," *Journal of Contemporary China*, no. 9, Summer 1995, pp. 35–55.

11. Li Zhisui, *The Private Life of Chairman Mao* (New York: Random House, 1994), p. 277.

12. Ibid., p. 507.

13. Some sources defined the Four Cleans more broadly, as politics, economics, organization, and ideology. I am indebted to Dr. William R. Heaton, Central Intelligence Agency, for this observation.

14. The events of this period are detailed in Richard Baum and Frederick C. Teiwes, *Ssu-Ch'ing: The Socialist Education Movement of 1962–1966* (Berkeley: University of California, Center for Chinese Studies, China Research Monographs, 1968).

15. See the supporting data amassed by Hong Yung Lee in *The Politics of the Chinese Cultural Revolution* (Berkeley: University of California Press, 1978).

16. The foreign policy aspects of the Cultural Revolution are discussed in more detail in Chapter 14.

17. Roxane Witke, *Comrade Jiang Qing* (Boston: Little, Brown, 1977), pp. 29, 38–39.

18. See ibid., pp. 3–4, and the photos between pp. 334–335.

19. For the official account, see *Peking Review*, April 9, 1976, pp. 3–7.

Suggestions for Further Reading

Jasper Becker, *Hungry Ghosts: Mao's Secret Famine* (New York: The Free Press, 1996).

Li Zhisui, *The Private Life of Chairman Mao* (New York: Random House, 1994).

Roderick MacFarquhar, *The Origins of the Cultural Revolution, 1: Contradictions Among the People 1956–1957* (London: Oxford University Press, 1974).

———, *The Origins of the Cultural Revolution, 2: The Great Leap Forward 1958–1960* (London: Oxford University Press, 1983).

———, ed., *The Politics of China: The Eras of Mao and Deng,* 2nd ed. (Cambridge, U.K.: Cambridge University Press, 1997).

Stuart R. Schram, *The Political Thoughts of Mao Tse-tung* (New York: Praeger, 1969).

Dali Yang, *Catastrophe and Reform in China* (Stanford, Calif.: Stanford University Press, 1996).

6 PRC Politics in the Post-Mao Era: 1976–2003

Interregnum: 1976–1978

Hua Guofeng, having claimed Mao Zedong's mantle by virtue of his conversation with the dying chairman, was duty-bound to preserve Mao's legacy. He pledged himself to "support firmly whatever decisions Chairman Mao had made, and to follow persistently whatever directives Chairman Mao had given." This pledge, referred to as "the two whatevers," would later cause Hua considerable discomfort.

Initially, however, Hua Guofeng's position seemed secure. In the confused and potentially volatile months before and immediately after Mao's death, Hua seemed to have at least the acquiescence if not necessarily the enthusiastic support of the major groups in the political spectrum.[1] These included, on the far left, the followers of the Gang of Four, led by Mao's widow Jiang Qing. Ideological zealots, they favored political incentives over material ones, and wished to realize true communism quickly. Another leftist group was composed of PLA officers who had been associated with the now-discredited Lin Biao and his Fourth Field Army. Military officers who had prospered while Lin was powerful tended to be clustered in those parts of the center and northern parts of the country that had been Fourth Field Army strongholds. They were concerned to protect the well-being of their members, and felt strongly that their former leader had been wronged.

A somewhat less extreme, but still left-of-center, group had formed around Marshal Ye Jianying, a member of the group known as Hakka.[2] Ye was strongly supported by his fellow Hakka and had an important regional power base in his native Guangdong province. In addition, Ye controlled the central military apparatus. While less fanatic than the aforementioned groups, they tended to be sympathetic to Mao's motives if not always the specific measures he had used to implement them. Yet another slightly left-of-center group seemed to have coalesced around Li Xiannian. Composed of those who had shepherded the PRC's government and economy through the Cultural Revolution with relatively minor problems from extremists, they favored economic growth in a Stalinist mode by emphasizing heavy industry and deemphasizing material incentives. The Middle East oil embargoes had badly disrupted world supplies in the 1970s, and the group saw opportunities for the development of the PRC's own impressive fossil-fuel resources. This view led to its adherents becoming known as the Petroleum Faction.

Somewhat to the right of center was a southern military–provincial grouping including among its members Wei Guoqing, an ethnic Zhuang (see Chapter 13) who had been first party secretary of his native Guangxi province and, later, governor of Guangdong.

Wei had quite literally been the person responsible for making the trains run on time in Guangxi during the Cultural Revolution. Since a large number of these trains contained Soviet arms and material intended to support the North Vietnamese war effort, it was of considerable interest to the central government that they pass through. However, from the point of view of Chinese leftists who wished to attack the PRC's powerholders, the Vietnamese communists' need was less important than their own desire for firepower to support their immediate domestic political agenda. Wei escaped the Cultural Revolution unpurged but with little affection for leftist causes. He was associated with the Third Field Army, as was the other major figure associated with this group, Xu Shiyou, the head of the Guangdong Military Region. While willing to modify Maoist policies where they did not seem to be producing results, they were not willing to risk social disorder and a crisis of confidence in the party and government by making drastic changes.

Furthest to the right was a group characterized by extremely bitter memories of the Cultural Revolution. Having suffered badly in it, and perhaps also in the antirightist campaign and Great Leap Forward, they were disillusioned with, and often hostile toward, Mao and Maoism. They distrusted mass mobilization as a tool to motivate the masses and preferred economic to political incentives. Their most prominent member was Deng Xiaoping.

Throughout all their interactions, an underlying issue was the principles under which the PRC would henceforth be ruled. Mao's death had meant the end of an era. Was the new era to be a continuation of the old, or to involve a reassessment of the changes of the past and a radical break with Maoism? Those who adhere to the former view are frequently described as ideologues or hard-liners. They wished to affirm Maoist radical values and methods. Those who wished to break sharply with the Maoist past are generally termed reformers, even though the reforms they wished to institute, including reduction of state subsidies and greater personal accountability in production, will strike foreign observers as more nearly like what would be referred to in the West as conservatism. Finally, there were a number of people who occupied various intermediate positions on the spectrum between ideological hard-liners and reformers, being in favor of some reforms under some circumstances.

There is a certain amount of flux in the membership of these groups, with leaders who are generally considered hard-line supporting some reforms and reformers occasionally endorsing ideologues' positions. Philosophical beliefs are influenced not only by the circumstances China finds itself in at a given time, but also by considerations of one's own power position. Some analysts believe that personal relationships are more important than ideological positions in determining the composition of these coalitions. They tend to argue against the use of any kind of policy-related labels.

The origins of these groups and their interactions fit in well with the central-regional model introduced in Chapter 1, in both its native-place and field-army variants. The events also fit in nicely with the analyses of the bureaucratic politics and palace politics schools. Although foreign policy was of lesser importance than internal considerations during this period, arguments over the method by which China should acquire foreign technology and on which, if any, foreign powers to rely, have overtones of the strategic interaction and political cultural schools. Ultimately, of course, there was a generational struggle going on as well.

The reader will also notice a reassertion of traditional Chinese values, including the importance of family and patronage ties, which resonate with the China-is-China-is-China paradigm. In the sense that ideological differences did not preclude alliances among different groups, the factional model seemed to apply as well. Since the system now permitted a limited form of competition among those who favored different policies, one may also see an incipient form of pluralism. As predicted by the communist neo-traditional paradigm, political competition took place more within the institutional framework set up by the party than it did along Western-inspired models of interest group articulation. However, none of these analyses could have predicted what was to follow.

Hua's acceptability to various groups as a compromise candidate was in certain ways a liability rather than an asset. Most importantly, he was faced with reconciling often incompatible demands from across the political spectrum and risked being attacked from all directions by those whose requests he could not satisfy. For example, victims of the Cultural Revolution and other leftist-inspired attacks demanded a thorough repudiation of its policies and reinstatement of their pre-purge status. At the same time, those who had profited by the campaigns were strongly resistant to attacks on the Maoist system, fearing a deterioration of their own status.

Just at the time of Mao's death, the Gang of Four, fearing for its future at the hands of military leaders it had previously dealt harshly with, had tried to take over, using the urban militia as its armed force. The military acted forcefully in support of Hua, easily defeating the militia. Less than a month after Mao's death, Hua arrested the Gang of Four. Saved from one group, he became more beholden to another. In July 1977, acceding to the wishes of Ye Jianying, Wei Guoqing, and Xu Shiyou, Hua rehabilitated Deng Xiaoping. Understandably reluctant to reinstate the man whose place he had so obviously taken the year before, Hua took this step only after Deng had written two letters, one pledging his support of Hua as the most suitable successor to Mao, and another admitting his own mistakes. Deng was then restored to his former positions of member of the standing committee of the politburo, vice-premier of the State Council, vice-chair of the Central Military Commission, and chief of the PLA's general staff.

Pledges notwithstanding, Deng immediately began to undermine Hua's position. He was able to revive the office of party general secretary, which had been defunct since Deng had held it at the outset of the Cultural Revolution. Deng used the position to take over the responsibility, formerly exercised by Hua as premier of the State Council, of overseeing the implementation of politburo decisions. At the same time, Deng began moving his supporters from positions they held in the provinces to the central government in Beijing. One Deng protégé, Zhao Ziyang, the first party secretary of Deng's native province of Sichuan, showed open contempt for Hua. His province did not participate in praise of Hua, and he practiced agricultural policies that were quite different from those sanctioned by Hua.

In addition to moving his people from the provinces into the center, Deng consolidated power in areas where he and his former mentor, Zhou Enlai, had been strongest, such as the foreign ministry. He made efforts to rehabilitate previously purged cadres, thereby earning the gratitude, and presumably the allegiance, of experienced and capable people. At the same time, Deng worked to purge or marginalize Hua's supporters. Hua tried to fight back, wrapping himself in the cloak of Maoist legitimacy and seeing that stories showing his love for the people and his ties with Mao appeared regularly in the official press. Observers noticed that he even began to comb his hair in the same style as Mao had.

Deng's supporters retaliated, accusing Hua of attempting to create a cult of personality. They also ridiculed him for the "two whatevers," implying that Hua was incapable of more than slavish imitation of Mao. Morever, they hinted strongly, Hua might have fabricated his alleged deathbed conversation with the Chairman. Deng counterposed Hua's pledge to follow Mao's principles whatever with a slogan of his own, "Seek truth from facts." This was derived from Mao Zedong's essay on the need to link theory with practice, which argued that when a theory did not prove consonant with practice, it was necessary to revise the theory. Apart from providing Deng Xiaoping with a cleverly indirect way to attack Hua, the slogan confirmed Deng's reputation as a pragmatist. Henceforth, he declared, practice would be the sole criterion of truth. Dogma was officially dead.

Finally, in December 1978, Deng decided to permit a degree of liberalization. Drawing his inspiration from a line in a Qing dynasty poem that began "Ten thousand horses stand mute," Deng argued that the repressive atmosphere of previous years had stifled the population's creativity and desire to work hard. Deng proposed to allow the people to actually exercise the freedoms of expression that the constitution had in theory already given them. The populace responded with enthusiasm, writing wall posters that contained vigorous denunciations of policies and leaders they disagreed with. Certain walls became the gathering places for poster-writers and those who wished to express their views orally. Known as Democracy Walls, they sprang up in many cities. By far the most famous was in central Beijing, not far from Tiananmen Square. In that many of the people who gathered at these walls demanded the removal of precisely those power-holders Deng wanted to get rid of, the decision to permit greater freedom of speech proved an effective weapon.

By early 1979, with its aims largely achieved, the movement was gradually cut off. It had been noticed that, not content with criticizing past leaders, critics had begun to make adverse comments about the present elite, including Deng. Wall-poster writers were first moved from central Beijing to a much less conveniently located park, ostensibly because they had been disrupting traffic. While this was indeed true, other government actions indicated that the leadership had more in mind than ensuring a smooth flow of vehicles through the heart of the city. Poster-writers were told to register their names and work units with public-security personnel, who would also monitor activities in the park. Finally, even this constricted avenue of expression was closed.

At the same time, the journals of dissent that had flourished during this period were ordered to cease printing; certain of their authors received severe prison terms.[3] The charges against them often seemed contrived and implausible. For example, Wei Jingsheng was accused of having passed secrets on China's war with Vietnam to a foreigner. Since Wei, an electrician, was an employee of the Beijing Zoo, it was difficult to imagine how he came to acquire military secrets. What was not controversial is that Wei had been an outspoken advocate of human rights and democratic reforms. He was sentenced to 15 years in prison. In 1980, the "four freedoms" clause, which allowed people to assemble, express their views, write wall posters, stage demonstrations, and (a "fifth freedom") hold strikes, was removed from the PRC's constitution.

Some analysts have interpreted Deng's sponsorship of the democracy movement as cynically manipulative: a tool to be discarded when it had served its purpose.[4] Others saw the crackdown not as evidence of a ruse but rather as an attempt to mold democracy into a less socially disruptive form. Yet a third view is that Deng was himself a reformer and in favor of democratic freedoms but had acceded to the wishes of party conservatives who feared that the movement was getting out of hand.

Deng Ascendant

With the cult of personality officially dead and Hua diminished in stature, the PRC seemed to be ruled by a five-person group. Deng and Hua were assisted by the aforementioned Ye Jianying and Li Xiannian, plus Wang Dongxing, the head of the country's security apparatus.[5] By the time the Third Plenum of the Eleventh Central Committee of the CCP was held in December 1978, the extent to which Deng had been able to exert his influence was clear. At this gathering, Deng reintroduced in a much more ambitious form the Four Modernizations program that had its antecedents in a program originally discussed some years earlier. It was revived by Hua soon after Mao's death, but after the Third Plenum, the program and its ambitious goal of bringing the PRC into the ranks of the more developed countries by the year 2000 became identified with Deng.

The primary focus of the Four Modernizations was economic and is discussed in Chapter 7. The sociopolitical ramifications of these economic reforms were, however, enormous. In order to encourage people to produce more, the leadership sanctioned economic incentives that would have been unthinkable under Mao. They were told that there was no shame in being rich, and, further, that it was all right for some people to become rich before others. Wealth could even be inherited. Free markets were sanctioned for agricultural goods, and productive factory workers could be awarded bonuses. Unproductive factories would be closed, with workers forced to find other employment. The media repeatedly reminded people that the "iron rice bowl"—guaranteed employment regardless of job performance—would be smashed.

Intellectually rigorous examinations were reintroduced as the criterion for admission to universities. At the same time, the requirement for political reliability was quietly downgraded. Under the new regime, "redness" was to be less important than "expertness." Rapid modernization would require knowledge of modern technology. To accomplish this faster, Deng announced an "open door" to the advanced countries of the world. Employing concepts that would have sounded familiar to proponents of the self-strengthening movement a century before, Deng announced that foreign trade was welcome, foreign technology could be purchased, and Chinese students would be sent to Western and Japanese universities. There were some innovations as well. Since increases in productivity would have a lesser effect if they had to be divided among a larger number of people, a stringent birth control policy was announced: The ideal family would have only one child, and no more than two was permitted.

In order to enlist the support of intellectuals, the Maoist characterization of them as "the stinking ninth category" was removed. Experts were not only no longer to be despised—their advice would be actively sought out. Major party and state ministries and commissions began to utilize specialists in advisory think tanks. The whole concept of progress through class struggle, which had been so important to the Maoist variant of Marxism-Leninism, was explicitly repudiated. Henceforth, cooperation rather than confrontation was to be the driving force of progress. A new state constitution, promulgated in 1982, deleted the 1978 constitution's definition of China as a "dictatorship of the proletariat" and replaced it with a description of China as a "people's democratic dictatorship." This meant a return to the language used in the original 1954 state constitution.

Class labels, such as *capitalist* and *landlord*, that had been awarded as long as 30 years ago and that had been hereditary, were removed. An investigation was promised into verdicts rendered during such mass campaigns as the antirightist movement of 1957 and the Cultural Revolution of the late 1960s; those discovered to have been wronged would have their verdicts reversed. Many famous figures were rehabilitated posthumously, including former head of state Liu Shaoqi.

Henceforth verdicts were supposed to be delivered according to proper legal procedures. Because the legal profession had all but disappeared by the late 1970s, codes would have to be drawn up and people trained to implement them. The codes would also cover business practices, since foreign companies were understandably reluctant to trade with a country that did not provide them with any means of redress for such problems as failure to deliver goods or for the delivery of substandard merchandise.

Constitutional guarantees and procedures would also be extended to the electoral system. In sharp contrast to the practice of the previous decade, party and state organs would henceforth meet at their scheduled times. Elections for the representatives thereto was to be by secret ballot. There would be more candidates than positions, although only in lower-level elections, at least at first. This would be a first step toward competitive elections. The CPPCC was revived. As the organ of the united front, it had disappeared during the Cultural Revolution when the whole concept of the united front came under attack for being tantamount to collaboration with bourgeois revisionism.

A separation was to be effected between party and government and between party and military. Revolutionary committees, which had replaced the organs of party and governmment during the Cultural Revolution and had then retained governmental functions after party organs reappeared, were also phased out. Communes lost their government functions and were subsequently dismantled completely. They, as well as the revolutionary committees, were replaced by standard, pre–Cultural Revolution governmental bodies.

A new, much more tolerant policy was announced with regard to religion. Services could again be held, and the government offered help in rebuilding churches, mosques, and temples that had been destroyed in the Cultural Revolution. It announced the creation of an institute for the study of religion and that it would subsidize a new edition of the Koran—the first to be printed, legally at least, in China since 1949. Policy toward ethnic minorities also became more tolerant.

While foreign observers described these changes as China's turn toward capitalism, Deng vigorously denied it, stating that his intent was to create "socialism with Chinese characteristics." What this meant was never explicitly stated, though the official media supplied a four-point summary, known as the Four Principles, of the new orthodoxy:

1. Acceptance of the leadership of the communist party
2. Adherence to Marxism-Leninism-Mao Zedong thought
3. The practice of democratic centralism
4. Following the socialist road

The careful reader will notice a number of problems with this definition. For example, there is a great deal in Deng's new program which ran precisely counter to Marxism, Leninism, and the thought of Mao. And how, exactly, could one follow the socialist road when many of the directional signals appeared to be written in capitalist language? Other problems in operationalizing Deng's principles soon appeared. Economic *decentralization* had uncomfortable consequences for acceptance of the *centralized* political leadership of the communist party. And promises for truly competitive elections at lower levels ran uncomfortably counter to the *practice* of democratic centralism. While the *principle* of democratic centralism stipulates that lower-level bodies should elect the members of higher-level bodies, in practice it had been just the opposite. Now, when the higher levels persisted in picking all the candidates for lower-level positions, there were sharp protests. Ambiguities and dissonances from reality notwithstanding, the Four Principles constituted the definition of the new socialism and became the standard against which loyalty was judged.

The Legacy of Mao

The large number of changes from Maoist theory and practice, plus the rehabilitation of so many people, including Deng, who had suffered under Mao, inevitably raised the question of the legacy of Mao. It would appear that Deng wanted an explicit repudiation of Mao, and that he was enthusiastically supported by a large number of other people who considered themselves to have been victimized under his regime. Several moves were made in this direction. The Mao mausoleum was closed for several months in 1979, and stories appeared in the official press describing the hardships of the workers whose homes had been razed in order to build the edifice. In that it was clear to all who had given the order to build the Mao mausoleum, this had the effect of tarnishing Hua as well as Mao. In August 1980 the Central Committee issued a directive banning all personality cults of all leaders, dead or alive. Since Mao's and Hua's pictures were the only ones that were regularly hung in public places, images of both rapidly disappeared from most offices and meeting halls. Several statues of Mao were dismantled, some of them toppled by angry crowds. While there was no overt official sanction of such acts, neither were the perpetrators apprehended and prosecuted, as would have happened only a few years before.

In November 1980, the Gang of Four was put on trial, with carefully edited excerpts of the proceedings made available for television broadcast. The Gang was charged with executing policies that were widely believed to have had the backing of Mao. A defiant Madame Mao argued this same position from the prisoners' dock. Characterizing herself as "Chairman Mao's dog," she described her role as barking when he told her to bark. Most politically aware Chinese seem to have understood the trial as an indictment of Mao. Foreign visitors who spoke with locals about the Gang of Four report that they pointedly held up five fingers, the last digit representing the chairman as unindicted co-conspirator.

There were also people who strongly disapproved of the idea of destroying Mao Zedong's reputation. Some of these were ideological hard-liners who had been advantaged during the period when such policies had prevailed. Significantly, however, others had not.

One elderly military man who had been extremely badly treated during the Cultural Revolution pleaded poignantly against the de-Maoification campaign. He worried that removing Mao from his place of honor would leave young people with nothing to believe in. This would, he predicted, provoke the kind of crisis of confidence that he had noted in many countries of the West, despite the high level of material well-being they had achieved.[6]

Eventually, a compromise was reached. The contributions Chairman Mao had made to the success of the Chinese revolution were affirmed, though he was judged to have made mistakes as well, particularly in his later years. The official verdict was that his record was 70 percent positive and 30 percent negative. The Mao mausoleum reopened, with a chamber containing Zhou Enlai memorabilia added. Pictures of Mao were rehung in public places, albeit in lesser numbers than before. The study of his works resumed, but more selectively and with less fervor. No longer idolized, Mao was at least considered worthy of a modicum of respect.

Political Realignment and Policy Readjustment

Politically, Deng Xiaoping moved steadily to consolidate his power. The same Third Plenum of the party's Eleventh Central Committee had, in addition to introducing a new, more ambitious version of the Four Modernizations, seen the resignation of several potential rivals, including public security minister Wang Dongxing. Wang, it will be remembered, had been considered a member of the five-person ruling group of the PRC.

The plenum also officially reversed the verdict on the Tiananmen incident of 1976, which had led to Deng Xiaoping's temporary purge. Since Hua Guofeng had been minister of public security at the time of the incident, he might well have been indicted in 1980 along with the Gang of Four. The question of indictment appears to have been seriously discussed. Allegedly, Deng declared that "Chairman Hua deserves to be defended" and had all references to the 1976 incident deleted from the trial. His price for this was Hua's resignation, which eventually did take place, though apparently not until after significant countermaneuvering.

In any case, Hua was replaced as premier by Deng's protégé, the former Sichuan party secretary Zhao Ziyang. Another Deng ally, Hu Yaobang, whose previous career had been concentrated in the Communist Youth League, took over as party general secretary. Deng Xiaoping himself took over Hua's position as head of the party's Central Military Commission. At the same time, Deng withdrew from his former position as head of the PLA's general staff department and replaced himself with yet another old ally from his Second Field Army, Qin Jiwei. Deng had thus installed his protégés in the top positions in party and government rather than taking either position himself. There was, however, no doubt who exercised ultimate decision-making. The PRC's official media referred to Deng as "the paramount leader," even though no position with this title existed on any organization chart. Actual power at the top of the PRC leadership was therefore not synonymous with theoretical power, as indeed it had not been under the latter part of Hua Guofeng's time in high office either.

This left Deng with two other members of the five-man team, Li Xiannian of the Petroleum Faction and marshal Ye Jianying, plus Wei Guoqing of the southern military faction. In 1980 a major scandal unfolded, involving the cover-up of the capsizing of an oil-exploration rig in the North China Sea a year earlier. Incompetence and mismanagement were blamed for the disaster. Suspicions that the release of this information at this particular time was politically motivated were reinforced when the scandal was *not* blamed on the remnant poison of the Gang of Four, as virtually everything else at that time had been. Several resignations of high-ranking members of the Petroleum Faction indicated that it, too, had now been weakened. Wei Guoqing was removed from his position as head of the PLA's General Political Department in 1982, after a spate of GPD publications took a markedly different propaganda line from that espoused by Deng. Given the strength of his regional and military power bases, Ye was decidedly more difficult for Deng to deal with. Though privately defiant, he did not publicly challenge Deng. As Ye was also nearly 90, Deng may have considered that time was on his side.

Meanwhile, the reforms that had been made were themselves causing problems. The ten thousand horses that had stood mute had definitely been energized, but the flaw in Deng's reasoning had been his assumption that the changes he introduced would cause all of them to rush forward in the desired direction. What actually happened was that, while some did rush forward, others hung back or charged off in a number of different directions, and a few even butted heads with each other. Economic decentralization meant wasteful duplication. For example, five areas decided to build cigarette factories when only one was needed, adversely affecting profits and sometimes leading to cutthroat competition. From the government's point of view, too much money was invested in the wrong kinds of projects: Localities had a decided preference for constructing upscale guest houses rather than less glamorous but more needed facilities such as fertilizer factories. Some areas refused to sell resources needed by others, preferring to use them locally. Others imposed levies on trucks passing through. If selling vegetables brought more money than selling pigs, large numbers of independent producers switched to raising vegetables, and there were shortages of pork. A policy that tried to limit families to just one child was most unpopular, particularly among the peasantry who form the great majority of China's citizens.

Deng's judgment that it was acceptable to be rich, and that it was all right for some to become rich before others, led to increasing inequalities of income and a concomitant increase in jealousy—the "red eye disease." Those with an entrepreneurial flair and the willingness to work longer hours than their fellows often did become comparatively wealthy, but not without dangers to themselves. One woman's neighbors destroyed all the eggs she had planned to sell; another's broke the legs of her milk cows, forcing her to kill them herself. Still other newly prosperous people found themselves victimized by cadres who exacted punitive "taxes." Moreover, not everyone who became rich did so because of intelligence and hard work. Some individuals prospered because they were able to exploit family or other connections—the ubiquitous *guanxi*. Others, who had access to vehicles and warehouses, could buy items cheaply in one area, smuggle them to another, and hoard them until scarcity drove the price up to net them the profit margin they wanted. Regional income disparities were also widened by the new policies: Nature had endowed some areas with better resources than others.

Another focus of jealousy was the children of high-ranking officials. It was noted that they constituted a disproportionate number of those who were selected to study abroad and that Deng Xiaoping's own son was among them. When and if they decided to return to China, these privileged sons and daughters of the powerful frequently obtained positions with access to foreign currency and travel to coveted destinations. Often such positions were connected with the PRC's newly founded foreign trading companies, where the occupants could exact lucrative bribes from companies desiring contracts or access to their influential parents. This aroused intense resentment from their peers who considered themselves at least as well qualified, and often were. The individuals thus favored were dubbed "the prince faction."

Many leaders became concerned with the rise of what they regarded as rampant materialism that led people to have little regard for other human beings. Examples that would support their claim abounded. A survey conducted at a Tianjin factory asked the question "What is your ideal?" A composite response went something like "I find revolutionary ideals hollow. Only visible and tangible material benefits are useful."

On the other side of the spectrum from materialism, the reforms also generated idealism of a sort that made some leaders equally uncomfortable. In 1980 and 1981, a series of disturbances took place on college campuses in different parts of the country. The proximate cause was a local communist party decision to delete from the ballot the name of a student who was a candidate for local office in Changsha. Arguing that elections in which the party vetted the candidates were not free elections, large numbers of students began to protest. Their demands soon moved beyond reinstating the student's name on the ballot and toward more fundamental issues like human rights and democracy.

The promise to investigate past judgments and, if warranted, to reverse verdicts, clogged the system. Enormous numbers of petitioners appeared. These included people who had been sent down to the countryside ten and twenty years before and were desperate to return. When their demands were not dealt with quickly, they were likely to demonstrate in front of party or government offices, and to publicly declare that they held their leaders responsible. A small army of peasants camped out in Beijing in the winter of 1979–1980, eager to present their grievances to the leadership. They also proved ready to talk to foreign reporters: Much to the annoyance of the elite, their pinched faces and sad stories were frequently featured by foreign news media.

Generally speaking, there was broad agreement within the leadership, and even the public at large, on what the country's problems were: inflation, corruption, nepotism, inefficiency, and low production levels. The status quo apparently being acceptable to no one, differences arose on how to deal with the problems. While previous factions and personal affiliations did not simply disappear, the policy differences of the 1980s seemed to coalesce around two points of view.[7] Leftists tended to hold the reforms responsible for the problems and to argue that recentralization of party and government controls was needed to curb these dangerous tendencies before chaos ensued. Reformers felt that many of the problems had arisen because the reforms had been partial; more reform was needed. They added that to rescind the reforms or to suppress people's right to criticize aberrations of the system would lead to worse problems and chaos. Both groups seemed to be in favor of the goals of the reforms. However, leftists tended to be more fearful of the consequences thereof. They wanted to move more slowly on implementing the reforms while acting faster to correct problems they saw as caused by them.

One should be wary of differentiating too sharply between the two groups, since the specific circumstances of China's situation at any given point in time could persuade some people who had been in favor of rapid reforms to opt for a more moderate pace, or vice-versa. And even the strongest pro-democracy activists were aware that there were many obstacles to overcome before they could bring about the sort of sweeping reforms they favored. For example, in the mid-1980s, a young man who would become a prominent human rights activist during the 1989 demonstrations attempted to survey public opinion in rural Gansu province. He abandoned the effort after discovering that most peasants were unable to read his questionnaires, much less fill them out. An interview with the richest, and one of the best educated, peasants in the area also yielded surprising results. Of course, said the patriarch with feeling, he knew who Chairman Mao was: the emperor. He had been a great emperor, and the new emperor, Deng, also seemed good. The peasant added emphatically that reform was good, and that he agreed with whatever the government did. Later, the frustrated interviewer told a fellow researcher that "if we gave these people the vote tomorrow, they would simply agree to surrender all their rights to the emperor."[8]

The crisis of faith that some had feared would accompany a repudiation of Mao seemed to have come about anyway. One small incident in 1981, involving a traffic accident between the mayor of Shanghai's limousine and a truck, may be indicative of attitudes toward authority. Seemingly indifferent to the matter of who was responsible for the crash, a crowd of bystanders quickly surged forward to form a barrier between the truck driver and the traffic police. In shouted consensus, they announced that a fitting punishment would be for the mayor to be crushed to death in his car.

It was as if the reformers had encouraged emancipation of the mind from the fetters of rigid and outworn dogma without providing a coherent new set of ideals. This, in turn, had caused many to pursue selfish materialistic goals or, alternatively, to adopt Western notions of freedom and democracy.[9] Both tendencies worried the leadership, and its emphasis switched from reform to readjustment to correct the imbalances caused by previous reforms.

One effort at alleviating the problems that had arisen involved introduction of a campaign against "spiritual pollution." Begun in October 1983, it attempted to counter rampant materialism by criticizing the emphasis on moneymaking. The campaign was also directed at those who had forsaken fine revolutionary traditions of plain living and austerity in favor of Western-derived notions of hedonism. These included wearing long hair, gold jewelry, bell-bottom trousers, tight blue jeans, and sunglasses. Also criticized were those who favored Western "vulgar" books, rock music, and pornography. The last category is rather broadly interpreted in China. It would include, though not be confined to, material that would generally be described in the West as simply bawdy, off-color, or even as art.

The lack of interest in singing patriotic songs in preference to "decadent" love songs from the West, Hong Kong, and (worst of all) Taiwan was greatly lamented. The protracted debate of the 1980s over how much to borrow from foreign industrialized states and how much to rely on China's indigenous resources and customs was an uncomfortable reminder to many observers of the abortive self-strengthening movement of a hundred years before. The twentieth-century debate about how to deal with distasteful customs and mores that accompanied foreign technology seemed to emphasize again what Yan Fu had pointed out in the nineteenth century: Western learning had an essence of its own, which proved impossible to separate from the practical uses to which China wished to put Western technology.

The anti-spiritual pollution campaign was not a success. Peasants, many of whom had been among the beneficiaries of Deng's encouragement of free-market policies, concluded that the new rhetoric was likely to portend a reversal of those policies. The possibility that they might be branded capitalists and persecuted, a concern that had been present ever since the new policies were introduced, now seemed imminent. Those Chinese who had developed a fondness for "decadent" Western clothing, hairstyles, and entertainment were loath to give them up. Foreign reaction ranged from amusement at all the sins that Western influence was held responsible for to apprehension that China's open door might be about to close again. An uncharacteristically blunt Japanese prime minister explicitly pointed out to the leadership that the PRC's frequent reversals of policy in the past had had a bad effect on the country's international image and had caused investors to lack confidence in the PRC. The strong implication of his words was that another policy reversal would have disastrous effects for China. In that peasant concerns about the movement were having a dampening effect on agricultural production, rural areas were exempted from the anti-spiritual pollution campaign only two months after it began. The campaign itself faded out a few months later, on Deng's orders.

Analyses of the reasons behind the origins and early demise of the anti-spiritual pollution drive differ. Some believe that it had been launched because the leadership agreed that it was necessary to reaffirm the four basic principles of the new system. Later, when critics of bourgeois decadence seemed to be going too far, they began to dismantle it. Another view is that Deng launched the campaign in order to preempt leftist demands for a more extreme antirightist campaign, such as that which followed the Hundred Flowers period of 1956–1957. This move would, it was believed, allow him to save the core of his reforms. It is also possible to view Deng's actions as maneuvering between the demands of leftist leaders on the one hand and the desires of an increasingly restive public opinion on the other. In this analysis, Deng's chief concern is seen as keeping himself in power rather than preserving a specific policy agenda.

Other problems addressed at this time included streamlining bureaucratic organs and the number of personnel who staffed them. Ambitious economic development plans had led to a proliferation of new offices and bureaus to oversee them. There was a good deal of redundancy and overlap among the different entities, causing lengthy delays in getting projects approved, turf fights, and various other inefficiencies. There was also a feeling that the aims of many of the reforms were being blunted by a large number of leftists, many of them elderly and poorly educated, who were entrenched in the bureaucracy. There was no established retirement age for senior cadres, many of whom were in their seventies and eighties. Below them, a large number of capable people had remained unpromoted for decades, their channels of advancement blocked and their enthusiasm dampened. Reduction in numbers and ages of personnel offered a way to solve some of these problems. Since it would be possible to have the cuts fall disproportionately on opponents of Deng's programs, the drive could be used to reduce factionalism and ease the path of reform as well.

The Twelfth Party Congress in September 1982 established the Central Advisory Commission as a way to retire some elderly senior leaders with honor. It did absorb some of these, but not necessarily with the desired effect. Several individuals agreed to leave their current positions for the advisory group, but not until they were able to select their own successor. Typically, this was someone who could be expected to do his mentor's bidding, and therefore the older leader continued to rule from behind the scenes. In the words of one frustrated reformer, ". . . elderly leaders still exercise tremendous power. They may not have a position, but their secretaries and their aides are now in positions of power. Those old guys just get on the phone and say 'do this.' "[10]

The handpicked successor was often the retiree's own son or daughter, thus swelling the ranks of the prince faction and, at the same time, giving credibility to the arguments of critics of that faction. Some elderly leaders would not resign at all. Ye Jianying, Deng's erstwhile ally and more recent nemesis, was reported adamant, saying that he did not believe in retirement and categorically refusing to do so. In that more people who did not possess formal power continued to exercise real power, the creation of the Central Advisory Commission and various other schemes to induce the elderly to retire widened the gap between theoretical responsibility and actual authority.

The retirements caused other problems as well. In his zeal to reduce the average ages of officeholders, Deng had passed over an entire generation in its sixties and late fifties, leading to grave disappointments and loss of morale. Moreover, a select group of Deng cronies, headed by Deng himself, remained at the center stage of power despite being in their late seventies or early eighties. A few were even promoted into higher positions. A newspaper that pointed out that Deng should resign his positions was promptly closed down. Deng had in fact made an effort to relinquish his position as chair of the Central Military Commission (though he did not suggest leaving his seat on the politburo) in favor of his protégé Hu Yaobang. Since Hu was party general secretary, this would have placed the party's top military position in the hands of the person who held the highest position in the party, as had been the case while Mao ruled, and also during the earlier part of Hua Guofeng's time in office. PLA leaders, arguing that Hu had no significant military experience, and apparently also feeling that he lacked good judgment, were able to block the move. This resistance from the military represented a significant weakness in Hu's position. While Deng certainly retained ultimate decision-making power with regard to the military, he was busy with many more pressing aspects of the administration of China. The actual day-to-day running of the PLA was in the hands of the Central Military Commission's general secretary, Yang Shangkun.

The mid-1980s were characterized by some events that allowed the reformers to claim success for their program, and by others that lent credence to the leftist critique thereof. For example, nominal personal income rose in 1985, but so did the inflation rate. Price rises triggered panic buying, which in turn caused shortages. Shortages encouraged black marketeering, speculation, and smuggling. Many of these illegal activities were organized by cadres or their children, thus further eroding the ordinary citizen's faith in the leadership. An elaborate $1.5 billion foreign exchange scam was uncovered on Hainan Island, with the island's highest-ranking official serving as ringleader. Trying to recover the total amount would have crippled the island's economy. Punishments were rather light, and therefore probably had little disincentive effect on others who might be contemplating similarly deft financial maneuvers.[11]

The removal from office of the leftist propaganda chief who had headed the campaign against spiritual pollution cheered reformers, as did the results of a special party conference held in September 1985. Ten of the politburo's twenty-four members resigned, including the doughty Ye Jianying. In what was believed to be Ye's price for departing, his son, Ye Xuanping, was named governor of Guangdong province shortly thereafter. The senior Ye had been a member of the even more select standing committee of the politburo as well; his departure from that body meant that the standing committee now numbered five, with the reformers Deng Xiaoping, Hu Yaobang, and Zhao Ziyang having a slight numerical edge over leftists Chen Yun and Li Xiannian. Here again, however, there were doubts as to how much the reform faction had gained. The procedures involved in the resignations were quite irregular. According to the party constitution, the resignations should have occurred at a party congress, not a conference, whose members are invited at the discretion of the party leader. The implication was that Deng felt he lacked broad consensus within the party to make these changes.[12]

A plenary session of the party Central Committee held right after the conference added six new members to the politburo, most of them younger and better educated than those they replaced. One, Hu Qili, had had long service in the Youth League and was considered a protégé of Hu Yaobang and a reformer. Although the two Hus shared a surname, they were not related. A second new politburo member was Li Peng, a Soviet-educated engineer. Although Li, orphaned at an early age, was the adopted son of Zhou Enlai, the widespread popular affection for Zhou did not accrue to Li. A leftist in most aspects, he was also a member of the prince faction. Both Hu and Li were considered rising stars in the party, and part of the "third echelon" who would eventually succeed Deng Xiaoping's second echelon of Hu Yaobang and Zhao Ziyang.

The same plenary session also featured a highly unusual (because it was so public) debate between Deng Xiaoping and the leftist economist Chen Yun. Deng, not surprisingly, had made a speech praising the results of his reforms and noting the increases in living standards that had resulted. Chen followed with a speech of his own, pointing out that the number of high-income households had been greatly exaggerated, and noting that the country's grain production had in reality gone down. In what is perhaps the most telling indication of the relative strength of the two sides, the official media printed both speeches, in order of presentation.

The disagreements between those who were more in favor of reforms and those who were less so were also mirrored in a debate on the relevance of Marxism to present-day problems. Initially, Marx seemed to be losing ground. In October 1984, Deng Xiaoping observed that China need not fear "a little capitalist stuff," and on December 7 an unsigned commentary in the official party newspaper *Renmin Ribao* stated that "one cannot expect that the works of Marx and Lenin, written in their times, will solve the problems of today." A few days later, however, the paper noted that it had made a mistake; the commentary should have said that the works of Marx and Lenin should not be expected to solve *all* of present-day China's problems. In March 1985, Deng stressed the need to heighten ideological vigilance lest the country's youngsters fall victim to capitalist ideas. Marx and Lenin had clearly regained official backing, with Deng's behavior interpreted as yet another of his tactical retreats in the face of criticism.

A rectification campaign was held in 1985, though carefully phrased to avoid the deleterious domestic and international concerns that had been aroused by the anti-spiritual pollution campaign of 1983–1984. Directed against "bourgeois-liberal tendencies" and "new unhealthy tendencies," it actually targeted rather old tendencies such as nepotism and cronyism in employment and promotion practices, spending public money on banquets and gifts to higher officials, and the misuse of foreign exchange. A follow-up campaign in 1986, the year of the tiger, aimed specifically at curbing corruption in high places. Despite its catchy slogan, "Beat the tiger [of corruption] in the year of the tiger," the campaign, like its predecessors, achieved few results.

Infighting between reformers and leftists continued. A foreign reporter who was arrested and later expelled from China during the summer of 1986 attributed his experience to a disagreement between reformers and state security bureau leftists. The latter had, he believed, chosen to make an issue of his failure to comply with one of their rules as a test case of strength.[13]

Uncertainty about whether the system would move backward, forward, or stay the same caused problems, too. The nation's peasant-oriented newspaper repeated a favorite slogan of its constituency, "Fear neither waterlogging nor drought, but a change in the party's policies."[14] Those who felt that they could make no predictions about the future were reluctant to invest in the present. While such attitudes were understandable, they had a dampening effect on development. Officials also worried about the rising incidence of disorder, with the population increasingly unwilling to accept their directives. In widely different parts of the country there were soccer riots, anti-Japanese demonstrations, Turkic Muslim protests against nuclear testing in Xinjiang province, and demonstrations against various official abuses of power. In Beijing in 1986, a crowd estimated at one thousand cornered a police vehicle, jeering at its occupants and threatening to overturn it.[15] The rather minor incident that had sparked this confrontation—a policeman had slapped a motorcyclist in an argument over a traffic violation—suggested the existence of a more serious underlying hostility toward police authority.

At the end of 1986, large student demonstrations began at the Chinese University of Science and Technology in Hefei, Anhui province. Despite an official attempt to suppress the news they soon spread to many other areas, including Shanghai and Beijing. On January 1, Beijing students assembled in Tiananmen Square, defying both an explicit ban against demonstrating and the freezing-cold weather. To further discourage the gathering, the police had sprayed water on the huge square, transforming it into a slick sheet of ice. Among the students' demands were greater democratization in general, and specifically, the return of the "four freedoms" clause that had been deleted from the constitution in 1980. After several weeks of uncertainty, the demonstrations were put down.

Leftists used their occurrence to support their argument that granting political freedoms would lead to chaos and disruption. Hu Yaobang, with his background in the Youth League and his association with the reform group, was blamed for mishandling the demonstrations, and resigned as party general secretary. A spate of anecdotes illustrating Hu's inept conduct in the office began to circulate. Some simply repeated previously known stories; others may have been fabricated. The common thread of the anecdotes reinforced the view that the PLA leadership, in blocking his appointment as head of the Central Military Commission, had held all along. Others of lesser renown were also relieved of their positions for complicity in the demonstrations. Among them was the now famous Fang Lizhi, the vice-president of the Anhui university where the demonstrations had begun. An eminent astrophysicist, he had also been vocal in support of democratization.

Deng's acquiescence in the dismissal of his longtime protégé Hu Yaobang was generally interpreted as yet another tactical retreat in the face of resistance. The commonly heard analogy was to chess: Deng had sacrificed a pawn, Hu, in order to save the king, himself and his reforms. Subsequent events seemed to bear out this hypothesis. Leftists of all ages, and elderly leftists in particular, seemed to gain in power.[16] The campaign against bourgeois liberalism was stepped up, and there was much talk about upholding the Four Basic Principles. Official pronouncements declared that adherence to the Four Principles had become "the central task of the political and ideological sphere." Deng himself sounded more leftist, calling, for example, for a restoration of the party's tradition of democratic centralism. He also spoke of "neoauthoritarianism," implying that steady progress toward economic development could best be ensured by a leadership with highly concentrated powers. Strong authority was necessary to remove hindrances presented by those who had vested interests in the old structure.

By April 1987, the tide had turned toward reforms. Deng again took the lead, telling a foreign visitor that a "leftist" tendency in the party was jeopardizing China's economic reforms. Zhao Ziyang, who had taken over Hu Yaobang's position on an acting basis, delivered several speeches with liberal overtones. In November, the party's Thirteenth Party Congress confirmed Zhao as general secretary and made him first vice-chair of the Central Military Commission, an honor never bestowed on his predecessor. Deng Xiaoping, Li Xiannian, and Chen Yun resigned from the standing committee of the politburo on grounds of their advanced ages and collectively entered the Central Advisory Commission. This left Zhao as the only holdover from the previous standing committee. He was joined by rising leftist star Li Peng, rising reformer star Hu Qili, plus Qiao Shi, a leftist who was chair of the Central Discipline Inspection Commission, and Yao Yilin, a leftist protégé of Chen Yun. Although the new standing committee had a three-to-two leftist edge, it contained no open critics of reform. Reformers were prominently represented in the politburo as well. These included Hu Yaobang. Because he had been demoted by the leftists partially because they thought he had been too lenient in his treatment of the students, the students now saw him as the champion of their cause. The deliberations of the congress indicated that reforms would continue to be made.

The Seventh National People's Congress, meeting in March and April 1988, continued the mixed signals sent by the Thirteenth Party Congress. Its communiqué stressed that reform was China's central task. At the same time, two elderly leftists with military backgrounds, Yang Shangkun and Wang Zhen, were selected as president and vice-president of the PRC, and Li Peng became premier. Li's speech focused on coping with inflation and declining grain production, both standard leftist themes.

A few months later, Zhao Ziyang, apparently with Deng's backing, launched an ambitious retail price reform. While completely in line with the end goal of reducing state subsidies and moving toward a free market, the reform produced the worst inflation in post-1949 China. The official figure, 18.5 percent, is believed to be less than half of the actual inflation rate, which some estimates placed at almost 50 percent. There were runs on banks, panic buying, and greatly increased social disorder. It would appear that, once problems became apparent, Deng characteristically opted for tactical retreat. Zhao, however, seemed determined to press on. During the summer he presented the politburo with a daring proposal to end all state price controls within four to five years, and furthermore proposed to devalue the currency in order to encourage the country's exports.

This scheme would have been ambitious under the best of circumstances. However, these were not the best of circumstances. Given the escalating inflation rate and level of popular discontent, Zhao's plan struck not only leftists, but some reformers as well, as unacceptably foolhardy. Sources close to Zhao later explained that Deng had pushed Zhao to do this, but shifted the blame to him when resistance was encountered. By the time of the Thirteenth Central Committee's Third Plenum in September, it became clear that price reform had been postponed indefinitely. Other solutions favored by leftists would also be pursued: efforts to cut back on capital construction, recentralize decision-making, and rectify ideology. Rumor had it that Zhao had been stripped of his responsibility for economic work. Though this was vigorously denied by official sources, Zhao's activities in the economic sphere did seem to have diminished at the same time that leftists Li Peng and Yao Yilin became more active. The diminution of Zhao's ability to influence economic policy, when added to the fact that he had never exercised much influence over the military, meant that his position was weak indeed. Official sources again spoke of the advantages of neo-authoritarianism.[17] While Deng Xiaoping had originally been seen as the authoritarian, neo-authoritarian theorists came to envision Zhao Ziyang as the strong force guiding reform. Deng appeared to become increasingly worried about the consequences of his own reform program, and to be siding with the leftists. This shift seemed to go unnoticed by foreign analysts, who perhaps considered it to be simply another temporary retreat. In the words of one disgruntled intellectual, Deng's admonition to seek truth from facts had been transformed to mean "seek truth from certain approved facts." Anti-Deng doggerel became increasingly common. One of the more popular ditties, sung to the tune of the hymn to Mao, *The East Is Red*, went:

> The west is red
> The sun has set
> A Deng Xiaoping has come
> He serves the privileged very well
> And tells the rest to go to hell.

While the leadership's effort to dampen inflation was popular, most of the other plans announced at the Third Plenum met with determined, if at first largely passive, resistance. In December, reformers convened a forum to commemorate the tenth anniversary of the Third Plenum of the Eleventh Central Committee in December 1978, at which many of the now postponed reforms had been introduced. Human rights became a major issue. Since the 1978 gathering had rehabilitated many of those leaders persecuted during the Cultural Revolution and reversed the verdict on the Tiananmen incident of 1976, participants used the 1988 forum to advocate reversing the verdict on those who had been convicted in the 1979 crackdown on the democracy movement. They also advocated borrowing Western democratic forms in order to build "socialist democracy."

Such pressures seem to have convinced the leadership to respond by digging in its heels rather than giving in. Protests in Tibet during March 1989, later alleged to have been instigated by the government, resulted in martial law being declared there. Intellectuals responded negatively, and called for greater freedom for all and the release of political prisoners. Students spoke openly of a large demonstration to commemorate the seventieth anniversary of the May Fourth movement in 1919. The atmosphere was rife with anticipation.

The Tiananmen Demonstrations, 1989

The sense that a time of reckoning was near may have been what convinced Hu Yaobang to come forward again. At a politburo meeting dedicated to the discussion of problems in education, Hu reportedly championed additional government support for that field—a stand that would have enormous appeal to his student backers. During this meeting, he suffered a heart attack; according to hearsay, the precipitant cause was an argument with a leading leftist. After a week in the hospital, Hu died. While the rumor that Hu Yaobang died as a result of an argument with a leftist over greater state aid to education seems suspiciously tailored to fit the students' cause, the important thing is that the story was believed by large numbers of people. Again flouting the ban on demonstrations, as they had in 1986–1987, thousands of students staged a sit-in at Tiananmen Square the night before Hu's memorial service was to be held at the adjoining Great Hall of the People. A few days later, on April 24, the students declared an indefinite boycott of classes, and announced the establishment of a preparatory committee for a national student federation. There was talk of founding unions for students and workers, on the model of Poland's Solidarity movement. Similar demonstrations were held, and similar demands made, in many other Chinese cities.

Zhao Ziyang, perhaps not realizing how serious the situation was, had departed on a week-long trip to North Korea the day before. His absence undoubtedly helped the leftist cause. Premier Li Peng and President Yang Shangkun, who was concurrently general secretary of the Central Military Commission, met with Deng Xiaoping, who approved a hard line toward the demonstrations. On April 26, *Renmin Ribao* published an editorial prohibiting the protests, which were deemed counterrevolutionary. It warned that troops would be sent in, if necessary, to quell the "chaotic disturbances."

The students, who generally considered themselves patriotic remonstrators in the traditional Chinese sense—carrying out their duty as educated citizens to press the government to right existing wrongs—were upset and insulted by the April 26 editorial.[18] A mass march of as many as a hundred thousand students surged into Tiananmen Square, meeting only token resistance from security forces. The students were supported by an estimated one million citizens of Beijing, many marching with them under the banners of their work units and making their own demands of the government. Newspaper reporters, for example, carried banners asking to be allowed to print the truth. The message, beamed by foreign news personnel to television sets around the world, unmistakably implied that they had been forced to print lies for the past 40 years. Needless to say, the government was not pleased.

Nor was this all. Placards denouncing inflation and official corruption joined those asking for freedom and democracy. Leaders were criticized by name, with Li Peng a favorite target. Deng Xiaoping also had a number of detractors, with one banner reading "It doesn't matter whether it is a black cat or a white cat if it is a bad cat." The party's monopoly of power was criticized as well: One poster, written in English as well as Chinese, proclaimed that "absolute power corrupts absolutely." The students began a hunger strike in support of their demands, again with the rapt attention of the foreign media. By mid-May, the entire population of Beijing seemed to support the demonstrators.

Although the leadership tried to keep news of the demonstrations from reaching other parts of the PRC, the U.S.-sponsored radio service Voice of America (VOA), which reported the events as they took place, has a wide audience all over China. Always acutely sensitive to foreign influence in Chinese politics, partially because of the experiences of the previous century, the leadership became very angry with both the VOA itself and the government that sponsored it. Chinese living abroad were also able to communicate the reports of foreign media to their friends and relatives in the PRC by telephone or via the country's still rather few facsimile machines ("truth from fax," according to one observer). In Hong Kong, many of whose citizens were apprehensive about the colony's scheduled reversion to PRC sovereignty in 1997, self-interest as well as ethical values led to strong support for the demonstrators' demands. Generous donations poured in from Hong Kong, Taiwan, and elsewhere, to the annoyance of the PRC leadership.

Soviet general secretary Mikhail Gorbachev's visit to Beijing, which should have provided the Chinese leadership with a triumphant conclusion to the Sino–Soviet dispute, was disrupted. Since the logical, and more impressive, route from the airport to the Great Hall of the People was blocked by several hundred thousand protestors, Gorbachev's car had to be rerouted through dilapidated back streets. This sent a clear signal that the CCP's control over its people was tenuous, which could only weaken the Chinese leadership's bargaining position with Gorbachev. Infuriated, Li Peng and Yang Shangkun lectured an unrepentant group of students on their behavior.

Zhao Ziyang, perhaps seeing an opportunity to regain some of his waning powers, or at least to prevent being blamed for inability to cope with the demonstrations, as his predecessor Hu Yaobang had been, attempted to play the intermediary between the protestors and the party-government hard-liners. He reportedly presented to the standing committee of the politburo a five-point proposal, involving such concessions to the demonstrators as launching an investigation into the finances of higher-level cadres and their relatives and abolition of their special privileges. Zhao's was said to have been the only vote in favor. At midnight on May 19, the day after Gorbachev left China, Premier Li Peng chaired a nationally televised meeting of several thousand party, government, and military officials. He announced that, in accordance with Article 89 of the country's constitution, the government had decided to declare martial law in most of Beijing. Zhao Ziyang was the only member of the politburo Standing Committee not present on the platform. As if to underscore the symbolism of his absence, Zhao's place was occupied by PRC president and party Central Military Commission general secretary Yang Shangkun.

The next two weeks were characterized by behind-the-scenes maneuvering. Some influential PLA leaders objected to the use of military forces against civilians, and Deng was reportedly using his powers of persuasion to enlist their support. Yang Shangkun was also able to call upon units considered part of his loyalty network, the "Yang family village." The process by which this took place left little doubt that the functioning of the modern Chinese state continued to be marked by a high degree of personalism.

Civilian resistance made it difficult for even those troops who wanted to enforce martial law to do so. Meanwhile, heat, exhaustion, and poor sanitary conditions in Tiananmen Square were rapidly depleting the ranks of demonstrators. In what seemed a desperate move to staunch the outflow, art students created a large styrofoam statue of a woman with a torch, dubbing it the Goddess of Democracy. Set up in the square, the figure, which bore a marked resemblance to America's Statue of Liberty, attracted a large number of people. However, foreign observers remarked that it was curiosity rather than a desire to protest that had drawn the crowds there. Needless to say, leftists, who were already leery of foreign "bourgeois" influence, did not react well to the arrival of the statue. Finally, in the early hours of Sunday, June 4, the troops attacked. In full view of foreign television cameras, tanks smashed barricades and soldiers fired into the crowds.

By morning's first light, the demonstrators were gone. The government claimed that only 300 were killed, none of them in Tiananmen Square itself; foreign and dissident Chinese figures ranged into the low thousands. Whatever the actual count, it was small in comparison to those who died in the Great Leap Forward and Cultural Revolution. The significance of the Tiananmen incident of 1989 lies not in the numbers killed but in the symbolism of the event. The image of tanks rolling toward unarmed young people and ordinary citizens protesting injustice was horrifying. The party's already tenuous claim to represent the people was weakened still further. Demonstrations in other cities were put down as well.

The failure of the Tiananmen demonstrators to achieve their goals weighed heavily on the survivors and their sympathizers, particularly after the victories of similar popular protests in the USSR and in Eastern Europe. They tended to blame themselves, probably unfairly. In one sense, the Chinese demonstrations, by encouraging others to voice their grievances openly, may have been the cry heard around the communist world. The demonstrators' situation was also different from that in the Soviet Union and eastern Europe. Deng Xiaoping's personal ties with the military appear to have been critical in winning over PLA leaders who were reluctant to move on the protestors. By contrast, Gorbachev had made many enemies within the Soviet military through years of budget-cutting. And the Romanian military did not support Ceaucesçu. Poland, unlike China, had an organized opposition, Solidarity, headed by the charismatic Lech Walesa. Factionalism within the ranks of the Chinese demonstrators was indeed a problem. And apparently no attempt was made to draw the peasants into the protest movement. Were the demonstrations to be held again today, the outcome might be very different. Neither Jiang Zemin nor Hu Jintao had or have the ties with the military and the personal authority that Deng Xiaoping enjoyed. And the peasantry, quiescent during the 1989 demonstrations, has become far more restive in subsequent years.

In the short run, the resolution of the demonstrations was a victory for leftists. The day after the Tiananmen incident Deng appeared, surrounded by his octogenarian support group, most of them (President Yang Shangkun and Vice-President Wang Zhen the exceptions) members of the Central Advisory Commission rather than holders of formal positions of authority. There seemed no better way to symbolize who was in charge in China. Clearly, the PRC had not yet managed the transition from the revolutionary generation to the successor generation.

Zhao Ziyang was replaced as party general secretary by Jiang Zemin, a former Shanghai party chief. Like premier Li Peng, Jiang was an engineer who had received training in the Soviet Union. Never very popular in Shanghai, Jiang may have come to the attention of party leftists after his efficient suppression of the 1986–1987 demonstrations there. He had also fired the editor of a Shanghai newspaper known for its willingness to test the limits of government censorship. Shanghai people felt that Jiang had not worked very hard to obtain their city's fair share of resource allocations from the central government, which may also have been a point in his favor from the point of view of central government leftists. However, Jiang had presided over a number of reforms in Shanghai, and could not simply be classified as a leftist.

Zhao was also deprived of his seat on the standing committee of the politburo, as was the committee's other reformer, Hu Qili. Three new appointments were made: Jiang Zemin, leftist party organization department chief Song Ping, and the popular former mayor of Tianjin, Li Ruihuan, considered a reformer. The six-man committee was thus less reformist than its predecessor, though certainly not monolithically so. The policies China pursued for the two years after the Tiananmen incident of 1989 were roughly in line with the composition of the standing committee: somewhat more to the left, but not without certain important countertrends. Initial fears that the open door to the outside world would be slammed shut were not borne out. Additional restrictions were placed on those who studied abroad: political reliability or "redness" had become more important. But the leadership clearly continued to value the skills that could be learned in foreign countries. It also continued to seek foreign investment and foreign tourism. Market reforms moved ahead, and stock exchanges were opened. Internally, the government became more repressive. Those who spoke out during the demonstrations were identified and apprehended. There were increased pressures toward ideological conformity, including a campaign to learn (yet again) from that selfless hero of the early 1960s, Lei Feng.

Domestically, the leadership continued to chart a course of economic reforms and political authoritarianism. Deng's well-publicized trip in early 1992 to areas of south China that had prospered through his reforms symbolized his decision to again speed up the pace of those reforms. In line with his wishes, the Fourteenth party congress, meeting in October 1992, called for the creation of a socialist market economy. The Western press immediately renamed this unusual hybrid "market-Leninism" (see Chapter 7). Deng Xiaoping and the surviving octogenarian leaders stressed the need for stability. The party congress abolished the central advisory commission, though this did not guarantee that the members thereof, with their powerful network of connections and protégés, would no longer influence decision-making.

Despite Deng's emphasis on rejuvenation, the average age of the Fourteenth central committee's members was up slightly, from 55.2 years in the Thirteenth central committee to 56.3. However, in the much smaller and more powerful politburo, this situation was reversed: the average age of its twenty full and two alternate members declined from 68.6 to 62.5 years. Thirteen had graduated from college, mostly in engineering and natural sciences, vis-à-vis only four in the previous politburo. The new politburo also had more of what might be called an "external orientation": the foreign minister and minister of foreign trade became members, as did the heads of five coastal provinces and cities.[19] Liu Huaqing, a military man loyal to Deng, joined the politburo's standing committee. Yang Baibing became a member of the politburo, though his formal ties to the PLA were severed at the same time he was appointed (see Chapter 9). Deng's motive was apparently to ensure that his chosen successor Jiang Zemin would not be deposed by a member of the Yang faction of the military. Yang Shangkun resigned as president of the PRC; shortly thereafter, his position was assumed by Jiang Zemin. Since Jiang remained party general secretary and head of the military commission, he had thus concentrated much of the formal political power of the PRC in his person.

While overt challenges to party and government authority continued to be harshly punished, the citizenry became increasingly assertive. A number of Beijing voters protested the slate of candidates offered to them in a 1991 local election by casting ballots for Zhao Ziyang, whose name was not listed. At the National People's Congress two years later, 11 percent of the delegates either voted against premier Li Peng or abstained. Since the delegates had been chosen partly on the basis of their loyalty, their actions represented a stunning rebuke. In Beijing during the closing months of 1993, leading democracy activists formed a "Peace Charter" group which called on the CCP to accept a multi-party system or face the only other alternative: violent change. Its members were promptly arrested.

Not all protest was violent or even overt. Although China's security apparatus had been regarded as so ruthlessly efficient that escape was hardly thought of, much less attempted, eight of the twenty-one June 4 dissidents on the government's most wanted list managed to flee to the West. Several years later, a cameraman with politically sensitive film was told by a public security officer:

> I could arrest you, but what for? I'll get some praise, but I won't get rich. And then, after some time, the situation will change. You will be exonerated and I'll be the one in trouble for having arrested you.[20]

The radio call-in show, a new phenomenon with potentially great impact on Chinese politics, appeared in a few urban areas. Callers showed remarkable frankness in criticizing local officials for what they considered poor performance of duty and in pointing out violations of environmental laws. They suggested ways to better handle problems from toll collection to garbage pickup. In Guangdong, officials began using public opinion polls to help them govern. People were also more willing to protest, sometimes violently, when they felt that their grievances were not being addressed. Each year brought a new record number of these disturbances. In the countryside, clan and religious leaders gained power at the expense of party organs. Power continued to drift away from the center, with regions and provinces becoming more important.

The "Third Generation" Assumes Power: China Under Jiang Zemin

By the mid-1990s, Deng Xiaoping's public appearances became more and more rare. Chinese and foreigners alike speculated on whether Jiang Zemin, Deng's heir apparent, could survive his mentor's demise. Qiao Shi, whose name had briefly been mentioned as Zhao Ziyang's successor before Jiang was appointed, remained powerful. His long-term ties with the public security apparatus gave him an important power base, which Jiang lacked. Moreover, Qiao employed his position as head of the National People's Congress to champion the role of that body in legislating reforms and instituting a rule of law. These positions were popular with many people who would not otherwise have favored the ex-security chief; there was speculation that Qiao was trying to build an additional base of support from which to challenge Jiang. Nor was he Jiang's only rival: Yang Shangkun, though formally retired, continued to tour the country and seemed to have a following.

Jiang Zemin, though his ability to act independently was surely constrained to some degree by Deng's presence, began to take a more active role in governance. For example, in a symbolic assertion of his authority over the military, he personally conferred promotions on generals. Jiang also paid ceremonial visits to various areas of the country, talking with officials, peasants, workers, and ethnic minorities about their problems and successes. He charged and subsequently convicted of corruption another powerful potential rival, Chen Xitong, head of the party apparatus in the city of Beijing. The mass media focused on the need for stability and loyalty to the party center, with Jiang as its core.

In early 1997, Deng Xiaoping slipped into a coma; he died on February 19. The army was reportedly put on high alert, but no incidents are known to have occurred. Possibly because his death had been expected for so long, mourning for Deng was subdued. Power successfully passed to the "third generation," as it was called. Curiously, the mass media scarcely mentioned the transition, but remained focused on the need for stability and loyalty to Jiang. Both themes had a defensive tone. Economic problems were looming. for example, in 1996, for the first time, subsidies to state-owned enterprises (SOEs) were greater than the amount they remitted to the state treasury, and the deficit was projected to worsen. In a major speech to the Central Party School in May, Jiang proposed to reorganize SOE ownership, criticizing the left by name in the process of doing so. The Fifteenth party congress, held in September 1997, was regarded as an important test for Jiang.

The result was a qualified victory for Jiang.[21] He had received support for a mandatory retirement age of 70 from the central committee, but with the year of birth and the month of June rather than one's actual birth date being used for purposes of calculation. This allowed Jiang Zemin to remain as General Secretary, but forced Qiao Shi to retire. Qiao withdrew, though a man regarded as his protégé, Wei Jianxing, succeeded Qiao as a member of the politburo and its standing committee. Admiral Liu Huaqing, in his 80s, also retired, meaning that there was no military representation on the standing committee. Jiang is believed to have wanted General Chi Haotian to replace Liu on the standing committee. Li Lanqing, a vice-premier of the state council with special responsibility for education, filled the vacancy. The other members remained the same.

Jiang also failed to revive the position of party chair, a post he had hoped to assume. If, as alleged, Jiang was trying to create a "Shanghai faction, his success was only partial. A number of Shanghainese thought to have Jiang's backing failed to receive enough votes to enable them to serve on the central committee; only one of Jiang's "gang" was elected to the politburo, with his vote tally being one of the lowest. Jiang's fellow standing committee member Zhu Rongji was also from Shanghai, but, because he was credited with bringing a "soft landing" to China's overheated economy in the mid-1990s, seemed to be regarded as more a rival for Jiang than a member of his clique.

The new standing committee had seven members: Jiang, Li Peng, Zhu, Wei Jianxing, Li Lanqing, Li Ruihuan, and Hu Jintao. (see Figure 6.1). Hu, who had been elevated to the standing committee in 1992 at an unusually early age, was regarded as the frontrunner

FIGURE 6.1   China's Top Leaders: Politburo Standing Committee, Elected September 1997

Name	Date of Birth	Place of Birth	Higher Education
Jiang Zemin	1927	Jiangsu	engineer
Li Peng	1928	Sichuan	engineer
Zhu Rongji	1928	Hunan	engineer
Li Ruihuan	1934	Tianjin	engineer
Hu Jintao	1942	Anhui	engineer
Wei Jianxing	1931	Zhejiang	engineer
Li Lanqing	1932	Zhejiang	? "technical background"

Source: Adapted from data in *Beijing Review* October 13–19, 1997.

to succeed Jiang. Members of the Fifteenth central committee, its politburo, and its standing committee were comparable in age to those of the Fourteenth, though better educated. Engineering was by far the best represented profession, with foreign analysts predicting that this would lead the standing commitee to seek pragmatic solutions to problems.

At the congress, Jiang spelled out in more detail the plan for economic restructuring he had initially mentioned at the Central Party School. The Ninth national people's congress, meeting in March 1998, decreed that 40 ministries would be reduced to 29 and half the state bureaucracy's 8 million jobs eliminated. Those who had watched the PRC's numerous previous efforts to prune its bureaucracy expressed skepticism, noting that, after an initial reduction, numbers of cadres had actually increased beyond the original levels. Plans also aimed at reorganizing the country's entire financial structure, including its banking system and investment institutions. State-owned enterprises were to be drastically restructured, privatized, merged, and, if all else failed, closed down.

The Three Representatives

Jiang abandoned, at least temporarily, a brief effort to establish "Jiang theory" and fell back on the study of Deng Xiaoping theory as a method of achieving consensus. Though treading very lightly on the subject for obvious reasons, he added that his mentor's theories must not be applied too rigidly. In 2000, Jiang introduced a new formulation designed to leave his ideological stamp on history, the "three representatives" (*sange daibiao*). The party, he claimed, represented the most advanced productive forces, the most advanced culture, and the fundamental interests of the broad masses of the Chinese people. Despite their innocuous sound, these words were political dynamite. For one thing, Jiang had not mentioned his mentor's Four Principles. For another, the phrase "most advanced culture" seemed to signal greater openness to modern Western culture. Finally, and most explosively, the "most advanced productive forces" included the capitalists, entrepreneurs, and educated classes that Mao Zedong had so despised.

Those with leftist leanings were shocked: With millions of workers being laid off in the economic restructuring and peasant incomes declining, the party was, in effect, turning its back on the workers and peasants that had brought it to power, and associating itself with bourgeois capitalism. Jiang's supporters countered that his theory represented an important ideological breakthrough, since now the party would represent the interests of all the people. To which a disgruntled official of a leading party institute in Beijing replied, "The theory is that the party can represent both the exploited and exploiters. How do you do that? Just because you say you do?"[22] Nonetheless, the country's media praised the "three representatives" extravagantly and often, advocating that they be the guide for doing virtually everything from educational reform to modernizing the military.

Civic Organizations

The number of nongovernmental organizations began to proliferate. In order to make sure that they do not escape control, all are required to register with the government. Some, however, manage to evade close supervision and behave with a degree of autonomy. Some do not register at all, and hence exist outside the law. One study of nongovernmental associations observed that, while there organizations might evolve from what the author terms "state corporatist" to "societal corporatist" modes of organization, it is high-status groups rather than ordinary people who are likely to be the principal beneficiaries of the evolution.[23] And, while some of these groups strongly favor the protection of individual liberties and democratic reforms, others advocate a variety of other positions including strong leadership and the suppression of any sort of freedom of expression that could cause social instability. Even so, the central government, fearing loss of control, became concerned.

In 1998, by which time there were 163,000 registered civic groups, Beijing passed more restrictive laws. One of those disestablished was Falun Gong, a society combining meditative elements of Buddhism and Taoism with traditional Chinese breathing exercises and certain martial arts techniques. In late April 1999, more than ten thousand of its members quietly gathered outside around the leadership compound of Zhongnanhai to request reregistration. Party and government appear to have been taken completely by surprise—the group's members had come from many different parts of the country, eluding the surveillance techniques that were supposed to prevent such organized movements. Falun Gong's timing was also sensitive, coming exactly 10 years after the Tiananmen demonstrations began. A crackdown resulted in the arrest and often brutal treatment of thousands of innocuous-seeming middle-aged and even elderly people, some of whom died as a result.[24] Other religions were targeted as well. By 2000, the total number of registered organizations had fallen by a fifth, with the 2001 edition of the China Law Yearbook stating that reasons for deregistration included redundancy, poor management, illegality, serious interference in social and economic order, and possession of a politically problematic nature. From the point of view of those who want to see a civil society emerging in the PRC, these trends are less than ideal.

Despite Jiang's concern with stability, a modicum of freedom was allowed. Both books critical of reform and books critical of the critics and demanding more reforms were tolerated. Prison conditions improved somewhat.[25] Some high-profile dissidents, most notably Wei Jingsheng and Wang Dan, were released, This, however, did not necessarily indicate a softer attitude toward dissent, since the dissidents were freed so that they could seek medical treatment abroad. Obliging such persons to leave the country meant ridding the PRC of high-profile potential troublemakers while simultaneously allowing American political leaders who championed their cause to claim that they have extracted a concession from their Chinese counterparts. Just after these dissidents were released, others were arrested, presumably to indicate that there were limits to the leadership's tolerance.

Changing Central-Local Relationships

At the same time, a fundamental restructuring of the relationship between the central government and its subordinate units was occurring. Scholars disagreed on what this meant for Beijing's ability to extract their compliance with its orders. Some saw provinces and localities as becoming more autonomous. Others pointed out that, despite having independent sources of revenue, even wealthier provinces and localities remained dependent on the center for budgetary subsidies. Since Beijing's ability to reduce or withhold such subsidies could result in serious budget shortfalls, it is an important lever in ensuring compliance. So too is the central government's ability to appoint and remove officials: Those regarded as loyal and reliable will have their careers advanced insofar as they obey Beijing's orders, while those who do not will be removed.[26]

Still, there are limits to the center's powers. Researchers have found that, although officials tend to be very responsive to orders from their immediate superiors, they are progressively less responsive to superiors at successive levels above them. Individual officials must also operate within their local bureaucracies, which often have interests and goals that differ from those of the center. Some sources of revenue, such as locally raised illegal taxes, can lower dependence on Beijing. To its dismay, the central government has discovered some villages and even small cities that operated quite autonomously from its control. While outright defiance of the central government risks almost certain punishment, such extreme behavior is highly unlikely and in fact unnecessary. Quiet deviation and rule-bending are less dangerous and more effective.

It is important to note that the decreasing control of the state does not necessarily mean an evolution toward pluralist government or civil society. Although this has happened in some areas, others have fallen under the control of dictatorial personalities referred to as "local emperors." Some of these are benign, though others are not.

At the lowest level of society, Deng's reforms also fundamentally changed the nature of central government control. The disbandment of communes led to a rapid erosion of the party's authority in rural areas. Crime rates rose, as did resistance to government policies such as tax collection and family planning. Certain tasks that the commune had taken care of were simply not being done. By the early 1980s, peasants in some areas began to experiment with various forms of self-government. The central government saw in these a way to relegitimate its authority in rural areas, allowing it to maintain social stability and raise revenue. In 1987, the National People's Congress passed a provisional law on village elections, revising and extending it in 1998. All of the country's 730,000 administrative villages must now conduct direct elections every three years.

There have been both successes and problems in the implementation of this reform. Elections have provided a safety valve for peasants who feel angry and exploited. They have introduced a standardized system of elections into a culture with very little prior experience in making political choices, thus fostering a new value system and awareness among peasants that they have some leverage in bargaining with party and government.

On the debit side, cadres have sometimes refused to allow individuals to exercise their constitutional right to run for office. In 1998, a democracy activist who knew the law and insisted on his rights was arrested, charged with endangering national security, and sentenced to three years in prison. Clan organizations, mafia-style "black gangs," and quasi-religious leaders exercise powerful pressures in many villages. Vote-buying occurs more often than the government would like. But there are also villages where the process works as it should, providing a valuable education in democracy.

Education in democracy is but a first step. One survey has found few indications that village democracy is challenging the local power structure. Villagers tend to select candidates who are acceptable to the local power elite. And, since corruption is often perpetrated by cadres at township or county level, it was difficult for even the most motivated village leaders to do anything to curb it.[27]

While extending suffrage upward from the village might prove helpful, Party leaders have said that they have no current plans to do so, and that it may not happen for 50 years or more. They may not have the final word on this, however. In 1999, in what may prove to be a milestone, the central government criticized a township election in Sichuan as unconstitutional—but, surprisingly, allowed the results to stand. Townships, the administrative level above the village, have much more power over such matters as taxation, road-building, running schools and hospitals, allocating central government funds and land use. Hence elections at this level would be more meaningful. Interestingly, provincial-level party officials supported the experiment, although they tried to keep it quiet.[28] In December 2001, the same township held another direct election for township magistrate, and there were reports that similar experiments were occurring in other parts of China. How widespread the sentiment is for expanding the electoral system upward is not known. But the old culture of deference and passivity in the face of higher authority has been changing.

Even this limited degree of democracy is not without consequences. Village heads are likely to feel more responsible to the people who elected them, and may therefore represent their opinions to higher levels more vigorously than village leaders who were chosen by higher levels. It will be harder for higher levels of government to extract compliance with unpopular policies. This is not always a matter of central government versus local-level interests: sometime peasants appeal to the central government for redress against exploitation and corruption at levels subordinate to Beijing. Doing so does not necessarily right the situation. For example, a letter sent to Zhu Rongji in 2000 describing local officials in Hubei as "locusts with insatiable appetites" engaged the premier's interest and action was taken. But as soon as higher level officials left, local party bosses retaliated against the complainer.[29]

In urban areas, elections have been occurring on an experimental basis since 1999, when 12 pilot cities were allowed to choose positions on urban residence committees. These constitute the lowest level of state power in cities. As with rural elections, these are sometimes reasonably democratic and sometimes far from it. With regard to the latter, lists of candidates may, for example, be prepared by an election committee controlled by the municipal government. Sometimes the committees have achieved results of significant importance to their constituents, such as getting the government to improve sanitation collection, close down a noisy karaoke bar, or improve street lighting. The authorities also hope that the committees will help them in reporting on, for example, the presence of illegal workers or members of banned religious sects.[30]

Shenzhen, the Special Economic Zone abutting Hong Kong, was chosen as the testing ground for a new municipal structure implemented in 2003. The local government will be divided into three divisions—policy-making, execution, and supervision, replacing the traditional communist government structure where there was no such division of power. Officials explicitly deny that this tripartite arrangement is comparable to the executive-legislative-judicial division of responsibilities that is common in Western governments. They hope the new arrangement will simplify a bureaucratic maze that seemed to work against problem-solving, and also help in the drive against corruption.[31]

The party itself is undergoing an evolution. Feeling that loss of party control might be reversed by having more members, particularly at the lower levels of society, authorities staged a recruitment drive that raised the number of CCP members from 50 million to 65 million in the decade ending in 2001. This still amounts to only 5 percent of the PRC's total population. Nor is it certain that the new recruits will help reimpose party control. Many joined because they believed that membership would result in economic or political benefits to themselves, rather than from ideological conviction. Younger and better educated than previous generations of members, they are unlikely to be as amenable to party discipline as their predecessors.

Another salient feature of Jiang Zemin's administration was a drive against corruption, the Strike Hard (*yanda*) campaign. Jiang's sincerity in doing so cannot be questioned—among other problems it causes, corruption means less tax revenue reaches the central government treasury—but Jiang was believed to have other motives as well. Arrested Beijing party leader Chen Xitong was not only corrupt, but one of Jiang's rivals: critics pointed out that Jiang had numerous other associates who were equally corrupt but nonetheless had not been investigated. The campaign against corruption in Xinjiang and certain other ethnic minority areas seemed a thinly disguised excuse for intimidating those minorities who were unhappy with Beijing's rule. Another facet of the drive against corruption was Jiang's July 1998 order to the People's Liberation Army to divest itself of its commercial empire. These efforts notwithstanding, corruption seemed to be becoming more rather than less entrenched in the political and economic system. Jiang came to power at a time of great difficulties for his country. Unlike his predecessors, he had no revolutionary credentials, and was regarded as lacking both vision and charisma. The Chinese populace has become more overtly cynical, as exemplified by a bit of doggerel that could be heard in widely separated parts of the country:

> Chiang Kai-shek led thieves and mugs
> Mao Zedong led peasant thugs
> Deng Xiaoping led a corrupt crew
> Jiang Zemin asks "What do we do?"

The common person's reaction to his plan to restructure the economy was no better:

> Mao Zedong wanted us to *xiafang* (do manual labor in rural areas)
> Deng Xiaoping wanted us to *xiahai* (jump into the sea of business)
> Jiang Zemin wants us to *xiagang* (be laid off)

The "Fourth Generation" Assumes Power

By the summer of 2002, there was intense speculation about the upcoming Sixteenth Party Congress. Five of the seven members of the politburo's standing committee (all, save the outspoken Li Ruihuan and heir-apparent Hu Jintao), would be ineligible to continue since they were over 70 years of age. Should the transition to what was called the "fourth generation" occur without major upheaval, this would be a milestone in CCP history as well as an important marker in the institutionalization of political power in the PRC. The media's incessant praise of Jiang Zemin and his three representatives, championed by the military, caused many to wonder whether Jiang would actually step down. Some interpreted this barrage of praise as no more than an attempt to congratulate Jiang at the end of his long career; others as a clear sign that he intended to stay on. When the party congress was postponed into November, the latter interpreted the delay as reinforcing their interpretation. Another view was that Jiang, having finally been granted his wish to visit President George W. Bush at his ranch in Crawford, Texas, wanted to attend as party general secretary rather than as a recent retiree.

In the end, Jiang did step down, as did all the other standing committee members except Hu Jintao. Hu assumed the title of party general secretary, though Jiang retained the position of chair of the party's central military commission. Some argued that this could open a division between the party and the gun, others that Jiang meant to hold the position only until the Tenth National People's Congress in March, when he would abandon his position as state president as well. Jiang's efforts to place himself among the great names of the party fell a bit short: The congress agreed unanimously to take "Marxism-Leninism, the thought of Mao Zedong, Deng Xiaoping theory and the three representatives" as its guide to action, pointedly not attaching Jiang's name to his contributions. The congress further resolved that the three represenatives would be a guiding ideology that the party must uphold for a long time to come—that is, not forever, as appeared to be the case for Marx, Lenin, Mao, and Deng's contributions. In his concluding report, Jiang announced the objective of creating a well-off (*xiaokang*) society by 2020. This task would, of course, fall to Hu Jintao to implement.

There were doubts about whether Hu, despite holding the position of party general secretary, would be able to wield the power associated with it. The unusually large new politburo standing committee had nine members—two more than its predecessor. Five and possibly six of them are regarded as allied with Jiang. Of these, Zeng Qinghong, though listed as number five in rank order (see Figure 6.2), is the most powerful member of the "Shanghai mafia." He is credited with important behind-the-scenes victories such as removing Jiang Zemin rivals Yang Shangkun and Qiao Shi from power. Shortly after the congress, Zeng was appointed head of the Central Party School, from which he can influence the management of party affairs, and is expected to become state vice-president.

The average age of the standing committee members is 61.1, about the same as that of the comparable group in the Fifteenth Party Congress. Curiously, there is no member young enough to be considered a member of the "fifth generation" and therefore being groomed for a top position. The absence of military leaders, as in the previous standing committee, may mean the institutionalization of a norm that the military should not have formal representation at the highest levels of political decision-making. All nine standing

FIGURE 6.2 China's Top Leaders: Politburo Standing Committee, Elected November 2002

Name	Date of Birth	Place of Birth	Higher Education
Hu Jintao	1942	Anhui	engineer
Wu Bangguo	1941	Anhui	engineer
Wen Jiabao	1942	Tianjin	engineer
Jia Qinglin	1940	Hebei	engineer
Zeng Qinghong	1939	Jiangxi	engineer
Huang Ju	1938	Zhejiang	engineer
Wu Guanzheng	1938	Jiangxi	engineer
Li Changchun	1944	Liaoning	engineer
Luo Gan	1935	Shandong	engineer

Source: Adapted from data in *Beijing Review* November 28, 2002.

committee members have an engineering background, leading many analysts to conclude that they are technocrats who are predisposed to seek pragmatic solutions to problems. Others point out that China has many engineers who did not rise to high political positions: The members of the standing committee attained their preeminence not because they are pragmatic problem-solvers but because they are the survivors of numerous bureaucratic battles and factional strife.

The results of the 10th National People's Congress of March 2003 led to continued speculation over what the perceived Jiang-Hu split would mean for the future. Jiang relinquished his position as state president to Hu Jintao, but remainded as head of both the state and party central military commissions. Zeng Qinghong became state vice-president. Neither move was popular with delegates to the congress. Jiang received only 92 percent of the votes for CMC chair—down from 97 percent at the 9th NPC. Zeng received 87.5 percent of the ballots cast, the lowest total for any major office since the NPC began announcing results. By contrast, Hu Jintao and the scholarly new premier Wen Jianbao won over 99 percent of the votes cast.

That said, no obvious differences over policy distinguish Zeng from Hu, both of whom consistently supported Jiang Zemin's programs while subordinate to him in the party hierarchy. It is possible that Hu's influence will grow as Jiang's wanes, somewhat as Jiang grew into his position as Deng Xiaoping's health declined. The leadership may remain collegial, or be characterized by intense internal rivalry as, in the absence of a strong leader, individuals struggle for preeminence. Unexpected challenges—for example, the threat of a major social upheaval, the need to make a difficult foreign policy decision, a major health or environmental disaster—could polarize standing committee and politburo members alike over opposing policy choices. With regard to the politburo as a whole, 14 of the 25 members, or 56 percent, have had provincial career roots, as opposed to 5 out of 24 in the Fifteenth National Congress, leading to speculation that one of these cleavage lines could be regional in nature.

The party's welcome to capitalists notwithstanding, Hu Jintao's early messages have been populist, emphasizing the need to address the decline in rural living standards and for cadres to pay attention to the needs of the people. In what can only be a conscious evocation of Sun Yat-sen's ideology (see Chapter 3), Hu announced a New Three Principles of the People: that "power must be used for the sake of the people; [officials'] sentiments must be tied to those of the people; and material benefits must be sought in the interests of the people." Whether reality will match rhetoric remains to be seen.

Conclusions

Both the legitimacy and the organizational efficiency of the Chinese Communist Party have eroded badly, particularly in the years since the death of Mao Zedong. Some of this was probably inevitable, given the passing away of the premier revolutionary leaders and the routinization of governing procedures and social rituals. Some could not have been so easily predicted, most notably the alienation of large numbers of people from the leadership caused by such upheavals as the antirightist campaign, Great Leap Forward, and Cultural Revolution. Deng Xiaoping's reform movement caused a further, and more rapid, erosion of both the party's organizational efficiency and its legitimacy.

More than two decades of limited, piecemeal reforms weakened the integrity of the previous system while not replacing it with one that most people think functions better. The previous system had been quite efficient at equitably distributing the products of scarcity; the new system was less efficient at distribution: it produced prosperity in some areas, but at the cost of producing great inequalities of income and status. Stability and predictability were undermined. A record post-1949 inflation, panic buying, hoarding of goods, and runs on banks ensued. These fed policy conflicts within the leadership, which in turn exacerbated popular doubts about the competence of the party to manage either the economy or the political system. The June 1989 demonstrations were simply the most visible of a series of social disruptions caused by partial reform.

The Deng leadership staked its legitimacy on an ambitious economic program. After several years of relative success, especially in the countryside, problems generated by the program threatened to overwhelm it. Jiang Zemin in turn staked his legitimacy on a massive effort to restructure the economy and end corruption. His success in both was limited, since the consequences of these reforms had sufficiently adverse short-term effects for so many people that they could not be fully implemented. As Deng's reforms entered their third decade, they appeared to be suffering from the law of diminishing marginal returns: the "easy" reforms—those that might be described as tinkering with the system without cutting deeply into the vested interests of powerful social and political groups—had all been tried. Although a thoroughgoing structural reform is regarded as crucial to future development, popular enthusiasm for further reform is low: too many people fear the consequences. Surveys indicate that most people prefer the Maoist iron rice bowl to an uncertain future. Much will depend on Hu Jintao's ability to move China toward the well-off society envisioned in Jiang Zemin's valedictory report.

The current situation may be only transitional. The PRC could regain developmental momentum, put more money into central government coffers, and regain the trust of the people. However, the difficulty that the party has had in reclaiming control of levers of power, political and economic, that have passed from its hands make such a solution less than likely. It is possible that there will be a continuation of the apparent present erosion of central control, with provinces and other subnational units increasingly able to bargain with Beijing for resources as well as increasingly able to follow policies guided by their own needs rather than those of the country as a whole. This increased pluralism may foreshadow the beginnings of a more democratic system if it is properly managed and guided. Indeed, some analysts perceive that China is developing the prerequisites for what they term a civil society (see Chapter 1), in which well-informed citizens form into independent social forces that exert pressure on the state for positive change.[32]

Others disagree. Initially, it was assumed that rising prosperity would create a middle class, and that the middle class would, in turn, provide the basis for democratization. At least so far, this does not seem to be happening. Chinese economist He Qinglian dismisses the middle class as an "academic bubble" which will not make significant demands on party and government. Since the people who might qualify as middle class have attained their status through relying on rich and powerful powerholders, they dare not challenge the structure they are beholden to. Moreover, given the widening disparity in incomes between the richest and poorest segments of society, it is debatable whether the middle class is growing at all. He Qinglian's analysis sees the development of a social pyramid, wherein a large number of poor support a small number of rich, rather than the diamond-shaped distribution of income that characterizes a middle-class society. Even the size of the middle class is uncertain: depending on definition, estimates range from 3.5 percent of the population to 18 percent.

Those who are skeptical that the PRC is moving toward pluralism and civil society point out that the greater willingness of people's congresses to challenge the writ of the leadership represents at best incremental change on a modest scale: an occasional outspoken speech; a minor, albeit highly publicized, rejection of a proposal; or a less-than-unanimous vote of approval. People's congresses, they note, are still at the rubber-stamp end of the spectrum of legislative types.[33] The private organizations that exist are organized along family lines. People accomplish their goals through a web of personal relationsips rather than through organizations founded on the basis of equality and consent-based rules. The Sixteenth Party Congress may have achieved a successful transfer of power, but a successful transfer of power does not necessarily mean that the polity itself is successful.[34]

While hopeful signs are present, there has also been a resurgence of some of the elements of traditional society that do not bode well for modernization. These include clan power, personalism, and social stratification. Rather than the Maoist ideal of "sharing weal and woe" with the common people, cadres are becoming more distant and oppressive. A folk saying describes the relationship between the officials and the people during the 1950s through 1970s as one of "fish and water"; during the 1980s as "oil and water"; and during the 1990s as "fire and water"—that is, having deteriorated from support to separation to explosive. Skeptics see the PRC evolving toward a socialist society with Confucian characteristics, or sometimes a Confucian society with socialist characteristics, rather than advancing toward civil society. In a variation on this theme, dissident writer Cao Jinqing envisions a China moving away from socialism but toward a uniquely Chinese style of bureaucratism rather than to Western-style liberal capitalism.[35]

This would seem to reinforce the China-is-China-is-China and communist neo-traditional analyses of PRC politics rather than the pluralist paradigm. There is also a possibility that, rather than continue along a relatively peaceful path of greater legislative and popular assertiveness or back toward a less ethical variant of traditional Chinese bureaucratism, the state could degenerate into chaos and a return to the China characterized by Sun Yat-sen as a sheet of loose sand.[36]

Notes

1. This analysis generally follows the argument made by Dorothy Grouse Fontana, "Background to the Fall of Hua Guofeng," *Asian Survey*, March 1982, pp. 237–260.

2. Descendants of ethnically Han Chinese refugees from northern China who had fled south at the time of the Jin (Jurchen) invasions of the twelfth century. Their dialect is believed to approximate standard Mandarin Chinese of that era and is very different from the languages spoken in the areas they moved to. Clannish and hardworking, they tended to monopolize certain trades. Intermarriage with the local population was exceedingly rare.

3. James D. Seymour, ed., *The Fifth Modernization: China's Human Rights Movement, 1978–1979* (Standardville, N.Y.: Coleman Press, 1980), provides a fuller discussion of this period.

4. See the Fontana article; also, Chu-yuan Cheng, *Behind the Tiananmen Massacre: Social, Political, and Economic Ferment in China* (Boulder, Colo.: Westview Press, 1990), pp. 50–51.

5. See, for example, Jürgen Domes, "China in 1978," *Asian Survey*, January 1979.

6. The text of his speech may be found in *Xinhua*, April 10, 1981, translated in *FBIS–CHI*, April 13, 1981, pp. K/6–K/18.

7. There is no consensus on what to call the first of these groups. Some people argue that the term *leftist* implies a greater degree of Marxist orthodoxy than many of these people have. Since it is leftist values that these people wish to conserve, they prefer to use the term conservative. The author has chosen to use "leftist" not out of personal conviction but because it seems to bother fewer people.

8. Quoted in George Black and Robin Munro, *Black Hands of Beijing: Lives of Defiance in China's Democracy Movement* (New York: John Wiley and Sons, 1992), pp. 99–100.

9. Lowell Dittmer makes this observation in "Modernization and Its Discontents: China in 1981," *Asian Survey*, January 1982, pp. 31–50.

10. Edward Gargan, "A Purged Chinese Intellectual Derides Talk of Liberalization," *New York Times*, February 11, 1988, pp. 1, 7.

11. John Burns, "China Reveals Major Scandal Among Top Island Officials," *New York Times*, August 1, 1985, p. 2; see also the articles published by *Renmin Ribao* between July 31 and August 10, 1985.

12. L. Ladany, "Deng's Grip on China Is Far from Secure," *Wall Street Journal*, September 30, 1985, p. 21.

13. "Reporter Links China Expulsion to Rift in Policy," *International Herald Tribune*, September 10, 1986, p. 2.

14. *Nongmin Ribao*, May 20, 1987, p. 1, in *FBIS–CHI*, June 8, 1987, p. K/16.

15. *Agence France Presse* (Hong Kong), June 11, 1986, in *FBIS–CHI*, June 12, 1986, p. K/1.

16. See Stanley Rosen, "A Year of Consolidation: China in 1987," *Asian Survey*, January 1988, pp. 35–55.

17. See, for example, Wen Jianming, "Debates Over Neo-Authoritarianism," *Guangzhou Ribao*, April 5, 1989, p. 3, in *FBIS–CHI*, April 12, 1989, pp. 16–17.

18. Andrew G. Walder, "The Political Sociology of the Beijing Upheaval of 1989," *Problems of Communism*, September–October 1989, p. 39.

19. David Bachman, "The Fourteenth Congress of the Chinese Communist Party," *Asian Update* (New York: The Asia Society, 1992), passim.

20. Richard Bernstein, "A Fugitive's Tale Sheds Light on China Today," *New York Times*, June 6, 1993, p. 27.

21. For more detailed summaries of the Fifteenth Party Congress, see Avery Goldstein, "China in 1997," *Asian Survey*, vol. 38, no. 1, January 1998, pp. 34–52; Li Cheng and Lynn White, "The Fifteenth Central Committee of the Chinese Communist Party," in *Asian Survey*, vol. 38, no. 3, March 1998, pp. 231–264.

22. Anonymous official, quoted by Erik Eckholm, "As China's Economy Shines, the Party Line Loses Luster," *New York Times*, November 4, 2002.

23. Jonathan Unger, "Private Business, the Chinese Government, and the Rise of New Associations," *China Quarterly*, no. 147, September 1996, pp. 795–819.

24. See Beatrice Leung, "China and Falun Gong: Party and Society Relations in the Modern Era," *Journal of Contemporary China*, November 2002, pp. 761–784 for an analysis of the movement and the reasons for its success.

25. James D. Seymour and Richard Anderson, *New Ghosts, Old Ghosts: Prisons and Labor Reform Camps in China* (Armonk, N.Y.: M. E. Sharpe, 1998), passim.

26. Andrew Wedeman, "Agency and Fiscal Dependence in Central-Provincial Relations in China," *Journal of Contemporary China*, March 1999, pp. 103–122.

27. David Zweig, "Democratic Values, Political Structures, and Alternative Politics in Greater China," (Washington, D.C., United States Insititute of Peace, 2002), p. 28.

28. Zha Qingjiu, "Democracy Shall Not Transcend the Law," *Fazhi Ribao*, January 19, 1999, p. 1.

29. See Minxin Pei's review of Li Changping's *Wo Xiang Zhongli Suoshihua* (I Told the Premier the Truth) in *Foreign Policy*, November–December 2002, pp. 82–83.

30. See the statements of Yawei Liu, Anne Thurston, and Elizabeth Dugan to the Congressional-Executive Commissiion on China's Roundtable on Village Democracy in China, July 8, 2002, http://www.cecc.gov; Erik Eckholm, "China's Neighborly Snoops Reinvent Themselves," *New York Times*, April 11, 2000, p. A3.

31. (No author). "Shenzhen To Become Testbed of Change," *South China Morning Post*, December 21, 2002.

32. Ma Shu-yun, "The Chinese Discourse on Civil Society," Research Note, *China Quarterly*, no. 138, March 1994, pp. 180–193.

33. Avery Goldstein, "Trends in the Study of Political Elites and Institutions in the PRC," *China Quarterly*, no. 139, September 1994, p. 721.

34. Bruce Gilley, "Smooth Power Transition is the Test of Progress," *South China Morning Post*, November 4, 2002.

35. I am indebted to Mr. David Cowhig, U.S. Department of State, for bringing Cao Jinqing's views to my attention.

36. John P. Burns, "China's Governance: Political Reform in a Turbulent Environment," *China Quarterly*, September 1989, pp. 481–518, and Michael D. Swaine, "China Faces the 1990s: A System in Crisis," *Problems of Communism*, May–June 1990, pp. 20–35, also argue along these lines.

Suggestions for Further Reading

Ding, Yijiang, *Chinese Democracy After Tiananmen* (New York: Columbia University Press, 2002).

John James Kennedy, "The Face of 'Grassroots Democracy' in Rural China," *Asian Survey*, May–June 2002, pp. 456–482.

Andrew J. Nathan and Perry Link, eds., *The Tiananmen Papers* (New York, Public Affairs Books, 2002).

Kevin J. O'Brien, "Agents and Remonstrators: Role Accumulation by Chinese People's Congress Deputies," *China Quarterly*, no. 138, June 1994, pp. 359–380.

Jonathan Unger, "Private Business, the Chinese Government, and the Rise of New Associations," *China Quarterly*, no. 147, September 1996, pp. 795–819.

CHAPTER

7 The Politics of the Economy

Introduction

Economics was the touchstone of the Chinese revolution: the substructure that, according to Karl Marx, determines not only the government but all else as well. Industrialization was a major priority for the new government, in order to bring the PRC into the ranks of the world's most advanced nations and to provide better living standards for the people of the country. However, party and government also wished to avoid many of the problems that have been associated with the industrialization process. In other countries, industrialization had frequently had the effect of exacerbating the differences between rich and poor. In the Western world, it was only after the industrial revolution had taken place that serious efforts were made to correct extreme inequities. Moreover, progress toward industrialization is rarely smooth; historical experience indicates that the more rapid the progress, the greater the strains generated within a society. The CCP's desire for social stability, albeit with certain salient exceptions such as the Cultural Revolution, was thus also a constraint on rapid industrialization.

In formulating its economic policies, the CCP had two goals: equality and prosperity. The first of these is idealistic, the second materialistic. In practice, it has proved difficult to pursue both simultaneously. In general, economic policy since 1949 has tended to emphasize either one or the other. The first tendency was more pronounced during Mao Zedong's leadership, the second under the leadership of his successors. However, economic policy both during the Maoist era and therafter has also been characterized by fluctuations between emphasis on one goal and the other. A rigid commitment to equality has typically resulted in dampening incentives to produce, leading to an economic downturn. At some point, party and government react to increasing scarcities by relaxing the commitment to equal distribution of resources, which fosters an upturn in production statistics but at the cost of increasing income differentials. One economist, referring to the repetition of this pattern under Mao's rule as the interplay of ideology and scarcity, likened its swings to that of the business cycle that early communists like Marx and Engels believed their approach would eliminate.[1] Although ideology is no longer an important factor in decision-making, structural problems in the economy have continued the cyclical pattern he described.

Jiang Zemin essentially carried forward and extended Deng Xiaoping's reforms, while seeking to correct the imbalances they engendered. There were successes—for example, inflation has been greatly reduced. But income gaps have widened, and corruption remains endemic. Hu Jintao's ability to cope with these will be a test of his competence as a leader.

The Early Years: 1949–1950

Initially, the party's chief economic tasks were, first, bringing the ruinous inflation of the late 1940s under control and, second, rebuilding the country's war-torn infrastructure and production facilities. Inflation was dealt with through a series of measures, beginning with revaluing the nation's currency to a more realistic rate in order to reduce the lure of black market currency transactions. It was further announced that anyone indulging in currency speculation would be punished. Several well-publicized executions convinced doubters that the new leadership meant what it said. Regional and other variant currencies were abolished; henceforth, everyone was to use the *yuan*, also known as the *renminbi*, or people's currency. The banking system was nationalized and placed under close party control. And the organs of a centralized state economic planning system based on the Soviet model were established.

Prices were fixed at what party and government considered a fair level, with penalties for those who violated the rules. Trading cooperatives were established to bring food into the cities. To curb panic buying and encourage people to save, the newly founded People's Bank established unit prices based on a market basket of commodities. Someone depositing a sum of money equal to one unit in a bank account was guaranteed that she or he would be credited with however much that unit had gone up to at the time of withdrawal, plus a small interest rate. If, by some miracle, deflation had occurred, the investor was also guaranteed the return of the amount he had deposited. People gradually gained confidence in the currency, and inflationary pressures subsided. Interestingly, this plan had originally been proposed by KMT economists, but their party had been too weak and corrupt to carry it out.

With internal peace at last attained, the railroads and irrigation works could be rebuilt. The cooperation of patriotic bourgeoisie, with their technical and managerial skills, proved invaluable at this time, as did the labor contributed by young men of the military. State farms were established, and factories rebuilt. By 1952, a semblance of normalcy had returned. Hence this is the year commonly used as a baseline from which to calculate production statistics.

The Socialist Transformation of Agriculture: 1949–1978

The Chinese communist revolution was in essence an agrarian revolution. The communists had spent more than 20 years working in rural areas, and with over 80 percent of the population engaged in agriculture at the time, Mao Zedong understandably viewed the peasant question as the central problem of the Chinese revolution.

To attract peasant support during the civil war, the CCP had called for land redistribution. After coming to power, the party proceeded to make good on this promise. Since another important goal of land reform was to overthrow the old ruling class in rural areas, class struggle was used as a tool in land redistribution. This in turn meant that precise criteria for the distinctions between one class and another were needed. By 1950, the rural population had been classified into six classes: landlords, semi-landlords, rich peasants, middle peasants, poor peasants, and laborers. Each of these was in turn subdivided into many other categories. The government attempted to dictate the criteria for determining these, but lines were difficult to draw, and rural cadres often made arbitrary judgments. Hence individuals who possessed the same amount of land might be classified quite differently in different localities.

Those who were designated landlords had their houses, furniture, and even personal possessions confiscated in a movement characterized by emotionally charged mass trials and immediate executions.[2] These events resulted in the elimination of the landlords and their prestige, and forged a bond between the party and the poor peasants. However, land reform actually had rather limited gains for the rural economy, neither increasing per capita landholding nor raising the rate of capital formation in agriculture.[3]

The land reform also created three new problems. The first came about because of the leadership's decision to grant equal shares of land to the family members of party workers, the armed forces, and the mass organizations, such as peasants' and women's associations. Having more than 50 million new landowners reduced the size of the average farm and the ability of the peasant to accumulate capital.

Second, land reform created new frictions, and did not end rural class stratification. Disputes arose, for example, over how to allocate responsibility for the draft animals that had been confiscated from landlords. Many were assigned to groups of peasants rather than to specific households. Since it was in the individual family's short-term interest to work the beasts as hard as possible and feed them as little as possible, a large number of animals died from lack of proper care. Also, a new rich peasant class began to arise. Not surprisingly, most of them were party members. Third, land reform led to severe food shortages in the cities. This occurred because, in contrast to the landlords, who would typically ship their grain to be sold in urban markets, newly landed peasants preferred to eat more themselves.

To deal with these problems and stop the resurgence of what it saw as capitalist tendencies in the rural economy, the leadership began to push the peasants toward collective arrangements. The first stage in this, mutual aid teams (MATs), began to be set up about 1951. Groups of peasant households were to help each other out by exchanging tools, draft animals, and labor power. These first teams usually consisted of three to five households and were temporary: after the busy period for farming, they would disband. Indeed, peasants in some areas had engaged in similarly informal practices for centuries. Later, the MATs were formalized, contained five to ten households, and became permanent, year-round arrangements.

Next came the formation of lower-level agricultural producers' cooperatives (APCs). Under this arrangement, land, farm animals, and farm implements were pooled, and a larger number of households, perhaps thirty-five, participated in each. Members retained the title to their land, which was entered into the account books of the APCs as a share of the household's capital contribution to the cooperative. Other capital assets like farm implements, transport vehicles, and draft animals were treated in the same way, remaining privately owned but under unified control. A certain amount of land, not to exceed 5 percent of the average household's total, could be retained for private use. Referred to as private plots, this land was worked by individual families which, within certain limits, could decide how to use it and how to dispose of what they produced on it.

The APCs' aggregate amount of agriculture and sideline production, the latter coming from such activities as handicrafts like weaving straw hats and baskets, would have a portion deducted to meet depreciation costs. The rest formed the cooperative's total income for the year. Part of this was paid to the state as taxes, and part went into reserve and welfare funds for the cooperative. The rest was distributed to the members as payment for work and the use of their land, animals, and tools. Payments for work were calculated according to the difficulty of the task and the number of days spent on it. Calculations were tallied in units called work points. An extremely physically demanding job might command ten work points a day; jobs that were considered easier got smaller amounts.

In theory, at least, the cooperatives had two major advantages over MATs. First, pooling land would eliminate the chief structural weakness of Chinese agriculture: small, uneconomic, and dispersed holdings. Simply removing the boundary lines between private holdings would create extra acreage for cultivation. Second, reducing the number of producing units would enable the government to exercise closer control over planning, investment, and consumption.

There were many negative aspects to the cooperatives as well. Management was foremost among them. Supervising 30 to 40 households took a great deal of planning, administration, and bookkeeping. Evaluating job performance in terms of work points was exceedingly difficult. A large number of tasks were involved, with legitimate differences of opinion existing on the matter of comparable worth. Whether a job was classified at, for example, eight work points per day or seven could make a substantial difference in one's yearly income. Also, the great majority of peasants were illiterate and therefore unable to cope with even the simplest bookkeeping tasks.

Although there was a great deal of resistance to joining the lower-level APCs, the leadership, after some wavering, decided in 1956 to forge on to higher-level APCs. After peasants joined one of these, their land and other principal means of production were transferred from private to collective ownership, and payments for land shares and other means of production were abolished. One's income thus depended wholly on accumulated work points. Members could, however, retain their small private plots and keep whatever they raised on them. The new units were also four to five times as large as lower-level APCs, averaging 158 households each.

By the end of 1956, almost 90 percent of the PRC's cooperatives were of the advanced type. Their proponents noted three major advantages to the new arrangement. First, the larger units facilitated land consolidation and the rational use of land better than lower-level APCs. Second, since land rent had constituted a significant part of rich peasants' income, the abolition of rent payments would increase the wages of poor peasants while lowering those of the rich, producing greater equality. Third, a higher level of collectivization was needed to carry out the massive water conservation campaign that party and government had scheduled for the winter of 1957–1958.

However, peasants were even more unhappy with the higher-level APC than they had been with its lower-level version. Many who had only recently realized their dream of becoming landowners reacted badly to seeing their property and animals snatched away again. The higher-level cooperatives also further separated individuals' level of productivity from the rewards they received, thus further dampening peasants' incentive to work hard. Peasant income declined. There was a drastic drop in pig production. Since pork is the staple meat in the Chinese diet, serious shortages of meat were reported in many urban areas. From the time of the inception of the collectives, most peasants had had doubts about their ability to raise their incomes and improve living conditions. As time went on, more and more of them became convinced that their doubts were justified.

The leadership, faced with yet another decision to retreat from collectivization or push forward, chose the latter. The result, touted by official propaganda as "fresh as the morning sun" and "the ladder to communist paradise," was the rural commune. As with other aspects of the Great Leap Forward, of which the commune was such an important part, the process of communization was characterized by extreme haste. An experimental model commune was organized in April 1958 in Henan province; in the closing days of August, the party directed that its example be generalized throughout China. By the end of September, more than 98 percent of peasant households had been included in the communes.

The huge size of the communes—averaging 5,000 households, or about 32 times as large as higher-level APCs—would allow them to command the resources of vastly greater amounts of land and labor. The commune was more than this, however, being described as "the basic unit of the social structure [of China], combining industry, agriculture, trade, education, and the military . . . it is the basic unit of social power." Whereas the original APCs had been organized purely for agricultural production, the communes merged peasants, workers, tradesmen, students, and militia members into a single unit to engage in afforestation, animal husbandry, and subsidiary occupations as well as agriculture. The communes also ran factories, banks, and commercial enterprises; handled credit and commodity distribution; did cultural and educational work; and controlled their own militia and political organizations. In terms of administrative functions, communes replaced townships, which had been of comparable size.

Under the commune system, private plots were abolished. In their zeal to eliminate private property, some cadres even took away peasants' wristwatches, alarm clocks, and cookware. Confiscating pots and pans meant that their former owners would be forced to eat in communal dining halls. Also, metal cookware could be melted down and contributed to the backyard blast furnaces the peasants were supposed to be setting up. The shortage of bookkeepers was solved by abolishing work points; henceforth, one was to contribute work to the commune to the best of one's ability and receive from it food and the other necessities of life. Under true communism, no work points would be needed; hence no one was needed to tally them.

As noted in Chapter 5, the result was disaster. Crops died through neglect, owners slaughtered their animals in preference to turning them over to the communes, cadres were attacked and public property sabotaged. Basic-level cadres, hard-pressed by unrealistically high production quotas, resorted to reporting inflated crop production statistics, which were then passed along to higher levels, who had a tendency to inflate them still further. At a party Central Committee plenum in August 1959, it was admitted that no one knew what production actually was. After bitter arguments among top leaders, the plenum agreed to rescind some of the more objectionable aspects of the Great Leap. For example, brigades rather than communes were given the responsibility for managing the reintroduced accounting system, and also for setting production targets. Since the brigade was comparable in size to the former higher-level APC, this was a distinct step backward for the party. Egalitarianism in income distribution was also abandoned, as was the slogan of "from each according to his ability, to each according to his need." Private plots were reinstated. But these measures were not taken quickly enough to save the situation.

As the agricultural crisis worsened in 1960, production teams, which were the level below brigades in the administrative hierarchy, were made the basic decision-making units determining output quotas and the distribution of resources. The teams were approximately equal to lower-level APCs in size. Communes themselves were reduced to about the size of the average marketing community in traditional China. Advocates of the China-is-China . . . school of political analysis interpreted this as confirmation of their views.

To stimulate peasant initiative, a system called "three guarantees and one reward" was instituted. Guarantees were provided to the recipients on output, time, and costs, and they would receive a bonus (reward) from the team if their output exceeded that which had been agreed to. In 1961, when the agricultural situation had become even more grim, a still more liberal policy, called the "three selfs and one guarantee," was instituted. It went further than its predecessor by directing that all communal land be distributed among individual households as "responsibility land," with each household agreeing to produce a certain amount.

The more idealistic members of the party elite bitterly resented this backsliding and, especially after the economy began to improve in 1962, there were arguments about whether and, if so, when to abandon these concessions to capitalism and forge forward toward communism again. During the early stages of the Cultural Revolution, with ideologues dominating the party elite, many of the concessions were in fact abolished. Mergers increased the size of communes. Poor and lower-middle peasants were told to assume power. In many areas, private plots were again confiscated, sideline occupations banned, and rural markets closed. Radicals called them "tails of capitalism."

Some communes moved from a three-level to a two-level system of management by making brigades rather than production teams the basic unit of accounting.[4] A major mass campaign was launched to publicize the achievements of Dazhai, a model production brigade that had adopted the two-level system. Dazhai was also lauded for having allegedly overcome all sorts of hardships, including poor land, drought, and invasions by predatory insects, to achieve impressive increases in production. The proper ideological outlook, one's "redness," was believed to be the key to success. In keeping with this notion, political attitude was added to hard physical labor as a criterion for allocating one's share of the collective income.

The result of these changes was rural unrest and agricultural stagnation. Clearly hoping to avoid the errors of the Great Leap Forward, the PRC's draft constitution of 1970 affirmed the three-level system of ownership, stating that the production team would be the basic unit of management. A 1971 Central Committee directive stressed the need to avoid "absolute egalitarianism," and emphasized that one's income would be based on one's work. The agricultural system that emerged from the Cultural Revolution thus closely resembled that which prevailed from 1962 to 1965. The agricultural distribution system was restored, though peasants, mindful of the disruptions of the past, remained apprehensive. Agricultural growth was disappointing, barely keeping up with the increase in population. In fact, per capita output of foodstuffs was below the levels of the early 1930s.

Industrial Policy in the Maoist Era

By contrast with the hesitations and retreats that characterized the collectivization of agriculture, the industrial structure was brought under state control more quickly, and with remarkably little resistance. At the time the CCP came to power, the urban economy was characterized by a relatively small modern sector, mostly dedicated to heavy industry, and a huge traditional or handicraft sector that used little or no mechanical power.

Modern Industry

The modern sector was concentrated in southern Manchuria, where it had been set up under the Japanese occupation, and in a few other coastal treaty-port cities such as Tianjin, Shanghai, and Guangzhou (Canton), and the Yangtze River port of Wuhan. It was mainly owned by the Chinese government (in this case, the KMT), and by a relatively small number of Chinese and foreign capitalists. There was no question that the CCP, as successor to the KMT, would take over its predecessor's enterprises. Certain other enterprises were taken over on the grounds that they had been owned by war criminals or collaborators, whether or not there was convincing evidence to substantiate these charges. Although direct expropriation could have been easily accomplished, it was not widely used. The party's tactics generally consisted of squeezing out private enterprise through tax pressures, credit rationing, capital levies, state competition, and union demands.

In order to avoid interruptions in production or sabotage of equipment, the party announced that it would retain not only the existing system of production of these enterprises, but also all technical and managerial personnel. A short while later, however, after consolidating its control, party leaders ordered a "democratic reform" campaign against "hidden counterrevolutionaries and feudal remnants." The real aim of this campaign was to remove former KMT officials from supervisory positions from which they might continue to exert influence, and to substitute people who were considered more loyal to the party and its goals. Several hundred thousand managers were thus replaced.

Some businesses were dealt with more gradually. At the end of 1950, new regulations set out the conditions under which the private sector would be allowed to operate. Businesses were required to submit their complete plans of production and sale for the approval of the relevant government ministry and to distribute their earnings according to specified categories like dividends and welfare funds. By the beginning of 1952, the "five-anti" campaign (see Chapter 5) had been launched against the capitalist class. Employees were encouraged to report their bosses to the authorities if they had been involved in any of the antis, and mass denunciation meetings often turned violent. The aim seems to have been to humiliate and demoralize businesspeople so as to reduce their resistance to absorption by the state. Massive fines were extracted from merchants and industrialists, some of whom committed suicide. For others, the fines depleted working capital to levels that made doing business nearly impossible. At this point, having their companies taken over by the state came as almost a relief. The fines also served as a convenient method of divesting the capitalist class of its savings, which the government could then use to finance its construction plans.

A process called rationalization provided the method for absorbing private firms. Under it, all of a city's privately owned firms engaged in the same business (for example, flour mills in Shanghai) were brought together under a single general management in order to coordinate their production plans and pool capital funds. These were then merged together into joint state-private concerns, with the state as senior partner. After taking an inventory and making an appraisal, the assets of the capitalists were turned into private shares, and the investment made by the government became state shares. In this way, the means of production came to be jointly owned by the capitalists and the state. The government also assigned its representatives to participate in and control management. The capitalists and their agents, who had previously held the responsible positions, now received their appointments from the government. Although they continued to participate in management, they no longer played a dominant role. In effect, the party had reduced the private capitalist to performing a bureaucrat's functions without actually assuming the full responsibilities of state ownership.

After joint operation of whole trades was established in 1956, the government announced that it would pay capitalists a fixed rate of interest on their shares of the enterprises, regardless of profit or loss during the period of joint operation. This was typically about 5 percent but amounted to an average of only 44 dollars a year per capitalist. Payment was to start on January 1, 1956, and end in December 1962. However, because of the difficulties caused by the Great Leap Forward, the government decided not to risk offending the recipients and to extend their interest payments into 1965. Over a million people were eligible for these payments, though a number of them decided not to take them. Their reasoning was that it would be better to sacrifice the small amounts involved than to risk being labeled capitalists. When the Cultural Revolution broke out in 1966, the payment of fixed interest ended, and many people were labeled capitalists even if they had forfeited their interest payments.

Handicrafts

Handicrafts people were, as mentioned above, spread throughout China. According to a 1954 survey, they totaled 20 million, 9 million of them full-time, and the other 11 million primarily peasants for whom handicrafts was a sideline occupation. The same survey found that handicrafts accounted for 17.4 percent of the PRC's gross output value and was thus an important part of the economic system. This sector supplied most of the items that enabled the average person to perform the chores of daily living more easily—things such as sandals, crockery, and sun hats. Hence disruptions in production in this sector would have had serious repercussions for the system as a whole.

The party proceeded by taking control of the supply of raw materials and the marketing of finished products, thus cutting off the connection of handicrafts with private commerce and substituting the state sector for it. The initial mechanism by which this was accomplished was the supply and marketing group. It was organized to buy raw materials from state commercial establishments and to sell finished products to them, and could also take orders for processing goods. Members of the supply and marketing group were independent handicrafts producers or small proprietors. They retained their former means of production, worked independently, and were responsible for their own profits and losses. From the party's perspective, the groups functioned to bring their members into a relationship with the state sector, and prepared the members for the party's next step, that of forming supply and marketing cooperatives.

Supply and marketing cooperatives functioned much as APCs had in the agricultural sector, even to being organized in lower- and higher-level versions. In the former, members received shares in proportion to the tools and equipment they contributed, but retained the ownership thereof. The cooperatives obtained raw materials and marketed finished products, with production itself remaining in the hands of individual members. Part of the profits was used to purchase additional means of production for the collective; part went to taxes and reserve and welfare funds. The rest was distributed to members in accordance with the labor they had contributed.

During the Great Leap Forward, many handicrafts cooperatives were transformed from collective ownership to ownership by the whole people, but this worked no better than the communes did to produce increased agricultural yields. Within a few years, the cooperatives reappeared in substantially their pre–Great Leap Forward form. Some were even further subdivided into family workshops. During the Cultural Revolution these workshops were branded "tails of capitalism"; they were banned and their members persecuted.

Also at the time of the Cultural Revolution, several other changes were made in industry in general. Their net effect was to dampen work enthusiasm still further; unlike certain other Cultural Revolution practices that were quickly discontinued, these changes remained in effect until after Mao's death. Perhaps the most important one was the discontinuation of bonuses that had been awarded to those that their work group had judged superior. Extra pay for overtime work was abolished as well. A temporary phenomenon of the Cultural Revolution, but one with lasting effects, was that workers were encouraged to struggle against their bosses. These measures, decided upon in order to further egalitarian goals, had devastating effects on productivity. Workers had no incentive to produce, and managers, fearing that their workers would denounce them, had no incentive to make them produce. They also had no rewards to offer employees to inspire them to work hard.

Many workers would simply show up at the factory in order to sign in and then pedal away on their bicycles. Some had obtained extended sick leaves from the factory doctor for largely imaginary ailments; they did not bother to show up at all. Other employees spent many hours at their workplace, since there was a severe housing shortage and factories were often more comfortable than their homes. Rather than actually work, however, they talked with fellow employees, played cards, or washed and mended their clothing. Since homes frequently lacked toilets and showers, employees availed themselves of factory facilities for these conveniences.

Because little was produced under these circumstances, goods were in short supply. Here, too, the factory facilities might come in handy. Machine-shop workers had access to tools and metal and could fashion cookware, using whatever materials were available. Sometimes this meant using expensive metals which could have been more productively employed, for example, in the manufacture of precision machinery. People who worked in plywood manufacturing factories brought home sheets of it for desks and tabletops. A widespread and pervasive underground trading system grew up: the plywood factory worker's tabletop for the metal worker's cookpot, and so forth. Highly illegal, such practices filled important needs for people; once started, the system was difficult to stop. Corruption was fostered in hundreds of ways. For example, the worker who wanted to stay away from work might present the factory doctor with gifts of useful items that the doctor could not easily otherwise obtain. In return, the doctor would certify that he or she was too sick to work. Both individuals gained from this transaction, although society as a whole suffered.

Maoist Economic Policies Assessed

Mao's economic policies achieved certain important goals. The Chinese economy was unequivocally freed from foreign domination, and the postwar inflation was quickly brought under control. In addition, the nationalization of the private banking system and unification of the monetary system enabled the government to suppress speculative activities and prevent the recurrence of inflation. Centralizing and unifying the currency had other benefits as well. They provided the basis for a national market in which the supply of money could be planned and its value stabilized. The state banking system enabled the central government to exercise a greater degree of control over the economy than had ever been the case before. This control enabled party and state to invest in the development of hitherto backward areas, generally in the country's hinterlands, that had not enjoyed the benefits of infusions of foreign capital prior to 1949. Shanghai's and Wuhan's surpluses could be used to develop Qinghai and Anhui.

By contrast, the socialist transformation of the economy had mixed results. It enabled a further development of a centrally planned economy. The government's large-scale purchases of food, textiles, and other basic necessities made possible effective rationing and distribution during times of crop failure. The socialist transformation also helped increase government revenue and accumulation. By buying out the capitalist sector, party and government could channel 95 percent of the after-tax earnings of private firms into the state treasury, part of which went into investment. Massive disruptions and unemployment were averted.

On the debit side, the fact that entrepreneurship was held in low regard could only inhibit the process of industrialization, as indeed it had when Confucianism held sway. Having so few incentives to produce more, people worked as little as they could. As noted above, *un*employment was not a major problem; *under*employment definitely was. In practice, it was nearly impossible to fire a worker. Overstaffed and undermotivated, Chinese enterprises generally produced the quantities assigned to them under the state plan's quota system, but were relatively unconcerned with the quality of the items, or their marketability. Investing money in backward hinterlands may have been good in terms of promoting equality, but it did not always make good economic sense: Better returns might have been realized by reinvesting coastal Shanghai's profits in Shanghai than in cold, arid, and remote Qinghai.

Moreover, the numerous rapid shifts in the party's conception of what was or was not ideologically acceptable had caused the average Chinese to become profoundly distrustful of the system and its leaders. Experience had taught that it was better to avoid responding to new signals, or at least to lag behind as far as possible. This mind-set, though perfectly rational in terms of individual experience, was nevertheless detrimental to economic development.

While Maoist policies were undertaken in support of egalitarian goals, in reality, they had an effect that was just the opposite: To get along reasonably well, one was forced to develop personal ties that were quite outside the system and, by most definitions of the word, corrupt. Those who succeeded best in this underground system were, not surprisingly, much resented. Their existence also led to widespread cynicism about the value of collectivism and egalitarianism, thus undermining popular support for those goals.[5]

Economic Policy Under Deng Xiaoping

When Deng Xiaoping returned to power, he was highly critical of the country's economic situation, saying it had stagnated under the Gang of Four and (unspoken but quite clearly implied) under Mao. The ambitious Four Modernizations program associated with his name was actually introduced by Deng's mentor, Zhou Enlai, at his last public speech in January 1975, though it was not widely publicized, much less acted upon. Hua Guofeng had also mentioned it in February 1978. In December, at the widely publicized Third Plenum of the CCP's Eleventh Central Committee, Deng reintroduced the Four Modernizations with much fanfare, and added to them a sweeping reform of the planning and management systems in industry and agriculture.

The original order of the modernizations put industry first, with heavy industry receiving priority over light industry. Second was agriculture; third, science and technology; and fourth, national defense. By March 1979, the order had been changed to put agriculture first, followed by light and then heavy industry. The priorities of science and technology and defense remained third and fourth, respectively.

The reform program had four major objectives:

- Instituting a contract responsibility system in agricultural areas
- Reviving individual businesses in urban areas
- Decentralizing a substantial amount of authority to state enterprises
- Reforming the irrational price system[6]

Agricultural Reforms

Deng, who had been criticized during the Cultural Revolution for condoning "capitalist" practices, now publicly championed the concept of material incentives. Henceforth, he announced, people would have to sell to the state only a certain, specified amount at state-set prices. Anything they raised or produced beyond these quotas was theirs to keep, or to sell on the free market. Local fairs and markets were not only condoned, they were encouraged. Specialized production—for example, planting tomatoes rather than grain, since they fetched a higher price—would also be condoned, provided it suited local conditions.

Dazhai, the production brigade that had been the model for all to emulate since 1964, was now condemned. Its leaders were accused of falsifying production records, misusing agricultural machinery, and having low labor productivity. It and other widely publicized models were reported to have had huge amounts of state funds funneled into them, giving the false impression that their accomplishments were the result of applying left-wing egalitarian policies.

To bolster agriculture, more credit was made available to it than ever before. In 1978 alone, state banks and credit cooperatives put an unprecedented 25 billion *yuan* at the disposal of production brigades. The share allocated to agriculture by state capital investment rose from 10.7 percent in 1978 to 14 percent in 1979. Even so, there were problems at the start. Peasants, whose past bitter experiences with their leaders' mercurial changes had made them extremely cautious, were concerned that the new policies might be aimed at ferreting out hidden rightists, which they would immediately be classified as if they tried the policies. Even if there were no ulterior motives, they reasoned, the policies might be changed in a year or two, and a campaign would be launched to cut off the "tails of capitalism"; that is, themselves.

Cadres, too, were resistant even when peasants were not. In one infamous incident that received extensive publicity, a cadre who was either ideologically opposed to heeding Deng's call for specialized production or fearful of its consequences for him personally, ordered an entire field of watermelons to be dug up and destroyed. The media seized this opportunity to point out what it portrayed as a basic fallacy of leftism: Not only was the peasants' cash crop gone, but it was too late in the season for them to plant another, more ideologically acceptable crop in its place.

For a time, the government tried to hold the unit of accounting at the team level, but by 1979 had acquiesced to peasants' strong preference for using the household instead. In that year it also agreed to a substantial increase in agricultural procurement prices that made production more profitable. The 1980 harvest, however, was hurt by poor weather.

By 1981, a combination of government reassurance and better weather ushered in a period of rapid growth. Grain production rose rapidly, by more than 5 percent per year. Several excellent harvests culminated in a record crop in 1984; China was actually a net exporter of grain in 1985. However, other problems came to the fore. Certain functions that had been performed by the communes were simply not performed at all after they had been dismantled. Disputes broke out over issues like water use. The problems of dividing up a collective's property among the households that had been its component parts replicated almost precisely those that had characterized the parceling out of landlords' possessions three decades before. Once again, many draft animals were assigned to several families, who overworked and underfed them. As before, many died.

Other problems concerned who received which items, and at what price. Who would get the contracts for running such potentially profitable entities as orchards and fishponds? Who would get which pieces of land? The main issue here was not how much land, since equality of size could be easily measured. Rather, it was which land. Plots with good soil that were close to water supplies, homes, and roads were obviously preferable to plots which did not possess these attributes. What was not clear and, by its very nature, could not be clear, was the method to parcel out plots of land, most of which had some but not all of the desired characteristics, among the large number of claimants. Cadres used different methods but found that whatever scheme they chose, some peasants would accuse them of favoritism. Even where they opted to draw lots, someone would accuse them of manipulating the process.

Cadres understandably felt resentful of Deng's reforms for putting them in this situation, which amounted to presiding over the dismantling of their own power and privileges. The team leader became the village leader, and peasants became more outspoken. However, many of the village leaders quickly perceived that there were advantages for them, too. For example, under the new system, the village retains ownership of collective property and businesses. This gave the village cadres the right to dictate the terms of land contracts and choose the people who would run village enterprises. In essence, the cadre might make himself or herself into a socialist landlord. They could arrange for themselves, their friends, and their relatives to get the best land and contracts at the lowest prices. Cadres could impose arbitrary taxes and manipulate the distribution of fertilizer or other commodities that the peasants needed.

Special relationships often grew up between the newly wealthy "ten-thousand-*yuan*" households—meaning those favored few whose yearly income equaled or exceeded ten thousand *yuan*—and the cadres. Cadres might receive expensive gifts from the affluent households, or even shares in their businesses. Punning on Karl Marx's theory of primitive capitalist accumulation, dissident economist He Qinglian refers to this process as "primitive socialist accumulation." Watching those who were advantaged under the Maoist system become those who were advantaged under the market system, less privileged individuals began to refer to them as the "never-left-out class."

If wealthy households were uncooperative, irregularities could be "discovered" in their accounting procedures or in the treatment of those they hired. A time-consuming investigation would follow, accompanied by much bad publicity. Some wealthy households were "persuaded" to donate one of their businesses to the town, out of gratitude for all that the party and government had done for them. The newly wealthy household's neighbors who had not become wealthy typically had little sympathy for them, and were unlikely to defend them against such treatment. Often, in fact, jealousy led such people to indulge in economically counterproductive activities. Prosperous families found themselves the targets of sabotage: Their warehouses could be burned, their animals maimed, and their vehicles immobilized.

Not all cadres were corrupt, and jealousy toward one's more affluent neighbors did not usually take such vicious forms. But the sum total of the several different types of behavior described here very definitely deprived some peasants of many of the benefits of Deng's new policies.[7] For others, knowledge of what might happen discouraged them from trying too hard to become wealthy.

Other concerns arose because of the uncertainties of agriculture in the new market economy. Wishing to avoid another grain surplus the size of that in 1984, the government lowered state grain-purchase prices for 1985. It also allowed peasants to produce the crops of their choice after fulfilling contractual grain obligations to the state, and relaxed state controls over the prices of nonstaple foods such as vegetables, fruit, and meat. Free market prices for these soared, and cash-crop production began to consume an increasing share of China's farmland, to the detriment of grain production. At the same time, low feed-grain prices caused by the large 1984 harvest encouraged many peasants to raise livestock. This in turn depressed meat prices, leading to shortages in 1987 and a return to pork rationing. Rationing of certain other commodities, such as sugar and eggs, also occurred due to imbalances in supply and demand.

After a few years of increased state investment in agriculture in the late 1970s, the state began a steady decline in its investments in this sector. Neither local government agencies nor peasants took up the slack. Rural officials typically preferred to develop profitable industries on farmland rather than make investments in agricultural infrastructure projects. Peasants continued to fear that changes in the central government's agricultural policies might deprive them of any benefits that might come from investments in the infrastructure. They therefore preferred to put their money into better housing and consumer goods. Rural industry boomed as a result of these decisions, taking a substantial amount of land away from agricultural production. As noted in the preceding chapter, the controversy within the leadership over how to deal with agricultural difficulties became public with the September 1985 exchange between Deng Xiaoping and leftist economist Chen Yun. It was to be an ongoing problem.

The Private Sector

In urban areas, Deng's reforms called for a rapid revival of the private sector. Under Mao, it had been despised as a remnant of capitalism. Even after the official rehabilitation of the private sector, many workers were reluctant to join it. It took some time to change the mindset that state-sector jobs were preferable to all others. Initially, a substantial proportion of those entering the private sector were ex-convicts, youth who had been in reform school, retirees, and others who had few options for employment. Some feared a change in the party line; others did not wish to leave the security of factory jobs where, even though one earned very little, the demands and risks were few. In essence, these workers had a guaranteed livelihood or, in popular speech, an "iron rice bowl." Others, some because they were unemployed and some because they had entrepreneurial personalities, decided to try their hand at such endeavors as running restaurants, beauty parlors, taxicab fleets, and bicycle repair shops. By the end of 1983, the private sector employed 17 million people and, as of 2003, this had risen to 27 million. Most of these businesses were in the service industry, sometimes referred to by economists as the tertiary sector of the economy, after agriculture and mining (primary) and manufacturing (secondary). Although typically charging higher prices than the state's, their services were actually available when those that in theory should have been provided by the state were not available. Typically, also, the quality of the service was superior. The output value of the service sector increased much faster than that of either industry or agriculture. As state-run enterprises declined in importance, the economic contributions of individual and collectively owned businesses burgeoned. The private sector had been legitimated. In 1998, an individual who owned a private company received the official designation of "model worker"—a startling departure from Maoist ideals.

More Responsibility for State Enterprises

The linchpin of economic reform, however, lay elsewhere: in the delegation of greater authority to individual enterprises in order to transform them into more independent units that would be responsible for their own successes and failures. With the iron rice bowl broken, the state would no longer subsidize factories or other enterprises that were unprofitable.[8] After a relatively short transition period, those that could not adapt to the new realities would have to go out of business.

Beginning in 1979, the government issued a number of directives and regulations designed to implement decentralization and the fiscal responsibility of enterprises. Administrative organization was to be simplified, with more decision-making power devolving to lower levels on the assumption that they were better positioned than Beijing bureaucrats to judge what was best. Many state-imposed mandatory quotas were lowered. Instead of requiring factories to turn over their profits to the state, taxes were levied. After-tax profits were to be retained by the factory for investment, expansion, and distribution as bonuses to deserving employees. To the carrot of returning profits to factories that produced them, a stick was added in the form of a bankruptcy law to enable the dismantling of those enterprises that persisted in running at a loss.

These reforms had a number of good effects. Factories did in general try harder to produce goods that people found attractive and wished to buy. Many workers put more effort into their jobs, and found themselves rewarded with more money and more consumer goods in the stores to spend it on. Clothes became more varied and stylish; they also fit the wearer better. A happy family pedaling its new refrigerator, washing machine, or television home on a trailer towed by bicycle became a common sight in major cities. Some lucky small children were given tricycles; a number of their parents and elder siblings acquired motorbikes. A few were even able to buy cars.

There were problems as well. In practice, it proved almost impossible to make the bankruptcy law work: A very large number of factories operated at losses, and forcing them out of business would turn a lot of unhappy workers out on the streets, with ominous potential for social unrest. Having to pay unemployment benefits to the workers would erase much of what might have been gained by ending the state subsidies that had kept the factory in business. Despite the wide publicity given to a few plant closings, as a general rule factories were allowed to keep operating. In 1991, Chinese economists reported that almost two-thirds of their country's 102,000 state-owned industrial enterprises were losing money.[9] At the same time, the PRC's finance minister stated that losses at state enterprises exceeded profits by a ratio of nearly eight to one. Subsidies to such factories absorbed nearly a third of government revenue in 1990.[10]

Bonuses, too, caused problems. Rather than being used as intended to reward outstanding workers, factories tended to divide the money equally among all workers, regardless of how hard they had worked. This reduced the efficacy of the bonus as an incentive. Economists complained that not only had the reforms failed to smash the iron rice bowl, but that everyone continued to "eat from the same big pot."

Reforming the Price System

The fourth of Deng's reforms, reforming the price system to reflect supply and demand rather than being artificially set by central government planners, was enormously difficult. To remove controls on prices overnight would have caused chaos, as low, state-set prices fluctuated wildly in search of market prices that were as yet unknown. Hence it was reasonable for the government to opt for a phased changeover instead. In 1983, a transitional two-tier price system was adopted: a government-set price for materials covered by the state plan and a negotiated price that was normally well above that of the government-set price. (For most agricultural products there was a third, or market, price determined by supply and demand that was usually even higher.) Unfortunately, the two-tier price system had the unintended result of encouraging hoarding and speculation. Individuals who were able to get access to goods at the low, state-set price bought up as much as they could and then held the commodities off the market until they could sell at high negotiated prices. Officials fulminated against such behavior, warning that economic crimes would be sternly prosecuted. Some people were indeed given stiff sentences, including execution, but hoarding and profiteering continued. These practices bid up the price of needed commodities, and caused serious economic inefficiencies.

Scarcities in basic raw materials caused other problems because, while government-controlled prices for coal, oil, iron ore, and many other mineral products continued to be far below their actual production costs, the products made from them could be sold at negotiated prices, which were very high. Hence, producers of these commodities could make huge profits—provided they could get the necessary raw materials. The situation was particularly serious with regard to coal, which supplies more than 70 percent of China's energy needs. *Xinhua*, the official news agency, reported on the strange phenomenon of dark shadows jumping over the high walls surrounding state guesthouses in the middle of the night. They were not thieves, the agency explained, but would-be coal purchasers who had heard that a cadre with coal to sell was staying at the guesthouse that night. Afraid to anger the official by disturbing his or her sleep, they would slip a note announcing their presence under the door, then wait outside hoping to be the first to see the cadre when he emerged from his room the next morning. When a coal auction was scheduled to take place, desperate buyers were known to have reserved the town's entire guesthouse for the night before. By paying for large numbers of empty rooms, they hoped to deprive potential competitors of a place to stay. Others simply offered bribes, which often became regarded by both parties as an acceptable way to do business.

Corruption in the railway system was reported to have assumed comparable dimensions since, once acquiring the raw materials, one needed a way to get them to the factory. Space was in short supply on the PRC's rickety, overcrowded railway system, and railway workers received fixed salaries that had not kept pace with inflation.

Guandao, or official corruption, was indulged in not only by high-ranking cadres but by their children, the "prince" faction, as well. Deng's open door policy toward trading with foreign countries encouraged many non-Chinese companies to seek contracts and joint ventures with the PRC. The government set up four special economic zones (SEZs), all of them on the PRC's southeastern coast, to facilitate attracting foreign investment. Later on, Hainan province was also made a SEZ, and a number of cities were accorded certain special provisions with regard to doing business with foreigners. Many overseas investors were indeed attracted by the lure of the Chinese market. However, cutting through the tangle of the PRC's overlapping bureaucracies, with their respective rivalries, seemingly inexhaustible supplies of red tape, and unpublished regulations proved a nightmare for foreign businesspeople. They discovered that access to the right top official, often through gifts to one of his or her children, could be the key to getting the right stamp, or "chop," of legitimization. Children of high-ranking officials were also prominent members of state trading corporations that supervised trade transactions with foreign countries. They were pleased to take advantage of offers to inspect the home offices of the foreign corporation with whom they might want to do business. Meals at gourmet restaurants and sightseeing expeditions could be charged to the corporation's expense account. For these princes and princesses, dealing with foreigners was the key to foreign travel, expensive consumer items, and the good life in general.

Although industry boomed, the practices described above led to shortages of energy and raw materials: Many factories could work only two to three days a week because they lacked such basics as power and water. Imports surged in the second half of 1988 as China turned to foreign suppliers for many of the things it could not supply domestically. These included sugar, cotton, and grain. The country's trade balance deteriorated. The government therefore decided to grant incentives to state trading companies to help exports. These measures did indeed lead to a rapid increase in exports but caused other problems. Because China's skewed domestic price structure severely underpriced raw materials and energy, trading companies rushed to export these commodities and sell them at international prices, which were much higher. Thus the companies made large profits by selling such items as coal, cotton, and silk at the very same time that domestic factories reported shortages of the same goods.

Rapid export growth also widened regional income disparities, which were already a source of debate within the leadership. In the name of economic efficiency, the government had for the past decade invested its money where it thought it could get the best returns, as opposed to the Maoist preference for redistributing funds away from more profitable coastal enterprises in order to bring about the economic development of the country's backward hinterland. Deng's policies meant that the coastal provinces forged ahead economically, while the hinterland fell further behind. By encouraging rapid export growth in 1988, the government exaggerated this trend. With their more modern factories, better-skilled work force, and access to the ports and rail lines that link China with the outside world, coastal provinces could more easily take advantage of central-government incentives to export than could those of the hinterland. This in turn gave coastal areas better access to credit and foreign exchange, more rapid gains in income, and greater independence from Beijing.

The interior provinces grew increasingly unhappy with this situation and retaliated by erecting trade barriers to protect themselves, aiming to prevent the more affluent coastal provinces from bidding up the prices for their coal, grain, and other products. In some areas, local authorities set up checkpoints at roads, railway stations, ports, or provincial borders to try to block the shipment of goods they had not specifically authorized. Local area banks limited their loans to, or raised interest rates for, enterprises that purchased goods from other regions. Local courts favored local interests in handing down their rulings.[11] This had the potential to destroy the national market that the communist party had established. The central government issued directives prohibiting various regionalist practices. Its officials made speeches pointing out that regionalism was not only bad for the country but that also in the long run it was even bad for the regions. There was no noticeable improvement in the phenomenon.

In the short run, however, inflation was a much more serious concern. The official inflation rate for 1988 was 18.5 percent, which is generally believed to understate the problem. Food prices rose more than 50 percent, causing serious difficulties for many: In China, unlike more developed countries, consumers spend more than 60 percent of their incomes on food. Panic buying and runs on banks were reported in many areas of China during the summer of 1988. Since consumer bank accounts amount to 27 percent of the PRC's gross national product, the government was concerned to stop the runs on banks as quickly as possible.

Reforming the Reforms

In September, a series of stringent measures was announced, their aim being to slow capital construction, restrict spending, and control inflation. For example, state investment spending was cut by 20 percent a year; credit ceilings for domestic banks were tightened, and interest rates raised on bank loans. Loans to private and rural enterprises were to be halted. The intent of these measures was to discourage bank-financed investment outside the state plan. Control over the production and marketing of certain steel products and nonferrous metals was recentralized. The central government also re-established its monopoly over the distribution of fertilizer, pesticides, and plastic sheeting to control speculation in farm inputs.

The central government also took steps to reassert its control over foreign trade. For example, it restricted the number of corporations authorized to import certain products and expanded the number of products subject to export licenses, quotas, and outright bans. The government also reduced the shares of foreign exchange that the PRC's five special economic zones were permitted to retain from their exports.[12]

The results of this elaborate retrenchment program were not what the government hoped for. Growth in capital construction spending did fall sharply but had its major impact on state enterprises: Rural enterprises grew three times as fast as state-dominated ones. Many factories were able to circumvent the government's credit controls by drawing on the resources of widespread nongovernmental financial institutions. This was particularly easy for those located on the PRC's southern coast, who had access to capital from Hong Kong and abroad. Inflation continued to increase, by more than 25 percent in the first half of 1989. The 1988 retrenchment was a vivid object lesson in how difficult it would be for party and government to reclaim the economic levers of power once they had been surrendered.

The rapidly rising inflation rate, the growth of inequalities in the distribution of income, and the pervasive nature of official corruption were major grievances expressed by antigovernment demonstrators at Tiananmen Square and elsewhere in the spring of 1989. While rejecting the marchers' calls for abstract rights like freedom and democracy, the government made serious efforts to address the economic issues they raised. Since the leftists had emerged victorious from the power struggle that accompanied the demonstrations, it is not surprising that the solutions proposed called for greater central-government control over the economy. A 39-point plan adopted in November 1989 went much further than the 1988 program. Some joint ventures that already had local or provincial control now had to apply to the central government for import-export licenses for previously uncontrolled items. The central bank withdrew large amounts of money from circulation. Officials accused private businesses of evading taxes, engaging in illicit activities, and causing income disparities. Some businesspeople were prosecuted for such activities and given stiff sentences; some corrupt officials were treated in the same fashion. Export industries received heavy subsidies at the same time that imports were severely restricted.

The collective effect of these measures, plus the economic sanctions imposed by some foreign countries on China after the government's bloody suppression of the demonstrations, was to plunge the PRC's economy into a steep downturn. On the positive side, inflation was brought under control, to a modest 4 percent. Export subsidies and import restrictions resulted in a doubling of the country's foreign exchange reserves, to over $23 billion, and there was now a trade surplus. However, the costs were high. Real gross national product grew at only 1.8 percent in the first half of 1990, losses in state enterprises were twice that of 1989, and unemployment soared. Large supplies of consumer durables piled up in warehouses, with potential buyers holding off purchasing due to economic uncertainties. The state taxation bureau was able to collect only half of what it had expected, partly because the economy had contracted and partly because widespread tax evasion continued.

The government subsequently rescinded certain measures, which seemed to help ease unemployment and encourage consumer purchasing a bit. The GDP grew by 5.2 percent in 1990 and 7 percent in 1991; the inflation rate in 1991 was a modest 2.9 percent. Party and government pronouncements continued to affirm both the need for structural reform and for economic retrenchment, thus reflecting their uncertainty about how to proceed. Pressures and counterpressures from leftists who preferred more central planning and reformers who preferred greater reliance on the market resulted in vacillating policies, as did pressures for recentralization of economic decision-making from the central government and counter-pressures for more leeway in economic decision-making from the provinces and local areas. Analysts described the Chinese economy as suspended in a state of disequilibrium.

In early 1992, Deng Xiaoping made a heavily publicized visit to several of the SEZs, praising their achievements and hence signalling that a new period of reforms was about to begin. Annual growth rates leaped upward into the 12 to 13 percent range. However, inflation again became a problem. In addition, the economic restructuring that was part of the reforms meant that a number of workers were dismissed. Worker unrest became a serious problem: In Tianjin, employees in a state-owned watch factory smashed equipment and fought with police after hearing that mass layoffs were imminent. In another city, a bank director's house was firebombed by a recently dismissed staff member.

In an effort to streamline the bloated and inefficient bureaucracy, officials were urged to "jump into the sea," meaning go into business for themselves as opposed to working for party or government. A number of them did, often helped to turn a profit by connections they had made in their previous jobs. This gave such individuals an advantage over those without connections in the bureaucracy, and led to complaints of unfair competition. Many other officials, not wishing to lose the subsidized housing that came with their jobs, took on new positions *without* quitting. Knowing that it would be difficult to dismiss them, they put in an absolute minimum amount of time on their official duties, thereby rendering party and government still less efficient.

Agriculture, too, had its problems. According to government figures, the income gap between rural and urban dwellers widened from 1:1.7 in 1985 to 1:1.24 in 1991, and continued to grow rapidly. Peasants were also being squeezed off their land. Between 1949 and 1991, China's total acreage under cultivation was reduced from 1.468 billion *mu* to 1.435 billion *mu*, while the number of rural laborers during the same period rose from 173 million to 428 million. Although the town and township enterprises which were first set up in the 1980s absorbed nearly 100 million rural laborers, this left over 150 million surplus laborers in the countryside, many of whom jammed trains and roads in search of work elsewhere. Efforts to stop what were called blind population shifts failed, and emphasis shifted to trying to better channel the "floating population" toward the jobs that could best help the country's economic development.[13]

To make matters worse, governments who were eager to devote resources to large-scale investment often found that they had no money left, and opted to pay peasants with IOUs. Other investment-hungry officials who wanted agricultural land for construction projects tried to either confiscate it or offered peasants less than they thought their land was worth. New kinds of taxes proliferated. A widespread lament was that "it used to be that the KMT was known for its numerous taxes and the CCP for its numerous meetings; now the CCP has even more taxes than it has meetings."

Despite these frictions, economic reforms continued. In October 1992, the Fourteenth Party Congress declared its intention to establish a "socialist market economic system." Commentaries explained this apparent contradiction in terms of using the advantages of capitalist market economies in order to develop socialized, large-scale production "while maintaining a balance of social and efficiency between the two."[14] Under the aegis of "market-Leninism," growth rates forged ahead.

By mid-1993, the problem was no longer an economy that had stalled, but rather one that appeared to be locked on overdrive. Prices soared, and people rushed to buy gold to preserve their savings, or to invest them in something that would outpace inflation. Investment fever threatened to get out of hand. More than a hundred thousand people lost money when the bonds they had been told would yield 24 percent interest turned out to be worthless. The head of the issuing company was apprehended, tried, and executed. Just as unsettling as the scheme itself was the revelation that the company had not acted in isolation: More than a hundred party and government officials were implicated, and journalists for official newspapers had been bribed to write articles that described the bonds favorably. It was also alleged that high-ranking party and government officials were guilty of insider trading on the Hong Kong stock market. Since they had advance knowledge of announcements from Beijing that could be expected to affect share prices in Hong Kong, such individuals were in a position to amass a fortune quickly.[15] Ordinary people found ways to evade tax assessments, which were officially estimated to cost the government over $15 billion each year.

Another problem that complicated the central government's economic planning was that it could not completely trust its statistics. Lower-level authorities who wanted to make themselves and their areas look good to higher levels falsified production records.[16] Concerned to eliminate what it perceived as widespread and pervasive exaggeration of production statistics, the government commended one county for its *truthful* reporting[17] and tasked investigative teams to fan out throughout the country to curb these practices.

In July 1993, the head of China's central bank was dismissed and replaced with popular vice-premier Zhu Rongji. Zhu announced an austerity drive which, despite his reputation as both clever and aggressive, lasted a mere four months. Deng Xiaoping had decided that the economy was not overheating, and by November, the party line again encouraged growth. Since the central government had surrendered so much power over the economy to provinces and local areas, Zhu's job may have been impossible from the beginning. While total tax revenue declined from 26.7 percent of total output in 1979 to 16.6 percent in 1993, the central government's share of that pie declined from 57 percent in 1980 to 38.5 percent in 1992, with provinces' share rising proportionately. This meant that the central government had less to redistribute to poor regions, which therefore relied less on Beijing, as well as less clout with the wealthier regions.[18]

A new fiscal system was introduced in 1994 that was designed to raise the central government's share of revenue to over 60 percent, but provinces resisted implementing it. In the same year, the government, reacting to peasants' anger at the many taxes that they were burdened with, ordered that levies on peasants should not exceed 5 percent of their incomes. Inflation again became a problem. Official figures, which are widely believed to underestimate the true rate, placed the 1994 rate at a post-1949 high of 21.8 percent; financial analysts were skeptical that the economy could achieve a "soft landing"—that is, that inflation could be lowered without provoking a severe economic downturn.

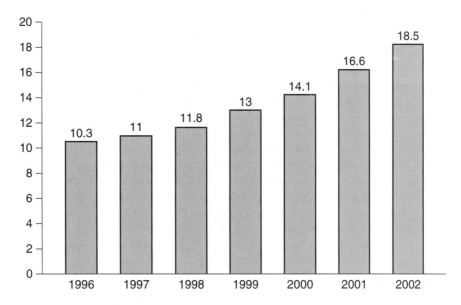

FIGURE 7.1   Tax Revenue as a Percentage of GDP
Source: State Administration of Taxation.

The government's plans were partially successful. By 1996, central government tax revenues had fallen to 10.3 percent of gross domestic product (GDP), though they had rebounded to 16.6 percent in 2001 and 18.5 percent in 2002. (See Figure 7.1.) In a stunning success for the government, the economy did achieve a soft landing, confounding expert predictions to the contrary. The inflation rate fell to 16.8 percent in 1995 and 8.3 percent in 1996 while GDP grew at satisfactory rates. Zhu Rongji, who was credited with having achieved this near miracle, utilized both administrative and market-based measures such as restrictions on investment, tightening credit, establishing prices controls and subsidies, releasing grain reserves to ease local food shortages, and subsidizing food shipments among provinces.

New Problems for Deng's Successors

At the time of Deng Xiaoping's death in February 1997, China's economic prospects looked bright. Foreign observers extrapolated healthy growth rates into the twenty-first century and issued glowing predictions for prosperity. All, however, was not well. As inflation dropped, so did economic growth rates. Initially, this did not appear to be a problem: even the lower rates were impressive, and the trade-off in lower inflation rates was welcome. Later, however, concerns grew about how long the downward trajectory would continue. GDP grew by only 8.8 percent in 1997, vis-à-vis an expected 10 percent, and the inflation rate, a modest 2 percent, had slipped into deflation by the end of the year. A World Bank report warned that, if reforms were not soon implemented, the result might be "sinosclerosis."

The leadership vowed that it would restructure, and promised an 8 percent growth in GDP for 1998, a rate it believed was the minimum figure necessary to create jobs for new entrants to the labor market and to reemploy those who would lose their existing jobs in the major restructuring effort that leaders knew had to be undertaken to keep the economy healthy. However, provincial officials, told that they must achieve an 8 percent growth rate, responded by reporting figures that were even higher. Zhu Rongji, who had become premier, sharply criticized them; in a process known as "wringing the water" from statistics, the official growth rate for 1998 was declared to be 7.8 percent. Zhu also introduced a massive fiscal stimulus package that included large public works projects as a way to keep the economy growing. This it did, although incurring large budget deficits as a result. Official growth rates were 7.1 percent in 1999, 8 percent in 2000, 7.3 percent in 2001, and 8.0 percent for 2002, with 7.5 percent predicted for 2003. By 2002, the government had decided that 7 percent was the minimum necessary for job creation and to avoid massive labor unrest. (See Figure 7.2.)

Some economists disputed the official growth rate statistics. One American expert calculated that actual growth in GDP since 1998 has been a maximum of 3.8 percent, and perhaps even less. In view of such indicators as declines in energy use, mass layoffs of workers, and widespread excess capacity in several industries, he suspects that the economy may actually have contracted in 1998–1999.[19] Others countered that, rather than overreporting growth rates, prosperous areas had deliberately underreported figures so as to reduce the amount of taxes they had to pay. They also point out the PRC has a massive underground economy, estimated at over $ 120 billion in 2002; if reported, it would raise GDP by several percentage points. Hence, they believe that officially reported figures are

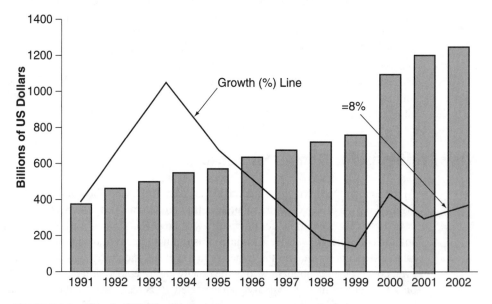

FIGURE 7.2   China's GDP Growth
Source: Calculated from data in *Beijing Review,* March 6, 2003.

essentially accurate. Still others argue that this debate about numbers is irrelevant, since the quality of economic growth is more important than the quantity thereof. For example, although building up inventories of unsaleable goods counts as economic growth, it does not represent an improvement in people's lives or the prosperity of the state. Moreover, current deficit spending is actually exacerbating the economy's structural problems, since it encourages ill-considered investment projects with poor returns.

Regardless of the true rate of economic growth, there were unmistakable indications of both prosperity in some areas and problems in others. When criticized for having authorized such a massive fiscal stimulus, Zhu Rongji replied that the national economy would have collapsed without it. Increasing labor unrest was also evident, as an estimated 60 million people who were displaced from their jobs as a result of restructuring looked for new positions. The government set up retraining centers, and some of those who lost their jobs have been successful in finding new ones. A few have even become better off. For example, one woman discovered a market for preparing and delivering meals to the homes of two-career couples who did not have time to shop and cook; she earned far more doing this than at the factory job she had been laid off from. Unfortunately, her story is not the norm. Moreover, the re-employment rate has been falling, from 50 percent in 1998 to 42 percent in 1999, 35 percent in 2000, and a mere 9 percent in 2001.

Pension funds proved inadequate. When factories defaulted on commitments to displaced workers—sometimes unavoidably because funds did not exist, at other times because corrupt managers had embezzled the money—tens of thousands of workers took to the streets in protest. These protests typically concerned a single factory and were suppressed, generally within a few days. The media are forbidden to report on labor unrest, thus limiting the possibilities that demonstrations will spread to other cities. One technique that the government has found successful involves undermining support for protest leaders by making minimal concessions like small cash payments to the rank-and-file. At the same time, officials attempt to divide the leaders of the demonstrations by buying some off and intimidating or arresting others. Demonstators who tried to organize a union independent of the government-controlled All China Federation of Trade Unions, were arrested. A Western journalist, reflecting on Karl Marx's call to the workers of the world to unite, since they had nothing to lose but their chains, commented that China's workers were trying to unite at the risk of being put in chains.[20]

Peasants fared still worse than workers. Their incomes, typically much less than those of city dwellers, fell from 1998 through 2000, rebounded slightly in 2001 due to increases in the prices of major farm products, and then began to decline again as a result of cheaper imports entering China after the PRC's admission into the World Trade Organization. A director of the PRC's State Statistics Bureau estimated the gap between urban and rural incomes in China as more than five to one, and perhaps even six to one.[21] Planners worried about millions of impoverished peasants flocking into the cities and thereby worsening unemployment problems there. By 2002, the Gini coefficient, an internationally recognized measure of income disparity in which zero represents perfect equality and one perfect inequality, had risen to 0.5. (See Figure 7.3.) Since 0.4 is considered the danger level, this was alarming—and all the more so in a country whose founding principles included the welfare of the workers and peasants. Corruption continued to be a problem: Leading Chinese analysts estimated that it had cost the economy an average of 14.5 to 14.9 percent of GDP annually from 1995 to 2001.[22]

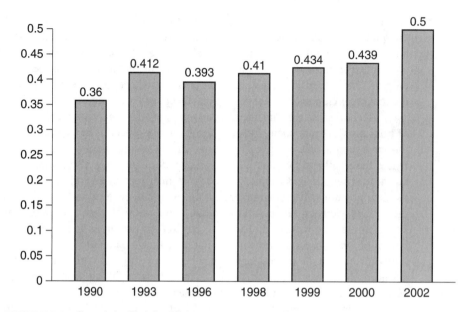

FIGURE 7.3   Growth in Gini Coefficient
Source: Compiled from world Bank data and other sources.

An attempt to reduce disparities between coastal and inland areas of the PRC, the "invest in the west" campaign, was begun in 2000. It received much favorable publicity but produced few substantive results. Foreign investors brought to the area were not impressed with the prospects for return on their capital. Domestically as well there was a good deal of privately expressed cynicism. Members of the CPPCC and National People's Congress worried about "empty words and wasteful duplication," as well as corruption reducing the effect of the money invested. A party member responded to questions about the campaign with a curt "just another opportunity for smart guys to get richer."[23] The disparities continue to grow.

In the course of extending credit to keep enterprises afloat and avoid exacerbating the unemployment rate, the PRC's banks amassed large amounts of nonperforming loans. Too often the criteria for loans were personal ties to government officials and bribery rather than creditworthiness. Such enterprises, many of them state-owned, were frequently unable to repay. Some enterprise managers did not comprehend the seriousness of the problem, arguing that, since state enterprises are using state funds, no actual losses were involved. The government admitted to 27 percent nonperforming loans, or more than twice the level regarded as safe by the Bank of International Settlements in Basel. Official figures are believed to greatly underestimate the actual number of nonperforming loans, but because China's banking system lacks transparency, it is difficult to be certain by how much. Experts have variously estimated the percentage of nonperforming loans at between 37 and 50 percent. Financial analysts have for several years expressed concern that the banking system might be on the verge of collapse.

In 1999, after a series of embarrassing defaults, the government set up four asset management corporations (AMCs) to take over and dispose of the banks' worst loans. One

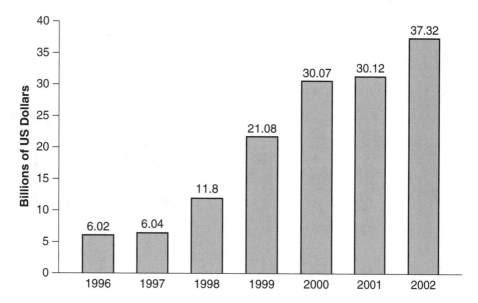

FIGURE 7.4 Growth in Fiscal Deficit
Source: National Bureau of Statistics.

hundred sixty nine billion dollars was removed from the books of the four state-owned banks that collectively hold over 70 percent of the PRC's deposits, and transferred to the AMCs. In return, the AMCs issued bonds worth $141 billion to the banks and added $28 billion in cash. The corporations were charted with selling the loans; however, the AMCs had difficulty finding buyers for even the least risky of the loans. Hence, many loans, instead of being sold for cash, were converted into stock in the bankrupt companies, allowing even the most inefficient of them to stay in business under government ownership. The AMCs then struggled to raise money for the interest payments on the bonds, and were unable to repay the country's central bank, which had loaned to them an amount that was several times the central bank's capital base. More money will have to be loaned to the banks, not only adding to the country's budget deficit but calling into question the health of the central bank itself.[24] (See Figure 7.4.) A frustrated economist observed that without reform of the state-owned enterprises, there could be no banking reform, but without banking reform, there could be no reform of state-owned enterprises.

Despite its economic difficulties, China remains an attractive destination for foreign direct investment. Financial decisionmakers are attracted by the size of the PRC's market, its apparent high growth rates, and their perception that in China they are apt to face few competitors with entrenched positions. (See Figure 7.5.) In 2001, the PRC surpassed the United States to become the world's number one recipient of foreign direct investment (FDI). While some of this FDI may have been from mainland companies opening subsidiaries abroad to pose as foreign investors in order to receive favorable treatment—so-called "round-tripping"—it could not all have been.

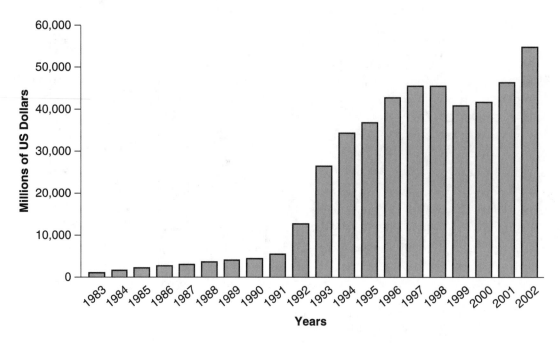

FIGURE 7.5   Utilized Foreign Direct Investment in China (all sources)

Conclusions

The Chinese economy has turned in a creditable performance over the past five decades, with development picking up markedly in the years after Deng Xiaoping assumed a leadership rule. However, by the time Jiang Zemin came to power, systemic flaws had become prominent and were threatening to end the upswing in prosperity. The social costs of reform were great, and conduced toward postponement. Yet, as economists warned, delay would increase the disruptions of the reform that must inevitably take place.

Even the lower estimates of the PRC's economic growth would be the envy of many countries. China is the world's fifth largest trading power, up from sixteenth place in 1990, which was already a rise of several dozen places only a decade before that. Its foreign exchange reserves rank second in the world. Some analysts believe that the PRC may within the current decade displace Japan to become the second largest economy in the world. Despite its irrationalities and other shortcomings, the system manages to feed and clothe 1.3 billion people, albeit at a fairly modest level for most. Nonetheless, serious structural defects continue to exist within the economy, with the potential to cause massive disruption and social unrest.

- *Among regions*: The eastern coast continues to forge ahead, leaving inland and western provinces behind. Average incomes in Shanghai are more than five times as large as those in Gansu province.
- *Between urban and rural areas*: While the rural population is 70 percent of the PRC's population, it has only 17 percent of the country's savings.

- *Among different industries, enterprises, and units*: Wages have risen fastest in power production and real estate, relatively slowly in agriculture, forestry, and fishing.
- *Among social strata*: The self-employed and owners of private enterprise receive higher wages than workers in state enterprises.
- *Among urban residents*: Citizens of Shanghai and Guangzhou earn far more than residents of "rust belt" cities such as those of Liaoning and Heilongjiang.
- *Within communities*: 80 percent of the money in rural savings accounts belongs to 20 percent of peasants; 50 percent of peasants have no savings at all, exacerbating resentments.

The transition from centrally planned to market economy is exceedingly difficult; differences of opinion continue to exist on the proper balance between central-government guidance and market regulation. While there is broad consensus within the current elite on the need to press on, there are important differences of opinion on the pace and timing of reform at the same time as a sense that something must be done, and soon. It is possible that the PRC can muddle through the current situation, as indeed it has in the past. But the possibility for significant instability cannot be ignored.

Notes

1. Alexander Eckstein, *China's Economic Development: The Interplay of Scarcity and Ideology* (Ann Arbor, Mich: University of Michigan Press, 1975).

2. For a fascinating eyewitness account of this, see William Hinton, *Fanshen* (New York: Vintage Books, 1966).

3. Chu-yuan Cheng, *China's Economic Development: Growth and Structural Change* (Boulder, Colo.: Westview Press, 1982), p. 67. Cheng's book contains an excellent in-depth analysis of events that can be only briefly summarized here.

4. See David Zweig, *Agrarian Radicalism in China, 1968–1981* (Cambridge, Mass.: Harvard University Press, 1989), for a summary of these actions.

5. See Andrew Walder, *Communist Neo-Traditionalism: Work and Authority in Chinese Industry* (Berkeley: University of California Press, 1986), Chap. 6, for an extended treatment of this issue.

6. Chu-yuan Cheng, *Behind the Tiananmen Massacre: Social, Political, and Economic Ferment in China* (Boulder, Colo.: Westview Press, 1990), p. 15.

7. Jean C. Oi's *State and Peasant in Contemporary China: The Political Economy of Village Government* (Berkeley: University of California Press, 1989), contains a fuller discussion of the points made here.

8. See Dorothy J. Solinger, *Chinese Business Under Socialism* (Berkeley: University of California Press, 1994).

9. James McGregor, "Closing of China's Bright Moon Plant Stands out as a Sunny Day in Annals of Beijing Reform," *Asian Wall Street Journal Weekly*, March 25, 1991, p. 5.

10. Sheryl WuDunn, "China to Raise Arms Spending Again," *New York Times*, March 27, 1991, p. A3.

11. *Xinhua*, November 22, 1990, in FBIS–CHI, November 23, 1990, p. 28.

12. U.S. Central Intelligence Agency, *The Chinese Economy in 1988 and 1989: Reforms on Hold, Economic Problems Mount* (Springfield, Va.: National Technical Information Service, August 1989).

13. You Hongbing, "Labor Tide Calls for Great Efforts to Develop Rural Employment Channel," *Liaowang* (Beijing), February 22, 1993, p. 3, in *FBIS–CHI*, March 16, 1993, pp. 53–54.

14. Geng Yuxin, "China Turns to Market Economy," *Beijing Review*, November 9–15, 1992, p. 7.

15. Hugo Gordon, "Communists Milk Colony's Stock Market," *Daily Telegraph* (London), March 19, 1993, p. 12.

16. (No author), "Bureau Complains of False Economic Statistics," *Zhongguo tongxunshe*, January 1, 1995, in *FBIS–CHI*, January 24, 1995, pp. 52–53.

17. "Hubei Town Submits Authentic Statistics," Hubei Radio, January 11, 1995, in *FBIS–CHI*, January 13, 1995, p. 91.

18. Laurence Zuckerman, "New Chinese Tax Rules Baffle Foreign Countries," *Asian Wall Street Journal Weekly*, January 10, 1994, pp. 1, 5.

19. Thomas Rawski, "What Is Happening to China's GDP Statistics?" *China Economic Review*, no. 12, 2001, pp. 347–354; "Where's the Growth?" *Wall Street Journal*, April 19, 2002.

20. Matthew Forney et al., "Working Man Blues: Labor in Lockstep Was the Core of China's Socialist Dream. Now It May Prove Beijing's Biggest Threat," *Time*, April 1, 2002.

21. Qiu Xiaohua, quoted in *Zhongguo Xinwen She* (Beijing), CPP200210210000060, October 21, 2002.

22. Wang Shaoguang, Hu Angang, and Ding Yuanzhu, "Behind China's Wealth Gap," *South China Morning Post*, October 31, 2002.

23. Author's conversations, August 30, 2000.

24. David Lague, "A Government Move to Clean Up Loans Backfires," *Far Eastern Economic Review*, November 14, 2002.

Suggestions for Further Reading

Anita Chan, *China's Workers Under Assault: The Exploitation of Labor In a Globalizing Economy* (Armonk, N.Y., M. E. Sharpe, 2001).

Gordon Chang, *The Coming Collapse of China* (New York: Random House, 2001).

Joe Studwell, *The China Dream* (London: Profile Books, 2002).

Marc Blecher, Dorothy Solinger, Yongshun Cai, William Hurst, and Kevin O'Brien, "China's Workers: Reform and Resistance," *China Quarterly*, June 2002, pp. 283–360.

Nicholas R. Lardy, *Integrating China Into the Global Economy* (Washington, D.C.: The Brookings Institution Press, 2002).

Ross Garnaut, Ligang Song, Yang Yao, and Xiaolu Wang, *Private Enterprise in China* (Canberra: Asia Pacific Press, 2001).

Crime and Punishment: The Legal System of the PRC

All societies attempt to regulate the conduct of their members, though they may differ widely in the sorts of behavior they condemn and sanction, the mechanisms through which judgments are made, and the punishments that are meted out. For example, one society may choose to encourage large families by providing incentives for childbearing and prison terms for the use or sale of contraceptives; another society, feeling that it is important to limit population growth, may employ an exactly opposite incentive/punishment scheme. Some societies prefer informal rules enforced by family and group sanctions; others rely on detailed written codes enforced by an elaborate hierarchy of courts and prisons. The types of punishment a society deems appropriate may vary as widely as ostracizing the offender at the one extreme to painful forms of execution at the other.

The Chinese communist leadership group in 1949 were the survivors of several decades of violent struggle against the KMT, warlords, the Japanese, and a number of internal rivals. None of these struggles was characterized by respect for legalities. These were not life experiences that predisposed the CCP leaders to believe in the sanctity of a court system, or in the notion that society could be bettered by reasoned appeals to the consciences of its rulers. Communist ideology, moreover, rejected the entire concept of the impartiality and inherent fairness of the legal system. To the contrary, the legal system was regarded as a tool in the hands of the ruling class—in China's case, feudal and bourgeois powers—to oppress and exploit the workers and peasants, and to inhibit the forces of progress.

Another factor predisposing the leadership against a formal legal system may not have been consciously intended: the traditional Chinese preference for informality in settling disputes and imposing sanctions. Also, like communism, the traditional Chinese legal system saw law as subordinate to a dominant political philosophy—in its case, Confucianism.

Mao Zedong was a fervent believer in the concept of permanent revolution. He was convinced that progress toward communism could be achieved only by continuous disruption of settled routines, lest the momentum of the revolution be lost and the evils of the old society reemerge. Violence was the order of the day, with Mao stating bluntly that the old society could not be transformed by genteel means. This attitude too militated against the development of a formal legal system, with its implications of predictability. Initially, therefore, the emphasis was on destroying the old legal system, with some rather violent alternatives imposed in order to cleanse its evils.

The PRC's legal system since 1949 can be analyzed in terms of the interplay between two models of law, the jural and the societal.[1] The jural model focuses on formal, elaborate, and codified rules enforced by a regular judicial hierarchy, while the societal model emphasizes socially approved norms and values. Indeed, both jural and societal influences were evident in the legal procedures developed in the communist-controlled base areas prior to 1949.[2] On the one hand, there was extensive use of the mass line in creating and enforcing consensus on ideological matters, and the techniques of mediation were employed in settling civil disputes. On the other, people's governments enacted a number of basic laws, and a formal judicial system that included courts, the rights to defense, and public trials was established.

Less Than Peaceful Coexistence of the Societal and Jural Models: 1949–1953

During the early years of the PRC, societal and jural models existed, as they had in Yan'an and the other base areas, in a complementary yet competitive manner. The government abolished all KMT laws and judicial organs and, under the aegis of the Common Program passed by the CPPCC in 1949, gradually set up a formal system of its own. As in the Soviet Union, a state organ called the procuracy (sometimes referred to as the procuratorate) was founded to investigate and supervise the judicial system. The procuracy is intended to oversee the actions of the public security (police) force that lead to arrests and prosecution and to ensure that public security investigations follow correct legal procedures. Assuming that public security personnel have observed correct procedures, the procuracy collects information on those to be tried, and acts as prosecutor in criminal trials.

One important feature of the post-1949 system that, at least until fairly recently, aided public security and procuracy in collecting information is the *dang'an*, or dossier, that is kept on every urbanite from the time she or he enters elementary school. There are generally two sets of identical dossiers: one at one's workplace and another at the public security bureau. Entered within are one's photograph, list of family members and relatives, school records and grade transcripts, date of entry into the Communist Youth League and CCP if one chose to opt for membership therein, promotions and level of work, performance and political evaluations. Any single piece of information or combination thereof can be vitally important to one's career prospects and to any investigation begun on an individual by the authorities. Depending on the party line at a given time, having a relative of bad class background, for example, can have severe consequences in terms of job assignment. Since there is no Freedom of Information Act, there is no guarantee that one can examine this dossier in order to point out a false entry or protest an unfair political evaluation. Residence registration, which required an individual to remain in a given area unless given specific permission to move or travel, was also a valuable tool in keeping track of people.[3]

In addition to the procuracy and public security organs, the new government established a three-tier judicial system—basic, intermediate, and supreme court levels—with one right of appeal. An estimated 148 laws and regulations were adopted from 1949 through 1953, of which the most important were the Marriage Law (1950), the Land Reform Law (1950), the Trade Union Law (1950), the Act for the Punishment of Counterrevolutionaries (1951), and the Act for Punishment of Corruption (1952).

At the same time, however, public security organs dispensed justice without reference to the procuracy, the court system, or the law. Arbitrary arrest and detention, forced confessions, and ad hoc punishments were regularly reported during this period. They were even celebrated in the literature and drama of the time—see, for example, the plot of *The White-Haired Girl*, discussed in Chapter 12.

During the countrywide mass campaigns such as the Three Antis and the Five Antis, land reform, and anticounterrevolutionary movement, hastily convened people's tribunals meted out revolutionary justice at mass trials. Mao Zedong stated that 800 thousand people deemed to be reactionaries and bad elements received death sentences at such trials; other estimates run in the millions. Many more people were sentenced to long terms of "reform through labor" under conditions so poor that only the exceptionally strong and fortunate survived. These methods were defended as absolutely necessary. Reactionary forces from the old society were considered to be very strong and simply biding their time before regrouping to attempt to strangle the infant new society. Only by completely destroying them could this comeback be prevented.

The Jural Model in Ascendance: 1954–1957

The promulgation of China's first state constitution in 1954 seemed to indicate the party's commitment to the institutionalization of its rule. The constitution established the National People's Congress (NPC) as the highest organ of state authority. The NPC, along with its standing committee, was vested with broad powers of legislation, amendment, and appointment. The constitution also established the State Council as China's chief administrative organ; it designated the State Council, the Supreme People's Court, and the Supreme People's Procuracy as comprising the central government structure. All three were made accountable to the NPC and its standing committee, which had the power to appoint or remove its officials. NPC deputies were protected against arrest and detention except by consent of the parent body or, when the NPC was not in session, its standing committee.

Organic laws for the people's courts and people's procuracies established separate hierarchies for each under the NPC and its standing committee. The people's courts, divided into basic, intermediate, and higher levels and headed by the Supreme People's Court, were given sole authority to administer justice. Similar tiers were created for the people's procuracies. Headed by the Supreme People's Procuracy, the various levels were collectively vested with supervisory power over the execution of the law. For the first time, albeit in limited form, the PRC seemed to accept the concept of judicial independence, with the constitution declaring "in administering justice, the people's courts are independent, subject only to the law." Courts were in fact, however, made responsible to people's congresses at corresponding levels. This was a clear contrast to earlier laws, which had subordinated courts to the leadership of the people's governments—that is, to the executive rather than the legislative authority—and therefore represented a significant step toward the jural model.

Other articles of the constitution guaranteed equality before the law, freedom of speech, of the press, of association, of demonstration, and of religion, as well as the right to work, to leisure, to education, and to social assistance. Explicit protection against arbitrary arrest was provided by an article declaring that "freedom of the person of citizens of the PRC is inviolable. No citizen may be arrested except by decision of a people's court or a people's procuratorate." An Arrest and Detention Act, promulgated in the same year, added concrete and detailed procedures to the guarantee. A large number of substantive and procedural laws and regulations were drawn up, often using Soviet codes as models.

Supplementing the work of courts and procuracies, a system of lawyers began to take shape. Colleges and universities established legal training programs to teach the new socialist legal philosophy and laws. By mid-1957, China had over 800 legal advisory offices, employing more than 2,500 full-time lawyers nationwide.

Though the legal situation during this period was a definite improvement over immediate postrevolutionary practices, both people's rights and judicial independence remained qualified. In keeping with the communist belief that law was a tool of the ruling class, those who had been designated reactionaries or class enemies had no constitutional rights whatsoever. The constitution's guarantee of equality before the law did not mean that legislation would be equally applied to all, regardless of class. Foreign analysts have pointed out that the idea of different rights for different classes resonates with the *li* and *fa* distinction in traditional China. So as well, they hypothesize, do the coexistence of societal and jural models.[4] However, it is exceedingly unlikely that the PRC leaders made any conscious connection between their conception of the law and that of traditional China.

As the post-1949 system took form, it became apparent that there was no presumption of innocence on behalf of the defendant: He or she who stood accused was presumed guilty unless the individual could amass strong evidence to the contrary. Moreover, a gap remained between written guarantees and actual practice. Even those fortunate few with impeccable class backgrounds might find redress difficult to obtain. Nonetheless, there could be no doubt that the mid-1950s showed a noticeable trend toward the regularization and institutionalization of the judicial system.

In 1956, at the Eighth National Congress of the CCP, Central Committee vice-chair Liu Shaoqi defended these changes. With the passing of the period of "revolutionary storm and stress," new relations of production had been established, which called for a corresponding change in methods. The existence of a complete legal system had become an absolute necessity in order to foster production. Individuals should understand that, as long as they did not violate the laws, their civil rights would be guaranteed. Interestingly, in light of future developments, Mao Zedong's speech at the same party congress warned of the evils of bureaucracy and the dangers of becoming isolated from the masses.

Resurgence of the Societal Model: 1957–1965

During the Hundred Flowers movement of 1957, lawyers and others involved in the judicial system spoke out against its defects. Their criticisms included gaps in laws and legislation, the lack of any benefit of the doubt for the accused, and aberrations in the administration of justice. One critic allegedly described his country as being without either laws or justice. The ensuing backlash of the antirightist campaign and frenzy of the Great Leap Forward effectively ended China's evolution toward a formal Soviet-style judicial system and substituted a highly arbitrary societal model.

Legal specialists, like all others who possessed professional expertise of any sort, were excellent targets for attacks on "so-called bourgeois scientific objectivism." They were accused of disregarding the class character of the law and of prattling about ridiculous concepts like equality for all, including counterrevolutionaries. The principles of relying on facts as the basis for trials and law as the criterion for making decisions were regarded as an abandonment of party policy. They were also seen as attempting to apply abstract legal concepts in isolation from the reality of the political context as a whole. The pre-1957 defense system, with its use of lawyers to represent the accused, was criticized as "protecting bad elements" and obscuring the distinctions between class elements and the people.

Judicial training programs at colleges and universities were curtailed. Codification programs were suspended, and legal research ceased. The legal profession itself was phased out. Teachers and students of law, as well as lawyers themselves, were sent to the countryside to engage in productive labor. Many prominent jurists, including four supreme court judges, were purged as rightists. Although the constitution itself remained in place, the court no longer functioned according to its constitutional mandate. If this caused any concern, it was never publicly stated.

Similarly, with its personnel under attack, the procuracy could no longer effectively question the legality of arrests and prosecutions by public security organs. Public security personnel gained much power as a result. So did party secretaries, who were empowered to decide cases and determine punishments without reference to relevant legal statutes. In effect, the judicial process became totally controlled by party committees and administered by public security organs.[5]

Another feature of this period was its renewed attention to the mass line in judicial work. Court trials continued to take place. However, they incorporated efforts to demystify the legal process through such methods as adding mass debates, bringing the courts directly to the people, using new rules and procedures designed to be more easily understandable, and carrying out justice on the spot.

The retrenchment years that followed the failure of the Great Leap Forward saw a partial, if less than energetic, return to some aspects of the jural model. For example, several codification projects were revived. But, in general, informal revolutionary norms prevailed.

The Societal Model Rampant: 1966–1976

Even this relatively strong representation of the societal model was not pure enough for Cultural Revolution ideologues. Their object seems to have been to destroy *all* formal laws and substitute party policy instead. The reasoning was that, since the CCP was the ruling party, its policy was ipso facto the law. A *People's Daily* article that appeared on January 31, 1967, was actually entitled "In Praise of Lawlessness." Although specifically advocating the destruction of *bourgeois* law, it indicated that what was meant by this term was the entire legal and constitutional structure of the party and the government. It was argued that this structure had kept the country's "bourgeois-capitalist" and presumably, therefore, merely pseudo-communist, leadership in power.[6] Many high-ranking leaders and hundreds of thousands of lesser beings were removed in complete disregard for constitutional procedures. Often it was alleged that they had "wormed their way" into the party in the 1920s and had been serving as minions of the KMT or the Soviets revisionists ever since.

Mao Zedong instructed his Red Guard followers to "smash the *gongjianfa*"—an abbreviation for the public security, procuracy, and courts, collectively, and therefore encompassing the entire judicial system. Bands of young Guards set to their task with enthusiasm, descending on *gongjianfa* offices, attacking their personnel, and destroying records. Not coincidentally, some of these records contained their own dossiers as well as those of friends and family members. The first vice-minister of public security, the chief procurator, and the president of the supreme court were all removed from office. Mass justice was the order of the day. It was sometimes dispensed at denunciation meetings so huge that they were held in sports stadia. The prosecutors might well be self-appointed; at other times, reports described those who conducted trials as revolutionary committees or military control groups. At least at some times and in some places during the Cultural Revolution, the army was empowered to perform *gongjianfa* functions. Presumably the military was called in to reimpose order on what had become a level of chaos that was unacceptable even to the surviving radical leaders.

By late 1968, the violent phase of the Cultural Revolution had abated to the extent that a new party constitution could be drawn up. It was adopted in April 1969. Foreign observers, noting that a new state constitution did not follow along, surmised (correctly, as it turned out) that high-level policy disagreements that would affect the drawing up of a constitution were taking place. After 1970, the PLA's control over law enforcement gradually receded, and in January 1975 a new state constitution was finally promulgated.

Reflecting radical influences, the 1975 constitution abolished the procuracy and deleted the 1954 constitution's protection of NPC deputies against arrest or trial without the consent of the NPC or its standing committee. Provisions concerning citizens' rights were drastically reduced, from nineteen articles to four. Among those conspicuously absent from the new document were freedom of residence, freedom to do scientific research, and freedom to create literary and artistic works. Since none of these had actually been truly free in the past, their deletions had little immediate consequence.

Surprisingly, in view of the attacks on religion during the Cultural Revolution, the 1975 document continued to guarantee the freedom to believe. However, it added the right *not* to believe and the right to propagate atheism. Certain other new rights were added as well, including the right to strike and the right to "speak out freely, air views fully, hold debates, and write big-character posters." The latter became known as the "four bigs," a short way of saying "the four big freedoms."

The procuracy, which had not functioned since the earliest days of the Cultural Revolution, was formally abolished by the 1975 constitution, and its functions were transferred to the ministry of public security. In view of the harsh criticisms leveled at public security organs during the Cultural Revolution, one must assume that the ministry had been thoroughly reorganized and revolutionized by 1975. The 1954 constitution's provision for judicial independence was dropped, and the courts were made subordinate to the control of the political leadership, as opposed to people's congresses, at corresponding levels. The 1975 document formalized the position of the mass line in judicial work and allowed for mass trials in major counterrevolutionary cases.

As of the time of Mao Zedong's death in 1976, most offenses and disputes were handled by extrajudicial institutions such as party committees and public security organs. In urban areas, many of the latter had come under the influence of radical elements who were positioning themselves for the post-Mao power struggle. They had been absorbing militia and even fire-fighting functions as well (see Chapter 5). The potential for abuse was clear, and official sources from this period record a number of instances of individuals receiving harsh sentences for real or imagined insults to pictures of Mao and of public security units imposing, rather rudely, their own notions of proper revolutionary clothing and hairstyles on ordinary citizens. Since urban public security units were also the foot-soldiers in a high-level ideological power struggle, punishments were often meted out to those whose political views were regarded as insufficiently orthodox. The verdict against Deng Xiaoping after the Tiananmen incident of April 1976 is merely the most spectacular of these.

Interestingly, foreign visitors to the PRC, perhaps reflecting a weariness with time-consuming attention to the fine points of law, its arcane jargon, and the too-frequent resort to the court system that characterize many Western societies, were generally favorably impressed with the Chinese system of justice.[7] It soon became apparent, however, that large numbers of Chinese did not share their views.

Law and Justice in the Post-Mao Era:
Return to the Jural Model

With Deng Xiaoping's return to power, the PRC's legal system abruptly changed its emphasis again, toward the jural model. Deng's reasons were partly economic and partly personal. From an economic point of view, Deng realized that Chinese entrepreneurs needed protection for both their individual rights and those of their businesses if they were to risk breaking so sharply from past practices. In addition, foreign companies required codes and other guarantees before they would feel comfortable investing in the PRC or trading with it on any significant scale. From a personal point of view, Deng wished to overturn the legal system that had twice in one decade punished him so harshly. Not surprisingly, one of the earlier verdicts to be reversed was that on the Tiananmen incident of April 1976. Henceforth, said the official directive, demonstrators were to be referred to as revolutionary heroes rather than counterrevolutionaries.

The rapid nature of the party's reversal of legal policy, though receiving overwhelming popular support, needed to be explained to the masses, who had for so long been indoctrinated with principles that were exactly the opposite of those that now prevailed. An early 1979 article in *Guangming Ribao*, a newspaper targeted at intellectuals, struggled to explain the erroneous nature of the "long-held viewpoint that party policy itself is law." After some rather tortured reasoning ("Laws, as national will, are assured of implementation under state compulsion. Party policy itself has no such character"), the author concluded that

> Simply equating party policy with national law would naturally encourage the use of commandism and imposing orders on others. People might freely put any kind of party policy in the form of law, abuse state power, and rely on the order of superiors to do things. Thus, they would neglect to do necessary patient and conscientious ideological work. One of the most directly harmful effects of equating party policy with state law in lawmaking work is to deny the necessity of legislation.[8]

This somewhat unconvincing rationalization notwithstanding, China in the period from 1978 to 1982 successively adopted two new state constitutions, codified a number of important laws, restructured its judicial system, reinstituted the legal profession, and gave renewed attention to legal research and legal education.

The New Legal System

In March 1978, a new state constitution was adopted, replacing that of 1975. More akin to the 1954 constitution than its immediate predecessor, the 1978 document restored the procuracy and required public security personnel to obtain the approval of the judiciary or the procuracy before making an arrest. Local procuracies and courts were made responsible only to people's congresses at corresponding levels, not to their executive organs as well, as had been the case in the 1975 constitution. The accused was again assured of the right to defense and to an open trial. Many of the freedoms promised by the 1954 constitution were also revived, though that concerning the freedom to change residence was not. The leadership did not want to encourage the several million people who had been sent out to rural areas over the past two decades to return to their original homes. Many were desperate to do so. Later in 1978, a party plenary meeting reaffirmed the independence of the judiciary and the equality of all people before the law, regardless of class background.

The demands placed on the new legal system by millions of people who felt wronged under the old one threatened to overwhelm the system. In the 18 months between January 1978 and June 1979, people's courts reportedly examined 708,000 cases and found that more than 166,000 of them had involved false accusations. These 708,000 were the fortunate ones: Court dockets became so crowded, and trained legal personnel were so few, that a large number of plaintiffs faced long delays. Suspicion grew that many cases might never be heard at all; some of the people who were affected believed it was because the authorities simply did not care about the persons involved. Others had reason to suspect that their cases were so potentially disruptive to the social structure of the area that officials did not want to deal with them. Those whose cases were heard but had not been decided in their favor became disgruntled because they felt they had been denied justice yet again.

Both those who were annoyed at not having their cases heard and those who believed their cases had not been heard properly began to exercise their constitutional rights to strike and demonstrate. Hundreds of thousands of people flooded into Beijing and other major cities seeking redress. Their plight was documented by the foreign media rather too often for the taste of the leadership. During the following year, the government responded by removing the "four bigs" and right to strike from the constitution. It was explained that these rights were, after all, a creation of the hated Gang of Four. Moreover, officials added, people's rights were now adequately protected in other ways; to put these rights in the constitution was rather like "adding legs to the picture of a snake"—completely unnecessary.

Others, however, argued that the leadership's actions showed that they regarded human rights not as a birthright but as merely *instrumental* or *bureaucratic*. As such, rights can be dispensed with whenever they do not seem to serve the needs of public policy. In fact, if one accepts the concept of human rights as instrumental, the public interest may *require* their suspension. In this case, and in those of subsequent mass demonstrations, it could be—and was—argued that China's major goal is economic development and the creation of national prosperity. Since demonstrations disrupt social stability and normal economic activities, they are inimical to the national interest and subversive in nature. Those who back such subversive activities are therefore counterrevolutionaries. A Western analyst who has spent many years researching this area concludes that the general public in China appears to accept the view that the value of human rights lies in their instrumentality.[9]

This retreat notwithstanding, the leadership continued its commitment to the institutionalization of a formal system of justice. The constitution adopted in 1982, and still in force, describes China as a "people's democratic dictatorship" rather than a "dictatorship of the proletariat." It not only reinstated the 1954 constitution's provision that no deputy to the NPC might be arrested or tried without the consent of the NPC or its standing committee, but added a clause exempting deputies from prosecution for speeches or votes at NPC meetings. People's courts and procuracies were not to be subject to interference by administrative organs, public organizations, or individuals, though it should be noted that, since the communist party is not one of these, it is not restricted by the provision.[10] The implication seems to be that, although the party has both the right and the duty to give general direction to lawmaking, it should not normally be involved in the day-to-day operations of the legal system. Party leaders have consistently described the concept of the separation of powers as bourgeois in origin and unsuitable for China. They have also pointed out that to have each branch of the government go its own way is conducive to inconsistent and confusing policies, with the potential for creating chaos.

The 1982 constitution also puts more emphasis on individual rights than its 1978 counterpart. Major new additions are the inviolability of the personal dignity of PRC citizens and the prohibition against insult, libel, false charges, and slander. Also prohibited are unlawful deprivation or restriction of citizens' freedom of person by detention or other means, and unlawful searches. Trials are to be public, except under special circumstances. However, the 1982 constitution also added new duties for citizens: They must safeguard state secrets and refrain from infringing upon the interests "of the state, of society, and of the collective, or upon the lawful freedoms and rights of other citizens." All of these have the potential to be used to restrict individual freedoms.

Conspicuous among the freedoms of the 1954 constitution that have not been reinstated is the right to change residence. The leadership, understandably concerned about the possibility of massive population movements disrupting the PRC's economic and social systems, presumably does not wish to give those who might be contemplating such moves a legal right to call upon. However, as will be seen in Chapter 11, tens of millions of people have been able to change their residences in the past decade even without a constitutional guarantee to back them up.

In 1986, concerned that many people were committing crimes out of a genuine ignorance of the new system, the government began an education drive to eradicate what it called "legal illiteracy." The legal education campaign, as it came to be known, employed radio broadcasts, lecturers being sent out to peasant areas during the slack farming season, and local art forms like ballad singing, storytelling, comic dialogues, and traditional clapper talks and cross talks. The last two have no exact counterparts in the West, but are roughly comparable to minstrel shows. Videotapes on the new legal system were also made and disseminated. The legal education campaign produced the huge statistical claims normally made for such productions: 640 million people had reportedly taken part by 1989.[11] What people actually learned from participation in the legal education campaign is not so easily measured, nor is whether and how much the campaign helped to dispel popular distrust of the legal system.

The 1982 constitution has been amended three times: in 1988, 1993, and 1999. In general, the additions were motivated by the evolution of the economic system begun by Deng Xiaoping. The 1988 revisions enhanced the legal status of those who engaged in private business, and sanctioned the transfer of land-use rights. The 1993 addition to the constitution also related to economic reform and opening up. Proposed just after Deng's tour of the Shenzhen Special Economic Zone (see p. 159), they made more explicit the commitment to reform and opening up. 1999's amendments gave legal protection to private enterprise, recognized the validity of multiple forms of ownership, declared that the government must use laws to rule the country, and added Deng Xiaoping Thought to the previous wording of the constitution which declared that the country "is ruled by Marxism-Leninism and the Thought of Mao Zedong." Analysts saw these changes as attempting to bolster private enterprises that could create jobs for the growing number of workers who were being laid-off by state enterprises.[12]

Legal Developments

Within the framework provided by Deng Xiaoping's instructions and the successive new constitutions, a large number of changes were made in the judicial system within a very short time. In addition to the Supreme Court and higher, intermediate, and basic-level people's courts, specialized courts have been founded to handle military, maritime, and railway matters, respectively (see Figure 8.1). The functions of the first two are obvious; the last has jurisdiction over criminal cases that occur along rail lines and aboard trains as well as cases of economic disputes related to rail transportation.

The main responsibility of the Supreme Court is to supervise the administration of justice by lower courts at various levels, and by the special courts. The Supreme Court actually considers very few cases. Since the PRC was founded, it has tried only the cases of

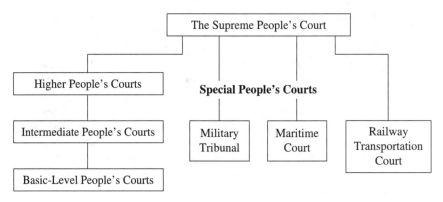

FIGURE 8.1   Organizational System of the People's Courts of the PRC
Source: Adapted from Zhang Min and Shan Changzong, "Inside China's Court System," *Beijing Review,* November 5–11, 1990, p. 16.

Japanese war criminals and a handful of others that are considered especially important, such as that of the Gang of Four.[13] China's Supreme Court is not empowered to determine the constitutionality of legislation or of government policies. Rather, it draws up explanations of how a given law should be interpreted or applied.

The Supreme People's Court and the Supreme People's Procuracy each publish a quarterly gazette containing interpretations of laws and model cases. Still, most research into the interpretation and application of laws is actually carried out by specialized institutes and published in books and journals sponsored by them. For example, the Legal Research Institute of the Chinese Academy of Social Sciences publishes a bimonthly review, and the East China Political–Legal Institute issues a similar publication monthly. The ministry of justice puts out a weekly update on its activities. Legal dictionaries have been published, and official legal gazettes appear regularly.

The Trial Process

People's courts at each level are composed of a president, vice-presidents, presiding judges, deputy presiding judges, and a number of ordinary judges. The first instance at people's courts may be handled by judges or by a collegiate bench formed jointly by judges and a people's jury. Judges receive no special training, nor is there an examination for them to take. On-the-job experience is considered important. Educational standards, though low, are improving. In 1995, only 5 percent of the PRC's judges had a four-year college degree of any sort; by 2002, nearly 10 percent had college degrees in law. Non-legally trained judges include demobilized soldiers, former clerks, and vehicle drivers. Whatever their backgrounds, Chinese sources describe judges' salaries and social status as low.[14]

Jurors, sometimes called people's assessors, may be elected by their people's congress or selected by their work units or other groups. They enjoy equal rights with judges, and can examine the files of a case, verify facts and evidence, and interrogate the parties to the case and all witnesses. They have the right to decide on a case, together with the judges, and to sign the court decision. Any citizen who has reached the age of 23 and is eligible to vote and stand for election may serve as a people's assessor. The presence of assessors is meant to ensure that judges do not reach biased or subjective decisions; it also aims at bringing to the ordinary person a sense of participation in the political process.

The accused has the right to a lawyer, and also the right to defend himself or to ask one of his relatives to do so. Until the late 1990s, a lawyer's loyalty was expected to be with the collective interests of the people rather than with his or her client. Once a case reaches the trial stage, the accused is assumed to be guilty. In fact, since leniency is frequently accorded to those who confess and show remorse, continued insistence on one's innocence is likely to produce a more severe sentence than admitting guilt would. The purpose of the courts is thus not to determine guilt or innocence but to decide on punishment. In the five years between 1987 and 1992, only 0.4 percent of cases resulted in acquittal; 34.5 percent of criminals received severe sentences, defined as those of more than five years to life and including execution, for which no separate figures were given; 63.3 percent were sentenced to terms of less than five years in prison or placed under detention and surveillance; and 1.4 percent were exempted from penalties.[15]

It is possible to appeal one's sentence by having it referred to a higher-level court, though in practice this is rarely done. If the procuracy finds errors in the judgment made by the lower courts, it can counter-plea. The court of second instance will then reexamine the case; its judgment is final. In sharp contrast to many foreign legal systems, justice is swift: Executions have been carried out within an hour of sentencing. Even when the sentence is appealed (in the case of the death penalty, an appeal is supposed to be automatic), the final disposition of the case may be accomplished within one week.

Although the constitution provides for public trial except under special circumstances, there are varying interpretations about what constitutes an open trial. Tickets are issued in accordance with the number of seats in the courtroom but may mysteriously have all been given out some time before the proceedings begin. Foreigners, including journalists, are not normally able to attend trials. In June 1998, courts were ordered to open to the nonforeign public; presenting an identity card was henceforth to be the sole prerequisite for admission. However, few people have thusfar actually exercised their right to attend trials, and judges seem uncomfortable with the presence of those who do.

Other departures from constitutional and criminal-code guarantees also occur. Although the government apparently intended its trial of the Gang of Four in 1980 to demonstrate China's commitment to a just legal system to the world, most international observers regarded the proceedings as carefully stage-managed to achieve maximum publicity for verdicts that had been predetermined. The trial of Democracy Wall dissident Wei Jingsheng had the same effect.

Several people who were arrested after the quelling of the spring 1989 demonstrations in Tiananmen Square appeared to have been beaten. And the trial of one dissident was accompanied by charges of blatant evidence-tampering. Lawyers complained that they had not been allowed to interview the witnesses for the prosecution. None of the witnesses appeared in court, and therefore could not be cross-examined. Several had been told to leave Beijing before the trial began. The witnesses' statements were contained on tape recordings believed to have been surreptitiously made by public security personnel and then edited. Even granting their admissibility as evidence, none of the statements on the tapes had characterized the activities of the accused as counterrevolutionary or seditious. He was nonetheless convicted, and sentenced to concurrent jail terms of thirteen years for attempting to overthrow the government and two years for making counter-revolutionary propaganda and instigation.

Mediation

The great majority of cases—on the order of 90 percent or more—are not handled by courts at all, but through the mediation process. There is widespread distrust of the court system, which is also perceived as being unnecessarily bureaucratic and slow-moving despite the speed with which it moves once a case is actually brought to trial. Many people also believe that there is a loss of face involved in resorting to the court system: Individuals should be able to resolve their problems among themselves, and an inability to do so may be perceived as a failing on their part. There is also the feeling that more serious cases, including physical violence and major theft, often arise out of less serious disputes that might have been resolved through mediation before tempers grew too short. These might include disputes within families, or among neighbors over the division of labor or property rights. Especially in urban areas, crowding is a serious problem. Three-generation families may occupy a one-bedroom apartment and share kitchen and toilet facilities with a number of other families. The frictions that may arise in such situations are easily imaginable.

Yet another reason for reluctance to resort to the court system is the attention that it may call to oneself. If an expensive object, such as costly jewelry or an imported wristwatch, disappears, public security personnel may decide to focus their attention on how the owner managed to obtain the item in the first place.

Mediation can be conducted by a variety of different groups. It is even applied during court proceedings, where it can be used as early in the process as immediately after the facts are investigated or as late as the court of second instance in handling appeals. Agreement may be reached with the help of one judge or the collegiate bench. After the litigants reach an agreement, a document is drafted specifying the terms. If agreement cannot be reached, or if one of the parties refuses to accept the mediation document, the court will make a judgment. Most mediation is conducted outside the court system, for reasons discussed previously. One's work unit, people's mediation committees, or street committees in one's neighborhood may take on the task. Street committees were typically composed of retired men and women who volunteered for the task—"energetic busybodies . . . who poke into all kinds of family disputes and tussles between neighbors."[16] While some people appear to genuinely appreciate the services they perform, others regard the presence of street committees as an unwanted intrusion. They are colloquially referred to by various names including "small feet inspection teams,"—not because they walk so quietly but because when they were founded in the early 1950s, most of the elderly women who formed the majority of their membership had had their feet bound as children—or "eight grannies with seven teeth."

Given the crowded living conditions in China, it is difficult to keep secrets. When neighbors fight, street-committee members will hear about it and step in to try to resolve differences. Disputes that are deemed serious and likely to have larger implications are recorded in a logbook kept in the street-committee office. Members also keep watch for robbers, stop children from misbehaving, conduct political study sessions to keep people abreast of new party policies, and try to mediate family quarrels. One street-committee member described her organization's goal as "educating people to live harmoniously and act peacefully."[17]

In one case, a man whose wife threatened to divorce him called on the street committee's services; within hours, a team of elderly women had assembled in the couple's apartment to discuss her grievances. On hearing that one of the wife's problems had been that she had had to perform her husband's tasks during his frequent business trips out of town, the ladies offered to help. They even bought heavy pails of coal and delivered them to the apartment. The committee also reminded the wife that she should try to settle her differences with her husband for the sake of the couple's three children.

In another instance, a foreigner visiting Shanghai noticed an elderly woman rush from her apartment to break up a street fight. She ordered the young toughs involved to meet with her immediately to resolve the dispute once and for all; they complied. The observer attributed a great deal of the neighborhood teams' success to the enforced immobility of urban life in China.[18] In a number of urban areas, the greater freedom of movement engendered by Deng Xiaoping's economic reforms led to loosened social controls. Some welcomed the greater degree of privacy, while others became uneasy because they felt less safe.

In addition to their mediation function, street committees served as adjuncts to public security work. For example, while public security personnel are not supposed to search one's home without a warrant, no such laws apply to street-committee members. They can arrive at any time to inspect an apartment for illegal goods or residents, and report their findings to the public security bureau.[19] Needless to say, serving as an informant can make one unpopular. Not only committee members but even public security personnel have suffered the wrath of their victims and those who sympathize with the victims. In 1991, the director of the Supreme People's Procurate urged that informers be protected against vengeful acts. In some cases, those informed upon had hired assassins in retaliation. Others had had life made difficult for them in various ways, referred to as "being given tight shoes to wear." Often this took forms which were very difficult to link directly to retaliatory behavior. There are, after all, many reasons besides a desire for revenge why a person might be demoted in rank or transferred to a less desirable area. Here as well mediation might be applied.

Experimental efforts are being made to update the neighborhood communities, staffing them with younger professionals rather than retirees. Several motives are involved. First, with the old work unit system and the social services it used to perform in decay, it is hoped that neighborhood committees can take over the tasks the work unit used to perform. A second reason is to put the communist party back in touch with people at the most basic level of society. And, finally, authorities want the committees to report on the activities of the country's increasingly outspoken and mobile population—informing them, for example, of the presence of illegal migrants, members of suspect organizations, or unusual occurrences of any sort.[20]

The Penal System

For those who are convicted, a number of different sentences may be applied. Several dozen crimes are punishable by death.[21] In addition to murder, these include bribing public security personnel, distributing pornography, luring women into prostitution, embezzlement, and damaging state property such as railways or dikes. Except for murder, where the death penalty is normally applied, only extreme instances of these crimes are actually punished by death. The majority of those executed are convicted of murder, rape, or robbery of large sums of money, estimated by one Western reporter at six thousand dollars or more. Political offenders are not normally executed, although at least one person is known to have received the death penalty for attacking a military vehicle during the PLA's suppression of the demonstrations during the spring of 1989. The usual method of execution is by a bullet to the back of the head; the family of the offender may be billed for the cost of the bullet. As will be seen on p. 188, the option of lethal injection has been introduced.

While some Chinese are critical of the legal procedures that lead to a sentence of execution, there is no objection to capital punishment in itself. Most people believe that it is necessary as a deterrent against serious crimes and are genuinely perplexed at hearing that in some other countries execution is considered a cruel and unusual punishment.

Those who receive lesser sentences may serve their time at a number of different institutions: prisons, labor reform discipline production detachments, reeducation-through labor camps,[22] juvenile-offender disciplinary camps, reformatories, and forced job-placement camps. According to the Chinese penal code, prisons are for those sentenced to death but who have a reprieve, counterrevolutionaries with sentences of five years to life, common criminals sentenced to terms of over ten years, and special cases including spies, foreign criminals, criminals with knowledge of classified material, and female criminals. The rest go to labor camps. Public security organs may also consign people to reeducation through labor *without* reference to the courts. Such administrative sanctions are commonly used for individuals who are considered politically or socially deviant. The latter include people who refuse to work or to comply with job transfers, and troublemakers who refuse to correct themselves despite repeated criticism.[23]

Special facilities are provided for juvenile offenders who are between the ages of 13 and 18. Offenders below the age of 13 are generally returned to their families, who are enjoined to keep them under better control. In exceptional circumstances, as when the parents are believed to be responsible for their offspring's aberrant behavior, children may be removed from their custody. The juvenile court system, which began in 1986, is less confrontational than that for adults. Defendants can remain seated while answering questions, and may talk with their guardians and attorneys during recesses. Minors receive more lenient sentences, and judges are supposed to visit them in prison to check on their rehabilitation.[24]

Thirteen percent of the PRC's criminals are in prisons, and the remaining eighty-seven percent in labor camps (*laogai ying*). However, in the opinion of a former political prisoner who spent 19 years in various penal institutions, this elaborate nomenclature hides a much simpler reality. Except in name, there is no basic difference between prisons and labor reform camps.[25] It is estimated that there are at least 3,000 penal institutions in the PRC. While these are found in all areas of the country, one province, Qinghai, had a disproportionately high number, and became known as China's gulag. Cold, arid, and frequently beset by tornadoes, the province is renowned for its harsh living conditions. Qinghai borders no foreign country, thus reducing the possibility of an escapee fleeing China and receiving asylum abroad. Its sparse population includes a number of ethnic minorities who are apt to be unsympathetic to any Han Chinese and therefore do not welcome immigrants, even involuntary ones.[26] Hence there are serious obstacles deterring even the most motivated from attempting to escape Qinghai's camps.

Although the government portrays its prisons as humane institutions aiming at rehabilitation while providing good nutrition, medical care, exercise, and job training, former prisoners describe a completely different situation. Conditions are believed to be worst for major political prisoners. China acknowledges holding over 3,000 individuals for political offenses; Amnesty International believes that this is a small fraction of those actually incarcerated for such crimes. Beijing's Qincheng Prison is home to a number of these, many held in solitary confinement for long periods in tiny, poorly heated, and dimly lighted cells on near-starvation rations and without access to medical care. There is an exercise yard but some prisoners are denied the use of it. The facilities at Beijing Number 2 prison, southeast of the capital, are reputed to be even worse. Dissidents transferred there from Qincheng after the 1989 demonstrations reportedly occupied cubicles of a little over

12 square feet, with only a bed, a cold-water tap, and an open sewer for a toilet. Their food allowance was a little over five dollars a month, and their only reading matter was that produced by state-run publishing houses. The warden rejected families' requests to provide more varied titles.

One 1989 dissident, Han Dongfang, was deliberately thrown into a cell packed with people suffering from contagious diseases. He contracted a drug-resistant strain of tuberculosis and appears to have been released for medical treatment only because the government realized that his death would have major international repercussions . . . and then only when his family agreed to pay the medical bills. Perhaps the most famous dissident of all, Wei Jingsheng (see Chapter 6), had his 15-year sentence reduced by half a year after a major international human-rights effort, but was promptly taken back into custody when he continued to advocate human rights. Also in poor health, Wei was eventually released in response to international pressure and sent out of China. Another outspoken member of the Democracy Wall era, Liu Qing, was incarcerated for 11 years. He spent the first six years in isolation, during which he was beaten regularly in an effort to get him to admit to crimes he did not believe he committed. During the remainder, he was forced to sit on a small stool from 8 A.M. to 9 P.M. He was beaten if he moved a muscle, or if he tried to speak to other prisoners. Liu believes that the scrutiny of journalists and diplomats had actually helped improve the treatment of prisoners in the Beijing area, and that cases much worse than his occur regularly in the countryside.[27]

If official statistics are to be believed, the PRC's prison population is not exceptionally large by international standards, when considered on a per capita basis. As might be expected, the population of prisons and camps can rise rapidly during periods of mass campaigns for political orthodoxy, and also after party and government have decided to crack down on crime. Reform is to be accomplished through two means: first, study of political materials approved by the CCP, followed by oral and written self-criticisms, and second, the performance of hard labor. According to official statistics, recidivism rates are very low, about 6 or 7 percent,[28] depending on the time period being reported. However, a Hong Kong magazine, citing detailed mainland sources, says that the actual figure is over 83 percent.[29]

The basic form of the prison system is based on Soviet legal codes dating from 1933, but in China prisons are economic enterprises as well. Each facility is expected to be not only self-supporting, but to produce a profit for the state. In the words of one commentator, "the Chinese *laogai* is the Soviet gulag with thought reform and a profit motive."[30] Because of their dual functions, camps are under dual administration. The ministry of justice has responsibility for prisoners in their role as prisoners, and the relevant economic industry has responsibility for whatever commodity the camp produces: coal, textiles, tea, and the like. In keeping with this production function, each camp has its own production plan, accounting and purchasing departments, and so on. There are even two names: for example, the Xi'an Municipal Number One Prison might simultaneously be the Chang'an (Long Peace) Chemical Company.

Since prisons and camps are expected to be economically profitable, their profit and loss statements are an important criterion determining the success of their administrators' careers. If the facility is profitable, a portion of the proceeds may be divided among the prisoners as a bonus and, of course, an incentive to future hard work. Prisoners who do not meet work quotas may be denied permission to write their families or receive visits from them. In more extreme cases, they can have their food rations reduced, or be placed in solitary confinement. Even illness may not be an acceptable reason for low production, since one's supervisor may take the position of "no work, no food."

Because prisoners can be made to work for little more than basic subsistence and cannot leave to take other work or threaten to go on strike, the products of their labor can be sold for very low prices. Several Western nations have laws against importing the products of what they term slave labor. The Chinese government has vehemently denied that it exports items produced by prisoners, though this can be disputed by reference to official PRC publications.[31]

In 1991, the use of prison labor for export production became a major issue between China and the United States. An American television crew was able to secretly videotape several encounters between Chinese administrators and Westerners purporting to be interested in importing their products. At one point, when a putative buyer asked what would happen if the quality of the merchandise were not good, the Chinese interpreter replied that there would be no problem: prisoners would simply be beaten until the buyer was satisfied with the product. Several foreign businesses also report being approached by camp administrators who proposed setting up a joint venture with their factory. The dual names of the facility could be useful here, since its innocuous-sounding enterprise name could be used on export documents rather than the prison name. There have also been persistent reports of "organ harvesting," that is, prisons selling the organs of recently executed inmates to wealthy individuals who need transplants. Prison officials state that the inmate has freely consented to become a donor; family members and human rights groups question whether the individual's permission was actually obtained and, if it were, whether it was truly voluntary. A 1998 study of prisons in three northwestern provinces found that the systems differed markedly from one another, largely because of decisions made by provincial governments. Its authors conclude that prisons have not produced profits, and also that rehabilitation is rare.[32]

Although prison sentences are for a fixed period of time, one's term may be extended unless one shows repentance. The rationale is that those who do not sincerely regret what they have done are likely to resume their objectionable activities if released, and it is therefore preferable to shield society from them until they do repent. Even when one is released, there is no guarantee of being able to return to society. Inmates may remain at the very same camp in which they have served their sentences, under a system known as *liuchang jiuye*, or forced job placement. With the stigma of a prison record in their dossiers, their former employers are reluctant to accept them back; other employers may not want them either. In a number of cases, the offense for which they were assigned to camps in the first place was nothing more than loitering and unemployment.[33] Since work units and dossiers are less potent in controlling one's destiny than they used to be, forced job placement is less prevalent than previously. Nonetheless, the aim of the "reform-through-labor" system would appear to be thwarted by the reality that, for many people, it is not possible to reenter society as a fully functioning member.

While the harsh punishments described here would certainly seem sufficient to deter most people from committing any proscribed acts, such has not been the case. During the era of Maoist austerity, possession of items of conspicuous consumption—even so modest as hair ribbons or bottles of foreign liquor—could mark their owners as bourgeois and therefore the objects of struggle sessions. Money and material goods were therefore dangerous. When Deng Xiaoping declared that it was acceptable for some people to become rich before others, and that it was no crime to live well, many people were tempted to take chances. For example, responding to the government's encouragement for the formation of group cooperatives in the service industries, small hotels proliferated. Some of these came to be used for gambling, prostitution, smuggling, or other illegal activities. Smuggling was likewise facilitated by the increased exchange of goods between China and other countries, and by the larger number of tourists and businesspeople entering and leaving China.

As mentioned previously, Deng's economic reforms caused dossiers to lose some of their effectiveness as a method of social surveillance. Those with needed skills found that entrepreneurial companies tended to care more for bottom-line profits than prior pecadilloes and might not bother to check their files. For the wealthy, bribing the right official to change their dossiers is another possibility. Not everyone is able to exercise these options, however, and maintaining an impeccable, or at least an innocuous, dossier is still a desideratum. In 1994, the government loosened several of the restrictions in its residence registration system. This was in some sense bowing to the reality that Deng's economic reforms had enabled large numbers of people to circumvent its intent (see Chapter 11). Nonetheless, the modifications weakened yet another of the government's mechanisms of control.[34]

With party and government controls attenuated, other organizations became more important. Secret societies, which had scarcely been mentioned since the early days of the communist government, reappeared and began to play a prominent role in criminal activities. Because many of these societies had branches in different parts of China as well as in foreign countries, they were able to coordinate the movement of large sums of money and large quantities of goods around the country and beyond its borders. Some of this money and goods were used to bribe officials at various levels to ignore the societies' activities. In 1993, the PRC's minister of public security created a furor when he admitted that the police maintained links with the notorious Triad society, and had once even enlisted its aid in protecting a Chinese leader traveling abroad.[35] So-called "black societies" have laundered money through the PRC in the form of foreign investment, and cooperated with the Russian mafia to prey on merchants in the Russian Far East.

The rising crime rate, which included a marked increase in violent crime, became a major issue, both to the leadership and the ordinary person. It is difficult to compare crime statistics, since many acts that are classified as offenses in China are not legally actionable in other countries. Nonetheless, there is consensus that even the higher crime rate in China is relatively low compared with that in many other countries. What is more important to people in China, however, is not the international standard but what they perceive as a deterioration in their own situation. There have been a number of crackdowns on crime, but the incidence of crime has continued to increase. One reason is that criminals are too often able to bribe the police and other authorities, including those at the highest levels of party and government. Sometimes corrupt officials receive a percentage of the profits, becoming, in effect, rent-seekers on criminal activities. Several of the bribers have argued convincingly that, given the irrational nature of the economic system and the attitude of the authorities they have to deal with, it is impossible for a business to prosper unless its owner pays off the authorities.[36]

The legal developments of the 1990s and early twenty-first century reflect cross-cutting pressures on decision-makers. One goal is to placate the complaints of human rights activists, both foreign and domestic; a second, which is often in conflict with the first, is to respond to public demands to deal with the rising crime rate. Finally, but not least in importance, reforms should be carried out without surrendering party control over the judicial process.

In 1991, a Civil Procedure law was passed which, among other provisions, allowed class-action law suits. These have been used with some success by, for example, persons who have suffered loss of health and income from factories that pollute the environment. While the ability to bring class-action suits is clearly advantageous for would-be plaintiffs, it must be pointed out that such suits are most likely to be successful when they simultaneously benefit the central government. Beijing has found it difficult to control local officials and factory managers, and is pleased to throw its influence behind such class actions. By contrast, a class-action suit by aggrieved democracy activists or relatives of those killed by the military in the Tiananmen Square demonstrations of 1989 is not possible, at least under current conditions.

A law on lawyers promulgated in 1996 established the basis for attorneys to move from being state-subsidized legal workers to independent professionals responsible to their clients and to the law. As part of this responsibility, clients who were harmed by their lawyers' incompetence could claim compensation. The law also stipulated that lawyers must set aside an unspecified portion of their time to provide legal aid services to the poor. Some progress has taken place, occasionally from unlikely areas. For example, lawyers in Hebei's poor, rural Qianxi county helped one woman obtain a divorce from her abusive husband and convinced the parents of another that they could not forbid her to marry a man they did not approve of. But lack of funding is a severe problem—the Qianxi case is unusual because its women's federation had obtained a small grant from the U.S. Ford Foundation to set up its legal aid work. China's justice minister predicts that it will be at least 15 years before the PRC has a comprehensive public defender system.

A new criminal procedure law also went into effect in 1996. In a signal advance, it proclaimed that no one was to be considered guilty until he or she had been convicted by a court. The law also gave defendants greater access to lawyers and abolished the procedure of *shoushen,* or "sheltering for examination," under which police had been able to detain people for three months and even, in practice, much longer without charging them with any crime. Originally devised to prevent transient suspected criminals whose status and residence were not known from leaving, *shoushen* was frequently misused and had been criticized by both Chinese and foreigners concerned with human rights. The reform was not quite all it appeared to be, however. Sheltering for examination was abolished, but police were given the right to hold suspects without charge for up to seven months or, if the case was "complicated," indefinitely. Also, there is no requirement that defendants be told that they have a right to counsel: most people do not know, and are not told. Police also retain the right to attend lawyer-client meetings "as necessary." And, the rule that no one was to be considered guilty until convicted notwithstanding, the conviction rate remained above 99 percent.

During the following year, amendments to the criminal law substantially limited the scope under which the death penalty could be applied. An official explained that, although some Chinese and many Westerners considered the death penalty unacceptable, it had been retained because the overwhelming majority of Chinese strongly backed it. The new law restricted the use of the death penalty for larceny, which accounts for between 30 and 40 percent of convictions in Chinese courts and hence also accounted for a high percentage of death sentences. As amended, only larceny at banks or financial institutions, or where valuable cultural relics are involved, or in "extremely serious" cases will result in execution. What is or is not a valuable cultural relic or an extremely serious case can be a matter for debate. When former Beijing party chief Chen Xitong was sentenced to 16 years for massive corruption, many citizens expressed outrage, feeling that this was excessively lenient. Since an ordinary criminal would have been executed for such acts, they argued that Chen, who had betrayed the trust of the citizens he was responsible for, deserved no less.

The crime of counterrevolution was abolished, although this could be considered more cosmetic than real, since one can still be charged with "endangering state security." When someone who insisted on his right to run for office despite the opposition of local party leaders was arrested and charged with endangering state security, it began to appear that the new law might not be a big improvement over its predecessor. Shortly thereafter, a democracy activist was sentenced to nine years in prison for "prying into state secrets," when he attempted to collect information on the country's political prisoners. United Nations' human-rights activists have urged the PRC to better define "endangering national security" to keep it from being misused.

From 1997 on, criminals were no longer paraded through the streets on their way to the execution grounds. They could also choose lethal injection in preference to the standard bullet, though this practice does not appear to be widespread.

The PRC's entry into the World Trade Organization in 2002 also occasioned an elaboration of legal codes. New laws covering insurance, copyright, and government procurement took effect in 2003, as did a civil law code to protect private properties. New offenses were also added to the criminal law, including prostitution, money laundering, insider trading, breaking into information networks, creating computer viruses, inciting ethnic hatred, and committing terrorist acts.

While applauding the sentiments behind the new laws, experts pointed out that there were problems in making them work properly. The president of the PRC's Supreme Court noted three major concerns:

- Local governments control the establishment, funding, and personnel of judicial organs, allowing them to interfere with judicial procedures. Because of this local protectionism, litigants from other areas find their cases postponed indefinitely so that "they disappear like rocks dropped into the sea." China's chief procurator lamented that law enforcement personnel from other areas have been attacked, beaten, and/or detained when they tried to investigate irregularities.
- Party and government officials treat the judiciary as an administrative body. For example, they obstruct investigations into construction irregularities for fear that it will affect approval of future projects and therefore harm economic development in their jurisdictions.
- The poor level of education and training of lawyers, procurators, and police results in low professional standards. Proper legal procedures are either ignored or circumvented.[37] In some cases, personnel have divulged confidential information to units or individuals that law-enforcement departments are investigating.

Given these circumstances, it is not surprising that the new laws do not function as human rights advocates wish them to. For example, although the 1996 Criminal Procedures Law adopts the presumption of innocence, expands the right to counsel, and increases the role of the courts so as to eliminate the prior practice of pre-trial determination of guilt, public security organs can detain for up to 30 days those "strongly suspected of wandering around committing crimes, of committing multiple crimes, or of forming gangs to commit crimes." The requirement for public security organs to inform detainees' families of the reasons for detention and the place of custody within 24 hours after the individual is detained may be waived if police believe it could hinder the investigation or if they have no way to notify the families. Police may also deny that the suspect is actually being detained, saying he or she is being "accommodated" (forcibly) in a guest house run by the police, for which the individual is required to pay room and board. The person thus accommodated is warned that, should she wish to protest, she risks being actually charged.

Also, although lawyers are now able to call witnesses, almost none wish to appear in court and many do not even want to be interviewed. Since lawyers have no way to make them cooperate, cross-examination is impossible and the entire investigative process may become a sham. Lawyers who become too insistent or too successful in unpopular cases may themselves be jailed on trumped-up charges that are difficult to disprove. They are especially vulnerable to such treatment in cases with high political salience, whether at central government or local level. Bar associations do exist, but they are weak and have thus-far been ineffective in protecting the professional rights of their members.

Additionally, reform-through-labor continues to exist. Since it is not considered a criminal procedure, it is not subject to any of the human rights safeguards of the Criminal Law and Criminal Procedures Law. Moreover, punishment under reform-through-labor can be more severe than if the offense were considered a criminal act. Currently, an estimated 300,000 people are being held in the PRC's nearly 300 reform-through-labor camps, at least a thousand of whom are supporters of the proscribed Falungong movement. They may be held for up to four years.

Although it is not legal, torture is used to extract confessions from recalcitrant suspects, some of whom are not guilty. It is impossible to tell how widespread this practice is. A number of factors of involved. Given popular concern with rising crime, police are more concerned with cracking cases than they are about abusing suspects. Second, given their meager training in investigative techniques and forensic science, the police have few other ways to get a suspect to confess. One expert, recalling the French chief inspector in the classic film Casablanca, refers to this as the Claude Raines theory of police work: round up the usual suspects and beat them until someone confesses. And, finally, so long as confessions extracted through torture remain admissible in court proceedings, laws forbidding torture will exist in name only.[38]

In announcing these new laws, party and government officials emphasized that they were not to be interpreted as a softening on attitudes on crime: the fight against lawlessness would be pursued vigorously. The "strike hard" campaigns that were introduced in 1996 put police under pressure to produce results, and civil liberties inevitably suffered. More than two thousand executions were reported in the course of a few months. Human-rights activists pointed out that this was yet another example of the subordination of law to politics: a crime was a crime whenever it was committed, and should carry the same sentence. The implication of the "strike hard" campaign was that crimes might have been prosecuted softly the year before the campaign, or would be prosecuted softly the year after it. The campaign also seems to have been used as a convenient tool to arrest and incarcerate those suspected of ethnic separatism, political activism, and practicing religion in non-state-sanctioned settings.

The average Chinese, however, regards the threat to her or his civil liberties as less worrisome than the rising crime rate. As a form of protest, against lawlessness, delegates to such bodies as provincial assemblies and even the National People's Congress have abstained or voted against the report of the judiciary and procuracy. Black marketeering continues to increase, as does the kidnapping of women. The kidnappers typically rape the women so they will be unacceptable as brides in their native areas, and then force them into prostitution or sell them to desperate farmers who have been unable to find wives in the more normal fashion. Children are abducted and sold to childless couples. Bus and railway passengers report being stopped at barricades set up by armed gangs, who then relieve them of their valuables. People on long-distance trains have had their tea drugged and wake to find themselves without wallets, jewelry, and baggage.

Organized gangs proliferated; in Nanjing, four gangs reportedly divided the city into "turf" for each. In some areas, villagers were turning to local strongmen to deal with their problems and disputes, completely circumventing the party apparatus. Secret societies also provided an alternate channel of authority and decision-making. Concern was expressed over the incidence of clan feuds. More and more often, clan heads and religious leaders were turned to as arbiters, sometimes even by the party organization itself. In Hebei, after peasants had refused to sell their harvest to the state and public security personnel proved powerless to persuade them, the authorities had to ask the help of the local priest. Not least among the justice ministry's problems was corruption in the police force and judicial system.

Nonetheless, the fact that more people have been using the courts to settle certain types of grievances indicates that there is a degree of public confidence in the system. For example, one factory successfully sued another for copyright infringement, and farmers won a suit against what they believed to be exorbitant levies by the township government. A writer whose works were censored by a state-run publishing house won compensation for damages, as did an actress when a magazine ran a photograph which superimposed her head above a nude body.

Conclusions

During the past 25 years, China has done much to establish the jural model of law, to stress rule by law rather than the rule of the party line or that of particular personalities, and to construct a more equitable and predictable system of criminal justice than has existed since the PRC was founded. The jural model is now firmly established; in contrast to the experience of the Mao years, it is unlikely to be reversed. Party control over the judicial system has weakened, and erosion is likely to continue. However, it should not be assumed that there will be an automatic evolution toward a Western-style legal system. There has been a shift toward a system with what one expert calls the basic elements of a thin rule by law, but little evidence of a rule of law that includes liberal democracy and gives priority to civil and political rights. He predicts that the PRC is more likely to evolve in a statist, socialist neo-authoritarian direction.[39] At least at present, China's legal system appears to more closely resemble the expectations of the communist neo-traditionalist model than pluralist expectations of liberalism.

Although Deng and Jiang's legal reforms are generally regarded as a significant improvement over the legal nihilist views of the Cultural Revolution, the instrumental-bureaucratic view of law runs counter to the legal relationship of state and society that a market-oriented economy and civil society would seem to require.[40] In several important respects, the PRC's legal system is not like that prevalent in the West. For example, the judiciary is not independent, the presumption of innocence for the accused is not well-established, decisions are made much more quickly and with fewer opportunities for review, and mediation plays a much greater role than in the West. The Chinese legal system, though successful in crushing human rights at its highest levels, may nonetheless be moving in the direction of producing an effective system of control over abuses of human rights by intermediate administrative officials.[41]

How important it is to have a universal legal system is a controversial matter among scholars. Some take a relativist position, saying that while the PRC's legal system would not be suitable for much of the rest of the world, it is nonetheless admirably suited to China. Others argue that human rights are mankind's birthright, not subject to restriction on the basis of alleged cultural differences.[42] Since each side feels very strongly about its views, this is not a controversy that can easily be resolved. What is clear, however, is that in many important ways, the current Chinese legal system does not live up to its own standards, as defined by its constitution and judicial codes. This is not to argue that aberrations of justice do not occur in other systems, but simply to state that the PRC's leadership seems to have actually supported the use of torture, tampering with evidence, and preordained verdicts in a number of trials involving sensitive political issues. And neighborhood committees are able to help public security personnel to circumvent the need for search warrants.

Other aspects of judicial miscarriage, which the government decidedly does not support but seems to have limited power to control, are the recent trend toward local authorities making their own law, especially in rural areas, and the increasing tendency of local courts to protect local interests regardless of the legal rights and wrongs involved. To the extent that these localist trends continue, China will be moving away from rather than closer to the equitable and predictable system of justice that Deng Xiaoping aimed to establish.

Notes

1. This model was first enunciated in Leng Shaochuan and Hungdah Chiu, *Criminal Justice in Post-Mao China: Analysis and Documents* (Albany: State University of New York Press, 1985). The analysis in this chapter closely follows Leng and Chiu's model.

2. Patricia E. Griffin, *The Chinese Communist Treatment of Counterrevolutionaries: 1924–1949* (Princeton, N.J.: Princeton University Press, 1976).

3. Nicholas D. Kristof, "Personal File and Worker Yoked for Life," *New York Times*, March 16, 1992, p. A4.

4. It is also possible to see links with the debate between Confucianists and Legalists on the merits of *li* and *fa*. See Ronald C. Keith, "Chinese Politics and the New Theory of 'Rule of Law,'" *China Quarterly*, March 1991, p. 116.

5. Jerome Alan Cohen, "Will China Have a Formal Legal System?" *American Bar Association Journal*, vol. 64, October 1978, p. 1511.

6. Quoted in Hungdah Chiu, *Chinese Law and Justice: Trends Over Three Decades,* Occasional Paper no. 7 (Baltimore: University of Maryland School of Law, 1982), p. 14.

7. See, for example, Victor H. Li, *Law Without Lawyers: A Comparative View of Law in China and the United States* (Boulder, Colo.: Westview Press, 1978), for a summary of these favorable views.

8. Sun Guohua, "The Relationship Between Party Policy and Law," *Guangming Ribao,* February 24, 1979, p. 3, in *FBIS–CHI,* March 6, 1979, pp. E/5–E/6.

9. The source has asked to remain anonymous.

10. The author is indebted to Professor Hungdah Chiu of the University of Maryland Law School for pointing this out.

11. Wu Naitao, "Disseminating the Law Among Citizens," *Beijing Review,* July 30–August 5, 1990, pp.17–20.

12. Ian Johnson, "Beijing Moves To Help Protect Private Enterprises," *Asian Wall Street Journal Weekly,* February 8–14, 1999, p. 4.

13. Zhang Min and Shan Changzong, "Inside China's Court System," *Beijing Review,* November 5–11, 1990, p. 16.

14. Yang Kaixiang, "A Comparative Study of Judges' Status," *Faxue (Legal Studies),* Shanghai, April 10, 1993, pp. 45–47.

15. Ren Jianxin, "Supreme People's Court Work Report," March 22, 1993, in *FBIS–CHI,* April 7, 1993, p. 18.

16. Sheryl WuDunn, "In the Cities of China, the Busybodies Are Organized and Are Busy Indeed," *New York Times,* March 13, 1991, p. A4.

17. Ibid.

18. This scene was reported by Professor James Nafziger.

19. Fox Butterfield, *Alive in the Bitter Sea* (New York: Times Books, 1982), p. 325.

20. Erik Eckholm, "China's Neighborly Snoops Reinvent Themselves," *New York Times,* April 11, 2000, p. A7.

21. Bao Suixian, "Reform of China's Death Penalty System," *Faxue,* June 10, 1993, p. 17.

22. Technically, reeducation-through-labor camps are not considered part of the penal system. I am indebted to Professor Hungdah Chiu for this information.

23. Hungdah Chiu, "China's Changing Criminal Justice System," *Current History,* September 1988, pp. 268–271.

24. Chang Hong, "Juvenile Justice: Change of Venue To Reduce Crime," *China Daily* (Beijing), April 22, 1992, p. 1.

25. Harry Wu, "*Laogai*: The Chinese Gulag," *Human Rights Tribune* (New York), vol. 2, no. 1, February 1991, p. 3.

26. There is one known exception to this, described in Wu Ning, *Red in Tooth and Claw* (New York: Grove Press, 1993), pp. 107–116.

27. Michael Kaufman, "Memories of Prison in China and Enduring for Democracy," *New York Times,* March 31, 1993, p. A17.

28. See, for example, *Xinhua,* September 17, 1991, in *FBIS–CHI,* September 18, 1991, p. 16.

29. Kung Wen, "Recidivism Rate of Released Criminals Under Reform or Reeducation Through Labor Reaches More Than 80 Percent," *Ming Pao* (Hong Kong), September 9, 1991, p. 9.

30. Steven W. Mosher, *Made in the Chinese Laogai: China's Use of Prisoners to Produce Goods for Export* (Montclair, Calif.: The Claremont Institute, 1990), pp. 1–2.

31. For example, the yearbooks of Yunnan province in 1986 and Guangxi province in 1987 specify which products are sold abroad and to what countries. The relevant sections are translated in *FBIS–CHI,* May 17, 1991, pp. 22–24.

32. James Seymour and Richard Anderson, *New Ghosts, Old Ghosts: Prisons and Labor Reforms in China* (Armonk, N.Y.: M.E. Sharpe, 1998), Chapter 7.

33. See, for example, Jay Mathews, "China Revives Labor Camp System," *Washington Post,* June 1, 1980, pp. A1, A27.

34. Kristof, "Personal File."

35. Nicholas Kristof, "China Police Are Linked to Gangs in Hong Kong," *New York Times,* April 9, 1993, p. A7.

36. Bruce Gilley, *Model Rebels: The Rise and Fall of China's Richest Village* (Berkeley: University of California Press, 2001) provides a generally sympathetic treatment of this issue. A similar argument is found in Seth Faison, "China's Paragon of Corruption: Meet Mr. Chu, a Hero to Some, an Embezzler to Others," *New York Times,* March 6, 1998, pp. C1;C4.

37. Daniel Kwan, "Judiciary Plans Changes to Counter Interference," *South China Morning Post,* December 10, 2002.

38. Murray Scot Tanner, Prepared Statement to Congressional-Executive Commission on China, July 26, 2002, www.cecc.gov

39. Randy Peerenboom, "The Long, Steady March of China's Legal System," *South China Morning Post,* January 6, 2003.

40. Murray Scot Tanner, "The Erosion of Communist Party Control over Lawmaking in China," *China Quarterly,* no. 138, June 1994, p. 401.

41. Margaret L. K. Woo, "Courts, Justice, and Human Rights," in William Joseph, ed., *China Briefing 1992* (Boulder, Colo.: Westview Press, 1993), p. 98.

42. Victor Li's *Law Without Lawyers,* cited in endnote 7, is an extreme example of legal relativism; Amnesty International argues for the universality of human rights and the incorporation thereof in a country's legal system.

Suggestions for Further Reading

United States Congressional-Executive Commission on China, *China's Criminal Justice System*, Round-table, July 26, 2002. Includes testimony by Jerome Cohen, Murray Scot Tanner, Veron Mei-ying Lung, and Jonathan Hecht. www.cecc.gov

Stanley Lubman, *Bird In A Cage: Legal Reform In China After Mao* (Stanford, Calif.: Stanford University Press, 2000).

Randy Peerenboom, *China's Long March Toward Rule of Law* (Cambridge, U.K.: Cambridge University Press, 2002).

Murray Scot Tanner, "The Erosion of Communist Party Control Over Lawmaking in China," *China Quarterly*, no.138, June 1994, pp. 381–403.

Qianfan Zhang, "The People's Court in Transition," *Journal of Contemporary China*, vol. 12, no. 34, February 2003, pp. 69–101.

9 The Role of the Military

Party and Army

Mao Zedong's statement that "political power grows out of the barrel of a gun" is indicative of the value he placed on the military as a means for bringing about the revolution. However, Mao also indicated that he considered the military a means to victory rather than an entity to be valued in itself: He immediately qualified the statement quoted above by adding "the party must always control the gun, the gun must never control the party."

This statement implies a clear-cut distinction between the party and the military that strongly overstated the cleavage between the two. Particularly in the decades before it came to power, the CCP was beset by powerful enemies, and sheer survival necessitated that the leadership be well versed in military strategy and tactics. Mao and most of the other high-ranking party leaders also held high military positions. Although some officers of the Red Army, as it was then called, had received formal military training, many had not. Of those who had received military training, a few had attended provincial military academies or been sent abroad to study, usually in Japan or the Soviet Union. Most of the rest had received short courses at the Whampoa Military Academy (see Chapter 3) or at Yan'an's Kangda military school. Typically, these were short courses of perhaps six months' duration, and the curriculum was heavy on political indoctrination.

Basically, the Red Army was commanded by amateurs, a situation not unlike that of the Confucian state the party leaders held in such contempt. What the proper sphere of the military should be after the party had come to power proved a troublesome question. The desire to have China assume a respected position in the ranks of world powers was, as proponents of the strategic interaction school discussed in Chapter 1 argue, an important factor in the communist leadership's calculation. Realization of this desire demanded a carefully trained and well-equipped professional army. Differences of opinion on the emphasis to be placed on training ideologically correct amateurs vis-à-vis technologically competent professional military members have been an ongoing theme of defense politics in the PRC and are a variant of the red-versus-expert debate introduced in Chapter 1.

Initially, the infant Chinese communist movement was uncomfortable with the whole concept of an organized professional military. It smacked of the warlords whose regimes they were so opposed to. Those CCP members who had read Marx knew that the revolt of the proletariat was supposed to come about spontaneously. Bitter experience soon taught the party that this was unlikely to happen. As noted in Chapter 4, CCP attempts at putsches were put down rather easily, with surviving party members fleeing to rural areas to avoid extermination. It was at this point that the party reluctantly accepted the need for a regular military organization.

When the Red Army was founded on August 1, 1927, and for several years thereafter, it was a ragtag group that included idealistic but untrained communists, deserters from warlord armies, some who had served in peasant militias, and bandits. Mao Zedong believed that the last category was the most numerous. His complaints about officers mistreating their troops, lack of discipline, and "the roving insurgency mentality" (banditry) indicate the difficulties of welding this disparate mass into a fighting force in support of communist goals. Communist leaders were concerned that the Red Army would degenerate into the warlord bandit force that formed an important part of its origins.

Despite this inauspicious start, the party was able to wrest power from its Kuomintang rivals in 1949. During the intervening two decades, the Red Army, renamed the People's Liberation Army (PLA) after 1949, had evolved into a well-disciplined force that provided effective support for the party's expansion on, and eventual control of, the Chinese mainland. In the process, it developed certain characteristics which are collectively referred to as the Maoist model. However, one should be aware that, first, the model evolved gradually in response to circumstances and, second, that leaders other than Mao played important parts in its development. Major elements of this model include:

■ *The military as an instrument for the achievement of political goals.* As such, the military must be unequivocally subordinate to the CCP. This is indicated by the statement that political power grows out of a gun, but that the party must always control the gun. After the founding of the PRC, soldiers were expected to assume responsibilities for organizing the masses and helping them to establish political power. Within the army, party control was exercised through a hierarchy of party committees headed by commissars, and paralleling the military chain of command at all levels.

■ *The relative importance of acquiring correct political views over the acquisition of advanced technology as a technique of army building.* A corollary of the primacy of political over military goals, this tenet is similar to biblical beliefs such as "If our hearts are pure, we will fight with the strength of ten thousand men." Sustained attention to military training or weaponry was criticized as "a purely military viewpoint," as opposed to correct views that emphasized the importance of people—that is, people with politically correct ideology—over weapons.

■ *Close relations between the army and the people.* Mao maintained that, without the support of the masses, the successful pursuit of war, like any other political action, is impossible. Comparing the masses to water and the army to fish, he noted that an army that fails to maintain rapport with the people will be opposed by the people. A military force that mistreats the people will dry up the water that supports it. A creed called "the three main rules and eight points for attention" was devised to train soldiers to treat the masses with honesty and respect. Soldiers were required to memorize it, and the creed was set to music to make it easier to remember. The three rules are:

1. Obey orders at all times
2. Do not take a single needle or piece of thread from the masses
3. Turn in everything that has been captured

The eight points are:

1. Speak politely
2. Pay a fair price for what you buy
3. Return everything you borrow
4. Pay for everything you damage
5. Do not hit people or swear at them
6. Do not damage crops
7. Do not take liberties with women
8. Do not ill-treat captives

Those who failed to live up to the standards of this creed were punished, sometimes severely. For example, the penalty for rape was often immediate execution. Military units were also expected to give aid to civilians in time of emergency.

- *The strategy of people's war.* The army, supported by paramilitary forces and a sympathetic populace, would lure the enemy deep into its territory until the invading force was overextended and dispersed. Communist troops would avoid the defense of fixed points, preferring highly mobile guerrilla-type tactics to isolate enemy units from one another. The element of surprise was considered crucial. When superior forces could be concentrated against dispersed units, communist troops were to surround and destroy them. When this could not be done, they were to withdraw and practice harassment tactics. If all went well, there would be a protracted period during which opposition forces became progressively more exhausted and demoralized. Eventually, the enemy would surrender.

- A *high degree of democracy within the military.* From the earliest days of the Red Army, Mao insisted that officers must not mistreat soldiers, and that officers should eat, sleep, work, and study alongside their men, "sharing weal and woe" with them. Nonetheless, Mao drew a distinction between democracy, of which he approved, and absolute egalitarianism, which he emphatically opposed. For example, he commented caustically on the folly of soldiers invoking the principles of democracy to prevent officers from riding horses in the performance of their duties when soldiers had to walk. Still, there are documented instances of officers and men discussing the merits and demerits of a given strategy in a nonhierarchical atmosphere of give-and-take. And, though distinctions were made between officers and men in terms of certain privileges, they were relatively small by comparison with other military organizations.

- *Economic functions of the military.* To minimize the costs of the military to society, the army was to strive for maximum self-sufficiency. Insofar as possible, units were to raise their own food, mend their clothing, knit their socks, and build and service their barracks. In addition to its military and self-maintenance duties, the army was to help build and maintain the civilian economy. During the early years of the PRC, military units played important roles in the agrarian reform movement, in carrying out irrigation projects, and in supervising factories and other industrial enterprises.

- *The army as a model for society.* In addition to being of the people and for the people, the army was to serve as a model for mass behavior. China's leaders likened their efforts to solve the country's economic and social problems to a battle, and enjoined citizens to emulate the army's energy, organization, discipline, and devotion to duty while launching a concerted attack on the evils of the old society. The slogan "every-one [should be] a soldier" referred to civilian personnel engaged in economic and so-cial reforms. Conversely, PLA members were expected to exemplify the virtues of so-cialist society and be models of collective behavior and self-reliance for the masses. The PLA was also expected to indoctrinate its members with socialist norms.

■ *Lack of clear distinctions between the military and civilian leaderships.* As men-tioned previously, a high percentage of the early leaders of the PLA had little or no formal military education. Also, political and military power were tightly inter-twined during the period of the civil war. This close connection between military and civilian administration continued for several years after the communist party came to power. The six Military and Administrative Regions into which China was divided after 1949 exercised both civil and military functions. When they were abolished a few years later, many military leaders assumed administrative duties. Subsequently, some who had received formal military training, and others who had not, assumed positions in the PLA, or in the party and government organizations supervising it.

While such career patterns of exit from and reentry into the military are far from the norm, they occurred often enough, and at a high enough level, to blur the distinctions be-tween the military and civilian elites. For example, Wei Guoqing, a military academy graduate, held several important military positions during the revolutionary war and for several years after it. In 1958, he became first party secretary of the newly founded Guangxi Zhuang Autonomous Region and was one of a handful of first party secretaries to survive the Cultural Revolution. In 1977, he returned to the PLA as head of its general po-litical department. Wei served in this capacity until 1982, when he was fired after differing with Deng Xiaoping on the loosening of restrictions on art and literature. During the Cul-tural Revolution, a majority of the members of the politburo and the party's central com-mittee were military officers. For a time in the late 1980s, China's president served simul-taneously as general secretary of the Central Military Commission; the country's vice-president was another old soldier.

Assessing the Maoist Model

Mao's followers claimed that his concept of the military and its relationship to society are revolutionary and that they represent a startling break with the past. These claims are often premised on a fallacious comparison: contrasting Mao's ideals with the reality of the badly degenerated civil-military relationships that characterized early twentieth-century China. A more valid comparison would be between Maoist ideals and the ideals of the classical Chinese tradition. Here one finds striking similarities between the Maoist model and con-cepts prevalent in China for millennia. For example, "The army is the fish and the people are the water" is first found in the works of Mencius, a disciple of Confucius who wrote in the third century B.C. Other "revolutionary" concepts derive from Sun Zi, the great mil-itary theorist who predated Mencius by several centuries. And the principle of isolating and surrounding an enemy to destroy him is basic to the ancient Chinese game of *weiqi*, better known in the West under its Japanese name *go*.

Civilian control of the military was also a firmly held value in traditional Chinese society. Much of the credit for putting down the rebellions that plagued nineteenth-century China belongs to scholar-statesmen who assumed command of armies although they lacked formal military training. They too believed that correct ideology (in their case, Confucianism) is more important than advanced technology. Traditional China also favored the idea that an army should be self-sufficient, insofar as possible. The notion that Chinese armies in outlying areas should raise their own food and provide for most of their other needs can be traced back as far as the first century A.D.

The Maoist military model is not simply a restatement of traditional Chinese attitudes toward the military; it represents the selective choice of certain elements from the past and the disavowal of others. One traditional attitude that was unequivocally rejected was the position of the soldier at the bottom of the traditional social hierarchy, in which scholars occupied the top position, followed by peasants and merchants. The elements of classical Chinese military tradition that Mao borrowed were combined in a blend which, although falling short of ingenious creativity, was innovative and well suited to the situation the party found itself in prior to 1949.

The Influence of the Korean War on the PLA

Although the CCP now portrays its military activities during the pre-1949 period as a series of heroic encounters against numerically and technologically superior Japanese and KMT forces, the Red Army actually devoted relatively little effort to fighting the Japanese. KMT mismanagement and the subsequent demoralization of its forces contributed at least as much to the communist military victory as the heroism of its soldiers. The chief formative influence on the military had been internal to the Chinese communist community. To borrow a phrase from eminent social scientist Samuel Huntington, the *societal imperative*, that which arises from the preeminent social forces, ideologies, and institutions of the community, had been the dominant force shaping the formation of the Red Army.

Following the founding of the PRC, the military, now renamed the People's Liberation Army, played an even more important domestic role. Soldiers contributed to the rehabilitation of China's battle-scarred economy. They also assisted in the land-redistribution process, set up state farms, and supported the collectivization of industry and agriculture. In addition to its economic functions, the army played an active political role. PLA work teams brought the party's message to areas that had had little prior exposure to communism, and helped to establish communist organs of political power. The army also guarded against the sabotage activities of anticommunist remnant groups, thus helping the party to consolidate power.

China's entry into the Korean War in late 1950 gave increased emphasis to external determinants in shaping the country's military. Needless to say, external military threats to the newly founded socialist regime had always concerned the party's leadership. But when Chinese communist soldiers, fighting beyond their country's borders for the first time, confronted United Nations forces, these concerns became increasingly salient. In Huntington's terminology, the *functional imperative*, which stems from threats to a society's security, gained importance relative to the societal imperative.

Committing some of their best units to battle, the Chinese leadership apparently anticipated a relatively quick and easy victory, feeling that their superior military doctrine could defeat the better-equipped enemy. After two months of initial successes, weaknesses in firepower, air support, logistics, and communications became painfully evident. PLA weapons and tactics were ineffective against the enemy's superior technology and mechanization, and the Chinese communist forces suffered heavy casualties. Morale plummeted. A new commander, marshal Peng Dehuai, was named, and the Chinese forces fell back to defensive positions. Additional troops were sent to reinforce them, and the Soviet Union increased its military aid and assistance. Eventually, the Korean War reached a stalemate.

This experience convinced many Chinese leaders, both within and outside the military, that a reassessment of the PLA's organization, strategy, tactics, and weapons was needed. Significant changes in the direction of specialization and professionalization took place within the Chinese military during the mid-1950s. When the PRC adopted its first constitution in 1954, Peng Dehuai was named the new government's first minister of defense. It was under his aegis that many of these changes occurred. They included:

- *The modernization of weaponry.* The Soviet Union sent substantial quantities of tanks, planes, artillery, and ordnance to China to aid the PRC during the last phase of the Korean War and for several years thereafter. Much of this equipment was obsolescent and supplied in smaller quantities than the Chinese leadership wanted. Nonetheless, it significantly upgraded the PLA's arsenal. With this material came several thousand Soviet military advisers to instruct the Chinese in its use, and to help the PRC to establish its own defense industry. The net effect was a strong Soviet influence over the development of the PLA.
- *Training and discipline.* The introduction of more advanced weaponry called for higher education for soldiers, and also required longer periods and more specialized kinds of training. Military personnel spent more time in these pursuits and less on economic development projects, whether on behalf of the society as a whole or for the benefit of the PLA itself. Increasing specialization also created a need for careful coordination of the many different specialties, which in turn required more elaborate procedures and tighter discipline. Training methods reflected the experience of Soviet advisers and placed greater attention on concepts that had not been a part of the Chinese experience and at times were even antithetical to Chinese concepts. For example, the Soviets emphasized highly mechanized and positional warfare. Also, their officers had the habit of treating enlisted men quite badly.
- *Rank system.* In early 1955, a rank system established 14 categories ranging from second lieutenant to supreme marshal. Officers were also classified into categories based on fields of specialization. Educational qualifications were established for entry into the various ranks, and a more formal system for entry into military schools was set up as well. Officers were required to wear the epaulettes and insignia of their rank, and a system of military honors was introduced. The establishment of ranks was accompanied by changes in the method of remuneration. The old system of providing military personnel with food and a small allowance to cover incidental expenses was replaced by one of cash payments based on rank. In 1960, the ratio between the pay of a marshal and that of a private was 160 to one.[1] This was far above the differences between

highest and lowest paid members of Western capitalist armies, and especially striking in a military that was proud of its egalitarian tradition.

- *Conscription.* A conscription law was devised and passed in mid-1955, regularizing the recruitment of military personnel. The law enabled whatever number of recruits had been decided upon to be selected from an already established pool of those who were eligible, rather than relying on volunteers as had been the previous practice.

These reforms improved the efficiency of operation and overall combat capabilities of the PLA. However, increasingly audible voices within the leadership and from the population at large complained that these advances in the PLA's ability to cope with external threat had come at the expense of ideological principles and were therefore detrimental to domestic social progress. External and internal imperatives, or red and expert points of view, were in conflict over the correct course of development for the PLA.

The Revolt Against Professionalism

Critics charged that the cherished socialist values of democracy and egalitarianism were being destroyed, arguing that conscription had sharpened distinctions between amateur and professional soldiers, and that the rank system had encouraged status distinctions and arrogant behavior among the officers. Establishing educational qualifications for officers meant that an increasing number of them were drawn from the bourgeois classes, to whom education had been more readily available and who tended to value it more. Not having risen from the ranks diminished their ability to understand the problems of the rank and file.

Officers who no longer ate with their troops were less motivated to deal with complaints of poor-quality food. And, while stricter discipline might increase efficiency in a battlefield situation, it also made officers less likely to ask for the opinions of their subordinates. In a clear violation of PLA tradition, some officers used physical force to discipline their troops. As officers gave less attention to their subordinates, they gave more to weapons procurement and maintenance, thus contradicting the principle of the primacy of people over weapons.

Relationships between the military and the civilian population had also become strained. Civilian homes and land had been requisitioned by the PLA for barracks and training grounds; peasants' crops sometimes fell victim to army maneuvers. Civilians resented displays of conspicuous consumption by more affluent military families, and some PLA members supplemented their incomes through black-market activities. Civilians also were angered by an increase in incidents involving soldiers' behavior toward local women.

Increasing specialization of functions led to a sharper distinction between military and political work within the PLA. Commissars complained that commanders made decisions without consulting them; officers retorted that, since commissars did not trouble themselves with military matters, their opinions were of little value. The number of party members in the armed forces declined during the late 1950s, and some units did away with commissars completely. Critics argued that this undermined the principle of party control over the military. Many of them also felt that the Soviet model was inappropriate for China, and blamed it for distorting the PLA's principles.

During the antirightist campaign of 1957, certain efforts were made to rectify these perceived distortions. These were massively escalated in the following year, as part of the Great Leap Forward. Officers were required to attend lengthy political study sessions, and an "Officers to the Ranks" program called for commanders to spend one month each year eating, sleeping, working, and passing their leisure time with ordinary soldiers. They were also assigned tasks like cleaning spittoons and latrines, caring for animals, and weeding crops, in order to lessen their arrogance and give them an understanding of their subordinates' point of view.

PLA members were reminded of the importance of good relations with civilians, and the army worked on behalf of economic development on an unprecedented scale. The media reported that the PLA contributed 59 million days to economic development in 1958 alone. Although this figure, like all other statistics from the period of the Great Leap Forward, is apt to be grossly exaggerated, there is no doubt that the PLA was heavily involved in nonmilitary activities, leaving little time for training. Simultaneously, the militia was raised to virtual parity with the PLA. The "everyone a soldier" movement of 1958 claimed to have enrolled over 200 million ordinary citizens in the militia. Maoist "reds" believed that allocating an important role to the militia would make the country better able to fight a true People's War while simultaneously undercutting the PLA's claims to a superior position because of its vaunted expertise in defense matters. The disparity between military and civilian living standards was redressed through such measures as lowering officers' pay and reducing the quality of the army's food and uniforms.

In 1959, defense minister Peng Dehuai, widely regarded as supportive of "expert" professionalist views, was dismissed after he reportedly criticized Mao for championing the Great Leap Forward. Peng was replaced by Lin Biao, who might then be considered to espouse "red" amateur positions. What actually happened is a good deal more complicated. Although Peng almost certainly resisted radical policies that he felt weakened PLA morale and combat capabilities, the proximate cause for his dismissal appears to have been his criticisms of the economic and social policies of the Leap—something a purely professional soldier would normally avoid commenting on. And it fell to Lin to regularize and reorganize the PLA into a force capable of ensuring the country's defense—a task that required substantial attention to professional criteria.

Secret Chinese military documents published in the PRC in 1961 and later made public by the U.S. Central Intelligence Agency reveal the devastating effect that the Great Leap had on the PLA. Widespread malnutrition and poor sanitary conditions caused debilitating diseases among young people who had been recruited partly because they were some of the country's most physically fit. Weapons maintenance had deteriorated, and accidents due to faulty equipment had risen. This was particularly noticeable in the air force, where equipment was expensive and hard to replace. Repudiation of the Soviet model had exacerbated strains in Sino-Soviet relations to the point that the USSR ceased giving military aid and withdrew its advisers to the Chinese military. This further compounded the problems of equipment replacement. PLA morale was dangerously low.[2]

By October 1962, the PLA had improved to the extent that it gained a decisive victory over Indian forces during a confrontation in the Himalayas. The Chinese triumph was made easier by India's poor planning and mismanagement. Nonetheless, the PLA successfully coped with long supply lines through difficult terrain inhabited by a hostile Tibetan population. There had been a major rebellion against Chinese rule in Tibet in 1959. However serious India's shortcomings, China's performance was impressive nonetheless. Lin had refurbished the PLA through a variety of measures, some consonant with concepts of redness and the societal imperative and some with those of expertise and the external imperative.

Reds, or amateurs, were pleased by Lin's vigorous efforts to reassert the party's control over the military, including strengthening the supervisory role of the party's Central Military Commission (CMC).[3] Commission directives revitalized the system of party committees within the military and restored commissars to a position of parity with commanders. The CMC also initiated an intensive campaign to instill a sense of political loyalty in the rank-and-file soldier. A "Five Good" movement admonished soldiers to excel in political thinking, military training, work style, fulfillment of tasks, and physical education; prizes were awarded to outstanding units and individuals. This was followed by a campaign to learn from Lei Feng, a young soldier who was martyred in the line of duty (if that is a proper description of someone who expired after a truck loaded with telephone poles backed into him). Excerpts from what was alleged to have been Lei's diary were published to inspire soldiers to emulate his many noble virtues.

Experts, or professionals, were pleased when the number of work days that the PLA was to devote to economic development was drastically reduced, leaving more time for training. The "Officers to the Ranks" program continued, but on a smaller scale and with a different purpose. Rather than lessening the distinctions between officers and common soldiers, the program now facilitated the transmission of directives from the top echelons to the bottom, and enabled officers to exercise better control. The militia was also reorganized so as to appeal to advocates of military professionalism: It was reduced in size and salience, directed more toward economic development than military activities, and subordinated to joint party-PLA control, as opposed to its position of virtual parity with the PLA during the Great Leap Forward.

Both amateurs and professionals could take comfort from Lin's pronouncements on the issues of people versus weapons and of democracy within the military. On the former, Lin declared that one should give unqualified preference to "people," while adding that cadres "should on the one hand oppose the purely technical viewpoint which departs from reality and on the other oppose the empty-minded politician who disregards techniques and professional operations." Lin applied the same sort of subtle modification to the concept of military democracy. Although Mao himself had carefully qualified the limits of democracy, persons acting in his name during the Great Leap Forward had not been equally fastidious. Lin, while strongly supporting the concept of military democracy, defined it so as to include the need for discipline and exclude egalitarianism and anarchism, thus encompassing both radical and professional views.

In 1964, the Chinese leadership indicated its approval of the military by launching a mass campaign to "learn from the PLA." Citizens were enjoined to apply the army's skill at being both ideologically correct and technically proficient ("both red and expert" was the slogan used) to their daily lives, and to the work of party and government organizations. Lin Biao had, it appeared, achieved a successful synthesis of the PLA's different roles.

During the next year it became obvious that the synthesis was more apparent than real. Mao decided that the "learn from the PLA" campaign had not been a success, and that in any case the army was insufficiently radical. In May 1965, in a move that was unequivocally proamateur and antiprofessional, the PLA's rank system was abolished. In the same year, the military's official newspaper began an attack on "bourgeois" intellectuals that proved to be the opening round of the Cultural Revolution. Significantly, it began with an attack on a play set in the Ming dynasty whose hero bore a striking resemblance to Peng Dehuai, Lin Biao's predecessor as minister of defense (see Chapter 12). All expertise, including military expertise, came under attack as bourgeois and anti-Maoist. Judging from the slogans being chanted, the correct ideological line no longer sought a blend of politically reliable people with superb training and advanced weapons: People counted; weapons and training did not.

Many PLA leaders came under attack, and the command structure was severely affected. Still, the military suffered less than most other institutions due to concern about external attack. China was literally surrounded by hostile powers at this time: The Soviet Union, India, and Taiwan all seemed menacing. Moreover, the United States maintained a large and growing military presence in Vietnam, just a few hundred miles from the Chinese border. Internal factors also tended to bolster the army's position. The chaos of the Cultural Revolution occasionally reached the point that the army had to be called upon to restore domestic order. Although the PLA was regularly enjoined to "support the left," its peacekeeping mission frequently put it on the side of the moderates. Radical ideologues were critical of the PLA's conduct at such times.

Lin Biao, whether through shrewd calculation of which way the political wind was blowing or from sincere conviction that this was the proper course of action at this particular point in time, strongly espoused leftist/radical causes in general and amateur views with regard to the military. He and many of his fellow Fourth Field Army members profited handsomely in terms of promotions. Nonetheless, the PLA's interventions on behalf of domestic order convinced other radicals that the army as a whole could not be counted on to support them. They began to organize the militia as a counterweight to the PLA. These activities were scarcely noticeable at the time, however.

The army emerged from the Cultural Revolution with greatly increased powers. Mao had ordered it to back worker-peasant teams when they entered the universities during the summer of 1968 and to quell student violence. The PLA ran study classes to "re-educate" Red Guards, and became a fixture on university campuses and in industrial enterprises. There was heavy military representation on the party and government organizations that emerged from the Cultural Revolution, and frequently a PLA man held concurrently the top party, government, and military positions in a province. The PLA's societal role had reached its zenith. In April 1969, the CCP's Ninth Party Congress adopted a new constitution that named Lin Biao as Mao's successor.

Although Lin was an avowed radical and apparently had an even more radical constituency, any further moves away from military professionalism were inhibited by deteriorating Sino-Soviet relations. Serious armed clashes on the eastern border began in March 1969 and spread to the western border in the summer. The PLA's military training increased, as did emphasis on the care and maintenance of weapons. Military budgets increased. In a number of cases, major defense plants were established in remote parts of China or removed from major cities and relocated to such areas, to make it more difficult for the USSR to destroy them. This was an exceedingly costly undertaking and, in light of the deficiencies of the transportation network in the country's outlying areas, made it much harder to get the products of these industries into the hands of the troops.

Lin Biao's death under mysterious circumstances in the fall of 1971 (see Chapter 5) was followed by a purge of officers loyal to him, many of them from his Fourth Field Army and presumably also radical in their views. This meant a concomitant increase in the power of moderates and professionals in the PLA. Such an explanation is consonant with an intensification of Shanghai radicals' renewed efforts to build up the militia as a counterweight to the regular army, beginning in 1973. In December of the same year, Mao Zedong rotated eight of the eleven military region commanders. Although the commanders assumed leading military positions in different regions, they lost the positions they had had in provincial party and government and were not given new ones. The transfers thus reasserted the party's control over the gun, and specifically over the moderates and professionals in the PLA who constituted most of the gun after the demise of Lin and his faction.

The radical-inspired reorganization of the militia had the same aim: Many of the People's Armed Forces Departments (PAFDs), through which the PLA exercised control of the militia, were abolished. Militia units were put under a new organization, the militia headquarters, which was subordinate to the party. The reorganized militia incorporated public security and fire-fighting functions. It was further strengthened through receiving substantial quantities of weapons, many of them produced by factories in Shanghai, the radicals' base of power. The new militia was urban-based, to take advantage of radical elements within the cities. Rural areas, which had typically been the mainstay of militia recruitment, tended to be less activist. In 1975, a new Chinese constitution gave the militia equal status with the PLA.

These moves did not go unnoticed by professionals. Deng Xiaoping, purged from his post as party secretary-general during the Cultural Revolution and rehabilitated only in 1973, became the symbol of resistance to radicals and the champion of military professionalism. In January 1975 Deng was named PLA chief of staff and appointed to the CMC as well. He bluntly characterized the army as a "mess" created by its "support the left" work during the Cultural Revolution, and pledged that the PLA would be prepared to fight future wars in terms of "iron and steel"—weapons. Deng also opposed the new-style urban militia, even sending the PLA to disband unruly militia elements in the city of Hangzhou during the summer of 1975.

Radicals interpreted these actions as negating the primacy of politics over the gun and of people over weapons. At this time, both Mao Zedong and Zhou Enlai were elderly and ailing, and the radicals' opposition to Deng and his policies was intensified by fears that he and his supporters might assume their positions. They were able to oust Deng from power in the Tiananmen incident in April 1976, in which the militia played a highly publicized role. But when Mao died a few months later, radicals' attempts to stage a militia-led uprising to put themselves in power failed dismally. Only in Shanghai did the militia's effort assume major proportions. The PLA aborted the uprising with ease, simultaneously destroying the power of radical leaders. The militia would never thereafter enjoy any kind of prominence, although it continued to exist in a reorganized form. Deng, apparently backed by professionals in the military, was rehabilitated during the summer of 1977, almost immediately assuming his old position of head of the PLA's General Staff Department and vice-chair of the CMC. Shortly thereafter, he became head of the CMC and relinquished his general staff position to a long-time protégé, Yang Dezhi.

The pendulum again swung in the direction of professionalism. Deng, his views clearly unchanged despite his past disgrace, instituted sweeping changes within the military. These included:

- *A reworking of strategic doctrine*, called "People's War Under Modern Conditions." Described as an adaptation of Mao's principles to modern times, the doctrine was characterized by greater attention to positional warfare, modern weaponry, and combined arms. The concept of luring an enemy deeply into China and then surrounding and attacking him was amended to include the possibility of forward defense: Many Chinese military strategists felt that, by the time an enemy had been lured deeply enough into the PRC for this to work, the enemy would have destroyed much of the country's vital industries and transportation nodes. China's "defensive counterattack" against Vietnam in early 1979 shows awareness that the enemy might have to be engaged in his own territory. The strategy is different enough from People's War that, in the opinion of many analysts, it ought to be considered wholly separate from it rather than as an adaptation. These analysts believe that the original name was retained mostly to emphasize continuity with the past, when in reality the doctrine represented a sharp break with past practice. In 1978–1979, when relations with the Soviet Union were strained, the PLA was told to prepare for an "early, major, and nuclear war" with the USSR. In 1985, by which time Sino-Soviet relations had improved, there was yet another change in strategy. The military was to expect, and train for, local, limited wars on the PRC's periphery.
- *More attention to training.* Troop training programs were ordered reorganized. Less time was to be given to political study sessions and more to the study of strategy and tactics. Training exercises were to be adapted to the sort of real-life situations combat troops might actually be expected to face, and to reflect the conditions of weather and terrain of particular geographic areas.
- *Efforts to acquire advanced weaponry.* Both foreign and indigenous sources were to be utilized. The National Defense Science, Technology, and Industry Commission was charged with supervising research and manufacturing for the PRC's seven ministries of defense building that dealt with defense production. Also, a number of military procurement missions were sent abroad to examine a wide variety of foreign weaponry and related items, including tanks, trucks, helicopters, warplanes, missiles, lasers, and computers.
- *Reorganization of the PLA into a smaller, younger, and more responsive force.* Plans were announced to cut the size of the military by one-fourth, or a million people. The number of military regions was reduced from eleven to seven, thereby cutting down on the number of headquarters and their personnel. The new military regions were authorized to command tank and artillery divisions and other specialized service branches; in the past, these branches had been directly under the armed forces supreme command. New regulations provided for the reinstitution of a rank system and set limits for time in grade. Older officers, many of whom were in their seventies, with some in their eighties and nineties, were encouraged, and in some cases forced, to retire. This would make it possible to promote younger, more vigorous people to command positions.

- *More stringent educational qualifications for the military.* Units at and above the corps level were ordered to sponsor classes to bring PLA cadres up to the level of senior middle school or technical middle school. Self-study was also encouraged: Those willing to enroll in night school, or in television or correspondance courses, were to be given assistance in doing so. Tests of general and specialized knowledge were to be administered. Those who could not or would not meet the required standards would either be denied promotion or be demoted. The Young Communist League was told to persuade outstanding college graduates to join the PLA.

  A three-tier system was created to train junior, midlevel, and senior officers, with more than a hundred military academies participating. The apex of the system is the National Defense University, which was founded in December 1985 by merging three PLA academies—military, political, and logistical. Each had previously been operated by the relevant general department of the PLA. Consolidating the resources and expertise of the formerly separate institutes was aimed at producing a more efficient instructional system. Another, though unstated, reason behind the decision to integrate the three academies may have been to reduce the departmental compartmentalization and attendant factionalism that the separate institutions tended to reinforce.

- *Reassertion of party and government control over the military, with the PLA more clearly separated from party and government.* There was a marked decrease in the number of individuals holding positions in either two or all three of the party, government, and military hierarchies. Statistical data show that there were 122 such individuals in 1960, 445 in 1973, and only 73 in 1982.[4] By 1990, there were no individuals with a primarily military background in the Standing Committee of the politburo, and very few in the politburo. A 1987 change in the party constitution dropped the requirement that the chair of the CMC must be a member of the standing committee.

The railway corps, heretofore under PLA control, was transferred to the railway ministry, and the capital construction corps was civilianized as well. The People's Armed Police was created from the PLA and charged with internal security functions that had heretofore been done by the army. The increased functional specialization that these more clearly differentiated military and nonmilitary roles allowed constituted a major step away from the amateur, "red," position and toward expertise.

Although these changes were startling, they did not represent a total break with the past. The military retained an important role in China's industrial enterprises. Indeed, the army's continued participation was considered vital to the success of the country's economic modernization. Encouraged by explicit party/government directives the PLA actually went into business for itself, in the form of large marketing enterprises for both civilian and military items. Many of their products were sold to other countries. There was no noticeable diminution of the PLA's charge to provide for its own food and other items; military units also regularly participated in mass tree-planting campaigns and other activities designed to help civilians and blunt the edge of civil-military tensions.

Not surprisingly, the magnitude and abruptness of Deng's innovations caused a number of problems. Advocates of old-style People's War pointed out that, given the weaknesses of the PLA's weaponry, a forward defense would expose the Chinese side to being outflanked and overrun. In addition, they contended, the disadvantages of positional warfare had been shown by the Red Army's ability to capture cities from the countryside during the war against Chiang Kai-shek.

Advocates felt that the Maoist conception of People's War retained its basic validity in the capital-poor labor-intensive Chinese context; they also saw a none-too-veiled attack on Mao as implicit in the revision of his military doctrine. More attention to troop training and to the acquisition of weaponry raised fears that troops were receiving less instruction in proper political attitudes. It was, moreover, expensive to develop and purchase technologically sophisticated weapons. China faced no imminent external threat, whereas its internal needs were many and urgent. The societal imperative, they believed, far outweighed the external imperative.

Military modernization was ranked lowest among Deng Xiaoping's Four Modernizations, and the amount of money that could be devoted to technological improvements fell far short of perceived needs. There was also the question of how much to procure indigenously and how much to acquire from foreign sources. Local design bureaus and those who feared dependence on external suppliers strongly favored the indigenous route; others pointed out that this path had proved slow and inadequate in the past. Arguments also existed over which kinds of weapons ought to receive priority.

Reorganization met massive resistance. Reducing the army by one million meant turning a large number of people out onto a civilian job market that could ill afford to absorb them. Officers had joined the military with the expectation of a lifetime career: To be demobilized unexpectedly caused anger and hurt as well as financial difficulties. There was also the matter of who got demobilized and who was allowed to stay. The ubiquitous *guanxi*, or connections, inevitably played an important role. Streamlining also involved merging certain units with other units, causing other problems. Typically, members served their entire career in the same unit, and strong loyalty networks developed. Those who were transferred into new units found that they were regarded with suspicion and treated as outsiders. In a few cases, soldiers who managed to retain their weapons after discharge formed bandit groups and preyed upon local populations. Officers who were told to retire because, at age 50, they were considered too old, noted that both the head of the CMC, Deng, and the CMC general secretary, Yang Shangkun, were in their eighties.

At the lower end of the military hierarchy there were very different problems: While older officers did not wish to leave the PLA, younger people did not wish to join. Deng's agricultural reforms had a strong disincentive effect on military service, since it was now more profitable to stay in the countryside. Moreover, draft-age youth were also marriage-age youth, and finding a suitable bride while serving in the 90-percent-male PLA was exceedingly difficult. The plight of bachelor soldiers was made more difficult because, since peasant men had higher incomes, young women and their families tended to consider them more desirable matches than poorly paid PLA members. For the first time in the history of the PRC, large numbers of peasant youth, heretofore the mainstay of the military, began to avoid the draft.

Commanders were not pleased at the thought of compensating for the drop in numbers of peasant youth by enrolling urban young people in their place. First, since more than 70 percent of the PRC's population is composed of peasants, the pool of urban youth was much smaller. Second, though recognizing that city youth were generally better educated than their rural peers, commanders felt that they were also too "soft" for the rigors of military life and too infected with bourgeois ideology to make good soldiers. Rural young people were inured to hardship and far less likely to pose discipline problems.

For their part, urban youth were as unwilling to join the army as their commanders were to have them. Prior to Deng's reforms, joining the PLA had been an important avenue of upward mobility for peasant youth—indeed, it was often seen as the only way that a young man could escape the tedium of his village. But joining the military gave fewer advantages to urbanites. Even city youth who were unemployed tended to regard waiting for a job as preferable to committing themselves to military service. Work units tried in various ways, including bribery, to keep their best workers while persuading PLA recruiters to accept social misfits, those with criminal records, physical weaklings, and illiterates. Individuals tried to bargain with recruiters: They would join if the military could provide them with something they desired. One might want to be taught a specific trade; another might demand a driver's license that he had otherwise been unable to obtain.[5] A number of young people simply refused to register for military service at all, and at least one county official resorted to staging surprise late-night visits to households he believed to harbor healthy young men who were eligible for induction.[6]

Some individuals and units solved their quality-of-life difficulties by illegal means. The military's greater access to such amenities as foreign exchange, vehicles, and storehouses facilitated such activities as smuggling. In one spectacular case, the apparent participation of most members of a division-level unit in Guangdong resulted in a large number of convictions, including that of both its commander and its commissar. The unit had been engaged in an illegal vehicle purchase-and-resale scheme that was discovered only when one of its members was robbed and murdered by the owner of a vehicle the officer was attempting to purchase. The scheme came to light almost accidentally, since the officers were able to conceal their comrade's death for several weeks.[7] Variations on this theme abound.

Problems also appeared in the effort to upgrade the educational qualifications of the PLA in order to prepare its members to take part in more complex training exercises and in the use of more sophisticated weapons. An article in the official military newspaper complained that "cadres are tired of studying and students are dropping out," thus having a bad effect on the already low scientific and cultural level of the PLA. Its author found two causes: First, military men were convinced that "the diploma craze has cooled down," and that studying was useless. Second, having noted that illiterates had become bosses and that middle-school dropouts had "made a windfall by engaging in illegal traffic," officers felt that since one needed only a little knowledge to succeed in commerce, it would be better to devote one's energy to establishing "unprincipled" connections than to waste time reading. Educated people, the author continued, were leaving the PLA in greater numbers than those who entered. Hence the educational situation was getting worse. It seemed doubtful that the "two twenty percents"—increasing the number of college-educated PLA cadres by 20 percent from 1985 to 1990 and by another 20 percent from 1990 to 1995—could be reached.[8]

In 1988, the PLA gave examinations to some of its officers, with alarming results. The commander of a regiment proved unable to read a map and, when asked to mark a specific location, was seven miles off target. A colonel, when asked what sort of arms the parachute troops of a certain country were likely to be equipped with, thought long and hard, eventually replying that he did not know.[9]

The existence of major problems should not obscure the fact that there were gains as well. Training exercises did become more sophisticated. Some weapons were upgraded, and in fact China became one of the world's largest arms exporters. Although the PRC's weapons were generally not state-of-the-art, they were very reasonably priced and found favor in many third world countries. Training programs were instituted to provide soldiers with skills that they could use in the civilian job market after demobilization, and the re-settlement of veterans began to receive more systematic attention. While the debate between amateurs and professionals continued, the PLA appeared to be moving in the direction of greater professionalism and increased capabilities.

The Effect of the June 4th Incident on the PLA

The declaration of martial law in May 1989 (see Chapter 6) brought the PLA directly into an internal political dispute. The leadership apparently judged the People's Armed Police incapable of handling the massive demonstrations of that time, and returned the military to internal security duties. In essence, the PLA was also being called upon to resolve a leadership struggle at the highest levels of party and government. This ran completely counter to the trend of separating and differentiating military from civilian administrative functions that Deng had been fostering for the previous decade.[10]

While Deng was strongly behind what seemed to represent a reversal of his own policies, there were definite indications that several of the commanders that he himself had appointed were not. A number of soldiers said openly, in front of television cameras, that the people's army must not be used against the people. Deng spent several days lining up support from the various military regions, and even then there were reports of skirmishing between different divisions. After the demonstrations had been crushed and the leadership crisis resolved, the newly reconstituted elite tried in a number of ways to ensure that this hesitation not recur. Collectively, these represented a step away from professionalism and toward the amateur model.

Awards were issued to servicemen who had acted strongly against the alleged handful of counterrevolutionaries who had instigated the subversive demonstrations, and there was a revival of the campaign to learn from Lei Feng (see page 127). Army newspapers also reiterated, again and again, the impossibility of separating the army from politics: The PLA was the party's own army and must take its direction from the party. Yet another technique to ensure loyalty was to encourage research on the Chinese communist military's glorious past when, at least as seen through the haze of nostalgia, right and wrong were easily distinguishable.

There were mixed results from these efforts. For example, the campaign to learn from Lei Feng was met with a fair degree of cynicism. It was widely believed to have been designed by president and concurrently military commission secretary-general Yang Shangkun to enhance the power of his faction. This included his younger half-brother Yang Baibing, who was head of the PLA's general political department. And certain of the research that was published on the PLA's glorious history came to less-than-idealized judgments about past campaigns.

After the PLA's suppression of the 1989 demonstrations, foreign analysts predicted first that the military would play a much more important role in high-level decision-making and, second, that the "Yang family village" would play a major role in that decision-making. There is little evidence to bear out the first prediction: Military leaders were not promoted to leading positions within party and government in any greater numbers than before, nor was there any indication that the military was exercising increased influence on policy in other ways.

The second prediction, on the power of the Yangs, ran afoul of the vicissitudes of Chinese politics. A mass transfer of high-ranking military personnel during the spring of 1990 did indeed reward a number of persons who were loyal to the Deng/Yang cause at Tiananmen, as well as promoting several people believed to have long-standing ties with the Yangs. However, just before the CCP's Fourteenth Party Congress in fall 1992, rumors began to circulate in the Hong Kong press that other high-level changes were to be made in the military with the aim of destroying the Yangs' power. Yang Baibing was accused of a variety of unacceptable actions, including having held a private meeting at a Beijing hotel to plan security arrangements for after Deng's death. Though none of these rumors has ever been confirmed, and several seem quite implausible, the Yangs' fortunes definitely took a turn for the worse. Yang Shangkun resigned as president of China and from his position on the military commission. Yang Baibing was replaced as head of the general political department and from the military commission.

Although Yang Baibing received a seat on the politburo, the Yangs' ties with their power base, the PLA, had been severed. A number of officers believed to be part of their "village" were also removed from their positions. Since there had been no hint of disloyalty to Deng Xiaoping himself, the most likely explanation for the purge is that the paramount leader wished to ensure that the PLA would remain loyal to his chosen successor, Jiang Zemin, after Deng's death. This hypothesis was confirmed when two elderly generals with no known factional bases of their own, Liu Huaqing and Zhang Zhen, replaced the Yangs on the military commission. Liu was appointed to the standing committee of the politburo as well, in what seemed to be a setback for Deng's plans to separate the military from the party. That it was felt necessary to reassign officers in order to deal with military factionalism bearing on the selection of the next civilian leader of China would also seem to indicate the persistence of a strong societal role for the PLA.

Pressures for increasing the PLA's functional role existed as well. The United States' performance in the UN-Iraq war of 1991 and the disintegration of the Soviet Union in the same year helped to focus the Chinese leadership's attention on the combat capabilities of the PLA. The sophistication of U.S. weapons seems to have come as a major shock to the Chinese leadership. Western military attachés report that PLA officers commented that they did not see how the PRC could ever catch up, and a foreign reporter described the war as dealing the final blow to the Chinese communist strategy of overwhelming an enemy with sheer numbers of troops.[11] A strategic reassessment shifted emphasis from limited regional conflict to "limited high-technology war." There was intense interest in the American military's Revolution in Military Affairs, in which networked computers combine with precision-guided weapons to destroy the enemy's warfighting capabilities. The PLA began to purchase arms from Russia, and continued to work with Israeli arms dealers.

The Military Under Jiang Zemin

With the Yangs' power diminished, Jiang Zemin worked to establish his control over the military. He created new billets for three-star generals (the PLA's highest rank) as commanders and commissars of the seven military regions, and personally conferred the awards. Jiang also visited military units throughout the country; the visits were well-publicized and described as showing his love for the troops and appreciation of the important work they were doing. Legislation on retirement ages passed under Deng Xiaoping's direction was scrupulously observed. In addition to creating a younger and presumably more vigorous and better-educated PLA, this also meant that, within a short period of time, all top military officers had been chosen by Jiang and could be presumed loyal to him. Jiang also continued the practice begun by Deng of transferring commanders and commissars among the military regions, to guard against individuals becoming entrenched with local power-holders, fearing that these ties would reinforce regional ability to modify or evade central government policies.

According to unconfirmed but persistent rumors, military commanders exacted a price in return for their loyalty to Jiang: a larger say in foreign-policy making. This greater influence is thought to be in the direction of a harder-line stance on disputed territorial issues such as the Spratly Islands and Taiwan. The impetus for increased tensions in the Taiwan Strait in 1995–1996, which included mainland missiles being fired into the strait and a series of menacing military exercises that looked as if they might be the prelude to a full-scale invasion of Taiwan, is believed (but not definitely known) to have come from PLA leaders.

Military budgets continued the increases that had begun in 1989. Considered in current dollars, defense expenditures rose 8.6 times between 1988 (21.53 billion *yuan*) and 2003 (185.3 billion *yuan*).[12] See Figure 9.1. Most of this happened during a period while, because of the disintegration of the Soviet Union, the defense budgets of the major powers were sharply reduced. The PRC's neighbors have expressed concern about China's intentions. Since the country faces no external threat and has many pressing domestic concerns that could be addressed with the money being spent on the PLA, there are worries that Beijing is bent on aggressive behavior. China has sought to calm these fears by explaining that increments in defense expenditure have barely kept pace with inflation. One cannot be certain of this for several reasons. First, official figures are generally believed to underestimate actual inflation rates, although it is difficult to say by exactly how much. Second, even if inflation rates were known to be accurate, they would not tell us how inflation impacted the defense sector. Third, the PLA received budget increments of 12.7 percent in 1997, when the inflation rate was about 2 percent, and 12.8 percent in 1998, when the economy was slipping into deflation. The argument that the PLA was being compensated for divesting its commercial empire is also less than convincing, since the double-digit increases that were reported for 1997 and 1998 occurred before the order to divest was given in July 1998.

Finally, the actual defense budget is much larger than the reported defense budget. For example, weapons purchases from the former Soviet Union were made from a separate budget under the State Council. The costs for other such large expenditures as nuclear research and development are hidden or otherwise unavailable. Some analysts believe that actual defense costs are as high as ten times recorded figures; most

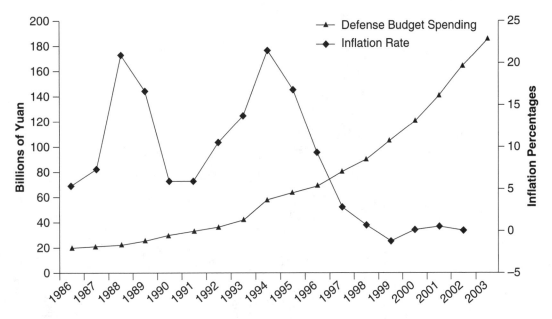

FIGURE 9.1   Recent Chinese Defense Budgets and Inflation
Source: Compiled from International Institute for Security Studies data.

estimates fall into the three- to four-times range. U.S. government sources have estimated the increment in actual defense expenditures at 5 percent per year since 1990. This is a substantial amount, although it tells us nothing about how well the money has been spent.

In the same period, China made major weapons purchases from Russia, including Sukhoi-27 and Sukhoi-30 fighter planes, Kilo-class submarines with advanced sonar systems, and Sovremenny-class guided missile destroyers equipped with sophisticated Sunburn anti-ship missile systems. Other systems were upgraded with Israeli help, to the extent that the U.S. government felt compelled to ask Israel to suspend the sales because of the threat to Taiwan.[13] A fourth general department, the general armaments department, also referred to as the general equipment department was established to deal with ongoing weaponry problems (see Figure 9.2). Military training exercises became more elaborate.

The PLA's journals contained many articles stressing the need to develop "information warfare" and "asymmetric warfare" in which one seeks out an enemy's weak points and, using an "assassin's mace" or killing blow weapon, attacks him through these vulnerabilities. In the case of the United States, these were judged to be its military's heavy reliance on high-technology weapons, and the American public's aversion to casualties. PLA analysts discussed the ability to seize control of a battlefield from a much more powerful enemy (unnamed, but presumably the United States) by inserting computer viruses into the opponent's communications systems. In a book entitled *Unlimited Warfare*, two senior colonels opined that, since the PRC was a poor country, it had to use whatever means it could. International military codes could be ignored since, they argued,

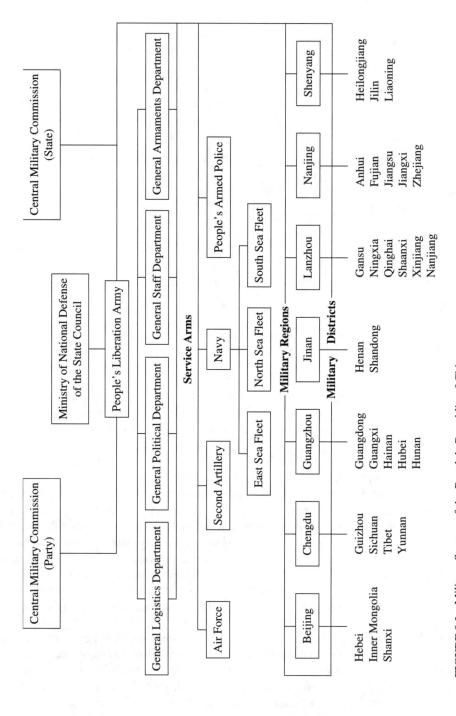

FIGURE 9.2 Military System of the People's Republic of China
Source: Adapted from U.S. Central Intelligence Agency. LDA 90–14715, August 1990.

Western powers had devised the codes in order to advantage themselves. Among the techniques they suggested were chemical and biological warfare, terrorism, and altering environmental conditions in order to produce changes in the climate of the enemy's territory.[14] Advocating the use of such techniques does not necessarily mean that the PLA is able to successfully use them. Most analysts believe that, although the PLA's combat capabilities are improving, it still has rather limited ability to project power beyond China's borders.

This concentration on the defense role of the military under Jiang indicated a reinforced trend toward functionalism and away from the PLA's societal role. At neither the Fifteenth Party Congress in fall 1997 nor the Sixteenth Party Congress in 2002 was a military representative named to the standing committee of the politburo. Although the military has other ways to express its views to party and government leaders, the fact that there is no serving military officer in the standing committee carries important symbolism.

At the national people's congress in 1998, Jiang announced that the PLA's numbers would be reduced by 500,000, to its current size of approximately 2.5 million. The cut was motivated by a desire for a "leaner and meaner" military: Fewer soldiers meant lower personnel costs, and more money to spend on upgrading weapons and training techniques. Most officers now have the equivalent of a college education, and are better able than their predecessors to utilize the more sophisticated weapons and techniques that are being introduced.

One very important societal function remained: the PLA's business empire. As mentioned above, Deng Xiaoping had encouraged the PLA to help in China's modernization effort through producing and marketing both civilian products and weapons. It did so enthusiastically, though the motive appeared to be profit rather than modernization. By the mid-1990s, products such as washing machines, refrigerators, and socks accounted for nearly 70 percent of defense-sector production. The military ran at least 10,000 businesses with profits of $5 billion to $10 billion a year. The growth of these businesses was accompanied by massive corruption. Many of the profits were not declared; therefore, no taxes were paid on them. In 1993, China's defense minister warned that, if such practices continued, the country's " 'Great Steel Wall,' [a common metaphor for the PLA] will self-destruct."[15] A Chinese Academy of Science report issued shortly thereafter argued that the PLA should be removed from business and return to its proper role of defending the country. Its author realized that this switch from the PLA's societal role to its functional role could not be accomplished without cost, and suggested that military industries should be purchased for a fair price, so that soldiers could concentrate on training.

In July 1998, as part of an anticorruption drive, Jiang Zemin actually took this action. The divestiture may have taken place more in form than reality: While less profitable enterprises were sold off, more successful ones appear to have changed ownership while remaining at least partially under PLA control. Eight to ten thousand enterprises, presumably including some of the most lucrative ones, were retained.[16] Still, that the order could have been given indicates that the PLA had advanced another step toward functionalism.

The military is nonetheless regarded as the *party*'s army rather than belonging to the state, and political qualifications, though far less stringent than in Mao Zedong's era, remain important. As faith in Marxism receded, patriotic considerations came to the fore as a focus of devotion.

Conclusions

Deng Xiaoping's military reforms, continued under Jiang Zemin and Hu Jintao, have succeeded in producing a younger, better-educated, and better-trained PLA with greater technical capabilities and improved weaponry. Rising military budgets and the purchase of advanced weapons and military systems from Russia and Israel have raised questions among many of China's neighbors as to the PRC's military intentions.

Despite predictions that the PLA would play a major role in the succession to Deng Xiaoping, and that Jiang Zemin would find it difficult to establish his authority with the PLA due to his lack of military experience, the transition from Deng to Jiang was accomplished smoothly. Jiang solidified his relations to the PLA to the extent that, before the fall 2002 Sixteenth Party Congress at which Jiang was to retire, military newspapers praised Jiang in such extravagant terms that observers both within and outside of China speculated that the PLA was spearheading a drive to keep him in office. Jiang's decision to sever the PLA's connections with its business enterprises was a bold stroke that could not have been undertaken by someone with less confidence in the military's loyalty to him. Whether it will accomplish its goal of reducing military corruption and allowing the PLA to better focus on its defense responsibilities remains to be seen. So as well does the question of whether Hu Jintao, who also lacks military military credentials, can establish his authority over the PLA.

The military hierarchy has become progressively more separate from party and government hierarchies; people like Mao and Deng, who combined military experience with party and government work are almost nonexistent. Although the PLA still performs a societal role in times of crisis—helping out the population in the aftermath of floods and earthquakes, for example—it is now firmly focused on its functional responsibilities. The military may thus develop a sharper sense of its interests as separate from those of party and government, and insist that its corporate voice be heard and accommodated by the system. A new party–government–military dynamic is likely to evolve.

Notes

1. Ellis Joffe, *Party and Army: Professionalism and Political Control in the Chinese Officer Corps, 1949–1964* (Cambridge, Mass.: East Asian Research Center, Harvard University, 1967), pp. 106–107.

2. See *Gongzuo Tongxun: The Politics of the Chinese Army: A Translation of the Bulletin of Activities of the People's Liberation Army*, trans. by J. Chester Cheng (Stanford, Calif.: Hoover Institution, 1966), passim, for the PLA's own view of this period.

3. The Central Military Commission was called the Military Affairs Commission at the time; I have used the present-day name for consistency and ease of recognition.

4. Data as presented in Monte Bullard, *China's Political-Military Evolution: The Party and the Military in the PRC, 1960–1984* (Boulder, Colo.: Westview Press, 1985).

5. Zhang Wenrui, Yang Yuwen, and Liu Bangguo, "The Great Changes and New Characteristics of Our Troops," *Qingnian yanjiu*, June 1986, pp. 19–23, trans. in *Chinese Law and Government*, vol. 20, no. 2, Summer 1987, p. 111.

6. Hangzhou Radio, September 21, 1988; in *FBIS–CHI*, September 27, 1988, p. 54.

7. *Ming Pao* (Hong Kong), November 6, 1985, in *FBIS–CHI*, November 7, 1985, pp. W/1–2.

8. *Jiefangjun bao* (*Liberation Army Daily*: Beijing), November 27, 1988, p. 1.

9. *Agence France Presse* (Hong Kong), October 24, 1988, in *FBIS–CHI*, October 24, 1988, p. 10.

10. *Jiefangjun bao*, October 1, 1989, pp. 1–2.

11. Sheryl WuDunn, "War Astonishes Chinese and Their Military," *New York Times*, March 20, 1991, p. A7.

12. International Institute for Strategic Studies, *The Military Balance, 2002–2003* (Oxford, U.K.: Oxford University Press, 2002), p. 298.

13. Slobodan Lekic, "United States Asks Israel to Freeze Defense Exports to China," Associated Press, Jerusalem, January 2, 2003.

14. Qiao Liang and Wang Xianghui, *Chaoxian Zhan* (War Beyond Boundaries) (Beijing: PLA Literature and Arts Press, 1999).

15. Li Chu, "Chi Haotian Personally Handles Smuggling Cases in the Military," *Cheng Ming*, September 1, 1993, pp. 20–21.

16. James Muvenon, testimony to U.S.-China Security Review Commission, December 7, 2001, in *Compilation of Hearing Held Before the U.S.-China Security Review Commission* (Washington, D.C., Government Printing Office, 2002), p. 821. At earlier hearings on June 14, 2001, former U.S. ambassador to China Joseph Prueher and former U.S. trade representative Charlene Barshevsky testified that the PLA had not fully divested its business empire. See *ibid.*, p. 106.

Suggestions for Further Reading

David Graff and Robin Higham, *A Military History of China* (Boulder, Colo.: Westview Press, 2002).

James Mulvenon, *Soldiers of Fortune: The Rise and Fall of the Chinese Military Business Complex* (Armonk, N.Y.: M. E. Sharpe, 2001).

Andrew Scobell and Larry Wortzel, eds., *China's Growing Military Power: Perspectives on Security, Ballistic Missiles, and Conventional Capabilities* (Carlisle, Pa.: Strategic Studies Institute of the Army War College, 2002).

David Shambaugh, *Modernizing China's Military: Progress, Problems, and Prospects* (Berkeley, Calif.: University of California Press, 2003).

U.S. Department of Defense, *Annual Report on the Military Power of the People's Republic of China*, July 2002. http://www.defenselink.mil/news/Jul2002/d20020712china.pdf

CHAPTER

10 Education

Education, broadly defined as both the transmission of cultural norms and expectations and as training in specific job-related skills, presents every society with difficult choices. In less-developed countries like China, limited financial resources and a lack of trained teachers place further constraints on the educational system. As a newly founded revolutionary state, the PRC had an additional difficulty: that of transforming many existing beliefs and practices.

Devising a System

The party faced decisions on whom to educate on what topics, and in what numbers. At one extreme, it could opt for providing large numbers of people with a relatively low standard of education. At the other, it could train a much smaller number of people in areas that would enhance the nation's prestige. For example, a few superbly trained medical scientists equipped with state-of-the-art laboratories and equipment could be expected to achieve major breakthroughs in disease prevention, thus adding to their country's luster. Similarly, a substantial amount of money devoted to educating and equipping nuclear physicists would allow the PRC to join the nuclear club, whose members had heretofore been a small number of Western powers. The former goal appealed to the egalitarian strain of Chinese communist ideology; the latter to adherents of the strategic interaction theory.

There were also questions about how much time in the curriculum should be devoted to the study of politics and ideology and how much to more substantive material like mathematics and foreign languages. How to treat China's past was a difficult question: Despite diatribes about the dead weight of tradition on the country's modernization and industrialization, to negate that tradition completely would leave the PRC without a national identity. The leadership was concerned with matters like what of the traditional to preserve and how to blend it with a still largely formless concept called socialist culture. Also at issue was whether to give preferential treatment, and how much, to the children of workers, peasants, and party members as opposed to those of the bourgeoisie and nonparty members. Every decision involved a trade-off that would benefit one or another social group. As in so many other aspects of policymaking in the PRC, arguments took the form of red-versus-expert polemics.

Initially, the party's task involved expanding and revising the educational system it had inherited from the republican government. Textbooks were rewritten to portray the communist party, and also the Soviet Union, in a more favorable light. The value of social-ist thought, the evils of capitalism, and the wisdom of Mao Zedong's views were taught in various degrees of sophistication, depending on the level of the educational institution in-volved. The importance of collective behavior was inculcated from the earliest years on. Textbooks stressed the value of the masses in making history rather than, as heretofore, giving credit to emperors and high-ranking ministers.

As in other areas of PRC policymaking, there was a heavy Soviet influence on the educational system. This included emphasis on mathematics, science, and technology, no-ticeable not only at the theoretical level but also in the founding of a network of vocational schools to train technicians. Many textbooks were simply translated from Russian into Chinese, some of them proving quite inappropriate and becoming the subject of numerous complaints. And at least some children of landlords were discriminated against by the ed-ucational system. However, in general, academic criteria were applied impartially during this early period, with relatively little emphasis on class background.

At the same time, the educational system was greatly expanded, the goal being to pro-vide schooling for all, including the children of the poorest peasants and factory workers. For adults, spare-time literacy classes were established; these might be held in the evening after factory work was done, or during the slack season in farming communities. Normal schools were set up in areas that had not previously had them, in order to train more teachers.

The government tried in various ways to make it easier for people to become literate. For example, it propounded the use of *baihua* in writing Chinese, which was closer to the way people actually spoke the language than the terse and more elegant *wenyan* previ-ously favored by scholars. It also popularized the use of a phonetic system known as *pinyin* so as to standardize the pronunciation of the Chinese characters across the country. The PRC's vast expanse includes a number of linguistic dialect groups and subgroups, several of which are mutually unintelligible. The new regime propounded the use of what is known in the West as Mandarin; since the communists had a very negative opinion of the old official class, they referred to the language as *guoyu*, the national language, or *putonghua*, meaning ordinary speech.

Basic lists of the most frequently used characters were drawn up, and books, news-papers, and magazines were urged to use only those. Eliminating a large number of com-plicated and seldom used characters would, of course, make it easier to learn how to read. The forms of some complicated characters were simplified: For example, a character writ-ten with eleven strokes of the pen might be reduced to four (see Figure 10.1). The standard for literacy was later established as the ability to recognize 1,500 characters (for peasants) or 2,000 characters (for workers and urbanites), to read simple popular newspapers and periodicals, keep simple accounts, and write simple statements.[1] It would appear that in earlier periods the ability to recognize 1,000 or 1,200 characters sufficed as the standard for literacy.

The literacy rate, estimated at about 25 percent in 1949 (not in itself bad for a de-veloping country) had more than doubled by 1955. That many of these people had not reached a very high level of literacy takes nothing away from the achievements of the government's efforts. Most of what the CCP government did was not its own invention: The use of *baihua* in preference to the literary language had been one of the demands of the May Fourth marchers in 1919. The *pinyin* system of transliteration had been de-

Original Character	Simplified Character	*Pinyin* Pronunciation	Meaning
寶	宝	bao	treasure
叢	丛	cong	crowd together
歸	归	gui	return
國	国	guo	country
蘭	兰	lan	orchid
龍	龙	long	dragon
慶	庆	qing	celebrate
勸	劝	quan	advise
無	无	wu	without
壓	压	ya	oppress

FIGURE 10.1   Selected Characters, Simplified Forms, and *Pinyin* Pronunciations

vised under the Kuomintang government; simplified characters had been used by writers in a hurry for at least a millennium. What was new and impressive was the energy and organization involved in putting these techniques together and popularizing them so widely.

A formal educational system evolved that was not very different from the one prevalent in the West. Six years of primary school were followed by three years of junior middle school, three years of senior middle school, and six years of university. This was supplemented by a variety of vocational and technical schools, the whole fairly tightly controlled by the ministry of education in Beijing. Chinese culture had always emphasized hard work and placed great value on education, so student motivation presented no particular problem. The main concern during this period seems not to have been over getting students to work hard but to keep them from ruining their health by studying too hard.

While it was impressive in many ways, there were complaints that this system was elitist. Frequently the most successful students turned out to be the progeny of the bourgeoisie who, being better-educated themselves, could more easily help their children to learn. Mao Zedong occasionally voiced strong anti-intellectual feelings, perhaps deriving from the days when he was looked down upon by Moscow-educated party bureaucrats who referred to him as a "dirt communist." The Hundred Flowers campaign of 1957 had the effect of reinforcing these anti-intellectual tendencies, since many of the most articulate criticisms of communist rule came from the more educated segment of society.

The Drive for Egalitarianism and Fall Back Toward Expertise

The ensuing antirightist campaign and Great Leap Forward aimed at broadening and flattening the educational system. In 1958 alone, the number of children in kindergarten reportedly increased from 1 million to 30 million; those in primary school from 64 million to 86 million; and enrollment in secondary schools from 7 million to 10 million.[2] While all statistics from this period should be regarded with skepticism, there is no doubting the almost explosive expansion of the system. Since it would have been impossible for resources and trained personnel to expand at the same rate, a concomitant decline in standards was inevitable.

At the same time, elitist education was sharply attacked, as was "so-called bourgeois scientific objectivism." A number of research projects were canceled in midcourse, since their aims were deemed too far from the country's primary goal, that of increasing production levels. Intellectuals were sent to the countryside to labor alongside peasants, both to reduce their arrogance and to narrow the cultural gap between city and countryside. Greater emphasis was placed on spare-time schools. Schools closed for a time so that faculty and students could participate in making steel in backyard blast furnaces.

Young people with peasant and proletarian background were given preferential admission to institutes of higher learning, and the ideological component of school curricula was increased. Teaching methods were changed to emphasize the dictum that education must serve the interests of the working class and that it must be integrated with productive labor. Politics was to take command. Although the slogan of the time was that every student was to be both red and expert, redness received far more attention than expertise. Academic standards declined markedly.

The failure of the Great Leap Forward was accompanied by a return to pre-1957 teaching standards. Academic achievement was again valued. Key schools were established, usually in major urban centers, and provided with exceptional resources, better trained teachers, and the most promising young students. The same criticisms of this educational system emerged as had during the antirightist campaign, adding fuel to the ensuing fury of the Cultural Revolution.

Redness Revisited: The Cultural Revolution

The theoretical debate on education during the Cultural Revolution centered on the need to suppress bourgeois and feudal attitudes in the pedagogical system, so that "the revolutionary successor generation" could be properly prepared to assume its role in the march toward communism.[3] However, most of the specific criticisms of the system as it existed in 1965 turned on less lofty issues. One was that children of poor and lower-middle-class peasant families found it very difficult to attend school, or to stay in if they managed to enter. Tuition fees, though minuscule by Western standards, were simply beyond the capacity of many poor peasant families. Often, the school was so far away that a child could not come home at night, so boarding fees would have to be paid as well. Examinations determined promotion; those who did not pass would have to repeat a grade, thus prolonging the time they spent away from productive labor and raising the cost to their parents. Age limits for each grade excluded those who might have to start late, or expelled those who could not pass a certain subject within a given period of time.

In cities, where parents had less need of their children's labor and schools tended to be within easy walking distance, the entrance exam for middle school was more likely to be the focus of discontent: Workers perceived that the children of the bourgeoisie and intellectuals were advantaged by virtue of their superior cultural levels. At the same time, the children of bourgeoisie and intellectuals resented the preferential treatment given the children of well-connected cadres. A vocal group argued that examinations themselves were ideologically improper, since they placed individual self-interest above anything else and thus endangered the collectivist values on which socialism was based. Examinations fostered the creation of a promotion-conscious elite, which reminded a number of people uncomfortably of the mandarins of yore.

Another prominent criticism was that course material was excessively abstract, with very long assignments and much emphasis on cramming and memorizing. Conversely, students were not taught to analyze. Also (and undoubtedly an irrefutable argument in the climate of the Cultural Revolution), they had little time to study the really important topic: the thought of Mao Zedong.

A third criticism was that, due to the tight control exercised by the ministry of education in Beijing, local needs were not taken into consideration. For example, school vacations in tea-growing areas of Zhejiang were set according to a schedule devised to be in harmony with the very different needs of rice-growing areas elsewhere. Villagers who had been assigned a bad teacher could do nothing to dismiss her or him, since the individual was considered a "cadre of the state."

An entire folklore grew up around the theme of the thin, pale-faced, near-sighted intellectual who really knew nothing about survival or productive labor. This image was invariably contrasted with the quick-minded and open-hearted "local expert" who, keen-eyed, fit, and tan from hard physical labor, knew how to grow rice and wheat from extensive practical experience, without regard to tedious scholarly discourses on hybrid seed strains.

For a time, no one could be sure of what was acceptable in teaching methods or content. Since students were enjoined to smash the old society and to exchange revolutionary experiences, most schools simply closed down. A number of students chose to denounce their teachers and school administrators as exemplars of the evils of the old society. They were "struggled against" and humiliated in various ways. Some were tortured to death; others committed suicide to escape further torment. All learned people, not just teachers, were targets of derision; Mao castigated them as the "stinking ninth category," the eight others of which included such obvious villains as capitalists. Bonfires were made of books deemed to be tainted with bourgeois thought, which nearly everything except the works of Mao was suspected of being. The educational system ceased to function. Though there was general agreement on the need to reopen schools, there was such a divergence of opinion on what ought to be taught, and how, that resumption of a normal academic schedule proved impossible for several years.

When schools began to function again in 1968, a number of changes were evident. Instead of an entrance examination, students were selected on the basis of recommendations. Political criteria became important, as did one's willingness to engage in productive labor for several years before applying to a university. Outstanding workers and peasants who were political activists would receive preferential admission to universities even if they had received only a junior middle school education, provided that they had been endorsed by their work units and party authorities. Though many such individuals were able to attend university under this new system, in practice it was corrupted in various ways. First, children of cadres found it easier to obtain the necessary official endorsements. And second, those sent down to the countryside could have their class labels changed to "peasant" at the end of two years. Hence, those university students who were classifed as peasants were often not really peasants. As always, it was easier for the well-connected to get their class designations changed.

The age limits for admission to various levels of the educational system were widened, and the curriculum was shortened. Six years of elementary school were to be compressed into five, and the three years each of junior and senior middle school combined into a single four-year segment. University would take just three years. The curriculum was simplified, and new teaching materials introduced. There was a noticeable bias against "bourgeois expertise": one group of students was reportedly writing its own textbook on organic chemistry. Illiterate but wise local peasants were brought in to lecture on growing crops. They were also assisting in writing textbooks. Other students were described as trying to discover the principles involved in inventing a radio.

Decentralization was another feature of the educational system to emerge from the Cultural Revolution. In rural areas, it became common practice for production brigades to run primary schools, with communes assuming responsibility for secondary education. In urban areas, primary schools might be run by street committees and secondary schools by factories. Teachers would be members of these units, rather than being moved from place to place by the state, and local people would be able to ensure that the curriculum was linked with reality. In rural brigades, which were habitually short of people able to keep accounts, teachers' arithmetical skills could be put to immediate practical use. By managing their own school finances, local areas would be free to abolish tuition fees and support schools in whatever ways they found most convenient—for example, payments in kind. Hence, more children would be able to receive an education.

There was a great deal of emphasis on integrating study with productive labor, though with varying ideas on how this should be done. For example, if schools were combined with factories, should the school have a separate administration or be run by the factory administration? Having students actually participate in productive labor proved a somewhat easier problem to deal with. The chancellor of a major U.S. university system, in China for a tour, described a group of elementary school children who were making a game of Chinese checkers. He watched with fascination as they cut sticks into cross- sections, painted the board, built cardboard boxes, fitted in the little chips, and sent the finished products off to a store to be sold. In a middle school he visited, students were making electrical turn signals for automobiles. They soldered wires, put on metal tapes, finished off the unit, and took the completed sets to an automobile factory. The chancellor was most impressed, though he made no mention of any precautions taken with regard to quality control.

With the examination system discredited as a means of evaluating student performance, a combination of other criteria took its place. Test results, homework, and a child's attitude toward study and labor were all taken into consideration. It became harder, though not impossible, to have a student repeat a grade. This could be done if the child did poorly in two of the three major subjects (political study, Chinese language, and arithmetic), if the parents agreed, and if the poor performance had been due to laziness. If a child failed because of ill health, the parents might be reimbursed for additional tuition costs.

For graduates of junior or senior middle school (in certain areas, even the former were considered intellectuals in the PRC's categorization at this time), the *xiaxiang*, or down-to-the-countryside, movement was intensified. They were urged to volunteer, with sanctions available for use against those who did not. The party's admonition to integrate themselves with the peasants was not especially popular with most young people, who felt that they had not spent so many years in school in order to waste what they had learned. Most found life in rural areas very harsh, with few diversions. Routes out of the countryside were also very few: One could find a job at an urban factory, join the military, or enter a university. None was easy or simple. Here again, however, the children of cadres had connections that eased the process.

Egalitarians Versus Experts: The Search for a Synthesis

Mao had decreed in July 1968 that college students should be selected from the ranks of workers, peasants, and soldiers. However, universities did not really begin reopening until 1970, and many not until 1971 or 1972. Almost immediately, there was a good deal of concern with the poor quality of the applicants. This, and perhaps the demise of the radical Lin Biao, led to certain modifications in the Cultural Revolution educational system. Toward the end of 1972 an examination system began to be reinstated. It was said to be a different kind of system in which, among other things, papers were jointly assessed by teachers, pupils, and members of the local Workers Propaganda Team, followed by a discussion with the examinee. Open-book examinations were also reported. As one indication of how far standards had fallen, a 1973 directive ordered that a student's academic accomplishments would henceforth have to be at least at the level of junior middle school before he or she could be considered for university entrance. Presumably a sufficient number of applicants had fallen below even this modest standard, or the directive would not have been issued.

Even these limited moves toward tightening academic standards caused controversy. People who favored more stringent educational requirements were pitted against those who felt that any reversal of the policies adopted during the Cultural Revolution amounted to a sellout of its principles, and those of the workers and poor and lower-middle-class peasants. When examinations were reintroduced there was an instant adverse reaction.

During the summer of 1973, the provincial newspaper *Liaoning Daily* published a letter from a young man named Zhang Tiesheng. A middle-school graduate who had been sent to the countryside, Zhang had clearly hoped to use admission to the university as his exit route, though his letter does not say so. After scrutinizing the content of the examination, Zhang concluded that he could not pass it and turned in a blank book. On the back cover, and in a subsequent letter to the provincial authorities, he wrote a note that soon reverberated throughout the country. Zhang's explanation for his action was that, because of his duties as leader of a production brigade, he had had no time to prepare for the examination. The main point is the converse of what Zhang stated: the implication that people who *had* done well on their university entrance examinations had probably been neglecting their obligations to productive labor. After a time, indicating that there was a split in the leadership on the examination issue, Zhang's letter was reprinted in *People's Daily*. Responding to this clear signal that the sentiments expressed in Zhang's letter had high-level backing, provincial radio stations took up the questions raised in it as well. The general tone seemed to be one of agreement with Zhang.

Nor was this the only example of disapproval of examinations. In January 1974, *People's Daily* published a letter from a middle-school student in Guangzhou (Canton). He complained that when he could not understand two problems on a mathematics exam and had asked the student next to him for help, the teacher had failed him for cheating. The young man complained that "Teachers are wrong when they say that one should not consult other people during an exam. The main task of the student is learning. Suppose a student does not understand a subject. With the help of another student, he now understands the subject. Is this not itself a kind of achievement?" Other students, even including primary-schoolers, took up the call, denouncing their teachers in the pages of major newspapers for discouraging group learning on tests.

This tug-of-war between reds and experts on educational matters continued for several years. The era of the Cultural Revolution was not without its research accomplishments. During it, Chinese scientists announced a major medical breakthrough in the laboratory synthesis of insulin. The country's nuclear program, which had first detonated a bomb in 1964, continued to make progress. And a satellite was launched in 1970, making China the third country in the world, after the Soviet Union and the United States, to have done so. But these advances occurred in small, well-protected areas. In general, educational levels fell sharply during the period from 1966 through 1978. An entire generation that could have been of immense value to the country's modernization was lost.

The Search for Academic Excellence

Deng Xiaoping's return to power and the priority he placed on economic modernization led to abrupt reversal of educational policies. Rather than serving ideological goals, the pedagogical system was to support economic ends. An examination given to would-be college entrants in 1978, and perhaps purposely designed to be difficult to prove Deng's point, revealed appallingly low levels of knowledge. Deng and his faction were openly derisive of the old system. Allowing students to write their own textbooks produced little of value, since they did not know enough about the content of the topics. Spending substantial amounts of time puzzling how to build a radio amounted to reinventing the wheel: One should be taught how to construct such a device with the idea of being able to add to and improve upon what was already known, not repeat it. The requirement that all students spend periods of time at productive labor distracted the most able ones from their main job of learning and lengthened the period of time before they accumulated sufficient skills to be truly productive to society. Mental labor, it was pointed out, was labor nonetheless.

Henceforth emphasis was to be placed on mathematics, science, and foreign languages; political study courses were downplayed and the requirement for productive labor at all levels modified. The new system was unabashedly elitist. Ninety-eight of China's then seven hundred fifteen tertiary level educational institutions received the designation *keypoint*, meaning that they were to have priority both in the choice of students from among those who had passed university entrance examinations and in the allocation of resources. In order to provide higher education with well-qualified candidates, keypoint schools were also established at primary and secondary levels beginning in 1978. Entrance to these schools was determined by intellectual ability, as tested by examination. They received more funds, more equipment, and the better-trained teachers. Universities established special ties with some of the best middle schools, with the aim of improving teaching at the secondary level and also of attracting that school's brightest students to attend their university. Technical middle schools, which had almost completely disappeared during the Cultural Revolution, were reinstated in order to provide qualified candidates for colleges of engineering and middle-level technicians.

Expertise was again honored, and redness downplayed. Zhang Tiesheng, the student who had so strenuously objected to university entrance examinations, was arrested on charges of hooliganism and sentenced to reform through labor. The designation "stinking ninth category" was removed from intellectuals, whose talents were now deemed absolutely necessary for their country's rapid modernization.

The new system also revived the track structure of the early 1960s that had been so heavily criticized during the Cultural Revolution. Its new incarnation was far more differentiated than the original.[4] From kindergarten on, children were rigorously tested and channeled to ordinary or keypoint schools, and to fast, average, or slow classes within those schools. Keypoint schools at primary and secondary levels were six years each, while ordinary schools were five years each, and the type of instruction at the former was more detailed than at the latter. Hence, a pupil from an ordinary school had almost no chance to be admitted to a keypoint school at a later stage.

In addition, nearly all keypoint schools were located in cities which are at county seat level or higher. They accepted only pupils who were registered residents thereof, thereby excluding rural and exurban children who amounted to nearly 80 percent of the PRC's school-age population. The assumption was that rural children would remain in the countryside and participate in production there. Ordinary middle schools would be turned into vocational schools, perhaps with a half-work, half-study system, and rural youth would be discouraged from seeking admission to senior middle schools and universities. This amounted to a deliberately discriminatory policy of cultivating an intellectual elite among urban youth while excluding rural children from the competition.

In urban areas, parents put tremendous pressure on their children to do well on examinations so that they could attend college. The odds were heavily against succeeding. One study showed that only 4.7 percent of those senior middle-school students who took the college entrance examinations passed, and that just one-half of 1 percent of the PRC's college-age students actually attended institutions of higher learning. By contrast, the figure for many developed countries is in the 20- to 30-percent range. Postgraduate study was still more exclusionary, and the opportunity to study in foreign countries even more difficult to obtain. With so much competition for so few places, and so much perceived as depending on success, there was a tremendous sense of disappointment among those who failed. Newspaper articles in the early 1980s contained frequent advice to such students not to feel bitter, and to try to help their country's modernization effort by working hard at whatever job the state deemed appropriate for them.

Other problems emerged. The party answered charges of elitism by pointing out that the previous nonexamination system had provided numerous opportunities for favoritism and "back door" cronyism: The examination at least provided an objective measure of success. With four-fifths of the population effectively excluded from this allegedly objective competition, it is unlikely that this argument convinced too many critics. Moreover, the "back door" continued to operate. It was noticed that a disproportionately large number of the people who were given permission to study abroad were the children of high-ranking officials. A surprisingly large number of Chinese students were able to point out that one of Deng Xiaoping's sons was studying physics at America's Rochester University. When the young man's wife had a child in the United States, the couple was widely suspected of having done so in order to receive preference in procuring American citizenship.

Some of these elitist policies were revised or phased out. For example, almost all middle schools are now six years, although there are experiments to have four-year junior middle schools in some areas to help train students for agriculture, plus a two-year senior middle school for those who wish to go on. Also, many cities now have key schools only at senior middle-school level. One is expected to attend the nearest junior middle school, although there are ways around this, including paying bribes and using connections. Linking admissions to payment is forbidden, but widely practiced. The sums of money involved can be very large. In 1995, a Beijing legal newspaper discovered that some key schools in Shanghai charged students entrance fees ranging from 30,000 to 50,000 *yuan*. Another school issued "educational stocks" that parents had to purchase before their child was admitted. Some institutions allowed grades to be purchased. Other research showed that in Beijing, as many as 50 percent of junior high students in some key schools were admitted through nonmerit based methods.[5] By the late 1990s, 36 percent of those sitting for college entrance exams passed, though the process had not actually become easier. A number of applicants were weeded out by a preliminary exam for graduation from high school. Parents often regarded a child's failure as their fault, to the extent that "educational schools for parents" proliferated. These essentially instructed parents in how to better prepare their offspring for the exams.

Despite the government's concerns, elitism and the role of money remained important. Visitors to institutions like the Shanghai Foreign Languages School and the Shanghai Number 3 Girls School were told that barely one in six members in the already select group of applicants was accepted. Teachers describe many of the students as only children whose parents and grandparents are focussed on their success. The twelve hours or more each day that these highly motivated students spend in the schools' well-equipped classrooms and laboratories typically result in outstanding test scores. Another form of elitism emerged for the children of the newly rich: private schools. Some kindergartens charged higher tuitions than universities. One Guangdong primary school, founded in 1993, charged tuition equal to the life wages of an ordinary worker. Its students dressed in designer uniforms and enjoyed the finest sports facilities in addition to a demanding curriculum. Teachers were housed nearby, in an attractive air-conditioned building.[6] Responding to resentment over the growing inequality of educational opportunities, officials tended to agree, while pointing out that this was an unavoidable consequence of the development of the commodity economy. The number of private schools continued to grow, reaching over 60,000 by the early years of the twenty-first century. Officials seemed to come to terms with their misgivings: In 2003, the national people's congress was even considering allowing private schools to make a profit.

Another obstacle in implementing a highly selective educational system was the low qualification level of most of the teachers. Reacting to principles established during the Cultural Revolution, even universities had taken in large numbers of poorly trained people. The socialist system made dismissal of workers in general nearly impossible; many of the individuals in question were additionally protected by party organizations because of their proletarian origin and party membership. Hence very little could be done about them.

The decollectivization of agriculture removed an important underpinning of rural schools: collective management. When the household became the unit of production, peasants found their children's presence at home more valuable, and many ceased to send them to school. The number of illiterates in China actually increased during the early 1980s. The government became concerned and, among other responses, it promulgated a nine-year compulsory education decree in 1985. However, as in other areas of policymaking, what is ordered from Beijing is not necessarily implemented at local levels. There was general dissatisfaction with the educational system, and dropout rates remained high. Only a quarter of 12-year olds were attending school, while 39 percent had already begun working. Little more than 12 percent of young people had intermediate-level education, and about 3 percent received higher education.[7]

Several reasons are involved. One is the perception (correct in many cases) that brainwork earns less than physical labor. Therefore, any effort spent studying is wasted. A second factor contributing to high dropout rates is that many businesses have taken to hiring children at wages that are very low, even by Chinese standards. This practice has been repeatedly condemned by the state education commission, but it continues.

A third reason was the rising cost of tuition, books, and other school expenses. Though regrettable, some of these increases were understandable. The high inflation of the mid- to late-1980s meant higher prices for books, electric power, food, and other school needs. When the central government basically ceased to subsidize primary education in the early 1990s, the situation grow worse. Since education budgets did not keep pace with the rate of inflation, many schools began increasing fees to make up the shortfall.

In some instances, however, the fee increases were so exorbitant that parents and government bodies began to suspect malfeasance; occasionally they were able to prove it. In urban areas, a parent's work unit might agree to pay the child's education fees. But in rural areas, where the entire burden fell on individual households, the impact was much greater. Moreover, peasants saw little benefit to be gained in terms of a better future for their children. Hence the number of rural dropouts began to rise. Parents who wanted to keep their children in school grew increasingly unhappy. Fees were assessed creatively: for fresh flowers, for watching the students' bicycles, for hard-working teachers, and so forth. In one Shaanxi village whose education budget had fallen short, thousands of children were banned from classes when their parents could not pay an additional 50 *yuan* ($6) levy on top of the usual fees.[8] In Guandong, a thousand people participated in a two-day protest against high tuition fees; five people received jail sentences of up to ten years for incitement to riot.[9]

Straitened educational budgets could be met by other means than raising fees, sometimes with disastrous consequences. In early 2001, an explosion destoyed a Jiangxi elementary school where children were assembling fireworks to earn money for the institution. The death toll exceeded forty.[10] In Gansu, education officials discovered that primary and middle school children were traveling two hours each way to work in cotton fields. Farmers paid the school authorities 0.4 *yuan* per kilogram of cotton—well below market rates. Similar programs were found to exist in the tea-raising areas of Anhui.[11]

Other problems contribute to the difficulties of remaining in school. Dilapidated buildings pose dangers to children, especially during the rainy season. According to figures from the Ministry of Education which are believed to understate the problem, an average of forty elementary and high-shool children die in school related accidents every day, ten of them from school building collapses.[12] While many of these structures are old, some were simply poorly constructed. Shoddy electrical wiring is frequently implicated as well. In late 2002, 21 children died and another 47 were injured when a stairway guardrail collapsed. Rescue efforts were hampered because the lighting system was not working. The school, not far from Beijing, was only three years old.[13]

Again, regional differences are important. Academic pressures can be intense in more affluent urban areas, but in poor areas, even key schools are not popular. There is no realistic chance to go on to a university and students prefer to apply to technical or specialist schools, or teacher-training institutions, because the state will give them jobs after graduation. Hence, academic senior middle schools cannot fill their quotas year after year.

When economic reforms made salaries in other professions more lucrative, teachers dropped out as well. One county in Guangdong province reported that 10.6 percent of its professional educational staff had resigned between 1986 and 1988. In neighboring Fujian, 148 schools were forced to suspend classes after 835 teachers left; nearly 3,000 children were deprived of instruction. Financial problems and poor working conditions were the primary reasons. The difficulties are most acute in schools run by rural communities. Not only are wages low, but teachers receive no bonuses, inadequate health allowances, and no other subsidies. The Chinese press has lamented that it is therefore impossible for teachers to maintain normal living standards. Worrisomely, most of the teachers who left were the core of the professional staff: the better educated younger and middle-aged teachers. To encourage more students to become teachers, the Ningxia Hui Autonomous Region's normal school lowered its minimum admission scores and signed contracts with first-year students, guaranteeing them specific job and district assignments after graduation. But less than one year after earning their diplomas, many still wanted to transfer to other jobs.

Most erstwhile teachers find jobs in business or transfer to office and technical departments in administrative units or enterprises. For those who live in prosperous coastal areas, or who are able to manipulate or circumvent their residence permits to emigrate there, the differences in salary can be striking, amounting to 30 to 50 percent more than their stipend as teachers. Educators willing to consider other, less traditionally prestigious occupations could earn even more. Former teachers who have become taxi drivers or bar girls can earn four to five times their previous salaries. One young woman who had decided on the latter profession noted that its working conditions were better and its hours more flexible.

Not only teachers' living standards but also their actual physical safety could be jeopardized by continuing in the teaching profession. During the mid-1980s, at least seven provinces issued circulars condemning violence against teachers—often by cadres or with their compliance. In Guizhou, a primary school teacher was seriously injured when three factory workers tied a rope around her neck, fastened it to a truck, and dragged her for 50 yards. The motive appeared to have been sport. The case received brief national attention when it was revealed that local authorities had dismissed charges against the young men.[14] A Beijing court sentenced two junior middle-school students to life imprisonment after they tortured and beat a young teacher to death with a bicycle chain. She had criticized them for truancy. Violence could also be committed by teachers against students. Officials deplored what they referred to as rising wave of vioence, attributing it to pressure on teachers to have their students perform well on exams causing them to overreact to minor instances of misbehavior. In one instance, a student was beaten to death for failing to properly clean his dormitory space, and another had his finger cut off for stealing a pair of shoes.[15] Sometimes the violence comes from outside the schools: "local hooligans," as the press refers to them, terrorize both students and teachers.

A final factor contributing to the high dropout rate applies mainly to urban areas. Schools reportedly concentrate on preparing students for college and ignore those who are less than outstanding academically. Feeling that they are regarded as backward, these students often lose self-esteem, begin to cut classes, and eventually cease to attend altogether. The children of migrant laborers are particularly discriminated against. Often unable to enter schools at all due to irregularities in their parents' residence registration, most are educated, if at all, in makeshift classrooms with poor facilities and unlicensed teachers. Those who are able to attend regular schools complain that they are shunned by their classmates. Again, the state education commission recognizes the problem and has urged schools to pay attention to the needs of all students rather than to just a select few. The results have been indifferent: There are more immediate pressures on these urban schools to have their best and brightest pass the exceedingly difficult university entrance exams.

Sometimes these pressures take the form of teacher-assisted cheating. The incentive for teachers and officials may be financial—they are paid for their services. Sometimes money is not the issue: The percent of exam-passers is one criterion in the evaluation of their job performance and they want to look better in the eyes of their superiors. In one county in Hebei province, 21 middle-school teachers and examination proctors were caught helping a student through his university entrance exam in a particularly inventive way. Student Wang, the younger brother of two senior party bureaucrats, used a tiny microphone hidden in his clothes to transmit the questions from the examination room to his two brothers, who recorded the questions and arranged for teachers to answer them. The teachers passed the answers to the proctors when the latter visited the men's room, and the proctors placed the answers on Wang's desk when they returned to the examination room. The fraud was discovered by accident, since the microphone signals were picked up by public radio, and several other teachers who were familiar with the content of the exam happened to be listening at the time. Teachers have also sold examination questions and transmitted them via pagers, or looked the other way when students hired substitutes to take their exams. The going rate for hiring a substitute exam taker is said to be between $2,000 and $2,500. The same amounts were quoted for purchasing admission slips to university, with the higher end price being required for the more prestigious institutions.

Well-placed relatives were also known to have bribed teachers to alter candidates' test results. Sometimes bribery was not even necessary: In August 2001, along with the list of incoming students, the website of Shanghai's prestigious Jiaotong University accidentally posted the names of high-ranking officials who had supported their applications.[16] Motivated young people who were bereft of useful connections could use other methods. For example, a group of students in Hunan enlisted the help of custodians with keys to the room where examinations were stored and copied them. Opinion polls reveal that clever cheats often receive the respect of their peers. Less than 40 percent of the students queried in a typical survey opposed cheating, while a somewhat larger number expressed opinions like "Cheating is a kind of ability," "It does not matter if you cheat occasionally," and "Cheating is not a significant [ethical] problem."[17]

Once students arrive at universities, through whatever means, they face different problems. Some are the unintentional consequences of other Deng reforms, which make it more profitable to be a businessperson than the sorts of jobs the university trains one for. Surveys show that intellectuals earn 90 percent less than the average urban worker, but they work longer hours each day. With less disposable income, their housing accommodations are correspondingly less comfortable. Demoralization was especially noticeable at the postgraduate level, where many students simply quit: In 1988, for the first time since Deng Xiaoping began his educational reforms, there were more openings for postgraduate study than there were applicants for the openings. Clearly these were the people that Deng's drive for expertise should have been producing. One former doctoral candidate explained that it had been impossible for him to live on his stipend; he planned to work in the Shenzhen Special Economic Zone and hoped to travel abroad.[18] In 1994, hoping to double the number of students enrolled in postdoctoral programs to 3000 by the year 2000, the government raised annual funding from the equivalent of $1,700 to $2,300 per year.[19] Intellectuals began to fare better, with professors salaries increasing several fold between 1990 and 2000. Unfortunately, teachers at lower levels did not share in these gains.

In discussing their futures, students frequently classify their options into three different categories: the red path, the golden path, and the black path. The red path refers to becoming officials and cadres. It is generally considered to be monopolized by the children of high-ranking cadres, since the leaders are able to secure the most favored places on the path for their progeny. There is also significant contempt expressed for this route. The golden path refers to the business world. While students approve of the fact that one can make money in this career, it is considered risky. Also, students add, to be successful in business, one must "enter by the back door" and have strong official backing.

The black path refers to study abroad. Of those who opt for this path, the great majority choose not to return. They have been criticized for depriving the country's modernization effort of their skills—in effect, biting the hand that fed them. According to official figures, of the 580,000 Chinese who studied abroad between 1978 and 2002, only 150,000, or less than 26 percent, returned home.[20] This was a decline from the approximately one-third of students who returned between 1978 and 1995, and occurred despite various measures to entice back elite students. In 1997, for example, Shanghai introduced measures to reverse the brain drain: employers would be allowed to pay salaries comparable with overseas firms. Housing and special bonuses could be added to the compensation package. These incentives were aimed primarily at specialists in cutting-edge technology and those with management expertise. They proved attractive to at least some Chinese who might otherwise not have considered going back.

The brain drain was not actually as disadvantageous to China as the numbers might suggest, since former students who settled abroad might return for visits and share the benefits of their expertise. Some set up joint ventures and arranged for their local personnel to receive training and for relevant technology to be transferred. And the downturn in the fortunes of dot-com companies in the industrialized world meant that many technologically trained Chinese would be available to staff the PRC's own burgeoning computer industry. Government warnings against "blindly worshipping a foreign degree" notwithstanding, foreign study is popular. In 2002, 300,000 Chinese students opted to study abroad.[21]

The matter of state-assigned jobs for university graduates caused considerable friction between students and state authorities. In 1987, more than 5,000 of 360,000 graduates were rejected by their designated employers, and the government abolished the system of guaranteed job assignments for new graduates. From the student's point of view, there were advantages and disadvantages to this: One might be assigned to a remote area and/or given responsibilities different from those one had trained for, but one was at least guaranteed a job. Officials defended the change, saying it would ensure that supply met demand. Under the previous system, too few students had elected specializations like English, computer software, accounting, and civil engineering, for which there was a need. And too many had opted for history and basic science, fields where there were many more qualified people than openings for them.

Two years later, the government reversed itself, saying that completely free competition for jobs was "still not a suitable option for China." Students had spent so much time during their senior year looking for jobs that their academic performance suffered. Moreover, if the state assigned graduates to jobs, it could be more confident that they went where they were most needed. During the period that the self-found job system was in force, larger and larger numbers of students had chosen to stay in urban areas, even those who had rural origins themselves. The education minister also candidly admitted that allowing students to find their own jobs had caused a marked increase in corruption and favoritism.[22] Although this was not something the minister could be expected to admit, transferring the responsibility for job arrangement back to the state would have the effect of transferring the focus of corruption back to it at the same time. Another, but unspoken, reason that the state took over the job-assignment system again was to control student behavior.[23]

A few years later, the state turned back the responsibility for finding work to the students themselves, bringing back familiar problems. The need to locate one's own employment brought back problems of favoritism in awarding jobs and reluctance to go to where one's talents were most needed. A Guangzhou newspaper applauded graduates who, unable to find other employment, joined the police force. The students had not selfishly insisted that they deserved a higher-status position, and their knowledge would surely improve the quality of law enforcement. It was later pointed out that the students had not been as altruistic as they had first appeared: moving elsewhere to take jobs that they had trained for would mean transferring their registration out of Guangzhou, which they did not want to do.

The feeling among students and intellectuals that the government was unresponsive to their difficulties was an important factor in the demonstrations in Tiananmen Square and elsewhere in China during the spring of 1989. Indeed, the immediate precipitant of the protests was the rumor that former first party secretary Hu Yaobang had died after suffering a heart attack in an argument with a leading leftist over the education budget. The demonstrators' agenda included the establishment of a student union, to allow them influence over an educational establishment that they perceived as badly in need of change.

The government's suppression of the protests was followed by restrictive measures to ensure that the educational system produced "trustworthy Marxists" loyal to party and government.[24] Student activists were sought out, apprehended, and given lengthy prison terms. The internal management system of the entire system, from primary schools through university-level institutions in major cities, was reformed to give greater influence to party committees. Mandatory military training was to be instituted, as it had been, for a brief period, after the student demonstrations of 1986–1987. In the case of Beijing and Fudan universities, this training, which was to include political study sessions in addition to marching and drills, would take the entire freshman year. Applications to these institutions dropped precipitously, and in 1993, the military training requirement was dropped. Gradually, the mood of distrust between students and party and government leaders abated.

In 1994, the government began a plan to have university students finance their own education. By 2000, all students had to pay tuition. They would also be able to find their own jobs. The expected problems arose. Although the fees are quite modest—averaging less than $550 a semester—they were beyond the means of an estimated 300,000 students, or about 10 percent of the total. Universities and colleges have been told to allocate 10 percent of tuition fees to provide scholarships for poor students, but this provision falls short of what is needed. A 2001 study revealed that less than a third of the 534,000 students who had applied for aid got it, and that most of them received less than the amount they had asked for.[25] During the following year, a father who was in despair because he could not pay for his son's tuition committed suicide.

For those who wanted a college degree but were unwilling or unable to take the time to attend an institution of higher learning, forged degrees could be purchased. In one celebrated instance, all of the education documents submitted by applicants for a local government vacancy were found to be forged. Those involved took considerable risks: Forgery is punishable by up to ten years in prison; sellers are treated as accomplices.[26]

It is difficult to tell how widespread these practices are, and one should be wary of generalizing on the basis of a few spectacular examples. Most Chinese schools, though extremely spartan in terms of equipment and creature comforts, are not hazardous to their inhabitants' lives. Most teachers do not assist their students to cheat, nor need either they or their students fear for their lives. Despite the increased obstacles to academic success, some motivated rural children manage to enter even the most prestigious universities and distinguish themselves in professional careers. And most students probably resist the temptation to cheat. But there is a consensus that the system is not functioning properly.

Plans for improvement exist, although progress has been slow. In 1993, the head of China's state education commission described the four major problems in basic-level education as insufficient funding, arrears in teachers' wages, dropouts, and the illegal charging of school fees;[27] nearly a decade later, its premier cited the very same issues.[28] Some ameliorative work has been undertaken: Project Hope, a fund to which Chinese and foreigners were invited to contribute, has enabled more than half a million rural dropouts to return to school since its founding in 1989. Unfortunately, project directors were discovered to be diverting funds away from their intended purpose, thus shortchanging the poor students who so badly needed help.

Major revisions in the basic educational system are underway. A two-stage program to improve rural education began in 2000. Its first two years concentrated on the central provinces, with the period from 2002–2004 to focus on the still more education-deficient western region. The program includes repair and rebuilding of schools, classes to upgrade teachers' skills, and free books. School fees are to be waived for children from poor families. In 2002, the State Council ordered country governments to take over the responsibility of providing nine years of compulsory education from township and village governments. Observers were skeptical, noting that corruption could siphon away funds meant for these improvements, and that the success of the reform was dependent on the uncertain goodwill and diligence of county governments.[29]

Another major innovation aimed at encouraging creativity and teaching children to think for themselves. This was to include livelier textbooks and new teaching methods designed to encourage dialogue between pupils and instructors. Introduced on an experimental basis in elementary schools in 2001, the new curriculum is scheduled to be implemented in all primary and secondary schools between 2005 and 2010. Success is far from ensured, however. These innovations will cost a great deal of money, which has so far not been allocated. An entire educational culture will have to be changed: both teachers and parents have expressed clear preferences for strict classroom discipline with rigorous homework assignments. And, as long as college entrance exams emphasize rote learning, teachers will continue to prepare their students by emphasizing rote learning. Provincial educational authorities are restricting the plan's provision for more freedom of choice in textbooks, since they want to protect provincial publishing houses. Finally, there are concerns about whether teaching children to challenge authority in the classroom will encourage a dangerous culture of dissent in society at large.[30] Those who are being taught to challenge their teachers while children may as adults feel free to challenge party, government, police, and judges.

Some of the pressure on university entrance exams has been abated through a combination of weeding out less qualified applicants at an earlier stage, and by an expansion of university enrollment that began in 1999. By 2002, 3.2 million of the 5.27 million students who took the exam, or about 60 percent, actually enrolled in tertiary-level institutions. About 15 percent of the PRC's college age population now has access to higher education; the government hopes to increase this to 23 percent by 2010. Of course, weeding out less qualified students at lower levels simply shifts the level of tension somewhere else. And the larger number of college graduates appears to have more trouble finding suitable jobs. Professors find some of the students substandard: In 2002, prestigious Beijing University instituted a new elimination system whereby 2 percent of undergraduates would be expelled due to poor academic performance.[31]

Some university administrators have recently seemed more willing to deal with student grievances, if perhaps only to head off an escalation of their protests. For example, student protests that began after a deadly traffic accident near a university in Anhui in 2003 ended quickly when city authorities promised to build a pedestrian bridge across a dangerous intersection where several of their classmates had been killed or injured.

Another educational reform involved consolidation of universities, since the previous system had encouraged a plethora of low-level facilities with overlapping departments and too many narrow disciplines. Between 1992 and 2000, 490 universities and colleges had been merged into 204, though there was general agreement that the PRC's universities were still far from the world-class institutions they aspired to be. Educators felt that universities needed to have legal status which would enable them to manage their own affairs, the ability to choose students in terms of potential rather than simply those with the highest examination scores, and a better way to attract the best teachers. Without these, the additional funding that all agreed was necessary would be wasted.[32]

As for forged diplomas, in 2001, authorities announced that all institutions of higher learning would be required to register their degrees, including those for correspondence schools and part-time courses. Each successfully completed degree would receive a 16-digit identification number, which would then be posted on the internet. Any certificates not so entered were to be considered bogus.[33]

Conclusions

The twists and turns of China's educational policies over the past five decades have been costly. Arguments between those who favor emphasis on political studies and a broadly egalitarian system vis-à-vis those who would prefer to emphasize technical specialization and are comfortable with a more elitist system have consumed precious time and creative energies and created much bitterness.

Nonetheless, the PRC's educational system has succeeded in changing a literacy rate of 25 percent to one of 91 percent, a significant achievement. Again, some skepticism is in order. A resident of Ningxia province provided a fascinating insight on this in a letter he wrote to *People's Daily* in mid-1985. His brigade had been honored as a model in the elimination of illiteracy, but the reality was somewhat different. The county had promised the brigade ten *yuan* for every person it made literate. Each year, the brigade reported that it had raised the literacy rate, eventually reaching 100 percent. The county gave the brigade its money and was praised by higher levels, which passed news of the county's success along to higher levels. Everybody was happy, but there was no improvement in actual literacy rates.[34] During the 1990s, interestingly, Ningxia was one of the areas where the number of illiterates was growing.[35] Moreover, standards for literacy can vary widely. A foreigner conducting research in one rural village in 2002 reports that in her area, it was the ablity to recognize the characters from one to ten.

According to the 2000 census, there are 87 million illiterates in China, with twenty million of them age 15 and over, up from 85 million a decade ago, though the population as a whole had grown as well (see Table 10.1). Moreover, the average educational level is 5.6 years nationwide, indicating that, while most people have learned to read, they do not possess a very high level of literacy. Only two-thirds of students complete primary school,

TABLE 10.1 Illiterate Population Aged 15 and Over by Sex and Region

Region	Percent of Total Population		
	Subtotal	Male	Female
National Total	9.08	4.86	13.47
Beijing	4.93	2.02	8.1
Tianjin	6.47	2.8	10.23
Hebei	8.59	6.47	10.76
Shanxi	5.68	3.21	8.31
Inner Mongolia	11.59	6.98	16.53
Liaoning	5.79	2.93	8.72
Jilin	5.74	3.46	8.12
Heilongjiang	6.33	3.68	9.08
Shanghai	6.21	2.35	10.28
Jiangsu	7.88	3.49	12.27
Zhejiang	8.55	4.35	12.92
Anhui	13.43	7.55	19.5
Fujian	9.68	5.57	13.96
Jiangxi	6.98	3.09	11.04
Shandong	10.75	5.53	15.98
Henan	7.91	4.25	11.67
Hubei	9.31	4.44	14.49
Hunan	5.99	2.76	9.45
Guangdong	5.17	1.72	8.6
Guangxi	5.3	2.07	8.85
Hainan	9.72	3.84	16.11
Chongqing	8.9	4.56	13.53
Sichuan	9.87	5.37	14.62
Guizhou	19.85	9.96	30.61
Yunnan	15.44	9.32	22.15
Tibet	47.25	34.38	60.47
Shaanxi	9.82	5.65	14.24
Gansu	19.68	12.04	27.81
Qinghai	25.44	15.69	35.87
Ningxia	15.72	9.47	22.25
Xinjiang	7.72	5.74	9.87

Source: 2000 Census

and despite the nine-year compulsory education plan promulgated in 1985, it is not actually compulsory. Although local governments spend as much as half of their budgets on education, they must still impose tuition fees high enough that 4 million children drop out each year because their families cannot afford to pay. Progress is unevenly distributed. Urban students are more than twice as likely to attend secondary school, and richer provinces spend 50 percent more per student than poorer ones. The gap between the western part of the country and the rest of it is even greater.[36] Especially in rural areas, males are more likely to be literate than females, and Han Chinese more likely to be educated compared to ethnic minorities. Ninety-two percent of China's illiterates live in rural areas, and seventy percent of them are women. The illiteracy rate in Tibet was 47.25 percent in 2000, up from 44.44 percent in 1990.

Expanding vocational training seemed to hold promise: In 1996, then-premier Li Peng expressed the hope that such training would help stem the falling literacy rate in certain rural areas. By 2010, it was hoped that ratio of vocational secondary schools to academic secondary schools would be 70:30. However, the plan has not been popular with students, due to the social stigma attached to blue-collar jobs. In 2001, only two candidates opted to take an entrance exam for technical education in northwest China, and Shaanxi province's vocational schools were able to recruit less than half the number they enrolled in 1995.[37] Officials continue to be concerned that the ability of the educational system to attract the best and brightest intellects and provide them with an atmosphere in which their talents can be nurtured and enhanced is sadly lacking. Both the quality of education and the study qualities of students are believed to have worsened. Academics blamed the deficiencies of the PRC's educational system for the decline in the country's international competitiveness. The Lausanne-based International Institute for Management Development's Global Competitiveness Report 2000 lowered the PRC's rating from 24 to 31, and from 13 to 28 in science and technology.[38]

While the red-versus-expert debate in education has been resolved in favor of expertise, post-Mao reforms have produced a marked pro-urban and elitist system that many Chinese find disturbing, and that has the potential for creating social unrest. A number of the problems of education in present-day China are due to lack of funding. More classrooms could be repaired. More generous salaries would enhance the prestige of teaching careers; better stipends would attract more postdoctoral students. The percentage of gross national product devoted to education in China in recent years has fluctuated within the middle to lower two percent range. According to United Nations data, this compares with 6.1 percent in the developed world, 4.1 percent in the developing countries, 4.6 percent in Asia as a whole, and 5.7 percent for all countries of the world. In other words, the PRC's investment for education is not only lower than the average international level, it is markedly below that of other developing countries. The leadership is aware that an inadequate educational system will hinder the country's economic development, but the numerous other claims on the central budget— many of them stemming from inadequate economic development[39]—place limits on how much can be spent on developing education. It is not a dilemma that can be easily solved.

Notes

1. *Xinhua*, February 25, 1993, in *FBIS–CHI*, February 25, 1993, p. 17.

2. Leo A. Orleans, *Professional Manpower and Education in Communist China* (Washington, D.C.: National Science Foundation, 1961), p. 18.

3. See Marianne Bastid, "Economic Necessity and Political Ideals in Educational Reform During the Cultural Revolution," *China Quarterly,* April–June 1970, pp. 16–45, for a detailed discussion of this period.

4. Marianne Bastid, "Chinese Educational Policies in the 1980s and Economic Development," *China Quarterly,* June 1984, pp. 189–219, has an excellent analysis of this period.

5. Stanley Rosen, "Education and Economic Reform," in Chris Hudson, ed., *The China Handbook* (Chicago and London: Fitzroy Dearborn Publishers, 1997), pp. 250–261.

6. Quinton Chan, "First 'School for Wealthy' Established in Guangdong," *South China Morning Post*, January 16, 1994, p. 7.

7. "Report Says Education Level of Young 'Worrisome,' " *Zhungguo tongxun she* (Hong Kong), February 25, 1993, in *FBIS–CHI*, March 3, 1993, pp. 31–32.

8. (No author) "Two Thousand Pupils Barred," *Agence France Presse* (Beijing), November 25, 2002.

9. (No author), "Five Jailed for Inciting School Children to Riot," *Straits Times*, January 3, 2002.

10. Craig Smith, "Chinese Leaders and Parents in Dispute over School Explosion," *New York Times*, March 8, 2001, p. A8.

11. Julia Han, "Report on Cotton-Picking Pupils Prompts Child Labour Warning," *South China Morning Post*, October 18, 2001.

12. Ma Guihua, "Forty Children Every Day," *South China Morning Post*, June 25, 2001.

13. (No author), "Twenty-One Chinese Children Die in School Accident," *New York Times*, September 25, 2002, p. A5.

14. *Xinhua*, September 5, 1985, in *FBIS–CHI*, September 9, 1985, p. K/21.

15. (No author), "Violence in Chinese Schools Increasing at Alarming Rate," *Agence France Presse* (Beijing), November 14, 2000.

16. Unsigned editorial, "Doubts About the Exam," *Asian Wall Street Journal*, August 21, 2001, p. 6.

17. *Xinhua*, August 25, 1988; in *FBIS–CHI*, August 29, 1988, p. 25.

18. Fang Fang, "Postgraduates Leave to Make Money, Go Abroad," *China Daily*, November 26, 1988, p. 3.

19. Xiao He, "State to Expand Post-Doctoral Work," *China Daily*, May 27, 1994, p. 3.

20. (No author), "China Has Sent 580 Thousand Students Studying Abroad," *Renmin Ribao*, January 28, 2003, http://english.peopledaily.com.cn/

21. (No author), "Statistics Show 300,000 Chinese Studying Abroad in 103 Countries," *Xinhua*, July 3, 2002.

22. *Xinhua*, January 10, 1991; in *FBIS–CHI*, January 11, 1991, p. 25.

23. I am indebted to Professor William Heaton, U.S.Central Intelligence Agency, for this observation.

24. Willy Wo-Lap Lam, "Beijing University's Party Leadership Strengthened," *South China Morning Post*, March 20, 1991, p. 15.

25. Julia Han, " 'Green Corridors' Proposed to Help Poorer Students Finance Education," *South China Morning Post*, September 3, 2001.

26. Pamela Pun, "Jobs Market Hit by Fake Degrees," *Hong Kong iMail*, July 28, 2001.

27. Li Lanqing quoted by *Xinhua*, August 24, 1993, in *FBIS–CHI*, August 26, 1993, pp. 28–30.

28. (No author), "Zhu Calls for Overhaul of Basic Education System," *South China Morning Post*, June 15, 2001.

29. (Unnamed staff reporter), "$6.8 Billion Boost for Rural Education," *South China Morning Post*, May 10, 2002; Josephine Ma, "Cut Payroll as First Step to Help Rural Schools", *ibid.*, May 18, 2002.

30. (No author), "Roll Over, Confucius," *Economist* (London), January 23, 2003.

31. (No author), "A New Elimination System: A Right Choice for Universities?" *Beijing Review*, October 24, 2002, pp. 21–22.

32. Zhang Zhiping, "Will Mergers Make Them World Class?" *Beijing Review*, September 11, 2000, pp. 7–8.

33. Raymond Li, "Education Authorities Go Online to Fight Fake Certificates," *South China Morning Post*, February 13, 2001.

34. Professor Stanley Rosen, personal communication, September 15, 1991.

35. Chen Yu, "Problems Facing Ningxia Education Work," *Ningxia ribao*, December 17, 1991, p. 2, in *JPRS-CAR*, March 11, 1992, pp. 32–33.

36. Wen Aiying, "Shangrila's Only Gift to Youth is Illiteracy," *South China Morning Post*, July 12, 2002.

37. Xie Hong, "Chinese Rejecting Vocational Education," *Straits Times*, October 15, 2001.

38. Raymond Li, "Weak School System Blamed for Drop in Global Ranks," *South China Morning Post*, March 30, 2001.

39. For example, the need for more roads and railroads, expansion of seaports and improvement of existing harbors. Water shortages also limit economic expansion: Plans to reroute water from one area to another will be very costly. There are, however, other expenditures, such as the steady rise in the military budget, that do not seem to be adequate justifications for such modest outlays on education.

Suggestions for Further Reading

C. Montgomery Broaded and Chongshun Liu, "Family Background and Educational Attainment in Urban China," *China Quarterly,* no.145, March 1996, pp. 53–86.

Min Weifang, "Economic Transition and Higher Education Reform in China," paper presented at Center on Chinese Higher Education, Columbia University, New York, January 24, 2002.

Suzanne Pepper, *Radicalism and Educational Reform in 20th Century China: The Search for a Developmental Model* (Cambridge: Cambridge University Press, 1996).

Stanley Rosen, "Education and Economic Reform," in Chris Hudson, ed., *The China Handbook* (Chicago and London: Fitzroy Dearborn Publishers, 1997), pp. 250–261.

Mun Tsang, "Education and National Development in China Since 1949: Oscillating Policies and Enduring Dilemmas," *China Review*, 2000.

Zhou Yan, "Brain Drain from Chinese Universities in the 1990s," *Journal of Contemporary China,* vol. 7, no.17, March 1998, pp. 103–124.

11 Quality-of-Life Issues: Health, Demography, and the Environment

The health of China's population is important not only in terms of the government's commitment to its people's well-being but also to that people's ability to enhance economic development. Good health is a factor in good productivity and, conversely, poor health contributes to poor productivity. Reducing infant mortality and lowering death rates may, however, cause problems of overpopulation: There are simply too many people among whom to divide the fruits of economic development. Moreover, a large population uses more resources and also creates more waste, leading to pollution and environmental degradation. Hence the issues of health, demography, and the environment are closely intertwined not only with each other, but with economic prosperity as well. With varying degrees of intensity over time, all have been of considerable concern to party and government.

Health

China's medical system was in very bad condition when the communist party took power in 1949. It was not unusual for hundreds of thousands to die in widespread natural disasters such as floods, droughts, and earthquakes, which were then followed by epidemics and famines. Most people had little understanding of the value of sanitation procedures. Infant mortality was very high, as was the incidence of infectious, parasitic, and hereditary diseases.

There were a few bright spots in this dismal picture. The KMT government founded a national health administration in the late 1920s, and health programs were an important part of the government's plans for rural reconstruction. The reports left by health care workers during the Republican era provide vivid insights into the frustrations experienced by this relatively small group of medically trained personnel trying to function in a vast countryside of ignorance and superstition.[1] China also had a number of missionary hospitals, jointly staffed by foreign and foreign-trained Chinese personnel. A few medical schools were set up in China as well. A grant from the Rockefeller Foundation made possible the establishment of Peking Union Medical College, which, among other activities, did research on the causes of China's most devastating diseases.

Impressive as these efforts were, they were mere drops in an ocean of need, and had in any case been adversely affected by the decades of fighting of the Sino-Japanese and Chinese civil wars. Most Chinese did not have access to modern medical facilities even where they did exist. Traditional Chinese medicine should be credited with some impressive achievements. Acupuncture has many admirers in developed countries, and some herbal medicines have been proved astonishingly effective. Many others, however, have at best a placebo effect. Diseases scarcely known in more developed countries ravaged millions of people. One example is schistosomiasis, a disease caused by the liver fluke. Using as its intermediary the snails that are ubiquitous in some waterways and rice paddies, the parasite slowly devours the internal organs of its victims and, if not properly treated, causes a prolonged and extremely painful death. It impacted one in ten persons south of the Yangtze River in the first half of the twentieth century.[2] Kala-azar disease, which attacks the liver and spleen, affected more than half a million persons, most of them in north China. It is spread by sandflies and reaches humans through the dogs the flies live on.

The communist government, though determined to improve this baleful situation, had limited resources to draw on and many other pressing problems. During 1949–1950, only 1 percent of total government expenditure was allocated to health care; during the subsequent five years, it never exceeded 2.6 percent. A three-pronged strategy was adopted. First, the emphasis was to be on preventive rather than curative medicine. Second, traditional Chinese medicine was to be employed where it was deemed useful. And third, medical education was to be established at different academic levels and supplemented by large numbers of paramedics. These approaches reflected practical considerations that were well suited to the PRC's resources.[3]

Teams were sent out to investigate the country's health problems and, where possible, give treatment. Certain diseases were targeted for special attention. Venereal disease, bubonic (black) plague, and malaria were treated free. Other treatments were not free, but efforts were made to set the costs at affordable levels.

The techniques of mass mobilization were employed in health care as in other areas. In 1952, the first "patriotic public health campaign" began, with the goal of teaching tens of millions of people the link between sanitation and good health. Lantern slides, posters, and theatrical performances spread the word. Mass movements were organized to clear away huge quantities of garbage, often the accumulation of many years. The people were instructed to kill mosquitoes and rats, and quotas were established for the number to be killed and turned in. This campaign was not without its own frustrations, as when cadres discovered that some people were raising rats and nurturing insects in order to have enough to meet their quota. But positive results greatly outweighed such disappointing episodes, and in general great progress was made. Patriotic public health campaigns became collective clean-up efforts for a week each spring and fall.

Prior to 1949, peasant families often lived together with, or in very close proximity to, their cattle, pigs, and chickens. Dilapidated animal shelters and manure pits were common sights in rural villages.[4] Government teams ordered or cajoled villagers to set up public latrines. Since manure was valuable as a fertilizer, more people were resistant to this particular form of communism than one might at first think. Peasants were taught how to put stone walls beneath the latrines, so that excrement would not pollute the drinking water supply through seepage into underground streams. They were also told how long waste matter should stay in the latrines before it could be used as fertilizer in the fields, since eventually the ammonia contained in waste matter would kill many parasites therein. Because peasants were reluctant to wait the necessary 15 to 30 days during spring planting season, when the demand for fertilizer was greatest, they were instructed to boil waste matter before putting it in the fields, or supplied with certain chemicals to add to it.

The mass campaign technique was also employed against specific diseases. For example, people were first given instruction on *how* schistosomiasis was spread, and then mobilized to drain the water of affected ponds and ditches and turn over the earth. They were advised that it was preferable to kill the snails by burning them with matches or pouring boiling water over them rather than in any way touching the creatures. Harsh but effective drugs were made available to those already infected with schistosomiasis, thus greatly reducing the numbers of sufferers.

Considerable effort was expended to ensure that swamps where malaria-carrying mosquitoes bred were drained. Here again, there was some resistance: Peasants in some areas regarded marshy areas as sacred and were reluctant to disturb the local deities whom they believed to reside there. As for kala-azar disease, government efforts resulted in dogs being removed from urban areas and their numbers greatly reduced in the countryside. Insecticides were employed against the sandflies that had lived on the dogs, and drugs were provided for those who had kala-azar.

Another major problem that post-1949 health programs concentrated on was infant mortality. Maternal and child health stations were established, and midwives were instructed to boil their instruments before using them. Traditionally, the midwife would either bite off the umbilical cord or sever it with an unclean knife, placing a bit of dung or a piece of unsterile cloth over the cut. Hence the relatively simple and inexpensive techniques of sterilization that party health workers introduced greatly reduced the number of deaths from tetanus and childbirth fever.

Initial efforts produced impressive results, though the cyclical nature of mass campaigns did not provide the kind of sustained effort that is needed for effective disease control. And, despite the CCP's commitment to amelioration of peasants' lives, the majority of China's health care facilities were located in urban areas. Even the more modern urban hospitals were, and remain, dirty by Western standards. Another problem was that medicine was in short supply. During the first decade of the PRC, the government's emphasis was on Western medicine, though traditional remedies continued to be used. For many people, traditional medicines were the drug of choice; others opted to use both types of remedy at once.

The Great Leap Forward, as part of its commitment to "walking on two legs," the traditional and the modern, attempted to raise Chinese medicine to equal status with Western. Though tremendous successes were claimed for the large-scale reintroduction of old remedies, they must be evaluated in the general context of the hyperbolic rhetoric of the Great Leap period. The Leap's slogan "more, better, faster, and cheaper" did little to improve the quality of medical care, and the famines that followed the collapse of its policies caused untold numbers of deaths as millions of malnourished people succumbed to diseases that they would normally have recovered from.

When economic conditions began to improve in 1962, health care improved as well, at least in the cities. The urban bias of the PRC's medical system had not escaped Chairman Mao's notice, and in 1965, as the country was approaching the Cultural Revolution, Mao expressed himself in a typically blunt way. His assessment of China's health care system is well worth reading (see the "Mao on Medical Care" box).

Mao's message was strongly populist, and the system hastened to comply. In most ways, the Cultural Revolution was not good for health care. One consequence of the chaos

Mao on Medical Care

Tell the Department of Public Health that it serves only fifty percent of the population of the country. These fifty percent consist of gentlemen; the broad peasant masses have no medical care—neither doctors nor medicine. The Department of Public Health does not belong to the people; it should be named the Department of Urban Public Health, Gentleman's Public Health, or City Gentleman's Public Health. Medical education should be reformed, because there is no need to read so many books. . . . Medical schools do not have to admit only senior middle-school graduates; it is quite proper to take in third-year children from junior middle schools. The main point is to raise their standrads during practice. The physicians trained this way may not be very competent, but they are far better than fake doctors and witch doctors. Furthermore, villages can afford them. More study only makes them stupid. The methods of check-up and treatment used in our hospitals now are quite unsuitable for the countryside; they are mainly for the cities. But China has more than 500 million peasants!

To allocate a great deal of manpower and resources to the study of difficult illnesses and to carry out penetrating research is to aim at the peaks, to detach [medical work] from the masses. The result is to ignore or to assign only small amounts of manpower and resources to the prevention or cure of common, frequent, widespead diseases. "Peaks" are not being abandoned, but they are going to receive less manpower and resources. The lion's share of manpower and equipment should be allocated to tackling the problems most urgently demanded by the masses.

There is another curious thing. When a doctor examines a patient, he always covers his mouth with a gauze mask, whatever the patient's illness. Is he afraid of passing germs to his patient? I think he is more likely to be afraid of his patient passing germs to him. He must make a difference here [between patients with infectious disease and those without]: to wear a mask under all circumstances is to build a barrier between him and his patients.

City hospitals should keep some doctors who have graduated after one or two years and are not very good. The others should all work in the villages. The "four purifies" [purify politics, organization, ideology, and economy] are basically completed. Their completion does not mean the completion of public health and medical work in the villages. Indeed, the focus of medical and public health work should be transferred to the villages.[5]

in party and government institutions was that little attention was paid to patriotic sanitation campaigns, regular inoculations, and the extermination of mosquitoes. Disruptions in rail service meant that medical supplies often did not reach their intended destinations. A major cholera epidemic broke out in 1967, the first such in many years. The Cultural Revolution's virulently antispecialist attitudes also resulted in most health care experts being forced to spend many hours in cleaning chores, to the detriment of the time they could spend on patient care. Some elitist research projects continued: During the height of the revolution's frenzy, Chinese doctors announced that they had successfully synthesized insulin, a first in world medical history. Many doctors were, however, sent to the countryside for varying periods of time. This might have improved the quality of rural medical care, as Mao had wanted. Unfortunately, doctors who had been sent down to the countryside were frequently not allowed to practice medicine but ordered to perform tasks designed to teach humility, such as slopping pigs or cleaning out latrines.

By far the most celebrated contribution of the Cultural Revolution to health care was the institution of "barefoot doctors." Neither barefoot nor physicians, they were actually a corps of paramedics with perhaps three to six months' training in relatively simple, but commonly needed, medical techniques. Following their training, the new barefoot doctors were expected to improve their qualifications with on-the-job experience supplemented by such additional training courses as might be made available. Certain barefoot doctors attained skill levels far beyond those generally associated with paramedics and were able to perform operations that included appendectomies and caesarean sections.

The barefoot doctors generally worked as part of a cooperative medical system set up by the production brigade to serve its members. Because the central and provincial governments gave very little financial support to rural medical care, most medical costs were paid by individuals, families, or the collective. Members of a production brigade could choose to have or not have a cooperative medical plan. If the answer were yes, each brigade member paid a small fee of a few *yuan* a year, and the brigade welfare fund subsidized the rest. Cooperative health plans differed widely in what they covered; generally speaking, prosperous brigades paid a higher percentage of the costs of illnesses, for a wider variety of illnesses. When brigades decided not to have a cooperative medical plan—nearly always because they were too poor to do so—the patient had to pay the entire cost of visits to the barefoot doctor, drugs, and hospital costs. Serious imbalances therefore occurred in the medical insurance system, with the best coverage generally belonging to those who least needed it.

A sick person was expected to see the barefoot doctor first. If the ailment proved beyond his or her capabilities, the barefoot doctor would refer the patient to better-trained individuals who worked at the commune clinic or hospital. When the system worked as designed, it was an inexpensive way to provide basic health care.[6] However, Western residents at a hospital in Hubei in 1980 noted that their patients, of both urban and rural backgrounds, regularly bypassed the screening system and were also adept at shopping among various hospitals when they felt that their care was inadequate. Moreover, although health care costs in China are reputed to be very low, they do not appear so when considered as a percentage of total income. For example, one patient in the Hubei hospital belonged to a collective insurance program that provided 70 percent coverage. Of a total bill of 508 *yuan*, he was thus responsible for 152.41 *yuan*, which was more than half of his yearly income.[7]

Particularly in rural areas, this system changed markedly with the dissolution of the commune system in the early 1980s. Collective medical insurance plans disappeared along with the collectives, and barefoot doctors were uncertain of their place in the new, incentive-based countryside. Their numbers declined sharply, and the emphasis of the health care system shifted from the prevention of illness toward treatment after the patient became ill. Many barefoot doctors were required to contract for farmland along with anyone else who was classified as a rural resident. Some became the equivalent of private practitioners, charging a fee for their services and taking a profit on the medicines they dispensed.

The official media began to complain that unqualified people in rural and urban areas alike were pretending to be doctors and charging exorbitant fees for bogus treatments and fake medicines.[8] The fake medicines were sometimes not mere placebos, but actually dangerous to the user. The government's attempts to clamp down had marginal results. For example, in 2001, 192,000 Chinese died from bogus or tainted medications. In response, the government closed down 1,300 pharmaceutical factories—half of the country's total—that it found to be turning out substandard products. In spite of this, the first half of 2002 saw 70,000 people die from the same cause.[9] And sometimes the government is actually complicit: A widely sold AIDS preventative, which apparently does no actual harm other than creating a false sense of safety, carries a permit number from the ministry of health.[10]

Another distinctly negative effect was the reappearance of diseases scarcely heard of in the PRC for decades. There was a widespread epidemic of hepatitis centered on Shanghai in the mid-1980s, followed by an outbreak of bubonic plague in Heilongjiang in 1988.[11] Diphtheria reappeared in Beijing in 1990, presumably because children were not being regularly immunized as they had been in the past.[12] Infant mortality rates began to rise, after a 40-year decline. Schistosomiasis was reported in eight provinces during 1990, after being nearly wiped out in the 1950s. Several provinces reported the return of other endemic diseases. The number of cholera cases rose; a 1993 epidemic affected almost 12,000 people in 12 provinces and claimed 142 lives.

When polltakers asked several thousand peasants what they feared most, the overwhelming majority replied that it was being sick. A separate survey of workers yielded the same answer. The previous state medical care system, modest as it was, had cost the state excessive amounts of money. The state's effort to make hospitals more self-reliant caused health care costs to rise by 20 percent and more each year from the 1990s onward, far in excess of the increase in GDP growth. Because hospitals were forbidden to raise fees for services, they covered the shortfalls in their budgets by overprescribing medicine and tests to patients who were covered by their enterprises. Since the enterprises, too, were now expected to be self-reliant, some ran out of money to even pay their workers, much less cover their medical costs. Cash-strapped hospitals turned away patients who could not pay deposit fees, sometimes with fatal results. A survey indicated that the average medical expenditure in rural areas was 1,532 *yuan* in 1998, but that 35. 5 percent of the rural population earned less than 1,500 *yuan* per year. Nearly half the the 60 million Chinese who live below the poverty line were put there by catastrophic medical expenses.[13] The average age of the population is rising, and older people typically have greater health needs than the young. Hence, the problems are expected to worsen just as a smaller number of working people are available to pay the costs. According to official figures, there was one retired person per 30.3 employees in 1978, but the ratio had fallen to 1: 3.7 in 1999 and, assuming a continuation of current trends, could reach 1: 2.4 in 2030.

To cope with the crisis in health care, the government experimented with a number of different schemes beginning from the mid-1990s, so far with little success. Because conditions in cities and the countryside are so different, there are separate plans for each. For urban areas, the latest version involves individuals paying 2 percent, and their employers 6 percent, of their salaries for health care. The worker's entire contribution and 30 percent of the employer's contribution will go into an individual health account for each worker. This is expected to be devoted primarily to pay outpatient fees and the cost of medications for the worker. The remainder of the employer contribution will go into a general medical trust fund. To end the practice of hospitals prescribing unnecessary or overpriced medications, hospitals are to be separated from pharmacies. Experts have pointed out that the proposed plan amounts to cost-shifting rather than cost-containment: Whereas recipients formerly received health care services for free, they now have to pay a fixed portion of their incomes to the fund as insurance against potential health problems. Moreover, the benefits the plan promises are quite limited, meaning that patients must pay the rest out of their own pockets. And, if hospitals cannot make up the shortfall in their expenses by selling medicine, they may choose to raise the fees they charge patients.[14]

For rural areas, a plan introduced by the health ministry in 2003 focuses on reinvigorating the health cooperatives that became ineffective after market reforms were introduced in the 1980s. The central government is to contribute 10 *yuan* annually to each participant in the co-ops in poorer inland provinces, though not in wealthier coastal areas. Regional governments and individuals enrolled in the health co-ops are to contribute at least as much as the central government. Specific targets include providing 90 percent of children with vaccinations for major illnesses, cutting maternal and child mortality rates by 20 percent from 2000 levels, and giving 75 percent of the rural population access to basic information on HIV/AIDS. But the ministry's plan did not address crucial issues of how the medical staffs would be paid or how the cost of medical care and prescription drugs might be met.[15] The ever-present scourge of corruption was apt to siphon funds away from their intended purpose, as it had with previous health plans, both urban and rural. One health care professional, when queried about the future of the system, replied with no trace of sarcasm that it was best to stay well.

During the 1990s there was a precipitous rise in the use of drugs—again, something that had been essentially eradicated in the 1950s. Party leaders showed immediate concern. The mass media reminded people of the events surrounding the Opium War of 1840 and pointed out the deleterious effects that drug use had, not only for individuals and their families but also for the strength of the country internationally. Rehabilitation centers were set up for addicts, and stiff new penalties enacted for drug dealers. Nonetheless, drug use continued to spread. Starting from Yunnan province, which borders Southeast Asia's Golden Triangle, drugs were brought into China by local ethnic minorities whose communications networks spread them throughout the provinces. Secret societies (see Chapter 2), which had also been essentially eradicated after 1949, reappeared as well and were heavily involved in the drug trade. An internal ministry of public security document noted that, among the numerous gangs involved, the Triad society had been particularly successful in bribing officials to ignore their activities.[16]

The same gangs were involved in prostitution, another revival from the ill-remembered days before 1949, and one which also facilitated the transmission of AIDS. Although prostitution is a crime according to the central government, some local governments view it as a source of revenue: For example, bar girls in the northeastern city of Shenyang pay taxes on the wages received from practicing their profession. According to one survey, less than 6 percent use condoms. Although it was estimated in 1998 that 90 percent of the PRC's 300,000 HIV-positive individuals had been infected through drug use, concern soon centered on unsanitary methods of blood donation that spread both AIDS and other serious diseases. So-called bloodheads paid desperately poor people to donate blood, centrifuged the pooled blood of many people to separate the components they wanted, and then returned the leftover pooled portion to donors. Thus the AIDS virus, as well as hepatitis and other diseases, quickly spread. In one of the most heavily impacted areas, Wanshou village in rural Henan, the infection rate was 65 percent. County officials, behaving much like bureaucrats in traditional China, tried to conceal the epidemic. In this case, they were abetted by the central government, which actually arrested several individuals who were trying to educate the population on how the disease was contracted and what measures they could take to protect themselves. A United Nations report of 2002 rebuked the Chinese government for its inaction, and warned that the PRC could expect 20 million people to be infected by the end of the decade unless immediate action were taken.[17]

These and other serious problems are continuing concerns for the PRC's health care system. One-third of the world's cigarette smokers live in China; 63 percent of the adult male population smokes, and people are starting to smoke at younger ages.[18] And lack of attention to developing safety standards for the workplace has resulted in a high incidence of occupation-related accidents. The World Health Organization's report for 2000 ranked the PRC 188 out of 191 countries in terms of the fairness of its health system, 144 for overall performance, and 138 in health care expenditure per capita.[19]

Such problems notwithstanding, the average life expectancy at birth in China is 71 years, compared to 42 in Afghanistan and Burkina Faso, 69 in Brazil, and 81 in Japan. The world average is 68. This is an impressive achievement for any country, and all the more so for a large developing country. Also, by the mid-1970s, the leading causes of death had shifted away from infectious diseases like dysentery and cholera and toward a pattern more like those of developed countries. By the late 1990s, cancer had become the leading cause of death in urban areas, and respiratory diseases in rural areas. Cigarette smoking and air pollution are major contributing causes. There is a nascent antismoking movement, though so far it has reached mostly younger people in large cities.

Not surprisingly, the type of medical care available differs sharply from that in more developed countries. Although the PRC's newly wealthy can purchase excellent health care, most people who need dialysis to survive, or a coronary bypass, or an organ transplant, will not get them: He or she will die. Enormous amounts of money are not generally devoted to caring for the very elderly when they are sick, as is the case in the United States. One reason for the PRC's impressive longevity statistics has more to do with lifestyle than medical care: Most people get plenty of exercise and have low-fat diets. They have been taught to drink tea or boiled water rather than trust suspect tap water. Relatively few people take drugs or consume large amounts of alcohol. The average Chinese is extremely unlikely to be murdered or killed in a car accident, though traffic safety is an increasing problem. And, finally, the PRC does not have a large underclass that lacks ready access to medical care.

This will not necessarily be the case in the future. Chinese sources complain that the newly prosperous are increasingly consuming rich foods, exercising less, and smoking and drinking more. In addition, the burgeoning "floating population" tends to flout rules and regulations on sanitation and health care as in other areas, thus facilitating the spread of disease. If the ambitious health care plans outlined above do not work, the millions of laid-off workers and increasingly impoverished peasants may in time take on the characteristics of an underclass. As noted above, problems with drugs and AIDS are growing, as are environmentally related diseases.[20]

Demography

Confucius considered a large population a sign of prosperity and contentment: an indication that the mandate of heaven lay securely on the dynasty. In addition, the Confucian family system encouraged the idea of large families. Imperial bureaucrats also were in favor of large populations, since more people would mean increased tax revenues. Thus, the government considered it important to keep an accurate population count. China conducted its first census in A.D. 2. Other censuses took place at irregular intervals thereafter. The population remained remarkably stable for over a thousand years, fluctuating between 37 million and 60 million in response to the presence or absence of natural disasters.

Starting from the early years of the Ming dynasty in the fourteenth century, China began a period of six centuries of population growth. Originally encouraged by the development of faster-growing varieties of rice, it was later also helped by the introduction of new types of food from America and technological innovations. New areas were opened to cultivation, and irrigation works were extended. Some Chinese began to worry about the Malthusian dilemma of land expanding arithmetically whereas population increased geometrically—much faster than new land could be put under cultivation, even where such land was available.

The century preceding the communist takeover was, as has been seen, characterized by dynastic decline, societal disintegration, civil war, and foreign invasion. With their attentions absorbed by a struggle for control, Chinese communist leaders were not so much concerned with the absolute size of the population as with the percentage of it that was under their jurisdiction. Karl Marx had, moreover, taken issue with Malthus, declaring that poverty was not caused by too large a population but by an unfair distribution of economic resources. Under socialism, these resources would be distributed equally, and all would prosper.

Despite the benign attitudes of Confucius and Marx toward a large population, the results of the PRC's first census, in 1953, came as a shock to the leadership. On hearing that China had 582.6 million people, Mao is reported to have wondered how there could possibly be that many. The country had been at peace since 1950 and this, together with the health care measures described above, led to a rise in the number of births while the mortality rate dropped sharply. A few voices, hesitant at first, began to question Marx's theory of population and advocate family planning. Accused by their critics of bourgeois Malthusianism, they denied that birth control had anything to do with Malthus. Rather, it was needed in order to protect the health of the mother, ensure that parents could give the best of care to each child they brought into the world, and allow them sufficient time to study and work hard in order to build socialism in China.

Beginning in 1955, China began to manufacture large quantities of contraceptives. However, even these quantities could meet the needs of only 2.2 percent of the couples of child-bearing age. And the quality of what was available was often poor. Condoms were unlubricated, intrauterine devices uncomfortable, and contraceptive foams and jellies unreliable. Those who wanted to practice family planning (and the overwhelming majority of people apparently did not) often had to resort to folk remedies. One of these involved the consumption of live, whole tadpoles. Three or four days after menstruation, a woman was to swallow fourteen of them, and ten more the day after. This was supposed to prevent conception for five years. Advocates pointed out that their formula had the advantages of being safe, effective (?), and inexpensive. Unfortunately, they admitted, it had the disadvantage of being feasible only in the spring—since the tadpoles would turn into frogs thereafter.

It is unlikely that this first effort to reduce births succeeded in significantly reducing fertility rates, with the possible exception of a few large cities.[21] It did, however, show the government how difficult population stabilization would be. Research began on better methods of contraception. China's doctors devised the vacuum aspiration method of abortion, which is both much simpler and much safer than the previously used dilation and curettage technique. It has since been adopted worldwide.

Led by eminent economist Ma Yinchu, who was also president of Beijing University, the movement for a family planning program gained momentum. Ma had originally planned to present a speech on the topic at the 1955 National People's Congress, but the adverse reaction he received from fellow representatives who previewed the text convinced him that it would be wisest not to. Finally, at the height of the Hundred Flowers campaign two years later, Ma decided that the time was right. The assembled delegates to the fourth session of the First NPC heard Ma contend that it was absolutely necessary for China to control its population in order to decrease consumption and thereby increase the accumulation of capital. He went on to say that, because the PRC's large population was basically unskilled, it would be inappropriate to rush into mechanization and industrialization; this would result in reducing the number of jobs and cause greater unemployment. Ma advocated shifting China's emphasis to light industry, which could absorb a larger labor force.[22]

Unfortunately for Ma, the Hundred Flowers began to wilt shortly after his speech. Among the many indictments issued against him, Ma was vilified for being a Malthusian, an anti-Marxist, and a poor economist. He was forced to relinquish his position at Beijing University. Undaunted, Ma continued to write papers, but was forbidden to publish them. The leadership had decided that a large population was actually good for production. It reasoned that everyone comes into the world with only one mouth, but two hands. A massive application of labor power would unleash the forces of production and the resulting huge expansion of agriculture and industry would refute conclusively the bourgeois notion that the growth of population would outstrip the growth of production. The media stopped encouraging birth control and began talking about the need for more people.

There is evidence indicating that the birth control effort begun in 1955 was not actually abandoned, but simply went underground. However, the starvation and malnutrition that followed the collapse of the Great Leap Forward did more to curb population growth than any government propaganda. They also discredited once and for all the notion that the larger the population, the better for production. By early 1962, there was renewed pressure for family planning. The "more, better, faster, and cheaper" slogan of the Great Leap was replaced by "later [marriage], longer [intervals between births], and fewer [children]." Young people were urged to postpone marriage until their mid- to late twenties and to have only two children, preferably spaced three to five years apart. Greater efforts were made to provide inexpensive and convenient contraceptives. The government also encouraged research leading to the development of a birth control pill.

In 1964, a family planning office was established under the supervision of the state council. Provinces and large cities set up guidance committees to coordinate propaganda work and the distribution of contraceptives. Their efforts were heavily focused on urban areas. Partly this was because urban areas were more likely to have modern medical systems and to be able to supply contraceptives and abortions. Partly it was because the party's control system was better in urban areas: Residents could be threatened with loss of jobs or withdrawal of other privileges more easily than in the countryside.

Various techniques were used. Some areas would issue ration coupons for up to three children; parents who insisted on having more would presumably have to feed everyone on proportionately less food. Neighborhood health stations kept track of menstrual cycles, methods of contraception, and previous births. Typically this information was posted on wall charts for the edification of all who were interested. Factories and work units were allocated quotas for the maximum number of births allowed; couples wishing to have a baby had to apply for permission. Should one couple conceive out of turn, another couple would have to be persuaded to postpone childbearing. This created tremendous pressure, from both one's superiors and one's peer group, to conform to the plan. The fact that there was, and continues to be, a shortage of housing in major cities undoubtedly also discouraged the creation of large families. Fertility seems to have declined rapidly in many cities from 1962 to 1966.[23] Unfortunately for China's overall population totals, the overwhelming majority of its citizens live in the countryside.

The family planning program, like most other officially sponsored plans, disintegrated during the Cultural Revolution. The period of time involved is, however, fairly short, and there is little evidence that any large number of births resulted. By 1970, official pressure for family planning was back again. New problems awaited. The large number of babies born in the early 1950s, before population planning measures became effective, had reached child-bearing age themselves, threatening an all-time high in births even if every couple were to agree to only two children. Agricultural production had been essentially stagnant, and Malthus's depressing theory began to seem more and more like an imminent reality.

The policies introduced by Deng Xiaoping to cope with population problems confirm his reputation as an action-oriented pragmatist. In December 1978, delegates to the Eleventh National Party Congress's Third Plenum were informed that only drastic curbs in population growth would enable the PRC to achieve the ambitious economic goals of the Four Modernizations plan. In January 1979, a policy of encouraging all couples to limit themselves to one child was announced. Initially, the hope was to keep the population level below 1.1 billion by the end of the twentieth century.[24] Eventually, it was hoped, the population could be stabilized at below 700 million. Ma Yinchu, aged 98, was rehabilitated and made honorary president of Beijing University.

A combination of incentives and penalties was introduced to ensure compliance. Families who pledged to limit their children to one were to receive free medical care for the child up to age 18, preferential admission to kindergarten and other child-care facilities, and free education. The child would be exempt from being sent to rural areas to work, and from military service. Its mother would receive extended maternity leave, and the family would get priority in obtaining housing. One-child families would even be made eligible for larger living quarters. A small cash subsidy and extra food rations would also be given to such families.

Those who did not agree to have only one child would be immediately disadvantaged, since they would be pushed further down the list for housing, kindergarten admission, and the like. Also, their child would be more likely to be sent to the countryside or selected for military service. For those who insisted on having three or more children, sanctions were imposed. Fines were levied, ranging anywhere from 5 percent to 15 percent of parental income until the children reached the age of 14 or 15. The rationale was that this sum was needed to compensate the state for the costs it incurred in educating and otherwise caring for excessive numbers of children. If the offending parents were cadres, they could be fired or expelled from the party. Billboards went up all over China featuring attractive parents admiring their adorable toddler (always a girl, in view of strong popular preferences for male children) and a caption that read variations of "Daddy, Mommy, and me" or "One child is best." This symbolized the image of the ideal family the government wanted its citizens to internalize.

The one-child policy worked quite well in China's large cities, where couples had already decided that one child was all they wanted, or were sufficiently indifferent to the idea of a second child that they found the government's incentives attractive. However the great majority of China's people do not live in large cities and, despite increasing urbanization, it will be many years, if ever, before they do (see Figure 11.1). The one-child policy was highly unpopular from the beginning. People were legitimately troubled by a number of questions that the architects of the new policy had left unanswered. Since the care of the elderly has traditionally fallen on their children, how could a married couple composed of two only children bear the burden of responsibility for four infirm parents? In terms of

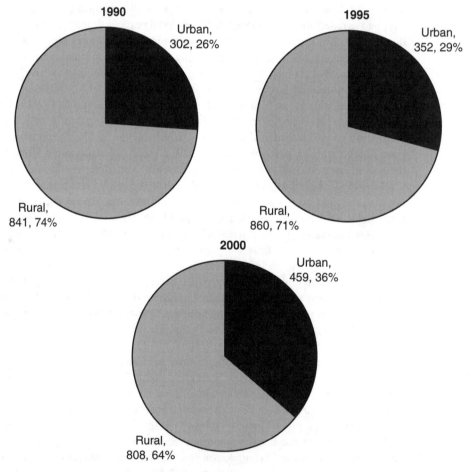

FIGURE 11.1   Increasing Urbanization, 1990–2000 (in millions)
Source: Compiled from State Statisical Bureau Data, 1990–2000.

the country as a whole, how could a small group of younger people support a huge elderly population and still achieve high economic growth rates? What about the psychological health of the child? With all the hopes of the family centered on the success of one small daughter or son, the burden might be too much to bear and adversely affect the child's mental health. Alternatively, it was argued, only children are apt to be spoiled brats. The image of a pampered and petted "little emperor" being fussed over by hordes of worshipful relatives quickly became prevalent. Military officers worried about the sort of recruit pool that the new policies would result in.

While many families were willing to stop at one child if that child were a son, nature did not grant that wish in slightly less than 50 percent of first births. The incentive was to try again and, if the second child were a girl as well, as many additional times as it took to produce a boy. There are sound economic reasons for preferring sons to daughters. Traditionally, when a woman marries, she goes to live with her husband's family, which then gains the use of her labor while her own family loses it. Since most men are physically stronger than most women, their labor is more highly valued. Also, despite the PRC's professions on equality of the sexes—Mao Zedong's "Women hold up half of the sky" is dutifully repeated every March in honor of Women's Day—females are frequently paid less than men for tasks that strike outsiders as the same. Although the law provides for equal pay for equal worth, the government's own surveys find that women receive only 70 to 80 percent of what men earn for the same work. Moreover, most women work in lower skilled and lower paid jobs than men.[25]

Horrifying stories followed attempts to impose the one-child policy strictly. The father of a four-year-old daughter threw her into a deep well when a soothsayer predicted that his pregnant wife would produce a son. (The girl died, the baby turned out to be another girl, and the unrepentant father was sentenced to several years in jail.) Other disappointed fathers of daughters or their families beat the mother, often to death, or insisted on a divorce. When it was announced that parents could have a second child if the first were nonhereditarily handicapped, there were reports of desperate parents maiming helpless children. Cadres under pressure to impose the one-child limit forced abortions on women who were late in pregnancy. The cadres in turn risked retaliation from relatives and friends of the women. Midwives in some areas kept a pail of water next to the delivery table, ready to drown newborn girls. Baby girls, and boys with birth defects, were abandoned, filling orphanages which had neither the money nor the staff to properly care for them. In the mid-1990s, a BBC television crew filmed the conditions under which these infants lived. It reported that certain children were consigned to "dying rooms" where they slowly starved to death.

Some couples did not register the birth of girls; others decided not to register their marriages. When wives got pregnant with a third child, the couple would often simply leave their area and visit distant relatives until the child was born. Alternatively, they could join the floating population. With the introduction of Deng's economic incentive system, people were no longer so tied to their units. The press regularly referred to villages of "excess birth guerrillas," composed of those who had set up communities of shacks on wasteland. One commentator wondered openly what must be on many people's minds: How long would it be before the excess birth guerrillas became the regular army? The floating population at that time was estimated at between 70 and 100 million, and growing. In 1991, the state family planning commission began issuing a series of increasingly stringent regulations to crack down on migrants' child-bearing. An unintended result of the confusing mass of rules and certificates the new regulations stipulated has been to deprive many migrant women of health care. More than three-fourths of all maternal deaths in Guangzhou in 2000 were migrant women.[26]

Nor do these techniques exhaust the tactics used by those who wished to evade the one-child policy. Women who had been fitted with intrauterine devices against their will paid physicians, and even witch doctors, to remove them. Those who had had sterilization operations arranged to have them reversed. These highly illegal acts were facilitated by the fact that there were now many private medical practitioners. In the countryside, where Deng's agricultural reforms had made the household the unit of production, peasants reasoned that it made sense to have more children to provide the family with more labor power. They regarded the fine for excess births as just another annoying tax, and either paid it or bribed officials to ignore the births. Since peasants built and owned their own homes, giving preference in housing to one-child families was no incentive. Nor was preference in school entrance, since most peasants did not aspire to long periods of education for their children.

The threat to remove cadres from their jobs or expel them from the party if they failed to set a good example for the masses was also less than completely effective. In the PRC's new incentive-based economy, being a cadre was no longer as desirable as it had once been, nor was party membership so esteemed. Even in the cities, results were less than hoped for. There was a tendency for the promised incentives to disappear.[27] For example, inflation wiped out the value of promised cash bonuses, even where they were paid. In a context where there was an acute lack of housing and nearly everyone held a one-child certificate, being given priority for housing meant little.

In short, the government had lost many of the economic levers over public behavior that it had once had. Faced with widespread passive resistance to the one-child policy, the leadership had to come to terms with the limitations on its ability to control population growth. The idea of *reducing* the population to 700 million—or at all—dropped quietly from the press. Instead, the media began to speak, none too confidently, of holding the population to 1.2 billion, and later 1.3 billion, by the year 2000,[28] rather than 1.1 billion—that is, 200 million more people than originally anticipated.

A series of directives issued in the 1980s and early 1990s alternated between tougher measures to ensure compliance and softer measures that permitted second births under certain specified conditions. Shifting emphases put cadres responsible for enforcing them in a particularly difficult position. In 1991, faced with widespread flouting of regulations, the government instituted draconian enforcement measures. Pregnant women were forced to undergo induced labor, which generally killed the fetus, and then sterilized. Huge fines were levied on the parents of out-of-plan children; sometimes their possessions were confiscated and their homes destroyed as well. At the end of 1993, a Henan court sentenced to death two hospital officials who had supplied falsified sterilization papers to 448 women; four other officials were sent to prison.[29]

One factor which helped the government's plan to reduce the birth rate was the introduction of ultrasound scanning machines, which allow prospective parents to know the sex of the fetus. Word about the new machines appears to have spread to even remote parts of the countryside, and in Deng Xiaoping's money-conscious society, it makes excellent economic sense for hospitals and even private practitioners to purchase them. A Chinese-made scanner costs a little over $1,000, and although the going rate for the brief procedure is $50 to $60, more than many farmers make in a month, couples are nonetheless willing to pay. Since scanners are also used to discover birth defects, the government cannot easily ban them. Many women who are told that the fetus is female immediately schedule an abortion. A Western anthropologist has commented that he can determine precisely the date that a town's ultrasound equipment arrived, because there will have been no baby girls born afterwards. When asked how they feel this skewed sex ratio will impact on their chances of having grandsons, people tend to reply that having grandsons depends on having sons first.[30]

The gender imbalance had ominous consequences. Although the 2000 census reports that the male to female ratio is 106.3 to 100, Chinese population journals place it at from 114 to 119 males per 100 females. (See Table 11.1.) If this is so, millions of young men will be unable to find brides. In a society where Confucian beliefs about the importance of producing a (male) heir remain deeply rooted, this could result in significant social tension. Another problem is the graying of society. Sociologists consider a society "aging" if more than 10 percent of its population is over 60, which was exactly the percentage in the PRC in 2002. If current trends persist, 400 million people, or 27 percent of the population, will be over 60 by the middle of the twenty-first century. Given the already

TABLE 11.1 Population by Age and Sex

Age Groups	Population			Percent of Total Population			Sex Ratio (Female=100)
	Total	Male	Female	Total	Male	Female	
Total	1,242,612,226	640,275,969	602,336,257	100	51.53	48.47	106.3
0–4	68,978,374	37,648,694	31,329,680	5.55	3.03	2.52	120.17
5–9	90,152,587	48,303,208	41,849,379	7.26	3.89	3.37	115.42
10–14	125,396,633	65,344,739	60,051,894	10.09	5.26	4.83	108.81
15–19	103,031,165	52,878,170	50,152,995	8.29	4.26	4.04	105.43
20–24	94,573,174	47,937,766	46,635,408	7.61	3.86	3.75	102.79
25–29	117,602,265	60,230,758	57,371,507	9.46	4.85	4.62	104.98
30–34	127,314,298	65,360,456	61,953,842	10.25	5.26	4.99	105.5
35–39	109,147,295	56,141,391	53,005,904	8.78	4.52	4.27	105.92
40–44	81,242,945	42,243,187	38,999,758	6.54	3.4	3.14	108.32
45–49	85,521,045	43,939,603	41,581,442	6.88	3.54	3.35	105.67
50–54	63,304,200	32,804,125	30,500,075	5.09	2.64	2.45	107.55
55–59	46,370,375	24,061,506	22,308,869	3.73	1.94	1.8	107.86
60–64	41,703,848	21,674,478	20,029,370	3.36	1.74	1.61	108.21
65–69	34,780,460	17,549,348	17,231,112	2.8	1.41	1.39	101.85
70–74	25,574,149	12,436,154	13,137,995	2.06	1	1.06	94.66
75–79	15,928,330	7,175,811	8,752,519	1.28	0.58	0.7	81.99
80–84	7,989,158	3,203,868	4,785,290	0.64	0.26	0.39	66.95
85–89	3,030,698	1,056,941	1,973,757	0.24	0.09	0.16	53.55
90–94	783,594	229,758	553,836	0.06	0.02	0.04	41.48
95–99	169,756	51,373	118,383	0.01		0.01	43.4
100 and over	17,887	4,635	13,242				35

Source: China Statistical Yearbook, 2002.

existing difficulties in enacting medical plans (see the previous section on health) and social security, this could place an intolerable burden on society.

According to the 2000 census, the annual growth rate in the preceding ten years was
10.07 per thousand, down 0.4 percent over the 1980–1990 period, with the population predicted to rise by about 10 millon per year over the next ten years, peaking at 1.6 billion in
2050. However, Chinese demographers privately estimate that 25 to 35 percent of births are
simply not reported, and that the true population growth rate is more likely between 2 and
2.3 percent.[31] The PRC would thus have about a hundred million more people than the census
indicates. These higher figures are supported by a statement from the state family planning
commission that only one in five of the PRC's 320 million families have a single child, and
also because far more children are reported to have been vaccinated each year than the census
bureau says are born each year. It is also noteworthy that, prior to the 2000 census, the government declared an amnesty on registering hitherto unreported children, though warning people
that they should not expect lenient treatment in future censuses. Even accepting the higher figure, it is a remarkable achievement for a developing country to have reduced its population
growth rate this far and so quickly. However, the present growth rate has troublesome implications for the government. For example, an equivalent number of jobs needs to be created each
year for new entrants to the labor market. As has been seen, there are a great many Chinese already unemployed or underemployed. Supplying housing and other amenities for such large
numbers of people takes additional land out of cultivation and is a drain on scarce resources.
Since births are lowest among educated professionals and highest among the poor and mar-
ginally literate, there are concerns that the quality of the population may decline.

Moreover, there is a distinct possibility that the government's ability to ensure compliance with its family planning regulations will erode still further. Chinese demographers privately express doubts about government claims that the populaton will peak in 2030 or at any
other date. They point out that, in the PRC's increasingly free-market economy, personal decisions made by individuals on the basis of their economic situation play a more important role
in determining fertility rates than any government fiat. Several family planning commission
reports over the past decade have expressed concern that programs are losing their effectiveness. In some cases, they have actually been counterproductive: The fines levied for over-plan
births have become an important source of income for local governments, who therefore have
no incentive to discourage them. In 2002, the central government announced that it was taking
responsibility for the collection of excess-birth fines away from local levels. But the order was
so vague on important details, such as how the fines would be collected, that analysts doubted
the new policy would be effective.[32] At about the same time, the family planning policy itself
began to relax: A law proposed in 2001 allowed provinces to make "reasonable arrangements
. . . according to law under certain legally set conditions" to have additional children.[33]

The Environment

China has traditionally been a country in which the population pressed hard against existing land and resources, resulting in a substantial amount of environmental degradation.
Even had they understood its causes better, people whose immediate survival was at stake
had little reason to be concerned about the environmental legacy they would impose on

future generations. The loess plateau described in Chapter 4 comprises 640,000 square kilometers of the upper and middle reaches of the Yellow River. It is believed to be the largest and most seriously eroded area in the world.

The CCP came to power dedicated to the goal of rapid industrialization, and showed little concern for environmental problems. For decades, party and government officials would not acknowledge that such problems even existed, much less try to deal with them. As late as 1972, a Western reporter who visited Guangzhou (Canton) and commented on the soot pouring from dozens of factory smokestacks was told that pollution was a product of rapacious capitalists who did not care what they did to the environment. Since China no longer had rapacious capitalists, the Chinese people did not need to be afraid of pollution.[34]

In fact, concern *did* exist. For example, a number of people were acutely aware that the Great Leap Forward had caused tremendous environmental problems. In 1958, large quantities of the country's coal were wasted in trying to make steel in backyard blast furnaces, forcing peasants in some areas to denude the countryside of trees and bushes in order to get enough fuel to survive the winter. In Tibet during the 1970s, an ill-conceived plan to substitute wheat for barley had exhausted the soil and caused famine. And people who lived near belching smokestacks complained about the soot. Responding to these and other concerns, in August 1973 the state council convened a national conference on environmental protection work.

In 1974, the Office of Environmental Protection was established under the state council, and similar units were set up at the provincial level in many parts of the country. However, establishing the national unit as an office meant that it did not have authority over subordinate levels the way a ministry or commission might. While the Office of Environmental Protection could coordinate and plan, it could not order compliance. The National People's Congress passed the PRC's first environmental protection law in 1979, though there were deficiencies in financing, personnel, and organization that made its provisions difficult to enforce.[35]

Environmental degradation became a matter of concern by the end of the 1980s, and continues to be so. Water pollution is considered the PRC's major problem, posing the greatest danger to the health of the population. China produces at least 40 billion tons of waste water every year, 80 percent of which is generated by industry. However, even large urban areas lack adequate sewage treatment facilities. Many waterways have become little more than transport canals for waste water. In 1998, a leading newspaper stated that most of the PRC's 500 rivers were polluted to the extent that they could not be used for drinking water. This was particularly so for rivers near large population centers, where the fish and plants that used to live therein have been reduced in numbers and, in some, completely eliminated.

In the case of Shanghai, millions of tons of human and industrial sewage are expelled into its waterways each day. One of these, Suzhou Creek, became devoid of dissolved oxygen in the water; as a result, neither animal nor plant life could survive in it. For several months of the year, when water flow is slow, the creek actually became toxic, smelling strongly of hydrogen sulfide (i.e., like rotten eggs). Periodic "red tides" which result in toxic seafood, threaten the city. Polluted drinking water has also been linked to a rise in hepatitis, stomach, liver, and intestinal cancers.[36]

In both city and countryside, drinking water supplies are increasingly contaminated by effluent from industrial sites as well. The promotion of small- and medium-sized industries in rural areas has helped to raise living standards but taken a heavy ecological toll. During the 1990s, 20 to 30 million peasants were displaced by environmental degradation—environmental refugees who have been forced to abandon land that can no longer support them. It is estimated that by 2025, at least 30 to 40 million more might need to relocate.[37] This presents the government with difficult problems of resettlement with implications for social stability. Many of the displaced have joined the floating population.

The countryside is not only susceptible to pollution from industrial sources, but also from agricultural runoff tainted with chemical fertilizers and toxic pesticides. In 1988, riots broke out near Beijing after officials, worried that a dam might break, released water from a local reservoir that had been affected by industrial waste. Crops were ruined, and many people developed unusual rashes. The most serious consequences may take a number of years to appear. Once underground water supplies have been polluted, they are virtually impossible to clean.[38] In Liaoning province, over a thousand drinking wells had to be abandoned in the 1980s because they were contaminated with hexavalent aluminum leached from mining, smelting, and industrial waste piles.[39]

The huge increase in the population of coastal China has resulted in shortages of surface water. Ground water has been used to make up the difference, thus causing a problem of sinking. In addition to causing structural damage to homes and businesses, the fact that the land level is dropping means that large coastal cities are more prone to flooding, particularly if the rise in sea levels that has been predicted actually occurs. The Chinese Academy of Sciences warned cities to take this sinking into account when drawing up their plans for development. The coastline in the Pearl River area has declined by 40 to 60 centimeters, and more along the coasts of Shanghai and Tianjin; Ningbo, a major port city, may sink below sea level by 2030.[40] Incursions of salt water inland lead to salinization of the soil, reduced crop yields, and further erosion.

The combination of these phenomena has devastating effects for both the health of the people as a whole and the income of those who earn their living through fishing. Water shortages are common in major cities at certain times of year, and factories have had to close down production lines for lack of water. If, as officials predict, the country's population peaks at 1.6 billion in 2030, water resources will have dropped to 1,760 cubic meters per capita, barely above the internationally recognized benchmark of 1,700 cubic meters. Environmental scientists warn that the country's water resources and farmlands are not keeping up with the demands placed on them, and worry that the ecological underpinning of Chinese society is fraying.

A massive South-North Water transfer project that will carry water from the Yangtze River in central China to the drier north began in 2003. It is expected to take 50 years to complete, and to cost nearly $60 billion. Experts have warned, however, that unless the water can be cleaned beforehand, the huge endeavor will simply have diverted sewage from one part of the country to another, at great expense to the central government's treasury and the Chinese taxpayer. Tianjin officials have privately expressed concerns that it may cost the city more to treat the water than is economically feasible.

Air pollution is also a growing concern. According to a World Health Organization (WHO) report released in 1999, nine of the ten cities in the world suffering from the worst air pollution are in China. WHO guidelines consider the maximum permissible amount of suspended particulates in the air to be 90 micrograms per cubic liter of air: Lanzhou has 700, and several other Chinese cities have nearly as much.[41] Much of this pollution is from sulfur dioxide, a by-product of coal combustion from industrial and electricity-generating facilities. About 75 percent of China's energy needs are met by coal, which is typically of low quality, untreated, and burned from relatively low smokestacks. All of these add to the amount of pollutants released into the air. Particularly in winter, a large proportion of urban residents suffers from bronchitis. High levels of sulfur dioxide are not only hazardous to health, but also contribute to acid rain, which results in lower crop yields and damage to forests. Nor is sulfur dioxide the only problem. Minamata disease, caused by mercury from a nearby factory, appeared in Guizhou province in 1998. Arsenic poisoning which was traced to the kind of coal burned for fuel affected several thousand people in the same province. Coal-washing, higher smokestacks, more efficient boilers, and switching to other forms of energy have been suggested, but they take time, money, and sustained attention. All are factors that have been in short supply.

Soil erosion and desertification are problems as well. One important contributing cause is deforestation. The forestry ministry has charged that overcutting and irrational consumption sharply decreased the growing stock, impoverished the quality of the timber available, and nearly exhausted supplies. Depletion was especially noticeable in mature stands of trees, which the ministry predicted would be completely cut in seven or eight years. By 1993, it was announced that the country had less than 2 million meters left, nearly all of it in remote areas or on the tops of mountains.[42] Reforestation drives have been conducted every spring since 1979, but despite annual glowing reports on numbers of trees planted, survival and preservation rates are poor. Sometimes the results are exactly the opposite of what is hoped for. Planting trees at the edge of deserts means that they cannot be sustained by natural rainfall and end up overdrawing from scarce groundwater reserves. They then evaporate the moisture through their leaves. Digging holes to plant the trees further damages already-scarred hillsides, and watering them takes precious water from already depleted rivers and lakes. Since tree belts generally consist of one species only, poplar, natural biocontrol mechanisms are absent, leaving the belts vulnerable to insect infestation. Depending on one's source, only 12 to 16 percent of the PRC's land area still has forest cover, compared with 33 percent in the United States, 35 percent in the former USSR, and 26 percent in India.

Efforts to solve one problem often end up creating another. For example, an electricity shortage in Qinghai province was helped when the Beijing government decided to build a hydropower station on the Yellow River. But the huge reservoir that had to be created as part of it lowered surrounding temperatures slightly and led to winds that eroded the nearby grasslands. The desert began to eat up the prairies that local herders relied on.[43] In 1993 an improperly maintained dam in the same province burst, causing several hundred deaths and huge property losses.

Another example, with the potential to be a far larger problem, is the government's decision to go ahead on the controversial Three Gorges project. This involves building a massive dam across the most scenic stretch of the Yangtze River. Proponents say that the dam will provide 84 billion kilowatt hours of "clean" electricity annually, raise the river's transport capacity four times while reducing transportation costs by one-third, and help channel water from the Yangtze basin to chronically water-short north China. Critics charge that, while the dam may alleviate flooding in one part of the Yangtze, it will increase flooding in other parts. Rare flora and fauna have already been destroyed by its construction, and there have been huge problems in resettling the more than a million people displaced by the waters. Corrupt officials have pocketed significant amounts of the compensation those displaced were to have received, and they have often been unable to find accommodations comparable to the homes they have left. The displaced have also encountered discrimination by natives of the areas they have been moved to. The area to be flooded includes dump sites, polluting factories, and grave sites which, if not cleaned beforehand, will cause the environment to deteriorate still further. Chongqing is bracing for an infestation of the rats that will flee the rising waters.

There is a also a serious possibility of landslides. The area surrounding the large reservoir that is part of the dam complex is characterized by loose-textured soil and frequent floods and rainstorms. As subterranean water levels rise, so do the incidence and size of landslides. As has happened elsewhere, the creation of such a large reservoir may induce earthquakes. Even if not, the ecological consequences will be catastrophic. The huge amounts of money (estimates range from $70 billion to $1 trillion) needed for the project could better be spent in other endeavors.[44]

The destruction of forests, use of marginal land for farming, intensive exploitation of agricultural land, and overgrazing of grasslands have contributed to increased soil erosion. In Inner Mongolia, the Gobi Desert has expanded as once-usable grassland deteriorates. Desertification has affected 28 percent of the PRC's land mass, and an additional 18 percent of the country is desertifying. Ninety percent of China's grasslands are deteriorating to various degrees.[45] This leads to reductions in soil fertility and agricultural production. The mass of sediment eroded from upstream is eventually deposited in downstream rivers and lakes. In Henan province, locals refer to the Yellow River as the *Shao He*, or burning river, since the dense silt causes fish to leap out in a vain search for air. The silt causes a rise in riverbed levels and a reduction of lakewater volume. As a case in point, Hunan province's Dongting Lake was once one of China's largest freshwater lakes. However, progressive sedimentation has severely reduced its ability to regulate the water level of the Yangtze River, thus restricting river transportation and shipping in many areas of lowland China. Sandstorms have become larger and more prevalent. One such storm bathed Beijing in an eerie Halloween-like glare in spring 2002, disrupting normal activities for several days.

When river beds rise, floods become more likely. The siltation of the Yellow River, "China's Sorrow," is an ongoing phenomenon. However, changes in the course of the Yellow River, which historically occurred every few hundred years, have become more frequent in recent centuries. In 1997–1998, the concern was rather different: With water being pumped out at double the recharge rate to serve industrial and human needs, the Yellow River was going dry. And, impossible as it must have appeared to those fleeing the disastrous Yangtze floods of summer 1998, a similar fate was predicted for that body of water. As floods become more likely in some areas, desertification increases in others.

Amid a growing feeling that environmental deterioration was proceeding unchecked, the State Council raised the status of the Office of Environmental Protection to commission level in 1984, and made it an agency in 1988. However, it had yet to attain ministerial level. In 1988 also, environmental norms were introduced in five areas: air pollution, water pollution, noise pollution, solid waste recycling and disposal, and urban "greenification." They were applied to 32 cities, with the officials thereof being warned that their annual performance evaluations would take their activities in the five areas into account.

There have been numerous attempts to expand the scope of environmental bureaus and clarify the division of responsibilities among the ministries and levels of government involved. In 2002, Beijing ratified the Kyoto Protocol on regulating greenhouse gas emissions, passed a new domestic law aiming at water conservation, and issued new regulations on pollution, energy use, and recycling. How much good this will do remains to be seen. Local environmental bureaus that are responsible for enforcing central government regulations are understaffed and often tied to the industries that they are supposed to regulate. Many state-run factories have a higher administrative classification than regional environmental agencies and can ignore warnings. The majority of the biggest polluters are state-run industries and factories that cannot realistically be shut down or severely punished.

A number of factories have included the cost of fines in their production costs rather than improve their ability to control pollution. Others simply ignore the regulations, reasoning that they cost too much to comply with, and that there is small risk of being caught. A sulphur dioxide reduction program that was supposed to reduce emissions by 10 percent over 2000 levels and improve the quality of the PRC's seven main waterways and lakes produced few results and, according to an internal Chinese document, the waters of the Yangtze and Yellow rivers have actually become dirtier. At present, interest in short-term profits and material benefits far exceeds concern for the environment.

When regulations are enforced, tragic consequences have ensued. For example, residents of one Lanzhou neighborhood complained repeatedly about a factory that was spewing hydrogen sulfide gas and obtained a judgment against it based on violations of the environmental protection law. The factory at first ignored orders to comply with emissions laws before producing again, sparking more protests. When, after repeated protests, the factory was finally closed, its angry workers turned on area residents at random, murdering two people in an exceptionally grisly fashion and injuring many more.[46]

Since China occupies a large proportion of the world's land area and has so many people, the PRC's environmental situation is important to the stabilization of the global environment as well. Data presented to the 1997 Kyoto environmental summit indicate that China is the world's second largest producer of carbon dioxide emissions, after the United States and just ahead of Russia, Japan, and Germany. Emissions are expected to be double that of the United States by 2050 if left unchecked. Should China remain an environmental "spoiler," the effects on the rest of the planet could be severe. For this reason, leaders of the international ecology movement have made efforts to persuade China to sign multilateral environmental agreements. Chinese leaders have been sympathetic but have argued that they have no money to enforce the statutes of such agreements. However, others point out that the PRC's decision to pursue enormously expensive and environmentally risky projects like the Three Gorges Dam and the South-North Water diversion project shows that ecology is simply not high on the government's agenda. The PRC currently spends about 0.7 percent of GDP on environmental protection, as against its own estimates that 2 percent is the minimum necessary amount.

International lending agencies have provided loans and credits for specific projects, such as to restore the loess plateau, but the amount of money that would be needed to even stabilize the PRC's environment is far beyond the ability of any domestic or international source to meet. Assuming that sufficient funds are made available, there are real questions as to how well they would be used. Corruption is serious: for example, "bean-curd" dikes built with watered-down concrete crumble, causing floods. In addition, poor coordination between central and provincial authorities makes water control much more difficult. Failure to coordinate efforts has been held responsible for exacerbating situations in which high waters turn into disastrous floods. Ministry officials also complain that many enterprise managers engage in "guerrilla warfare" with regulating agencies, and then go to great lengths to cover up what they have done so that they do not have to clean it up.

Thanks in part to government publicity, there is greater public awareness on environmental issues. Several cities, including Tianjin and Shanghai, have reported successes in controlling specific types of pollution. Shanghai leaders in particular are aware that a clean environment is important to their plans to continue attracting foreign investment, and have made real efforts to create such an atmosphere. Other cities exhibit varying degrees of concern. In addition, most are far less prosperous than Shanghai and therefore have fewer resources to devote to the environment. China has a nascent "green" movement. But, because officials are concerned that environmental concerns may provide the impetus for a potential prodemocracy crusade, the government carefully monitors their activities rather than lending encouragement. Nonetheless, the movement has burgeoned. Misgivings about the Three Gorges dam provided an important impetus, though certainly not the only one. As flood crests surged along the Yangtze in summer 1998, environmentalists charged that the deluges were the direct result of channeling funds that should have been spent on flood control. Those who supported the government's position countered that, had the dam been in place, there would have been no floods.

Conclusions

Better health care and a long period of peace have led to a sharp increase in China's already large population. Efforts to convince the PRC's citizenry of the need for family planning have had impressive results but have not succeeded in stabilizing the size of the population. Inevitably, this has taken a toll on economic growth. At the same time, efforts to better the living standards of this much larger number of people have led to intensive exploitation of existing resources and a worrisome deterioration of the environment. These, too, have taken a toll on economic growth as well as on the general health of the population. Party and government leaders are aware of the intricately intertwined issues of health, demography, the environment, and economic growth. The trade-offs among these issues are difficult to make and, in terms of public opinion, have potentially explosive consequences. The enormous nature of the task involved and the decreasing ability of the central government to exact compliance from its subordinate units and from the citizenry at large make it doubtful that these quality-of-life problems can be solved easily or soon.

Notes

1. Francis L. K. Hsü's *Magic and Science in Western Yunnan: The Problem of Introducing Scientific Medicine in a Rustic Community*, (New York: Institute of Pacific Relations, 1943) provides insights into the frustrations and the successes experienced by these public health personnel.

2. Mark Elvin, *The Pattern of the Chinese Past* (Stanford, Calif.: Stanford University Press, 1973), pp. 185–186.

3. Leo A. Orleans, "Health Policies and Services in China, 1974," Report to the Subcommittee on Health of the Committee on Labor and Public Welfare, United States Senate (Washington, D.C.: United States Government Printing Office, March 1974), pp. 1–2.

4. This is still (or perhaps again) common in rural areas.

5. Jerome Ch'en, *Mao Papers: Anthology and Bibliography* (Oxford, U.K.: Oxford University Press, 1970), pp. 100–101.

6. Judith Banister, *China's Changing Population* (Stanford, Calif.: Stanford University Press, 1987), p. 62.

7. Henderson and Cohen, p. 100.

8. *Jiefang ribao* (Shanghai), May 2, 1990, in *FBIS–CHI*, May 25, 1990, p. 35.

9. Wang Shaoguang, "The Problem of State Weakness," *Journal of Democracy*, January 2003, p. 40.

10. Matt Forney and Susan Lawrence, "Impotent Potions: 'Anti-AIDS' Elixirs Confound Regulators and Threaten Lives in China," *Far Eastern Economic Review,* August 6, 1998, pp. 64–65.

11. "Sixty Million Affected by Endemic Diseases," *China Daily*, October 12, 1988, p. 3.

12. John Kohut, "Officials 'Hush Up' Beijing Diphtheria Outbreak," *South China Morning Post*, February 17, 1990, p. 12.

13. (no author), "Chinese Farmers Face Financial Ruin If They Fall Ill," *Straits Times*, January 2, 2002.

14. Guo, Baogang, "Transforming China's Urban Health Care System," *Asian Survey*, vol. 43, no. 2, March / April 2003, pp. 305–403.

15. Josephine Ma, "A Rural Medical Scheme Aims to Cover up to 900 Million by End of Decade," *South China Morning Post*, January 15, 2003; Leigh Jenkins, "Rural Health Plan Finally Unveiled," *ibid.*, October 31, 2002.

16. "Four Distinct Features of Mainland Triad Gangs," *Ming Pao*, September 2, 1991, p. 8, in *FBIS–CHI*, September 9, 1991, pp. 30–31.

17. Elisabeth Rosenthal, "UN Publicly Chastises China for Inaction on HIV Epidemic," *New York Times*, June 28, 2002.

18. (no author), "Smoker Loses Fights Against Tobacco Industry: Raises Awareness," *AFP*, Hong Kong, September 19, 2001.

19. see www.who.int/country/chn/eng for this and other information relevant to the PRC's health care system; the report is summarized in Philip Hilts, "Europeans Perform Highest in Ranking of World Health," *New York Times*, June 21, 2000, p. A12.

20. Nicholas Kristof, "Chinese Grow Healthier from Cradle to Grave," *New York Times*, March 14, 1991, pp. A1; A6.

21. Banister, p. 148.

22. Leo Orleans, *China's Population Policies and Population Data: Review and Update*, United States House of Representatives, Committee on Foreign Affairs (Washington D.C.: United States Government Printing Office, 1981), p. 4.

23. Banister, p. 151.

24. *Xinhua*, February 13, 1980, in *FBIS–CHI*, February 15, 1980, p. L/11.

25. U.S. Department of State, Human Rights Practices 2002: China, p. 28. http://state.gov.drl/rls/hrrpt/2002/18239pf.htm

26. Human Rights in China Report, *Institutionalized Exclusion: The Tenuous Legal Status of Internal Migrants in China's Major Cities*, HRIC (London) November 6, 2002, p. 76.

27. Susan Greenhalgh, "The Evolution of the One-Child Policy in Shaanxi, 1979–1988," *China Quarterly,* April 1990, pp. 215–216.

28. Zhu Baoxi, "State Commission Plans To Limit Population Growth," *China Daily*, September 26, 1991, p. 3.

29. *AFP* (Hong Kong), December 1, 1993, in *FBIS–CHI*, December 1, 1993, p. 63.

30. Nicholas Kristof, "Peasants of China Discover New Way to Weed Out Girls," *New York Times*, July 27, 1993, pp. A1, A4.

31. For the 35 percent figure, see Leta Hong Fincher, "Hidden Millions Elude Census," *South China Morning Post*, October 3, 2000; for a U.S. Embassy report estimating one-third, see (no author) "PRC Census Misses One-Third of Births: Chinese Demographers Explain Why," www.usembassy-china.org.cn/english/sandt/fertl2b.htm; for the 25 percent figure, see (no author), "PRC Births 25 Percent Higher Than Official Count Says Vaccinator," www.usembassy-china.org.cn/english/sandt/vacc-pop.html

32. (no author), "Greedy Officials Bypassed as Fines for Illegal Births Revised," *AFP*, Beijing, January 22, 2002.

33. Sophia Woodman, "Draft Law Fails to Address Real Population Issues," *South China Morning Post*, July 9, 2001.

34. John Fraser, *The Chinese: Portrait of a People* (New York: Summit Books, 1980), p. 49.

35. Lester Ross, *Environmental Policy in China* (Bloomington, Ind.: Indiana University Press, 1988), p. 141.

36. (no author), "Spreading Red Tide Threatens Shanghai," *South China Morning Post*, May 30, 2002.

37. Elizabeth Economy, "Heading Off an Environmental Catastrophe," *South China Morning Post*, January 29, 2003.

38. Vanessa Lide, "The Perils of Pollution," *China Business Review*, July–August 1990, pp. 32–33.

39. Richard Carpenter, "China Fouling Its Nest, Say Environmental Scientists," *Centerviews* (Honolulu), July–August 1990, p. 5.

40. (no author), "Thirsty Ningbo May Sink Beneath Waves," *South China Morning Post*, May 8, 2002.

41. Reuters, "Nine of the World's Top Ten Worst-Polluted Cities in China: Report" *South China Morning Post*, January 25, 1999.

42. Wang Yonghong, "Forests Greening, but Mature Stands Few," *China Daily*, December 15, 1993, p. 1.

43. Nicholas Kristof, "Industry Fails as Cure-All for Western China," *New York Times*, September 4, 1991, p. 9.

44. An excellent summary of the debates surrounding the the Three Gorges project appears in "China Dams the Yangtze," November 2002, www.usembassy-china.org.cn/sandt/Dam-3G.htm

45. Liu Ying, "When Will We Not See Cattle and Sheep Everywhere in the Prairie?" *Keji Ribao*, November 19, 2001, p. 5.

46. Ran Xiaoling and Wang Hengzhan, "A Bloody Day of Sacrifice—A Murder Case Caused by Environmental Pollution," *Nanfang zhoumo* (Guangzhou), September 24, 1993, p. 5, in *FBIS–CHI*, September 27, 1993, pp. 29–33.

Suggestions for Further Reading

Guo, Baogang, "Transforming China's Urban Health Care System," *Asian Survey*, vol. 43, no. 2, March/April 2003, pp. 305–403.

Charles Horner, "Prescription for Chinese Reform," *Outlook*, vol. 2, no. 1, August 2000. (Indianapolis, Ind.: The Hudson Institute).

Human Rights in China Report, *Institutionalized Exclusion: The Tenuous Legal Status of Internal Migrants in China's Major Cities*, London, HRIC, November 2002.

Dorothy Solinger, *Contesting Citizenship in Urban China: Peasant Migrants, the State, and the Logic of the Market* (Berkeley: University of California Press, 1999).

United States Embassy, Beijing, "China Dams the Yangtze," November 2002. http://www.usembassy-china.org.cn/sandt/Dam-3G.htm

12 Conformity and Dissent: The Politics of the Arts and Journalism

Artist and Society in China

The relationship of the artist to society has been a thorny problem in modern China. As in most other civilizations, tensions exist between those who advocate the philosophy of art for the sake of art and those who believe in art as social criticism. There have also been familiar conflicts between art as entertainment and art aimed at bettering the mind and soul of its audience. An issue with particular salience in China has been that of how to treat past literary and artistic works, both foreign and those of traditional China.

"Serious" writers and artists tended to be quite critical of works done primarily for entertainment. For example, they referred contemptuously to the popular fiction that flourished in the first several decades of the twentieth century as "the Mandarin Duck and Butterfly School."[1] Particularly after the May Fourth movement, artists and writers attempted to grapple with the problems of what had caused China's abject weakness with regard to the West and how to remedy the situation. Typically, they found the roots of decay in Chinese civilization itself.

This is a recurrent theme in the works of Lu Xun, who is considered China's greatest modern writer. Lu's short stories directly criticized contemporary society and challenged his readers to struggle for a better China. In *The Diary of a Madman*, written in 1919, Lu Xun implies that, despite its professions of benevolence and righteousness, Chinese culture is cannibalistic. At the end of the story, the madman asks if perhaps there are still some children who have not yet become cannibals, and pleads that, if they exist, they must be saved. The protagonist of Lu's most famous work, *The True Story of Ah Q*, reacts to repeated bullying and humiliations by pretending that he has achieved spiritual victories. When people who are physically weaker than he cross Ah Q's path, he bullies them. However, since most of the people around him are stronger, Ah Q lives in a world of self-deception. He cheers himself up no matter how perilous the circumstances, assuming an air of superiority despite the obvious defeats he is suffering. Ah Q, of course, represents Lu Xun's view of China.

Another well-known writer chose his pen name, Ba Jin, from the Chinese transliteration of the first syllable of the Russian anarchist Bakunin and the last syllable of yet another Russian anarchist, Kropotkin. His novel, *Family*, is a scathing indictment of the Confucian kinship system and its deleterious effects on both individuals and the larger society. A number of other intellectuals added their voices as well. Though highly critical of the lingering vestiges of Confucian orthodoxy—the formal structure thereof having largely collapsed by the 1930s—there was little consensus on what should take its place. The communist party, believing that Marxist orthodoxy could succeed in strengthening China where Confucianism had failed, courted these writers and artists.

The Party, Art, and Social Protest

The party sponsored a number of artistic endeavors to help bring its message to the masses. Jiang Qing, who would later marry Mao Zedong, acted in guerrilla theater performances and films with left-leaning messages. Many writers and artists, some of them communists and others not, lent their talents to these endeavors. In 1930, the League of Left-Wing Writers was founded, its name purposely chosen to soften the appearance of communist control. Little effort was expended in trying to impose rigid ideological criteria on the works of its members: To do so might well have alienated many of them. Lu Xun himself made a speech in 1927, explaining

> But the writers at this revolutionary base, I am afraid, are inclined to stress a close bond between literature and revolution in the understanding that literature should be employed to propagandize, to promote, to incite, and to help fulfill the revolution. But I think writing of this kind will be very ineffective because good literary works have never been composed in accordance with other people's orders; rather, they are disinterested and an expression of the natural or spontaneous outpourings of the heart. [Works of propaganda] will have no literary value, nor any effect upon the readers. So, for the sake of the revolution, let's have more workers for the revolution and not be overworried about "revolutionary literature."[2]

While the CCP has lavishly praised Lu Xun and claims him as one of their own, it does not mention that he never joined the party. Moreover, since Lu Xun died in 1936, he never lived under communist rule. Many of his pronouncements, including the one cited above, indicate that Lu would have been very uncomfortable in post-1949 China.

After the Xi'an incident in December 1936, many left-leaning writers and artists made their way to Yan'an, where the party was pleased to make use of their talents in revolutionizing and propagandizing the masses. In May 1938, the Lu Xun Academy of the Arts was founded to train and nurture their talents. It was at Yan'an that the Yellow River Cantata was composed; the river is considered symbolic of China itself. The future People's Republic of China also acquired a national anthem at this time, "The March of the Volunteers," as well as many revolutionary songs designed to uplift the spirits and encourage arduous struggle in the name of the socialist cause. The stirring "The East Is Red" was another product of Yan'an. In this early manifestation of the cult of Mao, the chairman is compared to the sun in heaven. Its words are "The east is red, the sun has risen. China has produced a Mao Zedong. He works for the happiness of the people; he is the savior of the people." Literature, art, and music for the masses were also encouraged; "The Cowherd's Flute" and other such tunes date from this period.

The first of the revolutionary operas, *The White-Haired Girl*, was composed at Yan'an. Seemingly owing more to Russian ballet than to Chinese opera, it tells the story of a young woman whose hair turns white after being raped by a landlord. She flees to the hills after this sordid experience. The Red Army later liberates the area and puts the landlord on trial. The climax of the opera is the young woman's denunciation of the criminal, followed by the masses taking vengeance on him. When first performed, the drama reportedly so engaged the passions of the audience that, on at least one occasion, they had to be restrained from attacking the actor who played the landlord.

However, despite the production of a large number of politically correct works, tensions between art and politics became noticeable when artists began to criticize the shortcomings of the Yan'an government. As a case in point, in 1941 the young feminist writer Ding Ling published a short story called "In the Hospital." The protagonist, a young woman from Shanghai, is confronted with an administration which is composed of incompetent old cadres who do not know how to run the hospital and are indifferent to the needs of its patients or staff. Her attempts to correct the problems she sees result in her being slandered and censured. Finally, in frustration, the heroine leaves the hospital. Quite clearly, Ding Ling meant the hospital to symbolize Yan'an; what happens to the young woman represents the inability of the well-meaning individual to correct its problems.

A year later, Ding wrote a piece that was still more troubling to the authorities. Entitled "Thoughts on May 8," the essay was written in commemoration of Woman's Day. Ding pointed out the gap between the alleged emancipation of women under communism and the actuality of the discrimination they continued to face. Artists saw their criticism as *constructive*, since they were trying to correct defects in the system. However, party leaders were convinced that critical works were *destructive*, since they might have the effect of undermining the masses' faith in the party and its infallibility.

Ding Ling and others like her were forced to make self-criticisms during the *zhengfeng*, or rectification campaign. In May 1942, Mao Zedong delivered a speech at the Yan'an Forum on Art and Literature that laid down guidelines (albeit guidelines that could be interpreted either strictly or loosely) for literature, art, and journalism that have been in use ever since. Mao stated explicitly that there is no such thing as art for art's sake. It exists primarily for politics, and not for amusement or entertainment. Moreover, he maintained, all of the arts have a class character.

Post-1949 Control Mechanisms

Although relatively few artists were likely to be comfortable with these guidelines, the day-to-day tasks of survival in Yan'an, with its harsh climate and wartime conditions, mitigated the tensions between the party and its literary and artistic workers. After 1949, this was no longer the case. While many intellectuals sincerely wanted to, and did, serve the party loyally, they looked to their own ideals rather than to officially determined realpolitik for their themes. As a result, intellectuals were slowly pushed aside and attacked by the leadership and its career bureaucrats.

The party moved quickly to assert its control over the arts. During the summer of 1949, the All-China Federation of Literature and Art Circles (ACFLAC) was founded. One of the largest of the mass organizations, it was essentially a holding company for nine national organizations representing major branches of the arts. These included the Chinese Writers' Association, the Chinese Artists' Association, the Chinese Musicians' Association, the Chinese Filmmakers' Association, the Chinese Dancers' Association, the Chinese Dramatists' Association, the Chinese Balladeers' Association, the Chinese Folk Literature and Art Association, and the Chinese Acrobats' Association.

The organizations hold periodic meetings, at which their leaders convey party and government documents to the membership. There are discussions on the documents and on other matters of pertinence to the members' professional concerns. The associations also publish magazines which, at least prior to 1979, were considered the most prestigious in their respective fields. Those who did not conform to the party line would find it very difficult to have their work published by such journals. The associations also control the prizes that are so important to the prestige of writers and artists.

A small number of established older artists and writers draw their salaries directly from these professional organizations. The great majority, however, have as their work unit the troupe, film company, or magazine to which they belong. The units issue salaries, assign housing, control transfers, hold political study meetings, and so on, functioning very much as do other work units. The troupes, companies, and magazines are subordinate to their relevant professional associations and, ultimately, to the ACFLAC. Those who refuse to conform to the party line may be expelled from their units, meaning that they lose salary, housing, and the opportunity to practice their profession. Clearly these are powerful incentives to produce politically correct works.

Other, less drastic means are also at the government's disposal. For example, funding must be obtained before work can proceed on a movie. The script must first undergo several levels of approval, from that of party leaders at the film studio, to the provincial department of culture, to the propaganda department of the provincial party committee, or to the ministry of culture and the ministry of propaganda directly, if it is from a central-level company. When filming is complete, the movie will be scrutinized again. It may be rejected outright, or held indefinitely in a kind of limbo with no decision being rendered. Or it can be withdrawn after it has been released to theaters.[3]

For example, a movie that was made prior to the demonstrations in the spring of 1989 but released just afterward showed KMT troops spraying water on protestors to deter them. Anonymous voices in darkened theaters loudly pointed out that water pressure was benign compared to the tanks that the communist government had used at the Tiananmen demonstrations. The same movie also featured a scene in which the then-American ambassador was lecturing KMT leader Chiang Kai-shek on the need to treat students better; audiences saw unintended parallels with present-day China in this clip as well. The film was withdrawn for editing.

Similar scrutiny attends the production of other artistic works. Standards are not equally stringent for all the arts. Film and opera seem to be especially tightly regulated, perhaps because they reach such large audiences. Literature is less closely controlled *before* being printed. Writing is, of course, more of an individual endeavor and less dependent on subsidies or access to expensive, scarce commodities like sound stages and projection equipment. One's aberrant book can, however, be criticized *after* it appears. Music seems less closely regulated though, as will be seen, apparently innocuous choices of instrument and title have caused their composers a great deal of trouble during periods of ideological orthodoxy.

Given the risks of deviating from established orthodoxy, one may well ask how it is that anyone dares to do so. First, many writers and artists consider that it is their responsibility as intellectuals to protest social injustice. Second, it is not always clear where the limits of the permissible lie, and many writers and artists find it tempting to test the boundaries. Third, the party line has changed frequently, ranging from relative tolerance of a variety of points of view to rigid ideological orthodoxy. One can always hope that a work that is criticized at one point will later be tolerated. Perhaps its creator will even be praised for her or his courage.

Of course the converse is true also: A work that is initially praised may cause its producer problems later. A case in point is the film *The Story of Wu Xun*, which premiered in December 1950. Adapted from a true story, the plot dealt with a nineteenth-century peasant who was so poor that he could not afford an education. After thirty years of hard work, Wu Xun had prospered to the point where he could contribute his own money to establish schools for those who could not pay tuition. Eventually, he was able to persuade Qing dynasty officials to assist him in this endeavor. The producers portrayed Wu as a praiseworthy individual who had labored to strengthen China and help the poor. The film at first received excellent reviews. By the spring of 1951, however, the party line had changed. With Mao personally leading the attack, the movie was subjected to a barrage of criticism for its erroneous viewpoint that education and reform rather than class struggle and revolution could strengthen China. The purpose of this diatribe was not simply to correct an error in one work, but to provide other writers and artists with specific examples of what to produce and not to produce. Class struggle and revolution were in; charity and reform were out.

Party leaders favored socialist realism in literature and art; they explicitly rejected what they referred to as "the doctrine of the wavering middle." This meant that heroes had to be completely heroic. They must be without doubts that the course of action they had chosen was the correct one, no matter how adverse the consequences to themselves and their families. Conversely, villains had to be completely reprehensible. Writers who portrayed Japanese soldiers or KMT officials as worrying about the fate of the peasants or of their own families found themselves criticized.

Artists were to portray the workers and peasants as happy under all circumstances. Among the absurdities produced was a painting depicting several women telephone-repair workers atop a pole that was swaying precariously in an ice storm. In drawing their facial expressions, the artist chose not intense concentration or anxiety over the dangerous position they were in but broad, apple-cheeked smiles. The message, no matter how unrealistic, was that the women were pleased to be doing their bit for the masses and the state by repairing the downed lines. A short story had a herdsman singing to his sheep, telling them how lucky they were to live under communist rule, so that they were owned by the people instead of a landlord. No great amount of sophistication was needed to figure out that it was of little consequence to the sheep whether they were eaten by the people or by a landlord.

Such works may have had a certain appeal but were in general not well received by audiences. More relevantly, writers and artists did not wish to produce them. One writer, Hu Feng, became the target of a mass campaign in 1954–1955 for protesting what he referred to as "mechanicalism" in literature and predicting that if Marxism were used as a substitute for realism, artistic endeavors would be blocked and art itself destroyed. He and other writers associated with him disparaged Mao's Yan'an talks as discouraging creativity. Hu also was unwilling to use native folk styles in literature. He was criticized for insulting Chinese culture, for worshiping Western bourgeois ideology, and for misrepresenting Marxism-Leninism.

Repression and Reaction

Some writers responded by producing works that scrupulously conformed to the party line; others simply ceased to write. Party leaders were aware of, and unhappy about, this drop in quality and quantity of literature. During the Hundred Flowers campaign that began in 1956, writers and artists were encouraged to voice their grievances and, after an initial period of hesitation, began to do so. Predictably, they denounced the philistine attitudes of petty bureaucrats, and demanded to paint and write in styles other than socialist-realism. Writers asked for independent publishing houses. Musicians expressed their desire to play more Western music and to compose in more experimental styles. There were also demands for better pay and working conditions.

Whereas writers and artists regarded party supervision as interference by petty bureaucratic mentalities, party and government officials regarded literary and art workers as spoiled, arrogant people who worshiped creativity to the point of mysticism. Many bureaucrats found it difficult to see value in the products of the literary and art workers' output: Their usefulness could not be measured in the way that a bushel of rice or a new tractor could be. In the antirightist campaign and the Great Leap Forward that followed the wilting of the Hundred Flowers, vengeance was wreaked. Artists, writers, and musicians had their fees reduced drastically, sometimes by as much as 50 percent. The intent was to make them, and other intellectuals, comparable to ordinary workers in income level. In addition, thousands were sent to the countryside to learn about the lives of the peasants first-hand, so that they could portray rural life more realistically in their future compositions. This was not to be done through mere observation, but through actual labor. Intellectuals were assigned to feed pigs, shovel manure, and clean privies. While it is possible that this experience might have enabled musicians to better understand peasant folk tunes, artists to depict rural scenes more accurately, and writers to capture the flavor of peasant dialect, most of them believed that the real reason they had been sent to the countryside was to punish them for having spoken out.

The glorification of the amateur and denigration of expertise were important facets of the Great Leap Forward. At the same time that writers, musicians, and artists were ordered to learn from the peasants, peasants were urged to write, paint, and compose. Just as with industry and agriculture during the Leap, quotas were set for the production of songs, stories, and art work. And, just as in industry and agriculture, the quotas were raised again and again. Press releases spoke only of overfulfillment. Thousands of songs were produced, often with such catchy titles as "Carrying Manure up the Hill" or "Dance of the Mongolian Sheepherders." The government put its favorites on records and cassettes and made them available for export. Short stories, generally extolling the joy of hard labor or the valiant fight against Japanese and KMT aggressors, were not only made available domestically but also translated and sent abroad. Art became rigidly socialist-realist, with a heavy emphasis on folk forms such as paper cuts.

Despite the Leap's emphasis on folk forms, proletarianization of the arts, and the spirit of Yan'an, it was far less hostile to so-called bourgeois culture and to China's so-called decadent feudal past than the Cultural Revolution that was to come. During the Leap, which also placed great value on doing things in large collectives, huge singing groups performed Western choral music and enormous orchestras performed Beethoven's Ninth Symphony. In addition, there were concerts featuring ancient Chinese instruments.

The abject failure of the Great Leap Forward provided socially responsible intellectuals with an excellent issue to criticize. Since speaking out openly continued to be dangerous, oblique criticisms and metaphors were the weapons of choice. Veiling one's charges in the form of a short story or journal article that ostensibly dealt with the past became popular. Several examples of "using the past to ridicule the present" appear in Chapter 5. One of the most famous (or infamous) plays of the period, *Hai Jui Dismissed,* provides an excellent illustration of the genre. In actual fact, Hai Jui was simultaneously a censor and a governor during the Ming dynasty. A zealous official, he protested to the emperor about tax evasion by landlords in the Suzhou area and the deleterious effects that it was having on the peasants there. The Suzhou landowners, who had their own faction at court, began to conspire against Hai Jui. As a result of their machinations, the emperor dismissed him.[4]

In *Hai Jui Dismissed,* the protagonist is depicted as having brought the exploiters of the people to justice, returning land to the peasants that had been stolen by government officials, and then being dismissed from office by the emperor. Some of his language sounds curiously modern. For example, Hai Jui frequently sings about local officials appropriating people's land by force and making it difficult to farm. He also mentions large numbers of "wrongful judgments" that need to be straightened out, and warns the emperor that only when these problems have been solved can the land be returned to peace and prosperity.

Since the play's author, Wu Han, was a historian who specialized in the Ming dynasty, the discrepancies between the real Hai Jui and the Hai Jui of the play are unlikely to have been accidental mistakes. Most people's supposition was that the author was criticizing defense minister Peng Dehuai's dismissal in 1959, after Peng protested to Mao about the effects that the Great Leap Forward's communization (expropriation of peasants' land by the party) had. While people like Wu Han may have sincerely thought that they were helping the party by pointing out its mistakes, many party leaders did not appreciate their efforts.

Another subtle way to criticize was by using metaphor. For example, since party hagiography compared Mao Zedong to the sun, one could compose poetry ostensibly about the sun and its virtues for growing crops while adding a line about even the sun having spots. Art, too, could be used as a weapon. In December 1964 the back cover of the official journal of the Chinese Youth League contained a picture that at first glance was a typical exercise in socialist realism: a team of peasants harvesting grain. On closer scrutiny, one noticed Chinese characters formed by the way stubble in the painting's foreground had been cut. They read "Kill Mao Zedong" and "Long Live Chiang Kai-shek." In the background, one of a group of three red flags, which symbolized the then-current "three red banners" slogan, had fallen to the ground. The peasants were happily striding forward but were not actually following a shadowy and unhappy-looking figure at the head of the line. Embarrassed authorities quickly tried to recall all of the issues, but without success.[5]

Culture and the Cultural Revolution

While protest of this sort was widespread, it was scarcely the norm. In fact, protest was scarcely noticeable in the rising tide of the cult of Chairman Mao that began in 1962. "The East Is Red" replaced "March of the Volunteers" as China's national anthem and was also the title of a lavishly costumed and choreographed revolutionary opera composed in honor of the fifteenth anniversary of the founding of the PRC on October 1, 1964. The Cultural Revolution took this cult to an extreme, to the extent that nothing but the works of Mao could be considered safe reading. Classical Chinese literature was castigated for advocating the viewpoint of the ruling class and depicting "ghosts and beauties." Artists who painted traditional landscapes were condemned for not portraying the revolution.

Foreign works were no better regarded: Shakespeare's works were vilified for representing the ideology of the ruling class. Ideologues maintained that therefore they must not be allowed to spread their insidious poison around. Tolstoy's *Anna Karenina* had a "revisionist outlook," while Balzac's ideas were "ridiculous and false." Classical music "paralyzed revolutionary resolution." Beethoven's Ninth Symphony, originally envisioned as an ode in praise of freedom (*Freiheit*) but later slightly changed to joy (*Freude*) to avoid causing its composer political problems, was condemned as "infused with a concept of bourgeois humanist love." Bizet's opera *Carmen* was dismissed as "an attempt to sell the cult of sex and individualism"; the classical ballet *Giselle*, on the other hand, "completely and entirely stands on the position of the ruling classes."

The authors of protest literature and art were persecuted, often to death. Red Guards threatened to break the fingers of musicians. Both Western and premodern Chinese books, art, and music were attacked. Sometimes this posed dilemmas. For example, if both Western musical instruments and ancient Chinese musical instruments were proscribed, how could the new revolutionary operas be performed? Radicals who condemned the piano as a "coffin in which notes rattled about like the bones of the bourgeoisie"[6] did not realize that Madame Mao, a driving force in the Cultural Revolution and the impetus behind the revolutionary operas, had a fondness for the piano. When questioned about this apparent inconsistency, she reportedly replied "We have liberated the piano." While it is easy to satirize this statement, there is actually a serious point behind it. In effect, the Cultural Revolution's answer to the century-old problem of how to import Western technical knowledge without eroding Chinese values in the process was to detach European musical instruments and their techniques from the context in which they had been created.[7]

Despite the reprieve of the piano, cultural life during the Cultural Revolution was fairly limited. Troupes performed the same eight revolutionary operas over and over. Mao was the sole approved author of books. Stirring choruses of *The East Is Red* introduced each new segment of Radio Beijing, approximately every fifteen minutes, followed by an inspirational quotation from the Chairman. Artists, working in materials as diverse as oils, plaster, jade, and rose quartz, produced images of Mao greeting the worshipful masses of the world, Mao meeting ethnic minority children, and just plain Mao. Hit songs had titles like "Chairman Mao Is the Red, Red Sun in All Our Hearts" and "Chairman Mao Visits Our Village."

For some people, danger was preferable to boredom. The maker of a classical bamboo flute adorned his instrument with a protest poem written in Tang dynasty style; the flute had been exported to the West before the counterrevolutionary act was discovered. Amateur authors produced their own works by hand. After appropriating paper from their own or someone else's work unit, they would secretly write their stories—perhaps by flashlight, huddled under a blanket—a method that somewhat limited the length of the works. Sometimes eight or more people would share copying duties. The finished manuscripts could then be quietly passed around among friends. Participants risked severe punishment for either creating or reading works outside the officially approved topics, but they were not dissidents in the generally understood meaning of the term. Surviving copies of these manuscripts indicate that favorite topics were love stories, detective and spy thrillers, knight-errant fiction, and pornography. The values found therein are remarkably similar to those of popular fiction in the Qing and early Republican periods.[8]

When the furor of the Cultural Revolution had died down, cultural life became slightly more relaxed. Though China's rapprochement with the United States was driven by security considerations (see Chapter 14), cultural exchanges proved useful in thawing the climate of distrust that had existed between the two countries for more than 20 years. The cultural offerings that the United States decided to send to the PRC were designed to be as politically inoffensive as possible. But even sending a symphony orchestra meant that Western music was again played in China. And American theatrical companies would have had great difficulty in putting on plays that did *not* depict Western bourgeois society. Both these art forms had been viciously attacked during the violent phase of the Cultural Revolution.

Within the Chinese population itself there were stirrings of dissent. Protest wall-posters began to appear, calling for actual implementation of the rights and freedoms guaranteed by the constitution and obliquely criticizing the party and Mao. Typically, they were tacked up mysteriously in the dark of night and were signed with pseudonyms such as Golden Monkey and Li Yizhe. Golden Monkey was apparently never caught, but Li Yizhe, actually an acronym for part of the names of each of three students, received long prison sentences for attempting to exercise their rights.

Certain periodicals served to transmit the viewpoint of certain factions. For example, the Shanghai journal *Study and Criticism* represented the Shanghai-based radical faction. Literature and journalism now served as vehicles for a power struggle within the leadership. During the early 1970s, a campaign against Confucianism took several confusing forms. Apparently, the Shanghai radicals led by Madame Mao intended the campaign to be directed against Zhou Enlai, with his plausibly Confucian attributes of pragmatism and desire to bring harmony to a China that the Cultural Revolution had nearly torn apart. Zhou and his group fought back with long articles and essays denouncing very different aspects of Confucius in order to attack Lin Biao's followers and the Gang of Four. As a case in point, they praised Confucius's enemies, the Legalists, for having introduced universal law and unification—both antithetical to the radical agenda of arbitrary sentencing and class struggle.

A little later, in 1975, another denunciation campaign began. This one was directed against *Water Margin*, one of Mao's favorite novels since he was a child. Like the campaign against Confucianism, it too had Zhou Enlai as its target. By changing some details of *Water Margin*'s Robin Hood-like plot, the Gang of Four was in essence pleading that unless the king (Mao) took drastic action immediately, a reactionary and his followers (Zhou Enlai and Deng Xiaoping) would suppress his revolutionary generals (the Gang of Four) after the king's death. Ironically, with a few small modifications, the Gang accurately foretold its own defeat.

The Arts Under Deng Xiaoping

Restrained Dissent

The arts and journalism participated in the general loosening of social controls that accompanied Deng Xiaoping's rise to power. It was announced that the eight revolutionary operas would be withdrawn for a time, since they had been performed so often that people were bored with them. The official media urged artists and writers to portray life realistically, seeing not only "success, brightness, festive flowers, and children's laughing faces, but also the dregs of the past, the dark clouds, and the tears and sorrows of the ordinary people."[9] Within the strictures of the criteria proclaimed by Mao in his 1957 Hundred Flowers speech "On the Correct Handling of Contradictions Among the People," artists were to be free to create. These criteria included standards like being beneficial rather than harmful to socialist construction and strengthening rather than weakening the leadership of the CCP. In other words, they were ambiguous enough that they could be interpreted by different people in different ways.

Here, obviously, were new boundaries whose limits would have to be tested. First to respond were cartoonists, who produced scathing and sometimes lurid satires of Jiang Qing and her supporters. Cross-talk comedians poked earthy fun at the Gang of Four, drawing on humor that had flourished sotto voce for many years. These were soon joined by a form of writing that came to be known as scar literature, after the title of a short story that appeared in 1978. The protagonist of "Scar" is forced to repudiate her parents during the Cultural Revolution, when they are falsely accused of being counterrevolutionaries. Later, the young man she loves is forced to break off his relationship with her when he finds out about her parents' label. In essence, her life has been ruined by political and ideological power struggles.

The publication of this story encouraged many other writers to tell of their own family tragedies. Scar literature was acceptable to the new leadership, most of whom had themselves suffered terribly during the Cultural Revolution. It was also useful to their desire to repudiate Maoist radicalism. While scar literature was well received by the populace, it is unremittingly gloomy and is not considered artistically very interesting.

Protest Gains Momentum

Not long thereafter, some artists became more adventurous. In 1980, a play entitled *Unrequited Love* appeared and was later made into a movie entitled *Sun and Man*. It, like others that followed, was much more difficult for the leadership to accept. *Unrequited Love* deals with a Chinese artist who, although well established in the West, decides to return to China after the revolution to help build his country. At first, things go relatively well. Then, because of his "bourgeois" background and the taint of his stay in the West, the artist is persecuted. During the Cultural Revolution, he loses his job and his family, eventually escaping to a cold, arid plain where he must steal food to stay alive. The film poses the question "You love your country. But does your country love you?" As the action proceeds, the central character, dying, is stumbling seemingly randomly through the snow. The camera pans upward, and the audience sees that, rather than stumbling randomly, his path has traced a question mark. At this point, weakness prevents the protagonist from carrying on. He freezes to death as the sun, a symbol of Mao, shines on his body. In the final scene, a flock of birds flies overhead in inverted V formation. This happens also to be the shape of the Chinese character for mankind.

The movie was much criticized by the official media in 1981, and its author forced to make a self-criticism. But this suppression did not occur until the film had been widely circulated. Clearly *Sun and Man* went far beyond a criticism of the Cultural Revolution, daring to question the basic relationship between the party and the people who had tried their utmost on behalf of their country. As such, it typifies a second stage in the evolution of the arts under Deng. By suggesting that the evils and aberrations of society predate the Cultural Revolution, it implies that there are flaws in the basic nature of the socialist system itself.

Other artists expressed similar ideas. In a story entitled "Chen Huansheng Goes to Town," a peasant goes to market to earn the money to buy himself a hat. However, he becomes ill, and a party leader arranges for him to stay at the county reception center, even taking Chen there in his private car. Unfortunately, the bill for his stay is so high that Chen can no longer buy the hat that was the purpose of his visit. He convinces himself that really he is very fortunate since no one else he knows has been able to ride in a car or stay in such luxurious accommodations. The theme of people who persuade themselves that they are happy when in actuality they are being exploited is consciously reminiscent of Lu Xun's hero Ah Q. Here, however, the oppressor is the communist party. The story also draws its readers' attention to the gap in living standards between the city and the countryside—also a favorite theme of late nineteenth- and early twentieth-century Chinese writers—and between the luxurious life-style of the leaders and the poverty of the ordinary person.[10]

A play with a similar theme, entitled *Bus Stop*, concerns a group of people who wait for ten years for a bus that never comes. Again, the plot is metaphorical: The people represent China, and the bus the social transformation that they have been promised will solve their problems. *Bus Stop* had a brief run in Beijing, after which it was closed and severely criticized. To official chagrin, its author, Gao Xingjian, was awarded the Nobel prize for literature in 2000—the first Chinese ever to have received the honor.

The leadership also had its problems with the plastic arts. In 1979, a group of 30 avant-garde artists who called themselves the Stars organized a modern art exhibition in a Beijing park. As nonmembers of the official Beijing Artists' Association, they had had a difficult time securing permission to hold the exhibition. It included paintings in a variety of modern Western styles that had earlier been proscribed: French impressionism, abstractionism, and the nude. The fact that the exhibition could be held at all attests to the loosening of controls over art at this time.

What attracted the most interest among the show's large and varied offerings were wood sculptures done by a young former Red Guard named Wang Keping. One sculpture is done in the fashion of a Buddha, wearing a cap with a red star in place of the usual headdress. Whereas the traditional Buddha has both eyes closed, Wang's rendition, whose features bear a remarkable resemblance to Mao Zedong's, has one eye slightly open. This is, the sculptor explained, so that he can see who is worshiping him. Another powerful work, called "The Silent One," has one of its eyes blinded, implying a one-sided view. The silent one has no nostrils, and its mouth is plugged. Wang's "Art Judge" is hideously ugly since, its creator explains, in the PRC only the most ugly people are allowed to judge art. The judge has a heart growing on his cheek, so that his loyalty can easily be checked. The consistent theme of Wang's work is of arbitrary, unfeeling repression by a bureaucracy that has lost touch with the people.

In 1980, one of the Stars produced a large mural for the Beijing airport. It contained the figure of a minority-nationality woman celebrating the Water Festival in the traditional manner: nude from the waist up. The mural caused a minor sensation: Officials first hung a curtain over it and later boarded it over. Another boundary had been tested and, however briefly, breached.

In sharp contrast to the tight control of literature and journalism during the Maoist years, small journals and newspapers proliferated. Their contributors seemed to delight in provoking the leadership. For example, one of the ways the leadership sought to enhance the PRC's foreign exchange reserves was to set up "friendship stores," which sold certain goods only to foreigners, for hard currency. Ordinary citizens who sought to enter such stores were turned away by guards, often very rudely. How, one journal asked, did this differ from the sign "No dogs or Chinese allowed" that had allegedly adorned the entrance to a park in the foreign concession of Shanghai before the revolution?

The journal was ordered to cease publication and its editor was sent to jail. This temporarily reduced, but did not halt, the production of objectionable material from unauthorized sources. Particularly worrisome to the leadership was the degree of sympathy dissidents seemed to enjoy within the party. At a major speech delivered to 10,000 party cadres at the Great Hall of the People in January 1980, Deng Xiaoping asked rhetorically why it was that "certain secret publications" were printed so beautifully. Observing that their authors could not possibly possess printing plants, Deng concluded that the publications could not have appeared without the support of party members, and that many of these were apt to be cadres.[11]

Another worrisome development, from the leadership's point of view, was the "unhealthy" intrusion of romance into the new music, films, plays, and novels. Such stories might or might not be accompanied by overtones of political protest. Regardless, they proved very popular with the average citizen, whose chief emotional role model for years had been Lei Feng, the young soldier whose only love was for Chairman Mao (see Chapter 9). The government worried that too much attention was being paid to romance, and that this misdirection of energies would distract people from the much more important goal of building China's economy. Very little could be done to stop this development. Efforts at repression of domestic production simply enhanced the value of videocassettes—often pornographic—smuggled in from Hong Kong, or of tapes of love songs from various countries. The music of a young woman from Taiwan, Teng Li-chun (Deng Lijun in *pinyin*), was so sought after in the PRC that it gave rise to a popular saying: "The day belongs to Deng Xiaoping, but the night belongs to Deng Lijun."

Another genre of dubious value from the leadership's point of view was science fiction. In the abstract, this form of literature was valuable, since it promoted science and technology, which were collectively one of the four modernizations. However, as science fiction was actually written, the implications were frequently quite different. The description of life on other planets could, and often was consciously intended to, contrast with conditions in China. Not all of the criticism was subtle. What, one literary official wondered, was one to make of a story in which a group of aliens emerge from their spaceship and immediately begin to denounce socialism?

Experimenting with Capitalism in the Arts

In the early phase of Deng's reforms, the party tried to apply capitalist principles to literature and art through a contract system. For example, a troupe would be made responsible for its own expenses and could divide its profits among its members. This caused great difficulties in many cases. Performers were used to being met at train stations and taken to hotels where reservations had already been made for them. They were paid the same amount whether the audience was large or small. Now, for the first time, they had to worry about making such arrangements, cutting expenses, and selling as large a number of tickets as possible. In some troupes where expenses were high and money was lost on each performance, the contract system provided an incentive not to put on shows.

Alternatively, the troupe could cut expenses and do its utmost to attract paying customers. For example, performers could put on plays or musical performances with "unhealthy" romantic themes. They could wear provocative (from the government's point of view) clothing and move sinuously across the stage instead of standing in one place as proper revolutionary dignity demanded. Similarly, writers who were put on the contract system quickly discovered that detective stories, spy novels, and steamy romances sold better than works on politically correct topics. The contract system for literature and the arts was soon revoked.[12]

The Campaign Against Spiritual Pollution

Individuals and their objectionable works were sporadically repressed almost from the beginning of the post-Mao liberalization. Typically, this was more likely to have reflected differences among party members over what was acceptable than anger over the actual works and their creators. Within the leadership, ideological hard-liners were attempting to combat reformers, creating dangers for writers and artists. Their plight was aptly summed up by the traditional Chinese saying "When elephants fight, the grass will be trampled." As early as 1980, China's most famous movie actor, aware that he was dying of an incurable cancer, decided to speak openly. In an article headlined "If the Controls Are Too Rigid, There Can Be No Hope for Literature and Art," the actor lashed out at "meddling by nonprofessionals" and urged Chinese artists and writers to exercise control over the political system instead of being controlled by it.[13] Interestingly, the article appeared not in a wallposter or unofficial journal, but in *People's Daily*, the official newspaper of the party central committee.

By the end of 1983, ideological hard-liners had gained the upper hand, and there was a full-scale campaign against "spiritual pollution" that had an adverse effect on writers and artists. Several editors of *People's Daily* were dismissed on grounds that the paper was taking too independent a stance and "dwelling too much on leftist mistakes."[14] The avant-garde artists' group the Stars voluntarily disbanded, with many of its members eventually leaving the country. Separated from the emotional world that had inspired their work, the artists lost a great deal of their effectiveness. One observer lamented that the Stars no longer lit up the dark night, but had become hangers-on, sipping coffee in foreign salons.

The campaign against spiritual pollution was, however, short-lived, and the arts again flourished. Some things that had earlier been regarded as objectionable were now tolerated, albeit grudgingly, and only if discreetly rendered. One of these was the right of artists to use nude models. Literature continued to tweak the leadership and to incur its periodic ire. During the height of Deng Xiaoping's campaign to rejuvenate the leadership by forcing elderly party and government officials to resign, a youth newspaper in Shenzhen suggested that the octogenarian Deng set an example by doing so himself. The paper was immediately shut down.

Looming Confrontation

In 1985, a controversial play entitled *WM* appeared. The initials have a double meaning, one of which is "we"—*wo-men* in Chinese. *WM* also represents two persons, one turned upside down and the other standing upright, symbolizing the perversion of human nature and its return to normal. It is the story of seven young people, each with different origins and personalities, who are members of a collective household. The play is divided into four seasons, beginning with winter and ending with autumn. At the conclusion, in the harvest season, all the characters but one have gained something. But in essence, they have gained nothing. When they remeet, they discuss the same topic that they did while huddling together in their small house in the cold of winter: What is man? They come to the same pessimistic conclusion as before. The implication is that another winter is coming, and also that life is cruel to people whatever the season. Were this not bad enough from the government's point of view, the play included a number of actions that could be construed as deliberately offensive to the leadership, and possibly to good taste in general, such as using newspapers with Mao Zedong's portrait on them for toilet paper.

Writers also directed their attention to questions concerning the ethics of making money in an avowedly socialist society. One particularly probing, as well as amusing, example of this concerns a city that becomes obsessed with growing a type of orchid known as *junzi*, or "Confucian gentleman." Though the name is consciously satiric, such a variety of orchid actually does exist. Everyone's life becomes reoriented toward cultivating the flowers for export and personal gain. In the process, various Chinese character traits, some lovable and some not, are satirized.

As the craze for orchids builds, *junzi* orchid associations and branch associations spring up. People consult foreign-language gardening manuals. Neighbors drop in to talk about their plants. On the negative side, people begin to connive and murder to obtain the most precious black-flowered plants. Guards must be hired for protection; police deployments are reoriented to keep watch over prime orchid-growing turf. Doctors are distracted from the practice of medicine. One physician literally moonlights as a broker for speculative nighttime over-the-counter orchid transactions; another is urged by his son to give up his practice so that he can grow orchids full-time and make more money. In the end, the citizens turn into orchids.[15] The author, of course, is criticizing the government's policies for having created an obsession with making money while doing nothing to prevent the deterioration of the basic social services governments are normally expected to provide.

Other authors concentrated on the question of why, more than a century after beginning efforts to make China the equal of the West, the country was still internationally weak and economically poor. Their answer was not much different from that of Lu Xun: The defects were to be found in the Chinese character itself. One writer, advocating that China correct what he believed to be an excess of national pride, likened the Yellow River—a symbol of China—to a stream of urine. Another, based in Taiwan but well known on the mainland, wrote a book entitled *The Ugly Chinaman*. It complains, among other things, that the Chinese are too conformist, too loud, too cruel, too crass, and, above all, too willing to tolerate injustice.[16] Implicitly or explicitly, these critics argued for a greater degree of Westernization. Their solutions bear a close resemblance to the science and democracy solutions proposed by their counterparts a century earlier.

The producers of *Black Cannon Incident*, a 1986 film, were highly critical of the political control system. The plot revolves around an engineer named Zhao, who discovers he has left one of his chess pieces in a hotel room after a business trip. He sends a telegram to a friend which reads "Black cannon lost. Please look in room 301." Public security officials suspect Zhao of spying. Eventually Zhao is vindicated when party officials open a package mailed to him and find the miniature black cannon. But the officials still blame him for starting the incident by sending a telegram for something as cheap and inconsequential as a chess piece. In addition to the plot, the party and its officials are criticized in a number of ways. Security forces drive imported cars with flashing sirens and employ sophisticated equipment to harass ordinary people. Cranes, earthmovers, and mining trucks dwarf and threaten to crush the workers at the plant. And, in the final scene, Zhao is walking past a park where two small boys are setting up bricks like dominoes. The boys knock over the first brick, and set off a chain reaction that ends at Zhao's feet.[17]

The student demonstrations of December 1986 and early 1987 set off just such a chain reaction for the PRC's writers and artists. A number of journalists were dismissed and Liu Binyan, one of the most famous, was expelled from the communist party along with the highly articulate astrophysicist dissident, Fang Lizhi. A Shanghai newspaper, the *World Economic Herald*, that had been sympathetic to the students was nearly shut down. There was another effort to eradicate illegal publications. And a scheduled art exhibition from the United States was canceled when PRC authorities changed their minds about allowing two pictures to be shown. One was of Douglas MacArthur, who had been a commanding general in the Korean War, and the other of former Israeli prime minister Golda Meier.

Only temporarily daunted, China's writers and artists soon returned to heterodox themes. In 1988, a television drama caused considerable anxiety in official circles. Known abroad as *River Elegy*, the literal translation of the Chinese title is "Premature Death of a River." The river is the Yellow River, representing Chinese civilization, and the authors' implication is that it died at an early age. The message of *River Elegy* is the necessity of the Yellow River merging with the blue Pacific Ocean, symbolic of the West, and into which the Yellow River actually does flow. A year later, many of the same people who were associated with the creation of *River Elegy* were preparing *Sunrise in the Heart,* a similar epic in commemoration of the seventieth anniversary of the May Fourth movement. It was reportedly as critical of China in the past century as *Elegy* had been of the preceding millennia.

World Economic Herald continued to be obliquely critical of officialdom. For example, its Washington correspondent wrote about an unexceptional meeting between a member of the U.S. Congress and his constituents. Nowhere in the article was it stated that this sort of meeting would never occur in China, but many of the *Herald*'s readers would understand that that was the reporter's point. *Herald* reporters also conducted and published accounts of interviews with foreign ambassadors without obtaining government permission. In January 1989, the paper's editor compared his philosophy of journalism to playing ping-pong:

If you hit the ball and miss the end of the table, you lose. If you hit the near end of the table, it's too easy. So you want to aim to just nick the end of the table. That's our policy.[18]

The Tiananmen Demonstrations and Their Aftermath

In April the party decided that the *Herald* had missed the end of the table, banning it for supporting the student demonstrations that were taking place in many Chinese cities that spring. The sequel to *River Elegy* was canceled just before it was to appear. After the demonstrations had been put down, the expected repression began. In contrast to the spirited denunciations of artists and writers during prior periods of repression, the period that followed the quelling of the 1989 demonstrations was more akin to slow asphyxiation. The number of newspapers was reduced, and it was announced that no additional licenses would be granted. New guidelines were issued for art exhibitions. Film studios experienced sharp budget cuts. *Sister Jiang*, a politically correct opera first produced in the early 1960s but not seen in many years, reopened. The diary of selfless hero Lei Feng was republished. Stage and screen productions renewed their attention to Mao Zedong as a subject. And the PLA prepared to spend $21.3 million—far in excess of the cost of all 150 films made in China during 1989—to produce a three-part epic, *Great Strategic Battles*. At the same time, several of the PRC's most acclaimed directors had their latest works quietly but effectively banned.

Party leaders urged everyone to study the lessons of Yan'an, "when men were men and art was politics."[19] And a newly appointed leader of the Chinese Writers Association compared literature to groceries: In both cases the government should encourage what is nutritious and ban what is poisonous.[20] As one cynic observed, this is precisely the reason that, under socialism, both the best groceries and the best literature are found in the black market.[21]

There was considerable resistance to the party's new policies. For example, the first part of *Great Strategic Battles* contains a scene where it looks as if the valiant communist troops may be annihilated by KMT forces. Audiences cheered.[22] On the first anniversary of the June 4 incident, public security forces were deployed on university campuses to guard against demonstrations. The students threw small bottles, *xiaoping*, out of windows to symbolize their attitudes toward Deng Xiaoping, whose name is written with a different Chinese character and actually means "small peace." They also broadcast a Western rock hit which contains the lyrics "Every move you make, every breath you take, I'll be watching you." As the students knew, but the public security guards apparently did not, the group that had recorded it was called the Police.

Indigenous Chinese rock became, if anything, more bold after Tiananmen. Cui Jian, an ethnic Korean and former trumpeter in the Beijing Philharmonic, emerged as the nation's rock superstar. His lyrics are profoundly subversive. For example, one hit song laments that, while it is sad that there are so many problems before an unspecified "us," what is truly sad is that "we" will never be given a chance to solve them. Another, expressing Cui's view of the bureaucracy, is entitled the "Official Banquet Song." In it, a high-ranking cadre describes the different restaurants he frequents, closing with the lines "Anyway, it's not my money so eat, drink, and be merry." Whether Cui was allowed to continue to perform because he was too famous to arrest or whether the leadership simply paid no attention to his lyrics is a matter of speculation. Many months after the demonstrations, his radio and television appearances were curtailed. In May 1992, however, Cui reappeared performing for 10,000 wildly enthusiastic fans in Nanjing.

As before, periods of relative freedom alternated with periods of restrictive policy. However, repression was never as severe as it had been in the Maoist period. As mentioned previously, the attempt to achieve politically correct art and journalism that followed the suppression of the Tiananmen demonstrations met with considerable resistance. When Deng Xiaoping criticized the left during his 1992 visit to the Shenzhen Special Economic Zone, intellectuals were emboldened. For example, a fall 1992 adaptation of theater-of-the-absurd playwright Friedrich Dürrenmatt's *Romulus the Great* satirized Deng and the effect of his reforms. Set in ancient Rome at the time the barbarians (i.e., the West) are storming the gates of the capital (Beijing), emperor Romulus (Deng) announces that he intends to save the empire (communism) by destroying it. The only hope, he says, is to go into a business partnership with the barbarian tycoons, since the hard choice was between a catastrophic capitalism and a capital catastrophe. A theater-goer commented ruefully that her country had reached the point where the theater of the absurd seemed a straightforward description of the PRC's reality. The play closed briefly, but not because of censorship: The leadership requested a special performance be given for them in the Zhongnanhai compound where most of them lived.

In the mid-1990s, there was a new period of repression. In fall 1995, a neo-leftist "10,000 Character Memorial" appeared which called for the recentralization of a state-owned economy. Neo-leftists cited Marxism-Leninism to justify their calls for the reassertion of central party and government power; director of the propaganda department Ding Guan'gen called for the arts to serve socialism. A number of new books were banned by the party's propaganda department because of "serious problems in political and ideological inclination." Computer networks were required to register with the government, and those with political and pornographic content were declared illegal. A few months thereafter, the authorities blocked access to a hundred websites.

Also noticeable in this period was another ideological camp, the neo-conservatives. Like neo-leftists, they argued for strong state power, though unlike the leftists, they did so for practical rather than ideological reasons: a strong state, neo-conservatives believed, was needed to ensure stability. The alternative would be chaos. A third strain, neo-traditionalism or neo-Confucianism, argued that modernization was not the same as Westernization: The Chinese tradition, including the works of Confucius, provided the underpinnings of a uniquely Chinese form of modernization. Neo-traditionalists had much in common with the proponents of "Asian values" elsewhere in Asia. Nationalism was popular with all these groups. To some extent, this stemmed from a disillusion with the promise of the West: A number of its proponents had studied abroad and did not like some or many things they had seen there. Nationalism, as manifested in such works as *China Can Say No,* fit in with party and government's wishes until it threatened to disrupt relations with Japan and the United States. At this point, authorities moved to rein in the nationalists.

Fear of the consequences of globalization may also have been a factor influencing several of these groups. The neo-traditionalists, like their forebears a century ago, were particularly concerned with the effect of the outside world on what they considered the core values of Chinese tradition. Others were concerned that foreign ideas would erode socialist values.

Liberals, whose voices continued to be heard, countered that neo-traditionalists really knew nothing about the Chinese tradition or Confucius. They had been educated under a Marxist system, and were simply inventing a past that was useful for their purposes.[23] Liberals also attempted to refute the neo-leftists: A book called *Crossing Swords* strongly asserted the need for continued reforms and criticized the "10,000 Character Memorial" for opposing the PRC's interactions with Western capitalist states. Neo-leftists responded in a manner that would have been highly unlikely during the Mao era: by suing the authors of "Crossing Swords" for quoting the memorial without permission and for allegedly misrepresenting its contents. The economic reforms announced at the Fifteenth Party Congress and Ninth National People's Congress, as well as Jiang Zemin's visit to the United States and the U.S. president's return visit to the PRC, indicated that Jiang's views coincided with the liberals.

In short, by the late 1990s, many different schools of thought contended, and were fairly well tolerated by the leadership. The rift between the PRC's intellectual and political elites that was evident at the time of the Tiananmen demonstrations had narrowed considerably. Unlike the Mao years, people are able to criticize leaders and their policies in private with little fear of retribution. Academic journals may also contain articles that are quite critical, as long as they do not confront leading officials too bluntly. For example, it is usually acceptable to disagree with the effectiveness of a given policy, but not acceptable to call Politburo Standing Committee members idiots for foolishly proposing the policy. One technique that authors employ is to position heterodox thoughts in the center of their articles, wedged between ideologically correct introductions and conclusions. Academic journals, with their fairly limited readerships, are not normally carefully scrutinized by official censors.

Those who are tempted to test the limits of party and government tolerance are aware that risks remain. Heavy-handed Maoist tactics have been replaced by more subtle forms of coercion that induce people to censor themselves. The charges police bring against those they arrest tend to be vague. Often they will say "you yourself know what you did," and imply that they have much evidence to back up their claims. The individual is advised to confess immediately and beg for lenient treatment. Not knowing what the rules are, most people choose to err on the side of caution. One scholar describes this as the anaconda in the chandelier phenomenon. Although the anaconda rarely stirs, those below it are aware of its presence and move carefully even though they are unsure about what actions will cause the snake to strike.[24] For example, one website editor has voluntarily decided to exclude discussions of independent labor movements, the banned religious movement Falun Gong, and political parties from his site, but still worries that it may be closed down for upsetting the authorities in some way he cannot predict.[25]

Party and government want to use the media to achieve certain goals such as unearthing corruption, but do not want to have their own legitimacy undermined in the process. Since a good deal of corruption involves party and government officials, this puts journalists in a difficult position. In the words of a popular slogan that can be heard all over China, "if we do not root out corruption, the country will perish; if we do root out corruption, the party will perish." Reporters have described their solution to this as "swatting only at flies, but not hitting tigers," that is, attacking only low-level corruption. Obviously this technique does not address the root of the problem. Also, it is not risk-free: Sometimes the flies are protégés of tigers, who fear that allowing their subordinates to be investigated will implicate them as well; hence, they strike back against the reporters and publications. Although foreign reporters have seldom been arrested in recent years, their publications, including *Newsweek,* the *Economist,* and *Der Spiegel,* have been pulled from newsstands for including stories the leadership would rather not have its citizens know about.

In 1997, more than 10 percent of the PRC's newspapers were shut down, as well as several hundred journals. Party officials explained that the decision had been taken to avoid redundancy and upgrade quality. The surviving publications were grouped into media conglomerates or syndicates in order to maximize publishing efficiency and cut costs. Party and government had legitimate concerns about journalistic ethics: There were documented instances of reporters refusing to cover stories unless paid by the people or businesses they were to write about. In one well-publicized case, a favorable story about a company persuaded many people to invest in it: The company, which had in essence bribed the reporters to praise it, was actually financially weak. When it failed, investors lost hundreds of millions of dollars. Moreover, some self-styled artists really did seem to be pandering to the lowest standards of their audiences.

Liberals, however, argued that the press and journal cuts fell disproportionately on those who were critical of party and government policies. They also pointed out that investigative reporting had been hazardous to the health of the investigators. For example, public security personnel had threatened reporters if they did not surrender a videotape showing police abusing their power. Artists and journalists have been sued for producing critical works. The real motive behind the establishment of media syndicates, they suspected, was less to save money than to enhance official control. Syndicates can operate only print media, being forbidden to own television or radio outlets, and cannot cross provincial borders. Their establishment reinforces the hypothesis that post-Mao China is more apt to resemble the communist neo-traditional model than a civil society.

As the twenty-first century dawned, party and government stepped up efforts to control the internet. Certain search engines and websites were blocked; individuals who had expressed themselves too freely in chat rooms were arrested. Chinese hackers have devised ways to circumvent the blockages, prompting countermoves by officialdom to reblock them by other means. Falungong hackers have on occasion succeeded in inserting their own messages onto government websites and in hijacking satellite signals. It is not clear who will win these cat-and-mouse games, although officialdom would seem to have the more difficult task. While international rating agencies give low marks to press freedom in the PRC, several papers continue the "edge ball" tradition begun by the *World Economic Herald. Nanfang Zhoumo (Southern Weekend)* and *China Youth News* were nicknamed the "two chili peppers of south and north" for their willingness to report what party officials do not want them to. Both have faced dismissals of personnel and reorganizations meant to deter future journalistic activism. But other papers and journals have become more active.

Conclusions

Despite the efforts of party and government to retain control over literature, the arts, and journalism, China had by the 1990s achieved a degree of cultural pluralism that appears to be irreversible. Repressive periods alternate with periods of greater freedom; artists and journalists continue to test the limits of the leadership's toleration. Pressures for self-censorship indeed deter many would-be critics, but courageous individuals and publications who wish to speak their consciences forthrightly continue to come forth.

Whether these actions will be able to bring about a fundamental change in the system, as predicted by the civil society hypothesis, or will be shaped and co-opted by the system, as proponents of the communist neo-traditionalist theory predict, remains to be seen. Should the PRC's intellectuals, artists, and journalists issue a direct challenge to the leadership's power or try to forge alliances between themselves and workers and peasants, the current degree of toleration would quickly disappear. But it is possible that fundamental changes can be achieved gradually. Neither party nor government is monolithic, and influential segments in both are aware that listening to the criticisms of the PRC's literati and accommodating their suggestions are important to the country's social stability.

Notes

1. Both are traditional Chinese symbols of love. See Perry Link, *Mandarin Ducks and Butterflies: Popular Fiction in Early Twentieth-Century Chinese Cities* (Berkeley: University of California Press, 1981).

2. Quoted in C. T. Hsia, *A History of Modern Chinese Fiction, 1917–1957* (New Haven, Conn.: Yale University Press, 1961), p. 122.

3. Liang Heng and Judith Shapiro, *Intellectual Freedom in China After Mao* (New York: The Fund for Free Expression, 1984), pp. 79–85.

4. Summary provided by Professor Edward Dreyer, Department of History, University of Miami.

5. James R. Townsend, *The Revolutionization of Chinese Youth: A Study of Chung-kuo Ch'ing-nien*, China Research Monograph No. 1 (Berkeley: Center for Chinese Studies, 1967), p. 31.

6. Kraus, *Pianos*, p. vii.

7. Ibid., p. 202.

8. Perry Link, "Hand-Copied Entertainment Fiction from the Cultural Revolution," in Perry Link, Richard Madsen, and Paul Pickowicz, *Unofficial China: Popular Culture and Thought in the People's Republic* (Boulder, Colo.: Westview Press, 1989), p. 17.

9. *Xinhua*, September 5, 1979; in *FBIS–CHI*, September 12, 1979, p. L/17.

10. Liang and Shapiro, pp. 89–90.

11. The speech is reprinted in *Cheng Ming* (Hong Kong), March 1, 1980, and translated in *FBIS–CHI*, March 11, 1980, p. 12.

12. Liang and Shapiro, pp. 112–116.

13. Fox Butterfield, "Posthumous Plea by Movie Star Bids China Relax Control of Arts," *New York Times*, October 28, 1980, p. A3; Francis Deron, "*Renmin Ribao* Carried Actor's Plea for Artistic Freedom," *AFP* (Paris), October 8, 1980; in *FBIS–CHI*, October 9, 1980, p. L/9.

14. "China Said to Force Newspaper Editors to Quit Their Posts," *New York Times*, November 14, 1983, p. 5.

15. Translation in Jeffrey Kinkley, "Ideological Flux in Post-Mao Literature," paper presented to the Fourteenth Sino-American Conference on Mainland China, Columbus, Ohio, June 14, 1985.

16. Nicholas Kristof, "One Author Is Rankling Two Chinas," *New York Times*, October 7, 1987, p. 7.

17. Ann Scott, "Chinese Film Assails Official Abuses—And Wins Awards," *International Herald Tribune*, July 8, 1986, p. 8.

18. Nicholas Kristof, "Boldly, Paper Explores New Ground," *New York Times*, January 16, 1989, p. 5.

19. Paul Clark, "Money, Politics Bind China's Filmmakers," *Centerviews* (Honolulu), November–December 1990, p. 6.

20. Nicholas Kristof, "Chinese Writers are Told Not to Write Critically," *New York Times*, September 17, 1990, p. B3.

21. The cynic in this case is Professor Edward Dreyer.

22. Nicholas Kristof, "China's New Films: More Propaganda, Less Art," *New York Times*, August 1, 1991, pp. B1, B3.

23. Suisheng Zhao, "Chinese Intellectuals' Quest for National Greatness and Nationalistic Writing in the 1990s," *China Quarterly*, no. 152, December 1997, pp. 729–730.

24. Perry Link, "The Anaconda in the Chandelier: Censorship in China Today," in Gang Lin, ed., *Scholars Under Siege? Academic and Media Freedom in China*. Woodrow Wilson Center, Washington D.C., April 2002, pp. 3–7.

25. Yongming Zhou, "Expanded Space, Refined Control: The Intellectual Electronic Press in China," in *ibid.*, p. 19.

Suggestions for Further Reading

Merle Goldman, "The Potential for Instability Among Alienated Intellectuals and Students in Post-Mao China," in David Shambaugh, ed., *Is China Unstable: Assessing the Factors* (Washington, D.C.: Sigur Center for Asian Studies, 1998), pp. 111–121.

Shanthi Kalathil and Taylor Boas, *Open Networks, Closed Regimes: The Impact of the Internet on Authoritarian Rule* (Washinton, D.C.: Carnegie Endowment for International Peace, 2003).

Gang Lin, ed., *Scholars Under Siege? Academic and Media Freedom in China.* Asia Program Special Report No. 102, Woodrow Wilson Center, Washington D.C., April 2002.

Tonglin Lu, *Confronting Modernity in the Cinemas of Taiwan and Mainland China* (Cambridge, U.K.: Cambridge University Press, 2001).

Suisheng Zhao, "Chinese Intellectuals' Quest for National Greatness and Nationalistic Writing in the 1990s," *China Quarterly,* no. 152, December 1997, pp. 725–745.

13 Ethnic Minorities and National Integration

China's Minority Peoples

China's minorities in 1949, when the communist government first came to power, probably numbered less than 6 percent of the country's total population. Even now, after years of government pressure on the Han Chinese majority to practice family planning, while applying far less stringent restrictions to the minorities, the minorities constitute a bare 10 percent of the PRC's population. Moreover, there are 55 officially recognized minority groups and, although there is great variation in the sizes of the different groups, no one minority is especially large (see Table 13.1).

In spite of this relatively insignificant minority population, party and government have spent a great deal of time and energy, as well as money, on the minorities and the areas they live in. There are five basic reasons for this. The first is strategic. Most minorities live on or near China's land frontiers. Frequently, the border divides a group arbitrarily: Kazakhs live in both China and in the Kazakh republic of the FSU; Miao[1] in China, Thailand, Vietnam, Laos, and Burma; Mongols in China and the republic of Mongolia; and so forth. Hostile foreign powers might wish to make use of their own minority nationals to infiltrate the PRC and cause problems. There is also the problem of irredentism to consider: Mongolia might decide to claim the parts of China inhabited by Mongols, or the Kazakhs of Kazakhstan might want to include the PRC's Kazakhs in their state. Constant vigilance, as well as certain efforts to keep the minorities happy with their lives in the PRC, have seemed wise courses of action.

Second, most minority areas are sparsely populated relative to areas inhabited by Han Chinese. They therefore have the potential to absorb immigrants from overcrowded areas. Minority areas comprise well over 60 percent of the PRC's total land area. Third, a number of minority areas possess rich natural resources. Oil, coal, gold, and other minerals are located in different parts of the country inhabited by minorities. Eighty percent of China's meat, milk, and wool-supplying animals are also found there. Proper exploitation of these resources is important to raising living standards, and to economic development in general.

Fourth is the propaganda factor. Particularly during the Maoist era, the CCP maintained that its model of socialism had applicability in other areas of the developing world besides Han China. If the PRC could showcase its minorities as prosperous and contented, they could serve as living proof of the successes that the Chinese model of socialism would have for non-Han peoples. Conversely, having discontented and rebellious ethnic populations would be, and continues to be, an embarrassment for the PRC. Ethnically

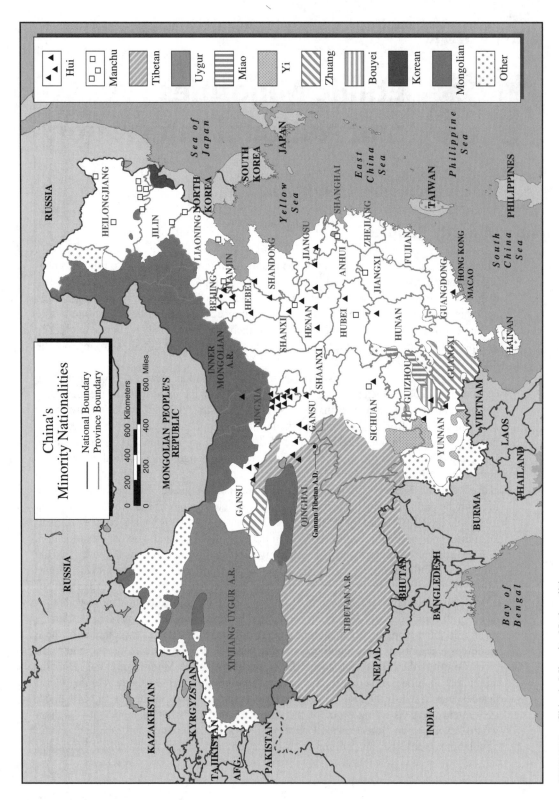

MAP 13.1 China's Minority Nationalities

based discontent could also compound China's strategic problems, in that dissident minorities would be more receptive to subversive influences from foreign powers.

A fifth reason is more recent: tourism. The Deng era was characterized by both its opening to the outside world and its ambitious plans for economic development. Many minorities wear colorful costumes of exquisite workmanship and possess rich artistic traditions. Some live in areas of breathtaking scenery. Thus, visiting minority areas has been popular with tourists, and provides a pleasant contrast with the somewhat drab appearance of many of the PRC's major cities. This has been an important source of foreign exchange for the government.

Additionally, even though minorities may total less than 10 percent of the PRC's population, this amounts to nearly 107 million people. Their numbers thus exceed the populations of most of the countries in the world, including France, Germany, and Great Britain. Hence, in spite of being a small part of the total population of the PRC, what China's media refer to as "the minorities problem" has occupied an important place in Chinese policymaking. Essentially, the minorities problem is one of *integration*: For reasons of defense, economic and social well-being, and national pride, the Chinese communist elite has attached considerable importance to, first, assuming jurisdiction over minority peoples and, second, obtaining their loyalties. This chapter examines the steps taken by the party and government to achieve integration and tries to assess the success of these efforts.

A few words on the concept of integration may be in order. There are many different methods by which to bring about the assertion of administrative authority and reorientation of loyalties. One might want to conceptualize these as arrayed on a continuum ranging from *assimilation* at one end to *pluralism* on the other. Assimilation involves the minorities being absorbed into the dominant group. In this process they lose their languages and other distinguishing characteristics, being in essence indistinguishable from the majority group. At the other end of the spectrum, in a pluralist system, minorities retain their languages as well as large parts of their culture and traditional ways of behavior. They accept the administrative authority of the government of the dominant group, and even participate in it. But they remain distinct from the majority group. Minorities policy in post-1949 China has vacillated between emphasis on pluralism and forced assimilation. During Mao's lifetime, these shifts were sudden and violent; under Deng and Jiang, there have been moves toward greater and lesser restrictions on the exercise of minorities' freedoms, with an underlying acceptance of pluralism.

Past Chinese governments have tried each of these extremes. Although there were wide variations over the long course of Chinese history and even, as has been seen, several non-Han dynasties, the dominant pattern in traditional China was pluralistic. It was also quite condescending. In the words of noted Ming dynasty philosopher–statesman Wang Yangming,

> Barbarians are like wild deer. To institute direct civil service administration by Han Chinese magistrates would be like herding deer into the hall of a house and trying to tame them. In the end, they merely butt over your sacrificial altars, kick over your tables, and dash about in frantic flight. . . . On the other hand, to leave these tribal chiefs to themselves to conduct their own alliances or split up their domains is like releasing deer into the wilderness. . . . Without watchers to guard the fences and prevent their goring and battling, they will leap the fences, bite through the bamboo screens, and wander far to trample the young crops. The presently established civil service aides are such guardians of the parks and fences.[2]

TABLE 13.1   China's Ethnic Minorities

Minority	Population (1990 Census)	Population (2000 Census)	Areas of Chief Distribution
Zhuang	15,489,630	16,178,811	Guangxi, Yunnan
Manchu	9,821,180	10,682,262	Liaoning, Jilin, Heilongjiang
Hui	8,602,978	9,816,805	Ningxia, Gansu
Miao	7,398,035	8,940,116	Guizhou, Hunan, Yunnan
Uygur	7,214,431	8,399,393	Xinjiang
Yi	6,572,173	7,762,272	Sichuan, Yunnan
Tujia	5,704,223	8,028,133	Hunan, Hubei
Mongol	4,806,849	5,813,947	Inner Mongolia, Liaoning
Tibetan	4,593,330	5,416,021	Tibet, Sichuan, Qinghai
Bouyei	2,545,059	2,971,460	Guizhou
Dong	2,514,014	2,960,293	Guizhou
Yao	2,134,013	2,637,421	Guangxi, Guangdong
Korean	1,920,597	1,923,842	Jilin, Liaoning, Helongjiang
Bai	1,594,827	1,858,063	Yunnan
Hani/Akha	1,253,952	1,439,673	Yunnan
Kazak	1,111,718	1,250,458	Xinjiang, Qinghai
Li	1,110,900	1,247,814	Hainan
Dai/Thai	1,025,128	1,158,989	Yunnan
She	630,378	709,592	Fujian
Lisu	574,856	634,912	Yunnan
Gelao	437,997	579,357	Guizhou
Lahu	411,476	453,705	Yunnan
Dongxiang	373,872	513,805	Gansu
Va/Wa	351,974	396,610	Yunnan
Shui, Sui	345,993	406,902	Guizhou
Naxi	278,009	308,839	Yunnan
Qiang	198,252	306,072	Sichuan
Tu	191,624	241,198	Qinghai, Gansu
Xibo, Xibe	172,847	188,824	Xinjiang
Mulam/Molao	159,328	207,352	Guangxi

In other words, Wang was advocating little more than supervision and control; efforts to force minority groups to behave like Han would be counterproductive.

KMT practice is harder to characterize, since the country was at war for most of its time in office, and the government exercised little or no control in the outlying areas where most minorities live. Its policy pronouncements, however, were stridently assimilationist in tone. Nationalism had become a potent force in China, and the KMT was in the vanguard; its very name means Nationalist Party. KMT leaders believed that, for minorities' own benefit, as well as in order to forge a strong and unified Chinese state, minorities should learn the Han language and Han ways.[3]

TABLE 13.1 *(continued)*

Minority	Population (1990 Census)	Population (2000 Census)	Areas of Chief Distribution
Kirghiz	141,549	160,823	Xinjiang
Daur	121,357	132,394	Inner Mongolia, Heilongjiang
Jingpo	119,209	132,143	Yunnan
Salar	87,697	104,503	Qinghai, Gansu
Blang/Bulang	82,280	91,882	Yunnan
Maonan	71,968	107,166	Guangxi
Tajik	33,538	41,028	Xinjiang
Primi/Pumi	29,657	33,600	Yunnan
Achang	27,708	33,936	Yunnan
Nu	27,123	28,759	Yunnan
Ewenki	26,315	30,505	Inner Mongolia
Gin/Jing	18,915	22,517	Guangdong
Jino	18,021	20,899	Yunnan
De'ang/Benglong	15,462	17,935	Yunnan
Uzbek	14,502	12,370	Xinjiang
Russian	13,504	15,609	Xinjiang
Yugu	12,297	13,719	Gansu
Bonan/Baoan	12,212	16,505	Gansu
Monba	7,475	8,923	Tibet
Orogen	6,965	8,196	Inner Mongolia
Derung/Dulong	5,816	7,426	Yunnan
Tatar	4,873	4,890	Xinjiang
Hezhen	4,245	4,640	Heilongjiang
Lhoba	2,312	2,965	Tibet

Source: Compiled from 1990 and 2000 Census Data

Ethnicity in Communist Ideology

Initially, the most important factor conditioning Chinese communist policy toward minorities was ideology. Karl Marx had believed that what appeared to be ethnic or nationality characteristics were actually just manifestations of the bourgeois-capitalist phase of society. When the dictatorship of the proletariat had been established, these manifestations of bourgeois society would wither away. What would emerge would be a homogeneous proletarian culture.

No coercion would be necessary to bring about this homogeneous culture, although there might be some resistance from a few diehard remnants of the aristocratic or bourgeois classes of the old society. They might have to be dealt with forcefully, but would constitute a relatively minor problem. In essence, the homogeneous society would come about automatically, with increasing levels of socialism and communism. It would be a blending of the best of all nationalities' customs and habits. Given this favorable ideological prognosis, a lenient policy toward minority cultures and ethnic identities seemed called for. If the new communist government could just take care of the diehard types, time and the increasing communization of the economy and society would take care of the rest.

Minorities Policy in Practice

The Early Years: 1949–1957

Ideology was reinforced by the practical situation in which the Chinese communists found themselves in 1949. There was a good deal of hostility between minorities and Han Chinese. The CCP had taken over most minority areas through military victory or because minorities leaders perceived armed resistance to be futile. The party elite was well aware that the hearts and minds of most minority peoples had yet to be won.

The party had trained a small group of minority cadres who were also communists, but there were not nearly enough of them to take care of the administrative and other work that the CCP felt it needed to do in minorities' areas. The leadership was aware that it did not know nearly enough about the various minorities to understand how to deal with them. Ignorance of specific ethnic groups' customs could cause grievous insult—for example, it might be extremely important to know whether a guest should sit to the right or the left of his host's campfire. Breaches of etiquette, however unintentionally committed, could cause lasting harm to the party's image and make the process of integration much harder. Also, lack of knowledge of the minorities meant that the party had little sense of what their problems were; conversely, possessing such knowledge would allow the party to approach them with suggestions for solution.

The people who were best equipped to enlighten the party's representatives, or cadres, and who also could be most influential in winning the trust of the minorities masses for the party, were typically the pre-1949 leadership elite of the minorities. Particularly in the case of the smaller and more primitive minority groups, headmen were the interpreters of the outside world to their constituencies and sometimes the only ones of their group who could speak Chinese. To approach the "exploited masses" directly, as the party had done in Han areas, was more apt to cause confusion and rejection than achieve the desired results. The fact that the party needed to work with traditional, pre-1949 elites was also conducive to a policy of tolerance and accommodation of differences.

Hence the Chinese communists fashioned a minorities policy that in essence resembled a pluralistic model of integration. Many of its elements were borrowed from the Soviet Union; a number of Soviet ethnologists served as advisers to the Chinese and assisted in research and data collection in minority areas. The PRC's situation was far different from that of the USSR, where nearly half the population were non-Russians. Also, a much higher proportion of the USSR's minorities were educated and economically developed to a level equal to, or higher than, that of Russians.

In accordance with Soviet doctrine, minorities were given so-called autonomous areas. Depending on the concentrations of minority populations involved, these areas could be created at province, prefecture, county, or township levels. These provided certain accommodations for the customs of the host nationality, and preferential treatment for them in selection for official positions. Minorities received the right to use their own languages, both spoken and written. In the case of those minorities who did not have a written language, the party promised to help them to devise one. Minorities were guaranteed the right to keep their traditional costumes and customs, so long as these did not interfere with production. In the majority of cases they could even keep their traditional leaders, as long as those leaders did not *actively* oppose socialism. This policy fit in well with the idea of a united front of cooperation with "patriotic" bourgeois upper strata in general, which was prevalent in the early days of the PRC.

The party organization most closely connected with minorities work was, and is, the United Front Work Department (UFWD) of the party Central Committee. Originally set up in Yan'an in 1944, the UFWD, before as well as after liberation, has been responsible for shaping the broad outlines of policy in minority areas in accordance with the party line. It is also in charge of other aspects of united front work concerned with the implementation of the People's Democratic Dictatorship, which Mao had deemed appropriate for China in this transition period from New Democracy to socialism. United front work departments also exist as sections of the party apparatus on the provincial level. At lower levels where no UFWD exists, the Rural Work Department of the local party organization may fill the task of political guidance of minorities.

At the central government level, broad guidelines from the UFWD are sent to the Nationalities Affairs Commission (NAC) of the State Council, which has responsibility for implementing them. Major pronouncements on minorities affairs are drawn up by the commission, then approved and promulgated by the State Council. The NAC is then charged with implementing them. Despite its subordination to the UFWD, the NAC, meeting every day and functioning as a regular ministry, has considerable powers. Nationalities affairs commissions also exist at provincial, prefectural, and county levels in areas with substantial minority populations (see Figure 13.1). Where minority populations are not large and their problems have been classified "uncomplicated," they may be handled by a department of civil affairs at the relevant level, with an office or a particular cadre designated as responsible.

The National People's Congress (NPC) has a nationalities committee. Composed of all ethnic minority delegates to the NPC, it has no real power, being confined to discussion and approval of measures decided upon elsewhere. In recent years, delegates have become much more open about voicing their grievances. Hence, their speeches give important information about problems in minority areas even though the delegates themselves have little ability to effect solutions. Also, the members' selection as NPC delegates provides an index of the party's assessment of their prestige in their own respective areas. For these reasons, the nationalities committee is considered an important factor in minority work.

Minorities were given assurances that socialist reforms would not be introduced until the minority masses wanted them. In addition, minorities received exemptions from certain other rules imposed upon the Han. For example, animals killed in connection with a ritual sacrifice were exempt from the slaughter tax. Muslim minorities whose customs included polygamy, and Tibetans, whose culture encouraged multiple husbands, were allowed to continue these practices. Where early marriage was a tradition, it could remain. The Yi could even continue to own slaves.

Meanwhile, the party made various efforts to speed up the transition period into socialism and the homogenization of proletarian culture. A network of "nationalities institutes" was established in order to educate minorities, and some Han Chinese, to do the

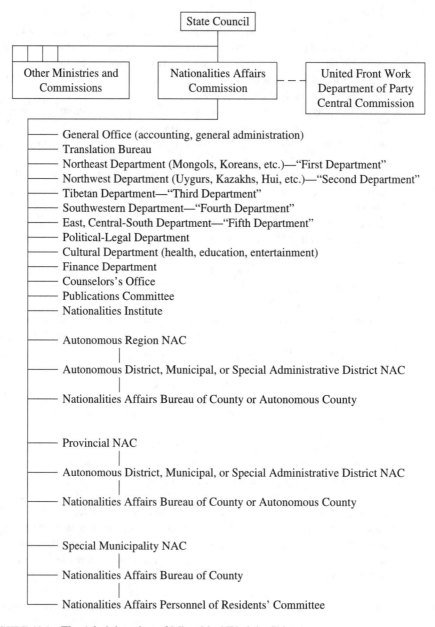

FIGURE 13.1   The Administration of Minorities' Work in China

party's work in minority areas. They were trained as teachers, administrative cadres, veterinarians, and even entertainers. Not surprisingly, all, including the curriculum the teachers were trained to teach and the entertainments that the entertainers were instructed in, carried a procommunist message.

Research teams, which included anthropologists and linguistics experts, among others, were sent out to live with the minorities and study them, learning their languages and customs. Health teams also visited minorities areas, as well as work teams generally composed of PLA members. These had a propaganda function in addition to their overt reasons for being. Doctors and paramedics dispensed pills and salves as gifts from the CCP and Chairman Mao; work teams dug irrigation ditches and reclaimed waste land with the same message. The emphasis during this period was on unity and patriotism. The teams also tried to build a positive image of the party and socialism; they did not emphasize ideology or sweeping social or economic reforms.

In general, the party seemed pleased with the results of these early efforts at social mobilization. The next step was to set up so-called people's governments in minority areas. These were established at different times in different minority areas during the early 1950s, consonant with the party's estimate of the receptivity of the target group. Such governments generally included a fair sprinkling of members of traditional minorities' leaders. In Tibetan and Mongolian areas, lamas were included; in the southwest, tribal headmen or headwomen.

Also included were as many minority-group activists as the party had been able to train. Some of these actually were from the stratum of society that the party considered exploited: the children of serfs or slaves who were bright, personable, and quick to absorb the party's message. Quite a few others, however, were the scions of the traditional elite, for whom cooperation seemed the best way to ensure their main goal: survival. For example, the numerous offspring of the Tibetan nobleman and archcollaborator Ngapo Ngawang Jigme were trained at the Central Nationalities Institute in Beijing and given various positions of responsibility when they graduated. Han Chinese administrators constituted a third group included in the memberships of the new people's governments. Nearly always party members and sometimes PLA members as well, they were the decisive elements of decision-making, whether or not they held the top positions.

Putting the more cooperative and prestigious members of the traditional minority elite into the new people's governments gave the party a way to allow traditional governmental structures to wither out of existence without actually abolishing them. Many of the traditional leaders themselves, and their prestige, remained intact. The party's motive seems to have been to maintain traditional symbols of power, thereby minimizing their resistance to change while gradually modifying the power structure they had represented.

Another attempt at symbol manipulation was the granting of the title *bator*, a Mongolian word meaning hero. It had been used by Uygurs and Kazakhs as well as Mongols to honor outstanding individuals among them, usually for valor on the battlefield. Henceforth, it was to be given to heroes of socialist labor.

Certain other gestures were made to accommodate minority sensibilities. For example, the names of many minority groups had been rendered into Chinese by characters containing the dog radical,[4] with clear intent to disparage the humanness of the particular group. Other groups were called not by the name they commonly called themselves, but by a pejorative term, such as Lolo for the group that knew itself as Yi. The party ordered an end to such practices, although of course changing long-standing habits was a more difficult task. Offensive place names were also changed; these had typically been given to commemorate Han conquests of "barbarian" areas or the suppression of rebellion therein. For example, Dihua, the capital of Xinjiang, was changed to its Uygur name, Urumqi.

The goal of introducing socialist reforms had not been forgotten; it was simply postponed until after the preliminary work had been done. Land reform in minority areas began only around 1952–1953, by which time it had been almost completed in Han Chinese areas. Efforts were made to research an area prior to introducing reforms, to ascertain whether the level of development was suitable. Target areas were chosen as test cases. Only after examining the problems caused by particular reforms and discussing remedies were the reforms generalized to surrounding locations. This was called the "point and area" system.

The result was a rather flexible reform process that was responsive not only to the differences between one minority group and another but also to the differences within minority groups. For example, Mongols whose main occupation was fixed agriculture, so-called sedentary Mongols, were judged ready for reforms, while Mongols who were nomadic herdsmen, or pastoral Mongols, were not. The Yi of Yunnan were ordered to emancipate their slaves, whereas the Sichuan Yi, who were found to be "less culturally advanced"—less sinicized—were not required to do so. Tibetan areas east of the Jinsha River underwent land reform in 1954, whereas land reform was not attempted west of the Jinsha.

In 1956 there was a speedup in agricultural collectivization in minority areas similar to that which had occurred in Han areas in mid-1955. But it, too, was carried out bearing in mind what a given minority would be receptive to. Those minorities who had already undergone land reform were moved up a stage in the approved socialist progression, to mutual aid teams. Those who were already at the stage of MATs got moved up to lower-level cooperatives, and so forth. In other words, the 1956 collectivization effort did not remove the differences between Han and non-Han areas, it simply raised them to a loftier level in the hierarchy of socialism.

Some events in the next few years were to cause dissatisfaction with this flexible system. Specifically, in 1956 and 1957, as part of a routine investigation of minorities work, and also in connection with the Hundred Flowers campaign (see Chapter 5), ethnic minorities were asked to express their opinions of party and government. What they said proved shocking. Some wanted to secede from China. Others said that they thought that the party's policies amounted to thinly disguised plans for assimilation. Yet a third group argued that the party was violating its own promise to allow dispensations from certain policies that ran counter to minorities' special characteristics. Collectivization, and socialism in general, they decreed, were incompatible with their customs and religions. The party's policy of autonomy was denounced as a sham, "as useful as ears on a basket." In actuality, they had no rights. Moreover, critics expressed the attitude that minorities who had joined the party or become cadres were traitors to their fellow ethnics, "jackals serving the Han."

The party responded much as it had to the Han Chinese who had been overly frank during the Hundred Flowers campaign. Some efforts were actually made to deal with certain grievances that minorities critics had raised: For example, where there were complaints of arrogance on the part of Han cadres, or where it could be shown that the language of the minority had been suppressed, there were attempts made at redress. However, an antirightist campaign was carried out in minority areas, as it was in Han areas as well. The campaign's main target was "local nationalism," which was deemed to be equivalent to antisocialism. The chief victims were some of the traditional leaders who were, in the party's estimation, proving to be stumbling blocks on the road to the reforms that the party wanted to introduce in minority areas. A number of traditional leaders were in fact replaced by young minority activists that the party had trained. Nonetheless, the campaign against local nationalism was far from a thoroughgoing purge. The united front continued in both theory and practice.

The Great Leap Forward and Its Aftermath: 1959–1965

However, the outpouring of grievances during 1956 and 1957 did seem to disabuse the party leadership of its idea that a policy that tolerated minorities' special characteristics would lead to a withering away of those special characteristics. This reassessment fed into a general mood of impatience with the pace of China's progress in areas besides minorities work, and led to that massive social and economic upheaval, the Great Leap Forward. The Leap's goals of increasing production, simplifying administration, eliminating bureaucratism and red tape, and achieving pure communism seemed ill-served by the congeries of special arrangements the party had made in minority areas. The existence of a number of different levels of collectivization, the issues of the timing of the introduction of reforms, the policies of cooperation with the traditional upper strata, respect for special characteristics, and encouragement of local languages were now seen as standing squarely in the way of progress.

Hence, in 1958 and 1959, areas that had had widely different levels of socialist reforms were hurriedly organized into communes. Often, several different nationalities were combined in these communes, including some that had very different economic levels and cultures. The mere mention of "special characteristics" was dangerous: It was regarded as equivalent to opposing socialism. Likewise, the policy of tolerating and even encouraging minorities languages changed. It was suddenly discovered that there was a high tide of enthusiasm for studying the Chinese language.

Also, all kinds of customs the party had tolerated became regarded as "decadent." What had been promised, the media pointed out, was that customs that were not detrimental to production could be kept. Clearly, festival days were detrimental to production, since people did no work on those days. So also was the ritual killing of animals, which reduced the food supply. Traditional turbans were counterproductive, since they were a waste of cloth. Moreover, many turbans were very heavy and apt to give headaches to wearers who were engaged in hard physical labor. A cloth cap or straw sun hat was superior. Colorful sashes were also declared counterproductive. Like turbans, they wasted material. In that many were intricately embroidered, they also wasted time that could have been spent in producing more necessary items. In addition, wearing such sashes prevented one from bending over freely while working in the fields. Wearing a belt would better serve the same purpose.

Research projects into minorities' languages, history, and cultures were terminated. Castigated as "bourgeois scientific objectivism," they too were considered a waste of time and money that could better be devoted to increasing production levels. For example, a dictionary compilation project that had amassed fifty thousand words was ridiculed since a few hundred, all relating to production, were all that were really needed. In their zeal to raise production, officials also took land that had been promised to herdsmen for pasture land and reclassified it as crop land. The people thus affected were reported to be very pleased with the changes. Even the Hui, who are Muslims, were said to be enthusiastic about joining communal mess halls, despite the fact that dishes containing pork were served there.

The Great Leap Forward produced a fiasco in minority areas, just as it had in Han China. There was one crucial difference: Ethnic minorities, unlike Han, perceived the Leap as being imposed on them by *outsiders* in an attempt to destroy their culture and ways of life. The party's abrupt swing to blatantly assimilationist policies was clearly at variance with its previous pronouncements that reforms would not be carried out except according to the desires of the minority masses, and by them themselves. It also ran counter to the role the party had set itself as protector of minorities cultures.

Beginning in early 1959, official publications started to admit that the gap between the party's promises and its performance in minorities areas had caused it to "lose the trust of the masses," and that "production had suffered to a certain extent." Minorities' resentment and resistance took many forms, ranging from passive resistance and small-scale sabotage to open revolt. The latter occurred in Tibet and Xinjiang provinces and among the Hui and Yi. In the case of the revolts in Tibet and Xinjiang, large numbers of refugees crossed over the borders into India and the Soviet Union, respectively. This created two hostile emigré communities on two different borders, both of them vigorously denouncing China's minorities policy as forced assimilation.

India, whose own relations with the PRC were strained by a nasty border dispute, tried to persuade the refugees to take a low profile. The Soviet Union, on the other hand, encouraged them to publicize their experiences, even providing increased radio programming in native languages and setting up a separate newspaper for the refugees. Interestingly, the new paper was allowed to use Arabic script, although the USSR had forced its own members of the same minority group to use the Cyrillic alphabet.

Ironically, the Great Leap Forward's drive for unity through uniformity of language, dress, and lifestyle had the effect of creating a heightened sense of awareness on the part of minorities of the differences between them and the Han, and to an increasingly stubborn desire among many of them to retain their separate natures. China was in very bad shape in 1959 as a result of the Leap, and the government had to concentrate on policies that would make it possible for people simply to survive. As in Han areas, these concentrated on repairing the damage done by the Great Leap. Ideology was a luxury that had to be forgone, at least temporarily. Land that had been taken from herdsmen was returned: most of it had been found unsuitable for cultivation anyway, just as the locals had pointed out in 1958, when the campaign started. Unfortunately, there were far fewer animals to graze on it. Many herdsmen had killed their livestock rather than turn the animals over to communes.

In general, communes that were set up in minority areas were disbanded in fact though not in name, as was the case in Han areas. In a few areas, however, communes had created such problems that even the name was discarded. These included those of the Dai (Thai), Yi, Lisu, and Tibetans outside the Tibetan Autonomous Region (TAR). Tibetans who lived *within* the boundaries of the TAR had not had communes imposed on them. Rumors that the harsh policies imposed in other Tibetan areas during the Great Leap Forward were about to be applied to them were one, but not the only, important cause of the March 1959 revolt.

In the case of communes that had comprised several different ethnic minorities, the reorganization specified that members of the more prosperous group would be guaranteed the income level they had had before entering the commune. Considerable resentment had been engendered when minorities with better farming skills had been combined with those of lesser abilities and the total incomes averaged. Hui were no longer obliged to eat in mess halls where pork was served.

Other accommodations made in the wake of the Great Leap included the rehabilitation of some members of the traditional elite who had been purged in the antirightist campaign. The research projects that had been canceled at the beginning of the Great Leap Forward were revived. It was explained that the previous work had been "only a beginning" and that "careful research and investigation has *always* been the basic method of Marxism-Leninism." Respect for minorities' special characteristics was also rehabilitated.

This backtracking on the rigid ideological positions that had been prevalent during the Great Leap Forward was similar to what was being done in Han areas, but the *degree* of backtracking seemed to be greater in minorities areas. During 1959 and 1960, there was a return to the pluralistic policies on integration that had characterized the period from 1949 through 1957. There was a bit of an attempt to tighten up some of the more lenient manifestations of this during what is known as the Socialist Education Campaign from 1962 to 1965, but it does not seem to have had much of an effect on policies in minority areas, and seemingly a good deal less than those in Han China.

The Cultural Revolution: 1966–1971

Although the period of the Cultural Revolution is officially 1966–1976, this periodization does not apply well to minorities policy. The major changes in minorities policy began in 1966, as elsewhere in China, but were substantially modified in 1971. Hence the period 1966–1971 is a more accurate time frame for the Cultural Revolution as it concerns minorities. As seen in Chapter 5, the Great Proletarian Revolution was a massive effort to wrench China away from the ideological laxity that had been induced by the failure of the Great Leap Forward and to return it to the path of orthodoxy. For minority areas, this meant the return to radical assimilationist policies.

Radicals demanded, and in many cases got, the purge of many of the administrators who had favored gradualism and pluralism. One party leader, a Han, was accused of actively seeking to disband minorities' communes; another, also a Han, was purged for "surrendering to" the upper classes of the ethnic minorities. It was apparently a shock to discover that "seventeen years after liberation, minorities chiefs and slaveowners [were] still riding roughshod over the peasants." The party leader of Inner Mongolia, Ulanhu, a Mongol who had been a CCP member since his youth in the 1920s, was accused of having encouraged the study of the Mongolian language and cultural heritage. He had thus promoted "national splittism" and impeded the development of unity among all nationalities. It will be remembered that encouraging the study of minorities languages and cultures was party policy at the time that the accused individuals were allegedly committing their heinous crimes.

Some of the charges were plainly fanciful. For example, Ulanhu was also accused of plotting to make himself emperor of a separate reunified Mongolian state. Since the Mongolian People's Republic was firmly under the protection of the much more powerful Soviet Union, and had moreover evinced no interest whatsoever in reuniting with its fellow Mongols in China, it is difficult to see how even the most imaginative plotter could have intended to proceed.

The radical assimilationists, aided by Red Guards, used an earlier statement of Mao on the minorities problem—"The nationalities problem is in essence a class problem"— as their rallying cry and interpreted it in the most extreme possible fashion. Since nationalities problems *were* class problems, they reasoned, and since class differences were to be done away with, nationality differences were likewise to be done away with. Consonant with this logic, Red Guards attacked the "four olds" in minorities areas. They called for an end to the united front, which they regarded as "class capitulationism," and demanded that concessions to minorities' special characteristics be terminated. Class struggle, they argued, must be introduced into minority areas; autonomous areas themselves should be abolished.

The radical assimilationists had some successes during the Cultural Revolution. For example, communes were begun in the Tibetan Autonomous Region, where they had never existed before. Communes were reimposed in other minority areas where they had been disbanded. And many of those the radicals referred to as "entrenched powerholders" in minority areas were indeed removed from office. But the net result of the Cultural Revolution could not have been entirely to their liking. Quite a few of the old guard in minorities areas, including nobles, headmen, and Living Buddhas, were retained. Some of the minorities' special characteristics were retained, and the autonomous areas were never abolished. Members of minority groups continued to be identified as such in the press.

Part of this failure to achieve assimilationist goals was the fear that pushing minorities too hard would jeopardize border defense. Part of it was simply that the goal was essentially unrealizable. In areas where radical supervision was strong, ethnic feelings went underground. For example, *Xinhua* news agency proudly reported that in Lhasa, the capital of Tibet, pictures of Mao Zedong had replaced pictures of the Dalai Lama in local homes. What it did not, and could not truthfully, report was that Mao had replaced the Dalai Lama in the residents' esteem. As soon as the pressure was off, the pictures of Mao were off the walls and the Dalai Lama's likeness again beamed down over Lhasa's citizens. Where radical supervision was sporadic or non-existent—which was often the case, since a number of minorities lived in remote, not easily accessible areas—the changes that were ordered could be, and were, ignored.

However, from 1968 through mid-1971, minorities were a low-key presence in the PRC. On the fairly rare occasions they were mentioned at all by the mass media, they were treated as Han by any other name. For any problems of livelihood and production, studying the works of Mao was the recommended solution. A story printed by *People's Daily* in this period is indicative of the general attitude expected of minorities. Aunty Renchin, an elderly Mongol who had been a beggar prior to liberation, was sent to Beijing for medical treatment. While on the way to a hospital, someone pointed out Chairman Mao's residence to her. Her treatment completed, she refused to take a car back to the train station but "doggedly walked" nearly two miles to Mao's home. There she sat down, gazing at the gates. Chanting *in Chinese*, she repeatedly wished Chairman Mao a long, long life.[5]

Return to Pluralism: 1971–1977

This situation changed markedly after mid-1971. It is impossible to prove causality, but the return to pluralism closely coincided with the decline from power of Lin Biao, heretofore regarded as Mao Zedong's heir apparent, and key members of his Fourth Field Army. From May to November 1971, several regional broadcasting stations resumed the programming in minority languages that had ceased in 1966–1967. Also, the media began to encourage people, both minorities and Han, to study minorities languages.

Books in minorities' languages began to be printed again. Party propaganda boasted that they sold for *less* than the same book in Han Chinese, because the party subsidized the costs. The party also took credit for saving the Mongolian language from dying out. This was ironic in view of the Inner Mongolian party secretary having been purged during the Cultural Revolution for having, among other crimes, urged people to study Mongolian. He was soon rehabilitated and cleared of all charges including, presumably, his plans to make himself emperor. The media gave much attention to the facts that the government was making special consumer goods available to the minorities and that restrictions were eased on religious practices.

There were some problems with minorities during this period. For example, in 1975 a directive that forced people to work on Fridays was issued. This being the Muslim holy day, riots among Muslims were reported from Xinjiang to Yunnan. Frictions continued to exist between various minorities and Han, occasionally bursting into violence triggered by some essentially minor incident. But basically the several years after mid-1971 saw a return to pluralistic policies, and minority-Han relations began to improve.

Post-Mao Minorities Policy

Deng Xiaoping extended this policy of toleration, with some innovations which had profound consequences for ethnic minority areas. This was more an indirect result than a conscious design of the new policies. As seen in Chapter 7, his paramount goal of creating prosperity could best be achieved by investing capital where it had the highest multiplier effect. In general, this meant in coastal cities such as Shanghai and Guangzhou or major river ports like Wuhan. Certain areas such as Shenzhen and Zhuhai received tax breaks and other perquisites designed to draw in foreign capital. None of these were in minority areas, whose inhabitants were told that they would have to adjust to the market economy: subsidies were replaced with loans. Just as in Han rural areas, minorities received the right to sell their goods on the free market.

The policy of nationalities problems being class problems was officially repudiated, it being explained that Mao had been "misunderstood." Differences between minorities and Han were henceforth to be understood as a function of income inequalities between the two groups. As living standards equalized, tensions would disappear. Overt differences between minorities and Han, such as language, dress, and customs, should not be expected to disappear in the near future, if at all. This went beyond the Mao era's periods of willingness to temporarily accommodate minorities special characteristics and toward a pluralist model of long-term acceptance of these characteristics. To help reduce tensions between

Han and non-Han, minorities were exempted to various degrees from the one-child policy imposed on Han. Their children also enjoyed easier access to higher education.

Reform Produces Problems

Various problems arose. With investment capital, both domestic and from foreign businesspeople, flowing into selected enclaves, economic redistribution now made these already relatively prosperous areas still wealthier; minorities areas fell behind. While the new rural policies increased food supplies in minority areas, they also reestablished the class inequities the communist party said it had come to rectify. Those who were disadvantaged by the reforms felt that the party was breaking faith with the masses. A study of Tibetan herders indicated that the newly prosperous families were precisely those who had prospered under the precommunist system. Replacing subsidies with loans had disadvantageous results as well, since minorities often did not understand how the loans worked. There was a tendency to borrow too much, make poor investment choices, and then be unable to repay the loans.

The inflation that encouraged burgeoning production in coastal areas proved disproportionately hurtful to minority areas as well. Typically, they had been the suppliers of raw materials to the manufacturing areas of the coast. Finished products were then available for purchase at value-added prices. When these prices rose sharply, minorities' sense that they were being exploited by the Han—a feeling that had been present long before the communist party ever existed—was reinforced. At one point, the Xinjiang Uygur Autonomous Region actually banned the "import" from other provinces of no less than 48 kinds of products including soap, bicycles, and color television sets. There was famine in Tibet and unrest in Xinjiang. In Tibet, a party policy of forcing people to plant wheat rather than the barley that the local population favored had proved unsuited to the climate. Transport aircraft were sent to evacuate Han. In Xinjiang, Han cadres were quietly withdrawn from the grass roots, a fact not revealed until late May 1998, when the withdrawal was linked to the beginnings of subversive religious activities there. In Yunnan, there were disputes over land and water rights. Minorities' land and rubber trees were illegally appropriated when plantations were established.

Efforts were made to deal with these problems. Tibetans were again allowed to cultivate barley; state subsidies were increased. Tibet was also exempted from certain taxes. Border minorities in general were encouraged to develop their economies through trade with neighboring countries. Hence, Tibetans began to trade with Nepal and India; Yunnan minorities with Laos, Burma, and Thailand; Xinjiang minorities with the Soviet Union; and Inner Mongolians with the Mongolian People's Republic and the Soviet Union. Tourism to minority areas began to be encouraged. The government also announced that foreign investment in minorities areas would be welcomed. While realizing that the investment potential was not as great as that in coastal areas, there was a good possibility that foreigners might wish to invest for essentially noneconomic reasons. For example, wealthy Saudis or Malaysians might wish to aid their co-religionists in China. Hu Yaobang, on the eve of his appointment as First Party Secretary, made an inspection visit to Yunnan to try to soothe the problems there.

Well-meant as these efforts were, there were serious side effects. Borders became more porous. Calls for increased trade, tourism, and foreign investment in minorities areas coincided with an upsurge of fundamentalist sentiments in the Muslim world. Those who came to invest were interested in how their fellow Muslims were treated, and often asked to tour mosques and religious schools. Spies could pose as businesspeople or tourists. Given that few Han administrators in minority areas had learned the local languages, foreign visitors could often converse freely with minorities while their guides remained oblivious to what was being said. Subversive materials, weapons, and explosives could be smuggled in, and letters and tapes alleging or documenting atrocities smuggled out. Yunnan's border trade included an upsurge of traffic in the Golden Triangle's most famous export product: opium.

Dai minorities were impressed with the affluent life-styles of their fellow Thai who came as tourists to Yunnan. The cultural and economic lure of Bangkok was apparently strong enough that when Thailand's state airline suggested opening a direct route from Chiang Mai to Jinghong, the capital of the Xishuangbanna Dai Autonomous Prefecture, Beijing initially refused. Investors from the Republic of Korea (ROK) similarly impressed their fellow Koreans in the PRC. Until the authorities began to keep close watch on them, Chinese Korean "tourists" simply disappeared after checking into their Seoul hotel rooms, finding it quite easy to find jobs in the then-booming South Korean economy. Chinese Koreans tried to enter the ROK on undocumented boats as well. ROK police also discovered a thriving marriage-of-convenience market involving elderly ROK males and young Chinese Korean women.

There were also complaints that the policies devised to develop the economies of minority areas primarily benefited the Han residents thereof. This was an especially sore point in Tibet, where the aforementioned tax exemptions resulted in a flood of Han migrants into the TAR to take advantage of them. Most of the peddlers in the tourist areas of Lhasa were Han from Sichuan. Western guests at the Lhasa Holiday Inn who spoke Tibetan to waitresses wearing traditional Tibetan clothing discovered that the young women were likewise Han. To make matters worse, nonmigrant workers brought in under government auspices to work at jobs that included weaving traditional Tibetan carpets received higher wages than did the Tibetans who worked alongside them. The authorities argued that these skilled workers would not have wanted to relocate to Tibet's harsh climate had they not been enticed by higher wages, and that they were enhancing economic benefits for all. Tibetans, however, felt that they were being made into second-class citizens in their own country, and that any Han who were brought in were taking jobs away from Tibetans.

Construction workers building pseudo-Dai structures in Jinghong, presumably for the benefit of tourists, were likewise Han migrant workers. In northwest China, Uygurs and Kazakhs complained that Han received preference for better jobs in "their" oilfields and elsewhere. The central government itself admitted that Han migrants had caused ecological damage in Xinjiang through careless use of the land. Environmental damage from Han misuse of the land has been an ongoing complaint among the Mongols of Inner Mongolia, dating at least as far back as the Great Leap Forward. As concerns about the environment in general have grown, so have the complaints.

Whether the benefits of these new economic policies were going primarily to the minorities in minority areas or to the Han in minority areas, the income gap between minority regions and Han China continued to grow. The average industrial and agricultural output in ethnic minority areas had dropped to 47.9 percent of the national average by 1989;[6]

nine years and many policy initiatives later, official sources admitted that the gap continued to widen. Only the Guangxi Zhuang Autonomous Region has managed to perform at a level comparable to the rest of Han China. The Zhuang had accommodated well to Han culture long before 1949; Guangxi has also benefited from its geographic location bordering on booming Guangdong province. According to a 1997 report, China's seven worst-performing provinces included all four remaining autonomous areas—Tibet, Ningxia, Xinjiang and Inner Mongolia—plus three other provinces, Gansu, Guizhou, and Qinghai, with large minority populations.[7]Authorities in Tibet complained that, once having lifted the poorest of its poor out of poverty, it was difficult to keep them from slipping back. Some areas experienced slight declines in minority education rates.

In any case, and contrary to the assumptions of party policy, narrowing the income and educational gap between minorities and Han will not necessarily end internationality tensions. People who are less focused on sheer survival may have more leisure to indulge their antigovernment feelings, and more money to finance the purchase of weapons. Better educational levels may stimulate interest in one's indigenous culture and enhance one's ability to learn more about it. A number of the Inner Mongolian dissidents who were arrested on splittist charges were graduates of the party's own institutes, where they had become interested in going beyond the officially sanctioned versions of Mongolian culture. The existence of tensions in a number of minority areas notwithstanding, it is only from Xinjiang and Tibet and, to a much lesser extent, Inner Mongolia, that serious disturbances have been reported in recent years.

External Factors

As for the effect of tourism, while some members of minorities profited from the presence of the outsiders and welcomed them, others felt that the central government was exploiting them on behalf of its desire for more foreign exchange. There were also complaints that the government was perverting and trivializing their culture. Indeed, many of the handicrafts marketed as minority-made are not authentic in style and not made by minorities. So-called "minority villages," in which foreign visitors are shown how several different minority groups live, have struck outsiders as more like theme parks or human zoos than authentic representations of minority life.

Within the Western world, the 1980s and 1990s also saw increased concern with human rights. Tibet in particular captured the imagination of large numbers of Westerners. Buddhism became the fastest-growing religion in the West, and adherents to its Tibetan variant spanned a range that included eminent scholars and prominent entertainers. The Beijing government pointed out that a Dutch woman who was wounded by Chinese police in their confrontation with Tibetan demonstrators was both active in human-rights organizations and had visited Tibet an unusually large number of times; if true, it would bolster the government's argument that she had come with subversive intent. Hollywood produced several films sympathetic to the Tibetan cause, and a U.S. congressman slipped into Tibet disguised as a tourist, later charging that the local culture was being systematically destroyed.

Turkish journalists posing as travel agents visited Xinjiang, photographed the ruins of mosques and Islamic schools, and published their findings in popular magazines. Some tourists were simply tourists, but nonetheless sympathetic to human-rights concerns and open to requests that they send in pictures of the Dalai Lama—possession of which is intermittently banned by the Chinese government—and take out documents detailing abuses.

These difficulties were compounded by the disintegration of the Soviet Union and its client states. States governed by ethnic groups with kin in China appeared on the PRC's borders. The Mongolian People's Republic, which had discouraged any "greater Mongolia" sentiments was replaced by a noncommunist republic that found it more difficult to repress such feelings. In addition, there was a revival of interest in Tibetan Buddhism, which had been the religion of most Mongols before communism. This was accompanied by an upsurge of interest in studying the Tibetan language. Despite Chinese protests, the Dalai Lama was invited to Mongolia and warmly received.

Repression Increases

The years 1988 through 1990, while these events were unfolding externally, were particularly difficult for Beijing's relations with its most restive minorities. In June 1988, the Dalai Lama addressed the European Parliament in Strasbourg. There he offered Beijing a compromise under which the PRC would have responsibility for Tibet's foreign policy while the TAR would have a popularly elected legislature and its own legal system. Beijing rejected the proposal, lashing out at the European community for hosting the Dalai Lama and at the Dalai Lama for "internationalizing" a domestic issue.

At this point, the central government appears to have decided to add the "stick" of increased repression to the "carrot" of its post-1979 policy of economic development as a solution to its minority problem. Police and military forces in the TAR were augmented with personnel sent in from outside the region. Monasteries were searched, and persons believed to be sympathetic to the Dalai Lama were arrested. Antigovernment demonstrations took place in December. In January, the normally placatory Panchen Lama said publicly that, although there had been progress in Tibet since the communists arrived, it came at too high a price. Four days later, it was reported that the heretofore healthy 51-year-old had died of a heart attack. Many assumed he had been killed for speaking out, and there were more protests. Martial law was declared in Lhasa in the spring, and continued for more than a year. During this time, the Dalai Lama was awarded the Nobel Peace Prize.

Also in the spring of 1989, Uygurs and Kazakhs attacked communist party headquarters in Urumqi with rocks and steel bars. The publication in Shanghai of a book containing defamatory statements about Islam was the major cause of the protest, though other, ongoing grievances were expressed as well. At the same time, Chinese Muslim (Hui) were causing problems in neighboring Gansu and Qinghai provinces, over other Islam-related issues. Their activities included attacks on rail lines, causing several suspensions in service. A government investigation produced evidence of collusion among Muslim groups in different provinces, as well as foreign support for their activities. A number of Han settlers who moved into Xinjiang's border with the former Soviet Union to provide a buffer against movements of minorities back and forth provided a further irritant in that area. Major protests occurred in Inner Mongolia as well; these seem to have been influenced by the growth of anticommunist sentiment in neighboring Mongolia.

After the Tiananmen disturbances and the fall of the Soviet Union, there were sharp crackdowns in all these areas. Inner Mongolia's leadership group was reorganized. Teams investigated monasteries in Tibetan areas and mosques and religious schools in Islamic enclaves. There were many arrests, some for matters that might have been considered relatively trivial a few years before. For example, members of two organizations to promote research into Mongolian culture, both of whom had tried to register themselves legally with the government, were accused of subversive and splittist intentions. In Tibet, people protesting economic problems, which would previously have been tolerated because the issues were not political, were arrested. A "strike hard" campaign against crime that began in the mid-1990s was used in minority areas to target separatism. Human rights advocates charged that the government was equating any expression of disagreement with government policies, no matter how innocuous, with separatism, and using the campaign to make arrests accordingly. Repression in Xinjiang became still more severe after the September 11, 2001 attacks on the World Trade Center and Pentagon. According to PRC sources, more than a thousand Taliban-trained Uygurs have infiltrated Muslim communities in China where they are disseminating fundamentalism and terrorist propaganda. Outside observers count between four and thirteen Uygurs trained by the Taliban, and believe that at least some of these come from the Uygur exile community in Pakistan that left Xinjiang in the 1930s.[8]

Official propaganda stresses that the problems are caused by a small handful of malcontents who are deceiving others. Most people are happy, and appreciate the many benefits party and government have brought to their previously backward areas. Han and minorities are interdependent: Each must help the other for the good of the country as a whole. Although the central government does extract resources from minority areas, it pays a fair price for these materials. Moreover, it also subsidizes the economies of many minority areas to a significant degree.

Certain concessions have been made to minorities within the context of these efforts at repressing expressions of discontent. For example, urban renewal plans for Beijing originally entailed the razing of an area inhabited by migrants from Xinjiang that was known, appropriately, as Xinjiang Village. The government then announced that it had decided to spare the village to avoid offending (or perhaps inciting to riot) its residents.[9] For the same reason, the central government resisted for several years ratifying an agreement between the Xinjiang and Guangdong provincial governments that would have allowed Guangdong to prosecute Xinjiang natives who ran a highly profitable smuggling operation near Baiyun airport.[10] And the revised criminal law introduced at the March 1997 National People's Congress stated that the author of any publication insulting or discriminating against ethnic minorities could receive a jail term of up to three years. The same law, however, provided for even harsher sentences of up to ten years for persons who "take advantage of national or religious problems to instigate the splitting of the state or undermine the unity of the state." The reprieve of Xinjiang Village proved temporary as well. It was demolished in 2001, on grounds that the layout of the area impeded traffic and created other unspecified nuisances. Many of the village's inhabitants moved to a different area of Beijing, which was then ordered demolished a year later.[11] However valid the government's motives, the people who lived there felt they were being targeted because of their ethnicity.

There are differences of opinion between party and government on the one hand and certain members of minorities on the other about what constitutes fostering the development of minority languages, cultures, and traditions—which party and government publicly favor—and what constitutes undermining the unity of the state and engaging in splittist activities. Most parties to these disputes understand that languages and cultures are not frozen in time but rather adapt to changing circumstances and changing perceptions of what is appropriate. The point at issue is that the central leadership reserves for itself the right to determine these changes. In actual practice, cultural development carried on by party and government *on behalf of* minorities seems to be acceptable, whereas cultural development carried out by minorities *on their own behalf* is not. Ethnic minority culture under the direct control of party and government is celebrated; all other manifestations thereof are regarded with utmost suspicion.

The issue of control can also be seen clearly in party/government attitudes toward local efforts to deal with alcoholism, heroin, and the HIV/AIDS problem that accompanies drug use. In 1997, Uygur students in Ili, one of Xinjiang's more secular areas, organized a campaign to get people to limit their consumption of liquor, and stores to limit sales to those with drinking problems. The government, acting on the assumption that fundamentalist Islam, which prohibits drinking alcohol, was behind the campaign, clamped down on the organizers. An estimated 5,000 students demonstrated against this, with perhaps 300 Uygurs killed when police moved against the demonstrators. In the previous year, Rebiya Kadeer, a successful Uygur businesswoman was arrested for subversive activities. Still in prison as of 2003, she had campaigned for women's rights and AIDS education and against heroin use.

In contrast to the marked shifts between accommodationist and assimilationist minority policies that characterized the early years of the PRC, a model has evolved that is pluralist in form but assimilationist in function. For example, as plans for a conference on Tibetan literature were being finalized in Beijing and the party was taking credit for rescuing lamaist ritual dances from extinction, one of the last neighborhoods of traditional Tibetan homes in central Lhasa was being destroyed. Several visitors remarked that only the Potala Palace now distinguished the city from one that might be seen anywhere in Han China. In Inner Mongolia, the central government proudly reported that it was refurbishing the mausoleum of Chinggis Khan[12] just weeks after rejecting the appeal of sentences meted out to Mongols who were active in a cultural organization.

The protection of language had limits as well. In an April 1998 speech, Xinjiang's party head, a Han, said that "we say the constitution provides that all nationalities have the freedom to use and develop their spoken and written languages, but this in no way means advocating the use of their own spoken and written languages." He went on to say that since it was impossible to promptly translate many things into minority languages, "it is a very urgent task for cadres of minority nationalities to learn and have a good command of the Chinese language." At the same time, Xinjiang University began phasing out Uygur-language instruction.[13] In 2000, the Han party secretary of Sichuan complained about having to teach minorities in their own languages saying, "the whole world is learning English. Why bother so much?"[14]

To be sure, cultural organizations may have agendas that are more subversive than they seem, choosing to cloak what the Chinese government would call splittist intentions with language classes or dancing lessons. The government charges that Tibetan monasteries have been used to store weapons, Islamic schools for preaching fundamentalist messages, and the Uygur festival *maixilaifu* as a meeting place for subversives. By 1996, the government had declared that religion would have to adapt itself to socialism rather than vice versa. It underscored this point by rejecting a candidate for the reincarnation of the Panchen Lama who had been approved by the Dalai Lama. The child simply disappeared and was replaced by a candidate approved by Beijing. The government also said explicitly that areas that were under control of the state and where religion must not intrude included education, family planning, burial arrangements, and the court system.

The central leadership sought as well to enlist the cooperation of border states in curbing dissident activities. This was one aim of the conference with Soviet successor states hosted by President Jiang Zemin in April 1996. More recently, Kyrgyz President Askar Akayev pledged his support against national separatism and religious extremists during a visit to Beijing, as have the heads of Kazakhstan and Tajikistan. Still, there is considerable support within those republics for the cause of Muslims in China, and no leader who depends on the support of his constituents to stay in power can afford to ignore this. The Nepalese government appears to be complying with Chinese wishes regarding dissidents fleeing Tibet, but its border guards are frequently successfully evaded or successfully bribed.

As government repression increases, dissident forces find ways around it. For example, one government effort involved sending work teams into rural areas where they were instructed to set up "joint-defense" teams to ensure public security. It was announced that the teams would apprehend not only dissidents but also those who were found to be harboring a suspect. Both would be punished. Dissidents struck back by assassinating not only those who joined the teams but also their family members. Even religious leaders who appeared to tolerate government supervision and their family members were targets of assassination.

Government propaganda made much of relatives who vowed to join the teams to avenge the memory of their loved ones, but one doubts that there were large numbers of such volunteers. Whether under al-Qaeda tutelage or not, Xinjiang dissidents moved beyond their province to set off car and bus bombs in Beijing and elsewhere. During times of official celebration or solemnity, including the reversion of Hong Kong in July 1997, the Fifteenth Party Congress in fall 1997 and the Ninth National People's Congress in March 1998, Beijing police were alerted to the possibility of violence by minority dissidents. Taxi drivers reported being warned against picking up suspicious-looking passengers, which many interpreted as anyone wearing minority dress or looking non-Han.

Party and government expressed concerns that there was simply indifference to its wishes at lower levels. There were repeated complaints that primary organizations showed "weak political sensitivity" and had "not exerted themselves in the struggle against national separatism and illegal religious activities." Worse, some officials actively sided with the dissidents. Contrary to the policy that party members should be atheists, they openly practiced their religious beliefs. Tibetan officials maintained lavish shrines in their homes and kept pictures of the Dalai Lama in plain view. A number of cadres whose children attended schools in India run by the Dalai Lama refused a party directive to bring them back.

Officials in Muslim areas proved similarly recalcitrant. In mid-1996, the Xinjiang regional party committee called for "sternly dealing with party members and cadres, especially leading cadres, who continue to be devout religious believers despite repeated education; instill separatist ideas and religious doctrines into young people's minds; publish distorted history; [issue] books or magazines advocating separatism and illegal religious ideas; or make audio or video products propagating such ideas."

These are startling statements, tantamount to admitting that the central government has lost a good deal of control over local levels in these areas. This being the case, it might seem logical to try to blunt the thrust of dissidents as well as accede gracefully to what seems to be happening anyway, by granting true autonomy to so-called autonomous areas. The Dalai Lama has consistently maintained that this would be sufficient for him to return. Some Inner Mongolia dissidents have indicated that this would be acceptable as well.

Genuine Autonomy as a Possible Solution

A law on regional autonomy was in fact devised as part of Deng Xiaoping's reforms. When discussions began on it in 1979, state vice-president Ulanhu, a Mongol leader who had been a party stalwart since the 1920s complained openly that "some communist party members hardly sound like Marxists on the question of minority nationalities."[15] The law was duly passed in 1984. Among its salient points was the stipulation that the administrative head of an autonomous region should be a citizen of the nationality or nationalities exercising regional autonomy in the area. The law also gave autonomous areas the power to administer local finances.[16] However, it said nothing about appointing ethnic minorities to leadership positions in the party hierarchy, which is far more crucial. And since the economies of many minority areas depend on state subsidies, which come under the purview of the State Council, there are limits on how financially autonomous they can be.

This analysis assumes that the autonomy law would be enforced. Three years later, Ulanhu was complaining of Han chauvinism blocking its implementation, and criticized higher levels for being unwilling to actually grant autonomy. He took note of minority fears that their areas could be overrun by Han migrants, whom they had no power to keep out.[17] In 1987, a prominent Tibetan with an impeccable record of cooperating with the party termed the lack of implementation of the autonomy law or its partial implementation "quite serious" and accused "some leading cadres" of never even having read it.[18]

Precisely a decade after, Ulanhu's son Buhe, who had essentially inherited his father's status, called for the autonomy law not only to be implemented, but extended as well. Obviously choosing his words carefully and expressing himself less bluntly than Ulanhu, Buhe argued that the autonomy law needed to be revised "in line with the market economy," urged the drafting of supplementary legislation, and said that only by rigorously enforcing the rights of autonomy could the unity of the ancestral land be realized. This was widely deconstructed to mean that only a more liberal and better-enforced autonomy law could hope to blunt separatist demands.[19]

Buhe's initiative occurred in the context of reports in the Hong Kong press that a long-standing struggle between the central authorities and the regions had erupted at the March 1997 meeting of the National People's Congress. In internal sessions with central leaders, representatives from ethnic minority areas had purportedly made proposals that could be characterized as "you give us autonomy and we guarantee you stability." Among their demands was that members of ethnic minorities be appointed heads of the communist party committees in the areas in which they allegedly exercise autonomy. Others included giving local leaders a greater say on contentious issues such as the numbers of Han

Chinese in their areas; the share of profits from the exploitation of the products of their bailiwicks; and the level and disposition of transfer payments and development funds from Beijing.[20] Regional leaders argued that, since the central government was willing to allow Hong Kong, whose population is Han Chinese, a significant degree of autonomy, they should have at least comparable powers. In fact, just the opposite had occurred. Long-standing plans to write more explicit guidelines on the practice of autonomy into law had been postponed as unrest increased in some minority areas.

There has been no indication that the central government is willing to accede to these demands, and it is not difficult to understand why. Even the modest degree of autonomy that minority areas have enjoyed in the years since Mao Zedong's demise has enabled a significant erosion of Beijing's control over those areas. The government fears that granting more autonomy would generate still more demands. What may appear to be reasonable calls for a devolution of decision-making may in fact prove the slippery slope toward gradual erosion of all government control and de facto independence. The risks of liberalization would seem to be greater than the risks of continued repression.

It has been argued that allowing Tibet, with its meager resources, forbidding climate, and hostile population to go its own way except for its foreign relations—that is, to reach an accommodation the Dalai Lama has already proposed—would end a huge financial drain out of the central government treasury as well as eliminate a festering human rights problem. From Beijing's point of view, however, this may appear foolish. Tibet has undoubted strategic value, which must seem all the more important in view of deteriorating relations with India. Western sympathy for Tibet aside, there have been few actual adverse consequences for Beijing as a result of its conduct there. Sustained attention from the international community is unlikely: there will be other causes to attract its attention. The Dalai Lama is in his sixties; when he dies, Beijing will install a successor, as it has with the Panchen Lama, and take great care to imbue him with its values.

Moreover, giving Tibet real autonomy would surely stimulate demands for comparable treatment from other areas. Xinjiang has important natural resources in addition to its strategic location, and its dissidents have never indicated that they would be willing to accept anything short of complete independence. Demands for the creation of an East Turkestan Republic (ETR) hark back to ETRs which had brief existences under the Qing dynasty and the Chinese Republic; they are unlikely to disappear with the current generation of dissidents. Inner Mongolian dissidents have said explicitly that they would be open to the idea of autonomy for the moment, but not necessarily that they would be satisfied with it in the long term.[21]

Beijing would also need to confront the problem of what to do with the Han in minority areas should they gain true autonomy. This would not be a great problem in the Tibet Autonomous Region. However, the TAR is surrounded by autonomous areas belonging to other provinces, but with substantial Tibetan populations. Tibetan dissidents claim these areas as well, though numerous Han now live there. In Xinjiang, Han comprise nearly half the population; in Inner Mongolia, they are the majority by perhaps six or seven to one. The trend has been to move in more Han to preserve stability and aid in economic development. Minority areas were also designated as receiving areas for at least some of the large numbers of people who have had to be relocated due to the Three Gorges dam project.

Conclusions

At present, it does not seem likely that the central government intends to deviate from its current policy of encouraging economic development and suppressing expressions of dissent in ethnic minority areas. It would be unwise to extrapolate an increase of ethnic tensions into the indefinite future. Like many other phenomena, they may be cyclical. But, given the difficulties that the Chinese economy faces over the next several years, instability in minority areas is likely to worsen, at least in the short term. Recent government work reports from Xinjiang and Inner Mongolia are not optimistic, with the word "grim" appearing more than once. Economic growth reports from Tibet are much better; the region has outperformed the country as a whole in recent years. But these are the results of massive infusions of capital from outside, and there is consensus that few Tibetans have benefited from the growth.

Party and government continue to maintain that ethnic tensions are an unfortunate legacy of the past that will disappear as prosperity comes to minority areas. In line with this, in October 2000, a campaign to develop the west, where most minorities live, was launched (see Chapter 7). Though presented as a humanitarian effort designed to raise living standards there, the campaign involved massive infrastructure and product extraction projects that local people fear will bring more Han in while moving their natural resources out. A cartoon in a Tibetan exile publication captured this attitude perfectly, depicting one of these infrastructure projects, the Golmud to Lhasa railway, as a dragon breathing fire toward the Potala Palace. Out of its mouth scrambled Chinese soldiers and settlers. Moreover, there have been severe environmental costs to past development projects. New and larger scale projects are liable to have still worse effects. Both Tibetans and Mongols have complained of worsening sandstorms from severe erosion. Most recently, a smelter in Qinghai is despoiling nomads' traditional pastures. These not only affect their grazing lands, but impact Han areas, and even foreign countries, as well. The spring 2002 sandstorm that inundated Beijing (see Chapter 11) also left deposits in South Korea, Taiwan, and Japan.

A revised national autonomy law introduced in 2001 in order to bring it into line with the campaign to develop the west was officially described as providing higher levels of support for minority regions in terms of policy, infrastructure, and finance. Critics, noting that the revisions enhanced the central government's involvement in all these areas, charged that the development program is based on the wider needs of the Chinese market rather than local needs or interests. They questioned whether development that is against the wishes of the local population should be considered development[22] To be fair to the central government, it is in a difficult position: Leaving the areas alone risks a widening of living standards with Han China; bringing in development opens it to charges of exploitation and the destruction of local cultures. Nonetheless, good or bad, many of the projects seem to have been carried out with unnecessary insensitivity to local feelings.

Despite the genuine efforts made to accommodate ethnic minorities within the framework of the PRC, the fundamental nature of the nationalities problem is little changed: Minorities who were content to be part of the Chinese empire have not been disruptive under the PRC. Those who were unhappy continue to be so. Neither pluralist nor assimilationist policies have succeeded in solving the nationalities problem. Dissident minorities do not have the strength to force the government to accept their demands for separatism or true autonomy. They will in all likelihood continue to press their demands through remonstrations and demonstrations. But in the absence of some fundamental change in the system as a whole, which would include pressure from segments of the Han majority such as peasants, workers, and intellectuals, it seems unlikely that minority unrest can win anything more than token concessions from the central government.

Notes

1. Called Miao in China, they are referred to as Meo elsewhere in Asia but prefer Hmong.

2. Quoted in Herold Wiens, *China's March to the Tropics* (Hamden, Conn.: Shoestring Press, 1954), p. 219.

3. See June Teufel Dreyer, *China's Forty Millions: Minority Nationalities and National Integration in the People's Republic of China* (Cambridge, Mass.: Harvard University Press, 1976), Chap.2.

4. One part of a Chinese ideograph, called the *radical*, frequently gives a clue to the class of words to which the ideograph belongs. For example, the heart radical will frequently be the radical in words denoting feelings, the water radical is part of the character for "flow," "river," and "flood," and so forth. Using the dog radical in characters for minority groups implied that they were a lower order of humanity.

5. *Renmin Ribao*, February 8, 1970, p.3.

6. (no author), "Economic Gap Widens in Minority Areas," *Xinhua*, August 25, 1989, in *FBIS–CHI*, August 28, 1989, p. 55.

7. Daniel Kwan, "East Still Outshines West for Industry," *South China Morning Post*, April 7, 1997, via the Internet.

8. Statement of Justin Rudelson to "Ethnic Minorities in China: Tibetans and Uighurs," Roundtable Before the Congressional-Executive Commission on China," June 10, 2002, pp. 23; 28–29. www.uscc.gov

9. This proved a temporary reprieve. In early 1999, it was revealed that the neighborhood had been razed anyway.

10. Daniel Kwan, "Guangdong, Xinjiang Agree to Combat Smuggling," *South China Morning Post* (Hong Kong), April 10, 1991, p.10. Guangdong lobbied Beijing for four years over this agreement; not until the central

government became alarmed at the rising drug trade in the area, Sanyuanli, did it finally agree.

11. Michael Jen-siu, "Beijing's Xinjiang Village Faces Demolition," *South China Morning Post*, November 26, 2002.

12. (no author), "$2.8 Million Facelift for Genghis Khan Tomb," *South China Morning Post,* April 8, 1997. No one actually knows where Chinggis Khan is buried; there is also a tomb to him in Mongolia. The Chinese structure was originally built in 1955. Its refurbishment was part of the preparations for the Inner Mongolia Autonomous Region's fiftieth anniversary. It was hoped that the celebrations would attract many tourists. Improvements included the construction of a statue of Chinggis on horseback, a sacrificial altar, a house for sacrifices, and landscaping.

13. (no author), "University Told to Stop Teaching in Uygur," *Agence France Presse*, May 30, 2002.

14. Josephine Ma, "Tibetans 'Wasting Money' on Donations to Monasteries," *South China Morning Post*, March 14, 2000.

15. Ulanhu, "Address to the Standing Committee of the Politburo," *Xinhua,* June 19, 1979.

16. See (no author), "Explanation of Law on Regional Autonomy for the PRC's Minority Nationalities," Beijing, State Council Bulletin No. 13, June 30, 1984, pp. 430–437, in *Joint Publications Research Service: China: Politics and Sociology,* 84–92, 331, December 1984, pp. 1–9.

17. (no author), "Ulanhu Calls for Cadres and the Masses to Study and to Implement the Law on Regional Autonomy for Minority Nationalities," *Renmin ribao,* September 30, 1987, p.1, in *FBIS–CHI,* October 7, 1987, p. 13. Underscoring Ulanhu's annoyance with this matter, the article had been delivered as a television address the evening before.

18. (no author), "Ngapoi Ngawang Jigme Interviewed," *Xinhua,* November 6, 1989, in *FBIS–CHI,* November 8, 1989, pp. 21–22.

19. See, for example, Buhe, "Legal Construction for Nationalities Essential to Rule of Law," *Qiushi,* no. 8, April 16, 1997, pp. 14–18, in *FBIS–CHI,* June 17, 1997; Zhang Minhua and Yin Hongdong, "Upholding and Improving the System of Regional Autonomy and Developing Nationality Solidarity: Interview with Buhe, Vice-Chair of the National People's Congress Standing Committee," *Xinhua,* April 21, 1997, in *FBIS–CHI,* April 23, 1997; for commentary on Buhe's arguments, see Agatha Ngai, "Appeal to Revise Law on Regional Autonomy," *South China Morning Post,* April 3, 1997, and Vivien Pik-kwan Chan, "Legal Push on Ethnic Policy to Improve Unity," *South China Morning Post,* April 8, 1997, via the Internet.

20. Willy Wo-lap Lam, "Warlords Make Their Play," *South China Morning Post,* March 19, 1997, via the Internet.

21. In the words of a 27-year-old China-born Mongol who heads a dissident organization based in Ulan Bataar, "the *first* thing we need to get is the freedom to express our grievances. . . at the *very least,* we need real autonomy. . . " (emphasis added). Quoted by Nicholas Kristof, "Restlessness Reaches Mongols in China" *New York Times,* July 7, 1992, p. A4.

22. Josh Schrei, "The Dark Side of China's Western Development Plan," *China Brief,* March 28, 2002, pp. 6–9.

Suggestions for Further Reading

Ethnic Minorities in China: Tibetans and Uighurs. Roundtable Before the Congressional-Executive Commission on China, June 10, 2002. www.cecc.gov

June Teufel Dreyer, "Assimilation and Accommodation in China," in Michael E. Brown and Sumit Ganguly, eds., *Government Policies and Ethnic Relations in Asia and the Pacific* (Cambridge, Mass.: The MIT Press, 1997).

———, "The Potential for Instability in Minority Areas," in David Shambaugh, ed., *Is China Unstable?:* *Assessing the Factors* (Washington, D.C.: Sigur Center for Asian Studies, 1998), pp. 123–141.

Dru Gladney, *Muslim Chinese: Ethnic Nationalism in the People's Republic* (Cambridge, Mass.: Harvard University Press, 1991).

Melvyn Goldstein, *The Snow Lion and the Dragon: China, Tibet, and the Dalai Lama* (Berkeley: University of California Press, 1997).

Colin Mackerras, *China's Minority Cultures* (New York: Longman, 1995).

CHAPTER

14 Foreign Policy

This chapter examines the determinants of foreign policymaking in China, its goals and mechanisms of formulation, and the different policies that have been chosen in pursuit of these goals.

Determinants

The factors that interact to influence the formulation of China's foreign policy are many and complex. Among the major determinants of the conceptual framework of the Chinese leadership are tradition, ideology, and perception of China's capabilities.

Tradition

As mentioned in Chapter 2, the traditional Chinese worldview saw China as the Middle Kingdom—the center of the world and the hub of civilization. The concept of the nation–state system, with sovereign states interacting as theoretical equals, was unknown. Imperial China considered other countries its cultural inferiors, in recognition of which they were expected to appear in the Chinese capital, make obeisance to the emperor, and present tribute. This consisted of costly gifts of local products—for example, lacquerware, incense, or exotic animals native to their area. In return, they received confirmation of their leadership over their own people as well as expensive gifts of Chinese workmanship. Reflecting its view of all other states as inferior, imperial China did not have a foreign ministry, but dealt with non-Chinese groups through its Board of Rites or Court of Colonial Affairs. The Chinese believed that their culture was superior in all respects: morally, materially, and aesthetically, and that it had universal validity.[1]

There have been certain resonances of these views in post-1949 China. Particularly during the 1960s, the reverence accorded to Mao Zedong reminded observers of that paid to the emperor. Mao's claim of a world communist movement based in Beijing with himself and his close associates as arbiters of what constituted true Marxism and who had committed the heresy of revisionism, is another case in point. So were Mao's disciples' claim that he had raised Marxist-Leninist thought to a higher level of validity, and their contention of its suitability for the rest of the third world. Richard Nixon's February 1972 visit to Beijing, during which Mao received the U.S. president in a formal state audience and presented him with a pair of panda bears, struck some Western observers as uncomfortably reminiscent of the tribute system, with Nixon unwittingly performing a symbolic kowtow.

However, the differences from tradition are at least as important as the parallels. Even at the height of the PRC's devotion to orthodox communism, the most fanatic pro-Maoist would have had to acknowledge that the universal belief system that their great leader stood at the apex of had its origins outside China: Neither Marx nor Lenin was a Chinese. The PRC's efforts to establish diplomatic recognition with other countries of the world on a reciprocal basis, and to participate in the United Nations and other world organizations, bespeak an acceptance of the multistate system. A persistent theme of Chinese foreign policy has been to win back the territories lost during the country's time of internal disintegration and humiliation by other powers. Rather than re-creating the previous universal order of the Middle Kingdom, it would seem that the traditionalist element of the PRC's foreign policy has aimed at placing the country in a position of international respect *within* a multistate order, thereby reversing the previous century's experience when it occupied a position of inferiority therein.[2]

China has, moveover, become a zealous defender of the concept of sovereign rights, the latter being an important underpinning of the multistate system. Ironically, this happened at a time when many of the originators of that system had begun to move away from strong views on state sovereignty.[3] In the mid-1980s, the PRC appeared to be softening its view of absolute sovereignty, as exemplified in its acceptance of limitations on its sovereignty over Hong Kong. While in general abiding by its agreement on Hong Kong, China moved back toward a position of absolute sovereignty after the Tiananmen demonstrations, the disintegration of the Soviet Union, and the Gulf War of 1991. The Chinese saw U.S. actions against Iraq as a big power bullying a small one. America's forcing Iraq to disavow its conquest of neighboring Kuwait had obvious parallels to the PRC's claims over Taiwan: This was not a precedent with which Chinese authorities were comfortable. They were still more uncomfortable with U.S. efforts to force the Yugoslav government to end its policy of ethnic cleansing in Kosovo in 1999: The United States bypassed the United Nations, working through NATO instead. Moreover, Kosovo, unlike Kuwait, was not even a sovereign state. Chinese analysts worried that America could use the argument it employed in the Yugoslav case—that human rights concerns took precedence over sovereign rights—to intervene if the PRC attempted to take over Taiwan. Beijing considers the Taiwan issue to be a domestic dispute rather than one between two sovereign states. Analysts worried that the United States might try to use the human rights issue to intervene in the restive autonomous regions of Tibet and Xinjiang as well. The authorities' fears were exacerbated when, unable to obtain UN Security Council authorization, American and British forces invaded Iraq in 2003 to bring about a change in government there.

A law passed by the National People's Congress in early 1992 unilaterally declared sovereignty over a number of territories that were claimed by the PRC as well as several neighboring states, and declared that the PLA would enforce these claims. China's media also became more strident in rejecting foreign criticism of its human-rights policy, arguing that it is an unjustifiable interference in the internal affairs of a sovereign state.

Both the soft and hard lines on sovereignty may be viewed as situational: The PRC's acceptance of limits on sovereignty was strongly conditioned by its desire to enter the U.S. capital market[4] and to make the prospect of unification with the mainland more attractive to Taiwan. In the early 1990s, the PRC's more immediate concern was to assert itself against what is perceived as foreign bullying. Moreover, despite rejecting other countries' human-rights policies, Beijing frequently rails out against those of other countries. Until relations with South Africa and Israel improved in the 1990s, the treatment of blacks in the former and of Palestinians in the latter were favorite targets.

Ideology

The analysis of international politics found in the works of Marx and Lenin forms one facet of the prism through which the Chinese leadership has interpreted world events. While there are differences between Marx and Lenin, and even differences in the writings of each that reflect changes in their thinking over the years, the worldview of what is generally referred to as Marxism-Leninism may be summarized as follows.

Imperialism is the highest, and last, stage of capitalism. Its successor, socialism, will be ushered in by an apocalyptic war among capitalist countries. The workers of the world will seize control of the means of production and arrange for an equitable distribution of the goods produced. Since previous wars were basically fought over the distribution of resources, putting resources in the hands of the workers will end national antagonisms and wars; the nation-state as we know it will disappear. Meanwhile, however, in order to facilitate the demise of imperialism and capitalism, socialist parties may support nationalist movements that are antiimperialist or serve to weaken imperialist and colonialist power.

By the time the Chinese communist government came to power, hopes that the advent of socialism in one country would set off a chain reaction in other countries had diminished. Although the rhetoric of "permanent revolution" remained, the demonstration effect had not occurred. The Soviet Union, the only country in which a socialist revolution had succeeded, found that its efforts to promote revolution elsewhere provoked hostile reactions against it which jeopardized the security of the state. This led to a realization that, in order to survive, a socialist state would have to choose carefully which nationalist movements to support and which to avoid. The concept of "socialism in one country first" justified a policy that allowed the national interests of the state to take precedence over the demands of proletarian internationalism.

A preoccupation with building China's own socialist institutions did not prevent its leaders from being concerned, from time to time, with internationalizing the doctrine. Mao's judgment, in 1957, that the East wind was prevailing over the West wind, and his advice to the Soviet Union to take advantage of this favorable situation, is one example. A second is the PRC's efforts, during the 1960s, to export the Chinese model of socialism. As memories of its own revolution receded and the PRC interacted more frequently with the international community, Marxism-Leninism lost salience to the motivations of pragmatic power politics. Ideological rhetoric notwithstanding, the latter had never been absent from Beijing's calculations. Marxist-Leninist thought categories remain. For example, the United States is frequently denounced as a "hegemonic power bent on a desire for world conquest." This has clear implications for Beijing's interpretations of U.S. actions which Americans might view as more benignly motivated.[5] Communist ideology has declined in importance, although it is not dead. In general, however, it has become less a guide for policy formulation than an instrument for after-the-fact rationalization of actions taken on the basis of other criteria. As the influence of communist ideology declined, nationalism came to the fore. Party and government may have consciously fostered nationalism to shore up their declining legitimacy in the aftermath of the suppression of the Tiananmen demonstrations as well as a decade of decidedly unsocialist economic reforms. Nationalism served to unify the citizenry behind the authorities while focusing on external threats to the PRC as opposed to divisive internal questions. It struck a responsive chord with many people.

Capabilities

The PRC has the world's largest military forces, backed by a still larger reserve/militia component. Since it also possesses the world's largest population, China has the ability to call up more reinforcements than any other state. However, this force lacks mobility, and its firepower is weak in comparison to that of most industrialized states. The military logistics system, though improving, remains weak. The navy has developed a blue-water capability which, although modest, has become worrisome to neighboring states with whom the PRC has territorial disputes. In-flight refueling of planes is only now being introduced; still, Chinese air force planes rarely venture far from their bases. The country's economy would be severely strained by a major confrontation. Since most of China's food is produced in three river basins, a nuclear attack on those areas could have devastating effects, for both long and short terms, on the country's ability to feed itself. However, this is unlikely to happen.

Under most conceivable circumstances, the PRC's military and economy are capable of sustaining the PRC quite well against outside attack and would make long-term occupation of the country impracticable. As no state currently has such intentions, this is a moot point. Economic and military vulnerabilities mean that the PRC is unable to project power any great distance beyond the country's borders. However, as shown by the missile and training exercises held in the Taiwan Strait in 1995–1996, it is capable of causing significant disruption and anxiety to China's neighbors and their allies.

Though of lesser importance in determining the limits of foreign policy, diplomacy and intelligence operations are also part of a nation's capabilities. The PRC's diplomacy is generally regarded as quite effective. Its intelligence services receive less high marks. A foreign intelligence agent describes the PRC's operations as inefficient, mired in red tape, and unable to keep secrets. There have indeed been successes. In one case, a Chinese employee of the U.S. Central Intelligence Agency, arrested in 1981, was found to have been passing secrets to communist party sources since 1944. In another, a French diplomat who fell in love with a performer in the Beijing opera was induced to provide classified information to the PRC for more than 15 years. He was eventually allowed to marry his love, who presented him with a son. Only after the couple's arrest by French counterintelligence did the diplomat learn that he had been set up: his "wife" was a male, and the child had been adopted. The publicity surrounding this operation inspired a Broadway show, *M. Butterfly*; a Hollywood movie; and a best-selling book.

Another factor contributing to the success of PRC intelligence operations is lax security in many of the areas it targets. A U.S. congressional committee report of 1999 faulted security lapses as a major factor in the ability of Chinese intelligence to penetrate

American weapons laboratories. The bipartisan committee's report revealed that China had stolen design information on, among other items, every currently deployed thermonuclear warhead in the U.S. ballistic missile arsenal.[6]

There have also been a number of clumsy failures. For example, at a trade show in Paris, members of a Chinese scientific delegation were caught dipping their neckties into a photo processing solution manufactured by the German firm Agfa. Their aim was presumably to analyze the solution and manufacture it themselves. A recent study concludes that the sheer numbers rather than the quality of Chinese operations enable a portion of them to succeed, since the target countries' counterintelligence and law enforcement agencies are simply overwhelmed. In addition, the fact that many of the PRC's collection activities concern mid-level technology means that they are not a major focus of concern for the foreign governments affected.[7]

Goals

China's foreign policy has shown underlying continuities, despite tactical shifts taken in response to international and domestic factors. These goals may be summarized as

- Preservation of China's territorial integrity
- Recovery of lost territories considered to be part of the PRC
- Recognition of the PRC as the sole legitimate government of China
- Enhancement of China's international stature

The Formulation of Foreign Policy

As with other aspects of high-level decision-making in China, the precise methods of formulating foreign policy are unknown. Newspapers do not discuss the merits or demerits of taking one position on the latest crisis in the Middle East versus another. There is no public discussion of debates within the leadership on whether to invade one country or extend diplomatic recognition to another. While there are many reasons for the Chinese leadership's reluctance to discuss the mechanics of foreign policy formation, the most important is probably the most obvious: There is little to be gained from revealing to potential international rivals anything that does not have to be revealed. It is also regarded as useful to present an image of a nation and leadership united behind a foreign policy decision, however dissonant with reality this image of harmony might be.

Certain information is known. Ultimately, of course, the responsibility for foreign policy decision-making rests with the supreme leader: Mao, then Deng—his lack of a formal title notwithstanding—and, after them, Jiang Zemin and Hu Jintao. Under Mao, the party's politburo and its standing committee were the principal loci of foreign policymaking. During the 1980s, however, they were superseded by the party secretariat and the State Council.[8] After the Thirteenth Party Congress in November 1987, the position of the party secretariat declined and that of the politburo standing committee again came to the fore. What these changes show, concludes an expert on the foreign policy bureaucracy, is that at the elite level of policymaking it is not so much institutions as individuals that are important.[9]

These individuals are relatively few in number, and simultaneously bear heavy responsibilities in a number of other areas. Since most foreign policy decisions cannot be intelligently made without reference to a wide variety of specialized information—for example, trade-flow statistics, knowledge of the power structure of another country, or information on the military capabilities of a potential enemy or ally—the standing committee must rely on other individuals and organizations for information and guidance.

A variety of support groups exists to provide this information and guidance. On important matters, a "leading small group" of top party, government, and party leaders may be formed to devise and consider various policy options. Such a small group exists to deal with Taiwan affairs. Within the party structure, the central committee has an international liaison office to provide data on foreign communist parties. On the governmental side, the most important organ concerned with foreign policy is the foreign ministry of the State Council. This ministry is divided into departments responsible for the study and analysis of given geographic areas of the world. It also has departments for other specialized functions, including consular affairs, foreign press information, international organizations, and treaties (see Figure 14.1). While in theory the international liaison department had responsibilities for relations between the CCP and other communist parties, whereas the foreign ministry was in charge of state-to-state matters, there was a good deal of overlap between them. Not surprisingly, the relationship had its frictions. A vice-premier who had at different times headed both, once revealed that, during the ascendancy of the Gang of Four, the ministry of foreign affairs had the habit of notifying the international liaison department only *after* delegations of communist parties from many foreign countries had already arrived.[10]

Externally, tensions also surrounded the use of the communist-party-to-communist-party channel. When China had formal diplomatic relations with a noncommunist state, the host government was understandably concerned about PRC support for subversive movements aimed at overthrowing that government.

These tensions between party-to-party and state-to-state channels have lessened in recent years. In the 1980s, PRC officials sharply reduced their support to insurgent communist parties in foreign countries. After the collapse of communism, the international liaison department began to host delegates from other countries' political parties, regardless of ideological affiliation. Thus, it might sponsor visits by members of the British Labour Party or Japan's Liberal Democratic party.

Other organizations subordinate to the State Council, such as the Ministry of Defense, the Finance Ministry, and the People's Bank, are concerned with foreign relations to varying degrees. In recent years, the PLA has reportedly become more assertive on foreign policy issues. A mass organization, the Chinese People's Association for Friendship with Foreign Countries, is responsible for a semiofficial channel, "people's diplomacy." This involves exchanges of sports teams as well as professional groups like surgeons, archaeologists, nuclear physicists, and businessmen. Theoretically, these activities take place between nongovernmental groups, although in practice they are closely monitored by the PRC leadership, and to some extent by the leadership of the other countries involved. "People's diplomacy" aims at the creation of goodwill for the PRC and is a means to influence domestic public opinion in a foreign country.

Chinese decision-makers also receive information relevant to foreign policymaking through other channels. Personnel of the official news agency, *Xinhua* (New China) who

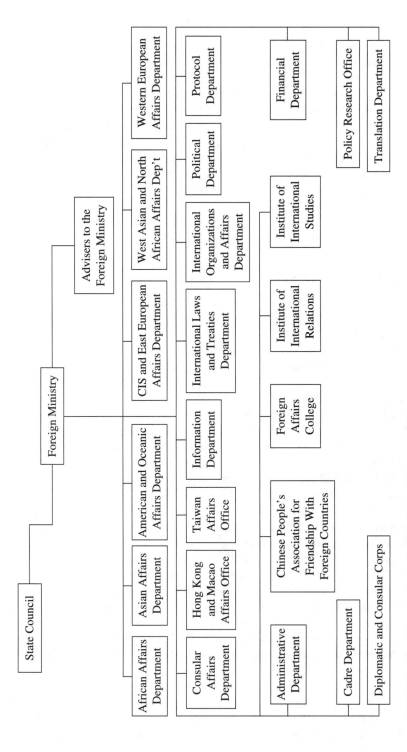

FIGURE 14.1 Organization of the Ministry of Foreign Affairs
Source: Adapted from U.S. Central Intelligence Agency, CR 85-10232, 1985.

are stationed in foreign countries are one such conduit. Intelligence operatives, some of whom may double as embassy or *Xinhua* employees, are another. Information is also received from Chinese who study or travel abroad or who maintain contacts with foreign sources. Several research institutes may be called upon for facts and analysis. These include the Chinese Academy of Social Sciences, the Shanghai Institute for International Affairs, and the China Institute of Contemporary International Relations. Just how carefully these academic experts are listened to by policymakers is questionable. The general consensus, which includes the experts themselves, is that their advice is not influential.

While precisely how these individuals and organizations impact on the foreign policy decision-making process is not known, a great deal about Chinese foreign policymaking can be learned from an examination of the strategies the PRC has adopted to effect its goals.

Chinese Foreign Relations: An Overview

The "Lean to One Side" Policy: 1949–1954

In 1949, the sweeping international changes desired by China's ambitious leaders seemed far off. Although many of the more distasteful provisions of the so-called unequal treaties forced on China during the nineteenth century had been abrogated in the course of two world wars, others remained. Hong Kong was still in the hands of the British; Macao was held by Portugal. The Soviet Union occupied many thousands of kilometers of land that Chinese patriots considered part of their country. Mongolia, effectively independent since 1911, had received international recognition after a plebiscite was held there in 1947. Tibet retained de facto independence. And the island of Taiwan was still held by the defeated KMT government under Chiang Kai-shek.

China's leaders began the task of restoring their country's greatness with limited resources. Exhausted by nearly 20 years of war and opposed by numerous hostile powers, the PRC could ill afford an adventuristic foreign policy. Claims to Mongolia, though not forgotten, had to be postponed, since the Mongolian People's Republic was a client state of the Soviet Union. Tibet was invaded only after a year's careful preparation. Subsequently, an agreement was signed that—while extremely distasteful to Tibetan nationalists— nonetheless promised a significant degree of autonomy to the area. Given its limited resources, the PRC wished to avoid actions that might serve as a pretext for foreign invasion.

The CCP's initial tendency was to seek normalization of relations with other countries, but to extend diplomatic recognition only to those nations who agreed to break relations with the KMT government. Not surprisingly, all of the communist countries immediately recognized the PRC. Britain, anxious to forestall Chinese claims on its lucrative Hong Kong colony, also quickly recognized the Beijing government. So did the Scandinavian countries, Switzerland, Israel (not reciprocated by the PRC), and six Asian states: India, Pakistan, Sri Lanka, Afghanistan, Burma, and Indonesia.

The PRC made overtures to the United States but received no answer. Within the United States, a debate raged over the merits of recognition. Those in favor of establishing diplomatic relations with the PRC argued that the CCP government controlled the Chinese mainland, and was therefore entitled to recognition regardless of what ideology it espoused. The Republic of China (ROC) was now confined to Taiwan, plus a few small islands. The advocates of U.S. recognition of the PRC had an ideological as well as a pragmatic reason for their views: They tended to look sympathetically on the CCP because of its plans to better the lot of the poorer segments of China's population and to point out that the KMT government had badly mismanaged the administration of the country.

Those opposed to normalization pointed out that the KMT government had been consistently pro-American, whereas the PRC, as a communist state, would be bound to side with America's archrival, the Soviet Union. Many of the KMT's problems in administering China had been caused or exacerbated by the war with Japan. Unlike the CCP elite, several KMT leaders had been educated in the United States. And, whereas the communist elite was atheistic and militantly antimissionary, many of the leaders of the KMT were practicing Christians who were appreciative, or at least tolerant, of missionary activities. There were a number of documented examples of victorious communists torturing or otherwise mistreating Americans, including diplomatic personnel and missionaries, who had stayed on in China. Some grounds also existed for distrusting the sincerity of CCP overtures to the United States.[11]

After due deliberation, the Truman administration articulated a policy it described as "let the dust settle": taking no action to support either KMT or CCP. This included the judgment that the fate of Taiwan was an internal matter of China; most people expected the island to fall to the CCP very shortly.

While the United States was biding its time, the PRC in February 1950 signed a Treaty of Peace, Friendship, and Mutual Assistance with the Soviet Union. The negotiations that preceded the conclusion of the treaty were protracted, requiring Mao Zedong's presence in Moscow for two months. This indicated that intense bargaining was taking place. Indeed, the treaty granted significant concessions to the USSR, in return for Soviet financial and technical assistance to the PRC. The concessions gave Stalin substantial leverage over the Chinese government. Subsequent events in Korea were to strengthen China's dependence on the Soviet Union.

In January 1950, U.S. secretary of state Dean Acheson defined a defense perimeter for America, excluding South Korea from United States responsibility. This convinced North Korean premier Kim Il-song that the United States would not actively intervene to prevent a North Korean takeover of the south, and he obtained Stalin's agreement to back the invasion. Their analysis that America would not intervene proved erroneous. Domestic critics of the Truman administration's China policy pointed to the Korean invasion as fresh proof of the same unbridled expansionism that had caused the Chinese mainland to be absorbed by the communist camp, and demanded immediate action.

Thus, North Korea's invasion of South Korea in June 1950 was met with determined U.S. resistance, channeled through the United Nations. An important consequence of the Korean confrontation was the abandonment of America's "let the dust settle" policy in favor of a policy of protecting Taiwan. President Truman, reasoning that a Chinese communist takeover of Taiwan would complicate the logistical problems of U.S. forces fighting in Korea, ordered the Seventh Fleet to "neutralize" the Taiwan Strait. In effect, this prevented the CCP government from invading the island.

The outbreak of the Korean War thus blocked the PRC from attaining one of its major foreign policy goals, and moreover one that had seemed easily within reach. It also hardened attitudes between the United States and China. U.S.–PRC animosity increased when, in October 1950, Chinese "volunteers" began crossing into North Korea to aid their fellow communists in fighting United States and United Nations forces. Foreign analysts at first believed that the PRC agreed to enter the confrontation only after strong prodding by the Soviet Union and when U.S.-UN troops began a rapid advance into North Korea, approaching the Chinese border.[12] More recent research into Chinese archives indicates that Mao's motivation was revolutionary rather than pragmatic. He believed an ideological confrontation with the United States was inevitable, and recognized the opportunity in U.S. intervention in Korea.[13]

Direct confrontation between U.S. and Chinese troops in Korea resulted in the war becoming a stalemate. In the course of prosecuting the conflict, the United States increased its aid to Chiang Kai-shek's government on Taiwan. A vigorous effort by the PRC in 1954 to take Taiwan, including the shelling of the offshore island of Quemoy (Jinmen), stiffened U.S. determination to protect the island. In late 1954, the United States signed a mutual defense treaty with Chiang's government. Given the importance the PRC attached to possessing Taiwan, this treaty was bad news. Mao appears not to have foreseen that intervention in Korea would doom his efforts to deal a final blow to Chiang.

The failure of the United States and China to create sufficient common ground for the establishment of diplomatic relations increased China's reliance on the Soviet Union. In part, this was due to the circumstances described previously. In part the increased dependence on the Soviet Union had been a response to the personality of Joseph Stalin. Becoming more paranoid with advancing age, he exacted fanatical loyalty from his followers. Stalin propounded the attitude of "whoever is not with us is against us," and, in general, his allies conducted their foreign policies accordingly.

China's trade and other relations during this period were overwhelmingly with other communist bloc countries. While the military strength evinced by Chinese forces in Korea increased international respect for the PRC, this was not necessarily accompanied by international diplomatic recognition. The United States, reminding the United Nations that China had fought UN troops in Korea, was able to block the PRC's bid to unseat the KMT government from membership in that body. On a state-to-state level, most nations continued to recognize Chiang Kai-shek's Taiwan-based government as the legitimate representative of China.

In addition to China's activities in Korea, the PRC also strongly supported Ho Chi-minh's struggle against the French in Indochina, sending arms and supplies to his Viet Minh. When accused by Western sources of being one-sided in his policies, Mao's often quoted reply was

> "You are leaning to one side." Exactly! . . . all Chinese without exception must lean to the side of imperialism or to the side of socialism. Sitting on the fence will not do, nor is there a third road.[14]

The Bandung Spirit: 1954–1957

Several events conspired to moderate the "lean to one side" policy. First, the death of Stalin in 1953 removed the principal force in favor of a monolithic communist bloc ranged against the outside world. Stalin's successors held a somewhat less confrontational view of the international scene. They favored a reduction of tensions, both within the communist bloc and between the communist countries and the noncommunist world.

Second, soon after Stalin's death, several causes of tension appeared to be resolved. In July 1953, a truce was signed in Korea, thus stabilizing the situation in Northeast Asia. And in 1954, the Geneva Conference met to determine the Indochina question. PRC diplomats led by premier Zhou Enlai played a major part in devising a truce that led to the partition of Vietnam and the inclusion of its northern half within the communist bloc.

Third, in the years after World War II, a number of colonies either became independent or received firm promises that independence would be granted in the near future. The relinquishment of so many colonies made imperialism seem less menacing.[15] In addition, most newly liberated colonies were concerned to avoid entanglement with either power bloc. A number of them announced that they would pursue neutralist foreign policies. Rather than ignore or antagonize so many countries who chose not to "lean to one side," it seemed wisest to move away from rigid insistence that whoever was not on the side of the communist bloc was against it.

In asserting this more outward-looking foreign policy, a primary focus of China's interest was its Asian neighbors. India, the largest of the Asian states espousing a neutral foreign policy, was an immediate recipient of Chinese attention. In June 1954, Zhou Enlai met with Indian prime minister Nehru to work out a basis for continuing relations between the two countries. From this meeting emerged the *Pancha Sheela*, or Five Principles, which were to be the cornerstone of Chinese diplomacy during the 1954–1957 period. These were

- Mutual respect for each other's territorial integrity
- Nonaggression
- Noninterference in each other's internal affairs
- Equality and mutual benefit
- Peaceful coexistence

Relations between China and India during this period were relatively harmonious despite the existence of a long-standing border dispute between the two countries, and the distaste of many Indians for China's forcible occupation of Tibet. Relations with Burma, with which the PRC also had a border dispute, improved as well. A Sino-Burmese border agreement followed in due course.

Both India and Burma agreed to remain aloof from the cold war and to maintain friendly relations with China. In return, the PRC agreed to refrain from aggression on the Indian and Burmese borders—both countries were having problems with independence-minded ethnic groups who inhabited border areas—and to negotiate on the delicate issue of the people of Chinese ancestry who live abroad. Known as Overseas Chinese, they are an important presence in most Southeast Asian countries. Overseas Chinese typically had higher income levels than the indigenous population, and often controlled important sectors of the economy of these countries. They had a tendency toward clannishness, to educating their children in separate, Chinese-language schools, and to remitting substantial portions of the profits from their businesses back to China rather than allowing the capital to remain in the countries where it was earned. In consequence, they were frequently much resented by the local population.

The sentiments symbolized by the *Pancha Sheela* and given concrete expression by China's improving relations with Burma and India led to the convening of an Asian-African conference at Bandung, a resort city in Indonesia. There, in April 1955, the PRC's emissaries renewed acquaintance with Asian diplomats and first made contact with representatives of African states. Zhou Enlai held extended talks with Egypt's president Nasser, which became the basis for closer relations between the two countries in later years. A number of other contacts were made which would prove useful in future years.

Bandung came to symbolize a political vision: that African and Asian states, since they shared common social and economic problems, should work together for the solution of these problems. Guided by the *Pancha Sheela* (subsequently expanded to ten principles) and based on mutual respect and opposition to colonialism, "have-not" countries with dissimilar social systems could not only coexist peacefully, but even prosper. Later, the PRC added Latin American states to this vision as well. Despite its own rather limited resources, China began a modest foreign aid program to encourage progress toward unity and prosperity.

China's conciliatory posture even extended to expressing willingness to discuss outstanding issues with the United States. The PRC won considerable goodwill during this period, and a number of countries broke relations with the Taiwan government to recognize the mainland regime.

China frequently invoked the Bandung spirit to encourage third-world states to support policies that the PRC favored. However, its lofty principles were never translated into effective institutions for coordination or implementation of these policies, and few actual problems were solved on the basis of the *Pancha Sheela*. Still, the "Bandung spirit" came to represent a striving for unity among third-world countries in an atmosphere of relaxed tension. As such, it demarcates an important period in the development of Chinese foreign policy.

Resurgent Nationalism and Isolation: 1957–1969

In emphasizing peaceful coexistence with third-world countries, China had muted rather than abandoned its revolutionary message. In 1957, the Chinese leadership reassessed its view of the international situation and decided that circumstances again favored revolutionary forces. The factors precipitating this reassessment included major scientific-technological breakthroughs on the part of the Soviet Union: the successful testing of an intercontinental ballistic missile in August 1957, and the launching of the world's first manmade satellite in October of the same year.

In November 1957, Mao Zedong made a famous speech signifying the change in his worldview. Asserting that an international turning point had been reached, he warned

> There are now two winds in the world: the East wind and the West wind. There is a saying in China: "If the East wind does not prevail over the West wind, then the West wind will

prevail over the East wind." I think that the characteristic of the current situation is that the East wind prevails over the West wind: that is, the strength of socialism exceeds the strength of imperialism.[16]

The metaphorical significance of Mao's words was clear: The communist states, led by the Soviet Union, should take advantage of their momentum over the capitalist world and pursue more aggressive revolutionary policies. Not to take advantage of this momentum might result in serious damage to the communist camp.

China's efforts to prod the Soviet Union into a more militant stance were unsuccessful. Khrushchev, who had assumed Stalin's leadership position after the latter's death, was faced with growing demands for better living standards from the Soviet populace. Adopting a more aggressive foreign policy would mean diverting funds from consumer goods to military purposes. The post-Stalin Soviet leadership was in addition more wary of the dangers of a confrontation with capitalism than the Chinese. While the PRC pursued peaceful coexistence with third-world countries, Khrushchev went even further, evincing willingness to coexist peacefully with capitalist countries as well.

Annoyed by the USSR's reluctance to capitalize on its revolutionary advantage, China assumed a more militant posture on its own initiative. The PRC's annoyance turned to anger when the Soviet Union refused to support its ally's more aggressive stance. For example, in 1958–1959, China adopted a harder line on Taiwan and resumed bombardment of the offshore island of Quemoy. Another disputed offshore island, Matsu, was shelled as well. Khrushchev, visiting Beijing, made a speech criticizing adventurism and mentioning Brest-Litovsk—an allusion to the treaty of Brest-Litovsk under the terms of which the newly founded, weak USSR had agreed to cede a large area of formerly czarist territory to Germany. The term had come to be understood as a synonym for a policy of trading space for time, and, in effect, Khrushchev was unsubtly lecturing China on the need to bide its time with regard to Taiwan. Mao was reportedly livid.

In another instance, the PRC decided to put pressure on India to resolve a complicated border dispute between the two countries. The Soviet Union not only refused to back its Chinese ally, but openly sought to improve relations with the Nehru government. Khrushchev's position was all the more irritating in that the weight of evidence tended to support China's position that the border had not been legally demarcated vis-à-vis the Indian government's contention that it had been.[17]

These and other accumulated disagreements between the PRC and the Soviet Union culminated in an open break between the two countries, permanently rupturing communism as a monolithic entity. The Sino-Soviet dispute had many causes. First, czarist Russia had incorporated a large amount of territory that the PRC claimed as Chinese, building cities, railroads, and ports on it. The USSR, despite promises to end the unequal treaties of its predecessor government, had never returned these lands.

Second, the Soviet government had ordered the infant Chinese communist movement to pursue policies which many CCP members felt to be unwise, and which had resulted in the death of many of their comrades, including Mao's wife and their two children. Third, Stalin had consistently supported CCP members other than Mao in Mao's drive for leadership of the party. He had also publicly criticized Mao's movement as little more than agrarian reform, describing the CCP as "margarine communists," or "radish communists" who were red on the surface but white inside.

Fourth, the Soviet Union had taken large quantities of material from northeast China during the USSR's occupation of that area after World War II. From the Chinese point of view, this amounted to looting a country that had been its ally. Moreover, the USSR continued to negotiate with Chiang Kai-shek long after it was clear that the CCP was winning its battle to control China. The Soviet Union sought to sell arms to Chiang in return for concessions in Xinjiang and elsewhere.

The Sino-Soviet Treaty of 1950 had granted aid to China when that country could not expect aid from elsewhere. Nonetheless, the terms of the agreement were hardly generous by international standards and included concessions to the Soviet Union in Xinjiang, Dalian (Port Arthur), and on the Chinese Eastern Railway. These concessions were canceled by Khrushchev in 1954, but not before Chinese pride had been hurt.

The Chinese leadership was also annoyed by the terms under which the Soviet Union had supplied the PRC with weapons to pursue the Korean War. They saw China as fighting on behalf of the socialist world in a war which would, among other ends, protect the Soviet Union. Yet the USSR not only supplied China with weapons that were obsolescent but required the PRC to pay for them as well.

More recently, the Chinese had been shocked when, at the Twentieth Congress of the Communist Party of the Soviet Union (CPSU) in 1956, Khrushchev had delivered a biting denunciation of Stalin. While the CCP had ample reasons for dissatisfaction with Stalin, its leaders were angry with Khrushchev's failure to consult them beforehand. The Chinese delegate to the CPSU had just finished a speech eulogizing Comrade Stalin, to the intense embarrassment of the Chinese leadership. More important in the PRC leadership's view was the long-run danger. As noted, the Chinese had excellent reasons for disliking Stalin themselves. But they were concerned that to publicly destroy the reputation of this symbol of unity of the communist bloc might cause its unity to disintegrate. Mao may also have feared that Khrushchev's denunciations of the cult of Stalin would subsequently be used to put pressure on Mao to eliminate his own personality cult.

To compound these other dissatisfactions with the Soviet Union, Chinese planners became increasingly convinced that the Soviet developmental model was not adequately serving the PRC's needs. The country's adoption of a radically different developmental scheme, the Great Leap Forward, was publicly ridiculed by Khrushchev.

Chinese and Soviet differences were expressed in rather muted form at first, with the Chinese propounding a strong, unified communist bloc and sharply criticizing its then most independent member, Yugoslavia. Implicit in Chinese diatribes against Yugoslavia was criticism of the Soviet Union for allowing its aberrant behavior to continue unchecked. Albania—which, because of irredentist problems involving a sizable Albanian minority group that had been incorporated into Yugoslavia—heartily endorsed China's indictment of Yugoslavia. The USSR responded in the same symbolic fashion: When the Chinese media attacked Yugoslavia, Soviet propaganda railed against Albania. The Soviet Union also made plain that it was withdrawing its promise to give China nuclear arms.

In the spring of 1960 a major turning point in the Sino-Soviet dispute, and for Chinese foreign policymaking in general, was reached. The PRC media, ostensibly in celebration of the ninetieth anniversary of Lenin's birth, began publishing a series of ideological articles with the collective title "Long Live Leninism." These differed from past Chinese pronouncements in that they no longer argued with Khrushchev about what the Soviet Union should do, but implied that he had betrayed the most fundamental beliefs of Marxism-Leninism and asserted that China must now assume leadership of the communist world.

The immediate consequences of this declaration were not to China's benefit. The Soviet Union abruptly withdrew its technicians and much of its aid, thereby hindering the PRC's economic development. With Albania a salient exception, communist states tended to side with the Soviet Union. In states where communist parties existed but did not govern, the communist party often split over the issue of the Sino-Soviet dispute, thus weakening its chances of coming to power. In general, the larger portion of these bifurcated parties remained loyal to the USSR, while the smaller splinter was pro-PRC. With Khrushchev's removal from office in October 1964, Sino-Soviet polemics abated somewhat, but the ideological differences between the two countries remained and, despite the wishes of the Chinese leadership, the unity of the communist bloc ceased to exist.

In the noncommunist world, China appeared threatening because of its diatribes against peaceful coexistence, insistence that wars were inevitable as long as imperialism remained, and denial of the possibility of peaceful roads to communism. Chinese actions exacerbated the fears aroused by its propaganda. In 1962, the PRC used military force against India with regard to the border dispute between the two countries. China's action was taken in response to documentable provocations on the part of India, and only after repeated warnings to the Nehru government.[18] Yet the PRC's decisive victory over India appeared to arouse more fear than admiration by world public opinion.

Other Chinese foreign policy actions were less successful. Although definitive proof is lacking, the PRC appears to have been involved in an attempted coup d'état by the Communist Party of Indonesia (PKI) in 1965. The Indonesian coup was put down by a coalition of generals; a bloodbath followed in which not only members of the PKI were massacred, but many thousands of noncommunist Overseas Chinese as well. Thousands more Indonesian Chinese were herded into detention camps and eventually deported to the PRC. The formerly pro-PRC government of Indonesia was replaced by one distinctly cool to China, and diplomatic relations between the two countries were suspended.

In the Middle East, China's support for the activities of the Palestinian Liberation Organization (PLO) annoyed the Egyptian government, as did China's efforts to wean Egypt away from its alliance with the Soviet Union. In Kenya, the popular nationalist leader Jomo Kenyatta resented Chinese support for his opposition party and declared "It is naive to think that there is no danger of imperialism from the East . . . this is why we reject communism."[19] And in Latin America, Fidel Castro complained of Chinese interference in Cuban affairs, asserting that he had not liberated his country from U.S. imperialism only to endure similar treatment from the PRC.[20]

A final rebuff occurred when China's efforts to have the Soviet Union excluded from a projected Afro-Asian conference in 1965 failed. The PRC announced that it would not attend a conference convened in disregard for China's views, and the gathering was postponed indefinitely. Chinese sources acknowledged these reverses, stating that "temporary setbacks" to the world revolution were to be expected. Because truth was on its side, the PRC, though presently outnumbered by the forces of imperialism (i.e., the United States and its allies), would yet triumph.

China's isolation reached an extreme during the Cultural Revolution, 1966–1969. During this period, radical leftists criticized the PRC's foreign policy for giving insufficient weight to world revolution. The PRC increased its encouragement of subversive movements in several countries, and groups of Chinese militants, most of them students, caused unpleasant incidents in a number of foreign states. As a result of these activities, the PRC's diplomatic relations with more than 30 countries were damaged. In addition, China's foreign policymaking apparatus was attacked by radicals who claimed that it had succumbed to subversive bourgeois influences from the foreigners with whom they interacted. Red Guards attacked foreign embassies, terrorizing their personnel and causing at least one death. They also sacked their own country's foreign ministry. With organs of decision-making near paralysis, the PRC recalled all its ambassadors save that to Cairo. The importance that China attached to the Middle East, and to Egypt's importance within the Middle East, is the most probable explanation for this exception. It also suggests that, despite the feverish ideological pronouncements of this era, some modicum of pragmatism remained.

Chinese leftists' feelings against the Soviet Union ran especially high. Militant extremists believed that China was in danger of contamination from Soviet "revisionism" and the USSR's tolerance of various invidious forms of capitalism. Thus it is not surprising that Soviet diplomats were a special target of extremist attacks, and that polemics against the Soviet government increased. The USSR's media responded by denouncing the turmoil within China as the product of insanity among the CCP elite. The Sino-Soviet dispute, quiescent since Khrushchev's fall in October 1964, became increasingly bitter. China denounced the Soviet invasion of Czechoslovakia in 1968 as a "monstrous crime," and there were rumors that the USSR was planning a preemptive strike against the PRC's nuclear installation in Xinjiang province, believed to contain China's only nuclear facility at that time.

Border tensions heightened, and there were minor incidents involving border guards and civilians of both sides throughout 1968 and early 1969. In March 1969, on a small island in the Ussuri River that was one part of the territorial disputes between the two countries, Chinese soldiers opened fire on a Soviet patrol. The Soviets retaliated in kind. Other clashes ensued on the border between China's Xinjiang and Soviet Kazakhstan, far to the west of the Ussuri incident. China's isolation from the international community was nearly complete, and even its territorial integrity seemed in jeopardy.

Global Power Politics: 1969–Present

1969–1989: Triangular Politics   China's actions on the Ussuri puzzled many foreign observers. To provoke hostilities against its more powerful neighbor at a time of domestic weakness over a long-standing claim to a tiny piece of land of no great value (the island is actually under water a good deal of the time) seemed absurd. Moreover, even if, as the PRC claimed, the démarche aimed to demonstrate that China would not be "bullied," the scenario seemed ill conceived. Soviet troops were well trained and showed themselves fully competent to deal with the PLA. Finally, it seemed pointless to provoke a major foreign policy crisis just a few weeks before the CCP's Ninth Congress was scheduled to open.

Some Western analysts believed the clash to be a natural outgrowth of the foreign policy excesses of the Cultural Revolution; others suggested that a local commander had simply exceeded his orders. A third explanation is that one faction of the highest echelon of the party's decision-making elite ordered the PLA to attack Soviet troops to force another faction of that elite to agree to a startling change in China's foreign policy: rapprochement with the United States.

In this scenario, Mao and Zhou Enlai interpreted the Soviet invasion of Czechoslovakia and the USSR's subsequent enunciation of the "Brezhnev doctrine"—that other socialist countries had the right to interfere when events within a socialist country were endangering the socialist community as a whole—as threatening the security of China. At the same time, the United States began to look less threatening. The Paris peace talks on Vietnam had begun, and a new president, Richard Nixon, had been elected. Part of Nixon's campaign rhetoric had included promises to reduce America's presence in Asia. Since the Soviet Union was far more menacing to the PRC than the United States, and since the United States was hostile to the Soviet Union while being approximately equal to it in strength, conciliatory moves toward the United States were indicated.

However, according to this line of analysis, the Mao-Zhou group was prevented from improving relations with the United States because they were opposed by Cultural Revolution radicals led by defense minister Lin Biao. Lin's group preferred to try to improve relations with the Soviet Union, reasoning that, despite its many faults, the USSR was still preferable to a capitalist state. Lin would in any case not have wanted to agree with a policy alternative suggested by Zhou Enlai, since Zhou was his principal rival for power. Because Lin Biao was defense minister, it was necessary to bypass him and give orders directly to the commander of the relevant military district, who was one of Zhou's supporters.

In this interpretation, then, the Ussuri clash was contrived to discredit those members of the Chinese elite who believed that a rapprochement with the Soviet Union was possible and to open the way for better relations with the United States. Chinese media, of course, described the clash as having been instigated by the Soviet Union. Lin Biao's demise in 1971, as he was allegedly fleeing to the Soviet Union, and the rapprochement with the United States that actually occurred in that same year, have been adduced as further evidence for this scenario.[21]

Whatever the truth of this hypothesis, and although Chinese propaganda continued to regularly denounce the machinations of both the United States and the USSR, the dominant faction of the post-1971 Chinese leadership clearly indicated that it considered the USSR the more dangerous of the two superpowers. However, the issue of U.S. support for Taiwan remained outstanding, inhibiting PRC moves toward better relations with the United States.

China responded favorably to President Nixon's relaxation of restrictions on trade and travel with the PRC, and in April 1971 Mao Zedong invited an American table-tennis team to tour China. With enthusiastic approval from Washington, the team accepted. Their widely publicized trip, which included meetings with high-ranking Chinese officials, was dubbed "ping-pong diplomacy." It formed the antecedent to President Nixon's own trip to Beijing in 1972.

Nixon's visit brought a further advance in the rapprochement process. After extensive talks, in February 1972 the two sides issued the so-called Shanghai Communiqué. This document affirmed their mutual desire to normalize diplomatic relations. It finessed the Taiwan issue by stating that "All Chinese on either side of the Taiwan Strait maintain that there is but one China and that Taiwan is a part of China. The United States government does not challenge that position."[22] However, the United States did not go so far as to state that it *agreed* with that position. There were awkward ethical and legal considerations for the United States to deal with. To break relations with its loyal Taiwan ally might call into question the sincerity of America's commitments to other allies. There was also the question of what to do about the U.S.-ROC Mutual Security Treaty. Moreover, a large number of native-born Taiwanese did *not* consider the island part of Chinese territory, and were vehemently opposed to unification with a mainland to which they felt no ideological or emotional affinity.

For the time being, the question of Taiwan was placed in abeyance. With the Shanghai Communiqué as a basis, relations between the United States and the PRC improved. In lieu of regular diplomatic representation, each side established a liaison office in the capital of the other. Trade between the two countries increased markedly, and contacts and exchanges took place in a number of areas, including technology, sports, and culture. Eventually, on January 1, 1979, China and the United States began full diplomatic relations. America agreed to end formal ties with the Republic of China on Taiwan, while declaring its intention to maintain cultural, commercial, and other unofficial relations therewith. The defense treaty was abrogated in accordance with its own provisions, which gave either party the option of terminating it after giving one year's notice. The Taiwan Relations Act, passed by Congress in April 1979, attempted to provide for the security of the island by declaring that the United States would sell its government such defensive weapons as were deemed necessary to keep a balance of power in the Taiwan Strait.

At the same time that Mao Zedong began seeking better relations with the United States, China's attitudes toward countries other than the Soviet Union also became a good deal more conciliatory. Ambassadors began returning to their posts in 1969, and the PRC not only formally apologized to foreign countries for what had happened to their embassies in Beijing during the Cultural Revolution but agreed to make restitution as well. This more accommodative posture enabled China both to reestablish relationships that had been broken off during the Cultural Revolution and to win new supporters. The PRC's acceptance as a legitimate member of the international community was given formal endorsement in October 1971, when the country was admitted to membership in the United Nations and made a permanent member of the UN Security Council.

Agreement on the PRC's right to UN membership was far from unanimous. Critics, citing the irresponsible acts of the Cultural Revolution period and quoting militant Chinese propaganda, predicted that the PRC would disrupt United Nations functions. These fears proved to be without foundation: Observers agree that China has been a responsible member of both the main bodies of the UN and of its specialized agencies. Beijing has used its UN membership to champion causes important to the less developed countries, including support for regulating multinational corporations, obtaining better control over technology transfers from advanced countries, and setting more favorable terms for repaying foreign debts. However, the PRC did not join the nonaligned bloc or, despite being an oil exporter, the Organization of Petroleum Exporting Countries (OPEC). While giving considerable rhetorical support to the New International Economic Order (NIEO), a favorite project of developing countries, China has joined the World Bank, the International

Monetary Fund, and the World Trade Organization (WTO)—all institutions of the "old international economic order."[23] The PRC's large size, wide variety of natural resources, and relatively well-educated population make it unique among developing countries. While frequently acknowledging its solidarity with the less developed world, the PRC tends to vote its own interests, which frequently run counter to those of the so-called third world. One observer has quipped that China's voting record at the UN makes it "a Gang of One."

In February 1974, Mao Zedong elaborated his views on the tripartite division of the world, saying, "In my view, the United States and the Soviet Union form the first world. Japan, Europe, and Canada, the middle section, belong to the second world. We are the third world. The third world has a large population. With the exception of Japan, Asia belongs to the third world. The whole of Africa belongs to the third world, and Latin America, too."[24]

The second world, Mao argued, had been dominated by the two superpowers in the past, but its members were now asserting their independence. Western Europe was especially important, since Soviet hegemonism was positioned directly opposite it. To safeguard independence and postpone war, the second and third worlds should form a united front against the superpowers. While specifically rejecting the role of superpower or hegemon, Mao clearly envisioned China as leader of this coalition against hegemony.

However, just as the PRC's stridently pro-third-world rhetoric did not always accurately describe its actual behavior, the three worlds theory translated into behavior that sought to weld the United States, the second world, and the third world into a united front against hegemony. After Mao's death in 1976, Chinese foreign policy became more unabashedly pragmatic in theory, as it had been in practice for several years before. There were significant gains for China.

Acceptance of certain generally agreed-upon norms in international law made it easier for the PRC to obtain loans and attract foreign investment. The existence of a number of tension-inducing issues notwithstanding, China was able to obtain substantial help from Japan to bolster its economic development plans. In 1978, the two sides ratified a Sino-Japanese Treaty of Peace and Friendship. The PRC also began to use its Muslim minorities to persuade wealthy Islamic states to invest in China. Settlements were negotiated with Britain to return Hong Kong in 1997 and with Portugal to rescind Macao in 1999. The process of negotiations was helped by the less militant rhetoric emanating from Beijing, and also by the PRC's willingness to grant a quasi-autonomous status to the areas in light of their unique historical and developmental situations. The category of special administrative region (SAR), granting some powers of self-government while Beijing would take over the SAR's foreign and defense functions, was written into the PRC's 1982 constitution. The SAR would also provide a mechanism for the absorption of Taiwan.

China's efforts to contain the Soviet Union suffered a setback when Vietnam, finally reunified under a communist government, decided to lean toward the USSR. The historical animosities between China and Vietnam that had been muted during Vietnam's struggle with the United States were rekindled. Vietnam's expropriation of the assets of its wealthiest citizens, a disproportionate number of whom were Overseas Chinese, brought charges of ethnic discrimination from the PRC. Vietnam replied that it was just doing what one should expect a communist state to do: destroying capitalism. Vietnam's December 1978 invasion of the PRC's ally, tiny Cambodia, proved the last straw. In February 1979, the PLA attacked across the two countries' disputed border, with the aims of forcing Vietnam to withdraw its troops from Cambodia and of "teaching it a lesson." Though the PLA did considerable damage, neither aim was fulfilled. Chinese casualties were quite heavy, and the cost of the attack hindered the PRC's modernization program.

Deng Xiaoping had anticipated that the Soviet Union would aid its Vietnamese ally, and made preparations against such an attack. Armed Soviet intervention proved unnecessary, though Vietnam must certainly have welcomed the USSR's moral support and material aid. Chinese propaganda put a positive spin on the Soviet Union's decision not to join the hostilities, boasting that the PRC had "touched the tiger's backside" with impunity. Nonetheless, soon after the confrontation, Vietnam rewarded the Soviet Union by granting it basing rights at strategically located Cam Ranh Bay. The USSR now had easy access to a warm water port located not far from China.

Shortly after its strike against Vietnam, the PRC abrogated the Sino-Soviet Treaty of 1950, accurately describing the agreement as having been a dead letter for nearly two decades. China argued that the treaty had been drawn up with the PRC in an inferior position, which was not only insulting to it but also no longer consonant with reality. Its leaders declared themselves willing to negotiate a new treaty on the basis of equality between the contracting partners. Talks, which began in an atmosphere singularly lacking in trust and harmony, were suspended by the Chinese after the USSR invaded Afghanistan in December 1979. The PRC then announced three preconditions for future negotiations: (1) The Soviet Union was to withdraw its troops from Afghanistan. (2) It was to cease support for Vietnam's occupation of Cambodia. (3) Soviet troops must be withdrawn from the Sino-Soviet border and from Mongolia.

Since neither past Soviet behavior nor the attitudes of the then-current Soviet leadership gave evidence that these conditions might be agreed to, prospects for better Sino-Soviet relations did not seem bright. However, by late 1981, China had begun to reassess its position. Several irritants in its relations with the United States had emerged. The PRC was unhappy with the amount of textiles it was allowed to export to the United States, dissatisfied at the pace of American technology transfer, and annoyed by continued U.S. support for Taiwan. In 1982, it was able to pressure the United States into agreeing to gradually reduce its sales of arms to Taiwan, but the communiqué said nothing about ending the transfer of military technology to the island.[25] With some help from the United States and other foreign countries, Taiwan began to design and build high-quality fighter planes and warships of its own. PRC leaders were also upset about the way in which American officials had handled the defection of a Chinese tennis player.

At the very least, Chinese officials reasoned, the threat of better PRC-USSR relations could be used as a lever to influence American policies in ways that would benefit China. Since the PRC at this point had better relations with both the United States and the USSR than the United States and the USSR had with each other, China was in a position to use the enmity between the two to obtain concessions from each.

Stressing that more cordial relations in no way modified the PRC's insistence that its three preconditions be met, China employed "people's diplomacy," exchanging sports and professional delegations with the USSR. Cross-border trade, which had almost ceased after 1960, picked up rapidly. Although this was barter trade, calculated in politically neutral Swiss francs, and mainly in items of lesser quality which would have poor marketability elsewhere, the renewal in exchange of goods was an important step toward normalization of relations between the two countries.

After Mikhail Gorbachev came to power in the Soviet Union, he actually did comply with Chinese demands with regard to Afghanistan, Vietnam, and troop deployments near the Chinese border and in Mongolia. Trade continued to grow, and Sino-Soviet relations were further institutionalized in a wide range of fields and at various levels of the two states' bureaucracies. Gorbachev announced his intention to visit China, the first Soviet head of state to do so in over 30 years. In terms of media attention, the drama of his May 1989 visit to Beijing was upstaged by the student demonstrations in Tiananmen Square. But in terms of putting a symbolic end to the Sino-Soviet dispute, it was significant indeed.

At the same time, however, China's ability to play the Soviet Union off against the United States was also waning. Gorbachev's policies included not only conciliatory gestures toward the PRC but increasing flexibility toward U.S. positions as well. This resulted in much better relations between the two superpowers. The brutality of the PRC leadership's actions against unarmed demonstrators at Tiananmen Square and elsewhere in China caused many people, including many Americans, to become disillusioned with the PRC. While Gorbachev's Soviet Union appeared less menacing and more deserving of American support than it had, Deng's China now appeared less benign, and less worthy of American solicitude.

Counterbalancing the Sole Superpower: 1989–Present The disintegration of the Soviet Union into 15 successor states made it far more difficult for the PRC to practice triangular diplomacy, confronting Beijing with a single superpower, the United States. This was not a situation the leadership was comfortable with, particularly in the years following the Tiananmen incident, when American sermonizing on human rights and the need for representative democracy intensified. Chinese sources predicted that a multi-polar international order would be the eventual outcome of the realignment of power caused by the USSR's collapse, and set about trying to aid its emergence. They envisioned a decline in American power, with the country then being balanced off by Japan, an increasingly united European Union, India, Russia, and the PRC itself. Chinese diplomacy thus encouraged greater distance between Japan and the United States, highlighted issues on which European countries disagreed with the U.S., and courted good relations with various Middle Eastern and Central Asian states.

Beijing's attempts to form a multilateral coalition against American hegemony while simultaneously threatening its neighbors produced mixed results. Some policymakers in these neighboring states viewed the PRC as an unstoppable economic juggernaut, and felt that placatory policies might therefore achieve more than confrontational ones. This attitude did not necessarily rule out tactics that involved resistance to Chinese expansion, nor efforts to form countervailing coalitions of their own against the PRC. Placatory policies included the regular exchange of visits by heads of state, their cabinet ministers, and members of parliamentary bodies, to and from China. Fishing treaties were signed and confidence-building measures discussed. The PRC, along with Japan and South Korea, was given dialogue partner status by the Association of Southeast Asian Nations (ASEAN), and Beijing began to explore the feasibility of a free trade agreement between China and ASEAN. China also established close relations with Russia, which soon became its leading supplier of advanced weaponry and an important trading partner.

Although concerned to counter American hegemony, Beijing's attitude toward the United States was not overtly hostile. It was the PRC that first approached America with the idea of a strategic partnership. U.S. President Clinton appeared to warm to the idea during his second term in office, perhaps in the belief that the best way to modify the PRC's belligerent behavior was to draw it into a condominium with the United States that would ensure global, or at least regional, stability.

Moves by regional neighbors that involved deterring the PRC from aggression included Indonesia's holding in 1996 its largest air, land, and sea military maneuvers in four years. Symbolically, they were held in Indonesia's Natuna islands, which had recently appeared on Chinese maps as part of the PRC's exclusive economic zone. Jakarta invited foreign military attaches to attend; China's attache declined to do so. Indonesia also ordered F-16 fighter planes from the United States. Beijing did not miss the significance of these moves: A spokesperson complained that Indonesia's attitude could "complicate" the situation in the South China Sea. Other Southeast Asian states took similar actions. Perhaps the most surprising development was the December 1995 signing of a mutual defense treaty between Australia and Indonesia, two countries whose relationship has historically been characterized by considerable friction. Some of these efforts to stem perceived Chinese expansion were undone by the Asian currency crisis that severely impacted several of the countries, and by internal turmoil in Indonesia.

Japan's reaction was more worrisome to Chinese leaders, who either did not see, or did not wish to acknowledge, the reasons for Tokyo's anxieties. In 1995–1996, in response to the United States granting a visa to Taiwan's president Lee Teng-hui so that he could receive an award from his alma mater, the PLA began nearly a year of war games and missile tests in the Taiwan Strait. Taiwan was a Japanese colony for 50 years, until the end of World War II, and Japanese companies have extensive investments on the island. Should China take over Taiwan, PLA naval patrols, already a concern for Japan, would become more intrusive. Tokyo approached Washington for an upgrade in the security relationship between the two, which included an agreement to cooperate in "dealing with situations in the areas surrounding Japan which would have an important influence in the peace and security of Japan." Beijing demanded Tokyo's assurances that the phrase "areas around Japan" did not include Taiwan; Japanese diplomats replied that, since the definition of areas surrounding Japan was situational rather than geographic, they could not give such assurances.

This, plus Japan's decision to join American efforts to establish a Theater Missile Defense system, led Beijing to reassess its opinion of the U.S.-Japan alliance. Heretofore, it had seen Washington as mitigating Japanese impulses toward a revival of militarism by including Japan under U.S. military protection. After these developments, however, it saw Washington as fostering the revival of militarism by encouraging Japan to become a partner in its plans to dominate the world.

Perceptions of the United States as determined to bring the world under its control were reinforced when an American-led NATO coalition began bombing the Yugoslav Republic in an effort to stop it from slaughtering an ethnic minority there (see p. 316). When one of the bombs landed on the Chinese embassy in Belgrade, Beijing refused to believe Washington's explanation that it was accidental. Angry mobs trashed the American embassy in Beijing, and the Chinese government publicly repudiated the idea of a strategic partnership between the two countries.

Only weeks after the signing of the agreement strengthening the U.S.-Japan alliance, Jiang Zemin convened the leaders of Russia and three Central Asian states in Shanghai to form a countervailing organization. Initially called the "Shanghai Five," the group was re-named the Shanghai Cooperative Organization when another Central Asian member joined. Among the issues discussed were border demarcations, border security and "a long-term convergence of strategic aims" that was generally interpreted as aimed at resisting undue U.S. influence. China regularly referred to Russia as its strategic partner. In July 2002, the two countries concluded a treaty—the first since the 1950 agreement between Mao Zedong and Joseph Stalin. Other potential allies were not neglected: There were proposals that the Sino-Russian partnership be expanded to include Iran and even India. Beijing argued for ending UN sanctions against Iraq, and helped to upgrade Baghdad's air defenses.

Post-9/11 Developments   Events set in motion by Muslim fundamentalists' attacks on the World Trade Center and Pentagon on September 11, 2001, led to yet another realign-ment of power, but in a direction that the PRC perceived as hostile to its interests. Beijing took several steps to assist Washington in its efforts to deal with terrorists. It helped to draft and pass resolutions in the UN Security Council and General Assembly that con-demned the attack, supported in principle attacks on the Taliban government of Afghani-stan, and promised to share intelligence with Washington that might lead to the appre-hension of terrorists.

The results of the September 11 attacks did not, however, lead to a united front against terrorism, but rather to a deepening of Chinese concerns that the United States was using the war against terrorism to expand its hegemonistic designs. After several members of the Shanghai Cooperative Organization offered support, including basing rights, to Washington, Beijing became concerned that the U.S. presence in Central Asia might be-come permanent, to the detriment of Chinese interests there. Moreover, Russian president Vladimir Putin also moved closer to the United States; in 2002, Washington and Moscow signed an arms reduction treaty and issued a joint declaration on the establishment of a new strategic relationship between them. Against Chinese wishes, Putin acquiesced in the abrogation of the Anti-Ballistic Missile Treaty, and Russia became a participant, though not an actual member of NATO—an alliance which was originally established to contain the Soviet Union. Chinese analysts assessed this as signifying "the complete assimilation of Russia into the American orbit," thereby upsetting the balance between the hegemonis-tic and antihegemonistic forces in the world.[26] Beijing saw U.S. plans to replace Saddam Hussein as an attempt to impose its notions of liberal democracy on yet another area of the world, as well as to take over Iraq's oil fields in order to benefit America.

China was likewise unhappy when President Bush's vow to pursue terrorists and whatever countries harbored them led to American military advisers being sent to several Southeast Asian states. More anxiety was generated by the mending of relations between India and the United States. These had been strained since India carried out nuclear tests in 1998. India's defense minister made clear at the time that fear of China had been behind his country's decision to develop a nuclear arsenal. Consonant with its policy of opposing proliferation, Washington initially responded by levying sanctions on India. By early 2002, however, Washington and New Delhi had agreed to conduct joint military training and India's president had made a speech to the U.S. Congress declaring that the two states were natural allies.

Sensing that post-September 11 trends had worsened its position, Beijing made efforts to shore up its diplomacy. China was an active participant at the ASEM (Asia-Europe) meeting held in Copenhagen in 2002, described as "a forum to balance U.S. power . . . these two parts of the world need each other not only to face up to an eventual 'pax Americana,' but also for a host of other reasons."[27] At the 2002 meeting of the ASEAN Regional Forum, the PRC tabled a security plan that members interpreted as a challenge to the United States. The plan's emphasis on enhancing trust through dialogue and promoting security through cooperation on the basis of the Five Principles of the People and "other universally recognized norms governing international relations" played on misgivings in several nations about American policy on preemptive strikes on territories believed to harbor terrorists.

In addition, Beijing continued to use the country's growing economic power to further its diplomatic ends. For example, the China National Offshore Oil Corporation signed a multi-billion dollar deal with Indonesia's state-owned oil and gas company to develop a large natural gas field, and bought a stake in a huge oil field in Kazakhstan. China also agreed to form a free trade framework with ASEAN in which the contracting parties pledged to begin cutting tariffs on certain products. It sought as well to capitalize on many states' reluctance to support America's desire to replace Saddam Hussein, in order to weaken U.S. influence in those states. Beijing continued to purchase arms from Russia, and conducted military maneuvers with several Central Asian states.

Conclusions

In terms of achieving major foreign policy goals, China's record contains several successes and a few failures. The PRC's territory has remained free from attacks, and the humiliating concessions made to foreign powers within China in the past have been abolished. China's international prestige has been restored. The country has attained membership in the United Nations, holds a permanent seat on the UN Security Council, and participates in a number of international financial organizations such as the International Monetary Fund, the World Bank, and the World Trade Organization. The PRC is the fifth largest trading nation in the world, up from thirty-first in 1980.

All but a handful of nations recognize the communist party as the legitimate government of China, and even those few count the PRC as an important force in international politics. China no longer aspires to a position of leadership over the third world, and indeed it occupies such an anomalous position in the third world that some have argued that it should not even be classified therein. Still, the PRC's statements on behalf of developing states are treated with respect. From a position of abject weakness during the century preceding 1949, China has come to be regarded as one of the more important powers in the world. Particularly when considered in light of the PRC's until recently modest military capabilities, this is a signal achievement.

As for recuperation of the territories China claims, the record is mixed. The PRC has achieved border settlements with several countries, including Burma and Nepal. It has established de facto control over substantial segments of its disputed borders with India and Vietnam. There has been a peaceful resolution of contending claims on what was formerly called the Sino-Soviet border, although it confirmed the loss of a substantial amount of territory that Chinese ideologues would have found unacceptable less than two decades ago. The PRC has regained Tibet, Hong Kong, and Macao.

However, there is an important distinction to be made between formal inclusion of a territory within the borders of the PRC and true absorption therein. More than 40 years after Chinese troops marched into Lhasa, the Tibetan independence movement remains strong—in fact, in the sense of having created a worldwide support network, the movement is much stronger than it was in 1950. The same can be said of Xinjiang.

In the Hong Kong Special Autonomous Region (SAR), there has been an accumulation of grievances such as a gradual erosion of civil liberties and a marked deterioration of the area's economy since it came under PRC sovereignty in 1997. This economic downturn was exacerbated when the Chinese government's misguided attempts to suppress information on a highly contagious form of pneumonia—SARS, or Severe Acute Respiratory Syndrome—led to an outbreak in Hong Kong that caused numerous deaths and a near cessation of the trade shows and tourist travel that are so important to the financial well-being of the SAR. Beijing's pessure on the SAR government to pass a controversial anti-subversion law may indicate its concern that the currently quiescent citizenry of Hong Kong may not remain so docile in the future.

Taiwan remains steadfastly independent, and has firm control of the offshore islands of Quemoy and Matsu. The ROC maintains a technologically sophisticated and well-trained military force that would make conquest difficult, as well as necessitate the killing of many of the same Taiwan Chinese brethren the PRC claims to have such solicitude for. Many schemes for peaceful unification, such as a "one country, two systems" idea, have been proposed but found unacceptable. Residents of the Republic of China on Taiwan are not attracted by the status of special administrative region pointing out that provisions for the self-government of SARS are ultimately dependent on Beijing's voluntary acquiescence. Moreover, the island's residents enjoy one of the highest living standards in Asia, including an income level many times that of the mainland. They also have a functioning democratic political system and a free press. Since the economies of the two countries are becoming more closely integrated, there are hopes that political integration will follow along, though there is scant evidence of this thusfar. As economic integration increases, so also has the Taiwanization (*bentuhua*) of the island, which emphasizes its cultural, linguistic, and ethnic differences from China. Hence, absorbing Taiwan into the PRC would be exceedingly difficult.

Mongolia seems unlikely to be recovered either. Residents of what was then called the Mongolian People's Republic reacted enthusiastically to the changes in their Soviet neighbor, holding free elections and choosing a new government. They are unlikely to be attracted by a China that has become more internally repressive since the 1989 demonstrations. Influence might even be said to have gone in the opposite direction: China's Mongol minority has been attracted by the liberalizing influences across the border in the renamed republic of Mongolia. In addition, the freer intellectual climate in Mongolia has included a revival of the area's traditional lamaist Buddhist religion. This is the faith of most of Tibet's population as well, and there has been increased interest in the study of the Tibetan language in Mongolia. Mongols' sympathies are likely to lie with the Tibetans in their ongoing conflict with Chinese rule. Many Mongols continue to be concerned that their country may become an economic colony of China.

In the course of the past four decades, Chinese foreign policy has moved from a position of dependence on the Soviet Union to one in which the PRC formulates policy independently, in accordance with its perception of Chinese needs and capabilities. The PRC's foreign policymakers have shown considerable skill and flexibility in bringing about relatively smooth shifts in strategy in response to perceived changes in the international climate. In contrast to rhetoric that has often been militant and prorevolutionary, China's international actions have generally been rather circumspect, indicating careful forethought and shrewd calculation of both adversary capabilities and foreign public opinion. Exceptions to this are associated with the Cultural Revolution period and with certain aspects of the 1978–1979 dispute with Vietnam.

It may be asked whether China will regress to militance and irrational behavior in the international sphere. In theory, of course, anything is possible. However, analysts generally agree that the web of interactions linking China with the outside world has now enmeshed the PRC in the international community to such a degree that only the most catastrophic and unlikely circumstances would allow the country's return to isolationism. Interdependence and practical considerations will almost certainly characterize the PRC's relations with the other nations of the world.

While the PRC's foreign policy has been described as pragmatic, one must bear in mind that perceptions of what is pragmatic are shaped by ideological and cultural factors. The Chinese have been careful to justify their foreign policies in terms of both Marxist-Leninist and traditional Chinese principles. There is no necessary contradiction between these factors. The principles of international power politics may be expressed with clarity through the use of Marxist dialectics as well as through traditional Chinese principles such as using barbarians to control barbarians and avoiding encirclement by one's opponents.

In sum, Chinese foreign policy since 1949 is characterized by both continuity and change. Strategy has varied according to China's perception of international forces, and in order to achieve the fixed goals that have lent continuity to the PRC's foreign policy. During the half-century since the founding of the PRC, many of these goals have been attained. In the process, foreign policy has evolved in a manner in which the PRC's international responses can be fairly described as pragmatism with Chinese characteristics.

Notes

1. See, for example, the discussion of Chinese foreign relations in John Fairbank, Edwin Reischauer, and Albert Craig, *East Asia* (Boston: Houghton Mifflin, 1973), pp. 195–204.

2. This argument follows that of Benjamin I. Schwartz, "The Chinese Perception of World Order, Past and Present," in John K. Fairbank, ed., *The Chinese World Order: Traditional China's Foreign Relations* (Cambridge, Mass.: Harvard University Press, 1968), pp. 276–288.

3. I am indebted to Dr. James D. Seymour, East Asian Institute, Columbia University, for this observation.

4. Jean-Luc Domenach, "Ideological Reform," in Gerald Segal, ed., *Chinese Politics and Foreign Policy Reform* (London: Royal Institute for International Affairs, 1990), p. 19.

5. David Shambaugh, *Beautiful Imperialist: China Perceives America, 1972–1990* (Princeton, N.J.: Princeton University Press, 1991), p. 301.

6. Report of the Select Committee on U.S. National Security and Military/Commercial Concerns with the People's Republic of China (Washington, D.C.: U.S. Government Printing Office, 1999), passim.

7. Nicholas Eftimiades, *Chinese Intelligence Operations* (Annapolis, Md.: Naval Institute Press, 1994), pp. 113–114.

8. A. Doak Barnett, *The Making of Foreign Policy in China: Structure and Process* (Boulder, Colo.: Westview Press, 1985), p. 25.

9. Shaun Breslin, "The Foreign Policy Bureaucracy," in Segal, *op. cit.*, pp. 117–119.

10. "Ji Pengfei Talks on PRC Future Foreign Policy: Part 4," *Chung Pao* (Hong Kong), March 13, 1980, in *FBIS–CHI*, March 18, 1980; p. U/6.

11. Edwin W. Martin, *Divided Counsel: The Anglo-American Response to Communist Victory in China* (Lexington, Ky.: University of Kentucky Press, 1986), pp. 39–54. Martin, a U.S. Foreign Service officer in China at the time, bases his analysis on American and British diplomatic archival material.

12. See Allen S. Whiting, *China Crosses the Yalu* (New York: Macmillan, 1960).

13. Chen Jian, *China's Road to the Korean War: The Making of the Sino-American Confrontation* (New York: Columbia University Press 1994), passim.

14. Mao Zedong, "On the People's Democratic Dictatorship," in *Selected Works of Mao Tse-tung*, vol. 4 (Beijing: Foreign Languages Press, 1961), p. 415.

15. Although a few hard-liners within the Chinese leadership seem to have reasoned that this was a good time to push imperialist powers still harder.

16. Quoted in *Peking Review*, September 6, 1963, p. 10.

17. See, for example, Neville Maxwell, *India's China War* (New York: Pantheon, 1971), passim.

18. See, for example, the analyses contained in ibid., and Allen S. Whiting, *The Chinese Calculus of Deterrence: India and Indochina* (Ann Arbor, Mich.: University of Michigan Press, 1975).

19. Quoted in Bruce Larkin, *China and Africa 1949–1970* (Berkeley: University of California Press, 1971), p. 215.

20. The full text of Castro's statement may be found in *Peking Review*, February 25, 1966, pp. 14–22.

21. This argument is made by Roger Glenn Brown, "Chinese Politics and American Policy," *Foreign Policy*, Summer 1976, pp. 3–23.

22. "Joint Communiqué," February 27, 1972, in *Peking Review*, March 3, 1972, p. 5.

23. For a detailed analysis of the dichotomy between Chinese words and deeds, see John F. Copper, "The PRC and the Third World: Rhetoric Versus Reality," *Issues and Studies* (Taipei), March 1986, pp. 107–125.

24. *Peking Review*, November 4, 1977, p. 11.

25. "China, US Issue Joint Communiqué," *Beijing Review*, August 23, 1982, pp. 14–15.

26. Ching Cheong, "U.S.-Russia Summit Worries China," *Straits Times*, May 31, 2002; Zhou Shuchun, "September 11th Accelerates Change of World Order, Intensifies U.S. Unilateralism and Russian Tilt to West," *Liaowang*, no. 23, June 3, 2002, pp. 10–13.

27. Eric Teo, "ASEM: A Forum to Balance U.S. Power," *Straits Times*, October 2, 2002.

Suggestions for Further Reading

James Mann, *About Face: America's Curious Relationship with China from Nixon to Clinton* (New York: Knopf, 1999).

Denny Roy, *China's Foreign Relations* (Basingstoke, U.K.: Macmillan, 1998).

Eberhard Sandschneider, "China's Diplomatic Relations with the States of Europe," *China Quarterly*, March 2002, pp. 33–44.

Alfred D. Wilhelm, Jr., *The Chinese at the Negotiating Table* (Washington, D.C.: National Defense University Press, 1994).

Quansheng Zhao, "China and Major Power Relations in East Asia," *Journal of Contemporary China*, November 2001, pp. 663–682.

CHAPTER

15 Conclusions

Any assessment of how successful the Chinese communist political system has been presents problems of what weight to assign to the various criteria of success. For example, those who place high value on the criterion of a government's ability to keep the peace, or that of satisfying its citizens' minimal needs for existence, will make a judgment very different from those whose greatest concerns are issues like human rights and freedom of the press. Another problem is how to assess the government's spectacular failures, primarily the Great Leap Forward and the Cultural Revolution. Should one consider them as aberrations of the system and therefore discount their disastrous effects, or as evidence of fatal structural flaws in the system itself? In addition, every political system has both its backers and detractors, and one would normally want to consult the opinions of Chinese themselves as to how successful they feel the system has been. Carefully used, opinion polls can tell us much about changes in citizens' views of their government over time. Only in the last decade, however, has the PRC begun to use opinion polling, and there are limitations on what may be concluded from local samples.[1] Additionally, researchers have noticed that respondents have a tendency to give what they perceive to be "correct" answers based on their understanding of official policy.[2] Moreover, no data are available for the past. Therefore, both we and, for that matter, the country's leaders, are deprived of the guidance they might provide.

Party and government deserve credit[3] for feeding and clothing nearly a quarter of the world's population on a mere 7 percent of the world's arable land. The average Chinese has a lifespan of more than 70 years, putting the PRC nearly at the level of more developed nations and well ahead of many developing areas. Though one can quibble with the claimed literacy rate of over 90 percent, there is no doubt that a markedly higher proportion of China's population is literate than prior to 1949. Thousands of miles of railroads and highways have been built, and the country's industrial base has been greatly expanded. The PRC has developed a nuclear deterrence capability, and sells a variety of military equipment to the third world. It is regarded as a major actor in international affairs. China is a respected member of the United Nations and a permanent member of the UN Security Council.

All of these are important achievements. On the other hand, in the 1950s, economic conditions in China, Japan, Korea, Taiwan, and Southeast Asia were quite similar. Since then, living standards in many of these neighboring countries have risen much faster than in the PRC. Moreover, compared to citizens in most of these states, the average Chinese is far more constrained in what he or she can say and to whom. Freedom to associate with whom one wishes, to state one's grievances, and to practice one's religion are also restrained in various ways, constitutional guarantees notwithstanding. So is the right to a fair and public trial.

The Chinese communist party came to power with clearly articulated goals of equality and prosperity for the society it wished to create. For a time, the party enjoyed relatively solid support from the people in whose best interests it claimed to rule. Since the best path to the goals the CCP espoused was not at all clear, there was a good deal of social and economic experimentation. Loyalty to the party, to Marxism-Leninism, and to Mao Zedong's interpretation of Marxism-Leninism was not merely encouraged but demanded. There was a tendency for all of these to be subsumed into a demand for absolute and unswerving loyalty to the person of the supreme leader himself. While Mao's desire for self-aggrandizement was certainly a factor in the growth of this personality cult, it was also a way to smooth over the strains of modernization and industrialization. There appeared to be a genuine belief that, however difficult the problems of the present, the emergence of a classless society was inevitable: The communist cause would triumph in the end. Meanwhile, peasants and workers were regarded as the most worthy classes. And loyalty, both to the person of Mao and to communist doctrine, was rigidly enforced.

Society became highly politicized. In no society, and particularly not in one as large as China, can this be done equally and uniformly. Some individuals are more receptive to political messages than others, and urban areas are more readily accessible to the bearers of political messages than are remote rural areas. But the party and its bureaucrats, or cadres, made every effort to inculcate its doctrines both widely and deeply across the country.

The cult of personality that developed around Mao, and the style of rule that characterized his leadership, seem to fit the eminent German sociologist Max Weber's description of charismatic rule. According to Weber, the norms and practices developed under this leader, who generally eschews past practices and makes his own rules, will gradually become accepted ways of behavior and decision-making. Hence, the stage of government after charismatic leadership is called the transition to institutionalization. In Weber's paradigm, bureaucracies will grow up to enforce these norms and staff the institutions. The third and final stage described by Weber is that of rational rule legitimization, a process he called the "routinization of charisma." The result is a modern, bureaucratic state.[4]

Most social scientists assumed that China would follow the path outlined by Weber in its quest for modernity. However, Mao strenuously resisted routinization and the bureaucratization of his revolution. The mere mention of bureaucracy aroused painful memories of the mandarinate of Mao's childhood. He was concerned to keep society from settling into comfortable rules and routines, which Mao saw as undermining the progress toward creating the type of society that had been his life's work. The best way to do this was, in Mao's own words, to have the country in a state of permanent revolution until the advent of the classless society. Periodic economic and social upheavals, most notably the Great Leap Forward and the Great Proletarian Cultural Revolution, were designed to further this end.

Unfortunately, the widespread economic and social disruptions they caused also led many Chinese to have doubts about the party's ability to govern them and to improve living standards. A contemporary German social scientist, Jürgen Domes, noted that not a routinization of charisma but what he termed a "transitional crisis system" had evolved. In such a system, conflict may not be expressed openly. The signs that a society is experiencing this condition include the appearance of differences in terminology among leaders, removals of leaders from office, expulsions from the party and, occasionally, an open rift within the party.[5]

The ascent of Deng Xiaoping to de facto leadership was characterized by a pragmatic reworking of communism. "Socialism with Chinese characteristics" was defined as including a definite commitment to modernization and to the raising of living standards, as well as an acceptance of the need for laws and regulations to govern conduct. The PRC seemed well on its way to Weber's stage of rational rule legitimization. Particularly in the first few years after Deng's plans began to be implemented, there were marked improvements in living standards.

However, these were accompanied by rapidly increasing differences between rich and poor, in terms of both individual persons and geographic regions. If Deng's reforms made some people and areas wealthier, they made others relatively poorer, comparatively speaking. In the words of one Chinese dissident,

> . . . were one to single out one factor conditioning workers' support for communist regimes, it would be an expectation of protection from insecurity, inequality, and uncertainty by a strong welfare state. Deng Xiaoping gambled on being able to compensate Chinese workers with greater prosperity in exchange for any erosion of security, equality, and certainty . . . the gamble failed.[6]

Escalating inflation, arguments within the leadership elite, and uncertainty about the future of reform undermined stability and further weakened many people's faith in their government and leadership. These phenomena indicate that China continued to closely conform to Domes' definition of a transitional crisis system.

Abolition of the communes and decentralization of economic decision-making, although good for raising production, led to deterioration of the capabilities of central-level institutions. Generally, no compensatory mechanisms emerged to fulfill important services they had provided. The system appeared to be becoming less rather than more capable of coping with problems. In a number of areas, political development had been replaced by political decay. There was a resurgence of traditional forms and patterns of authority. This retraditionalization included the revival of the power of clans, religious figures, and secret societies as well as that of village leaders who were chosen by consensus within the village rather than by the party. The position of women, whom Mao poetically described as "holding up half the sky," deteriorated in a number of ways. When economic restructuring occurred, for example, females were disproportionately likely to be among the first workers to be laid off. Local and regional protectionist tendencies in the economy and even in the court system caused problems for the further development of a nationwide market directed by the party from the capital city. Decentralization and market reforms also strengthened centrifugal forces in ethnic minority areas.

Deng's economic reforms eroded the party's clientist networks in the workplace.[7] Individuals, groups, and regions became increasingly assertive vis-à-vis party and central government. Sometimes, as in the cases of tax assessment and mandatory retirement ages, they engaged in extensive bargaining, thereby causing significant modifications in the policies.[8] Occasionally, meaningful proportions of the citizenry were able to passively resist or completely ignore the central government's directives. The one-child policy is the best-known example of a widely scorned directive. Party and government's inability to extract compliance with its directives is especially striking in the case of the hundred million people who comprise the floating population.

Deng several times attempted to determine the succession to the highest offices of government and party, but those he chose proved unable to maintain their positions. He forced a number of other high-ranking people to retire but many of them, like Deng himself, were able to exercise considerable influence without benefit of formal position. In effect, power became divorced from responsibility. The advent of classless society was no longer seen as inevitable. In fact, it seemed less attainable than ever and, except for a minority of individuals, so did the prospect of the good life. As the Deng era progressed, large numbers of people became convinced that, however much the new system differed from Mao's, it was no better in its ability to produce equality and prosperity.

By the mid-1980s, widespread disaffection with the status quo began to permeate various sectors of society: Peasants, workers, professionals, students, and military men expressed their grievances in disparate and, at least initially, disconnected ways. Many, particularly the students and intellectuals, demanded what amounted to a broadening of political participation. The guardianship of the elite no longer seemed adequate. This situation has many similarities to that described by Harvard social scientist Samuel Huntington as *praetorian society*: a politicized society in which not just the military but other social forces, such as students, bureaucrats, and the clergy participate as well. A praetorian society lacks effective political institutions. Power comes in many forms and is fragmented. No agreement exists among its groups on the legitimate and authoritative methods for resolving conflict.[9]

Huntington contrasts praetorian society with institutionalized polities, in which most political actors agree on the procedures to be used for the resolution of political disputes, such as the allocation of offices and the determination of policies. For example, offices may be assigned through election, heredity, examination, drawing lots, or some combination thereof. Policy issues may be resolved by hierarchical processes, petitions, hearings, appeals, majority votes, or consensus. The crucial factor is the existence of general agreement on what those means are, and that the groups participating in the political process recognize their obligation to employ those means.

In a praetorian society, each group employs the means that reflect its peculiar nature and capabilities: the wealthy bribe; students riot; mobs demonstrate; and the military uses force. In the absence of accepted procedures, all these forms of direct action are found in the political scene. *Radical* praetorianism, Huntington continues, has its social roots in the gap between the city and the countryside. The city replaces rural areas as the main focus of political action and becomes the continuing source of political instability. The stronger influence of the city in the political life of the society leads to greater political turbulence. In a radical praetorian society, the city cannot furnish the basis for governmental stability. The extent of the instability depends on the extent to which the government is able and willing to use the countryside to contain and pacify the city. If the government can build a bridge to the countryside—if it can mobilize support from the rural areas—it can contain and ride out the instabilities of the city.

This characterization seemed to accurately describe the PRC at the time of the 1989 demonstrations. Rather than being mobilized in *support* of the government, however, the rural areas simply gave the leadership the margin of *passivity* it needed to ride out the crisis caused by widespread demonstrations. The rural areas are, however, not without their own problems, and cannot automatically be counted upon to remain passive in the future. It should be remembered that Deng Xiaoping's educational reforms concentrated almost wholly on the large cities, allowing the countryside to go its own way so long as it produced the requisite amount of food to nourish the population and support the government's modernization programs. The number of rural semi-literates and school dropouts has increased. And coastal cities rather than the rural hinterland garnered most of the benefits of Deng's reform programs. In terms of modernization and industrialization, the party has in effect turned its back on the peasant class that brought it to power. As a result of efforts to restructure and rationalize the economic structure, workers have fared little better. The alliance between China's new entrepreneurs and the CCP symbolized by Jiang Zemin's Three Representatives is yet another indication that the twenty-first-century CCP no longer accords the workers and the peasants the same degree of respect as the party's founders. Although the country's leaders would disagree, many Chinese feel that the party has betrayed the interests of those who brought it to power.

Nonetheless, there have been no large-scale demonstrations in the decade and a half since the Tiananmen incident, and the PRC no longer resembles a praetorian society. Jiang Zemin's assumption of office as a result of the Tiananmen upheaval rather than through regularly established selection processes is an example of the transitional crisis system. Yet the smooth transfer of power after Deng Xiaoping's death and the transition from Jiang to Hu Jintao in 2002–2003 may indicate that routinization is occuring—despite evidence of considerable maneuvering beforehand and Jiang's holding onto military power and packing the Standing Committee of the Politburo with his supporters. An orderly transition to the "fourth generation" of post-1949 leaders does not, however, mean that there is consensus on how China should and will evolve in the future. In a country as large and diverse as the PRC, with changes occuring at all levels of society, it is difficult to distinguish linear movements from cyclical movements and trends from countertrends. One can find evidence for whatever conclusion one's hopes or biases conduce toward. Among the commonly heard scenarios are

- Party and government will reimpose Beijing's control over society.
- The present government will be overthrown and replaced by a popularly chosen reformist regime.
- There will be an evolution toward a more liberal regime that is market-oriented and tolerant of a variety of political views.
- Party and government will remain in a kind of paralysis as power continues to devolve to provinces and regions with a range of variations within each.

Historical prediction is always difficult and fraught with errors. A mere two decades ago, anyone who predicted the dismantling of the Berlin Wall and the fall of the Soviet empire would have been laughed at as a misguided idealist. China, as the PRC government frequently points out, is very different from Europe, and one cannot assume that it will replicate developments there. This said, certain developments seem more likely than others.

The first scenario closely resembles the neo-authoritarian paradigm that Chinese media began to publicize about 1988. With party and state firmly in control again, mechanisms will be established to substitute for those functions that were lost when Deng's reforms were introduced. System decay, to use Huntington's terminology, will be halted. Economic development, adherents of neo-authoritarianism argue, needs a firm guiding hand. Market reforms must be introduced gradually and be closely monitored by the central government to correct for such unwanted side effects as inflation and maldistribution. This guided economic development, and ultimately the country as a whole, could only be hurt by disruptive demonstrations and calls for pluralistic decision-making. Therefore, demands for political liberalization must be firmly rejected.

There is some evidence that this has been happening. Although China after the Tiananmen incident had a ruling elite that appeared unstable, politically backward-looking, and internationally isolated, Jiang Zemin was able to maintain the leadership position for which Deng Xiaoping had chosen him. The PRC's economy grew rapidly, and the country quickly reintegrated into the global system. Analysts who espouse this scenario find other indications that party and government have been relegitimated including

- The routinization of leadership succession
- An increase in meritocratic criteria for social mobility
- Institutions that have become more specialized in their functions, and are therefore able to perform their responsibilities more effectively
- The growth of institutions for political participation—for example, village elections—that have strengthened the party's appeal to the public[10]

Other scholars see this as overstating what has happened. For example, Jiang Zemin's ability to retain military power and arrange for the appointment to the Politburo Standing Committee of persons known more for their loyalty to him than their competence indicates that there are limitations on the routinization of leadership succession and the application of meritocratic criteria for promotion. These aberrations are not, they point out, isolated phenomena. And increased functional specialization of bureaucracies does not necessarily mean better government, as shown by the miscarriages of justice that occurred during the "Strike Hard" campaign. Finally, while village elections have often improved governance in rural areas, the party will not tolerate any actions there that contravene its policies. It has invalidated the election results of candidates that it believes might challenge party authority and resorted to a variety of methods to impose or reimpose its control.[11] Moreover, repression has not actually been mitigated; it has simply become more subtle—able to operate below the scrutiny of international monitoring agencies or, in the manner of the anaconda in the chandelier metaphor described in Chapter 12, induce individuals to exercise self-censorship.[12]

The second scenario, that the present government will be overthrown, is predicted by those who believe that an accumulation of problems is causing pressures that will lead to an explosion of anger against the current form of government. At least one analyst sees China's entry into the World Trade Organization as the catalyst for this explosion: Farmers who cannot compete with more efficient agricultural systems elsewhere will rise up against the authorities; displaced workers will join the protests. Runs on the fragile banking system will provide the final blow. Democracy will follow.[13]

Unfortunately for proponents of this scenario, however unpopular the party and state leaders may be, they have effectively prevented the articulation of alternative formulations of government, at least in any organized and aggregated form. In other words, it is conceivable that the government will be overthrown, but more difficult to imagine that the overthrowers will seek to replace the basic social structure of society. This is not to say that a group with a more democratic agenda could not seize power, as it did in parts of Eastern Europe and the former Soviet Union. But many of these leaders are having trouble holding their countries together and maintaining a degree of pluralistic decision-making in the midst of economic chaos and tendencies toward political anarchy. These problems would be compounded for a similar group trying to seize control in the PRC, which has many more people and is even poorer.

A Chinese economist describes the situation in today's PRC as volcanic stability. Underground fires, deriving from labor unrest, displaced peasants, and a rapidly deteriorating environment, are smoldering dangerously just below the surface. They could erupt and rage out of control at any time. While nearly all Chinese can feel the heat, none are more sensitive to it than the elite, whose privileged positions are threatened by these forces. They believe that maintaining the status quo through repression is the best way to cope. Eventually, however, the leadership's "fire-brigade" techniques will prove inadequate, and the CCP's rule will be consumed in the resultant conflagration. The proponent of this theory does not believe that democracy will be the necessary outcome of the cleansing by fire.[14]

One analyst has likened China's dilemma today with that existing in the late Qing dynasty. There is a crisis of meaning that is very similar to that of a century ago, except that now it is Marxist orthodoxy that has collapsed rather than Confucian orthodoxy. This threatens the social order and causes economic, political, and cultural problems that are exacerbated by contact with the West. And, as in the past, this sense of crisis and urgency has led to "quick-fix" proposals for radical and extreme change. These reflect only limited consideration of practical realities, and have very little hope of success.[15]

The third scenario, that of an evolution toward a more liberal regime, has great appeal. The economic pluralism that market reforms have encouraged will generate pressures for political pluralism and eventually lead to liberal democracy. Analysts who are hopeful that the process of evolution is under way point to signs that a *civil society* has been developing in the PRC. As noted in Chapter 1, this term refers to the sphere of independent activity outside the structure of the state and party. Marxist-Leninist systems aspire to total control of a society, aiming at comprehensive domination of all aspects of economic, political, and social life. Groups such as labor unions, youth organizations, and medical associations are to be controlled by party and state and subsumed under them. In a civil society, by contrast, these and other groups have their own agendas, which may differ from those of party and state and exert influence on parties and governments to implement their proposals.

The past two decades have indeed seen a proliferation of new forms of association. However, state and society are intermingled within them, thus blurring the distinction between civil and not-civil society. Some organizations are "caged"—very dependent on the state, with little or no autonomy. Others are partially state-controlled, with some autonomy. Still others—which are illegal—possess genuine autonomy, but their members must be concerned with arrest and incarceration. It has also been pointed out that the civil society paradigm focuses too heavily on formal associations, neglecting the networks of personal connections between state officials and members of society. These informal relationships further blur the public-private distinction that is central to the civil society paradigm.[16]

State institutions responded to the new socioeconomic environment resulting from the reforms by refusing to surrender control of the old mass organizations while trying to create or co-opt new social organizations. These organizations may be described as corporatist with a Chinese form, and are more reminiscent of Walder's communist neo-traditionalist paradigm than that of civil society. However, the corporatist groups appear to be a relatively small section of the extant organizations, and official control over them could gradually decline. Nonetheless, in the near term, the evolutionary process is likely to be accompanied by a good deal of economic and social disruption, which will cause great discomfort to the ruling elite, who will in turn be strongly tempted to crush it.

It has been pointed out that an evolution toward civil society will not necessarily lead to liberal democracy: Even the illegal autonomous groups are divided on the issue of political reform. Some do indeed want liberal democracy. But some want to return to Maoist politics. There are a variety of positions in between, and little discourse among the holders of these positions. At the other extreme, ethnic separatists advocate the dissolution of the current political system; they have not advocated democracy even for their areas.

Certain key counterelites who could potentially challenge the current communist leadership, most notably the new private entrepreneurial class, show little interest in meaningful political change. Their interests are closely tied to the stability of the process of market reform under the auspices of the current authoritarian government. Some dissidents have argued that the two groups—political and economic elites—have a common intrest in exploiting and repressing the peasants and workers. Hence, market forces are conducing toward an incorporation of society rather than a liberation of society.[17] In this view, it is not simply party/government repression that keeps economic freedom from generating political freedom, it is that the type of capitalism that has developed in the PRC does not lend itself to generating demands for freedom. China has developed relation-based capitalism, in which the interests of entrepreneurs are protected not by institutions but by special relationships with those in power. Hence entrepreneurs not only do not demand autonomy but actually fear it, since their persons and their business activities will no longer be protected.[18]

Those who espouse the fourth scenario, paralysis within the central government as power devolves to lower levels, see state capacity continuing to deteriorate. Leaders from Deng Xiaoping through Hu Jintao have strongly backed continued reform and announced ambitious plans to effect it, but party and government's ability to extract compliance with their directives continues to erode. Authoritarian power, already fragmented, will become more so. One advocate of this position describes the PRC as in a crisis of governance. He points out that an intrusive state is not necessarily an effective state. Among other factors,

- Grassroots party organizations have deteriorated markedly.
- Lawlessness, including the incidence of violent crime, is increasing.
- Public finances are in chaos.
- The central government has insufficient regulatory capacity.
- Issues of identity are not fully resolved, particularly in certain ethnic minority areas, thus posing a threat to territorial integrity.[19]

At the same time, local forces continue to gain strength and, as long as they do not directly challenge the central authorities, are rarely challenged by the central authorities. For the time being, at least, the clientelist networks that arose from the institutional framework established by the party function well enough to bind state and society together, albeit not in the manner originally envisaged by the CCP leadership.

Others disagree, arguing that state capacity is actually on the rebound. The central government's ability to appoint officials to posts and rotate them at will prevents the emergence of personal fiefdoms. Moreover, party and government have been working to make the organs of government more effective. Restructured fiscal and tax systems have given central authorities a stronger revenue base. Regulatory institutions have been improved, and efforts are being made to curb bureaucratic abuses of power.[20]

What this means for the future is problematic. For now, China more nearly represents the communist neo-traditional model than that of an emerging civil society. There is a fair degree of consensus on the problems that the PRC faces. The real question on which analysts differ is whether the reforms described here will be sufficient to ameliorate social tensions, or whether they will prove to be too little and too late. There is a great deal of inertia in the Chinese system, and party and government have shown themselves resilient in the face of challenges. The CCP has survived predictions of cataclysm and collapse before, and may yet muddle through again. Thusfar, its efforts to make minor adjustments to the system while portraying chaos as the alternative to its rule and itself as the standard-bearer of Chinese nationalism have proved persuasive to a sufficient number of people to keep the party in power. Should the leadership's strategy of maintaining one-party rule through market reform prove sustainable, the PRC will have evolved a new variant of development that can fairly be called modernity with Chinese characteristics.

Notes

1. Melanie Manion, "Survey Research in the Study of Contemporary China: Learning from Local Samples," *China Quarterly*, No. 139, September 1994, pp. 741–765, discusses the pitfalls of generalizing from available data.

2. Edward Friedman, "How to Understand Public Opinion in China," in Gang Lin, ed., *China's "Credibility Gap": Public Opinion and Instability in China* (Washington, D.C.: Woodrow Wilson Center Asia Program Special Report No. 104, August, 2002), p. 17.

3. Two readers of this manuscript have questioned exactly how much credit the government deserves for this. One maintains that it is the Chinese people who deserve credit for feeding themselves, noting that no one gives the warlords credit for feeding those under their jurisdiction during the warlord period, for example. Another suggests that Deng's government deserves credit for leaving the farmers alone more than Mao did, so that they can get to the business of raising food.

4. Max Weber, *The Theory of Social and Economic Organizations*, trans. A. M. Henderson and Talcott Parsons (New York: Oxford University Press, 1947), passim.

5. This theory is explained in detail in Jürgen Domes, *The Government and Politics of the PRC: A Time of Transition* (Boulder, Colo.: Westview Press, 1985), pp. 249–253.

6. Shaoguang Wang, "The Role of Chinese Workers," in Hao Jia, ed., *The Democracy Movement of 1989 and China's Future* (Washington, D.C.: The Washington Center for Chinese Studies, 1990), p. 99.

7. Andrew Walder, "A Reply to Womack," *China Quarterly*, no. 126, June 1991, p. 339.

8. See, for example, Melanie Manion, "Policy Implementation in the People's Republic of China: Authoritative Decisions Versus Individual Interests," *Journal of Asian Studies*, vol. 50, no. 2, May 1991, pp. 253–279, and June Teufel Dreyer, "The Demobilization of PLA

Servicemen and Their Reintegration into Civilian Life," in Dreyer, ed., *Chinese Defense and Foreign Policy* (New York: Paragon House, 1989), pp. 297–330.

9. Samuel P. Huntington, *Political Order in Changing Societies* (New Haven, Conn.: Yale University Press, 1968), passim.

10. Andrew Nathan, "Authoritarian Resilience," *Journal of Democracy*, vol. 14, no. 1 (January 2003), pp. 6–17.

11. Bruce Gilley, "The Limits of Authoritarian Resilience," *Journal of Democracy*, op. cit., pp. 18–26.

12. As noted in Chapter 12, the phrase was coined by Professor Perry Link of Princeton University.

13. Gordon Chang, *The Coming Collapse of China* (New York: Random House, 2001), passim.

14. Qinglian He, "A Volcanic Stability," *Journal of Democracy*, op. cit., pp. 66–72.

15. Geremie Barmé, "Travelling Heavy: The Intellectual Baggage of the Chinese Diaspora," *Problems of Communism,* January–April 1991, p. 96.

16. This analysis follows the arguments made by Gordon White, Jude Howell, and Shang Xiaoyuan, *In Search of Civil Society: Market Reform and Social Change in Contemporary China* (Oxford: Clarendon Press, 1996), pp. 213–216.

17. Dorothy Solinger, *China's Transition from Socialism: Statist Legacies and Market Reforms* (Armonk, N.Y.: M. E. Sharpe, 1993), p. 259.

18. Lawrence W. Kaplan, "Why Trade Won't Bring Democracy to China," *The New Republic*, July 9, 2001.

19. Shaoguang Wang, "The Problem of State Weakness," *Journal of Democracy*, op. cit., pp. 36–42.

20. Dali L. Yang, "State Capacity on the Rebound," *Journal of Democracy*, op. cit., pp. 43–49.

Suggestions for Further Reading

"China's Changing of the Guard," *Journal of Democracy,* vol. 14, no. 1, January 2003. Articles on Andrew Nathan, Bruce Gilley, Bruce Dickson, Shaoguang Wang, Dali Yang, An Chen, Qinglian He, Gongqin Xiao, Minxin Pei.

Yijiang Ding, *Chinese Democracy After Tiananmen* (New York: Columbia University Press, 2001).

Joseph Fewsmith, *China Since Tiananmen* (Cambridge, U.K.: Cambridge University Press, 2001).

John Fitzgerald, ed., *Rethinking China's Provinces* (London: Routledge, 2002).

Gordon White, Jude Howell, and Shang Xiaoyuan, *In Search of Civil Society* (Oxford: Clarendon Press, 1996).

Useful Websites

The following list is not meant to be definitive, but only to suggest likely avenues for further research. Many of the sites contain links to other sites of interest.

www.straitstimes.asia1.com.sg   Singapore's leading English-language newspaper.

www.cecc.gov   Congressionally established commission that sponsors hearings and roundtable discussions on major issues of human rights and related topics.

www.chinesenewsnet.com   Duowei Chinese news service.

www.chinadaily.net   China Daily (subscription only).

www.china-embassy.org   PRC embassy in Washington, D.C.

www.chinatoday.com   China Today.

www.cna.com.tw/eng   Central News Agency, Taiwan, ROC.

www.cnd.org   China News Digest.

www.cpirc.org.cn   China Population and Information Research Center.

www.fmprc.gov.cn   Ministry of Foreign Affairs, PRC.

www.hkstandard.com   Hong Kong Standard.

www.ncuscr.org   National Committee on U.S.-China Relations.

www.pbc.gov.cn/english   People's Bank of China.

www.peopledaily.com.cn/english/index.htm   People's Daily (Beijing), in English translation.

www.pku.edu.cn   Peking University.

www.scmp.com   South China Morning Post (Hong Kong).

www.sina.com/news   sina.com   Chinese news service.

www.stats.gov.cn/english   PRC State Statistical Bureau.

www.taipeitimes.com   Taipei Times, Taiwan, ROC.

www.undp.org/missions/china   United Nations Development Program/China.

www.uscc.gov   Congressionally established commission that sponsors hearings and discussions on economic and security matters.

www.usembassy-china.org.cn   American embassy in Beijing; particularly useful on environmental and trade issues.

www.xinhua.org   PRC official news agency.

Index